Global Information Systems

Global Information Systems

The Implications of Culture for IS Management

D. E. Leidner and T. R. Kayworth

AMSTERDAM • BOSTON • HEIDELBERG • LONDON
NEW YORK • OXFORD • PARIS • SAN DIEGO
SAN FRANCISCO • SINGAPORE • SYDNEY • TOKYO

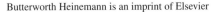

Butterworth Heinemann is an imprint of Elsevier

Butterworth-Heinemann is an imprint of Elsevier
Linacre House, Jordan Hill, Oxford OX2 8DP, UK
30 Corporate Drive, Suite 400, Burlington, MA 01803, USA

British Library Cataloguing in Publication Data
A catalogue record for this book is available from the British Library

Library of Congress Cataloguing-in-Publication Data
A catalogue record for this book is available from the Library of Congress

ISBN: 978-0-7506-8648-8

For information on all Butterworth-Heinemann publications
visit our web site at www.elsevierdirect.com

Typeset by Charon Tec Ltd., A Macmillan Company.
(www.macmillansolutions.com)

Printed and bound in Hungary

08 09 10 11 12   10 9 8 7 6 5 4 3 2

Contents

---

[1] The first three articles take a national perspective of culture and the last one an organizational perspective.

List of Contributors

Maryam Alavi, Emory University, Atlanta, Georgia, USA. Chapter 10

Soon Ang, Nanyang Business School, Singapore, China. Chapter 16.

Sebastian Barajas, Deloitte Consulting,New York City, USA. Chapter 6.

Angel Cabrera, Thunderbird, Glendale, Arizona, USA. Chapter 6.

Elizabeth F. Cabrera, University Carlos III of Madrid, Madrid, Spain. Chapter 6.

Kenneth J. Calhoun, Slippery Rock University, Slippery Rock, Pennsylvania, USA. Chapter 11.

Sven Carlsson, Lund University, Lund, Sweden. Chapter 12.

Myun Joong Cheon, University of Ulsan, Ulsan, Korea. Chapter 11.

Martha Corrales, Monterrey Institute of Technology, Monterrey, Mexico. Chapter 12.

Joyce Elam, Florida International University, Miami, Florida, USA. Chapter 12.

Kamal El-Sheshai, Georgia State University, Atlanta, Georgia, USA. Chapter 9.

Roberto Evaristo, University of Illinois at Chicago, Chicago, Illinois, USA. Chapter 13.

Robert Galliers, London School of Economics, London, UK. Chapter 7.

Jody Hoffer Gittell, Brandeis University, Waltham, Massachusetts, USA. Chapter 1.

Carole E. Hill, Georgia State University, Atlanta, Georgia, USA. Chapter 9.

Norton Hoffman, IBM Global Services, Armonk, New York, USA. Chapter 8.

Jimmy C. Huang, University of Houston, Houston, Texas, USA. Chapter 7.

Michelle L. Kaarst-Brown, Syracuse University, Syracuse, New York, USA. Chapter17.

Sherif Kamel, The American University in Cairo, Egypt. Chapter 5.

Shivraj, Kanungo, George Washington University, Washington DC, USA. Chapter 14.

Nancy Katz, Harvard University, Cambridge, Massachusetts, USA. Chapter 1.

Timothy R. Kayworth, Baylor University, Waco, Texas, USA. Chapter 10.

Mark Keil, Georgia State University, Atlanta, Georgia, USA. Chapter 3.

Robert Klepper, Southern Illinois University, Edwardsville, Illinois, USA. Chapter 8.

Dorothy L. Leidner, Baylor University, Waco, Texas, USA. Chapters 10 and 12.

Karen D. Loch, Georgia State University, Atlanta, Georgia, USA. Chapters 5 and 9.

Ramiro Montealegre, University of Colorado at Boulder, Colorado, USA. Chapter 3.

Susan Mary Newell, Bentley University, Waltham, Massachusetts, USA. Chapter 7.

Ojelanki Ngwenyama, Virginia Commonwealth University, Richmond, Virginia, USA. Chapter 4.

Peter Axel Nielsen, Aalborg University, Aalborg, Denmark. Chapter 4.

Shan-Ling Pan, National University of Singapore. Chapter 7.

Leslie Perlow, Harvard University, Cambridge, Massachusetts, USA. Chapter 1.

Gregory Rose, Washington State University, Pullman, Washington, USA. Chapter

Sanjeev Sadavarti, Indian Institute of Technology Bombay, Mumbai, India. Chapter 14.

Sandra Slaughter, Georgia Tech University, Atlanta, Georgia, USA. Chapter 16.

H. Jeff Smith, Miami University, Oxford, Ohio, USA. Chapter 3.

Yadlapati Srinivas, Indian Institute of Technology Bombay, Mumbai, India. Chapter 14.

Detmar W. Straub, Georgia State University, Atlanta, Georgia, USA. Chapters 5, 9 and 13.

Bernard C.Y. Tan, National University of Singapore, Singapore, China. Chapter 3.

James T.C. Teng, University of South Carolina, Columbia, South Carolina, USA. Chapter 11.

Roger Tomlin, University of Oxford, England, UK. Chapter 15.

Geoff Walsham, University of Cambridge, Cambridge, UK. Chapter 2.

Introduction: An Overview of Culture and IS

Since the emergence of IS as an academic discipline, researchers have observed that the deployment of information technology (IT) in organizations seems to follow no predicable pattern. Rather, the dynamics of IT adoption and use, and the outcomes of such use in organizational settings, were seen to be largely dependent on a host of variables external to the technology itself. One such variable – culture – has been identified by some as a key management variable to be considered in the successful deployment and management of IT in organizations (Cash et al., 1994; Lucas and Baroudi, 1994).

Given the focus of this book on IT and culture, it is essential to first introduce the concept of culture and, in particular, to identify the myriad of ways this construct has been conceptualized.[1] Such an introduction will provide a lens for the reader, as they read the ensuing articles, that may interpret culture very differently in terms of how it is actually defined as well as the levels at which culture is actually studied (e.g. national, organizational, sub-culture, individual).

To begin this introduction, it is important to ask ourselves what culture actually is. The answer to this question is not an easy one since culture has been viewed in sundry ways, including as ideologies, beliefs, basic assumptions, core values, important understandings, the collective will, norms and practices, symbols, rituals, and myths (Sackman, 1992; Delong and Fahey, 2000; Hofstede, 1998; Burchell et al., 1980; Pettigrew, 1979). So, our first point is that there is no single, universally accepted definition of culture.

Regardless of its definition, most agree that culture is a useful construct for explaining social group behaviors based upon their particular cultural interpretations of various events, objects, and stimuli. Theories of culture are critical to the IS field in that they present the view that IT artifacts and the information they generate are symbolic in nature (Robey and Markus, 1984)

---

[1]One early account lists 164 definitions of culture (Kroeber and Kluckhohn, 1952).

and hence subject to the various cultural interpretations. Such a view provides an alternative to the notion of technical determinism and suggests that technology is socially constructed based on particular social groups' assumptions, beliefs, or values. As social groups enact information technologies in different ways, these varied interpretations will lead to different behavior patterns in how such groups adopt and use IT, thereby leading to different outcomes of such use. Consequently, theories of culture may be helpful in explaining why IT use in firms often results in what seems to be contradictory consequences (Robey and Azevedo, 1994; Robey and Boudreau, 1999).

One definition we find useful is by Edgar Schein (1985a, 1985b) who defines culture in terms of 'basic assumptions, shared beliefs, or values'. Schein argues that culture exists at three levels: basic assumptions, values, and artifacts and creations. Basic assumptions exist at the core level of human existence and represent the belief systems that individuals have towards human behavior, relationships, reality, and truth. They represent interpretive schemes that are used to perceive situations and that form the basis for collective action. These assumptions are formed over time; they are passed along to new members, and they remain largely preconscious or invisible to the group's members.

At the next level lie values that represent espoused beliefs identifying what is important to a particular group. For organizations, corporate values form the foundation of corporate culture and provide a basis for appropriate behavior (Deal and Kennedy, 1982). According to Schein, values tend to be much more visible than assumptions with individuals being able to articulate their particular sets of values. Values are often characterized in terms of polar opposites such as 'task-orientation' vs. 'results-orientation' cultures.

At the third and most visible level of culture are artifacts and creations. Artifacts and creations may include such things as art, technology, and visible and audible behavioral patterns. While these manifestations of culture are quite explicit, they may also be among the more difficult to interpret. Consequently, one finds a dearth of mainstream research examining IS phenomenon based upon cultural artifacts and creations.

To summarize, culture may be very implicit in the form of basic assumptions (e.g. assumptions regarding information technology and the information it produces) while at the same time it may be very explicit in the form of visible artifacts and creations (e.g. technology artifacts). Additionally, culture can be reflected in individual values that represent knowable espoused beliefs (e.g. collaborative values). To date, IS culture research has been heavily slanted in favor of a 'values perspective' to the study of issues at the intersection of technology and culture. As such, much of the extant IS culture research focuses on the identification of particular sets of value orientations at the national, organizational, or sub-unit levels to examine how variations in such values affect particular IT outcomes. This trend is evident in the selection of this book's readings that focus heavily on a values perspective of IS culture research. To a much lesser extent, IS culture research has examined the role of basic assumptions in shaping various IT outcomes. Two notable examples of this are Kaarst-Brown and Robey (1999) and Kaarst-Brown (2005).

Defining culture on the basis of values or basic assumptions, researchers have examined an abundance of IS-related phenomenon addressing such questions as: How does culture influence patterns of IT adoption and diffusion? How does culture influence the way IT is managed in organizations? How do cultural differences influence the systems development process? How can variations in patterns of IT use and subsequent organizational outcomes be explained through cultural values? The common thread among these and other IS culture studies is that researchers seek to explain variance in IT-related dependent variables based upon differences in culture as either an independent or moderating variable.

While there are differences in the definition of culture, we also see dissimilarity across studies regarding the level at which culture is studied. Essentially, IS culture research has evolved over two distinct streams that examine culture's influence at the national level[2] as well as at the organizational or sub-unit levels (Leidner and Kayworth, 2006). While these two streams have experienced little overlap, they both share a focus on defining the cultural values that distinguish one group from another and how differences in values influence certain IT-related outcomes. The great majority of IS cross-cultural studies to date have relied extensively on Hofstede's (1983) taxonomy characterizing national culture along the value dimensions of power distance, uncertainty avoidance, individualism–collectivism, and masculinity–femininity.[3]

Studies using these dimensions generally involve subjects from two or more countries with very distinctive value sets (e.g. China vs. USA) and examine how differences in one or more of these value orientations might explain variations in one or more IT-related outcomes. Such studies have been helpful in deciphering how differences in national culture may help to account for differences in IT use, adoption, and IT use outcomes. Other popular conceptualizations of national culture used in cross-cultural IS research have included: time orientation (Hofstede and Bond, 1988), monochronism vs. polychronism (Hall, 1983), context (Hall, 1976) and locus of control (Smith et al., 1995). While most cross-cultural IS studies rely on some existing conceptualization of national culture (e.g. Hofstede, 1983), other studies such as Hill et al. (1998) rely more on evidence from field research to develop qualitative assessments of culture.

---

[2]This is typically referred to 'cross-cultural' research.
[3]See Leidner and Kayworth (2006: 361) for a more complete taxonomy of national cultural value frameworks.

Recently, some criticism has been leveled at Hofstede's dimensions of culture (Myers and Tan, 2002; Ford et al., 2003) with some arguing that it is overly simplistic and outdated. One criticism is over the underlying assumption of homogeneity of national culture that is implicit to Hofstede's work. In reality, specific countries may consist of various regional sub-cultures. Secondly, Hofstede's data on cultural values was collected close to thirty years ago. Over this period of time, it is likely that values have changed, particularly as the world has undergone globalization. In spite of these criticisms, research based on Hofstede's cultural values remains popular given the intuitive appeal of these dimensions as well as the body of prior research that has been built upon this tradition.

The second major stream of IS culture research examines the intersection of IT and culture from the standpoint of organizational culture.[3] Similar to the cross-cultural tradition, this line of inquiry has, to a great extent, taken a values-based approach to studying how organizational values (e.g. espoused beliefs) influence how social groups adopt and use IT, as well as subsequent organizational outcomes of such use. However, unlike the body of cross-cultural IS research, organizational IS culture research does not always assume homogeneity of culture at the organizational level. This is evidenced by a growing body of IS research investigating how distinctive sub-unit cultures within given organizations may influence IT-related outcomes. From the organizational literature, Martinson and Myers (1987) do an excellent job of describing these two views of organizational culture in terms of the *integration* and *differentiation* perspectives. Further discussion on each of these perspectives is provided below.

The *integration* perspective regards organizational culture as a homogeneous set of values that act as 'an integrating mechanism or social or normative glue that holds together a potentially diverse group of organizational members (Martinson and Myers 1987: 624).' One of the drawbacks to this perspective of organizational culture is that it cannot explain the presence of conflict in firms with homogeneous sets of values. Furthermore, this portrayal of organizational culture does not tolerate ambiguity in values. Thus, organizational values are valid only to the extent that they are widely shared across the enterprise. A good example of IS culture research from the integrationist perspective is a study by Ruppel and Harrington (2001) who use Quinn and Rohrbaugh's (1981) competing values framework to explain how different types of organizational values account for different patterns of intranet adoption across companies.

In contrast to the integrationist perspective, the *differentiation* perspective embraces the notion that most organizations are composed of different sub-cultures, each with their own views of the world based upon distinctive sets of values embraced by each group. Regarding this view, Rose (1988) comments: 'while it is empirically possible for an organization to exhibit a homogenous organization culture, this appears to be the exception rather than the rule'. Thus, a more realistic view may be one that considers organizations as mini societies – multi-cultural in nature; each with distinctive, competing, and potentially overlapping sub-cultures.

This differentiation perspective is useful for explaining how different sub-cultures within the same firm (e.g. engineers vs. sales people) may adopt and use IT differently based upon their respective sub-culture values. Furthermore, the differentiation perspective holds promise for explaining the conflict that often occurs among different sub-cultures (e.g. users and developers) within the same firm as well as across firms. One good example of such IS culture research from this differentiation perspective is found in Huang et al. (2003). While there have been a number of such studies from the differentiation perspective, most studies at the intersection of organizational culture and IS do so from the integrationist perspective.

While IS culture research has focused almost exclusively on culture's influence on IS, there has been a more recent trend in research examining how the adoption and use of IT may actually influence culture (Leidner and Kayworth, 2006). In one recent example, Doherty and Perry (2001) showed how the implementation of advanced data warehousing technology actually transformed an organization's culture in terms of values related to customer service, flexibility, and empowerment. This stream of research has practical significance through examining how technology might be deployed as an intervention to shape a firm's values consistent with management's wishes. Such research examining technology's influence on culture appears relatively unexplored, particularly at the national level.

Research on IS and culture is not without its challenges. First is the fact that studies at the intersection of IS and culture must address a construct that may exist at one or more levels (e.g. sub-unit, firm, national) simultaneously. In addition to determining the level of culture one is studying, researchers must also agree upon how culture should be best conceptualized; whether it be in terms of basic assumptions, values, tangible artifacts or one of the many other ways that culture has been defined. Given these conceptual challenges, a final challenge has to do with how culture is actually measured. In spite of these challenges, we believe the potential rewards to be gained from IS culture research are well worth the effort of grappling with these types of challenges.

In *Global Information Systems*, we provide readers with a cross-section of articles that we believe capture the complexities of IS culture research we've discussed. These readings provide some excellent examples of studies examining the IS phenomenon at different levels of culture (organizational, sub-unit, national culture) using various conceptualizations (e.g. basic assumptions, values) and different means to measure the culture construct. Many different national cultures are featured in the readings, including China,

Egypt, Hong Kong, Hungary, India, Jamaica, Korea, Mexico, Peru, Saudi Arabia, Sweden, Singapore, Turkey, the United Arab Emirates, the United Kingdom, and the United States. It is our hope that upon completion of this book, readers will have a much better grasp of the role played by culture in the development, adoption, use and management of IS. Enjoy the book!

References

Burchell, S., C. Clubb, A. G. Hopwood, J. Hughes, and J. Nahapiet (1980), "The Roles of Accounting in Organizations and Society," *Accounting, Organizations, and Society*, Vol. 5, No. 1, pp. 5–27.

Cash, J., R. Eccles, N. Nohria, and R. Nolan (1994), *Building the Information-age Organization: Structure, Control and Information Technologies*. Homewood, IL: Irwin.

Deal, T. E. and A. A. Kennedy (1982), *Corporate Cultures: The Rites and Rituals of Corporate Life*. Addison-Wesley.

DeLong, D. W. and L. Fahey (2000), "Diagnosing Cultural Barriers to Knowledge Management," *Academy of Management Executive*, Vol. 14, No. 4, November, pp. 113–127.

Doherty, N. F. and I. Perry (2001), "The Cultural Impact of Workflow Management Systems in the Financial Services Sector," *The Services Industries Journal*, Vol. 21, No. 4, October, pp. 147–166.

Ford, D. P., C. E. Connelly, and D. B. Meister (2003), "Information Systems Research and Hofstede's Culture's Consequences: An Uneasy and Incomplete Partnership," *IEEE Transactions on Engineering Management*, Vol. 50, No. 1, February, pp. 8–25.

Hall, E. T. (1976), *Beyond Culture*. Anchor, Garden City, CA.

Hall, E. T. (1983), *The Dance of Life: The Other Dimension of Time*. Anchor, New York, NY.

Hill, C. E., K. D. Loch, D. Straub, and K. El-Sheshai (1998), "A Qualitative Assessment of Arab Culture and Information Technology Transfer," *Journal of Global Information Management*, Vol. 6, No. 3, pp. 29–38.

Hofstede, G. (1983), "The Dimensions of National Cultures in Fifty Countries and Three Regions," in J. B. Deregowski, S. Daiurawiec, and R. C. Annis, Eds. *Explications in Cross-Cultural Psychology*. Swets and Zeitlinger, the Netherlands.

Hofstede, G. (1998), "Identifying Organizational Subcultures: An Empirical Approach," *Journal of Management Studies*, Vol. 35, No. 1, pp. 1–12.

Hofstede, G. and M. H. Bond (1988), "The Confucius Connection: From Cultural Roots to Economic Growth," *Organizational Dynamics*, Vol. 16, No. 4, pp. 4–21.

Huang, J. C., S. Newell, R. Galliers, and S. L. Pan (2003), "Dangerous Liaisons? Component Based Development and Organizational Subcultures," *IEEE Transactions on Engineering Management*, Vol. 50, No. 1, February, pp. 89–99.

Kaarst-Brown, M. L. (2005), "Understanding an Organization's View of the CIO: The role of underlying assumptions about IT," *MISQ Executive*, Vol. 4, No. 2, pp. 287–301.

Kaarst-Brown, M. L. and D. Robey (1999), "More on Myth, Magic and Metaphor: Cultural Insights into the Management of Information Technology in Organizations," *Information Technology and People*, Vol. 12, No. 2, pp. 192–217.

Kroeber, A. L. and C. Kluckohn (1952), *Culture*. Vantage, New York.

Leidner, D. L. and T. R. Kayworth (2006), "A Review of Culture in Information Systems Research: Toward a Theory of Information Technology Culture Conflict," *MIS Quarterly*, Vol. 30, No. 2, June, pp. 357–399.

Lucas, H. C. and J. Baroudi (1994), "The Role of Information Technology in Organizational Design," *Journal of MIS*, Vol. 10, No. 4, March, pp. 9–23.

Martinson, D. and J. Myers (1987), "Cultural Change: An integration of three different views," *Journal of Management Studies*, Vol. 24, pp. 623–647.

Myers, M. D. and F. B. Tan (2002), "Beyond Models of National Culture in Information Systems Research," *Journal of Global Information Management*, Vol. 10, No. 1, pp. 24–32.

Pettigrew, A. M. (1979), "On Studying Organizational Cultures," *Administrative Science Quarterly*, Vol. 24, pp. 570–581.

Quinn, R. E. and J. Rohrbaugh (1981), "A Competing Values Approach to Organizational Effectiveness," *Public Productivity Review*, Vol. 5, pp. 122–140.

Robey, D. and A. Azevedo (1994), "Cultural Analysis of the Organizational Consequences of Information Technology," *Accounting, Management, and Information Technologies*, Vol. 4, No. 1, pp. 23–27.

Robey, D. and M. Boudreau (1999), "Accounting for the Contradictory Consequences of Information Technology: Theoretical Directions and Methodological Implications," *Information Systems Research*, Vol. 10, No. 2, pp. 167–185.

Robey, D. and M. L. Markus (1984), "Rituals in Information Systems Design," *MIS Quarterly*, Vol. 8, No. 1, pp. 5–15.

Rose, R. A. (1988), "Organizations as Multiple Cultures: A Rules Theory Analysis," *Human Relations*, Vol. 41, No. 2, pp. 139–170. ,

Ruppel, C. P. and S. J. Harrington (2001), "Sharing Knowledge through Intranets: A Study of Organizational Culture and Intranet Implementation," *IEEE Transactions on Professional Communication*, Vol. 44, No. 1, March, pp. 37–52.

Sackmann, S. A. (1992), "Culture and Sub-Cultures: An Analysis of Organizational Knowledge," *Administrative Science Quarterly*, Vol. 37, pp. 140–161.

Schein, E. H. (1985a), *Organizational Culture and Leadership*. Jossey-Bass, San Francisco, CA.

Schein, E. H. (1985b), "How Culture Forms, Develops and Changes," in R. H. Kilmann, M. J. Saxton, and R. Serpa and Associates, Eds. *Gaining Control of the Corporate Future*, Jossey-Bass, pp. 17–43.

Smith, P., F. Trompenaars, and S. Dugan (1995), "The Rotter Locus of Control Scale in 43 Countries: A Test of Cultural Relativity," *International Journal of Psychology*, Vol. 30, No. 3, pp. 377–400.

Part One

The Role of Culture in IS Development

This first part of the book focuses on the role played by culture in the development of IS. Research on IS development considers the challenges of IS design and development, the different development approaches used as well as the outcomes of the methods, the motivations and incentives of IS developers, and issues concerning IS developer productivity. Considerable work has focused on the cultural differences observed across different software development teams and approaches. A common finding across studies is that cultural variation explains different approaches towards software development and that an approach that works well in one cultural context may not work so well in another.

For example, Dagwell et al. (1983) found that systems designers' approach towards end users varied across four nationalities (USA, UK, Australia, and Sweden): Australian and Swedish designers favored a more people-oriented approach to IS development whereas US and UK designers favored a more process and efficiency orientation. Likewise Kumar et al. (1990) found that the Danish designers emphasized people-related issues in ISD projects more than their Canadian counterparts, who emphasized technical issues.

This part comprises four papers on the role of culture in IS development. The first three of these examine culture from a national perspective whereas the final paper examines culture from an organizational perspective. Of the articles looking at national culture, the following nations are included: China, Hungary, India, Jamaica, Singapore, and the United States.

The first article, by Perlow, Gittell, and Katz, describes the approaches to software development employed by software development teams in India, China, and Hungary. Having spent time observing the different teams onsite, the authors were able to get detailed information on how much time the team members spent interacting with one another, and for what purpose, as well as how much time, and for what purpose, they spent interacting with the leader. The article demonstrates the dramatic difference in how the project leader interacts with the team members in the different cultural environments as well as the differences in how the team members interact with one another. Moreover, the reward structures and work hours are shown to be quite different.

The Walsham (2002) article – the second in this part – considers the consequences of cross-cultural software development teams. In Walsham's paper, the interactions of Indian and Jamaican software developers are described, as the team members try in vain to complete an urgently needed software application. The differences in leadership style, in work habits, and in the very meanings associated with timetables and deadlines are shown to be stark across the two cultures. As a result, the developers from both cultures are challenged to adapt to the other.

In the third article in this part, Tan, Smith, Keil, and Montealgre (2003) address the question of information gathering and dissemination during software projects. Specifically, they are curious as to whether national culture influences the degree to which unfavorable project information (such as being behind schedule and or over budget) is shared upwards in the hierarchy. Such information has important implications for whether doomed software projects are continued, or recognized as troubled and stopped or adjusted. The cultures they consider are Singapore, and the United States where the United States is an 'individualistic' culture and Singapore is considered to be 'collectivist'.

The final paper in this section examines organizational culture and its influence on CMM. The capability maturity model (CMM) has been part of a trend towards software development improvements over the past decade and is used by companies around the globe. Yet software development projects continue to fail at an alarming rate.

Ngwenyama and Nielsen (2003) uncover the core assumptions about organizational culture that are embedded into CMM and explain why CMM might not be successful in all organizations.

With the increasing use of offshore development practices (Carmel and Agarwal, 2002; Kaiser and Hawk, 2004) as well as cross-cultural software development teams, it is essential to understand how value differences in culturally diverse software development teams may influence the systems development process and outcomes. Moreover, as software process improvements, such as CMM, become common, it is likewise important to understand how these are accepted, or rejected by, an organization's culture. The four articles in this part help expand our understanding of these points.

References

Carmel, E. and R. Agarwal (2002), "The Maturation of Offshore Sourcing of Information Technology Work," *MIS Quarterly Executive*, Vol. 1, No. 2, June, pp. 65–78.

Dagwell, R., R. Weber, and R. Kling (1983), "Systems Designer's User Models: A Comparative Study and Methodological Critique," *Communications of the ACM*, Vol. 26, No. 11, November, pp. 987–997.

Kaiser, K. and S. Hawk (2004), "Evolution of Offshore Software Development: From Outsourcing to Cosourcing," *MIS Quarterly Executive*, Vol. 3, No. 2, June, pp. 69–82.

Kumar, K., N. Bjorn-Anderson, and R. King (1990), "A Cross-Cultural Comparison of IS Designer Values," *Communications of the ACM*, Vol. 33, No. 5, May, pp. 528–538.

Ngwenyama, O. and P. A. Nielsen (2003), "Competing Values in Software Process Improvement: An Assumption Analysis of CMM From an Organizational Culture Perspective," *IEEE Transactions on Engineering Management*, Vol. 50, No. 1, February, pp. 101–111.

Perlow, L., J. H. Gittell, and N. Katz (2004), "Contextualizing Patterns of Work Group Interactions: Toward a Nested Theory of Structuration," *Organization Science*, September, pp. 520–536.

Tan, B. C. Y., H. J. Smith, M. Keil, and R. Montealegre (2003), "Reporting Bad News about Software Projects: Impact of Organizational Climate and Information Asymmetry in an Individualistic and Collectivist Culture," *IEEE Transactions on Engineering Management*, Vol. 50, No. 1, February, pp. 65–77.

Walsham, G. (2002), "Cross-Cultural Software Production and Use: A Structurational Analysis," *MIS Quarterly*, Vol. 26, No. 4, December, pp. 359–380.

1 Contextualizing Patterns of Work Group Interaction: Toward a Nested Theory of Structuration

Leslie A. Perlow, Jody Hoffer Gittell and Nancy Katz

Abstract: The focus of this article is the patterns of interaction that arise within work groups, and how organizational and institutional factors play a role in shaping these patterns. Based on an ethnographic study of groups across three national contexts, we describe the variation in patterns of interaction that we observed. We further suggest how different patterns of interaction form mutually reinforcing systems with aspects of the organizational context. In addition, we suggest how these mutually reinforcing systems are perpetuated by aspects of the broader institutional context. Our findings point toward a nested theory of structuration, expanding structuration theory to multiple levels simultaneously. In turn our findings have theoretical and practical implications for better understanding and managing interaction patterns among group members.

Introduction

How does work get done in groups? Why does similar work get done differently in different places?

To address these questions, we must explore what people actually do at work. As Stephen Barley and Gideon Kunda (2001, p. 90) aptly describe: "The dearth of data on what people *actually* do – the skills, knowledge, and practices that comprise their routine work – leave us with increasingly anachronistic theories and outdated images of work and how it is organized". Moreover, if we want to understand how work gets done, we cannot strip away the context. Rather, we must contextualize our findings to better understand the phenomenon we observe (e.g., Johns 2001, Rousseau and Fried 2001). Also, we must consider how factors at multiple levels of analysis shape and constrain the phenomenon we study (Kozlowski and Klein 2000, Hackman 2003).

Back in the 1950s, researchers at the MIT Group Networks Laboratory established that variation in patterns of communication among group members affects group functioning and performance (Bavelas 1950, Leavitt 1951, Shaw and Rothschild, 1956). However, by the 1970s, this stream of research had been largely abandoned (Monge and Contractor 2001). Along with several other researchers (i.e., Argote et al. 1989, Brown and Miller 2000, Sparrowe et al. 2001, Cummings and Cross 2003), our purpose is to revive research that explores patterns of work group interaction. Moreover, we are interested in expanding the scope of this research to include both the national *and* organizational context in which these patterns emerge.

Prior research that explores the effects of contextual factors has tended to focus on either macrocontextual variables and how they affect organization structure (e.g., Hamilton and Biggart 1988, Maurice et al. 1980), or on organization-level factors and how they affect aggregate measures of group functioning and performance (e.g., Stokols 1981, Seers et al. 1995, DeMatteo et al. 1998). Some researchers have further explored how differences in cultural profiles, based on individuals' value orientations (Hofstede 1980, House et al. 1999), affect how people behave in groups (Mann 1980, Earley 1993, Bond and Smith 1996). Missing in these studies is an exploration of the patterns of work group interaction. Moreover, missing in these studies is an exploration of how the multiple different levels of context affect each other, as well as the patterns of work group interaction.

Our research is unique in its multilevel focus on interaction patterns and both the organizational and national context in which these patterns exist. We further chose to focus on the patterns of helping as a type of interaction pattern because of the central role of helping behavior in completing the work of the software engineering teams we studied. Using what Hackman (2003) calls "informed induction," we further identified the structures located at each level that appeared to most powerfully explain our local phenomenon, patterns of helping. We found that the reward structures can both explain and be explained by the patterns of helping. In turn, this mutually reinforcing relationship between the reward structures and helping patterns can itself be explained by elements of the larger institutional context.

Our analysis suggests a nested theory of structuration, extending structuration theory across multiple levels of analysis simultaneously. This nested theory of structuration further sheds light on alternative theories of fit – contingency, configuration, and congruence – suggesting how the underlying mechanism of mutual influence associated with structuration theory may explain how fit is achieved in these alternative theories. Our analysis also illustrates the value of unpacking aggregate measures, be they cultural or group aggregates, to better understand how work really gets done. In the end, our findings have theoretical and practical implications for better understanding and managing interaction patterns among group members.

Methods

Given how little is known about patterns of interaction within work groups and their relationship with the organizational and national contexts in which they exist, we engaged in close observation and built grounded theory. We studied software engineering as a type of work because, characteristic of knowledge work, software engineering includes both an individual and an interdependent component (Perlow 1999). Furthermore, the work is open-ended, creative, individually styled, and very demanding (Barley and Orr 1997). It cannot be standardized or fully planned out in advance (Bell 1973). Moreover, as it turned out, individuals – even on the components of their work for which they were individually responsible – often got stuck and needed help. We could therefore isolate a particular type of interaction – getting help on individual work – and explore how patterns of helping varied across groups.

We sought to hold constant the nature of the work as much as possible, while varying the context. Toward this end, we explored three teams of software engineers doing similar work at similar stages in the work process, but in very different cultural contexts.[1] We studied software engineers working for three partnerships, each a venture with the same American-headquartered multinational corporation. These partnerships were located in three distinct national contexts – Bangalore, India; Shenzen, China; and Budapest, Hungary. We refer to the three sites studied as follows: (1) *Cco* (all company names are pseudonyms), the joint venture located in Shenzhen, China; (2) *Ico*, the joint venture located in Bangalore, India; and (3) *Hco*, the *strategic partnership*, with longer-term plans to form a joint venture, located in Budapest, Hungary.

To further choose the three sites, we looked for teams who were comparable in terms of performance. These regions were home to some of the fastest-growing, most technically advanced software development industries in the world (IDC 1995, NASSCOM 1997). Moreover, each of the local organizations we studied had been chosen by the headquarters for an alliance because of its reputation for being technically advanced in its region. The teams we studied were further chosen by senior managers at each location as being among their highest-performing teams of software engineers. Additionally, members of the U.S. headquarters helped to select the three teams studied to ensure highly comparable work assignments.

Research sites

Physically, the offices looked quite similar. The Cco office was immaculate, air conditioned, and well lit. Cco engineers sat in cubicles in wide-open spaces with managers around the edges in closed offices. Like Cco, Ico was clean, well lit, and air conditioned. Ico engineers also sat in cubicles; however, their workspace was configured in honeycombs, rather than rows. At Hco, the entire company was not all co-located. Rather, Hco was spread out around the city of Budapest, with groups of 5 to 25 engineers working at each location. The team studied worked by itself a few blocks from the head office, sharing two big open rooms plus a small kitchen. Their office was also clean, well lit, and air conditioned.

In addition, the three teams had similar compositions. The Cco team consisted of a project leader and four engineers: The project leader was male, as were two of the engineers. The Ico team consisted of a project leader and five engineers: The project leader was female, as was one of the five engineers. The Hco team consisted of a project leader and four engineers: The project leader was male, as were three of the four engineers. Across the three teams, the engineers ranged in age from 22 to 30 years old; the average age was 25 at both Cco and Ico, and 26 at Hco. The project leaders at Cco and Ico were 28; the Hco project leader was 29. All engineers and project leaders were natives of their respective countries. Additionally, all members of these three teams had four-year degrees from top technical universities in their countries. The project leaders had all been engineers; they simply had a few more years of experience in the software industry than the engineers that they managed.

Nature of work

In each case, the team worked to provide a collective deliverable to a single customer. The work was moderately interdependent in the sense that individual components could be completed relatively independently of each other prior to being integrated into a finished product. In all three cases, the project leader divided up the work among the engineers such that each engineer was assigned his or her own independent tasks to perform based on his or her area of specialty. We observed each project after the work had been assigned and as engineers worked on completing their individual deliverables. At a later date, each of the engineers' individual components would be integrated and delivered to the customer.

Cco. The team we studied at Cco was working on part of the internal development of a banking system for a high-technology manufacturer located in Shenzhen. The project was scheduled to last a total of eight months. During the first two months, the project had focused on documenting the user requirements. The following four months were spent coding. The project leader had divided the coding task into 10 modules to be completed in sequence. Each of the four engineers on the team was assigned a part of each module. The project leader was responsible for integrating different components completed by each of his engineers. The plan was to complete these 10 modules by the end of the sixth month, leaving two months to test the code before delivering it to the customer. We collected data during the three weeks spanning the end of the fifth and the beginning of the sixth month. The period observed involved engineers working independently, but each on different aspects of the same module.

Ico. The team we studied at Ico was working for a company in Germany that had developed a home banking system for the Internet. The project was to develop Internet security plug-ins that checked for viruses. It had started six months prior to our arrival, with three engineers identifying the programming needs of the customer in Germany. After three months, these engineers had returned to India with a set of work requirements. At this point, five engineers plus a project leader worked on-site in India. The engineers each had separate tasks, the output of which they provided to their project leader upon completion. When we arrived, the engineers had already been back in India for two months, and had about three months more work to do.

Hco. The team we studied at Hco was working to computerize the information technology system for a hospital in Debrecen, Hungary. The project, including installation and training, was scheduled to last two years and had begun six months prior to our arrival. When we arrived, the team was in the midst of developing new features for the information technology system. The project leader had spent long hours dividing up the work as he thought would best suit the skills and abilities of his four engineers. He would later be responsible for integrating their work and interfacing with the customer.

The nature of the tasks carried out by the three teams studied can be characterized as "complex" and "uncertain" (March and Simon 1958, Thompson 1967). The software-engineering tasks allocated to individual engineers were complex in the sense that novel solutions were required as new problems emerged. Complexity reduces the preprogrammability of tasks and increases information requirements, thus increasing task uncertainty. The tasks were uncertain in the sense that the information required to perform the tasks was greater than the information possessed by any one individual engineer at any given point in time, requiring both new learning and the sharing of knowledge among engineers and the project leader.

Data sources

Data for this study were drawn from observations, interviews, and tracking logs conducted by the first author.

Observations. In each location, the selected team of software engineers was observed on a daily basis. The first author was usually present from the time the engineers arrived until they left, observing them at work in their cubicles, at meetings, and in hallway conversations. She typed field notes throughout the day, as time permitted, and for several hours each night. She was on-site for eight weeks at Ico, six weeks at Hco, and three weeks at Cco.

Consistent with the process of inductive theory building (Glaser and Strauss 1967), by the time she got to Cco she already knew what she had found at Ico and Hco, which enabled her to collect comparative data more efficiently. In contrast, when she started at Ico, she had little idea what she would find at Hco or Cco, so her data collection effort had to be broader, and therefore her stay more lengthy.

At each site, the first author had an office near to where the software engineers worked. This location enabled her to close the door and have confidential conversations with the engineers. Often engineers would come into her office, shut the door, sit down, and update her on events that had occurred. At both Hco and Cco, because English was not spoken among engineers at work, it was more difficult to capture the full meaning of meetings and interactions observed. The first author often had to reconstruct content by asking multiple individuals their interpretations of events. She did this in interviews, hallway conversations, and informal discussions with engineers in her office. At both Hco and Cco, about 75% of the engineers spoke English and almost all of them understood it; English is the international language of software development. Still, a translator was always available to assist with any difficulties encountered while communicating.

Interviews. In addition to observing work, the first author interviewed a range of people at each company. She first interviewed each member of the software team, including all engineers, their project leader, and their manager. Initial formal interviews lasting one to two hours provided background information about team members as well as an understanding of team members' perceptions of their work. During these interviews, questions were asked about the individual's work history, work at the present company, life outside of work, and career goals.

To obtain a richer understanding of the work environment, additional interviews were conducted with other individuals at each site, including both other managers and other engineers. These interviews provided supplemental information on individuals' perceptions of their work, company, and industry. At Ico, an additional seven senior managers, 14 managers, and 18 engineers were interviewed. At Hco, an additional three senior managers, seven managers, and nine engineers were interviewed. At Cco, an additional four senior managers, six managers, and six engineers were interviewed.

Tracking Logs and Debriefing Interviews. To better understand how individuals spend their time at work, each member of the selected teams was asked to keep a log of what he or she did on one randomly chosen day. On these days, individuals were asked to track their activities from when they woke up until they went to bed. The team members were asked to wear a digital watch that beeped on the hour, and at each beep to write down everything they had done during the previous hour. Team members were encouraged to write down interactions as they occurred and to use the beeps as an extra reminder to keep track of their activities. The day after a team member tracked his or her activities, a debriefing interview was held. In these interviews, the individual was asked to talk through his or her log sheet, reviewing all interactions in which he or she had engaged, including who had initiated each interaction, for what purpose, and with what outcome. Data from 10-tracked days at Ico, 6-tracked days at Hco, and 6-tracked days at Cco were collected.

Analyses

To analyze the data collected at each site, we followed the guidelines suggested by Glaser and Strauss (1967) and Miles and Huberman (1984), developing empirically grounded sets of categories capturing how people related to one another in the process of getting the work done (e.g., types of interactions, people involved, sequencing) and the context in which it occurred (e.g., reward, family, educational, mobility, and political systems). We followed an iterative process, first developing hunches, then comparing those ideas to new data from the site, and further using the new data to decide whether to retain, revise, or discard the inferences. We came to recognize that the key interaction, which occurred among engineers and their project leader once the work was divided up and individuals were each focused on their own deliverables, was that of helping. At all three sites, individuals often encountered problems on their deliverables and would turn to others for help. However, we noted that who they tended to turn to and who willingly reciprocated varied across the three sites. Below, we first document the observed variation in patterns of helping that emerged among teammates in the process of doing their work. We next document the reward structures and the elements of the larger institutional context that appear to play a role in shaping these helping patterns.

Patterns of helping within work groups

We first describe the helping patterns observed within each of the three work groups studied. We then present data from the daily tracking logs, which corroborate the patterns identified.

Cco

At Cco, engineers narrowly focused on their own work responsibilities, interacting with their project leader as necessary. Cco engineers frequently approached the project leader to clarify assignments and to ask for help. For example, one Cco engineer noted, "If something is not clear, I will always confirm it first." Furthermore, engineers approached their project leader for help in doing the work itself. For instance, at one point a Cco engineer started working on a piece of code but found a bug in it. The engineer informed the project leader of the problem and they spent half an hour discussing the problem, trying to understand it so they could correct it. In contrast, Cco engineers rarely communicated with their peers about work-related questions. We refer to this pattern of helping as "managerial centered." In this system, the core helping interaction was between engineers and their project leader. (Refer to Figure 1.1a.)

Ico

In contrast to the managerial-centered pattern of helping at Cco, the Ico project leader was more removed from the day-to-day technical questions arising in the work process. When problems arose, engineers depended on each other for help. They requested help based on a peer's area of expertise. As one engineer explained, "When I get stuck, I turn to other engineers on the team, friends at the company, or as a last resort, surf the net." For example, when one Ico engineer needed help on a problem related to the UNIX system, he turned to another engineer. The other engineer had a reputation for being the office expert on UNIX. The Ico engineers knew each others' strengths and felt at ease both asking for and providing help. Moreover, if engineers found members of their team could not help, they asked a batch mate – someone who entered Ico at the same time that they had entered – or they would call a classmate at another company – often a competitor – for assistance. Indeed, peer input was so valued at Ico, engineers would wait long periods of time for such expertise. For example, one Ico engineer spent the better part of two days waiting for a peer to assist with her code. She relied on his expertise so much that she did not try to proceed without him. Whether she could have created an alternative solution on her own was not

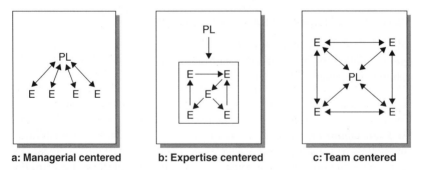

a: Managerial centered   b: Expertise centered   c: Team centered

Figure 1.1   *Patterns of helping within work groups*
Notes. E = Engineer. PL = Project Leader.

clear. What was clear was that she never considered the possibility of exploring other ways to address the problem.

There was far greater interaction among engineers at Ico than at Cco. Ico engineers turned to each other whenever they were not sure how to proceed, or when they wanted the benefit of someone else's expertise in a given situation. We refer to this pattern of helping as "expertise centered." In this system, the core helping interaction was between engineers based on areas of specialized knowledge in which they could provide help. (Refer to Figure 1.1b.)

Hco

At Hco, the project leader was more involved in addressing technical questions than at Ico, and the engineers were more involved than at Cco. Work assignments at Hco were not defined more broadly than at Cco or at Ico; however, Hco engineers frequently discussed problems with whomever happened to be available, whether their project leader or a peer engineer. For example, when one engineer had a bug in his code, he discussed the problem with a peer who knew little about this type of problem. Together, they explored possible origins. They looked at the source code and spent over an hour exploring how to fix the bug. When engineers would discuss a problem, often others in the office would overhear the conversation and find that they too had something to contribute. Consequently, they would join the conversation. Frequently, all four engineers and the project leader would become involved. As a result of such frequent, more general interactions, engineers at Hco had a broader sense than Cco or Ico engineers of what each was doing and what problems each faced.

Because Hco engineers appeared more willing – and, as part of the process, became more able – to assist each other on tasks not specifically assigned to them or within their particular areas of expertise, the Hco work process was often independent of specific individuals. Even the project leader and the engineers were closely interchangeable. When the project leader left for vacation when his team was busy finalizing the product for installation, one engineer explained: "I have extra work this week because [the project leader] is away. We each develop certain functions, and it is easier if there is a problem for me to work on those functions I have developed and for him to work on the ones he developed ... but if a problem arises and the one of us responsible is away, the other one can always figure out a solution." When asked if he would ever contact the project leader on vacation, he responded, seemingly quite surprised by the question, "No. I can figure it out." Similarly, the project leader could easily step in for an engineer who was having a problem, and peer engineers often stepped in for each other as well. We refer to this pattern of helping as "team centered." In this system, helping occurred, more generally, between all members of the team. (Refer to Figure 1.1c.)

Table 1.1   *Patterns of helping within work groups*

	Cco	Ico	Hco
Role of project leader	Provider	Overseer	Team player
Role of engineer	Specialist	Specialist	Generalist
Dependent on whom for help	Project leader	Peer engineer	Project leader or peer engineer

In sum, the patterns of helping varied across the groups studied in three core ways. First, the role of the project leader varied from that of provider to overseer to team player. Second, engineers were either specialists or generalists. Third, the person on whom an engineer depended for help on work-related questions/problems was the project leader, a peer engineer, or whoever was available. Table 1.1 summarizes these differences.

Corroborating evidence

The daily tracking data corroborate the existence of the three different patterns of helping. According to these data, Cco engineers spent the smallest fraction of their workday interacting (13%), with the vast majority of this interactive time spent with their project leader (81%). Indeed, no time was spent in team meetings and hardly any with individuals beyond the team (2%). (Refer to Table 1.2.) These time allocations support our observation that at Cco helping existed primarily between the project leader and each engineer, and not among peer engineers.

In contrast, the daily tracking data indicate Ico engineers spent more of their workday interacting (26%). Furthermore, most of this time was spent with other engineers (55%), rather than with their project leader (13%). When engineers did meet as a team with their project leader, the purpose was to update their project leader on their progress to date (10%). In addition, Ico engineers allocated almost a quarter of their time to interactions with individuals outside the team (22%).[2] These time allocations highlight the limited technical assistance Ico engineers received from the project leader and emphasize Ico engineers' reliance on each others' expertise, even when such expertise lay outside the team or even company.

Finally, the daily tracking data indicate that Hco engineers spent an equivalent percentage of work time to Ico engineers interacting (26%). However, these interactions were divided among the project leader and peer engineers more equally than they were at Ico. Indeed, the allocation of Hco engineers' interactive time consistently fell between that of Ico and Cco for each type

Table 1.2   *Composition of interactive time*

	Cco	Ico	Hco
Fraction of total work time spent interacting	0.13	0.26	0.26
Fraction of interactive time spent on			
• Managerial interactions	0.81	0.13	0.54
• Engineer interactions	0.17	0.55	0.31
• Group meetings	0.00	0.10	0.09
• Other interactions	0.02	0.22	0.06

of interaction. Hco engineers spent more time interacting with their project leader than Ico engineers, but less time than Cco engineers did. Furthermore, Hco engineers spent more time interacting with peers than did Cco engineers, but less time than Ico engineers. Hco engineers also spent more time interacting in team meetings than Cco engineers did, and just slightly less than Ico engineers; however, the purpose of these meetings was quite different at Hco, compared to Ico. At Hco, team meetings were discussions about how to address a particular problem that one or more members of the team faced, as opposed to an update on each individual's status. Overall, the Hco engineers' time allocations support our observation that helping was more evenly distributed between the project leader and engineers and among the engineers themselves.

It is interesting to note that had we only observed aggregate measures of time spent interacting, the Ico and Hco teams would appear to be identical. However, when we unpacked the aggregate measures and observed the patterns of helping, we found important differences between Ico and Hco. Further, these differences turned out to be part of a reinforcing relationship with the reward structures in each context, which we describe below.

Reward structures

In each case, the nature of the work was similar in terms of complexity, uncertainty, and interdependence. Differences in the nature of the work, therefore, cannot explain the observed variation in patterns of helping. Variation in the criteria that governed the distribution of rewards as well as variation in the nature of the rewards that were given, however, can explain the observed variation in helping patterns. Below, we describe where each team falls in terms of the criteria for rewards (refer to Figure 1.2), and then we describe the nature of the rewards themselves. In the following section,

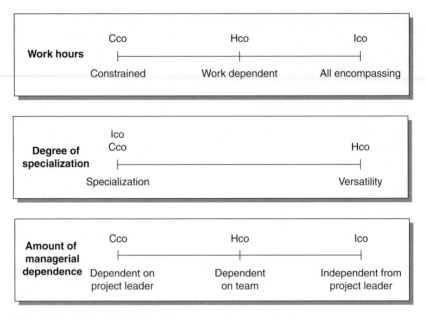

Figure 1.2   *Criteria for rewards*

we describe *how* reward structures, in turn, can explain and be explained by the observed variation in helping patterns.

Criteria for rewards

At all three sites, the criteria for rewarding engineers involved hours worked, the level of specialization, and the degree of managerial dependence. The criteria varied from short to long work hours, from specialization to versatility, and from managerial dependence to managerial independence.

Work hours

Cco. At Cco, engineers were evaluated based on their work within fixed temporal boundaries; how hard they worked was more important than how long they worked. Cco engineers were expected to work eight hours starting between 8:00 and 9:00 A.M. and ending between 5:00 and 6:00 P.M., with an hour for lunch. At Cco, engineers rarely were expected to work much beyond 6:00 P.M., or on the weekends.

As one Cco engineer stated, "Hours do not matter. If I worked more hours, I wouldn't be any more successful." Another engineer explained that it is "your way of working … your efficiency … not the sheer number of hours one puts in. We don't get rewarded for hours. Longer hours [beyond an eight-hour day] will not result in a higher evaluation." As one project leader confirmed: "Hours worked are not important for evaluation." Rather, as one manager put it, "We judge engineers based on how hard they work [while at work] and their native talent."

Ico. At Ico, the core workday – 9:00 A.M. to 6:30 P.M., – was referred to as "mandatory time." Ico engineers were expected to begin their workdays around 9:00 A.M., but end closer to 7:00 P.M., and often as late as 10:00 or 11:00 P.M. In addition to long workdays, weekend work was regularly expected. Saturday was typically considered a full workday, with individuals expected to arrive around 10:00 A.M. and leave about 6:00 P.M. One engineer explained: "There is great pressure to spend the entire day in the office on Saturday whether or not you have work to do."

At Ico, it was important to managers that their engineers demonstrated a commitment to work, "a mindset" as one manager referred to it, "a willingness to do whatever in response to the job." Managers modeled the desired behavior. For example, the team's manager (i.e., the project leader's manager) was described by one of his engineers as "ambitious and extremely hard working." This manager often stayed late into the evening and routinely worked long hours on Saturdays. Moreover, he seldom took time off from work between Monday and Saturday. One of his engineers noted: "I don't think he has taken a single day off this year."

Ico managers expected their engineers to be like themselves, willing to work at all times. Rather than regulating fixed hours, the managers ensured that work got done by rewarding long hours. One project leader described his team's efforts in glowing terms: "[They] want to excel and know when to set their priorities ... [they] never go on leave ... and I never ask any of my staff to do this. It comes from within them."

Hco. At Hco, engineers typically worked from 9:00 A.M. until 6:00 P.M., sometimes 7:00 P.M. The senior manager estimated total [expected] work hours to be "five, eight-hour days a week ... but everyone works at least 10% more than a 40-hour week." Moreover, work hours were expected to vary with work demands. Engineers were expected to put in long hours when the work required it.

The project leader explained, "People are evaluated on their output, not on the amount of time they put into their work.... The team has a whole range of skill levels. Those with higher skills will take a shorter amount of time to complete the same task." The manager confirmed, "I don't evaluate people based on long hours. It is hard for me to even know if people are working or not because they can, and many of them do, work from home." He added, "I can get a lot more done at home. I work at home whenever I can." It is important to note that, unlike Cco or Ico engineers, Hco engineers had the technical capabilities (i.e., computers, faxes, and cell phones) and the physical space to work at home. Moreover, because engineers were evaluated on output, not hours, Hco engineers had the flexibility to decide whether to work at home. They could also choose when and how long they worked at the office. One engineer explained: "I decide for myself when I must devote more time to keep up with deadlines. I decide not just when I should work, but which projects are urgent or critical and where I prefer to do my work ... I decide where and when by myself."

Rewards for specialization

Cco. Cco managers rewarded engineers with strong technical backgrounds who could rapidly adapt to a continually changing technological world. Cco wanted engineers who would make an effort both at work and outside of work to learn and advance their areas of expertise. Managers evaluated engineers based on their ability to "catch on to new technology.... We want people who take advantage of ongoing training and learning opportunities so they stay current." Engineers were rewarded for bringing the needed set of skills to a project – often from a specific area of rapidly advancing technology.

Ico. Engineers at Ico were also expected to provide a set of skills to their team, and they too were expected to stay up to date on their skills. According to one manager, "Engineers must constantly be developing the skills needed by the client.... It is essential to stay current."

Hco. At Hco, managers valued people who showed a desire to work hard to achieve a goal. However, rather than focusing on people's existing knowledge, managers focused on what people could learn in short periods of time. The project leader explained that, when hiring, "What matters is not that one is familiar with how the work is done, or the language in which we program, but that one can pick it up quickly.... I look for people who want to do the work and want to learn." The focus at Hco was on understanding the whole project and being able to help whoever needed help, rather than developing an in-depth understanding of a particular part of the project and staying abreast of current trends only in that specialized area. Hco engineers were rewarded for being generalists, rather than specialists.

Rewards for managerial dependence

Cco. Cco engineers were encouraged to consult with their project leader whenever necessary to complete their deliverables. Cco managers rewarded engineers who were cautious and avoided taking risks that might lead them down the wrong path. According to the project leader, "If people do not fully understand, they should clarify their questions." He explained that he did not value people working independently, trying to develop a program by themselves. He preferred that an engineer approach him frequently with questions and updates.

Ico. At Ico, engineers were expected to work independently from their project leader and to seek help from their peers as needed. "Ultimately," the project leader explained, "the more support I provide an engineer, the lower rating I will give him in his yearly appraisal…. At some point, you need to become independent." Unlike Cco, where the project leader encouraged his engineers to turn first to him when there was a question or problem, the Ico project leader encouraged engineers to do as they were told and work among themselves to solve technical problems.

Hco. At Hco, individuals were rewarded not only for being committed to gaining a broad understanding of the project, but also for being willing to do whatever was needed to contribute to the *team's* success. When engineers needed help, they were expected to turn to whoever was available, whether that person was their project leader or another engineer. Hco project leaders willingly provided assistance and expected this same willingness of their engineers. As the project leader stated, "If someone has the time, I expect it of them to help." The manager explained, "Anything impeding the group's progress is worthy of a group member's time." The project leader noted: "We are all in the same boat. We must work together. We must depend on each other to succeed."

Nature of rewards

In the above subsection, we described the three core criteria on which engineers were evaluated. However, not only do the criteria for rewards vary across the three sites studied, but the rewards themselves vary as well.

Cco. At Cco, engineers received salaries that were comparable to other "top-flight" software houses in China. In addition, engineers were paid extra for the rare request for overtime work. The project leader and the manager evaluated engineers every three months. Bonuses were paid based on these assessments. Promotions were evaluated every six months. High-performing engineers were further rewarded with more challenging work assignments that enabled them to further develop their technical skills on the job, as well as more opportunities to engage in training sessions outside of work.

Ico. At Ico, engineers received compensation comparable with the rest of the software industry. Engineers also received a certain amount of money, based on performance, placed in an account, which they could then allocate among benefits including medical insurance, company car, housing loan, or refrigerator. Engineers were evaluated once a year by their manager in conjunction with their project leader, on a 1 to 5 scale, where 5 is "unsatisfactory performance" and 1 is "far exceeds expectations, needs no supervision, and doing work of next level." Salary, benefits, and promotions depended on one's ratings. High-performing engineers also received more challenging work assignments that enabled them to further develop their skills, and projects that would likely take them abroad, to Europe and, most desirably, to the United States.

Hco. At Hco, salaries were top-end for the software engineers in Hungary. However, there was no "extra" money at Hco to further motivate engineers. There were no bonuses. The manager explained, "I need to find other ways to motivate (besides money). There is no extra money for bonuses or raises." There was only an implicit promise that, if the company did well, "they will create a stable environment for their futures and a place where they know they will have a good job." This was seen as a valuable promise, given that most engineers currently had multiple unemployed friends and family members.

Reward-helping systems

As noted above, the observed helping patterns differed in three core ways: (1) role of the project leader, (2) role of the engineer, and (3) dependencies between project leader and engineers and among engineers. Our findings, elaborated in the previous section, further suggest that reward structures vary as they pertain to: (1) work hours, (2) degree of specialization, and (3) amount of managerial dependence. In this section, we describe *how* differences in reward structures appear to reinforce the patterns of helping, while the patterns of helping appear to reinforce the differences in reward structures.

While interconnections appear to exist between each of the three character- istics of the helping patterns and each of the three ways in which the reward structures vary, we have chosen for the sake of clarity and brevity to describe only three of these nine relationships in the paper. We describe the following relationships between aspects of the reward structures and helping patterns: (1) work hours and role of project leader, (2) degree of specialization and role of engineers, and (3) amount of managerial dependence and core helping interaction (i.e., between project leader and engineers, or among engineers). It is important to keep in mind that we are only exploring a subset of the multiple interconnections that appear to exist. Further, it is important to note that even the three relationships we do describe are not independent from each other, but are themselves highly interrelated. We describe them as three distinct mutually reinforcing relationships only to simplify the explanation, while still providing sufficient evidence to document that reward structures and patterns of helping appear to be highly interconnected, each reinforcing the other. In each case, through their mutual reinforcement, reward structures and helping patterns form a distinct type of reward-helping system.

Cco

At Cco, the project leader acted as the central provider of help. Cco engi- neers were specialists who were expected to seek out their project leader as necessary to get their jobs done. At the same time, the reward system valued engineers for completing their assigned work during short but intensive work hours, for maintaining areas of specialization, and for getting help from the project leader to ensure optimal time use. (Refer to Figure 1.3a.)

The first mutually reinforcing relationship on which we focus revolves around the role of the project leader and the hours worked. Having the project leader act as the central provider of help required that the work got done in the hours that the project leader was at work. It also required that engineers were present during those hours. The project leader was therefore encouraged to reward engineers for all working the same short, but tightly regulated, schedule. In turn, when engineers worked only those short and tightly regulated hours, there was pressure to maintain a system of helping that took advantage of the fact that engineers were all present during the same overlapping hours, but also that ensured the work got done in this constrained time period. This set of requirements reinforced the project leader's role as the

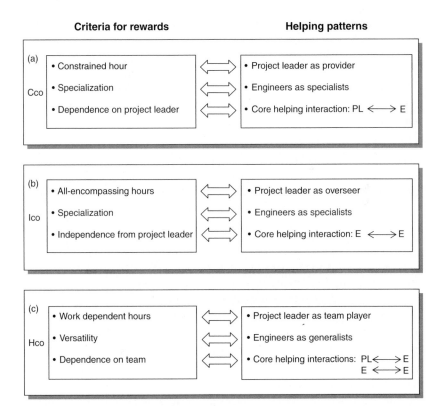

Figure 1.3   *Mutually reinforcing relationship between rewards and helping patterns*

central source of help, with the project leader focused on ensuring that the work got done as efficiently as possible.

The second mutually reinforcing relationship we focus on revolves around the engineers' role as specialists and the degree of specialization rewarded. At Cco, patterns of helping based on specialization reinforced a system that rewarded engineers for being specialists. Because the work required specialists, the project leader wanted to encourage engineers to be specialists. Rewarding specialists reinforced a system that revolved around the use of specialists to get the job done. Moreover, the engineers, rewarded for being specialists, put pressure on their project leader to provide them with work opportunities where they could act as specialists and further hone their areas of specialization.

Finally, the third mutually reinforcing relationship we focus on revolves around the dependencies between the project leader and engineers and the amount of managerial dependence rewarded. At Cco, the central dependency was between the project leader and the engineers, and the reward system valued engineers for being dependent on their project leader. A system that revolved around engineers seeking help from their project leader reinforced the valuing of engineers so they would remain dependent on their project leader. At the same time, encouraging engineers to be dependent on their project leader reinforced that the core helping interaction was between engineers and their project leader, and not between peer engineers.

Ico

At Ico, the project leader was more removed from the process than at Cco, and engineers completed their work with limited help from the project leader. Engineers depended on each other, based on their areas of specialization. At the same time, the reward system valued engineers for working all-encompassing hours independently from their project leader. (Refer to Figure 1.3b.)

In terms of the first mutually reinforcing relationship, at Ico the helping patterns did not include the project leader. Not having the project leader involved in the day-to-day execution of tasks allowed the project leader to spend time involved in other aspects of the work; however, it also meant that the project leader was not focused on ensuring the completion of work during a tightly constrained workday. The helping patterns at Ico reinforced a reward system that valued work hours being long and all encompassing, rather than short and rigid as at Cco, to ensure that the work got done. At the same time, because long hours were rewarded, there was less pressure to develop patterns of helping that ensured that work got done in a constrained number of hours. Instead, the rewarding of long hours reinforced the existence of helping patterns where the project leader did not need to spend a great deal of time acting as the primary source of help.

In terms of the second mutually reinforcing relationship, at Ico patterns of helping were based on specialization. As at Cco, this reinforced a rewarding of specialists to ensure that engineers would maintain the necessary specialization to do the work. And, rewarding specialists reinforced helping patterns based on areas of expertise.

Finally, in terms of the third mutually reinforcing relationship, the patterns of helping were between engineers rather than with their project leader, and managerial independence, not dependence, was rewarded. A system that depended on engineers seeking help from each other and not from the project leader reinforced valuing engineers for helping each other and not turning to the project leader. At the same time, rewarding independence from one's project leader reinforced the existence of patterns of helping between peer engineers, and not the project leader.

Hco

At Hco, the project leader and engineers worked together as a team with overlapping skills, helping each other as necessary. Hco engineers were rewarded based on their versatility and willingness to help whomever needed help to make sure that the team would succeed; they were evaluated based on output, not hours. (Refer to Figure 1.3c.)

At Hco, the first two mutually reinforcing relationships were particularly highly interrelated. The project leader's role was neither that of the central provider of help nor that of an overseer, but rather that of a team player. At the same time, the engineers were generalists, not specialists. The project leader and the engineers were therefore more easily substitutable, and did not all need to be at work during the same overlapping hours to ensure that each could complete his or her own deliverables. This emphasis on the team rather than particular individuals doing particular work reinforced the rewarding of engineers for getting the work done rather than working a fixed set of overlapping hours. Because team members, in turn, were not always there during the same overlapping hours, it forced them to develop ways of working that enabled them to make progress even if they were not all present. Rewarding hours based on getting the work done, rather than long hours, therefore reinforced a pattern of helping that revolved around everyone being able to help each other. Moreover, versatility was also rewarded, reinforcing team members' willingness to develop as generalists rather than specialists.

Furthermore, in terms of the third relationship, the patterns of helping at Hco existed between engineers and the project leader as well as among engineers, and dependence on the team was rewarded. Developing a pattern of helping with both the project leader and other engineers reinforced a dynamic where the project leader and the engineers were rewarded for being dependent more generally on the team than on anyone in particular. At the same time, rewarding people for being dependent more generally on the team rather than on any one particular individual reinforced patterns of helping among all of the members of the team.

Elements of institutional context

Given the cross-cultural nature of our data, we are able to further consider how these reward-helping systems were shaped by the larger context. What we observed was a tight link between the institutional context and the reward structures, which is highly consistent with existing literature (e.g., Maurice et al. 1980, Lincoln and Kalleberg 1990). In each of our three cases, government policies and family values appeared to shape the types of hours rewarded. The education and mobility systems appeared to influence whether engineers were rewarded for being specialists or generalists, and the mobility systems further appeared to shape the nature of the rewards that were offered.

Hours worked

At each site, rewards for hours worked were not only part of the mutually reinforcing relationship between the rewards and helping patterns; these rewards were further reinforced by government policies, and work and family values.

Cco. At Cco, work hours were short and rigid. Indeed, the Chinese government discouraged overtime – beyond five, eight-hour days a week – and required that engineers be paid extra for overtime work. Expressing a perception shared across engineers and managers at Cco, one manager explained: "The Government is concerned that it is not healthy for the workforce to overwork." Moreover, Cco engineers expressed a strong preference not to work overtime unless it was absolutely necessary to meet a deadline. As one engineer explained, "I work only eight hours a day, but I work very hard during those eight hours. I am very busy at work in order to avoid overtime." Cco engineers did not want work to dominate their lives. One engineer said, "I define success more broadly as a 'happy life' and one in which I don't need to always worry about tomorrow." Married engineers with children talked about their desire to maximize the amount of time that they could spend with their families. One engineer with a nine-month-old described, "My husband and I recently moved so I would be closer to our daughter when I am at work. We have a live-in babysitter, but I want to be close…. I want to maximize the time I can spend with my daughter."

Ico. At Ico, work hours were long and all encompassing. Ico engineers accepted the importance of these long work hours. One engineer commented, "There is a sense of commitment among the engineers that they will work as hard as necessary to get the job done. People don't complain, realizing that they must work – sometimes even through the night – until things are finished." Ico engineers believed work should come before all else, including family. They relied on their social networks to manage household chores and childcare responsibilities. One engineer, six months pregnant, explained: "I am not sure about the time I will be able to spend with my child. I would still be willing to accept on-site assignments if they are short, not more than six months. My in-laws and my parents will take care of the child." (Note: On-site assignments are overseas postings.) Indeed, with this type of support from relatives, Ico engineers apparently could devote themselves to work without feelings of conflict. One engineer described her parents as caregivers: "They raised me. I have no concerns.... I only feel responsible that my children are well brought up. I do not have to do it."

Hco. At Hco, work hours were the most responsive to work demands. More like Cco than Ico, neither engineers nor managers at Hco wanted to bow completely to the pressures of work. As one engineer explained, "Success in life means success at work, while also having a family and raising children." Individuals respected and protected each other's family time, developing ways to cover for each other so that neither the team's progress nor the individual's flexibility was hindered. Moreover, at Hco they stressed the importance of finding ways to balance success at work not only with time to appreciate their family, but also their culture and history. According to the senior manager: "One's job is critically important, but as a human being, there are other more important things ... culture and family. There are other things in life that matter besides money." On two different occasions, members of the Hco team insisted on taking the first author to concerts, explaining this was a critical part of who they were and how they worked.

Development of specialization

At each site, rewards for specialization were also a core part of the mutually reinforcing relationship between rewards and helping patterns. The rewards for specialization appeared to be further reinforced by elements of the larger institutional context. Specifically, both the education and mobility systems appeared to reinforce the rewards for specialization.

Cco. Cco managers suggested that the importance of specialists was supported by an educational system that trained individuals to be specialists. As one manager explained, comparing education in the United States and China: "In the U.S., the education system is focused on developing one's imagination. In China, the goal is to pour knowledge into a child's mind. We are not taught to think broadly, but to memorize the relevant facts."

Furthermore, the external labor market rewarded Cco engineers for being specialists. Cco engineers lived under a Communist system, where everyone was ensured a job. The issue for Cco engineers was whether they had a "good job," which to them was defined as working for a private firm, not the government. Engineers obtained "good jobs" based on having expertise in an area in which a firm needed to hire. To ensure that they always had a good job, engineers wanted jobs that would provide them with advanced technology tools, so they could continue to learn while working. They also wanted jobs that provided them with the time and opportunity to learn outside the job, both on their own and by attending training seminars.

If engineers did not receive developmental opportunities, they would move to a new organization. About a quarter of new engineers left within their first year at the company. Of the 40 people in the division studied, five had left the previous year and three had already left during the first six months of the current year. To retain their engineers, Cco managers felt immense pressure to provide engineers with opportunities to develop as specialists.

Ico. The reward-helping system at Ico, like the one at Cco, revolved around specialists, and was reinforced by both the education and mobility systems in India. Ico engineers, like Cco engineers, were trained as specialists and perceived that they could achieve their greatest career potential by developing marketable areas of expertise and switching jobs to increase opportunities. When engineers had skills in areas that they considered to be critical and in demand (whether at the company or elsewhere), they felt strongly about continuing to work in those areas to further develop their expertise.

Like Cco engineers, Ico engineers continually searched for jobs with better development opportunities and higher pay. One Ico engineer explained, "There is no loyalty. It is very different from my parents' generation where you worked at one company until retirement. I have already worked at four companies [she was 26 years old]. What is most important is my growth as an individual." Ico engineers had even more job offers within their country and abroad than Cco engineers, because of the strength of the software market in India and the engineers' greater freedom to enter and leave their country. According to the human resource manager, "Turnover at Ico is 22% a year." Like at Cco, Ico managers therefore experienced much pressure to find ways to accommodate engineers' desire for opportunities to further develop their areas of specialization, especially if they wanted to retain the most technically qualified engineers.

Hco. Unlike the reward-helping system at Cco and Ico that revolved around specialists, the system at Hco revolved around generalists. The centrality of generalists was reinforced by an education system that trains generalists. As one manager explained:

> There is something very unique about the Hungarian way of thinking. It is very colorful....
> Our language itself is more complex. Individuals must think very hard and deep about
> the words they choose to convey accurate meaning... contrast that with the narrow yes/no

form of the English language... the English dictionary is much thinner than the Hungarian dictionary.... From an early age, we come to have a greater sensitivity to problems... to understand them more broadly.

Moreover, the mobility system in Hungary produced generalists. Unlike Cco and Ico engineers, for whom job opportunities abounded, at Hco there was a looming fear of unemployment. As one manager explained:

> For 40 years of Communist rule, you were sent to jail if you didn't have a job and no one lost their job unless there was a real problem. To not have a job took on a very serious meaning. Today, with all the changes in the environment, many people find themselves without a job, but they haven't changed their idea of what it means to be unemployed, and so they don't know how to handle it. It gets them totally down. People know so many others who are unemployed that it is terrifying for them. It could happen to them or their families at any time.

Hco engineers perceived that their greatest job potential would be realized if Hco succeeded and they were part of that success. As a result, Hco employees were loyal to the company and eager to be part of its growth. When one engineer was asked where he wanted to be in 10 years, he responded, definitively, "at Hco." Engineers envisioned their future as highly connected to Hco's success, and as a result actively pursued opportunities to be part of the team, work together, and help and cover for each other to ensure the company's success. At the same time, because of the breadth of understanding of the project that the engineers developed, Hco managers invested heavily in keeping their engineers. Part of the way in which the project leader made such an investment was by working collaboratively with his engineers, reinforcing that they all were important members of the team working collectively to ensure the completion of the final product.

Nature of rewards

Beyond finding that elements of the institutional context appeared to affect the criteria for rewards, we further found the mobility system influenced the nature of the rewards. At Ico, where there was the most job mobility and engineers were single-mindedly focused on finding work that expanded their skill base so they could maintain mobility, Ico managers rewarded top-performing engineers with the most challenging work assignments – which in turn enabled them to learn the most in the process of doing their work. In contrast, at Hco, where job mobility was low and the foremost issue for engineers was job security, the reward for high-level work was a greater sense of job security. Moreover, at Hco, because job security ultimately involved not only one's own performance but the performance of one's teammates – so the company stayed in business – there was a much greater emphasis on team work and being a team player. Finally, at Cco, where job mobility was much greater than at Hco, but more limited than at Ico – mostly because of the fewer opportunities to go beyond their own country – high performance was rewarded by opportunities to develop skills that would in turn be useful for the company. Letting engineers spend long periods of time outside the workplace, while highly valued by the engineers, was perceived to be less risky at Cco than at Ico because Ico engineers would most likely leave upon returning from their training experience, while Cco engineers were more likely to continue to work for the organization. Cco could therefore afford this investment because the engineers were more likely to add value to the company when they returned.

Discussion and implications

We have conducted a multilevel exploration of software-engineering teams performing similar tasks at Cco, Ico, and Hco. We have found differences in helping patterns among engineers, as well as with their managers. We have further found that these patterns of helping appear to be part of mutually reinforcing relationships with the organization reward systems and, moreover, that these reward-helping systems are further reinforced by elements of the larger institutional context.

In the language of contingency, configuration, and congruence theorists, we have identified "fit" between multiple components: helping patterns, reward structures, and elements of the larger institutional context. As Schoonhoven (1981) pointed out, the underlying idea behind such theories of fit is that somehow the presence of one organizational structure enhances the impact of the others. When there is a lack of fit, the presence of one organizational structure undermines the impact of the others.

Contingency theory posits that organizational structures are most effective to the extent that they fit with the nature of the task and the requirements of the external environment (e.g., Lawrence and Lorsch 1967, Galbraith 1977). Configuration theory posits that organizational structures are most effective to the extent that they fit with each other, in the sense that they are working in the same direction and not at cross-purposes (e.g., Ichniowski et al. 1997). Congruence theory posits that organizations are most effective to the extent that the structures fit with each other, as well as with the nature of the task and the external environment (e.g., Nadler and Tushman 1997). Congruence theory further posits that organizations, to be effective, should achieve fit between their internal structures and the types of people who are hired, as well as with the informal culture of the organization (e.g., Tushman and O'Reilly 1997).

In this paper, we document "fit" with a key additional component. The components between which we find fit include institutional structures, organizational structures, *and* patterns of work group interaction. While the other theories include several of these components (particularly congruence theory, which is the most inclusive), none of them consider patterns of work group interaction as one of the components with which fit is achieved.

Furthermore, the primary mechanism for achieving fit among the various components differs in our data from that of contingency, configuration, and congruence theories. In each of those theories, fit is achieved through the design choices made by managers regarding the adoption of various components. Organizations whose managers choose components that fit together well are expected to thrive, while organizations whose managers make the wrong choices are expected to be less effective, and even to fail. In our data, by contrast, fit does not appear to occur simply due to managerial choice regarding various organizational practices. Rather, fit appears to occur through a process of mutual influence, where the components themselves shape the forms each other takes. In other words, work group interactions and organization practices shape each other (i.e., reward-helping system). That is not to suggest that managerial action does not play a role in shaping organization practices, but only that these practices are themselves part of a mutually reinforcing relationship that is beyond the manager's *direct* control.

Given these differences between our data and theories of contingency, configuration, and congruence, both in terms of the core components in need of fit and in how such fit is achieved, we turned to structuration theory to further understand our findings. What is unique about structuration theory as a theory of fit is the treatment of workplace interactions as a distinct organizational component in need of fit, and the process of mutual influence between workplace interactions and organizational structures as a distinct mechanism for achieving fit (Giddens 1984).

According to structuration theory, agents act within the constraints of structures in such a way that either reinforces or undermines those structures. In particular, structuration theorists have suggested that the form and meaning of prescribed structures are produced and reproduced through emergent interactions, and that the likelihood and content of emergent interactions are influenced by prescribed structures (e.g., Ranson et al. 1980). In addition, structuration theory has been specifically applied to patterns of interaction in work groups (e.g., Poole et al. 1996). Moreover, Pentland (1992), in a study of software support hot lines, has gone so far as to document how types of helping behaviors, in particular, both reflect and enact major structural features of the organization.

It is important to note that according to structuration theory, managerial choice does play a role in the adoption of organizational structures (Orlikowski and Yates 1994). However, while the structures can result from managerial choice, the patterns of interaction themselves do not result directly from managerial choice. Rather, the patterns of interaction are shaped by the structures that managers and others have chosen to implement in a particular workplace. These patterns of interaction, shaped by the organizational structures, in turn reinforce or alter the organization structures.

Applying structuration theory to our data sheds light on structuration theory as well as on alternative theories of fit (i.e., contingency, configuration, and congruence). Our data illustrate how the process of structuration may occur on multiple levels simultaneously, with each level of the mutually reinforcing relationship between action and structure itself in a mutually reinforcing relationship with structures at the next level. In other words, we found that patterns of interaction and elements of the organizational context appeared to create a mutually reinforcing relationship, which itself, as an entity, appeared to be reinforced by elements of the larger institutional context. And, in conjunction with theorizing by Barley and Tolbert (1997), we would expect that this relationship with the broader institutional context not only shapes but also is shaped by what goes on within the organization. Moreover, Feldman (2003) has documented how individuals' patterns of interaction or routines themselves shape and are shaped by individual action, which she notes are embedded in a process of shaping and being shaped by the organizational context. Taken together with existing literature, our findings therefore suggest a nested theory of structuration. Individual action and patterns of interaction mutually reinforce each other, and further are part of a mutually reinforcing relationship with elements of the organizational context (reward structure in our case). In turn, this relationship (the reward-helping system in our case) is itself further part of a mutually reinforcing relationship with elements of the larger institutional context. (See Figure 1.4 for a graphical depiction of this nested theory of structuration.)

There are, however, some important limitations of our theorizing stemming from the cross-sectional nature of our data. We are unable to provide compelling evidence that the reward-helping system shapes the institutional context; our data effectively suggest only how the institutional context shapes the reward-helping system. Moreover, we can only suggest the existence of a mutually reinforcing relationship between reward structures and helping patterns; we do not have the data to document its existence. Future research, ideally using longitudinal data, would benefit from further exploration into the existence of each of the multiple mutually reinforcing relationships illustrated in Figure 1.4.

Still, the nested theory of structuration suggested by our data raises important possibilities for better understanding alternative theories of fit, namely contingency, configuration, and congruence. Although structuration theory does not directly address the question of fit between organizational structures, the mechanism posited by structuration theory for achieving fit between organizational structures and workplace interaction – that of mutual influences – may help to explain whether organizational structures fit with each

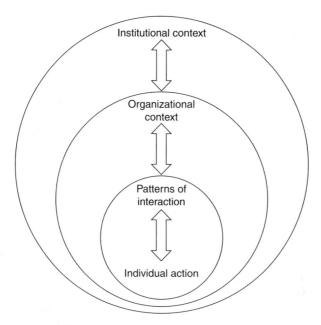

Figure 1.4   *Nested theory of structuration*

other. As Schoonhoven (1981) has pointed out, there has not previously been a theoretical rationale for why some organizational structures fit together, or enhance each other's impact, while other organizational structures lack fit. However, from a structuration standpoint, organizational structures would be said to fit with each other to the extent that they reinforce and are reinforced by the same patterns of interaction. In other words, for two organizational structures to fit with each other, they both must simultaneously be in their own unique mutually reinforcing relationship with the same pattern of interaction.

The nested theory of structuration suggested by our data also has implications for research that draws aggregate-level conclusions at either the group or cultural level of analysis. When aggregate measures are considered, important differences are overlooked. For instance, given the fraction of time spent interacting across the three sites, one would expect great similarity between Ico and Hco, and much larger differences with Cco, where half as much time was spent interacting. However, moving down a level to explore patterns of interaction, we have documented three distinct patterns of helping: expertise centered, team centered, and managerial centered, respectively.

This same critique of aggregate measures is also relevant to research that depends on aggregate measures of the cultural context. If one were to look at differences in cultural value orientations of the engineers we studied, as is typically done in cross-cultural comparative research (e.g., Hofstede 1980, Earley 1993), one would again predict different patterns of behavior from those that we observed. In terms of cultural value orientations, Hungary has been found to be the most individualistic and hierarchical of the three countries studied (Fiske et al. 1998, House et al. 1999). However, we found Hco to be the least hierarchical and the most collectivist in work orientation. We further found that Hco engineers were willing to help their colleagues because their job mobility was highly constrained, and they viewed their career success as dependent on the success of their firm. The institutional context therefore appears to have shaped the reward-helping system in a way that differs from that which the individualistic, hierarchical cultural-value orientations of Hungarians would predict.

This finding is consistent with a purely structural explanation of behavior, which finds social structures, not cultural values, are the antecedent of workplace dynamics (Bendix 1956, Dore 1973, Cole 1985). However, while cultural-value orientations in Hungary alone cannot explain patterns of helping at Hco, they may still play a role in shaping the institutional context, which in turn appears to play a central role in shaping the reward-helping systems. The Hungarians' individualistic cultural-value orientation, in conjunction with their education and mobility system that values generalists, means that to be successful as an individual, one must be a generalist. Helping others therefore becomes an essential component of one's own individual success. Cultural-value orientations should therefore, perhaps, be conceptualized as an additional outer ring in our nested theory of structuration, depicted in Figure 1.4. This proposition is consistent with a study of free riding in the United States and Japan, where Yamagishi (1988) found that, when comparing the behaviors of members of different cultures, one must focus on both value orientations and the institutional context. We are similarly suggesting that both value orientations and institutional context may influence behavior.

The nested theory of structuration emerging from our research also has important implications for better understanding and managing interaction patterns among group members, such as team learning (e.g., Edmondson 2002), coordination (e.g., Faraj and Sproull 2000, Gittell 2002), and knowledge sharing (e.g., Cummings and Cross 2003, Borgatti and Cross 2003), as well as helping (e.g., Burke et al. 1976, Lees 1997). What our nested theory of structuration suggests is that to sustain or change any of these patterns of interaction requires not just understanding the patterns of interaction themselves, but also the organizational, institutional, and cultural contexts that enable and constrain them.

Moreover, when team members are separated by space, time, organizational, and even cultural boundaries as they are in global virtual teams (Maznevski and Chudoba 2000), our nested theory of structuration suggests that managing interaction patterns presents additional challenges. Drawing on our data to construct a hypothetical example, suppose a global virtual team was formed comprising engineers from Cco, Ico, and Hco. Cco engineers would tend to look to their team leader for help, rather than to their peer engineers. If the team leader was from Ico, he or she would perceive the Cco engineers as lacking sufficient initiative to either solve problems on their own or to seek help from their peers with the appropriate expertise. The reverse problem would occur for Ico engineers with a Cco team leader. Hco engineers, on the other hand, would tend to look to anyone on the team for help, regardless of his or her area of expertise, meeting with resistance from Ico engineers who were accustomed to helping only in their particular area of expertise and from Cco engineers who expect engineers to seek help from their team leader rather than their peers. Similar conflicts would arise around rewards for work hours and rewards for specialization.

Even if the team leader was able to develop a common set of rewards for all members of the virtual team, those rewards would come into conflict with at least some of the institutional contexts in which team members lived and worked, as well as with some of the team members' pre-established patterns of interacting. What would happen next would depend on which force won out. If the change in the rewards dominated, and it affected enough people, it might begin to affect both people's patterns of interaction as well as their institutional context, shaping both to be more consistent with the new reward system. However, there would be great resistance to changing the reward system in those contexts in which the change was at odds with old patterns of interacting. Both the institutional context and individual repetition of old ways of interacting would likely undermine such a change or cause people to leave the organization.

In taking a multilevel approach to the study of how work gets done, we have highlighted a set of mutual, interconnected relationships that appear to shape and constrain patterns of work group interaction. Whether one strives to better understand patterns of interaction among group members such as team learning, coordination, knowledge sharing, or helping in a given context or across multiple contexts, our findings suggest that it is insufficient to explore these patterns in isolation, or even to just include the organizational, institutional, and cultural contexts in which these patterns occur. Rather, understanding the interconnections that exist across these multiple levels is essential to effectively sustain or change the patterns of interaction in play in organizations.

Acknowledgments

Work on this paper has been supported by a grant from the William Davidson Institute to the first author. The authors greatly appreciate the help of all the participants involved. Deborah Ancona, Lotte Bailyn, Allen Bluedorn, Robert Cross, Jane Dutton, Martha Feldman, Mauro Guillen, Casey Ichniowski, Nitin Nohria, Jeffrey Polzer, Michael Tushman, John Van Maanen, John Weeks, Leigh Weiss, and the participants at the University of Michigan ICOS, Wharton Labor Lunch, MIT OSG Seminar, and Harvard OB Research Seminar offered invaluable advice and suggestions.

Endnotes

[1] A data collection was done by the first author. However, for ease of exposition, we do not make this distinction in the text except in the data sources section.

[2] When Ico engineers needed help, they would often turn to their batch mates, others who had joined the company at the same time as them, or their classmates from university, who frequently worked at a competitor company.

References

Argote, L., M. E. Turner, and M. Fichman (1989), "To centralize or not to centralize: The effects of uncertainty and threat on group structure and performance," *Organ. Behavior Human Decision Processes*, Vol. 43, No. 1, pp. 58–75.

Barley, S. R. and G. Kunda (2001), "Bringing work back in," *Organ. Sci.*, Vol. 12, No. 1, pp. 76–95.

Barley, S. R. and J. E. Orr (1997), "Introduction: The neglected workforce," in S. R. Barley and J. E. Orr, Eds. *Between Craft and Science: Technical Work in U.S. Settings*. Cornell University Press, Ithaca, NY, pp. 1–9.

Barley, S. R. and P. S. Tolbert (1997), "Institutionalization and structuration: Studying the links between action and institution," *Organ. Stud.*, Vol. 18, No. 1, pp. 93–117.

Bavelas, A. (1950), "Communication patterns in task-oriented groups," *J. Acoustical Soc. America*, Vol. 22, pp. 725–730.

Bell, D. (1973), *The Coming of Post-Industrial Society*. Basic Books, New York.

Bendix, R. (1956), *Work and Authority in Industry*. University of California Press, Berkeley, CA.

Bond, R. and P. B. Smith (1996), "Culture and conformity: A meta-analysis of studies using Asch's line judgment task," *Psych. Bull.*, Vol. 119, No. 1, pp. 223–240.

Borgatti, S. P. and R. Cross (2003), "A relational view of information seeking and learning in social networks," *Management Sci*, Vol. 49, No. 4, pp. 432–445.

Brown, T. M. and C. E. Miller (2000), "Communication networks in task-performing groups: Effects of task complexity, time pressure, and interpersonal dominance," *Small Group Res.*, Vol. 31, No. 2, pp. 131–157.

Burke, R. J., T. Weir, and G. Duncan (1976), "Informal helping relationships in work organizations," *Acad. Management J.*, Vol. 19, No. 3, pp. 370–377.

Cole, R. (1985), "The macropolitics of organizational change: A comparative analysis of the spread of small group activities," *Admin. Sci. Quart.*, Vol. 30, No. 4, pp. 560–585.

Cummings, J. N. and R. Cross (2003), "Structural properties of work groups and their consequences for performance," *Soc. Networks*, Vol. 25, No. 3, pp. 197–210.

DeMatteo, J. S., L. T. Eby, and E. Sundstrom (1998), "Team-based rewards: Current empirical evidence and directions for future research," in Barry M. Staw and L. L. Cummings, Eds. *Research in Organizational Behavior*, Vol. 20. JAI Press, Greenwich, CT, pp. 141–183.

Dore, R. (1973), *British Factory-Japanese Factory*. University of California Press, Berkeley, CA.

Earley, P. C. (1993), "East meets West meets Mideast: Further explorations of collectivistic and individualistic work groups," *Acad. Management J.*, Vol. 36, No. 2, pp. 319–348.

Edmondson, A. C. (2002), "The local and variegated nature of learning in organizations: A group-level perspective," *Organ. Sci.*, Vol. 13, No. 2, pp. 128–146.

Faraj, S. and L. Sproull (2000), "Coordinating expertise in software development teams," *Management Sci*, Vol. 46, No. 12, pp. 1554–1568.

Feldman, M. S. (2003), "A performative perspective on stability and change in organizational routines," *Indust. Corporate Change*, Vol. 12, No. 4, pp. 727–752.

Fiske, A. P., S. Kitayama, H. R. Markus, and R. E. Nisbett (1998), "The cultural matrix of social psychology," in D. T. Gilbert, S. T. Fiske, and G. Lindzey, Eds. *The Handbook of Social Psychology*. McGraw-Hill, New York, pp. 915–981.

Galbraith, J. (1977), *Organization Design*. Addison-Wesley, Reading, MA.

Giddens, A. (1984), *The Constitution of Society*. University of California Press, Berkeley, CA.

Gittell, J. H. (2002), "Coordinating mechanisms in care provider groups: Relational coordination as a mediator and input uncertainty as a moderator of performance effects," *Management Sci.*, Vol. 48, No. 11, pp. 1408–1426.

Glaser, B. G. and A. L. Strauss (1967), *The Discovery of Grounded Theory: Strategies for Qualitative Research*. Aldine, New York.

Hackman, J. R. (2003), "Learning more by crossing levels: Evidence from airplanes, hospitals, and orchestras," *J. Organ. Behavior*, Vol. 24, No. 8, pp. 1–18.

Hamilton, G. G. and N. W. Biggart (1988), "Market, culture, and authority: A comparative analysis of management and organization in the Far East," *Amer. J. Sociology*, Vol. 94, pp. S52–S94.

Hofstede, G. (1980), *Culture's Consequences*. Sage Publications, Beverly Hills, CA.

House, R. J., P. J. Hanges, S. A. Ruiz-Quintanilla, P. W. Dorfman, M. Javidan, and M. Dickson, 170 GLOBE Country co-investigators (1999), Cultural influences on leadership and organizations: Project Globe. Unpublished manuscript, University of Pennsylvania, Philadelphia, PA.

Ichniowski, C., K. Shaw, and G. Prennushi (1997), "The effects of human resource management practices on productivity: A study of steel finishing lines," *Amer. Econom. Rev.*, Vol. 87, No. 3, pp. 291–313.

IDC (1995), Overview of the Hungarian Software and Services Industry. IDC, Kronberg, Germany.

Johns, G. (2001), "In praise of context," *J. Organ. Behavior*, Vol. 22, No. 1, pp. 31–42.

Kozlowski, S. W. and K. J. Klein (2000), "A multi-level approach to theory and research in organizations: Contextual, temporal, and emergent processes," in K. Klein and S. Kozlowski, Eds. *Multilevel Theory, Research, and Methods in Organizations: Foundations, Extensions, and New Directions*. Jossey-Bass, San Francisco, CA, pp. 3–90.

Lawrence, P. R. and J. W. Lorsch (1967), *Organization and Environment: Managing Differentiation and Integration*. Harvard Business School Press, Boston, MA.

Leavitt, H. (1951), "Some effects of certain communication patterns on group performance," *J. Abnormal Soc. Psych.*, Vol. 46, pp. 38–50.

Lee, F. (1997), "When the going gets tough, do the tough ask for help? Help seeking and power motivation in organizations," *Organ. Behavior Human Decision Processes*, Vol. 72, No. 3, pp. 336–363.

Lincoln, J. R. and A. L. Kalleberg (1990), *Culture, Control, and Commitment: A Study of Work Organization and Work Attitudes in the United States and Japan*. Cambridge University Press, Cambridge, U.K.

Mann, L. (1980), "Cross-cultural studies of small groups," in H. C. Triandis and R. W. Brislin, Eds. *Handbook of Cross-Cultural Psychology*. Allyn & Bacon, Boston, MA, pp. 155–209.

March, J. and H. Simon (1958), *Organizations*. John Wiley & Sons, New York.

Maurice, M., A. Sorge, and M. Warner (1980), "Societal differences in organizing manufacturing units: A comparison of France, West Germany, and Great Britain," *Organ. Stud.*, Vol. 1, pp. 59–86.

Maznevski, M. L. and K. M. Chudoba (2000), "Bridging space over time: Global virtual team dynamics and effectiveness," *Organ. Sci.*, Vol. 11, No. 5, pp. 473–492.

Miles, M. B. and A. M. Huberman (1984), *Qualitative Data Analysis: A Source Book of New Methods*. Sage Publications, Beverly Hills, CA.

Monge, P. R. and N. S. Contractor (2001), "The emergence of communication networks," in F. M. Jablin and L. L. Putnam, Eds. *The New Handbook of Organizational Communication: Advances in Theory, Research, and Methods*. Sage Publications, Thousand Oaks, CA, pp. 440–502.

Nadler, D. A. and M. L. Tushman (1997), *Competing by Design: The Power of Organizational Architecture*. Oxford University Press, New York.

NASSCOM (1997), *The Software Industry in India: Strategic Review 1997–98*. NASSCOM, New Delhi, India.

Orlikowski, W. and J. Yates (1994), "Genre repertoire: The structuring of communicative practices in organizations," *Admin. Sci. Quart.*, Vol. 39, No. 4, pp. 54l–l574.

Pentland, B. (1992), "Organizing moves in software support hot lines," *Admin. Sci. Quart.*, Vol. 37, No. 4, pp. 527–548.

Perlow, L. A. (1999), "The time famine: Towards a sociology of work time," *Admin. Sci. Quart.*, Vol. 44, No. 1, pp. 57–81.

Poole, M. S., D. R. Seibold, and R. D. McPhee (1996), "The structuration of group decisions," in R. W. Hirokawa and M. S. Poole, Eds. *Communication and Group Decisionmaking*. Sage Publications, Thousand Oaks, CA, pp. 114–146.

Ranson, S., B. Minings, and R. Greenwood (1980), "The structuring of organizational structures," *Admin. Sci. Quart.*, Vol. 25, No. 1, pp. 1–17.

Rousseau, D. M. and Y. Fried (2001), "Location, location, location: Contextualizing organizational research," *J. Organ. Behavior*, Vol. 22, No. 1, pp. 1–13.

Schoonhoven, C. B. (1981), "Problems with contingency theory: Testing assumptions hidden within the language of contingency "theory." *Admin. Sci. Quart.*, Vol. 26, No. 3, pp. 349–377.

Seers, A., M. Petty, and J. Cashman (1995), "Team-member exchange under team and traditional management," *Group Organ. Management*, Vol. 20, No. 1, pp. 18–38.

Shaw, M. E. and G. H. Rothschild (1956), "Some effects of prolonged experience in communication nets," *J. Appl. Psych.*, Vol. 40, pp. 218–286.

Sparrowe, R. T., R. C. Liden, S. J. Wayne, and M. L. Kraimer (2001), "Social networks and the performance of individuals and groups," *Acad. Management J.*, Vol. 44, No. 2, pp. 316–325.

Stokols, D. (1981), "Group x place interactions: Some neglected issues in psychological research on settings," in D. Magnusson, Ed. *Toward a Psychology of Situations: An Interactional Perspective*. Lawrence Erlbaum Associates, Hillsdale, NJ, pp. 393–415.

Thompson, J. D. (1967), *Organizations in Action*. McGraw-Hill, New York.

Tushman, M. L. and C. A. O'Reilly (1997), *Winning Through Innovation: A Practical Guide to Leading Organizational Change and Renewal*. Harvard Business School Press, Boston, MA.

Yamagishi, T. (1988), "Exit from the group as an individualistic solution to the free rider problem in the United States and Japan," *J. Experiment. Soc. Psych.*, Vol. 24, No. 6, pp. 530–542.

Questions for discussion

1 If you were an IT manager at a large national bank thinking of outsourcing the development of a new loan management software would you choose to outsource to a software development team in India, China, or Hungary?

2 Would your own location make a difference? If so, in what way? What other factors would affect your choice of a location?

3 How might you expect a cross-cultural software development team to function? Suppose a team consisted of members from India, China, and Hungary. What problems might you expect to arise?

4 If you were a software developer, which of the three software development teams would you prefer to work on?

5 Do you feel that one of the three teams exhibited "best practice" behavior more than the other two? If so, which one and why?

2   Cross-Cultural Software
Production and Use:
A Structurational Analysis[1]

Geoff Walsham

Abstract: This paper focuses on cross-cultural software production and use, which is increasingly common in today's more globalized world. A theoretical basis for analysis is developed, using concepts drawn from structuration theory. The theory is illustrated using two cross-cultural case studies. It is argued that structurational analysis provides a deeper examination of cross-cultural working and IS than is found in the current literature, which is dominated by Hofstede-type studies. In particular, the theoretical approach can be used to analyze cross-cultural conflict and contradiction, cultural heterogeneity, detailed work patterns, and the dynamic nature of culture. The paper contributes to the growing body of literature that emphasizes the essential role of cross-cultural understanding in contemporary society.

Introduction

There has been much debate over the last decade about the major social transformations taking place in the world such as the increasing interconnectedness of different societies, the compression of time and space, and an intensification of consciousness of the world as a whole (Robertson 1992). Such changes are often labeled with the term globalization, although the precise nature of this phenomenon is highly complex on closer examination. For example, Beck (2000) distinguishes between *globality,* the change in consciousness of the world as a single entity, and *globalism,* the ideology of neoliberalism which argues that the world market eliminates or supplants the importance of local political action.

Despite the complexity of the globalization phenomena, all commentators would agree that information and communication technologies (ICTs) are deeply implicated in the changes that are taking place through their ability

[1]Michael D. Myers was the accepting senior editor for this paper.

to enable new modes of work, communication, and organization across time and space. For example, the influential work of Castells (1996, 1997, 1998) argues that we are in the "information age" where information generation, processing, and transformation are fundamental to societal functioning and societal change, and where ICTs enable the pervasive expansion of networking throughout the social structure.

However, does globalization, and the related spread of ICTs, imply that the world is becoming a homogeneous arena for global business and global attitudes, with differences between organizations and societies disappearing? There are many authors who take exception to this conclusion. For example, Robertson (1992) discussed the way in which imported themes are *indigenized* in particular societies with local culture constraining receptivity to some ideas rather than others, and adapting them in specific ways. He cited Japan as a good example of these *glocalization* processes. While accepting the idea of time-space compression facilitated by ICTs, Robertson argued that one of its main consequences is an exacerbation of collisions between global, societal, and communal attitudes. Similarly, Appadurai (1997), coming from a non-western background, argued against the global homogenization thesis on the grounds that different societies will appropriate the "materials of modernity" differently depending on their specific geographies, histories, and languages. Walsham (2001) developed a related argument, with a specific focus on the role of ICTs, concluding that global diversity needs to be a key focus when developing and using such technologies.

If these latter arguments are broadly correct, then working with ICTs in and across different cultures should prove to be problematic, in that there will be different views of the relevance, applicability, and value of particular modes of working and use of ICTs which may produce conflict. For example, technology transfer from one society to another involves the importing of that technology into an "alien" cultural context where its value may not be similarly perceived to that in its original host culture. Similarly, cross-cultural communication through ICTs, or cross-cultural information systems (IS) development teams, are likely to confront issues of incongruence of values and attitudes.

The purpose of this paper is to examine a particular topic within the area of cross-cultural working and ICTs, namely that of software production and use; in particular, where the software is not developed in and for a specific cultural group. A primary goal is to develop a theoretical basis for analysis of this area. Key elements of this basis, which draws on structuration theory, are described in the next section of the paper. In order to illustrate the theoretical basis and its value in analyzing real situations, the subsequent sections draw on the field data from two published case studies of cross-cultural software development and application.

There is an extensive literature on cross-cultural working and IS, and the penultimate section of the paper reviews key elements of this literature, and shows how the analysis of this paper makes a new contribution. In particular, it will be argued that the structurational analysis enables a more sophisticated and detailed consideration of issues in cross-cultural software production under four specific headings: cross-cultural contradiction and conflict; cultural heterogeneity; detailed work patterns in different cultures; and the dynamic, emergent nature of culture. The final section of the paper will summarize some theoretical and practical implications.

Structuration theory, culture and IS

The theoretical basis for this paper draws on structuration theory (Giddens 1979, 1984). This theory has been highly influential in sociology and the social sciences generally since Giddens first developed the ideas some 20 years ago. In addition, the theory has received considerable attention in the IS field (for a good review, see Jones 1998). The focus here, however, will be on how structuration theory can offer a new way of looking at cross-cultural working and information systems. The rest of this section develops this analysis. A summary of key points is provided in Table 2.1.

Structuration theory is described by Giddens as an "ontology of social life" or, in other words, a description of the nature of human action and social organization. At the heart of the theory is the attempt to treat human action and social structure as a duality rather than a dualism. In other words, rather than seeing human action taking place within the context of the "outside" constraints of social structure (a dualism), action and structure are seen as two aspects of the same whole (a duality). This device is achieved in part by a careful redefinition of the meaning of structure. Giddens defines structure as:

> Rules and resources, recursively implicated in the reproduction of social systems. Structure exists only as memory traces, the organic basis of human knowledgeability, and as instantiated in action (1984, p. 377).

The crucial point here is that structure, defined in this way, is seen as rules of behavior and the ability to deploy resources, which exist *in the human mind itself,* rather than as outside constraints. (This distinction is often misunderstood in the IS literature which draws on structuration theory; see Jones 1998.) The actions, therefore, of an individual human being draw on these rules and resources and, in so doing, produce or reproduce structure in the mind. So, for example, a manager who reprimands an employee for arriving late at the workplace is drawing on the concept of the start time of an employee, the rule that the employee should arrive before or at this time, and

Table 2.1   *Structuration theory, culture, and ICTs: some key concepts*

Structure	• Structure as memory traces in the human mind • Action draws on rules of behavior and ability to deploy resources and, in so doing, produces and reproduces structure • Three dimensions of action/structure: systems of meaning, forms of power relations, sets of norms • IS embody systems of meaning, provide resources, and encapsulate norms, and are thus deeply involved in the modalities linking action and structure
Culture	• Conceptualized as shared symbols, norms, and values in a social collectivity such as a country • Meaning systems, power relations, behavioral norms not merely in the mind of one person, but often display enough systemness to speak of them being shared • But need to recognize intra-cultural variety
Cross-cultural contradiction and conflict	• Conflict is actual struggle between actors and groups • Contradiction is potential basis for conflict arising from divisions of interest, e.g., divergent forms of life • Conflicts may occur in cross-cultural working if differences affect actors negatively and they are able to act
Reflexivity and change	• Reproduction through processes of routinization • But human beings reflexively monitor actions and consequences, creating a basis for social change

the perceived ability for the manager to deploy the human resource represented by the employee, and thus to reprimand the employee for being late.
In carrying out this action, the manager and the employee have the structure
of these rules and resources reinforced in their minds as standards of appropriate behavior.

In order to develop a more detailed analysis of the duality of structure, as
defined above, Giddens introduced three dimensions concerned with systems
of meaning, forms of power relations, and sets of norms. Human action and
structure in the mind are composed, according to structuration theory, of elements of each of these dimensions but, as the example of the manager and
the employee above demonstrated, the dimensions are inextricably inter-
linked. So the power to reprimand is linked to the concept of starting time
and the norm of what it means to be late. This may seem obvious, but norms
of behavior such as this vary widely between cultures. In our analysis later
in the paper, it will be seen that it is precisely some of these differences "in

the mind" as to what is appropriate behavior that can cause conflict in cross-cultural working.

Culture, at its most basic level, can be conceptualized as shared symbols, norms, and values in a social collectivity such as a country. In Giddens' terms, systems of meaning, forms of power relations, and norms of behavior have a more widespread currency than *merely* within the mind of one person. Giddens defines these as *structural properties,* namely "structured features of social systems stretching across time and space." He comments that social systems should be regarded as widely variable in the degree of *systemness* that they display, and he says that they rarely have the sort of internal unity which may be found in physical or biological systems. In other words, related to the focus of this paper, national cultures are composed of many different people, each with a complex structure in their mind, none of which can be thought of as fully shared. For example, there will be all sorts of nuance as to how individuals view lateness, even within the same cultural context. Nevertheless, it will be argued in this paper that the structural properties of cultures often display enough systemness for us to speak about shared symbols, norms, and values, while recognizing that there will remain considerable intra-cultural variety.

There have been a number of attempts to incorporate information systems within the theoretical framework of structuration theory (e.g., DeSanctis and Poole 1994; Orlikowski 1992). Giddens himself makes little direct reference to information technology in his development of the theory, so that the IS researcher is left to his or her own devices. This paper draws on the conceptualization in Walsham (1993, p. 64), where he argues that:

> A theoretical view of computer-based information systems in contemporary organizations which arises from structuration theory is that they embody interpretative schemes, provide coordination and control facilities, and encapsulate norms. They are thus deeply implicated in the modalities that link social action and structure, and are drawn on in interaction, thus reinforcing or changing social structures.

In other words, IS are drawn on to provide meaning, to exercise power, and to legitimize actions. They are thus deeply involved in the duality of structure.

There is one further element in structuration theory, which has not been widely referred to in the literature, and certainly not in the IS literature, that is of considerable theoretical value in the study of cross-cultural working. This is Giddens' discussion of conflict and structural contradiction. He defines and discusses these concepts as follows:

> By conflict I mean actual struggle between actors or groups...whereas contradiction is a structural concept.... Conflict and contradiction tend to coincide because contradiction expresses the main "fault lines" in the structural contradiction of societal systems (1984, p. 198).

Conflict is thus real activity, while contradiction can be thought of as the *potential basis* for conflict, arising from structural contradictions within and between social groupings. Giddens elaborates on this:

> contradictions tend to involve divisions of interest between different groupings or catego-
> ries of people… . Contradictions express divergent modes of life and distributions of life
> chances...If contradiction does not inevitably breed conflict, it is because the conditions
> not only under which actors are aware of their interests but are able and motivated to act
> on them are widely variable (1984, pp198–199).

This theorizing has immediate application to cross-cultural working and IS. Contradictions include "divergent modes of life," which can be taken to include cultural differences. They *may* result in conflict if actors feel that the differences affect them negatively, and they are able and motivated to take positive action of some sort. We will see examples of this in the later empirical material.

Structuration theory appears at first sight to be focused on reproduction of structure in the mind, and broader social structures within societies, through processes of routinization of activity and thus reinforcement of existing structures. However, Giddens also emphasizes human knowledgeability, and the way in which human beings reflexively monitor their own actions, that of others, and consequences, both intended and unintended. The latter provides an example of the basis for social change as well as social stability. If a human being takes action and he or she subsequently views the unintended consequences of this as negative, then it is likely that different action will be taken in similar circumstances in the future, with related changed structure in the mind. The following empirical sections will analyze stability and reproduction, but will also focus on change processes.

Software production in a cross-cultural team

This section is the first of two designed to illustrate the value of the theoretical basis described above, and focuses on a cross-cultural software development team. Software development in the context of a more globalized world is no longer carried out exclusively within the country that needs it, using citizens from that country, but is increasingly outsourced through nonlocal arrangements such as body-shopping and global software outsourcing (Lacity and Willcocks 2001), and the use of global software teams (Carmel 1999). The case below provides a specific example of this in a Jamaican insurance company, with the cross-cultural element being the extensive involvement of a team of Indian software developers. The description of the case below draws from papers by Barrett and Walsham (1995) and Barrett et al. (1996), but the structurational analysis is new.[2]

Case description

The case concerns a Jamaican general insurance company, called Abco, which formed part of a broader Jamaican conglomerate, called the Jagis Group. Jamaica is located in the high risk catastrophe region of the Caribbean, but the capital base of general insurers in Jamaica is insufficient for high risk insurance coverage, such as that caused by earthquake and hurricane. Jamaican general insurance companies thus rely on worldwide reinsurers, who underwrite some of these high risks. In 1988, Hurricane Gilbert swept through Jamaica, paralyzing business activities on the island for a couple of months. At Abco, computer records were lost, and claims were made on policies that did not exist on the batch system.

After the hurricane and other world catastrophes, reinsurance not only became a problem to obtain, but reinsurers started to demand better quality information from companies such as Abco on risks and levels of exposure.

Responding to this crisis, the Jagis Group's chairman led an investigation as to how IT/IS could be used to provide superior quality service to clients through improved claims handling, as well as providing reinsurers with the more detailed risk and exposure information that they required. The decision was made to develop a new general insurance information system, called Goras. A leading management consultancy was commissioned to conduct the requirements study and a group software development company, Gtec, was set up within Abco in order to strengthen existing information technology skills. In March 1990, an Indian software expert, Raj, and other experienced Indian software developers were recruited from software houses in India to form the top management group of Gtec.

After the requirements study, bids were invited for the job of carrying out the software development, and Gtec was selected. However, in the initial stages of development, it became clear that additional expertise in insurance systems was needed, and a selected team of Jamaicans from the Jagis Group was seconded to the project as insurance consultants, including Roberts, the MIS manager of Jagis. The initial stages of the project were marked by some enthusiasm, at least by team members at the programmer level. Drawing from their experience on past development projects, Indian developers provided guidance to the

---

[2]Readers should refer to the earlier published material for details of the research methodology and data collection methods. As a member of the research team, the author had access to all the field notes from the study and has chosen quotes from these as appropriate to illustrate the theme of the current paper, and the new theoretical analysis carried out here.

Jamaican members on software development issues. There were weekly awards for the "most helpful member" and "project champion," and cash incentives for meeting deadlines. A key developer at Gtec reflected later:

> Looking back at it now, it was well organized. Every Monday, a memo came out specifying the deliverables and bonus structure for the week. There was a bonus on top of your salary if you met deadlines…but it was so hard to make your deadlines… . Though teams were compliant, deadlines were rather stringent, if not unreasonable.

As time went by, conflict started to develop between the Indians and the Jamaicans, particularly at the senior and team leader levels. Raj was viewed by the Jamaicans as having an autocratic approach as he would "lay down the law which was not to be questioned." In contrast, the senior Jamaican on the project team, Roberts, viewed an appropriate management style with Jamaicans as being more consensual:

> If there is a problem to be solved, we would sit down and solve it… . It was not a sort of hierarchy… . It was a team effort, meet and discuss each project.

Resentment by the Jamaican software developers at all levels had deeper roots than specific conflicts on management style, since some of the locals believed that Indians were not needed in the first place. A key Gtec developer expressed this sentiment:

> The Abco MIS staff felt the whole project had been taken away from them … . They were the natural group to be utilized to develop a new general insurance system for Abco. Instead [the management consultancy] who were a bag of Indians again were asked to do the functional requirements and the initial design. Later on, Gtec was formed, staffed by Indians in all the senior posts, and responsible for the Goras project… . The Indians had been given power over the Jamaicans.

There are, of course, two sides to these cross-cultural issues. Raj, for example, was critical of the more laid-back attitude the Jamaicans had to deadlines, regarding their formal working hours as being all they were prepared to offer to the project:

> With the Indians, there is no discussion once the deadline is agreed; they will work until 9 p.m. every night, weekends if necessary to have it on my desk at the stipulated time. However, with the Jamaicans, this is not the case. If the worker recognizes that they cannot meet the deadline, they will call me up and give some excuse as to why they need more time…they expect me to understand and accommodate.

Raj also felt that there were significant cultural differences in the way that project activities were coordinated. In India, that task was handled by the project manager whose job was "walking around and seeing how people are progressing," coordinating and administering activities, while in Jamaica project coordination was seen by him to be inherently problematic. Raj attributed this to Jamaicans' inability to "link hands and do parallel work." To illustrate this point, he offered an analogy of Jamaica's performance at international athletics events:

> They are fantastic runners...they only miss out on medals at international relay races because at the interchange of the baton, it is dropped or it is passed too late outside the permitted exchange...there is no training to coordinate and keep things moving.

In contrast, a Jamaican member of the software team viewed the Indian approach to coordination as representing an adult-child mentality, related also in his mind to the Indian caste structure:

> The strict deadlines seemed impossible, and I was not used to the interpersonal relations of the closely knit teams. . . . I was reluctant to fully integrate myself into the environment which was different to what we [Jagis MIS staff] were used to. . . . It was a school room attitude, with someone senior to me telling me to do as he says. . . . It was hard to relate to their caste system where hierarchy and status were so important.

These comments relate to differences in deep-seated cultural attitudes to hierarchy and authority that were recognized on the Indian side also, but of course with a different emphasis on their merits and demerits. Raj gave his view of Jamaicans' attitudes in these areas as follows:

> Everybody treats everybody as equal. The boss is viewed as a supervisor but at the same time they expect to be treated as equal. If something is due at the end of the month, don't intervene [as the boss]...the attitude is, "I will tell you if the job is done or not, then we reset the date and keep going. . . . If you feel performance is bad, then fire me with redundancy pay". . . . They don't want a monitoring system. . . . It is demeaning to them if the boss asks about progress of activities in between tasks.

The above quotes from the case study may be thought to reflect racial stereotyping on the part of some of the Indian and Jamaican software developers and managers.[3] They have been reproduced here to exemplify some of the

---

[3]A reader of this section may indeed believe that some of the organizational members were engaging in racial or ethnic stereotyping. Regardless of whether this is or is not the case, we need to make it clear that any such stereotyping reflects the values of those particular organizational members. It does not necessarily reflect the values of other organizational members and it does not reflect the values of the researcher who is reporting the organizational members' words. Such stereotyping also does not reflect the values of the editorial policy of the journal publishing the research. We believe it is the responsibility of researchers to report, rather than to cleanse or censure, the data that they collect, where such data include the subjective interpretations that are constructed and held by the organizational members themselves. *MIS Quarterly* stands behind the author of this study in reporting his data, although this does not amount to any endorsement of the organizational members' own opinions.

Michael D. Myers, Senior Editor

broader issues and problems, which were interpreted by some participants to have arisen from the different cultural backgrounds of the team members. However, not all members subscribed to these views in a simple way, and the importance of individual diversity and difference within the national groups was recognized. For example, the project approach reflected the personality of Raj, in addition to elements derived from his cultural background, and this did not pass unnoticed, demonstrated by his removal from the role in the later history of the case study, as described below.

But first, how successful was the initial project in the cross-cultural team environment? The development of Goras started in 1990. The original plan envisaged a year for completion, but there were significant delays and major project cost overruns. The acceptance testing done by end users showed substantial inadequacies in the design, but the system was finally delivered by Gtec to Abco in August 1992. After further quality assurance, user testing, and system modification, a first attempt at implementation was made in December 1992. The implementation was not a success. System performance was poor in terms of time taken to carry out tasks, and users were critical of the restricted functionality of the new system, partly due to incomplete data conversion from the old system.

In January 1993, a new CEO of Gtec was appointed, also an Indian expatriate. Raj stayed on as technical director, "preferring to work on technical issues rather than organizational ones." The responsibility for further development of the Goras system and user acceptance testing and training was switched to the Jagis group, although Gtec continued to make a technical input. By 1995, the Goras system had still not been fully implemented, but new deadlines were in place for implementation later that year. An increased emphasis had been placed on user involvement. One of the Jagis staff described this involvement:

> Testing started in July [1994] with live data from users. Each module is being tested module-by-module and then issue forms are created which then involve a lot of work on the part of MIS [staff] to implement the required changes.

Five years after project inception, there was general optimism about successful project implementation, but it still remained a promise rather than a reality.

Structurational analysis

Structure

This subsection analyzes the Abco case using the theory articulated earlier. Key points of the analysis are summarized in Table 2.2. Structure "in the mind" and its links to action, according to structuration theory, can be analyzed through

Table 2.2   *Jamaica–India software development case: structurational analysis*

Structure	• Different meaning systems: metaphor of teamwork as a school room attitude or international relay races • Different views of appropriate power relations: Indians too autocratic; Jamaicans too equal for project control purposes • Different norms of behavior: attitude to time deadlines on software projects
Culture	• Strong degree of systemness in terms of different cultural attitudes of Indian and Jamaican groups • But important to note that individual difference also matters • Culture of IS development also different in the two national groups: high productivity/strict deadlines versus working closely with end users/application backlog
Cross-cultural contradiction and conflict	• Structural contradiction arising from different cultural backgrounds • Resulted in conflict since these affected all participants directly, and they had the ability to act: e.g., to enforce deadlines or to resist them
Reflexivity and change	• Increasing recognition on all sides that cross-cultural issues were important, and needed to be managed • Pragmatic actions taken on roles and responsibilities, reflecting changed structure on the part of both Jamaican and Indian participants

the dimensions of meaning, power, and norms. Cross-cultural interaction is likely to involve basic differences in these dimensions, and the development of information systems in a cross-cultural team can bring these differences into stark contrast. With respect to meaning, metaphors of teamwork used by Abco and Gtec staff can be used as an illustration. A Jamaican software developer described the Indians' approach as a "school room attitude," linked in the mind of this person to the Indian caste system. In contrast, the Indian project leader used the metaphor of international relay races as a way of illustrating his view that the Jamaicans were incapable of working together in a coordinated way.

Turning to the second structural dimension, the case study shows radically different views of appropriate personal and power relations. The Indian team leader was viewed as autocratic by the Jamaican staff, whereas the senior Jamaican staff member thought that an appropriate management style in Jamaica was consensual. In contrast, the Indian team leader felt that the Jamaicans were too equal to make project monitoring and control effective. Related issues arose with respect to the third structural dimension of norms of behavior, for example, with respect to time deadlines for software projects and a sense of urgency. The Indian team leader was critical that the Jamaicans would go home at the "normal" leaving time, whereas the Indian team members would work evenings and weekends if necessary to meet deadlines.

Culture

The above analysis, in order to make some general points, has downplayed individual differences within the Jamaican and Indian groups. This can be justified on the grounds that there was some consistency of the responses from within each cultural group which supports the argument that there was a strong degree of systemness operating here. In other words, the indigenous elements of Jamaican and Indian national cultures were sufficiently strong in the minds of the individuals concerned to influence their behavior in a broadly similar way to other members of their own culture and, equally importantly, for this to be perceived as such by members of the other culture. However, as noted in the case description, individuals also matter, and the personality of Raj was given as one example of this.

In addition to the influence of national culture, the word *culture* is often as a metaphor (Morgan 1986) for shared values and attitudes within a specific organization or other form of social grouping: In the Abco case, Barrett and Walsham (1995, p. 30) highlighted how the culture of IS development was different in the two countries:

> While occupational cultures for Indians and Jamaicans alike originated from software development, the impact of the local work culture at Indian software houses and the insurance company respectively were significantly different. The norms of an Indian software house include high productivity and profitability, the software development being driven from a specification under strict project deadlines. The norms of an insurer's MIS department in Jamaica involve application development by MIS personnel working closely with end users with a backlog of applications being quite acceptable.

Cross-cultural contradiction and conflict

Contradiction reflects differences in structural principles, according to structuration theory, such as those arising from different cultural backgrounds. However, conflict is an actual struggle, and we have seen that significant struggle did indeed take place in the case. It was argued earlier that this is likely to occur, first, if the differences affect actors negatively. With respect to the Jamaicans, they felt the force of the structural contradictions in cultural attitudes in a very direct way through Indian approaches to project monitoring and control, attitudes to deadlines and working hours, and what they viewed as excessively hierarchical approaches. The Indian management team, in particular the overall team leader, viewed these as the right way to approach software development, and the Jamaicans' attitudes as largely negative to the goal of effective project monitoring and control. The second condition for actual conflict to arise along the fault lines of the structural contradictions is that the participants have the ability to act to support their perceived position. The Indian management team had the recognized authority to control the project and to make the rules, such as time deadlines. On the other hand, the Jamaican team members were able to resist in various ways, such as giving reasons why more time was needed for a particular software task. In addition, the removal of Raj from the CEO role in the later history of the project can be taken to reflect the resistance of some of the software team members to his leadership.

Reflexivity and change

The analysis so far has focused on the way in which structure in the minds of actors in cross-cultural interaction affects the way they think and behave, and the way in which they perceive others from a different culture, which may result in disagreement and conflict. However, as noted in the earlier theoretical section, human beings reflexively monitor actions and their consequences, creating a basis for social change. In other words, structure and culture are not immutable. This can be illustrated in the Jamaica–India software development project, in that there was an increasing recognition on all sides that cross-cultural issues were important and that they needed to be managed effectively. This resulted, in the later years of the project, in various actions being taken to mitigate the problems which had occurred. These actions included shifting the role of Raj away from organizational issues to a primarily technical role, and giving increased responsibility for human issues such as user involvement to the Jamaican MIS group. These actions not only reflected a pragmatic interest in getting a better job done, but also changed attitudes, or structure in the mind in Giddens' terms, on the part of the Jamaican and Indian participants.

Technology transfer of GIS software

A second way in which software is involved in cross-cultural interaction is through the transfer of IS across borders to different cultural environments from that in which it was initially developed. This technology transfer phenomenon is not a new one, but it is increasingly common in the context of globalization. For example, major software packages such as enterprise resource planning systems have spread extremely rapidly across much of the world, particularly in large organizations, over the last decade (Davenport 1998). The case described in this section will provide a specific example of the technology transfer of another global technology, namely that of geographical information systems (GIS). In particular, the case looks at the transfer of GIS from the United States to India. The description of the case below draws from the paper by Walsham and Sahay (1999), but the structurational analysis is new.[4]

Case description

The case concerns attempts to develop and use geographical information systems (GIS) to aid district-level administration in India. In particular, the focus is a set of GIS projects that took place under the umbrella of the Ministry of Environment and Forests (MOEF) of the government of India over the period 1991 through 1996. The technical work to develop the systems was carried out by scientists in a range of institutions, including two remote sensing agencies, three research groups within universities, and three other scientific agencies concerned with forestry, space research, and the study of science and technology in development. The systems were intended to be used by district-level administrators. The MOEF initiated 10 GIS projects in January 1991, in collaboration with the eight scientific institutions, with the aim of examining the potential for using GIS technology to aid wasteland development. Wastelands are categorized as degraded land that can be brought under vegetative cover with reasonable effort, and land that has deteriorated due to lack of appropriate water and soil management.

The initiation of the project in 1991 can be traced back to two earlier events. In 1986, the government of India started the National Wastelands Identification Project, involving the mapping of the distribution of wastelands across the various states of India. Detailed maps were produced on a 1:50,000 scale for 147 selected districts using remote sensing techniques. The existence of these maps provided a basis for considering how to develop and manage these wastelands. The stimulus for the possible application of GIS to this issue was provided by a chance meeting of some GIS experts from Ohio in the United States with Indian government officials, in the context of a general USAID mission to India in 1989. This was followed by a visit of an Indian expert team to see GIS installations in the United States in 1990, and then the eight scientific institutions in India were invited by the MOEF to test the efficacy of GIS in wasteland management, using specific districts as research sites.

Phase I of the projects took place over the period 1991 to 1993, and the staff of the scientific institutions saw the objectives to be primarily technological,

---

[4]See footnote 2 above.

involving the production of working GIS systems based on real data from the field sites in their particular districts. The detailed models and systems developed by the institutions tended to reflect their view of themselves as scientific research and development centers. For example, there was a heavy reliance on data obtained by sophisticated remote-sensing techniques, reflecting the nature of the interests of the typical research scientist in these institutions. There was less emphasis on other socio-economic variables relevant to wastelands management, such as population and livestock data. In addition, and of crucial importance to later development of the project, many of the scientists involved in the project saw their institutional mandate to be limited to the development of technology rather than to its transfer to administrators at the district level.

Although the Phase I projects were completed in early 1993, proposals for continuation were not submitted until about a year later, and then only by five of the original eight institutions. This period of transition from Phase I to Phase II was characterized by uncertainty about the objectives and nature of the continuation phase. The project director saw it as involving the transfer of the developed systems to the district level so that they could be used for real management applications. However, the project managers in the scientific institutions did not view their staff skills or resources to be adequate for this task in most cases. The institutions asked for further funding largely to provide more hardware and software, whereas the project director felt that the institutions should concentrate on using the existing equipment and on its transfer to the field.

Eventually, five institutions agreed to terms for Phase II and these continuation projects were authorised by the MOEF. Soon after this, the project director left the MOEF and transferred to another institution, and there was very limited further central direction of the Phase II projects. Despite this lack of coordination from the center, all of the five Phase II projects went ahead, in different ways and with different levels of success in terms of the stated project goals. However, by the end of the project in 1996, although some efforts had been made in some of the sites toward transferring the technology to the district level, there were no actual working systems receiving real use.

Structurational analysis

At one level, this project can be thought of as another example of a failed technology transfer effort, all too common in the history of aid agencies and their attempts to promote the use of western-origin technologies in Third World contexts. One could argue, for example, of the need for improved training and education, or institutional development. While acknowledging that these may be relevant, the theoretical basis of this paper can be used to analyze more underlying reasons. A principal argument will be that information technologies such as GIS, developed in the western countries, can be thought to reflect and embed western values. These may not be compatible with deeply-held beliefs and attitudes in other cultures such as India. Key points of the analysis in this section are summarized in Table 2.3.

Structure and culture

As with the case study in the previous section, it is not possible to analyze in detail the individual perceptions and actions of the many project participants. Rather, the analysis here aims to aggregate to the level of groups who can be taken to broadly share similar structure in the mind. Three such groups consist of the U.S. GIS specialists and USAID personnel, the Indian scientists concerned with GIS development, and the Indian district-level administrators. With respect to the three structural dimensions of meaning, power,

Table 2.3   *GIS technology transfer case: structurational analysis*

Structure	• GIS embody systems of meaning, such as the representation of space through maps; provide resources: and encapsulate norms, such as the high value of coordinated activity • However, these may clash with the structure in the mind of actors in the different cultural interest groups
Culture	• [U.S. personnel] GIS as appropriate spatial technology; provides means of deploying financial resources; promotes good development • [Indian GIS scientists] GIS as lead-edge technology; provides means of gaining financial resources; is suitable for a scientific institution • [District-level administrators] GIS as alien technology; requires them to provide data; but need not affect normal job role
Cross-cultural contradiction and conflict	• Interests not threatened in Phase I • Some conflict in interim phase between GIS project director and scientific institutions – some of the latter withdrew • Passive resistance in the form of nonuse by district-level administrators in Phase II
Reflexivity and change	• Increasing awareness of maps and map-based systems in India • Resulting in subtle shifts in perception, but major social change over longer time horizons is made up of such minor shifts • Some current evidence of successful use of GIS for land management in India, reflecting changed attitudinal rigidities

and norms, the first group took the view that GIS was an appropriate technology to help with spatial issues, that they had the power through financial resources to sponsor its application in India, and that computer-based applications such as this were the right way forward for development in India. The Indian scientists saw GIS as a new lead-edge technology which they wished to learn about, that the USAID-sponsored project was a way to obtain the necessary resources, and that this fitted their mandate as a scientific institution. Finally, the Indian district-level administrators thought that GIS technology was something outside their experience, that they were required to provide data for the systems, but that the norms of carrying out their own job in the usual way still applied.

There is clear structural contradiction here, and an analysis of this can be sharpened by looking carefully at the technology itself and the way in which it can be thought to embed structural properties in terms of meaning and norms, and to provide political resources. With respect to meaning, GIS are a way of representing space through the explicit device of maps, a common enough concept in western societies. However, India is not a map-based culture. Typical Indians will rarely, if ever, use maps in their daily life. A GIS project leader in the National Informatics Center (NIC), one of the other institutions in India trying to introduce GIS, said:

> The most difficult part of GIS introduction is getting people to think spatially. There is no simple strategy here. A first step would be to motivate NIC's own people. They must start thinking spatially first.

This remark misstates the core of the issue. It is not that Indians do not think spatially, but that they do not in general use external conceptualizations of space, namely maps, as key aids to spatial awareness. District-level administrators, for example, those concerned with forestry management, are well aware of spatial distributions of trees in their areas. However, they do not normally conceptualize this in terms of maps, whether computer-generated or not.

Sahay (1998, p. 181) linked Indians' conceptualization of space to fundamental aspects of their identity. He argued that Indians view space as basically "in-here," subjective and inherent to the person, rather than "out-there" as some objective entity.

Sahay summarized the lack of fit between GIS technology and these aspects of Indian cultural identity as follows:

> The objective reality depicted in GIS software is interpreted to represent a disconnection of space from place, a relationship that allows interaction between absent others. In contrast, in Indian society, a strong relation is seen to exist between notions of space and place arising out of political, cosmological, religious and social considerations. These differences between subjective considerations and objective reality (of the GIS) seem to contribute to the discomfort which some Indians feel in relating to the notion of a GIS map.

Sahay added that the purpose of a GIS reflects a sense of being able to control space and nature through technology. This need to dominate nature is also not a concept that comes naturally for many Indians, who typically see themselves as part of nature rather than standing outside of it.

A second feature of GIS technology can be seen as reflecting an organizational norm in western societies that places a high value on coordinated activity. The multi-layered nature of GIS systems, where data on different characteristics are brought together as overlays in the same map-based system, assumes that management issues will be addressed in a coordinated way. For example, the management of land resources in any country involves a wide range of disciplinary specialities, including agriculture, forestry, wildlife management, and many others. However, in India, these issues have typically been handled in relative isolation by the different agencies involved. Over 20 separate government agencies operate at the district level in India, each dealing with a particular functional area, and reflecting the wider governmental funding structures that are built around departmentally-based schemes. An employee in a non-governmental organization operating at the district level in India described this as follows:

> The main problem is the compartmentalism of activities. Different departments do not speak to each other. There is a problem of attitude, people do not want to do things. The crux of the problem is not technical but that of sustained coaxing. The district level engineer says that he is interested only in dams, the agricultural scientist in soils, the forester in trees. Everyone says that I am fine and no one sits and talks with each other. There is extreme compartmentalization. There is a mental barrier among the people.

This feature of compartmentalism of role in India is not a simple matter of inefficient bureaucratic organizations, but reflects some deeply-held cultural beliefs. Indian society has traditionally been stratified on functional lines with caste as the basic structural feature. Hinduism, the religion of the majority in India, emphasizes a social framework that embodies caste rituals, and these have governed the lives of most Indians for hundreds of years. One of the sacred Hindu texts, the *Bhagavad Gita,* says:

> And to thy duty, even if it be humble, rather than another's, even if it be great. To die in one's duty is life: to live in another's is death.

The compartmentalism of role and activity was a clear feature of the GIS projects. Most of the GIS scientists viewed their goal as producing accurate scientific models for the GIS, which they then expected the district-level administrators to use.

The GIS can be viewed, therefore, as embodying systems of meaning such as the representation of space through maps, and encapsulating norms such as the need for coordinated action. The systems were thus aligned to the interests and structures in the mind of the U.S. personnel, and can be thought of as *actors* (Walsham and Sahay 1999) introducing those ideas into an Indian context. Another way of expressing this is that the systems provided a political resource for an attempt to use western ideas in Indian district-level administration. No value judgement is being made in this paper about whether this attempt was a "good thing" or not. The point being made here is that there was a marked structural contradiction between the values embedded in the technology and those in the minds of local actors, particularly the district-level administrators.

Cross-cultural contradiction and conflict

Structural contradiction, according to the theory in this paper, does not necessarily result in conflict. Conditions under which conflict is likely to occur are when actors feel that their interests are affected negatively, and when they are able to act to counter this. The relatively smooth nature of Phase I can be explained in that, although the GIS scientists were not map users themselves in their daily lives, they did not feel their interests threatened by the technology. Indeed, it provided a resource for them to learn about a leading-edge technology, with positive career connotations. Although the district-level administrators were, in some cases, required to provide data for the GIS, this did not compromise their normal way of working. The interim period between Phases I and II did, however, start to manifest some conflict, notably when the GIS scientists felt that they were being asked by the project director to carry out a role which was not theirs, namely working closely with the district-level administrators to implement the systems. Some institutions withdrew from Phase II as a consequence.

Phase II itself saw little overt conflict, despite the stark structural contradictions between the values embedded in the technology and those in the minds of the Indian participants. Yet, there was real potential for some participants to be affected negatively. For example, the district-level staff were having alien systems imposed on them, which they saw as of little value. However, forms of resistance are many and subtle. The district-level staff did not, in general, reject the systems or undertake any form of direct action. Rather, they simply did not use the systems – action in the form of inaction, a type of passive resistance. This provides a nice illustration of what Giddens (1984) calls the "dialectic of control," namely the ways in which the seemingly less powerful manage resources in such a way as to exert control over the more powerful.

Reflexivity and change

This passive resistance to the GIS on the part of district-level staff can be taken as an example of reproduction of structure, but change is also inherent in the human actors' reflexivity here. India is not a static culture and there is an increasing awareness of maps and map-based systems in India, not least since private Indian software companies in places such as Bangalore have been very successful in selling their services as GIS developers in the world software market. Structures in the mind do change overtime, even with respect to such a fundamental issue as the conceptualization of space. Changes in culture are often imperceptible over short time periods, but major social change over longer time horizons is made up of such minor shifts.

As an example of longer-term shifting attitudes in the development and use of GIS in India, Puri (2002) describes ongoing efforts to use GIS for land management in the Indian state of Andhra Pradesh. He argues that some indications of successful use are now discernible, in contrast to the earlier work described by Walsham and Sahay (1999). Puri ascribes the later success to shifts in earlier "attitudinal rigidities," and gives examples of new approaches: GIS scientists assuming ownership of implementation as well as development of systems; increasing consultation with local departments and people; and nodal district agencies managing implementation action plans. Puri's research provides a valuable reminder that longitudinal studies of several years length, as carried out by Walsham and Sahay, may still not be long enough to detect the effect of shifting individual attitudes, or structure in the mind, which can aggregate overtime to major shifts in national or subgroup cultures.

Theorizing cross-cultural working and IS

In order to assess the contribution the structurational analysis of this paper can make to the study of cross-cultural software production and use, or more generally to cross-cultural working and information systems, it is necessary to examine the existing literature in this latter domain. A good starting point is the widely-cited work of Hofstede (1980, 1991), which describes cultural difference in terms of scores on five dimensions: power-distance, individualism, masculinity, uncertainty avoidance, and long-term orientation. Myers and Tan (2002) noted that much of the literature concerned with cultural and cross-cultural issues in the IS field has relied on Hofstede's work. They analyzed 36 studies from the cross-cultural IS literature, and noted that 24 of these used some or all of Hofstede's dimensions.

While the work of Hofstede, and that of similar style such as Trompenaars (1993), has the merit of alerting us to the importance of cultural difference, it can also be criticized as rather crude and simplistic. Myers and Tan note that the very concept of *national culture* is problematic on several grounds. These include the heterogeneity within a given nation-state and the difficulty of relating national cultural values to work-related actions and attitudes. They propose that IS researchers should adopt a more dynamic view of culture – one that sees culture as contested, temporal, and emergent. The rest of this section will examine why such issues are important to the study of cross-cultural working and IS, and what the structurational analysis of this paper has to offer. The discussion is organized under the four headings of cross-cultural contradiction and conflict, cultural heterogeneity, detailed work patterns, and the dynamic nature of culture. Key points in this section are outlined in Table 2.4, summarizing limitations of Hofstede-type studies and related contributions from a structurational analysis.

Cross-cultural contradiction and conflict

Hofstede-type studies describe intercultural differences in the selected aggregate variables, and these can be taken as reflecting *contradictions* between different cultures. However, no analytical tools are provided by such studies as to how to analyze whether, and if so how, such contradictions result in actual *conflict,* physical or otherwise. For example, people from different cultures may coexist quite easily despite such differences, but in other cases the differences seem to cause major difficulties. In trying to analyze possible conflict in cross-cultural working and IS, such as in software production and use, the aggregate national variables are of little use.

The structurational analysis in this paper offers a way of addressing the question of both structural contradiction and conflict. It has been argued that conflicts may occur in cross-cultural working if differences in structures in the mind are perceived to affect actors negatively, and they are able to act to resist or oppose these negative impacts. This was illustrated in the Jamaica–India case by identifying differences in cultural views about approaches to teamwork, forms of appropriate power relations, and attitudes to time deadlines. These contributed to conflict since they affected all participants in the software project directly, and in ways that were largely perceived to be negative. Opposition or resistance was possible, and detailed ways in which this occurred were described in the case.

The GIS case also illustrated the value of a structurational analysis of cross-cultural contradiction and conflict, although in a slightly different way. Three cultural subgroups were identified, with rather different structures in the mind with respect to GIS systems, but no significant conflict occurred in Phase I of the project. This was explained by an analysis of the specific interests of the three groups, which were not negatively affected by the GIS project, although they had different views concerning its merits. However, in Phase II, some resistance did occur, for example when the Project Director wanted the GIS scientists to become involved in local-level implementation, something which they viewed as outside their remit.

Cultural heterogeneity

By treating the concept of national culture through the use of scores on particular dimensions, as is the case in Hofstede-type studies, the implicit

Table 2.4   *Cross-cultural working and IS: contribution of different theories*

Topic	Hofstede-Type Studies	Structurational Analysis	Examples in Jamaica Case	Examples in GIS Case
Cross-cultural contradiction and conflict	Describe aggregate differences between cultures But provide no link to conflict	Detailed way of relating contradiction and conflict	Differences in cultural views about teamwork, power relations, time deadlines Resulting in conflict since perceived negatively and resistance possible	Three different cultural subgroups with different attitudes to GIS Resulted in resistance in Phase II only, when participants perceived negative consequences
Cultural heterogeneity	No description of heterogeneity	Can be used to analyze differences in cultural subgroups and even individuals	Some analysis of individual difference related to the Indian project director	Analysis of different attitudes of Indian scientists and district-level administrators from the same national culture
Detailed work patterns	Aggregate cultural variables do not easily translate to effect on work patterns	Meaning systems, power relations, norms already targeted at the detailed work level	Example of approaches to control of subordinates	Example of different ways of representing space
The dynamic nature of culture	Normally treated as static	Can analyze reflexivity and change	Increasing recognition over time of importance of cross-cultural issues Example of negotiated culture	Recent work indicates some shift away from the attitudes that characterized the earlier studies

assumption is that national culture shows a strong homogeneity. However, there is much evidence against this view of the world. For example, India provides a good counterexample. Its one billion people come from many and varied cultural, racial and religious backgrounds, speak hundreds of different languages, and exhibit enormous variety at different hierarchical levels within the society. Within western countries, there is an increasing heterogeneity of history and background, not least due to the existence of ethnic subgroups (see, for example, Appadurai 1997).

An interesting example of work in the IS field which goes beyond the simple attribution of national cultural characteristics is that of Korpela and his colleagues (Korpela 1996; Korpela et al. 2000). Korpela criticized the approach of taking West Africa, an area equal in size to Europe, as one culture characterized by Hofstede's aggregate variables such as low individualism and a high acceptance of an unequal distribution of power. In contrast, Korpela pointed out that the country of Nigeria, for example, is a colonial creation and contains many different groups with "sharp cultural discontinuities." One such group is the Yoruba people, numbering some 20 million. Although there are differences within this large group itself, Korpela drew on the extensive literature on the Yoruba to highlight five aspects of the Yoruba cultural heritage that are distinctive. The work of Korpela and his colleagues used these characteristics to illuminate complex issues of IT development problems in the health sector in Yorubaland.

So, what does structurational analysis offer to the study of cultural heterogeneity and its impacts on IS? If we look back to the case studies of this paper, such an analysis does not require that cultures are regarded as homogeneous, but rather that one should be looking for a measure of systemness or homogeneity within particular social groupings. A good example is provided by the GIS case study. As we saw earlier, the sub-cultures of the GIS scientists and the district-level administrators, both composed solely of Indian nationals, had radically different attitudes toward the GIS and their value. For example, the first group viewed the GIS as providing ways for them to work with lead-edge technologies and systems, whereas the second group viewed the GIS as alien technology of little relevance to their role. A structurational analysis opens up the possibility of examining the heterogeneous systems of meaning, power relations, and norms of different social groupings within the same national culture.

The Jamaican case study did not analyze cultural heterogeneity within the two national groups directly, but aspects of it can be seen through the discussion of the role of the initial project director, Raj. His interest in organizational issues was limited, and the quotes from him in the text show his tendency to racial stereotyping of the Jamaican software employees. He was later moved to a role dealing with technical issues, leaving the way open for a new Indian CEO with a rather different management and cross-cultural approach. Space and resource limitations provide a natural barrier to case analyses which treat every project participant as an individual person with a different mixture of attributes, but structurational analysis can, in principle, be used to analyze cultural heterogeneity down to the level of subgroups, or even individuals.

Detailed work patterns

A further criticism of the use of Hofstede-type national cultural character-istics as a basis for analysis of cross-cultural working and IS is that there is normally a poor link between these characteristics and detailed work-related attitudes and actions. It is one thing to know how the people of a country score on masculinity or uncertainty avoidance, but another to know how this translates into the details of systems development processes, or attitudes to particular technologies. In terms of cross-cultural working, it is not neces-sarily the case that similarities in national characteristics imply similar work-related patterns. For example, Khare (1999) describes radical differences between Indian and Japanese work patterns, in areas such as commitment to their organization and attitude to time, despite similarities between India and Japan in terms of their scores on individualism, long-term orientation, and power-distance (Hofstede 1995).

In order to analyze detailed patterns in cross-cultural working, it is nec-essary to go away from the high level of national characteristics to a more detailed focus on behavior at the micro-level of the group or organization. For example, in the general management literature, Lam (1997) described a fascinating longitudinal study of cross-cultural working between Japanese and British engineers. Her detailed analysis demonstrated how differences in educational background, bases of skills, and approaches to coordination of work resulted in very different attitudes to knowledge sharing by the two cultural groups, and thus major problems in cross-cultural working. In the IS literature, a limited number of authors have carried out cross-cultural studies from this perspective of a detailed analysis of work patterns and attitudes. For example, Trauth (1999, 2000) examined the management of IT workers in an American–Irish cross-cultural work environment as part of a detailed lon-gitudinal study of the information economy in Ireland. Barrett et al. (1997) described cross-cultural working on software outsourcing from U.S. to Indian companies, examining detailed work patterns in areas such as forms of part-nership and coordination mechanisms.

The structurational analysis described in this paper can offer a valuable theoretical underpinning for studies of this latter type, which otherwise tend to be somewhat anecdotal in nature. Such an analysis, as we have seen, focuses on meaning, power, and norms within particular work groups and how these affect particular work patterns and behavior. For example, in the

Jamaica–India case, we saw how the Indian managers of the project were used to hands-on approaches to control subordinates, whereas this was viewed as reflecting an "adult-child" approach by one of the Jamaican participants. In the Indian GIS case, we saw how the different ways of representing space between the U.S. developers and the Indian users resulted in passive resistance to the implementation of the technology. The insights from these studies could not have been obtained by a high-level analysis of cultural dimensions. It may be possible, in theory, to make a connection between Hofstede-type dimensions and detailed work patterns and attitudes, but such an analysis is not easily found in the literature. A structurational analysis, with its focus on meaning, power, and norms, is already targeted at the detailed work level.

The dynamic nature of culture

A final area of weakness of the cultural dimensions approach to cross-cultural working is that culture is not static. For example, we have seen quite dramatic changes in many societies over the last few decades in areas such as attitudes to gender, the environment, race, sex, family life, and religion. In the context of globalization, with increasing contact between different societies, it is increasingly difficult for any group to remain isolated and uninfluenced by other cultures. Thus, in the domain of cross-cultural working, we need theories that reflect change as well as stability, and that are attuned to shifts in attitudes and actions as well as their continuance.

An example of such work in the cross-cultural management literature is that of Brannen and Salk (2000) on *negotiated culture.* They used the case example of a German–Japanese joint venture to show how the attitudes of the two cultural groups shifted over time as they engaged with each other in collaborative work activities. The groups negotiated a compromise between themselves in areas such as styles of decision making and attitudes to time off on weekends and holidays, resulting in a hybrid culture for both groups. This is not saying that the two groups became homogeneous, but that they both shifted in their attitudes from their initial cultural starting point. In the IS literature, Sahay and Krishna (2000) described a similar process in some ways, although they did not use the term *negotiated culture.* They described a case study of a software outsourcing venture over a period of several years from a Canadian multinational to an Indian software house. At first, cultural contradiction produced some conflict, but the authors argued that, later, the relationship "showed signs of maturing" based on both sides gaining an increased understanding of the other's culture. Again, this did not result in the parties becoming the same in terms of attitudes and values, but it certainly supports the view of workgroup culture being dynamic and emergent, and not derived in a static manner from national cultural characteristics.

Although neither of the above studies used a structurational analysis, this would have provided a theoretical framework within which to embed their analyses. Structuration theory, in addition to analyzing structural reproduction, emphasizes reflexivity on the part of human actors and thus changes in structure in the mind. This was analyzed in the earlier case studies under the heading of reflexivity and change. In the Jamaica–India case, we saw this reflected in an increasing recognition over time of the importance of cross-cultural issues, and the necessity for actions to be taken to address such issues. Job roles were changed, people were moved to different positions, and the India–Jamaica team started to function rather better. The negotiated culture concept fits quite well here.

In the Indian GIS case, longer-term attitudinal changes are needed if people working at the local level, such as district-level officials, are to embrace technologies such as GIS in their day-to-day work, or if GIS scientists are to perceive their role as involving implementation as well as technical development of systems. Although such changes are hard to trace in detail in the complexity of a context such as India, the earlier structurational analysis of the case drew on some recent work to indicate, at least in some areas, a shift away from the attitudinal rigidities which had characterized the earlier reported case studies. Indian culture, as with all other societies, is dynamic and emergent, and a structurational analysis can offer insights on such change processes.

Conclusions

In the more globalized world of the 21st century, working with information and communication technologies is increasingly taking place in a cross-cultural context, but we are short of good theory to analyze such phenomena. A recent article by Goodall (2002) argued that this applies to the cross-cultural management literature more generally, namely that "we are short of both rich descriptions of cross-cultural interaction, and theoretical explanations of the same." The primary contribution of this paper has been to provide such a theoretical basis, drawing from structuration theory, which was used to analyze cross-cultural software production and use. The theorization goes beyond the relatively simplistic Hofstede-type studies which dominate the IS literature to date. In contrast to such studies, it was shown in the preceding section that a structurational analysis can accommodate elements such as the links between structural contradiction and conflict, cultural heterogeneity, an analysis of detailed work patterns, and the dynamic and emergent nature of culture.

The theory has been illustrated using two empirical examples only, with a focus on software production and use, but it could be used to analyze any case study involving cross-cultural working and IS. Viewed from a more critical perspective, however, any theory illuminates some elements of particular case situations and is relatively silent on others. Structuration theory is no exception, and as noted by Giddens (1984) himself, the use of structuration theory does not preclude the use of other theories in tandem with it. For example, Walsham and Sahay (1999) drew on actor-network theory to analyze elements of the GIS case other than those discussed in this article. In particular, they focused on the detailed processes of human reflexivity, technical adaptation and network building involved in the case. The structurational analysis in this paper can be supplemented with other specific theories, as appropriate to the particular domain of interest.

Moving finally to the issue of IS practice, what conclusions can be offered? The paper lies squarely within the literature which considers that globalization, facilitated by ICTs, is not leading to simple homogeneity of culture and approach. While it has been argued that culture is not static, the relatively enduring nature of cultural norms and values results from processes of reproduction of structure in the mind. Thus, there is a need for practitioners to be highly sensitive to cultural difference when working in a cross-cultural context. Sensitivity to other cultures does not imply the need for practitioners to change their own attitudes and values to those of the other culture. What is needed is some understanding, and ideally empathy, for the attitudes, norms, and values of others. This offers the possibility of mutual respect between cross-cultural partners and the opportunity for a move toward a more negotiated culture of cooperation.

A detailed discussion of ways in which this can be achieved is beyond the scope of the current paper. However, some broad approaches are worth mentioning in conclusion. Cross-cultural education and training can be achieved through such means as reading, formal courses, and on-the-job facilitation. With respect to the latter, open discussions about difficult cross-cultural issues can be valuable starting points to increased understanding in cross-cultural teams. While technologies, such as GIS, have features that reflect their cultural origins, technology has a degree of *interpretive flexibility* (Pinch and Bijker 1987), and can be adapted and used in different ways. For example, Braa (1997) used the metaphor of *cultivation* to describe the process of adapting Scandinavian technologies and approaches to the different context of the development of South African health information systems. In our more globalized world, cross-cultural working is increasingly common, and the information systems field needs to increase its understanding of the problematic issues involved and approaches to resolving them. It is hoped that this paper makes a modest contribution to these goals.

Acknowledgments

The author would like to thank the senior editor, Michael Myers, who was particularly helpful in guiding the paper through the review process. He is also grateful to the anonymous referees and associate editor for their helpful and constructive comments on the earlier drafts of the paper.

References

Appadurai, A. (1997), *Modernity at Large: Cultural Dimensions of Globalization*. Oxford University Press, New Delhi, India.

Barrett, M., A. Drummond, and S. Sahay (1996), "Exploring the Impact of Cross-Cultural Differences in International Software Development Teams: Indian Expatriates in Jamaica," in J. D. Coelho, W. Konig, H. Kromar, R. O'Callaghan, and M. Saaksjarvi, Eds. *Proceedings of the Fourth European Conference on Information Systems*. Portugal, Lisbon.

Barrett M., S. Sahay, and B. Hinings (1997), "The Process of Building GSO Relationships: The Experience of a Multi-National Vendor with Indian Contractors," in K. Kumar and J. I. DeGross, Eds. *Proceedings of the Eighteenth International Conference on Information Systems.* Atlanta, GA.

Barrett, M. and G. Walsham (1995), "Managing IT for Business Innovation: Issues of Culture. Learning and Leadership in a Jamaican Insurance Company," *Journal of Global Information Management*, No. 3:3, pp. 25–33.

Beck, U. (2000), *What is Globalization?*. Polity Press, Cambridge, UK.

Braa, J. Use and Design of Information Technology in Third World Contexts with a Focus on the Health Sector: Case Studies from Mongolia and South Africa, Unpublished Ph.D. Thesis, Department of Informatics, University of Oslo, Oslo, Norway, 1997.

Brannen, M. Y. and J. E. Salk (2000), "Partnering Across Borders: Negotiating Organizational Culture in a German-Japan Joint Venture," *Human Relations*, No. 53:4, pp. 451–487.

Carmel, E. (1999), *Global Software Teams*. Prentice-Hall, Englewood, Cliffs, NJ.

Castells, M. (1998), *End of Millennium*. Blackwell, Oxford, UK.

Castells, M. (1997), *The Power of Identity*. Blackwell, Oxford, UK.

Castells, M. (1996), *The Rise of the Network Society*. Blackwell, Oxford, UK.

Davenport, T. H. (1998 July-August), "Putting the Enterprise into the Enterprise System," *Harvard Business Review*, pp. 121–131.

DeSanctis, G. and M. S. Poole (1994), "Capturing the Complexity in Advanced Technology Using Adaptive Structuration Theory," *Organization Science*, No. 5:2, pp. 121–147.

Giddens, A. (1979), *Central Problems in Social Theory*. Macmillan, Basingstoke, UK.

Giddens, A. (1984), *The Constitution of Society*. Polity Press, Cambridge, UK.

Goodall, K. (2002), "Managing to Learn: From Cross-Cultural Theory to Management Education Practice," in M. Warner and P. Joynt, Eds. *Managing Across Cultures: Issues and Perspectives*, 2nd ed. International Thompson Business Press, London, pp. 256–268.

Hofstede, G. (1980), *Culture's Consequences: International Differences in Work-Related Values*. Sage, Beverly Hills, CA.

Hofstede, G. (1981), *Cultures and Organizations: Software of the Mind*. McGraw-Hill, New York.

Hofstede, G. (1995), "Managerial Values," in T. Jackson, Ed. *Cross-Cultural Management*. Butterworth-Heinemann, Oxford, pp. 150–165.

Jones, M. R. (1998), "Structuration Theory," in W. L. Currie and R. D. Galliers, Eds. *Rethinking Management Information Systems: An Interdisciplinary Perspective*. Oxford University Press, Oxford, UK, pp. 103–135.

Khare, A. (1999), "Japanese and Indian Work Patterns: A Study of Contrasts," in H. S. R. Kao, D. Sinha, and B. Wilpert, Eds. *Management and Cultural Values: The Indigenization of Organizations in Asia*. Sage, New Delhi, pp. 121–136.

Korpela, M. (1996), "Traditional Culture or Political Economy? On the Root Causes of Organizational Obstacles of IT in Developing Countries," *Information Technology for Development*, No. 7:1, pp. 29–42.

Korpela, M., H. A. Soriyan, K. C. Olufokunbi, and A. Mursu (2000), "Made-in-Nigeria Systems Development Methodologies: An Action Research Project in the Health Sector," in C. Avgerou and G. Walsham, Eds. *Information Technology in Context: Implementing Systems in the Developing World*. Ashgate Publishing, Aldershot, pp. 134–152.

Lacity, M. C. and L. P. Willcocks (2001), *Global Information Technology Outsourcing*. Wiley, Chichester, UK.

Lam, A. (1997), "Transfer in Global Cooperative Ventures Embedded Firms, Embedded Knowledge: Problems of Collaboration and Knowledge," *Organization Studies*, No. 18:6, pp. 973–996.

Morgan, G. (1986), *Images of Organization*. Sage, Beverley Hills, CA.

Myers, M. D. and F. B. Tan (2002), "Beyond Models of National Culture in Information Systems Research," *Journal of Global Information Management*, No. 10:1, pp. 24–32.

Orlikowski, W. J. (1992), "The Duality of Technology: Rethinking the Concept of Technology in Organizations," *Organization Science*, No. 3:3, pp. 398–427.

Pinch, T. J. and W. E. Bijker (1987), "The Social Construction of Facts and Artifacts," in W. E. Bijker, T. P. Hughes, and T. J. Pinch, Eds. *The Social Construction of Technological Systems*. MIT Press, Cambridge, MA, pp. 17–50.

Puri, S. K. (2002 May), "Building Networks to Support GIS for Land Management in India: Past Learnings and Future Challenges," in S. Krishna and S. Madon, Eds. *Proceedings of the IFIP WG9.4 Working Conference on ICTs and Socio-Economic Development: Balancing Global and Local Priorities*. Bangalore, India.

Robertson, R. (1992), *Globalization; Social Theory and Global Culture*. Sage, London.

Sahay, S. (1998), "Implementing GIS Technology in India: Issues of Time and Space," *Accounting, Management and Information Technologies*, Vol. 8, No. 2–3, pp. 147–188.

Sahay, S., and Krishna, S. "A Dialectical Approach to Understand the Nature of Global Software Outsourcing Arrangements," Working Paper, Indian Institute of Management, Bangalore, 2000.

Trauth, E. M. (2000), *The Culture of an Information Economy: Influences and Impacts in the Republic of Ireland*. Kluwer Academic Publishers, Dordrecht, Netherlands.

Trauth, E. M. (1999), "Leapfrogging an IT Labor Force: Multinational and Indigenous Perspectives," *Journal of Global Information Management*, No. 7:2, pp. 22–32.

Trompenaars, F. (1993), *Riding the Waves of Culture*. Nicholas Brealey, London.

Walsham, G. (1993), *Interpreting Information Systems in Organizations*. Wiley, Chichester, UK.

Walsham, G. (2001), *Making a World of Difference: IT in a Global Context*. Wiley, Chichester, UK.

Walsham, G. and S. Sahay (1999), "GIS for District-Level Administration in India: Problems and Opportunities," *MIS Quarterly*, No. 23:1, pp. 39–66.

Reproduced from *MIS Quarterly*, December 2002, pp. 359–380. Reprinted with permission from the University of Minnesota.

3 Reporting Bad News About Software Projects: Impact of Organizational Climate and Information Asymmetry in an Individualistic and a Collectivistic Culture

Bernard C. Y. Tan, H. Jeff Smith, Mark Keil and Ramiro Montealegre

Abstract: The reluctance of people to report bad news can be a major contributor to the phenomenon of runaway software projects. If senior managers receive bad news sooner, they may be able to prevent runaway software projects through corrective action. Two factors that are known to impact predisposition to report bad news are organizational climate (whether reporting bad news is likely to result in reward or punishment) and information asymmetry (whether hiding bad news is likely to be possible over time). Using matching experiments in an individualistic (United States) and a collectivistic culture (Singapore), this study investigates how the individualism–collectivism dimension of national culture may moderate the impact of organizational climate and information asymmetry on human predisposition to report bad news. The results revealed that individualism appeared to amplify the impact of organizational climate on predisposition to report bad news (compared to collectivism) whereas collectivism appeared to amplify the impact of information asymmetry on predisposition to report bad news (compared to individualism). When deciding on whether to report bad news about software projects, people from an individualistic culture seemed to be more sensitive to organizational climate whereas people from a collectivistic culture seemed to pay greater attention to information asymmetry. These results have useful implications for practice and research involving cross-cultural software project teams. Beyond these implications, these results add a cultural dimension to our existing knowledge on software project management.

I. Introduction

Failure is a common occurrence in the realm of software development. A widely reported study of 23 000 software projects showed that only 26% of the projects were delivered on-time, on-budget, and with the promised functionality. The remaining 74% were either canceled before the development cycle was completed or were delivered late, over budget, or with less functionality than was originally promised [50].

Traditionally, researchers have attempted to reduce the probability of software project failure through better project management techniques and more user involvement in the development process. This is sound advice for dealing with technical risks. However, software project failure may also arise because of factors pertaining to organizational culture. One major cause of software project failure is the reluctance of people to report bad news about a project and its status. While evidence of failing may be apparent to people involved in a project, this information may not be communicated up the hierarchy [23] or may be substantially distorted in the communication process [19], [21]. As a result, senior managers who have the authority to remedy the situation are unaware of the true status. This reduces organizational ability to prepare for a project failure and, when the failure eventually comes, increases the size of the loss [18].

Statistics regarding the prevalence of such a phenomenon are elusive, but several publicized incidents of software project failure have suggested that nonreporting or distorted reporting of project status contributed to the difficulties e.g., [12], [35], [54]. In one of the few field studies to consider this phenomenon, Keil and Robey [24] discovered that information systems auditors are frequently reluctant to report bad news about project status due to factors pertaining to organizational culture. This is particularly interesting, considering the fact that reporting true project status is a key role of auditors. If auditors are reluctant to report bad news, it is plausible that programmers, systems analysts, and project leaders would be even less willing to report bad news about software projects.

Given that human reluctance to report bad news can be detrimental to software projects, senior managers should be interested in learning which factors may promote or inhibit such a phenomenon in an organization. As discussed by Smith and Keil [45], [46], people may be influenced by dozens of factors when deciding whether or not to report bad news about software projects. Two likely factors pertaining to organizational culture are organizational climate and information asymmetry. *Organizational climate* refers to the communicated expectations regarding the reporting of bad news about software projects. Such expectations are often manifested in the way organizations treat people who report bad news (e.g., reward, thank you note, no action taken, discouragement message, or punishment). *Information asymmetry* refers to the extent to which status information about software projects can be hidden. Whether information asymmetry is sustainable or not depends upon the extent to which the projects are being monitored (lax monitoring helps to sustain information asymmetry). By manipulating these two factors in an experiment, Keil et al. [25] showed that both factors affected human intention to report bad news. However, given that this study was conducted solely in the U.S., it is not known whether (and to what degree) the findings would apply in other national cultures [2].

National culture is the collective mindset that distinguishes people of one nation from another [17]. The management literature has clearly established that differences in national culture are reflected in human decisions and practices [9], [10], [52]. Hence, when deciding whether or not to report bad news about software projects, the degree to which people may be influenced by organizational climate and information asymmetry may be contingent upon their national culture. The objective of this study is to add a cultural dimension to our existing knowledge on software project management. Specifically, this study investigates how national culture may moderate the impact of organizational climate and information asymmetry on human predisposition to report bad news about software projects.

The remainder of the present paper is organized as follows. Section II covers the background materials while Section III derives the hypotheses for testing. Section IV presents details of the methodology used. Section V analyzes the data collected. Section VI discusses the implications of the findings for practice and research while Section VII concludes by emphasizing the key contributions.

II.   Background

Previous research models associated with reporting of software project status [25], [45]–[47] have been grounded in the whistle-blowing literature. While there has been some debate on the definition of whistle-blowing [20], a widely embraced viewpoint is that whistle-blowers disclose information about organizational dysfunction to persons or organizations who may be able to address the problems [8, p. 824]. In the context of this study, organizational dysfunction is associated with resources being devoted to software projects that are not delivering the outcomes that were intended when the resources were allocated. Whistle-blowing theory assumes that whistle-blowers "lack the power and authority" to handle the situation and must, therefore, "appeal to someone of greater power or authority" [31, p. 31].

The premise of whistle-blowing theory is that people choose to disclose (or not disclose) information due to personal, project team, and organizational factors. In a general context, Miceli and Near [31] reviewed the body of theoretical and empirical work on whistle-blowing and identified dozens of factors that could have causal relationships with human decisions to report bad news. Smith and Keil [45], [46] extended the Miceli and Near [31] framework by including additional causal variables, some outside the whistle-blowing literature, that may be salient in the specific context of software projects.

In spite of this emerging theoretical development, empirical evidence on whistle-blowing in software projects appears to be very limited. In one study, Smith *et al.* [47] conducted an experiment in which perceived behavioral immorality (i.e., deception by a superior) and perceived impact from project loss were manipulated. Both these factors significantly impacted the intention of subjects to report bad news. In another study, Keil *et al.* [25] manipulated two aspects of organizational culture (organizational climate and information asymmetry). Four treatment scenarios and questions for manipulation checks were developed. In a 2×2 factorial controlled laboratory experiment that involved 122 subjects, organizational climate and information asymmetry were found to impact the intention of subjects to report bad news.

In the present study, we choose to extend the model by Keil *et al.* [25] (by testing it in a cross-cultural context) for several reasons. First, among the many factors identified by Smith and Keil [45], [46] for their potential impact on human intention to report bad news, organizational climate and information asymmetry appear to be two of the most important ones. Second, unlike personal factors that cannot be controlled (e.g., moral development and risk propensity), organizational climate and information asymmetry are aspects of organizational culture that can be influenced to some extent by managerial actions. Therefore, findings related to such factors may guide managerial actions. Third, the relationship between organizational culture (organizational climate and information asymmetry) and national culture is an important research issue that has rarely been explored [6].

Only one other study has examined differences associated with whistle-blowing behavior across cultures [4]. In that study, which did not examine how various factors might impact reporting decisions, all subjects were given the same third-person scenario and asked if an accountant had a responsibility to report irregularities to various entities. The present study is the first cross-cultural study that attempts to identify factors affecting reporting intention in any context (not just in the context of software projects).

Organizational climate

Organizational climate determines the extent to which people have an incentive to shirk because their interests diverge from those of the organization. In many instances, the organizational climate is such that people perceive serious reprisal risks for reporting bad news. Such risks can take the form of job loss or other adverse impact on career prospects. This gives people an incentive to keep bad news to themselves even when it is not in the best interest of the organization to do so.

Theoretical arguments within the whistle-blowing literature suggest that such an organizational climate has a significant impact on perceived responsibility to report bad news. Through formal and informal communication as well as organizational stories, cues that guide behavior are transmitted to members of an organization. When there is a history of reprisals against whistle-blowers, people are likely to consider this as a signal regarding reporting responsibility [31, p. 153]. In an examination of the perceived personal obligations of first-level managers to blow the whistle, Keenan [22] found that "fear of retaliation" within the organizational climate played a great part in reducing perceived obligations. However, when organizations have a climate in which people are expected to report bad news (or are even rewarded for doing so), people would assess their responsibility based on these cues and, thereby, be more obliged to report bad news.

One other body of literature offers some insight into these causal relationships. In the 1970s, a small number of studies were conducted on the "mum effect." The "mum effect" label captured the notion that people are generally reluctant to transmit unpleasant messages [34, p. 39]. Several studies examined this phenomenon, primarily in dyadic contexts and outside of organizational boundaries, so the unit of analysis differs from that in the whistle-blowing literature. Nevertheless, the "mum effect" literature also suggested that a fear of retribution reduces felt personal responsibility to report bad news to another party (see reviews in [5] and [53]). As demonstrated by Keil *et al.* [25], in a study conducted within the U.S., an organizational climate that was conducive for reporting bad news could reduce the reluctance of people to do so.

Information asymmetry

Information asymmetry can also influence human intention to report bad news. In some organizations, software projects may be so tightly monitored that it would be difficult for people to hide bad news from others for long. This is a situation where information asymmetry cannot be sustained. In other organizations, the monitoring of software projects may be more lax and there may be opportunities for people to hide bad news from others over a long period of time. This is a situation where information asymmetry can be sustained.

When information asymmetry cannot be sustained, people are likely to believe that bad news ought to be reported because nothing can be gained from hiding such information. They may also fear that, by not reporting the bad news, others may quickly arrive at the conclusion that they are deliberately trying to cover up problems. However, when information asymmetry can be sustained, people are likely to believe that delaying the reporting of bad news can help to buy more time so that the software project can be turned around. Under such circumstances, they may conclude that there is less of a need to report bad news. In a study conducted within the U.S., Keil *et al.* [25] found that sustainable information asymmetry could increase the reluctance of people to report bad news.

National culture

Based on responses from about 120 000 subjects in 50 countries, Hofstede [16] deduced a model of national culture comprising four dimensions. Each country is given a relative score on each dimension based on a mathematical formula. Although some scholars [11] have criticized the questions and mathematical formula used by Hofstede [16], the validity and stability of the cultural dimensions have been confirmed by many other researchers [39], [42], [49]. These cultural dimensions have also been shown to possess explanatory power in information systems studies, e.g., [13], [26], [36], [43], [51], [52], [57].

So far, the most important and stable dimension in cross-cultural psychology has proven to be individualism–collectivism [41], [48], [52], [55]. *Individualism* pertains to nations in which ties between people are loose and people focus on their own needs [17]. In such a culture, people tend to put personal interests above team interests [9]. People take their actions independently of what others think and base their self-understanding on these personal actions [10]. *Collectivism* pertains to nations in which people are integrated into cohesive groups, which take care of them in exchange for unquestioning loyalty [17]. In such a culture, people tend to put team interests above personal interests [9], [10]. They base their self-understanding on how others around them react [10], largely because they consider themselves members of cohesive groups [1]. Along this dimension of national culture, Singapore is found to be much more collectivistic than the U.S. [17].

III.   Hypotheses

In an individualistic culture, people tend to behave largely in accord with their personal interest, with team interest being subordinated [9], [10]. In such a culture, when the organizational climate is conducive for reporting bad news (because those who report are known to receive rewards for their behavior), many people are likely to embrace reporting behavior. By reporting bad news promptly, they can further their personal interest by trying to be "positive" people and thereby reaping personal rewards. However, in such a culture, when the organizational climate is not conducive to reporting bad news (because those who report are known to receive punishment for their behavior), many people are unlikely to embrace reporting behavior. By hiding bad news, they can avoid being seen as "negative" people and, thereby, avert personal punishment.

In a collectivistic culture, people tend to let their personal interest be subordinated to team interest [9], [10]. In such a culture, even when the organizational climate is conducive for reporting bad news, many people may not embrace reporting behavior. Rather than going for personal rewards, they may report the bad news only if they believe the reporting decision is good for their project team (e.g., brings about team rewards). Likewise, in such a culture, even when the organizational climate is not conducive to reporting bad news, many people may not shun reporting behavior. Rather than trying to avoid personal punishment, they may embrace reporting behavior if they believe the reporting decision is good for their project team (e.g., allows the team to address its problems). Together, these arguments suggest that people in an individualistic culture may be more willing to report bad news than people in a collectivistic culture if organizational climate is conducive. However, people in an individualistic culture may be less willing to report bad news than people in a collectivistic culture (the opposite result) if organizational climate is not conducive.

Hypothesis 1: The impact of organizational climate (conducive versus not conducive) on predisposition to report bad news about software projects would be stronger in an individualistic culture than in a collectivistic culture.

In a collectivistic culture, people tend to put project team interest before personal interest [9], [10] when deciding whether or not to report bad news. In such a culture, when information asymmetry can be sustained (perhaps due to lax monitoring of software projects), many people are likely to shun reporting behavior. By hiding bad news, they can promote their project team interest by giving it time to facilitate project turnaround. However, in such a culture, when information asymmetry cannot be sustained (perhaps due to tight monitoring of software projects), many people are likely to embrace reporting behavior. By reporting bad news promptly, they can further their project team interest by diffusing the possibility that others would later accuse their project team of attempting to hide bad news.

In an individualistic culture, people tend to put personal interest before project team interest [9], [10] when deciding whether or not to report bad news. In such a culture, even when information asymmetry can be sustained, many people may not shun reporting behavior. Rather than trying to further their project team interest, they may embrace reporting behavior if this helps to promote their personal interest (e.g., frees themselves from the possibility of having to share the blame should the bad news become known in the future). Likewise, in such a culture, even when information asymmetry cannot be sustained, many people may not embrace reporting behavior. Rather than trying to advance their project team interests, they may shun reporting behavior if their personal interest is at stake (e.g., risks themselves to the possibility of having to shoulder more than their fair share of the blame). Together, these arguments suggest that people in an individualistic culture may be more willing to report bad news than people in a collectivistic culture if information asymmetry is sustainable. However, people in an individualistic culture may be less willing to report bad news than people in a collectivistic culture (the opposite result) if information asymmetry is not sustainable.

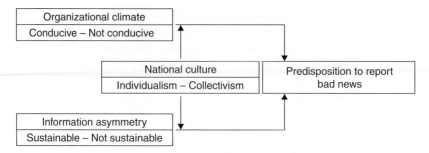

Figure 3.1   *Research model*

Hypothesis 2: The impact of information asymmetry (sustainable versus not sustainable) on predisposition to report bad news about software projects would be stronger in a collectivistic culture than in an individualistic culture.

Fig. 3.1 depicts the research model of this study. Hypotheses 1 and 2 suggest that individualism–collectivism would moderate the impact of organizational climate and information asymmetry, respectively, on human predisposition to report bad news about software projects.

IV.   Methodology

A key objective of this study was to test and advance a cross-cultural theory that could explain reluctance to report bad news for different populations of people. Given that internal validity would be a critical issue when testing theories, we used laboratory experiments to achieve precision of measurement and control over extraneous variables, so that causal relationships between constructs in the research model could be established [7]. Matching laboratory experiments were conducted in two distinct national cultures. Results were pooled to obtain a $2 \times 2 \times 2$ factorial design with three independent variables: organizational climate (conducive versus not conducive), information asymmetry (sustainable versus not sustainable), and national culture (individualism versus collectivism). The dependent variable was predisposition to report bad news.

Scenario

In the scenario given to the subjects (see Appendix), each subject was asked to play the role of a software project leader in System Solution Corporation (SSC), a large consulting firm. He/she was leading Project Y (a software project to build a new order processing system for a client organization). In

Table 3.1   *Operationalization of organizational climate*

Treatment	Conducive	Not Conducive
Context	Encourage information disclosure	Discourage information disclosure
Scenario given to subjects	The company expected them not to misrepresent or withhold information concerning the state of affairs existing or expected regarding any aspect of a project. In a previous case, a project leader who disclosed negative project information was commended and shortly thereafter received an expected promotion.	The norm in your company is that project leaders are expected to keep negative project information to themselves and not to inform either their supervisor or the client. In a previous case, a project leader who disclosed negative project information was severely reprimanded and denied an expected promotion in spite of a very strong track record.
Questions for manipulation check	*OC1*: SSC management expects its project leaders to report major project problems to their supervisor. *OC2*: My career at SSC is likely to be negatively impacted if I report Project Y's system problems to my supervisor (reverse scale). *OC3*: If I decide to inform my supervisor of Project Y's system problems, SSC management will react positively to my decision. *OC4*: If I inform my supervisor about Project Y's system problems, I will get into trouble with my supervisor (reverse scale).	

the middle of Project Y, he/she discovered a serious problem with the software system under development. If not addressed, this problem would have a significant negative impact on the ability of the client organization to process orders correctly.

This scenario was developed by Keil *et al.* [25] and was subjected to an iterative series of pilot tests and refinements in that study. Two authors of the present paper had extensive software project management experience and could assess the realism of this scenario.

Operationalization of organizational climate

Organizational climate was varied at two levels: conducive and not conducive to reporting bad news. The conducive condition was operationalized using a context that emphasized the importance of information disclosure. The not conducive condition was created using a context that discouraged information disclosure (see Table 3.1). As shown in Table 3.1, the manipulation for organizational climate was checked using four questions (OC1–OC4) taken from Keil *et al.* [25]. Each question was anchored on a seven-point scale ranging from "strongly disagree" (1) to "strongly agree" (7). These four questions had a Cronbach's alpha of 0.80 for this study. The scores for these questions were averaged for the manipulation check (see Section V – *Manipulation and control checks*). A higher score indicated an organizational climate that was more conducive for reporting bad news.

Operationalization of information asymmetry

Information asymmetry was varied at two levels: sustainable and not sustainable. The sustainable condition was operationalized using a context that allowed subjects to hide bad news for some time. The not sustainable condition was created using a context that would not allow subjects to hide bad news (see Table 3.2). As shown in Table 3.2, the manipulation for information asymmetry was checked using two questions (IA1 and IA2) taken from Keil *et al.* [25]. Each question was anchored on a seven-point scale ranging from "strongly disagree" (1) to "strongly agree" (7). These two questions had a Cronbach's alpha of 0.52 for this study.[1] The scores for both questions were averaged for the manipulation check (see Section V – Manipulation and control checks). A higher score indicated a context where information asymmetry was sustainable.

Operationalization of individualism–collectivism

Hofstede [17, p. 53] provided individualism–collectivism scores for more than 50 countries. The scores range from 6 to 91 with the average being 43. High scores are associated with individualistic cultures while low scores are associated with collectivistic cultures. The U.S. has a score of 91 (highly individualistic) while Singapore has a score of 20 (highly collectivistic). Although Hofstede's [16] data were collected in the 1970s, recent studies (e.g., [41], [48], [52]) have provided support for Hofstede's [16] data by showing that Singapore is much more collectivistic than the U.S. These findings lend validity to the claim that national culture is fairly stable in a temporal sense.

In this study, individualism and collectivism were operationalized by conducting matching experiments in the U.S. and Singapore, respectively (see Table 3.3). Differences between these two countries on individualism–collectivism have been found to be very salient in prior studies, e.g., [52], [57]. Other than cultural differences, the U.S. and Singapore shared several

---

[1]Since the Cronbach's alpha was low, the result of the manipulation check for information asymmetry was confirmed using separate analyses for IA1 and IA2 (see Section V – Manipulation and control checks).

Table 3.2   *Operationalization of information asymmetry*

Treatment	Sustainable	Not Sustainable
Context	Subjects can hide bad news for some time	Subjects cannot hide bad news
Scenario given to subjects	The client would not detect the problem for a period of five months and that, in one month, you would receive a promotion to another division of the company where there was very little chance that anyone would hear about the ultimate success or failure of this project.	The problem would become visible to everyone immediately when the software system was delivered to the client.
Questions for manipulation check	*IA1*: Project Y's system problems will become apparent almost immediately after the system is turned over to the client (reverse scale). *IA2*: Whether or not I tell my supervisor about Project Y's status, the system problems will come to light very soon anyway (reverse scale).	

Table 3.3   *Operationalization of national culture*

Treatment	Individualism	Collectivism
Country	United States	Singapore
Description	Ties between people are loose and people focus on their own needs. People tend to put personal interests above team interests. People take their actions independently of what others think and base their self-understanding on these personal actions.	People are integrated into cohesive groups, which take care of them in exchange for unquestioning loyalty. People tend to put team interests above personal interests. They base their self-understanding on how others around them react because they consider themselves members of cohesive groups.
Question for manipulation check	*IC1*: Work with people who coopera well with each other.	

common characteristics. First, citizens of both countries are educated in English. Second, both countries are economically developed. Third, the software industry plays a key role in the economy of both countries. As shown in Table 3.3 the manipulation for individualism–collectivism was checked (see Section V – Manipulation and control checks) using a question (IC1) taken from Hofstede [16]. The question was anchored on a five-point scale ranging from "of no importance" (1) to "of utmost importance" (5). A higher score indicated collectivism while a lower score indicated individualism.

Operationalization of predisposition to report bad news

Predisposition to report bad news (the dependent variable) was measured using three questions (RR1 to RR3) taken from Keil *et al.* [25] (see Table 3.4). Each question was anchored on a seven-point scale ranging from "very unlikely" (1) to "very likely" (7). These three questions had a Cronbach's alpha of 0.75 for this study. The scores for these questions were averaged to obtain the dependent variable. A lower score indicated greater reluctance to report bad news about the software project.

The procedure

Subjects in each treatment condition were told that this was an experiment on business decision-making and that their answers would remain anonymous. They were reminded that their participation was voluntary and those who did not wish to participate could leave. All subjects chose to participate in the experiment. Subjects in each country were randomly assigned to one of the four treatment conditions (obtained by varying organizational climate and information asymmetry).

Table 3.4   *Operationalization of reluctance to report bad news*

Questions for measuring dependent variable	*RR1*: How likely are you to go directly to your supervisor to inform him/her of the system problems on Project Y?
	RR2: If you inform your supervisor about the system problems on Project Y and he/she does not act to remedy the problem or inform the client, how likely are you to inform his/her supervisor about Project Y's problems?
	RR3: If you inform your supervisor and his/her supervisor about the system problems on Project Y but neither acts to remedy the problem or inform the client, how likely are you to inform a senior executive about Project Y's problems?

During the experiment, subjects received a copy of the scenario corresponding to their respective treatment condition. They were asked to read the scenario and complete a questionnaire that measured their likelihood of reporting the bad news about their project (RR1 to RR3). Subjects also responded to a series of questions for manipulation checks (OC1 to OC4, IA1, IA2 and IC1). They then provided their demographic information for control checks.

The subjects

A total of 354 subjects (162 citizens of the U.S. and 192 citizens of Singapore) participated in this study.[2] The subjects were working professionals who were attending graduate (masters-level) classes part-time in the evenings. They were enrolled in information systems courses at a large university in their respective countries. Subjects in the U.S. had an average age of 27.7 years, an average work experience of 5.5 years (2.5 years on software projects), with 56% males and 44% females. Subjects in Singapore had an average age of 24.0 years, an average work experience of 3.4 years (2.1 years on software projects), with 60% males and 40% females.

Many empirical studies have used student subjects in decision-making tasks, e.g., [44] and, specifically, decisions associated with project management, e.g., [15], [26], [47]. While some researchers have argued that the use of student subjects could limit the generalizability of the results to organizational decision-makers, other scholars have provided support for using students as surrogates for managers, e.g., [7], [37]. In this study, the issue of generalizability was addressed by using (graduate student) subjects who were full-time working professionals with experience on software projects. These subjects should be capable of grasping the business and political aspects of the scenario. Their demographic characteristics were close to those of a project leader (the role prescribed in the scenario). Thus, this subject pool appeared to be appropriate for this study.

V. Analyses

Manipulation and control checks

Results of manipulation and control checks that were stronger than the 5% level were considered significant. For the manipulation of organizational climate, subjects assigned to the treatment of conducive organizational climate (mean = 4.31, std. dev = 1.01) scored significantly higher on the manipulation

---

[2]The responses of 58 other subjects in the U.S. experiment and eight other subjects in the Singapore experiment were dropped from this study because these subjects were not citizens of the U.S. and Singapore, respectively. The 354 responses used were all obtained from citizens of the U.S. and Singapore.

check (OC1–OC4) than subjects assigned to the treatment of not conducive organizational climate (mean = 2.28, std. dev. = 1.37) (t = 15.61, $p < 0.01$). For the manipulation of information asymmetry, subjects assigned to the treatment of sustainable information asymmetry (mean = 4.13, std. dev. = 1.48) scored significantly higher on the manipulation check (IA1 and IA2) than subjects assigned to the treatment of not sustainable information asymmetry (mean = 2.24, std. dev. = 1.30) (t = 12.71, $p < 0.01$).[3] For the manipulation of individualism–collectivism, subjects from the collectivistic culture (Singapore) (mean = 4.43, std. dev. = 0.63) scored significantly higher on the manipulation check (IC1) than subjects from the individualistic culture (U.S.) (mean = 4.19, std. dev. = 0.67) (t = 3.43, $p < 0.01$). The manipulation of the three independent variables appeared to be successful.

Control checks were carried out on subject demographics for each country. Mann–Whitney tests showed that the gender ratio of subjects in each country did not differ significantly across the different treatments for organizational climate and information asymmetry. F-tests showed that the age and work experience of subjects in each country did not differ significantly across the different treatments for organizational climate and information asymmetry.

Hypothesis tests

Table 3.5 presents the descriptive statistics for the dependent variable. Table 3.6 shows the results of an ANOVA test on the dependent variable. Given that the dependent variable could not simultaneously fulfill the homogeneity and normality requirements of the ANOVA test, all significant results found were confirmed with nonparametric tests. Results of statistical tests that were stronger than the 5% level were deemed significant.

The ANOVA test revealed main effects due to organizational climate (F = 24.47, $p < 0.01$) and information asymmetry (F = 25.24, $p < 0.01$). In addition, there were two-way interactions between organizational climate and individualism–collectivism (F = 4.15, $p < 0.05$) and between information asymmetry and individualism–collectivism (F = 4.33, $p < 0.04$). Interpretation of the interactions should take precedence over that of main effects [27].

The interaction between organizational climate and individualism–collectivism was examined by separating the individualism (U.S.) data from the collectivism (Singapore) data. For the individualism data, organizational

---

[3]Since the questions for this manipulation check had low Cronbach's alpha (see Section IV – *Operationalization of information asymmetry*), this result was confirmed using separate analyses for IA1 and IA2. Subjects under the treatment of sustainable information asymmetry (mean = 4.76, std. dev. = 1.89) scored significantly higher on IA1 than subjects under the treatment of not sustainable information asymmetry (mean = 2.23, std. dev. = 1.50) (t = 13.97, $p < 0.01$). Subjects under the treatment of sustainable information asymmetry (mean = 3.51, std. dev. = 2.01) also scored significantly higher on IA2 than subjects under the treatment of not sustainable information asymmetry (mean = 2.26, std. dev. = 1.73) (t = 6.28, $p < 0.01$).

Table 3.5   *Mean (std. dev., sample size) of dependent variable*

National culture	Information asymmetry	Organizational climate	
		Conducive	Not conducive
Individualism	Sustainable	5.20 (1.23, 39)	4.35 (1.61, 40)
(United States)	Not sustainable	5.41 (1.08, 40)	4.61 (1.44, 43)
Collectivism	Sustainable	4.53 (1.56, 45)	4.55 (1.58, 50)
(Singapore)	Not sustainable	5.62 (0.94, 47)	5.13 (1.18, 50)

Table 3.6   *Results of ANOVA test on dependent variable*

Source of variation	DF	SS	F	P
Organizational climate (OC)	1	24.47	13.49	0.001**
Information asymmetry (IA)	1	25.24	13.91	0.001**
Individualism–collectivism (IC)	1	0.38	0.21	0.648
OC × IA	1	1.23	0.68	0.410
OC × IC	1	7.54	4.15	0.042*
IA × IC	1	7.86	4.33	0.038*
OC × IA × IC	1	1.82	1.00	0.318
Error	346	627.71		
Total	353	696.25		

$^{**}p < 0.01$, $^{*}p < 0.05$, R-squared $= 9.84\%$

climate had a significant impact on the dependent variable ($t = 3.85, p < 0.01$). This result was confirmed using a Mann–Whitney test (Chi-squared $= 3.54$, $p < 0.01$). Subjects under the treatment of not conducive organizational climate (mean $= 4.49$, std. dev $= 1.52$) were significantly more reluctant to report bad news about their software project than subjects under the treatment of conducive organizational climate (mean $= 5.30$, std. dev $= 1.15$). For the collectivism data, organizational climate had no significant impact on the dependent variable ($t = 1.22$, $p < 0.23$). Subjects under the treatment of not conducive organizational climate (mean $= 4.84$, std. dev $= 1.41$) were slightly (but not significantly) more reluctant to report bad news about their software project compared to subjects under the treatment of conducive organizational climate (mean $= 5.09$, std. dev $= 1.39$). *Individualism appeared to amplify the impact of organizational climate while collectivism appeared to dampen the impact of organizational climate.* Hypothesis 1 was supported.

The interaction between information asymmetry and individualism–collectivism was investigated similarly by separating the individualism (U.S.) data from the collectivism (Singapore) data. For the collectivism data, information asymmetry had a significant impact on the dependent variable ($t = 4.26$, $p < 0.01$). This result was also confirmed using a Mann–Whitney test (Chi-squared $= 3.65$, $p < 0.01$). Subjects under the treatment of sustainable information asymmetry (mean $= 4.54$, std. dev. $= 1.56$) were significantly more reluctant to report bad news about their software project than subjects under the treatment of not sustainable information asymmetry (mean $= 5.37$, std. dev. $= 1.09$). For the individualism data, information asymmetry had no significant impact on the dependent variable ($t = 1.03$, $p < 0.31$). Subjects under the treatment of sustainable information asymmetry (mean $= 4.77$, std. dev. $= 1.48$) were slightly (but not significantly) more reluctant to report bad news about their software project than subjects under the treatment of not sustainable information asymmetry (mean $= 5.00$, std. dev. $= 1.33$). *Collectivism appeared to amplify the impact of information asymmetry while individualism appeared to dampen the impact of information asymmetry.* Hypothesis 2 was supported.

VI. Discussion and implications

The main effects for organizational climate and information asymmetry in the ANOVA test reinforce prior research [25] by showing that both factors impact human predisposition to report bad news about software projects. Thus, this study provides evidence that the key relationships shown by Keil *et al.* [25] hold, to some extent, in both an individualistic and a collectivistic culture. But more importantly, this study shows that the individualism–collectivism dimension of national culture moderates the impact of organizational climate and information asymmetry on human predisposition to report bad news about software projects. The causal relationship between organizational climate and predisposition to report bad news appears to be stronger in an individualistic than in a collectivistic culture. Conversely, the causal relationship between information asymmetry and predisposition to report bad news appears to be stronger in a collectivistic than in an individualistic culture.

The model presented in Table 3.6 explained about 10% of the variance in human predisposition to report bad news about software projects. There is clearly room for more research in this area. The findings of this study provide a foundation upon which further research can be built.[4] Some useful practical

---

[4]In a similar context involving software projects, early empirical studies on the escalation of commitment phenomenon could explain no more than 15% of the variance in human decisions. Nevertheless, these early studies provided a foundation for subsequent empirical studies that could explain more than 40% of the variance in human decisions [26].

implications based on these findings and some ways to extend the research model, so as to account for more of the variance in human predisposition to report bad news, have been presented in the following section.

Implications for practice

From the perspective of senior managers, the sooner bad news about a software project is received, the higher the probability that either corrective action can be taken or the software project can be canceled so that valuable resources can be channeled to better alternative uses. From the perspective of clients, early corrective action on the software project may also allow them to have earlier delivery of the final software product. In general, by creating an organizational climate that encourages early reporting of project information (both positive and negative) and by having a system that reduces the probability that project information can be hidden for long periods, senior managers can encourage bad news about software projects to be brought to their attention sooner. This reduces expenditure of valuable resources on failing software projects [25] and allows faster delivery of final software products.

Adding to prior research findings, results of this study suggest that paying careful attention to the cultural context can improve the likelihood of problems about software projects being reported earlier. It is worth noting that, even within a national culture, there would still be some variance across the citizenry on a cultural dimension [10], [17], [48]. Even when software projects must be staffed from within a single national culture, senior managers can conceivably use such variance to their benefit. They can populate software project teams with employees who seem to have somewhat different personal orientations on a cultural dimension (e.g., individualism–collectivism). In many instances, senior managers may have the opportunity to create cross-cultural software project teams. They can then intentionally put together employees from different national cultures so as to alleviate problems (factors causing human reluctance to report bad news) associated with specific national cultures. Alternatively, senior managers can institute additional mechanisms to address the issues pertaining to the culture from which many of their employees are drawn. In light of the moderating impact of individualism–collectivism identified by this study, two specific issues deserve the attention of senior managers.

First, people from individualistic cultures appear to be particularly sensitive to organizational cues regarding perceived retribution from reporting bad news. Researchers have noted that, if the organizational unwritten norms suggest that "bad news gets you killed," this deters many employees who might otherwise provide input to superiors [22]. While this relationship between retribution and reporting of bad news is not unique to individualistic cultures, it appears to have special salience within such cultures. Hence, some lessons may be learned from the U.S. federal government efforts, over a 15-year period, to increase reporting of wastefulness and malfeasance by employees. The Civil Service Reform Act of 1978 created a structure (e.g., "hotlines") to encourage employees to report accurate information (including bad news). Eleven years later, the Whistleblower Protection Act of 1989 was introduced to prohibit retaliation against employees who reported accurate information (including bad news) and a special federal office was established to provide the necessary protection to employees [31, p. 223], [31, pp. 1–3], [33, pp. 1–2]. Two surveys of federal employees, conducted 12 years apart (in 1981 and 1993), provided encouraging feedback. The percentage of employees willing to report illegal and wasteful activities jumped from 30% to 50% [32], [33]. Although there may be other factors at play, it seems reasonable to infer that these efforts had some impact on the tendency of employees to report accurate information (including bad news). Thus, especially in individualistic cultures, it seems that a nonretaliatory message can be especially useful. To add to these measures, senior managers may also include some employees with a collectivistic background to software project teams that otherwise are primarily consisted of employees with an individualistic background.

People from individualistic cultures also appear to be sensitive to promises of rewards for reporting accurate information (including bad news). Often targeted at those who report illegal or immoral behavior, some organizations give cash rewards to employees who come forward. Federal law also provides for such rewards under certain circumstances (e.g., reports of physicians defrauding Medicare). Other organizations give written commendations to employees when they report improper behavior [31, pp. 299–301]. Although the reporting of negative project information is not exactly the same as whistleblowing on illegal activities, it is plausible that many of these techniques can be useful in encouraging the reporting of accurate information (including bad news), particularly in individualistic cultures.

Second, people from collectivistic cultures appear to be particularly susceptible to perceptions of sustained information asymmetry when it comes to reporting bad news. People may be disinclined to report bad news about software projects if they believe that they can help their project team by giving it more time to get the projects back on track. Yet senior managers would usually prefer to be aware of emerging difficulties so that a resource re-allocation decision or a project cancellation decision can be taken. Senior managers can proactively address this matter, to some extent, by adding some employees with an individualistic background to software project teams that otherwise are primarily consisted of employees with a collectivistic background. As another alternative, senior managers in collectivistic cultures can appeal to employees' sense of corporate identity to move their reference point from their project team to the overall organization. This way, the employees may put organizational interests above that of their project team and, thereby, be more willing to report bad news about software projects.

People from collectivistic cultures also seem to be particularly eager to report accurate information (including bad news) under conditions of unsustainable information asymmetry. Therefore, in collectivistic cultures, senior managers must recognize that increased monitoring of software projects is an especially prudent investment of resources. If employees believe that project information would become known quickly, they would be very willing to report accurate project information (including bad news). Thus, the key is to increase the perceptual probability that project information will come to light soon.

Implications for research

Although this study provides new and useful insights regarding the reporting of bad news about software projects, the model presented in Table 3.6 was able to explain only about 10% of the variance in reporting intention. This suggests that much work remains in our quest to better understand human predisposition to report bad news about software projects. Other than national culture and organizational culture, project team culture and individual cultural beliefs [6] may also affect human predisposition to report bad news about software projects. Along this direction, several specific extensions seem appropriate.

First, researchers may consider the project team (rather than the individual, as in this study) as the unit of analysis. There are no doubt many situations in which the entire software project team is aware of the project status and the team may make a group decision on whether or not to report bad news. One interesting feature of project teams is that they create an opportunity for "diffusion of responsibility." Some of the earliest research on bystander intervention concluded that individuals were less likely to offer assistance when they were part of a large group of bystanders than when they were alone [30]. In an organizational analogy, first suggested by Dozier and Miceli [8], one could surmise that as the number of team members who are privy to the bad news about their software project increases, so each individual would feel less personal responsibility for reporting the bad news. Additionally, if such project teams consist of some members who have an individualistic orientation and other members who have a collectivistic orientation, the team dynamics may prove especially interesting. On the one hand, both orientations may be so dominant that the team embraces the individualistic sensitivity toward organizational climate as well as the collectivistic sensitivity toward information asymmetry. On the other hand, both cultures may neutralize each other so that the team loses both the individualistic sensitivity toward organizational climate and the collectivistic sensitivity toward information asymmetry. In reality, little is known about how project team culture may emerge from such team dynamics and impact human predisposition to report bad news. This is a fertile ground for additional research.

Second, to the extent that people may be guided by their ethical disposition [3], [38] when deciding whether or not to report bad news, it may be useful to investigate the propensity of people for ethical reasoning or their level of moral judgment development [28]. Third, researchers may want to consider the inclusion of some other variables related to project management. Given that people vary in their perceptions of time urgency [29], this factor may be a good candidate for investigation in future work that considers the time pressure associated with software projects. Related studies on software project management have examined the risk propensity of people as a factor affecting project management decisions (e.g., [26], [47]) so this factor may also impact reporting decisions. There is also reason to believe that the "locus of control" [40] of a person (the degree to which a person believes that events are under his/her control) can influence his/her assessment of reporting intention [31]. Finally, demographic variables may affect human assessments of reporting intention [46]. All these factors are aspects of individual cultural beliefs that potentially affect human predisposition to report bad news about software projects and can be studied in the future.

Limitations

It has already been noted that the results of this study could be strengthened by the inclusion of other variables that may help to explain the variance in reporting behavior. The three independent variables examined here, while important, clearly do not tell the entire story. It should also be noted that this study used graduate students as subjects. Although these subjects were full-time working professionals with some experience on software projects and demographic characteristics close to those of a project leader, it was still a sample of convenience. To increase the confidence that the results of this study would apply to specific populations of project leaders, it is necessary to select a sample from the target population of project leaders and administer this study to that sample of project leaders.

Consistent with other studies that examined software project management decisions involving organizational factors (e.g., [14], [15], [56]), the experiment conducted in this study took a necessarily narrow focus so as to attain a high degree of internal validity. The experimental manipulations (especially the manipulation on organizational climate) were strong. Although such strong manipulations can strengthen treatments and, thereby, help to increase the internal validity of an experiment, it may also cause subjects to simply adhere to treatments without making a behavioral decision. In reality, project team leaders may not be so clear about whether the organizational climate is conducive or not, or whether the information asymmetry is sustainable or not. The scenarios were simple with limited decision options. Project team leaders may have decision options that were not considered in this study.

Further, there are doubtless other organizational and political factors that may also influence decisions on whether or not to report bad news about software projects. These factors have not been investigated here. Indeed, some of these factors may not lend themselves to experiments. However, these factors can be examined through field studies using interpretivist methodologies (e.g., ethnographic studies).

Like many prior cross-cultural studies in the field of information systems, e.g., [10], [52], [57], this study included only one individualistic culture (U.S.) and one collectivistic culture (Singapore) in its sample space. Obviously, the findings of this study can be strengthened in terms of generalizability if these findings can be replicated in other individualistic and collectivistic cultures. This study attempts to enhance internal validity by using only responses from citizens of the U.S. and Singapore (see Section IV – The subjects). Nevertheless, citizens within each country (especially the U.S.) may still differ widely in terms of their cultural beliefs because they have different ethnic origins and therefore different cultural values. This is a threat to internal validity.

VII.   Conclusion

The present study is the first cross-cultural study that identifies causal factors affecting reporting intention in any context (not just in the context of software projects). It adds a cultural dimension to our knowledge on human decision-making involving software projects. Specifically, it demonstrates that a dimension of national culture (individualism–collectivism) moderates the impact of two aspects of organizational culture (organizational climate and information asymmetry) on human predisposition to report bad news about software projects. These findings have useful implications for the management of increasingly common cross-cultural software project teams and provide a foundation for pursuing further research involving cross-cultural software project teams.

Increasingly, software development efforts (both in-sourcing and out-sourcing) are crossing national and cultural boundaries. For the most part unconsciously, project team leaders and members bring their own cultural values with them as they make project-related decisions. Specific cultural values may cause some project team leaders and members to be more vulnerable than others in certain project decision situations (e.g., whether or not to report bad news about software projects). A better understanding of the relationship (direct or moderated) between cultural values and the project decision-making process or outcome can be particularly valuable for the management of cross-cultural software project teams. This study represents a first step in improving our understanding in this important area and we hope it will stimulate other studies along this direction.

Appendix

Scenario 1 (Not Favorable Organizational Climate, Sustainable Information Asymmetry)

You are a system development project leader in a large consulting firm, System Solution Corporation (SSC). For the past six months, you have been project leader for Project Y, the development of a new order processing system for an important client. The client is expecting that you will turn the system over to them this month, as scheduled. It is very important to the client that this schedule be met so that the client will be able to complete a phase-in period before their peak order season, which is still five months away.

You have just discovered, somewhat by accident, that Project Y has a problem due to system limitations. You are the only person who is aware of the system's behavior and its possible negative consequences. There is no reason you would have been expected to know of these limitations. And, unless you tell others, no one will ever know that you were aware of the problem. Because of the system limitations, it is almost certain that the system performance during peak order season will be unacceptable. This will have a significant negative impact on the client's ability to process orders.

If you implement the system now, as scheduled, there is no way that either the client or your management could learn of the technical problems for **at least five months**. Performance problems will only become apparent during the peak order season when the volume increases. In addition, in **one month**, you are being promoted to a job in another division of the company in an overseas location. (SSC is comprised of several autonomous divisions that act almost as separate companies and there is almost no interaction between managers in the different divisions.) **It is very unlikely that your career path will ever return you to your present division and there is very little chance that anyone in your new division will ever hear about the ultimate success or failure of Project Y**.

On multiple occasions you have observed situations in your company where critical information concerning the current or expected state of a project was withheld from the client. **The norm in your company is that project leaders are expected to keep negative project information to themselves – not to inform either their supervisor or the client**. In one case of which you are aware, a project leader who disclosed negative project information was severely reprimanded and denied an expected promotion in spite of a very strong track record. And there is an unconfirmed rumor that, in another such case, the project leader who disclosed negative project information was later fired after being "set up" on some fabricated charges unrelated to the project.

Scenario 2 (Favorable Organizational Climate, Sustainable
Information Asymmetry)

You are a system development project leader in a large consulting firm,
System Solution Corporation (SSC). For the past six months, you have been
project leader for Project Y, the development of a new order processing system for an important client. The client is expecting that you will turn the system over to them this month, as scheduled. It is very important to the client
that this schedule be met so that the client will be able to complete a phase-in
period before their peak order season, which is still five months away.

You have just discovered, somewhat by accident, that Project Y has a problem due to system limitations. You are the only person who is aware of the
system's behavior and its possible negative consequences. There is no reason you would have been expected to know of these limitations. And, unless
you tell others, no one will ever know that you were aware of the problem.
Because of the system limitations, it is almost certain that the system performance during peak order season will be unacceptable. This will have a
significant negative impact on the client's ability to process orders.

If you implement the system now, as scheduled, there is no way that either
the client or your management could learn of the technical problems for **at
least five months**. Performance problems will only become apparent during
the peak order season when the volume increases. In addition, in **one month**
you are being promoted to a job in another division of the company in an
overseas location. (SSC is comprised of several autonomous divisions that
act almost as separate companies and there is almost no interaction between
managers in the different divisions.) **It is very unlikely that your career
path will ever return you to your present division and there is very little chance that anyone in your new division will ever hear about the
ultimate success or failure of Project Y**.

Through its company policies and its actions, your firm strongly emphasizes the importance of ethical conduct in all dealings with others – including
clients and employees. The company code of ethics includes the commitment "not to misrepresent or withhold information concerning the state of
affairs existing or expected regarding any aspect of a project." The Employee
Handbook that you were given when you joined the company clearly
describes how to behave when projects do not proceed as expected – employees are to report this information to their supervisor. If the employee's supervisor does not act to remedy the problem or inform the client, the employee is
to inform their supervisor's supervisor. **You are confident that if you inform
your supervisor about the system problems on Project Y, your supervisor
will immediately inform the client and work actively with them to determine the best course of action**. In one case of which you are aware, a
project leader who disclosed negative project information was commended
and shortly thereafter received an expected promotion.

*Scenario 3 (Not Favorable Organizational Climate, Not Sustainable
Information Asymmetry)*

You are a system development project leader in a large consulting firm,
System Solution Corporation (SSC). For the past six months, you have been
project leader for Project Y, the development of a new order processing system for an important client. The client is expecting that you will turn the system over to them this month, as scheduled. It is very important to the client
that this schedule be met so that the client will be able to complete a phase-in
period before their peak order season, which is still five months away.

   You have just discovered, somewhat by accident, that Project Y has a problem due to system limitations. You are the only person who is aware of the
system's behavior and its possible negative consequences. There is no reason you would have been expected to know of these limitations. And, unless
you tell others, no one will ever know that you were aware of the problem.
Because of the system limitations, it is almost certain that the system performance during peak order season will be unacceptable. This will have a
significant negative impact on the client's ability to process orders.

   Although neither the client nor your management is currently aware of the
performance problem, **this problem will be immediately visible to everyone
as soon as the system is turned over to the client**. A performance test is
part of the turnover process to the client and the current version of the system
will not pass the performance level requirement.

   On multiple occasions you have observed situations in your company where
critical information concerning the current or expected state of a project was
withheld from the client. **The norm in your company is that project leaders are expected to keep negative project information to themselves – not
to inform either their supervisor or the client**. In one case of which you are
aware, a project leader who disclosed negative project information was severely
reprimanded and denied an expected promotion in spite of a very strong track
record. And there is an unconfirmed rumor that, in another such case, the project
leader who disclosed negative project information was later fired after being "set
up" on some fabricated charges unrelated to the project.

*Scenario 4 (Favorable Organizational Climate, Not Sustainable
Information Asymmetry)*

You are a system development project leader in a large consulting firm, System
Solution Corporation (SSC). For the past six months, you have been project
leader for Project Y, the development of a new order processing system for an
important client. The client is expecting that you will turn the system over to
them this month, as scheduled. It is very important to the client that this schedule be met so that the client will be able to complete a phase-in period before
their peak order season, which is still five months away.

You have just discovered, somewhat by accident, that Project Y has a problem due to system limitations. You are the only person who is aware of the system's behavior and its possible negative consequences. There is no reason you would have been expected to know of these limitations. And, unless you tell others, no one will ever know that you were aware of the problem. Because of the system limitations, it is almost certain that the system performance during peak order season will be unacceptable. This will have a significant negative impact on the client's ability to process orders.

Although neither the client nor your management is currently aware of the performance problem, **this problem will be immediately visible to everyone as soon as the system is turned over to the client**. A performance test is part of the turnover process to the client and the current version of the system will not pass the performance level requirement.

Through its company policies and its actions, your firm strongly emphasizes the importance of ethical conduct in all dealings with others – including clients and employees. The company code of ethics includes the commitment "not to misrepresent or withhold information concerning the state of affairs existing or expected regarding any aspect of a project." The Employee Handbook that you were given when you joined the company clearly describes how to behave when projects do not proceed as expected – employees are to report this information to their supervisor. If the employee's supervisor does not act to remedy the problem or inform the client, the employee is to inform their supervisor's supervisor. **You are confident that if you inform your supervisor about the system problems on Project Y, your supervisor will immediately inform the client and work actively with them to determine the best course of action**. In one case of which you are aware, a project leader who disclosed negative project information was commended and shortly thereafter received an expected promotion.

Acknowledgment

The authors would like to thank the Special Issue Editor and the four anonymous reviewers for their many constructive comments and suggestions on earlier versions of this paper.

References

[1] M. H. Bond, K. Leung, and K. C. Wan (1982), "How does cultural collectivism operate? The impact of task and maintenance contributions on reward distribution," *J. Cross-Cultural Psych.*, Vol. 13, No. 2, pp. 186–200.

[2] N. A. Boyacigiller and N. J. Adler (1991), "The parochial dinosaur: Organizational science in a global context," *Acad. Manage. Rev.*, Vol. 16, No. 2, pp. 262–290.

[3] F. N. Brady and G. E. Wheeler (1996), "An empirical study of ethical predispositions," *J. Bus. Ethics*, Vol. 15, No. 9, pp. 927–940.

[4] R. G. Broody, J. M. Coulter, and P. H. Mihalek (1998), "Whistle-blowing: A cross-cultural comparison of ethical perceptions of US and Japanese accounting students," *Amer. Bus. Rev.*, Vol. 16, No. 2, pp. 14–21.

[5] M. C. Conlee and A. Tesser (1973), "The effects of recipient desire to hear on news transmission," *Sociometry*, Vol. 36, No. 4, pp. 588–599.

[6] R. B. Cooper (1994), "The inertial impact of culture on IT implementation," *Inform. Manage.*, Vol. 27, No. 1, pp. 17–31.

[7] G. DeSanctis (1989), "Small group research in information systems: Theory and method," in *The Information Systems Research Challenge: Experiment Research Methods*. Harvard Bus. School, Cambridge, MA, pp. 53–82.

[8] J. B. Dozier and M. P. Miceli (1985), "Potential predictors of whistle-blowing: A prosocial behavior perspective," *Acad. Manage. Rev.*, Vol. 10, No. 4, pp. 823–836.

[9] P. C. Earley (1993), "East meets west meets mideast: Further explorations of collectivistic and individualistic work groups," *Acad. Manage. J.*, Vol. 36, No. 2, pp. 319–348.

[10] ――― (1994), "Self or group? Cultural effects of training on self-efficacy and performance," *Administ. Sci. Quart.*, Vol. 39, No. 1, pp. 89–117.

[11] M. Erez and P. C. Earley (1993), *Culture, Self-Identity and Work*. Oxford Univ. Press, Oxford, U.K.

[12] D. Frantz (1989), "B of A's plans for computer don't add up," *LA Times*, June, pp. 1–8.

[13] M. J. Garfield and R. T. Watson (1997), "Differences in national information infrastructure: The reflection of national cultures," *J. Strat. Inform. Syst.*, Vol. 6, No. 4, pp. 313–337.

[14] A. Harrell and P. Harrison (1994), "An incentive to shirk, privately held information and managers' project evaluation decisions," *Account. Org. Soc.*, Vol. 19, No. 7, pp. 569–577.

[15] P. D. Harrison and A. Harrell (1993), "Impact of 'Adverse selection' on managers' project evaluation decisions," *Acad. Manage. J.*, Vol. 36, No. 3, pp. 635–643.

[16] G. Hofstede (1980), *Culture's Consequences: International Differences in Work-Related Values*. Sage, Newbury Park, CA.

[17] ――― (1997), *Cultures and Organizations: Software of the Mind*. McGraw-Hill, New York.

[18] C. L. Iacovou and A. S. Dexter (1996), "Explanations offered by IS managers to rationalize project failures," in *Proc. Academy of Management Conf.*, Cincinnati OH, Aug. 11–14, p. 552.

[19] M. C. Jensen and W. H. Meckling (1976), "Theory of the firm: managerial behavior, agency costs and ownership structure," *J. Financial Econ.*, Vol. 4, No. 3, pp. 305–360.

[20] P. B. Jubb (1999), "Whistleblowing: A restrictive definition and interpretation," *J. Bus. Ethics*, Vol. 21, No. 1, pp. 77–94.

[21] C. Kanodia, R. Bushman, and J. Dickhaut (1989), "Escalation errors and the sunk cost effect: An explanation based on reputation and information asymmetries," *J. Account. Res.*, Vol. 27, No. 1, pp. 59–77.

[22] J. P. Keenan (1995), "Whistleblowing and the first-level manager: Determinants of feeling obliged to blow the whistle," *J. Social Behav. Personality*, Vol. 10, No. 3, pp. 571–584.

[23] M. Keil and D. Robey (1999), "Turning around troubled software projects: An exploratory study of the deescalation of commitment to failing courses of action," *J. Manage. Inform. Syst.*, Vol. 15, No. 4, pp. 63–87.

[24] ――― (2001), "Blowing the whistle on troubled software projects," *Commun. ACM,* Vol. 44, No. 4, pp. 87–93.

[25] M. Keil, H. J. Smith, S. Pawlowski, and L. Jin (2001), *Why didn't somebody tell me? Climate, information asymmetry and bad news about troubled projects.* Georgia State University, Atlanta, GA.

[26] M. Keil, B. C. Y. Tan, K. K. Wei, T. Saarinen, V. Tuunainen, and A. Wassenaar (2000), "A cross-cultural study on escalation of commitment in software projects," *MIS Quart.*, Vol. 24, No. 2, pp. 299–325.

[27] G. Keppel (1991), *Analysis and Design: A Researcher's Handbook.* Prentice-Hall, Englewood Cliffs, NJ.

[28] L. Kohlberg (1981), *Essays on Moral Development (Volume 1): The Philosophy of Moral Development.* Harper & Row, San Francisco, CA.

[29] F. J. Landy, H. Rastegary, J. Thayer, and C. Colvin (1991), "Time urgency: The construct and its measurement," *J. Appl. Psych.*, Vol. 76, No. 5, pp. 644–657.

[30] B. Latane and J. M. Darley (1968), "Group inhibition of bystander intervention," *J. Personality Social Psych.*, Vol. 10, No. 3, pp. 215–221.

[31] M. P. Miceli and J. P. Near (1992), *Blowing the Whistle: The Organizational and Legal Implications for Companies and Employees.* Lexington, New York.

[32] "Merit systems protection board, whistleblowing and the federal employee," United States Merit Systems Protection Board, Washington, DC, 1981.

[33] "Merit Systems protection board, whistleblowing in the federal government: An update," United States Merit Systems Protection Board, Washington, DC, 1993.

[34] E. C. O'Neal, D. W. Levine, and J. F. Frank (1979), "Reluctance to transmit bad news when the recipient is unknown: Experiments in five nations," *Social Behavior Personality*, Vol. 7, No. 1, pp. 39–47.

[35] E. Oz (1994), "When professional standards are lax: The CONFIRM failure and its lessons," *Commun. ACM.*, Vol. 37, No. 10, pp. 29–36.

[36] I. P. L. Png, B. C. Y. Tan, and K. L. Wee (2001), "Dimensions of national culture and corporate adoption of it infrastructure," *IEEE Trans. Eng. Manage.*, Vol. 48, pp. 36–45.

[37] W. Remus (1986), "Graduate students as surrogates for managers in experiments on business decision making," *J. Bus. Res.*, Vol. 14, No. 1, pp. 19–25.

[38] J. Rest (1973), "The hierarchical nature of moral judgment: A study of patterns of comprehension and preference of moral stages," *J. Personality*, Vol. 41, No. l, pp. 86–109.

[39] S. Ronen and O. Shenkar (1985), "Clustering countries on attitudinal dimensions: A review and synthesis," *Acad. Manage. Rev.*, Vol. 10, No. 3, pp. 435–454.

[40] J. B. Rotter (1966), "Generalized expectancies for internal versus external control of reinforcement," *Psych. Monographs*, Vol. 80, No. 1, pp. 1–28.

[41] S. H. Schwartz (1994), "Beyond individualism-collectivism: New cultural dimensions of values," in *Individualism and Collectivism*. Sage, Newbury Park, CA, pp. 85–119.

[42] V. J. Shackleton and A. H. Ali (1990), "Work-related values of managers: A test of the Hofstede model," *J. Cross-Cultural Psych.*, Vol. 21, No. 1, pp. 109–118.

[43] B. Shore and A. R. Venkatachalam (1995), "The role of national culture in systems analysis and design," *J. Glob. Inform. Manage.*, Vol. 3, No. 1, pp. 5–14.

[44] S. B. Sitkin and L. R. Weingart (1995), "Determinants of risky decision-making behavior: A test of the mediating role of risk perceptions and propensity," *Acad. Manage. J.*, Vol. 38, No. 6, pp. 1573–1592.

[45] H. J. Smith and M. Keil (2003), "The reluctance to report bad news about software projects: A theoretical model," *Inform. Syst. J.*, Vol. 13, No. 1, pp. 69–95.

[46] ——— (2001), "The reluctance to report bad news on troubled software projects: A theoretical model," Wake Forest University, Winston-Salem, NC.

[47] H. J. Smith, M. Keil, and G. Depledge (2001), "Keeping mum as the project goes under: Toward an explanatory model," *J. Manage. Inform. Syst.*, Vol. 18, No. 2, pp. 189–227.

[48] P. B. Smith, S. Dugan, and F. Trompenaars (1996), "National culture and the values of organizational employees: A dimension analysis across 43 nations," *J. Cross-Cultural Psych.*, Vol. 27, No. 2, pp. 231–264.

[49] M. Sondergaard (1990), "Hofstede's consequences: A study of reviews, citations and replications," *Org. Stud.*, Vol. 15, No. 3, pp. 447–456.

[50] "CHAOS: A recipe for success," Standish Group Int. Inc., West Yarmouth, MA, 1999.

[51] D. W. Straub (1994), "The effect of culture on IT diffusion: E-mail and fax in Japan and the United States," *Inform. Syst. Res.*, Vol. 5, No. 1, pp. 23–47.

[52] B. C. Y. Tan, K. K. Wei, R. T. Watson, D. L. Clapper, and E. R. McLean (1998), "Computer-mediated communication and majority influence: Assessing the impact in an individualistic and a collectivistic culture," *Manage. Sci.*, Vol. 44, No. 9, pp. 1263–1278.

[53] A. Tesser and S. Rosen (1975), "The reluctance to transmit bad news," in *Advances in Experimental Social Psychology*, Vol. 8. Academic, New York, pp. 193–232.

[54] R. Tomsho (1994), "Real dog: How greyhound lines re-engineered itself right into a deep hole," *Wall St. J.*, Oct. 20, pp. Al–A6.

[55] H. C. Triandis (1995), *Individualism and Collectivism*. Westview, Boulder, CO.

[56] B. Tuttle, A. Harrell, and P. Harrison (1997), "Moral hazard, ethical considerations and the decision to implement an information system," *J. Manage. Inform. Syst.*, Vol. 13, No. 4, pp. 7–27.

[57] R. T. Watson, T. H. Ho, and K. S. Raman (1994), "Culture: A fourth dimension of group support systems," *Commun. ACM.*, Vol. 37, No. 10, pp. 44–55.

Reproduced from *IEEE Transactions on Engineering Management*, Vol. 50, No. 1, Feburary 2003, pp. 65–77. Reprinted with permission from IEEE.

About the authors

Bernard C. Y. Tan received the Ph.D. degree in information systems from the National University of Singapore (NUS), in 1995.

He was a Visiting Scholar with the Graduate School of Business, Stanford University, Stanford, CA from 1996 to 1997 and with the Terry College of Business, University of Georgia, Athens, in 1992. He is currently an Associate Professor and Head of the Department of Information Systems, NUS. He has served on the editorial board of *MIS Quarterly* and is currently serving on the editorial boards of *Information and Management, Journal of the AIS, Journal of Global Information Management* and *International Journal of Distance Education Technologies*. His research work has been published in IEEE TRANSACTIONS ON SYSTEMS, MAN AND CYBERNETICS, IEEE TRANSACTIONS ON ENGINEERING MANAGEMENT, IEEE TRANSACTIONS ON PROFESSIONAL COMMUNICATION, *MIS Quarterly, Information Systems Research, Management Science, Journal of Management Information Systems, Communications of the*

ACM, ACM Transactions on Computer-Human Interaction, ACM Transactions on Information Systems, International Journal of Human-Computer Studies, Information and Management, Decision Support Systems and European Journal of Information Systems. His current research interests include cross-cultural issues, computer-mediated communication, knowledge management, and electronic commerce.

Dr. Tan has won research and teaching awards at NUS.

H. Jeff Smith received B.S. degrees in computer science and mathematics from North Carolina State University, Raleigh, the M.B.A. degree from the University of North Carolina, Chapel Hill, and the D.B.A. degree from Harvard University, Cambridge, MA.

He is currently an Associate Professor of Management with the Babcock Graduate School of Management, Wake Forest University, Winston-Salem, NC. He was with the International Business Machines (IBM) Corporation for several years in the area of software development. His research interests include societal and regulatory issues associated with strategic uses of information technology and organizational impediments to successful implementation of information technology applications. His research has appeared in *California Management Review, Communications of the ACM, Harvard Business Review, MIS Quarterly, Organization Science, Sloan Management Review* and other journals. He is also the author of *Managing Privacy: Information Technology and Corporate America* (Raleigh, NC: Univ. North Carolina Press, 1994).

Dr. Smith received the 1994 Donald McGannon Book Award for Social and Ethical Relevance in Communication Policy Research (administered by Fordham University).

Mark Keil (M'02) received the B.S. degree from Princeton University, Princeton, NJ, the M.S. degree from the Sloan School of Management, Massachusetts Institute of Technology, Cambridge, and the Ph.D. degree in management information systems from the Harvard Business School, Harvard University, Cambridge, MA.

He is currently a Professor of Computer Information Systems (CIS) in the J. Mack Robinson College of Business, Georgia State University, Atlanta. His research interests include software project management with particular emphasis on identifying and preventing software project escalation. His publications have appeared in such journals as IEEE TRANSACTIONS ON ENGINEERING MANAGEMENT, *MIS Quarterly, Sloan Management Review, Communications of the ACM, Journal of Management Information Systems*, and *Decision Support Systems*. He has also served as an Associate Editor for *MIS Quarterly*, and as Co-Editor of *The DATA BASE* for Advances in Information Systems.

Dr. Keil currently serves on the Editorial Board of IEEE TRANSACTIONS ON ENGINEERING MANAGEMENT.

Ramiro Montealegre received the B.S. degree in engineering from the Francisco Marroquín University, Guatemala City, Guatemala, the M.S. degree in computer science from Carleton University, Ottawa, Canada, and the Ph.D. degree in business administration in the area of management information systems from the Harvard Business School, Harvard University, Cambridge, MA.

He is currently an Associate Professor of Information Systems at the University of Colorado, Boulder and a Visiting Professor at the Instituto de Empresa, Madrid, Spain. He has been an Invited Lecturer at Case Western Reserve University, Cleveland, OH; IAE Business School, Buenos Aires, Argentina; the Instituto de Centro América de Administración de Empresas (INCAE), Costa Rica; and the Instituto Tecnológico y de Estudios Superiores de Monterrey, Mexico. His research interests include the interplay between information technology and organization transformation in highly uncertain environments. He has been involved in studying projects of organizational change in the U.S., Canada, Spain, Mexico, and the Central and South American regions. His research has been published in IEEE TRANSACTIONS ON SYSTEMS, MAN AND CYBERNETICS, IEEE TRANSACTIONS ON COMMUNICATIONS, INFORMATION & MANAGEMENT, *Organization Science, MIS Quarterly, Sloan Management Review, Journal of Management Information Systems, Information Technology & People,* and other journals.

Questions for discussion

1   Why do so many software projects go over-budget, or are late, or lack the promised functionality?
2   Among the members of the project development team, excluding the auditors, who do you think should be responsible for reporting the true status of the project (even if it is bad news)? Why?
3   Why might the project manager (or whomever is responsible) choose not to report bad news to his/her superior?
4   Besides national culture, what might influence a person's decision to report, or withhold, bad news about a software project?
5   What do you think could be done to encourage people to report bad news earlier?
6   What types of "bad" news would be "good" to report? What types of "bad" news might be better to conceal?

4 Competing Values in Software Process Improvement: An Assumption Analysis of CMM From An Organizational Culture Perspective

Ojelanki Ngwenyama and
Peter Axel Nielsen

Abstract: The capability maturity model (CMM) approach to software process improvement is the most dominant paradigm of organizational change that software organizations implement. While some organizations have achieved various levels of success with the CMM, the vast majority have failed. In this paper, we investigate the assumptions about organizational culture embedded in the CMM models and we discuss their implications for software process improvement (SPI) initiatives. In this paper, we utilize the well-known competing values model to surface and analyze the assumptions underlying the CMM. Our analysis reveals contradictory sets of assumptions about organizational culture in the CMM approach. We believe that an understanding of these contradictions can help researchers address some of the difficulties that have been observed in implementing and institutionalizing SPI programs in organizations. Further, this research can help to open up a much-needed line of research that would examine the organization theory assumptions that underpin CMM. This type of research is important if CMM is to evolve as an effective, organizational change paradigm for software organizations.

I. Introduction

During the last decade, software process improvement (SPI) has emerged as the dominant approach for improving quality and productivity in software development organizations. Inspired by the work of Humphrey [15]–[17], a large body of knowledge on SPI has become available including specific models such as SPICE [7], the European bootstrap model [22], the capability maturity model (CMM) [33]–[35], quality improvement process [27], and quality software management [49]. The CMM and its SPI implementation methodology, IDEAL, are the most widely known and are used by software companies all over the world. The theoretical foundations of SPI approaches (specifically CMM) are rooted in the technical perspectives of cybernetics and total quality management. Ever since its first presentation, CMM has been extremely influential on software engineering practices around the world. The model has served as a framework for software process and quality improvement efforts in thousands of software organizations and the resources expended on CMM-based SPI are in the billions of dollars [9]. Despite the large investments of resources, the failure rate for SPI programs is high – too high many would say. The most recent report from the Software Engineering Institute puts the rate of failure at around 70% [45]; a prior report [44] showed equally dim results.

There are several possible explanations for the high rate of failure. Several researchers have suggested that CMM does not effectively deal with the social aspects of organizations. Johansen and Mathiassen [18] argue that CMM needs a more managerial focus. Nielsen and Nørbjerg [31] argue that CMM needs to be supplemented with socially oriented theories in order to address organizational change issues and organizational politics. Aaen *et al.* [51] argue that the scale and complexity of the organizational change proposed by CMM necessitates a managerial rather than technical approach. We agree that the CMM-SPI paradigm lacks an awareness of the social nature of organizations, but we also believe that assumptions about organizational culture embedded in CMM constitute a fundamental issue. In general, the CMM–SPI paradigm holds a rational and mechanistic view of organizations. The risk is that this mechanistic view reduces software organizations to little more than input–output processes governed by technical rules. The primary objective of the CMM is to achieve "optimal repeatable processes for software development" [32], [33]. Although the SPI paradigm is an attempt to change how software professionals think and act in their everyday organizational activity [50], researchers and proponents of SPI have yet to incorporate the organizational culture perspective in their work. The fundamental conjecture of this paper is that SPI is an intervention in the organizational culture with the objective of changing it. In this regard, SPI theory and practice cannot ignore the body of knowledge about organizational culture. As Lundberg puts it: "Organizational culture determines much of what we can do as we attempt to manage change" [24].

In this paper, we investigate the core assumptions about organizational culture embedded in the CMM models. Our motivation for conducting this study stems from our experiences in longitudinal (1997–1999) studies of CMM–SPI implementation conducted in four companies. During these studies, it became clear to us that contradictory assumptions within the CMM models were presenting difficulties to the implementation teams. We believe that a clear understanding of the core assumptions of CMM–SPI can help both researchers and implementers understand the limitations of the paradigm.

The research presented here can help researchers to reconceptualize the CMM–SPI models in order to address not only the cultural contradictions, but also blind spots in organizational change that inhibit successful implementation. It can also help managers using current CMM models to anticipate implementation problems and to design solution strategies for overcoming them. In this paper, we utilize the well-known competing values model to surface and analyze the assumptions underlying the CMM. Our analysis uncovers two distinctly different and contradictory sets of assumptions about organizational culture in the CMM approach. We believe that these contradictions can lead to significant problems in implementing and institutionalizing SPI programs in organizations. The rest of the paper is organized as follows. In Section II, we review the basic concepts of organizational culture and outline the framework and method for our analysis. We use this in an analysis of the assumptions in the CMM about organizational culture. In Section III, we present the research findings. In Section IV, we discuss our findings and conclude with some ideas for future research into CMM-based SPI.

II.   Organizational culture

Our primary objective is to surface and analyze the assumptions about organizational culture that are embedded in the CMM. Some of these assumptions are explicitly addressed in the CMM, while others are not explicated and we need to go beyond the claims made by its developers and proponents. To assist in surfacing the assumptions, we look particularly for inherent contradictions and hidden meanings in the CMM texts. Specifically, we are interested in surfacing contradictory assumptions about organizational culture present in the text. We use the competing values in organizational culture framework as a lens for examining the CMM documents. Before we outline the competing values framework, we will briefly overview some basic concepts of organizational culture.

   Although there is a growing body of literature on organizational culture, there is no formal definition of the term [14], [43]. Definitions of organizational culture range from mentalist (mental models) to social constructivist (social structures) views. Hofstede, for example, views organizational culture as "the collective programming of the mind which distinguishes the members of one organization from another" [13]. Louis views organizational culture as "the tacit, shared, and coherent understandings among members about who and what matters; how, what, and why things get done as they do" [23]. Others view organizational culture as social structures (symbols, norms, shared meanings) that influence an actor's lived experience and sense-making about organizational realities [12], [28], [30], [37], [46]. Although there are different conceptualizations of organizational culture, most authors agree that it is the basis upon which organizational actions are constructed and enacted [1], [13], [36], [43].

Smircich [46], for example, suggests that organizational culture can be viewed as a cognitive–social structure that is partly embedded in the minds of organizational members and partly externalized in specific symbolic activities, shared values, norms, and understandings. Such structures are built up over time via socialization and lived experience in the organization and society [2]. From this perspective, organizational culture is viewed as cognitive and social structures that circumscribe and determine the potential and the options in organizational action. Other researchers view organizational culture as the ground of organizational action and its manifestations as various levels of organizational reality. Schein [42], [43] distinguishes three levels of organizational culture: artifacts, values, and underlying assumptions. In Schein's conceptualization [43, p. 252], *artifacts* are "visible organizational structures and processes;" *values* are "strategies, goals and philosophies;" and *underlying assumptions* are "unconscious, taken for granted beliefs and habits of perception, thought and feeling." Lundberg [24] also distinguishes between three levels of organizational culture: manifest, strategic, and core. In Lundberg's conceptualization, the *manifest* level is composed of "symbolic artifacts, language, stories, ritual activity, and patterned behavior." The *strategic level* is composed of strategic beliefs. The *core level* is composed of ideologies, values, and assumptions. Schein's conceptualization has been criticized for its shallowness and augmented by other theorists such as Marcoulides and Heck [26] and Grundy and Rousseau [8]. It is generally agreed that what is most visible in organizational culture are "symbols of identification," such as logos, ritualistic activity, patterns of behavior, and communication (jargon, slogans, etc.). These symbols are simply a reflection of deeper levels of culture, such as core values, ideologies, and assumptions [40], [41]. Some theorists have suggested that the stronger the integration between layers of culture, the stronger the culture is [6], [36] and the more difficult to change [24].

Framework for analysis

In this research, we take the view that organizational culture can be interrogated via *organizational artifacts*, such as: (1) visible organizational structures and processes; (2) values and underlying assumptions; and (3) symbols [24], [40], [41], [43]. We are not suggesting that organizational culture is static – we take the view that organizational culture is emergent. We view the cultural process as a continual enactment within a context of cognitive and social structures that circumscribe and determine the potential and options in organizational action. We share Smircich's [46] view that organizational culture is a cognitive-social structure. On the manifest level, organizational structures, processes, and symbols are carriers of organizational culture. On the core level, organizational members share beliefs, values, and understandings, which guide their actions.

We have selected the competing values framework of Quinn and McGrath [38] and its extensions as the lens through which we examine the artifacts of the CMM paradigm. The reasons for choosing this framework are as follows. First, the framework focuses on the problems of organizational change and this is certainly relevant to understanding SPI. Second, the framework focuses on how the values of the different schools of organization theory are embodied in management practice and through that we can analyze the organization theories that underpin the CMM. Third, the competing values framework provides the lens through which we can observe and analyze the contradictions of organizational culture embedded in the CMM paradigm of organizational change.

We are aware that any type of framework of organizational culture types can be seen as an objectification that can limit understanding of a dynamic and emergent organizational practice. It can also provide a set of *concepts* to help us understand how certain organizational cultures enable or constrain organizational changes. Our interest is in the latter; we are interested in interrogating SPI in general and CMM in particular from an organizational culture perspective with a view to understanding the strengths and limitations of SPI theory and practice.

Quinn and McGrath [38] described and characterized four organizational culture forms: Hierarchical, Rational, Consensual, and Developmental (see Table 4.1). These four forms are rooted in four schools of organization theory: Internal Process, Rational Goal, Human Relations, and Open Systems. For a detailed historical analysis of these four schools of organization theory and the basis for these competing values see [30]. The four organizational culture forms that derive from these schools can be characterized by their core beliefs, routines, and symbolic representations of key aspects of organizational life. The prototypical hierarchical culture is the military, but it can be found in many other organizations. The prototypical rational culture is the production plant oriented to economic measures, productivity, and efficiency. The consensual cultures are oriented toward cohesion, group maintenance and morale. Authority rests with the group, decision-making is participative, and power derives from ability to cultivate and maintain relationships. Consensus cultures are open to change, but require agreement of the group members. The leadership style focuses on team building and a high degree of commitment to group process is expected of members. The development culture is oriented to growth and its organizational purpose is human development. The leadership style is open and empowering, decision-making is people-oriented, and power is based on deeply held values. Change is embraced as the natural evolution of things. As stated earlier, these are

Table 4.1 *Competing values in organizational culture [38]*

Aspect	Hierarchical	Rational	Consensual	Developmental
Organizational orientation	Stability and control	Productivity and efficiency	Cohesion and morale	Flexibility, adaptability and readiness
Organizational objectives	Execution of regulations	Pursuit of objectives	Group maintenance	Growth and development
Organizational structure	Routine tasks and technology; formal rules and policies	Complex tasks; Responsibilities based on expertise	Complex tasks; Collaborative work groups	Complex tasks; Collaborative work groups
Base of power	Knowledge of organizational rules and procedures	Competence	Ability to cultivate relationships	Values
Decision making	Top-down pronouncements	Goal-centered, systematic and analytical	Participatory, deliberative	Organic, intuitive
Leadership style	Dominance, conservative, cautious	Rational achiever, goal oriented	Team builder; concerned, supportive	Idealistic, risk oriented, empowering
Compliance	Monitoring and control	Contractual agreement	Commitment to process	Commitment to values
Evaluation of members	Adherence to rules	Level of productivity	Quality of relationships	Intensity of effort
Orientation to change	Resistant (orientated to maintaining the status quo)	Open to goal driven change	Open to change	Change is embraced as part of growth

ideal types. Organizations may exhibit these cultures to varying degrees or be a mix of cultures [47].

Method of analysis

Our methodology for uncovering the assumptions embedded in the empirical materials was based on content analysis [20], [25]. For this analysis, we selected the authoritative documents of the CMM, SW-CMM 1.1, and P-CMM 2.0, the latest versions published by the Software Engineering Institute (SEI),

Carnegie-Mellon University, Pittsburgh, PA. The background for the CMM can be found in the late 1980s U.S. Department of Defense project for evaluating which software developing companies could be expected to deliver high-quality software on time and within budget. Humphrey has explained the philosophical foundations of CMM in [16]. The first version of CMM was published and used by SEI in 1990. From SEI's interaction with software developing companies and from the documentation readily available on their website, the CMM became the most influential framework for improving software processes. A revised version 1.1 was authored by Paulk and others and published in 1993 in two significant technical reports: [33], which provides the rationale and the overview and [35], which gives detailed descriptions of the maturity levels and the key process areas. These two reports were later compiled into a book [34]. Curtis and others published the People CMM (P-CMM) addressing similar improvement of human resources in 1995 in its first version [3], [4]. A version 2.0 of SW-CMM has been underway since 1995, but its release has been cancelled and the scope of CMM has later broadened considerably. However, the core documents of SW-CMM are still [33], [35] and Version 2.0 of P-CMM [5].

Our analysis of these documents followed a three-stage process:

1) identifying themes around the terms suggested in the competing values framework;
2) exhaustive searching for empirical observations on the themes;
3) analysis and interpretation of the findings.

We started this research with significant knowledge of the CMM gained from participation in a longitudinal (1997–1999) action research project on the implementation of CMM-based or CMM-inspired SPI in four software companies. In this regard, we were able to enter at Stage 2. Using keywords defined from Table 4.1, we conducted an exhaustive iterative search of the documents. The procedure for Stage 2 is as follows.

1) The three documents are available in PDF format. We stripped them of all meta-data by sending them to pdf2txt@adobe.com. The resulting ASCII texts were loaded into ATLAS/TI without modification.
2) We searched the text matching key words derived from the four culture types. For example, from Table 4.1 in the category of Organizational Structure, we derive the key words: (a) Responsibilities; (b) Group; (c) Role; (d) Complex Task; (e) Competence. We used the key words to search the documents and when matches were found we coded the term for all occurrences of it in the text. E.g., all occurrences of "goal" and "goals" where coded with "goal." We found 638 instances of the term *Responsibility*, 1980 instances of the term *Group*, 254 instances of the term *Role*, 5 instances of the term

Complex, and 1736 instances of the term *Competence*. Table 4.5 illustrates part of the results from the search process.

3) The coded sentences were then read. By reading the sentences we were able to find new search terms and repeated Step 1.
4) One of the authors read all the overview chapters of the three documents to find additional search terms. These were used and Steps 1 and 2 were repeated.
5) For each of the three documents, we ran a count of frequencies of word occurrences. Frequently occurring words were selected based on whether they were judged to be significant either in one of the four culture types or in one of the CMMs. Steps 1 and 2 were repeated for significant terms.
6) We then retrieved segments of text from the documents based on logical relationships between codes, e.g., the sentences coded with "effective" and "goal."

Through this iterative search, reading, and rereading the text excerpts in context, we were able to uncover empirical evidence of assumptions of organizational culture relating to the four types in the competing values framework outlined in Table 4.1. The main themes of our findings are:

1) both CMMs, SW-CMM in particular, are predominantly rational and lead to organizational cultures of the rational form;
2) SW-CMM suffers from some internal contradictions as it shares many aspects with the hierarchical culture type; SW-CMM turns gradually hierarchical at higher levels;
3) P-CMM suffers from an additional, significant, main contradiction between the rational and the consensual culture forms; SW-CMM and P-CMM are mutually inconsistent;
4) both CMMs, P-CMM in particular, express allegiance with the developmental culture form as an end but not as a means.

In the next section, we discuss each of the findings and outline the present significant contradictions for organizational change within the CMM paradigm.

III.   Research findings

According to Paulk *et al.,* SW-CMM is a framework that describes the key elements of an effective software process [33, p. O-7]. In the CMM, "capability" refers to "the range of expected results that can be achieved" [35, p. O-10]. As part of CMM software development, organizations are characterized as *immature* and *mature* (see Table 4.2). According to SW-CMM, software

Table 4.2   *Characterization of immature and mature organizations [33]*

The Ad Hoc (Immature) Organization	The Mature Organization
• Software processes are generally improvised during the course of the project.	• Software processes are defined and communicated to both existing and new employees.
• Even if software processes have been specified they are not rigorously followed.	• Work activities are carried out according to the planned process.
• The organization is reactionary and the managers are fire fighters.	• Roles and responsibilities are clear throughout the project and across the organization.
• Schedules and budgets are not based on realistic estimates and are routinely exceeded.	• Schedules and budgets are based on historical performance and are realistic.
• Product functionality and quality are often compromised to meet hard deadlines.	• Expected results for cost, schedule, functionality and quality of the product are usually achieved.

development in immature organizations is accomplished by improvisation as opposed to adherence to rules. Software functionality and quality are often compromised to meet deadlines. Schedules and budgets are not based on realistic estimates and are routinely exceeded. However, in mature organizations, software development is carried out according to planned and well-defined processes in which roles and responsibilities are clear. Schedules and budgets are realistic and based on historical data; cost expectations are met and product quality is achieved. In the SW-CMM the *immature* organization is the suboptimal organization that does not follow the rules of "good" software development practice and, thus, falls into difficulty. As an antidote to the "problems of immaturity," "the CMM describes an evolutionary improvement path from an *ad hoc*, immature process to a mature, disciplined process" [35, p. O-7]. The evolutionary improvement path is a five-level model: Level 1 is the immature stage and Levels 2–5 describe what the maturing software development organization needs to focus on in order to achieve that level of maturity.

1) *Initial.* The software process is characterized as *ad hoc* and occasionally even chaotic. Few processes are defined and success depends on individual effort and heroics.

2) *Repeatable.* Basic project management processes are established to track cost, schedule, and functionality. The necessary process discipline is in place to repeat earlier successes on projects with similar applications.

3) *Defined.* Management and engineering activities are documented, standardized, and integrated into a family of standard software processes for the organization. Projects use a tailored version of the organization's standard software processes for developing and maintaining software.

4) *Managed.* Detailed measures of the software process and product quality are collected. Software processes and products are quantitatively understood and controlled.

5) *Optimizing.* Continuous process improvement is facilitated by quantitative feedback from the process and from piloting innovative ideas and technologies.

The fundamental conjecture of the CMM is that organizational change, along the trajectory of maturity levels, means improving the efficiency and effectiveness of software production, with Level 5 being the pinnacle of software development capability – the mature organization.

CMM: the rational ideal

Our analysis of the CMM documents reveals that while the proponents espouse the idea that CMM would lead to a dynamic, flexible learning organization, the core assumptions of the CMM paradigm are based on rational rule-governed organization structures that are oriented toward stability, control, and productivity. SW-CMM defines an organization that develops software as a set of processes (i.e., software processes) that can be monitored and controlled to achieve optimal output. This process view of organizations is the fundamental premise of the rational bureaucratic organization (Table 4.1, [38], [39]).

The underlying assumptions about organizational culture in SW-CMM are very much of the rational culture type. The *organizational orientation* in SW-CMM is that of increasing software developers' productivity as well as the organized efficiency and produced quality.

"At Level 5, new and improved ways of building the software are continually tried, in a controlled manner, to improve productivity and quality. Disciplined change is a way of life as inefficient or defect-prone activities are identified and replaced or revised" [33, p. 38].

"[A]s a software organization matures, costs decrease, development time becomes shorter, and productivity and quality increase" [33, p. 41].

The task of developing reliable software is a complex task which is reflected in the organizational structure. The primary organizational unit is the project and all effort directed at getting a software organization to Level 2 deals with managing the project.

"An objective in achieving Level 2 is to institutionalize effective management processes for software projects, which allow organizations to repeat successful practices developed on earlier projects" [33, p. 27].

The *organizational structure* is also created around different roles and groups with separate responsibility and specialized expertise. Special groups are established for software quality assurance, software configuration management, software engineering process, and quantitative process management, among others.

"There is a group that is responsible for the organization's software process activities, e.g., a software engineering process group, or SEPG" [35, p. O-15].
   "Roles and responsibilities within the defined process are clear throughout the project and across the organization" [33, p. 19].

The software engineering group, for example, has in SW-CMM definite and explicit responsibilities at Level 2, e.g.,

"The software engineering group reviews the project's proposed commitments" [35, p. O-33].

The scope and responsibilities of the groups vary considerably depending on expertise:

"Some groups, such as the software quality assurance group, are focused on project activities and others, such as the software engineering process group, are focused on organization-wide activities" [35, p. L3-4].

The SW-CMM is goal seeking in several ways. In the documentation, the term "goal" plays a significant role. The two main documents [33], [35] add up to more than 500 pages. The term "goal" occurs 344 times making it one of the 20 most used significant words. First and foremost, the whole idea of the CMM is a goal-seeking one where the ultimate goal is the Level 5 organization, but where subgoals are formulated in terms of Levels 2–4. The goals for the improvement are set by the CMM.

"To achieve lasting results from process improvement efforts, it is necessary to design an evolutionary path that increases an organization's software process maturity in stages. The software process maturity framework...orders these stages so that improvements at each stage provide the foundation on which to build improvements undertaken at the next stage" [33, p. 22].

It is also goal seeking within each of the processes. For each key process area there is a set of goals. A goal is defined as:

"The goals summarize the key practices of a key process area and can be used to determine whether an organization or project has effectively implemented the key process area. The goals signify the scope, boundaries and intent of each key process area" [35, p. O-11].

These goals are set by the SW-CMM, e.g., for the key process area Intergroup Coordination at Level 3 the goals are:

> "Goal 1: The customer's requirements are agreed to by all affected groups.
> Goal 2: The commitments between the engineering groups are agreed to by the affected groups.
> Goal 3: The engineering groups identify, track and resolve intergroup issues" [35, p. L3-85].

Decision making in CMM is also based on the rational culture form. Decisions are driven by goals and in decision-making goals are pursued in a systematic and analytical way.

> "In a mature organization, managers monitor the quality of the software products and customer satisfaction. There is an objective, quantitative basis for judging product quality and analyzing problems with the product and process" [33, p. 19].

Further, each key process is evaluated based on a set of predefined measurements and a set of verification activities. For example, the intergroup coordination process at Level 3 is evaluated by the following measurements and verification activity.

> "Measurement 1: Measurements are made and used to determine the status of the intergroup coordination activities" [35, p. L3-93].
> "Verification 3: The software quality assurance group reviews and/or audits the activities and work products for inter-group coordination and reports the results" [35, p. L3-94].

Compliance is, to a large extent, based on meeting commitments. Commitments are common in the formulation of key process areas.

> "Goal 3: Affected groups and individuals agree to their commitments related to the software project" [35, p. L2-12].

Humphrey, in providing the philosophical underpinning of the CMM, explains commitment and commitment discipline in the following way:

> "The foundation for software project management is the commitment discipline.... Commitments are not met by reviews, procedures, or tools, however; they are met by committed people" [16, p. 69].
> "In simplest terms a commitment is an agreement by one person to do something for another" [16, p. 70].
> "Commitment is a way of life. Committed organizations meet their large and their small commitments" [16, p. 71].

This attitude coincides with the idea of compliance as contractual agreement as defined in the rational culture type. In the SW-CMM, many commitments are made – they form a hierarchy, they are sometimes made informally (but not lightly), and they are often made formally and documented, hence, making it easier to observe compliance and noncompliance.

Based on a similar analysis of P-CMM, we found that it too leads to a dominant rational culture type.

SW-CMM: the hierarchical ideal

In SW-CMM, a software process is a set of activities, methods, practices, and transformations that developers use to develop and maintain software and the associated products, e.g., project plans, design documents, code, test cases, and user manuals [35]. Further, SW-CMM defines "software process maturity [as] the extent to which a specific process is explicitly defined, managed, measured, controlled, and effective" [33, p. 4]. Some of the key features of the CMM process view that clearly reflect the hierarchical culture are: (1) an orientation to stability and control; (2) precise job definitions; (3) clear lines of authority; and (4) strict policies and management controls. Table 4.4 shows the organizational structures required by SW-CMM. As Paulk *et al.* explain, the SW-CMM "provides software organizations with guidance on how to gain control over their processes for developing and maintaining software and how to evolve to a culture of software engineering and excellence" [33, p. 5]. From this perspective, the SW-CMM espouses an organizational culture form in which people and processes are treated mechanistically like a machine, for which the operation and performance can be quantified, measured, and controlled. These assumptions are evident in the SW-CMM's overview of itself:

> "The key process areas are categorized ... into three broad categories: Management, Organizational and Engineering processes. The Management process category contains the project management activities as they evolve from planning and tracking at Level 2, to managing according to a defined software process at Level 3, to quantitative management at Level 4, to innovative management in a constantly changing environment at Level 5. The Organizational process category contains the cross-project responsibilities as the organization matures, beginning with a focus on process issues at Level 3, continuing to a quantitative understanding of the process at Level 4 and culminating with the management of change in an environment of continuous process improvement at Level 5. The Engineering process category contains the technical activities, such as requirements analysis, design, code and test, which are performed at all levels, but that evolve toward an engineering discipline at Level 3, statistical process control at Level 4 and continuous measured improvement at Level 5" [35, p. O-26].

In more detail, there are several elements of SW-CMM that share its assumptions about organizational culture with the hierarchical culture type. The orientation is toward stability and control.

> "The first responsibility and the focus of Level 4, is process control. The software process is managed so that it operates stably within a zone of quality control" [33, p. 17].
> "At Level 2, the customer requirements and work products are controlled and basic project management practices have been established. These management controls allow visibility into the project on defined occasions" [33, p. 21].

The SW-CMM requires considerable knowledge of organizational rules and procedures in terms of standard processes, though these are more general than what is often seen in hierarchical culture types. Decision-making, thus, also has elements of top-management pronouncement in the way the standard software process is common to all projects. The project decides its own defined software process, but within the limits of the standard software process.

"Projects tailor the organization's standard software process to develop their own defined software process, which accounts for the unique characteristics of the project. This tailored process is referred to in the CMM as the project's defined software process.... Because the software process is well defined, management has good insight into technical progress on all projects" [33, p. 12],

There are also elements of measuring compliance by monitoring and control. All key process areas stipulate measurement and verification activities. For example, the measurement and verification activity for the key process area "Software Configuration Management" at Level 2 is:

"Measurement 1: Measurements are made and used to determine the status of the SCM activities" [35, p. L2-87].
    "Verification 1: The SCM activities are reviewed with senior management on a periodic basis" [35, p. L3-87].

Another aspect of CMM that reflects the hierarchical organizational form is its fascination with rules. In the more than 500 pages of SW-CMM documentation and 735 pages of P-CMM documentation, what stands out is pervasiveness of rules. There are detailed descriptions of key process areas with: goals, activities, measurement, and verification. These detailed descriptions are formal rules, procedures, and policies to be followed, they also stipulate a large number of organizational rules and policies that establish and enforce the organizational structures.

The elements of the hierarchical culture type are present but not dominant at the lower levels of SW-CMM. The higher the level in SW-CMM the more the hierarchical culture type is imposed on the software processes. At Levels 2 and 3, the rational culture type is imposed as part of the evolutionary, staged change activities though there are definitely elements of the hierarchical culture type. At Levels 4 and 5, there is a drift away from the rational culture type toward more and more of the hierarchical culture type.

P-CMM: the consensual ideal

The P-CMM is a framework for guiding organizations in attracting, developing, motivating, organizing, and retaining the talented people needed to continually improve their software development [5]. However, the organizational culture that P-CMM prescribes is based on the human relations approach to management that is contradictory to the SW-CMM rational machine view of the organization. The management and leadership styles of the P-CMM and the SW-CMM models are diametrically opposed. The management and leadership styles embedded in the SW-CMM descriptions reveal an orientation to monitoring, control, and rule compliance. The style suggested in P-CMM involves mentoring, coaching, and team building. Further, decision-making processes in the SW-CMM are closed and roles and responsibilities explicitly defined, while the processes suggested by P-CMM are participatory and open.

According to Curtis *et al.* [5], the strategic objectives of P-CMM are:

1) improve the capability of the software organization by increasing the capability of its workforce;
2) ensure that competences for developing software are organizational rather than individual;
3) align the motivations of individuals with those of the organization;
4) retain the human assets of the organization.

P-CMM outlines a similar five-level evolutionary model for assessing the organization and implementing improvements. According to P-CMM, the worst-case scenario of Level 1 is that managers do not accept responsibility for developing their employees. They put little effort into evaluating job candidates and the performance of employees; consequently, employees are disgruntled and the capability of the organization is undermined. The P-CMM remedy for this problem is the five-level model.

1) *Initial.* The software organization's capability is unknown since there is no effort to measure it. Individuals are motivated to pursue their own agendas since there are few incentives to pursue the organization's objectives.
2) *Repeatable.* Instill basic discipline into workforce activities. Eliminate problems that keep people from being able to perform their responsibilities effectively. Establish a foundation of workforce practices that can continually improve the workforce.
3) *Defined.* Identify primary competences and align with workforce activities. Adapt the workforce practices to develop specific skills and competences that the organization needs. Identify best practices and tailor them to the organization.
4) *Managed.* Quantitatively manage organizational growth in workforce capabilities and establish competence-based teams. Collect and analyze performance data to evaluate competence.
5) *Optimizing.* Continuously improve methods for developing personal and organizational competence.

In line with the structure of SW-CMM, P-CMM defines a set of key processes that must be implemented for each level of maturity before moving on to the next. The processes are categorized into four areas: (1) developing capabilities; (2) building teams and culture; (3) motivating and managing performance; and (4) shaping the workforce. P-CMM suggests that the path to developing capabilities starts with delivering training in oral and written communication, followed by systematic assessments of competence requirements and implementing organizational structures for competence development. The model also suggests mentoring and coaching as important activities for developing the capabilities of the employees. Prescriptions are given for developing a participatory culture and team building. Table 4.3 summarizes the processes that the organization must implement to achieve each level of maturity in the P-CMM scheme.

In many respects, P-CMM exhibits fundamental assumptions of the consensual organizational culture type (see Table 4.1). The following aspects of

Table 4.3   *Key processes for developing organizational capabilities [5]*

Maturity levels	*Developing individual capabilities*	*Building workgroups & culture*	*Motivating & managing performance*	*Shaping the workforce*
5 Optimizing	Continuous Capability Improvement		Organizational Performance Alignment	Continuous Workforce Innovation
4 Managed	Competency Based Assets	Competency Integration	Quantitative Performance Management	Organizational Capability Management
	Mentoring	Empowering Workgroups		
3 Defined	Competence Development	Workgroup Development	Competency Based Practices	Workforce Planning
	Competency Analysis	Participatory Culture	Career Development	
2 Repeatable	Training and Development	Communication & Coordination	Compensation	Staffing
			Performance Management	
			Work Environment	
1 Initial				

the consensual culture type are all part of the core idea of P-CMM: group maintenance as an organizational objective, the organization structured around collaborative workgroups, decision-making to be participatory, and the leadership style based on team building. At Level 2, we find the key process area Communication and Coordination where the purpose is:

"To establish timely communication across the organization and to ensure that the workforce has the skills to share information and coordinate their activities efficiently" [5, p. 141].

At Level 3, there is the key process area Participatory Culture. The purpose of Participatory Culture is to create the ability to participate in decision-making.

"The open communication established with Communication and Coordination practices at the Managed Level creates a foundation for developing a participatory culture. A participatory culture provides an environment in which competent professionals are fully able to exercise their capabilities" [5, p. 379].

At Level 4, there is the key process area Empowering Workgroups with the purpose:

"To invest workgroups with the responsibility and authority for determining how to conduct their business activities most effectively" [5, p. 141].

The development and management of individual and organizational competences also play an equally important role in P-CMM. The primary vehicle for developing individual and organizational competence is the workgroup.

"The purpose of Workgroup Development is to organize work around competency-based process abilities" [5, p. 347].

However, is this really a departure from the rational model of the workgroup espoused in SW-CMM? Close observation reveals that, in principle, the same rational culture assumptions about organizational structure are operating here. Some might argue that the team organization and goal-oriented structure of the SW-CMM software organization suggest a consensual or developmental organizational form. However, the underlying context of P-CMM tells a different story. At first sight the concepts "team work" and "participatory decision making" belong to the consensual culture type where the idea of process is also strong. However, this is not the same in SW-CMM. The key process areas are first and foremost defined by their goals. Goal-driven behavior – in particular adherence to predefined goals – belongs to the rational culture type and can never be a core idea of the consensual culture type. Also, in the consensual culture type compliance is measured by commitment to process and that seems to be a core idea in SW-CMM as well. However, we have already seen that compliance in SW-CMM is measured by contractual agreement, i.e., that commitments are met. The consensual culture's idea of a process is that the process itself ensures the right outcome. This is similar to democracy, where there is a particular focus on the process through which agreement and consensus is reached and without an ideology about which is the right outcome. Such participatory ideas are essential in consensual cultures but are foreign to SW-CMM. Such ideas about consensual processes are not common in P-CMM. The workgroup structure defined in P-CMM is created based on explicit rules.

It makes sense that SW-CMM and P-CMM should be considered as one "voice." They were both developed at the SEI, both are official publications of the SEI, and one person was a coauthor of both SW-CMM and P-CMM. Also in the P-CMM, we find the following:

> "The People CMM employs the process maturity framework of the highly successful Capability Maturity Model for Software ... as a foundation for a model of best practices for managing and developing an organization's workforce" [5, p. vi].

P-CMM contains a major inner contradiction in adhering both to the consensual culture type and to the rational culture type together with SW-CMM. Thus, SW-CMM and P-CMM are also mutually inconsistent.

Tensions of developmental and hierarchical cultures

Although the process view is dominant in CMM, it also espouses a developmental culture for the software organization. Paulk states that the CMM-based SPI approach "should build an organization that can dynamically adapt to a rapidly changing, even chaotic, environment; an organization that knows what business it is in and pursues software projects aligned with its strategic business objectives; a learning organization that explicitly, rather than implicitly, captures knowledge; an organization managed by facts rather than intuition, while still valuing creativity; an organization that empowers its most crucial asset: its people" [32]. Although the P-CMM prescribes team building and a participatory culture, the hierarchical structures of CMM work processes with their explicitly defined role responsibilities and strict management control are contradictory to building trust upon which a developmental culture thrives.

There are also a few elements of P-CMM that suggests that it contains elements of a developmental culture. These have to do with empowerment of individuals. However, when viewed in the context of the super structure of the CMM paradigm, they seem contradictory. For example, the SW-CMM documents suggest that:

> "A disciplined process, then, empowers the intellect, while regimentation supplants it" [16, p. 13].

However, in SW-CMM the term "empower" is mentioned twice. First, in an activity in the key process area Change Process Management at Level 5:

> "Activity 1: A software process improvement program is established which empowers the members of the organization to improve the processes of the organization" [35, p. L5-37].

Paulk *et al.* mention this again in their Appendix where some of the activities of Change Process Management are repeated [35]. Empowerment and the orientation toward flexibility, adaptability, and readiness could be inherent in SW-CMM without the term "empower" being used, but this is not the case. Humphrey, for one, is aware of the fine balance between discipline and regimentation, but even so, neither he nor SW-CMM advocate any processes through which the software developers and their projects are given power, resources, means, and responsibilities for making their own decisions about their own activities. On the contrary, at Level 3 and above, the standard software process is organization-wide. There is no indication that any key process area or any aspect of SW-CMM, even in a generic way, resembles the developmental culture type. Decision-making is not organic and intuitive; it is goal-centered, systematic, and analytical. Compliance is not measured by commitment to value. Change is not part of growth; it is driven by a desire to increase flexibility, adaptability, and readiness without jeopardizing productivity.

> "At Level 5, new and improved ways of building the software are continually tried, in a controlled manner, to improve productivity and quality. Disciplined change is a way of life as inefficient or defect-prone activities are identified and replaced or revised. Insight extends beyond existing processes" [33, p. 22].

While there is the claim that SW-CMM leads to more creativity and empowerment, the assumption shows a different picture.

The P-CMM, on the other hand, presents an elaborate vision of the empowered group culture, but in a way that enforces its adherence to the consensual culture type. At Level 3, the P-CMM has a key process area called Empowering Workgroups.

> "Practice 4: Empowered workgroups are delegated the responsibility and authority to determine the methods by which they will accomplish their committed work" [5, p. 451].

That means that within the limits of the standard process in general, and specifically the commitments made, a workgroup functions with some autonomy. In that sense, it belongs to the developmental culture type. No other aspect of the P-CMM belongs to the developmental culture type. The key process area Empowering Workgroups, thus, puts emphasis on the group and the group's processes in a way that strengthens its consensual culture. The workgroup becomes a dominant organizational structure, but decision-making while participatory is based on systematic and deliberative application of rules.

IV. Conclusion

The design ideal of CMM is the rational bureaucratic learning organization that is flexible. It is not surprising to find that the CMM models (SW-CMM and P-CMM) contain several major organizational cultural contradictions in their core assumptions. Both models, and SW-CMM in particular, are designed on the basis of rational ideal and lead to organizational cultures of the rational form. SW-CMM suffers from some internal contradictions as it shares many aspects with the hierarchical culture type; SW-CMM turns gradually more hierarchical at higher levels. P-CMM suffers from an additional contradiction as its core elements are designed with major elements of both the rational and the consensual culture forms. In their core assumptions, the SW-CMM and P-CMM are contradictory and antagonistic. Both express allegiance with the developmental culture form as an end but not as a means, as they adopt a rational-hierarchical process view. While we agree that "value conflicts" are inherent in organizational change initiatives [19], [21], we believe that these inconsistencies and contradictions are not simple and may not be easily overcome. Further, managers of software organizations seeking guidance in the CMM not only run the risk of being confused at a theoretical level but also have to face the inconsistencies and contradictions in practice.

If we could come to terms with the inconsistencies and contradictions per se, the pervasive, massive task of SPI practice adds profoundly to the size of the problems to face. The scale and complexity of organizational change that an immature organization must implement to become a mature organization is simply breathtaking [48], [51]. According to CMM, becoming a mature/optimal software development organization requires fundamental change across several dimensions of the organization:

1) core processes;
2) software development technologies;
3) management and control procedures;
4) planning;
5) work group organization;
6) roles and responsibilities;
7) power and authority structures;
8) skills and knowledge.

The pervasive change in terms of scale, complexity, and depth of the organizational change required by SW-CMM is too much to outline in this paper.

Therefore, we have chosen to summarize its basic elements in Table 4.4 and outline some of it in very brief detail. Level 1 is the starting point of the CMM scale; this is the immature organization. In order to move to Level 2, the Level 1 organization must undertake profound organizational changes in each of the eight dimensions. For example, the organization must implement business processes, formal procedures, and supporting technologies for the six key processes: requirements management, project planning, project tracking and oversight, subcontract management, quality assurance, and configuration management. It must also implement organizational policies and management, controlling, and tracking procedures for each of the key processes. CMM is quite ambitious as a change approach; it attempts to change all aspects of the organization structure and culture (cf. Table 4.4). On the symbolic level, CMM-based SPI seeks to change the activities and patterned behaviors of developers. On the level of structure, it seeks to change norms, conventions, customs, rules, and procedures for doing and managing software development.

CMM's adherence to the rational culture type makes it less effective as an approach to deal with such scale and complexity of SPI. These limitations of CMM and their consequences for informing SPI practice may be lessened, but probably never alleviated completely. We believe that CMM can benefit from a more thorough understanding of the organization theory (design, culture, and change). One direction for extending the CMM would be to incorporate a framework of organizational change that can guide the change process more effectively. However, even this extension to CMM would still leave the question of reconciling the organizational design and cultural contradictions that are embedded in CMM. The question of how to reconcile the core assumptions of the rational culture and those of the developmental cannot be resolved by simply improving the organizational change strategy. This would require adopting a different strategy. We outline two such strategies, but whether either of them is effective we shall leave for future research.

In the first strategy, we believe that CMM might benefit from being supplemented with a rational and dynamic approach to handle the main contradictions in SPI practice. The contradictions between distinctive paradigms in information systems development have received much attention, (e.g., [10], [11], [21], [48]). In that perspective, the dilemmas facing CMM are not new and are not reconcilable. Nevertheless, Klein and Hirschheim [21] suggest a rational decision-making approach to choose between competing values and design ideals. Their approach serves the primary purpose of extending the decision-making well beyond the traditional technical issue. If we transfer that idea to CMM and outline it in terms of culture types, we would need to supplement CMM with an approach where we could for a particular software organization choose a specific balance between the organizational culture types. In one organization, we could end up with a main focus on implementing the rational culture type improvement while in another organization we

Table 4.4 Dimensions of organizational change required by CMM [51]

Change Aspects	Change Objective CMM Level 2	Change Objective CMM Level 3	Change Objective CMM Level 4	Change Objective CMM Level 5
Core Business Processes	Requirements Management (RM), Project Planning (PP), Project Tracking & Oversight (PTO), Subcontract management (SM), Quality Assurance (SQA), Configuration Management (SCM)	Organization Process Focus (OPF), Organization Process Definition (OPD), Training Program (TP), Integrated Software Management (ISM), Software Product Engineering (SPE), Intergroup Coordination (IC), Peer Reviews (PR)	Software Quality Management (SQM), Quantitative Process Management (QPM)	Process Change Management (PCM), Technology Change Management (TCM), Defect Prevention (DP)
Product/ Process Technology	Tools and techniques to support the work in RM, SPP, SPTO, SSM, SQA, and SCM; A configuration management library.	Tools and methods defined and integrated to support work in OPF, OPD, TP, ISM, SPE, IC, PR, Software Process Database; Library of process-related documentation.	Tools to support quantitative process management; Support for collecting, recording, and analyzing data; Tools to support predicting, measuring, tracking, and analyzing the quality of products; Measurement program in place.	Tools to support defect prevention activities, technology change management and SPI; Support for collecting and analyzing data needed to evaluate technology changes; Appropriate data on the software processes and products are available; Records of SPI activities.

(Continued)

Table 4.4 *Continued*

Change Aspects	Change Objective CMM Level 2	Change Objective CMM Level 3	Change Objective CMM Level 4	Change Objective CMM Level 5
Management & Control procedures	Measurements performed and used in core processes; Activities and work products are reviewed – by senior management – by project manager – by SQA group	Manage project in accordance to defined process; Measurements performed and used in core processes; Activities and work products are reviewed. – by senior management – by project manager – by SQA group	Define, monitor, and revise project's quantitative quality goals; Measure, analyze, and compare the quality of the project's software products to the products quantitative quality goals; Measurements performed and used; Activities and work products are reviewed – by senior management – by project manager – by SQA group	Measurements are made and used; Activities and work products are reviewed by – senior management – project manager – SQA group
Planning	Software project planning, Quality planning, Configuration management planning, Resource planning	SPI planning; Training planning; Peer reviews planning	Plan for quantitative process management; Project's software quality plan	Plan for defect prevention activities; Document and track defect prevention data; Plan for technology change management
Work Group Organization	Software engineering groups in place	Staff groups, Software engineering groups	Quantitative process management group	Members of the organization participate in SPI teams

Tasks	Tasks defined and linked into documented procedures for project management, e.g. – develop project plan – estimate the size, effort, cost – perform formal reviews – define and plan work to be sub-contracted – prepare SQA plan – prepare SCM plan – control changes to baselines	Tasks defined, linked, and integrated into a standard process. Tasks are performed in accordance to a defined process, e.g. – develop and maintain organization's standard software process – develop and maintain organization's training plan – a waiver procedure for required training tailor standard software process to project's defined software process – develop and revise project's software plan – identify, negotiate, and track critical dependencies between engineering groups – perform peer reviews	Perform tasks in accordance to documented procedures, e.g. – develop software project's plan for quantitative process management – collect measurement data – analyze project's defined software process and bring it under quantitative control – establish and maintain the process capability baseline – develop and maintain project's software quality plan	Perform tasks in accordance to documented procedures, e.g. – conduct causal analysis meetings – incorporate revisions resulting from defect prevention activities to the organization's standard software process and the project's defined software process – select and acquire technologies for the organization and software projects – incorporate appropriate new technologies into organization's standard software process and the projects' defined processes – develop and maintain a plan for SPI – handle SPI proposals – implement the improvement
Roles	Particular project manager roles defined, Special groups or functions established for SQA and SCM	Special staff groups established with organization-wide responsibilities e.g. a SEPG to define and improve organization process and a training group to educate and train organization members.	Quantitative process management group; Individuals implementing and supporting software quality management	An organization-level team to coordinate defect prevention activities; A project-level group to coordinate defect prevention activities; A technology change management group

(Continued)

Table 4.4 Continued

Change Aspects	Change Objective CMM Level 2	Change Objective CMM Level 3	Change Objective CMM Level 4	Change Objective CMM Level 5
Power & Authority	A senior manager with authority to take oversight actions in SQA: A board with authority for managing the project's software baselines.	Senior management sponsors and oversees SPI		Management participation in defect prevention activities; Senior management sponsors and oversees the organization's activities for technology change management and SPI; Establish a SPI program which empowers the members of the organization to improve
Coordinating Mechanisms	Written organizational policies for implementing RM, SPP, SPTO, SSM, SQA, SCM: Documented procedures for project management. Standard reports are made available; Project plans.	Written organizational policies in place for 1) coordinating software process development and improvement activities, 2) developing and maintaining a standard software process, 3) meeting its training needs, 4) planning and managing the software project using the	Written organizational policies in place for 1) measuring and quantitatively controlling the performance, 2) analyzing the process capability, 3) managing software quality; Project's software quality plan	The organization follows a written policy for 1) defect prevention activities, 2) improving its technology capability, 3) implementing SPI; The project follows a written organizational policy for defect prevention activities; Periodic meetings to review and coordinate implementation of

	organization's standard process, 5) performing the software engineering activities, 6) establishing interdisciplinary engineering teams, 7) performing peer reviews; Standard process defined, tailored and used by projects	Orientation to members, e.g. – goals and values of quantitative process management – reports documenting the results of software – project's quantitative process management activities	action proposals; TCM group works with software projects; The SPI group; The SPI plan
			Feedback to members, e.g. – status and results of the organization's and project's defect prevention activities – new technologies – status and results of the SPI activities
Skills & Knowledge	Groups and project management positions staffed with competent people, Orientation to members, e.g. – role, responsibilities, authority, and value of the SQA group – technical aspects	Staff groups and projects staffed with competent people, Orientation to members, e.g. – SPI activities – training program – team work	

Table 4.5   *Illustration of search terms and some citations in support of the rational culture type*

Search Terms and Frequency	Some Excerpts From The Documents
Orientation: Productivity and efficiency Productivity (60), efficiency (94), quality (502)	At Level 5, new and improved ways of building the software are continually tried, in a *controlled* manner, to improve *productivity* and *quality*. Disciplined *change* is a way of life as *inefficient* or defect-prone activities are identified and replaced or revised. [33, p. 38] as a software organization matures, costs decrease, development time becomes shorter, and *productivity* and *quality* increase. [33, p. 41]
Organizational objectives: Pursuit of objectives Objective (786)	An *objective* in achieving Level 2 is to institutionalize *effective management* processes for software projects, which allow organizations to repeat successful practices developed on earlier projects. [33, p. 27]
Organizational structure: Complex tasks, responsibilities based on expertise Responsibility (638). group (1980), role (254), complex (5). competence (1736)	There is a *group* that is *responsible* for the organization's software process activities, e.g., a software engineering process *group*, or SEPG [35, p. O-15] *Roles* and *responsibilities* within the *defined process* are clear throughout the project and across the organization. [33, p. 19] The software engineering *group reviews* the project's proposed *commitments*. [35, p. O-33] Some *groups*, such as the software *quality* assurance *group*, are focused on project activities, and others, such as the software engineering process *group*, are focused on organization-wide activities. [35, p. L3-4] While questions can appropriately be raised about the size and *complexity* of current systems, these are human creations, and they will, alas, continue to be produced by human beings (with all their failings and creative talents. ... [T]he *complexity* of our systems is increasing, which will make the systems progressively more difficult to test. [16, 13] The purpose of Workgroup Development is to organize work around *competency*-based process abilities. (Curtis *et al.* 2001, p. 347)

Decision-making: Goal-centered, systematic, and analytical
Result (561), goal (683), quality (502), monitor (72), measure (563)

To achieve lasting *results* from process improvement efforts, it is necessary to design an evolutionary path that increases an organization's software process maturity in stages. The software process maturity framework orders these stages so that improvements at each stage provide the foundation on which to build improvements undertaken at the next stage. [33, p. 22]

The *goals* summarize the key practices of a key process area and can be used to determine whether an organization or project has *effectively* implemented the key process area. The *goals* signify the scope, boundaries, and intent of each key process area. [35, p. O-11]

Goal 1: The customer's requirements are agreed to by all affected *groups*.
Goal 2: The *commitments* between the engineering *groups* are agreed to by the affected *groups*.
Goal 3: The engineering *groups* identify, track, and resolve inter*group* issues. [35, p. L3-85]

In a mature organization, *managers monitor* the *quality* of the software products and customer satisfaction. There is an *objective*, quantitative basis for judging product *quality* and analyzing problems with the product and process. [33, p. 19]

Measurement 1: Measurements are made and used to determine the status of the inter*group* coordination activities. [35, p. L3-93]

Verification 3: The software *quality* assurance group *reviews* and/or audits the activities and work products for inter*group* coordination and reports the *results*. [35, p. L3-94]

Compliance: Contractual arrangement
Commitment (384)

Goal 3: Affected *groups* and individuals agree to their *commitments* related to the software project. [35, p. L2-12]

The foundation for software project *management* is the *commitment* discipline. ... *Commitments* are not met by reviews, procedures, or tools, however; they are met by *committed* people. [16, p. 69]

In simplest terms a *commitment* is an agreement by one person to do something for another. [16, p. 70] *Committed* organizations meet their large and their small *commitments*. [16, p. 71]

Orientation to change: Open to goal-driven change
Change (535)

At Level 5, new and improved ways of building the software are continually tried, in a *controlled* manner, to improve *productivity* and *quality*. Disciplined *change* is a way of life as inefficient or defect-prone activities are identified and replaced or revised. Insight extends beyond existing processes. [33, p. 22] could well end up with a main focus on implementing the consensual and developmental culture types. That would not in itself remove the cultural inconsistencies and contradictions, but it would create a process through which these could be explicitly addressed and handled.

In the second strategy, we believe that CMM might benefit from a different perspective for the organization and management of software development. It is accepted that software development is a nonroutine complex undertaking requiring high levels of competence and a flexible organizing structure. That is why CMM not only has hierarchical and rational culture elements, but also the consensual elements. The fundamental issue for software organizations is how to achieve a balance between control and goal-orientation on the one hand and change and flexibility on the other hand – between the rational culture and the developmental culture. The current CMM focus on controlling the processes of software development can easily lead to a level of bureaucratization of software organizations that is less flexible than desired. While no one would suggest that software processes should not be defined, there needs to be some flexibility in their implementation and execution. There is another perspective for organizing and managing software development that may offer some possibilities for moving CMM out of its current process model. This organizational form, the professional bureaucracy, has been thoroughly researched and discussed by Mintzberg [29]. It has been found to provide a high level of flexibility coupled with specialization and predictability of outputs. The professional bureaucracy focuses on standardization of skills and indoctrination of the professional. Professional bureaucracies are based on trust and competence and have been highly successful in specialized work such as surgery, engineering, scientific research, and so on. Professionalization of software engineering would offer a tradition, standards and a culture that is well entrenched and recognizable without regard to the particular organizational setting.

References

[1] M. Alvesson (1987), "Organizations, culture and ideology," *Int. J. Stud. Manage. Org.*, Vol. 17, pp. 4–18.

[2] P. L. Berger and T. Luckmann (1966), *The Social Construction of Reality: A Treatise in the Sociology of Knowledge*. Anchor, New York.

[3] B. Curtis, W. E. Hefley, and S. Miller (1995), "Overview of the people capability maturity model," Software Eng. Inst., Carnegie-Mellon Univ., Pittsburgh, PA, CMU/SEI-95-MM-01.

[4] ——— (1995), "People capability maturity model," Software Eng. Inst., Carnegie-Mellon Univ., Pittsburgh, PA, CMU/SEI-95-MM-002.

[5] —— (2001), "People capability maturity model (P-CMM)," Software Eng. Inst., Carnegie-Mellon Univ., Pittsburgh, PA, CMU/SEI-Ol-MM-001.

[6] T. E. Deal and A. A. Kennedy (1982), *Corporate Cultures: The Rites and Rituals of Corporate Life*. Addison-Wesley, Reading, MA.

[7] K. E. Emam, J.-N. Drouin, and W. Melo (1998), *SPICE: The Theory and Practice of Software Process Improvement and Capability Determination*. IEEE Computer Society, Los Alamitos, CA.

[8] L. K. Grundy and D. M. Rousseau (1994), "Critical incidents in communicating culture to newcomers: The meaning is in the message," *Hum. Relat.*, Vol. 47, pp. 1063–1088.

[9] J. Herbsleb, D. Zubrow, D. Goldenson, W. Hayes, and M. Paulk (1997), "Software quality and the capability maturity model," *Commun. ACM,* Vol. 40, pp. 30–40.

[10] R. Hirschheim, J. Iivari, and H. Klein (1998), "A paradigmatic analysis contrasting information systems development approaches and methodologies," *Inform. Syst. Res.*, Vol. 9, pp. 164–193.

[11] R. Hirschheim, H. Klein, and K. Lyytinen (1996), "Exploring the intellectual structures of systems development: A social action theoretic analysis," *Inform. Org.*, Vol. 6, pp. l–64.

[12] G. Hofstede (1981), "Culture and organizations," *Int. Stud. Manage. Org.*, Vol. 10, pp. 15–41.

[13] —— (1991), Culture and Organizations: Software of the Mind. New York: McGraw-Hill.

[14] G. Hofstede, B. Neuijen, D. D. Ohayv, and G. Sanders (1990), "Measuring organizational cultures: A qualitative and quantitative study across twenty cases," *Administ. Sci. Quart.*, Vol. 35, pp. 286–316.

[15] W. S. Humphrey (1988), "Characterizing the software process," *IEEE Software*, Vol. 5, pp. 73–79.

[16] —— (1989), "Managing the Software Process". Addison-Wesley, Reading, MA.

[17] —— (1992), "Introduction to software process improvement," Software Eng. Inst., Carnegie-Mellon Univ., Pittsburgh, PA, CMU/SEI-92-TR-007.

[18] J. Johansen and L. Mathiassen (1998), "Lessons learned in a national SPI effort," in *Proc. EuroSPI'98*. Gothenburg, Sweden.

[19] H. Klein (1987), Design ideals and their critical reconstruction, In: *Proc. TIMS,* Toronto, ON, Canada, pp. 12–26.

[20] H. Klein and D. Truex (1996), "Discourse analysis an approach to investigating organizational emergence," in B. Holmqvist, P. B. Andersen, H. Klein, and R. Posner, Eds. *Signs of Work*. Walter de Gruyter, New York.

[21] H. K. Klein and R. Hirschheim (2001), "Choosing between competing design ideals in information systems development," *Inform. Syst. Front.*, Vol. 3, pp. 75–90.

[22] P. Kuvaja, J. Similä, L. Krzanik, A. Bicego, S. Saukkonen, and G. Koch (1994), *Software Process Assessment & Improvement – The Bootstrap Approach*. Blackwell, Oxford, U.K.

[23] M. R. Louis (1981), "A cultural perspective on organizations: The need for and consequences of viewing organizations as culture-bearing milieux," *Hum. Syst. Manage.*, Vol. 2, pp. 245–258.

[24] C. C. Lundberg (1989), "Working with culture," *J. Org. Change Manage.*, Vol. 1, pp. 38–47.

[25] P. Manning and B. Cullum-Swan (1994), "Narrative, content and semiotic analysis," in N. Denzin and Y. Lincoln, Eds. *Handbook of Qualitative Research*. Sage, Newbury Park, CA.

[26] G. A. Marcoulides and R. H. Heck (1993), "Organizational culture and performance: Proposing and testing a model," *Org. Sci.*, Vol. 4, pp. 209–225.

[27] F. McGarry, R. Pajerski, G. Page, S. Waligora, V. Basili, and M. Zelkowitz, *Software process improvement in the NASA software engineering laboratory*, *Software Eng. Inst.* Pittsburgh PA: Carnegie-Mellon Univ, 1994, Tech. Rep.CMU/SEI-94-TR-22.

[28] J. C. H. Mills and A. J. Mills (2000), "Rules, sensemaking, formative contexts and discourse in the gendering of organization culture," in N. M. Ashkanasy, C. P. M. Wildrom, and M. F. Peterson, Eds. *Handbook of Organizational Culture & Climate*. Sage, Newbury Park, CA, pp. 55–70.

[29] H. Mintzberg (1992), *Structure in Fives: Designing Effective Organizations*. Prentice-Hall, Englewood Cliffs, NJ.

[30] G. Morgan (1997), *Images of Organization*, 2 ed. Sage, Newbury Park, CA.

[31] P. A. Nielsen, J. Nørbjerg (2001), "Software process maturity and organizational politics," in *Realigning Research and Practice in Information Systems Development: The Social and Organizational Perspective, Proc. IFIP WG 8.2 Conf.*, B. Fitzgerald and N. Russo, Eds., Boise, ID.

[32] M. C. Paulk (1996), "Effective CMM-based process improvement," in *Proc 6th Int. Conf. Software Quality*. Ottawa, ON, Canada.

[33] M. C. Paulk, B. Curtis, M. B. Chrissis, and C. V. Weber, "*Capability maturity model for software, Version 1.1, Software Eng. Inst.*", Pittsburgh, PA: Carnegie-Mellon Univ, 1993 Tech. Rep. CMU/SEI-93-TR-024.

[34] M. C. Paulk, C. Weber, B. Curtis, and M. B. Chrissis (1995), *The Capability Maturity Model: Guidelines for Improving the Software Process*. Addison-Wesley, Reading, MA.

[35] M. C. Paulk, C.V. Weber, S.M. Garcia, M.B. Chrissis, and M. Bush (1993), "*Key practices of the capability maturity model, Version 1.1, Software Eng. Inst.*", Pittsburgh, PA: Carnegie-Mellon Univ. CMU/SEI-93-TR-025.

[36] T. J. Peters and R. H. Waterman (1982), *In Search of Excellence: Lessons From America's Best-Run Companies*. Harper & Row, New York.

[37] A. M. Pettigrew (1979), "On studying organizational cultures," *Administ. Sci. Quart.*, Vol. 24, pp. 570–581.

[38] R. E. Quinn and M. R. McGrath (1985), "The transformation of organizational cultures: A competing values perspective," in P. J. Frost, L. F. Moorre, M. R. Louise, C. C. Lundberg, and J. Martin, Eds. *Organizational Culture*. Sage, Newbury Park, CA, pp. 315–334.

[39] R. E. Quinn and J. Rohrbaugh (1983), "A spatial model of effectiveness criteria: Toward a competing values approach to organizational analysis," *Manage. Sci.*, Vol. 29, pp. 363–377.

[40] A. Rafaeli and M. Worline (2000), "Symbols in organizational culture," in N. M. Ashkanasy, C. P. M. Wilderom, and M. F. Peterson, Eds. *Handbook of Organizational Culture & Climate*. Sage, Newbury Park, CA, pp. 71–84.

[41] V. Sathe (1985), *Culture and Related Corporate Realities*. Irwin, Homewood, IL.

[42] E. H. Schein (1985), *Organizational Culture and Leadership: A Dynamic View*. Jossey-Bass, San Francisco, CA.

[43] ———, "What is culture?," in *Reframing Organizational Culture*, P. J. Frost, L. F. Moore, M. R. Louise, C. C. Lundberg, and J. Martin, Eds. Newbury Park, CA: Sage, 1991, pp. 243–253.

[44] "Process maturity profile of the software community," Software Eng. Inst, Carnegie-Mellon Univ., Pittsburgh, PA, 1997.

[45] "Process Maturity Profile of the Software Community," Software Eng. Inst., Carnegie-Mellon Univ., Pittsburgh, PA, 2002.

[46] L. Smircich (1983), "Concepts of culture and organizational analysis," *Administ. Sci. Quart.*, Vol. 28, pp. 339–358.

[47] H. Trice and J. Beyer (1984), "Studying organizational cultures through rites and ceremonials," *Acad. Manage. Rev.*, Vol. 9, pp. 653–669.

[48] D. Truex, R. Baskerville, and H. Klein (1999), "Growing systems in emergent organizations," *Commun. ACM,* Vol. 42, pp. 117–123.

[49] G. M. Weinberg, *Quality Software Management*. New York: Dorset House, 1992–97, vol. 1 (1992), 2 (1993), 3 (1994), 4 (1997).

[50] K. E. Wiegers (1996), *Creating a Software Engineering Culture*. Dorset House, New York.

[51] I. Aaen, J. Arendt, L. Mathiassen, and O. Ngwenyama (2001), "A conceptual MAP of software process improvement," *Scandinavian J. Inform. Syst.*, Vol. 13.

Reproduced from *IEEE Transactions on Engineering Management*, Vol. 50, No. 1, February 2003, pp. 101–111. Reprinted with permission from IEEE.

About the authors

Ojelanki Ngwenyama received the Diploma from Humber College, Toronto, ON, Canada, the B.G.S and M.S. degrees from Roosevelt University, Chicago, IL, the M.B.A. degree from Syracuse University, Syracuse, NY, and the Ph.D. degree in computer science from The Thomas J. Watson School of Engineering, State University of New York, Binghamton.

He is currently a Professor of information systems and the Director of the International Scholars Program at Virginia Commonwealth University, Richmond, VA. He is also an Extraordinary Professor in the Department of Informatics and a Member of the Board of Directors of the School of Information Technology, University of Pretoria, Pretoria, South Africa; a Research Professor with University of Jyväskylä, Finland; and a Visiting Research Professor with Aalborg University, Aalborg, Denmark. His research focuses on organizational issues of information technology and software development and use. He is a coauthor (with L. Mathiassen and J. Pries-Heje) of the book *Learning To Improve: Software Process Improvement In Practice* (Reading, MA: Addison-Wesley, 2001). He is currently an Associate Editor for *MISQ* and a member of the Advisory Board of the *Scandinavian Journal of Information System*. His papers have appeared in a wide range of international journals.

Dr. Ngwenyama has been a member of IFIP Working Group 8.2 since 1986.

Peter Axel Nielsen received the M.Sc. degree in computer science from Århus University, Århus, Denmark, and the Ph.D. degree in information systems from Lancaster University, Lancaster, U.K.

He is currently an Associate Professor of computer science at Aalborg University, Aalborg, Denmark. He is also a Visiting Research Professor with Agder University, Kristiansand, Norway, and a Visiting International Research Scholar with Virginia Commonwealth University, Richmond, VA. His research interests include action research on software development practice and development of object-oriented methodologies, software engineering, and social and organizational aspects of software development. Currently, he is engaged in research on software process improvement.

Dr. Nielsen is a Member of the IEEE Computer Society and a Member of the IFIP Working Group 8.2.

Questions for discussion

1   What do you think are the core benefits and risks involved in an SPI program? Is there any risk mitigation program? If yes, how can it be carried out?
2   As stated in the article, there is high rate of failure for SPI programs. What do you think is the cause of this failure besides those reasons discussed in the article?
3   If the SPI itself still has a high failure rate, is it possible that the SPI program, including CMM, can help improve software development? Why?
4   Who do you think should be responsible in leading the implementation of an SPI program in the organization? And what should be done first to improve both SPI and software development?
5   What is the similarity and difference of the P-CMM and SW-CMM? And how would you make the best utilization of both programs together?

Questions for discussion

Part Two

The Role of Culture in IS Adoption and Diffusion

This second part of the book concentrates on the role played by culture in the adoption of IS – just because an IS is successfully developed does not imply that it will be successfully adopted. Research on IS adoption and diffusion examines the phenomenon of how information technology becomes accepted and institutionalized in the adopting group's work processes. As it pertains to culture, work in this area has focused mainly on examining how different types of value orientations either facilitate or hinder the success of IT adoption efforts. Such research has been conducted examining cultural values at both the national and organizational levels as well as at the organizational sub-culture level. Two of the articles in this section address the question of IS adoption and diffusion at the organizational level (Cabrera et al., 2001; Hoffman and Klepper, 2000) while the remaining two do so at the cross cultural (Loch et al., 2003) and organizational sub-culture (Huang et al., 2003) levels.

One of the main themes in this particular stream of research has to do with the notion of 'cultural fit'. Cultural fits means that groups will be more likely to adopt and use a given information technology if the values embedded in the technology fit those values of the group or society in which the technology will be used. For example, lack of fit becomes particularly apparent when western-developed technologies (e.g. group support systems) are embedded in non-western cultures whose particular values may clash with the values implied in the technology itself. Therefore, information systems that closely fit the culture they are to be embedded in will more likely be adopted, whereas technology that lacks 'fit' will often be rejected or not used as intended.

Drawing on this theme of cultural fit, our first reading by Loch et al. (2003) examines culture specific factors that either inhibit or facilitate diffusion of the internet in the Middle East region. More specifically, these authors investigate how individual's level of exposure to technology developed in other countries (technical culturation) will lead to higher levels of internet usage. While Loch et al. (2003) examine cultural fit at the cross-cultural (Middle Eastern) level, our second article by Cabrera et al. (2001) examines how certain organizational-level work values influence the success of a technology innovation within a single large Turkish bank. They conclude that successful technology innovations require either the technology be designed to fit the organizational culture or that culture be designed to fit the behavioral requirements of the technology.

Our third reading by Huang et al. (2003) draws from Martinson and Myers (1987) *differentiation* perspective of culture to show how clashing values among organizational sub-cultures might influence the adoption of IT. In this single firm case study, the authors used creative metaphors to describe the existence of various sub-cultures within a given firm. Based on their analysis of sub-cultures, they conclude that these sub-cultural differences actually hindered the information sharing and collaboration that was required to effectively implement component-based development (CBD).

Such sub-culture differences help to illustrate that corporate-wide efforts to implement integrative solutions like CBD might be complicated by the existence of various firm sub-cultures each with different value preferences and orientations. To the extent that these different sub-cultures have competing values, then conflict may result. A similar study by Von Meier (1999) involving organizational sub-cultures has examined work group sub-cultures' interpretations of proposed technological innovations. Results showed two different occupational sub-cultures (engineers vs. operators) had entirely different cultural interpretations of proposed technologies and as a result experienced conflict and resistance to adopting certain technologies.

In our fourth reading, Hoffman and Klepper (2000) draw from Goffee and Jones (1996) to examine what types of organizational values are more conducive to enabling technology assimilation to occur. The focus is less on cultural values embedded in the technology and more about identifying which organizational culture allows innovative activities associated with technology assimilation to thrive. They conclude that organizational cultures characterized as 'mercenary' in nature (low sociability and high solidarity) are more likely to experience success in infusing information technologies into their respective environments.

Readings from this section provide evidence that cultural values (national, organizational, or sub-culture) may predispose certain social groups towards either favorable or unfavorable IT adoption and diffusion behaviors. It is clear from this theme of research that the degree of fit between social groups' culture and cultural assumptions embedded in IT has emerged as an important construct for studying IT adoption and diffusion. Furthermore, the presence of different organizational sub-group cultures with competing values must be considered as a potential source of conflict in firm's IT adoption and diffusion processes.

References

Cabrera, A., E. F. Cabrera, and S. Barajas (2001), "The Key Role of Organizational Culture in a Multi-System View of Technology-Driven Change," *International Journal of Information Management*, Vol. 21, No. 3, pp. 245–261.

Goffee, R. and G. Jones (1996), "What Holds the Modern Company Together?," *Harvard Business Review*, Vol. 74, No. 6, Nov–Dec, pp. 133–148.

Hoffman, N. and R. Klepper (2000), "Assimilating New Technologies: The Role of Organizational Culture," *Information Systems Management*, Vol. 17, No. 3, pp. 36–42.

Huang, J. C., S. Newell, R. Galliers, and S. L. Pan (2003), "Dangerous Liaisons? Component Based Development and Organizational Subcultures," *IEEE Transactions on Engineering Management*, Vol. 50, No. 1, February, pp. 89–99.

Loch, K. D., D. W. Straub, and S. Kamel (2003), "Diffusing the Internet in the Arab World: The Role of Social Norms and Technological Culturation," *IEEE Transactions on Engineering Management*, Vol. 50, No. 1, February, pp. 45–63.

Von Meier, A. (1999), "Occupational Cultures as a Challenge to Technological Innovation," *IEEE Transactions on Engineering Management*, Vol. 46, No. 1, pp. 101–114.

5 Diffusing the Internet in the Arab World: The Role of Social Norms and Technological Culturation

Karen D. Loch, Detmar W. Straub and Sherif Kamel

Abstract: Drawing on the theoretical work of Hill *et al.* and Straub *et al.*, this study examines culture-specific inducements and impediments to using the Internet in the Arab world. Research questions were (1) to what extent does the process of technology culturation affect the acceptance of the Internet (2) to what extent do social norms (SNs) affect the acceptance of the Internet?

Of the two research methods employed, the first was a quantitative field study of knowledge workers. The instrument measured the extent to which respondents and their organizations are influenced by advanced technology cultures. Using partial least squares (PLS), the first of two models tested links between SNs; technological culturation and Internet usage for each respondent. The second model investigated links between technological culturation and Internet utilization for the respondent's organization. Findings show strong support for both models, explaining, respectively, 47% and 37% of the variance. The second method was a qualitative analysis of respondents' free-format comments. These findings reinforce the quantitative findings, on the one hand, and reveal additional cultural barriers that still need to be studied, on the other. Findings identify how culture can both inhibit and encourage technological innovation and how Arab cultures can move their economies more quickly into the digital age.

Introduction

The regional setting is dynamic. Internet use and the general demand for information technology (IT) hardware and services in the Middle East are growing, with a projected market value of $8.9 billion by 2005 [1]. Egypt, Saudi Arabia, and the United Arab Emirates (UAE) accounted for 59% of 2001 demand and as much as 64% of the future forecast. In 2001, the launching of Egypt's first free Internet service provider Noor illustrated wide commitment to market opportunities. It is no wonder that the Internet and burgeoning world of e-commerce and Net-enhancement are viewed as engines of economic growth for Egypt in the 21st century, and why Arab countries such as Egypt are exemplars of how to leapfrog [2] into the IT era [3]. While it is easy to ride this wave of enthusiasm for innovations such as the Internet, failing to understand the factors that influence diffusion at the micro level is still a threat. Past experience shows that technology diffusion is not a straight-forward process [4].

Based on prior theoretical work, our field study gathered quantitative and qualitative data from Arab knowledge workers and top and middle-level managers, nearly all of whom were Internet-savvy. We examine the acceptance of the Internet by the respondents themselves as well as their perceptions of organizational acceptance.

Literature review

A question frequently asked is whether a country's culture – understood as unconscious values, beliefs, and behavioral patterns as well as manifest political regimes – is favorable to IT adoption [5]. Culture is thought by many scholars to have a bearing on outcomes. It follows that if cultural beliefs and attitudes toward technology were better understood, then the technology itself, which, in this study, was the Internet, might be better adapted to the behavioral patterns of the adopting country, rather than the traditional approach of force-fitting the culture to the technology.

To investigate this research domain, we drew on theoretical work of Hill *et al.* [6],[7] and Straub *et al.* [4], as shown in Figure 5.1. In 1994, Hill *et al.* [7] first presented their approach, known as cultural influence modeling, by arguing that culture-specific beliefs, technological culturation, and national policy/infrastructure affect systems outcomes. Past empirical studies support the contention that both cultural beliefs and technological culturation significantly affect the transference of IT to Arab cultures [4],[6],[7]. Thus, we felt that it would be reasonable to posit similar results with respect to a specific technology such as the Internet.

What are the constructs and linkages in this theoretical base? Briefly, culture-specific beliefs (CB) and values are thought to be surrogates of culture that have a downstream effect on the use of information systems and, in the case of the current study, the Internet. Culture is demonstrated through social actions and becomes crystallized in social institutions, via the creation of social norms (SN) [8]. Nearly two decades ago, Bertolotti [9] suggested that the culture of a country or region greatly affects the acceptance of a technology through its beliefs and values on modernization and technological development. Prior to that, Kransberg and Davenport [10] argued that "an advance in technology not only must be congruent with the surrounding technology

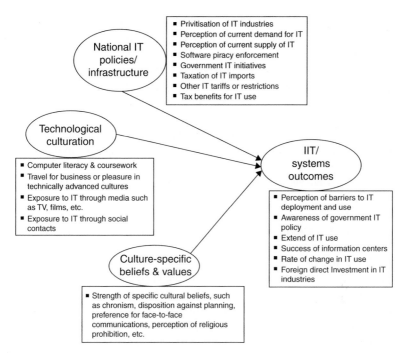

Figure 5.1   *Cultural influence modeling and IT transfer based on Straub* et al. *[4] and Hill* et al. *[6]*

but ***must also be compatible with … existing economic and other cultural and social institutions*** [italics and bolding added]." Corea [11] argues this point from a slightly different perspective, stating emphatically that "information and communication technologies should be self-cultivated rather than imported." Escobar [12] recognizes the interactive relationship between technology and culture, one influencing the construction and reconstruction of the other, and vice-versa.

Whereas the theory base we have discussed uses the CB construct, we chose to take an alternate path in this study, examining the effect of the traditional construct of SNs on systems outcomes. One important distinction between this study and past studies cited is this substitution of the more general construct of SNs for a CB variable measurement, such as sense of time, or face-to-face versus electronic meeting. SNs are typically defined as social pressure on an individual to perform, or not to perform, some behavior [8]. The closer the affinity of the individuals with their reference group, the more likely the individuals are to perform according to reference group expectations [13].

Closely related to, but distinct from, cultural beliefs is the phenomenon of technological culturation (TC). This latent construct refers to the cultural exposure and the experiences that individuals have with technology originally developed in other countries. Straub *et al.*'s representation of this construct [4] assumes that (1) technology is not a neutral agent, but rather (2) technology reflects embedded cultural-specific beliefs and values as a result of where (and by whom) it was developed. When all is considered, technological culturation translates into a greater acceptance of a new technology, even if there are cultural barriers. The theory base for this effect is not only the anthropological literature (for review of this literature, see [12] and [14]–[18]) but also the work on the impact of familiarity/trust on brand acceptance in the marketing and management literatures [19]–[23].

This conceptualization differs from the traditional social science construct of "acculturation." In anthropological studies, "acculturation" refers to the assimilation by members of one society of the values and beliefs of another [24]. While these earlier acculturation studies assumed that more developed countries unilaterally "give" new technology to lesser-developed countries, this is not the prevailing scholarly view of this construct at this time. Modern anthropologists attempt to glean insights into the process of the interactive relationship between technology and culture [14],[25]–[27]. The assumption is that the cultural and social lives of respondents influence attitudes toward and use of technology. The theoretical framework introduced by Straub *et al.* [4] assumes that Arabs continually negotiate their technological world within the context of their social and cultural world and that the contact between these worlds is transforming in nature. In short, technology is not force-fed through the social mechanism of technological culturation, but its benefits are made clear, and adaptation of cultural norms and values to be able to receive some of these benefits will lead to higher levels of adoption, albeit not necessarily universal adoption.

In the IT arena, TC occurs when people become informed or educated about networks, computer systems, and application software from another culture. These are technologies that are not presently assimilated into their own cultures. The relevant experiences of TC range from formal experiences such as long-term studying in a technically advanced culture or informal experiences such as travel abroad and through a network of family and friends.

Besides focusing on new perspectives on these relationships, the current study also contributes to the emerging literature by exploring a new context for the theory. The context of Hill *et al.* [7] was general computer usage in the Arab world as was the subsequent work by Rose and Straub [28] and Straub *et al.* [4]; none of these focused specifically on Internet usage, as in the current study.

Two research questions were the focus of our inquiry: (1) To what extent does the process of technological culturation affect the acceptance of the Internet? (2) To what extent do SNs affect the acceptance of the Internet?

Research models

We conceptualize two models for explaining cultural impacts on Internet acceptance. These are shown in Figures 5.2 and 5.3, with latent constructs being represented in bubbles and indicator variables, or measures, in rectangular boxes. The first model predicts systems outcomes consistent with the work of Hill *et al.* [6], Hill *et al.* [7], and Straub *et al.* [4].[1]

The research project had some elements that are exploratory and some that were confirmatory. It is exploratory in that this is the first use of this specific field study methodology in this specific research domain. The organizational model is likewise exploratory, especially in the addition of the SN construct. The individual model has been tested before, however, in Straub *et al.* [4].

Having a clear linkage to culture, SNs are another critical antecedent of system usage although they are more generic than the culture-specific beliefs that are modeled in Straub *et al.* [4]. SNs are clearly related to culture or are even a component of it, according to Zaheer and Zaheer [29]. For similar arguments, see [30]. Our view is that CB and TC represent a set of cultural

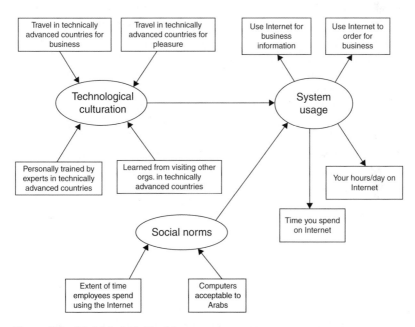

Figure 5.2 *Model 1: Individual Internet acceptance*

[1]PLS can represent both formative and reflective constructs, the difference between which will be discussed. For the moment, it is only important to note that reflective measures point outward from the construct while formative measures point inward. If one measure is formative, then the entire construct has to be treated as a formative construct.

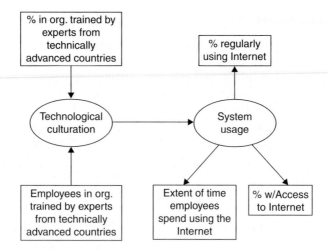

Figure 5.3   *Model 2: Organizational Internet acceptance*

obstacles. SN is a more generic representation of CB as part of this set of cultural obstacles. In our instrumentation, two questions tap into the SN construct. In accordance with the suggestions of Straub [31], we devised measures to draw on referent groups. Each question presumes a referent group, in which, depending on the strength of his/her affinity with that group, it is more or less likely that an individual will conform to the norms of the referent group. One question considers peers in the workplace as the referent group; the second question stresses Arab society as a referent group.

Organizational-level effects of cultural antecedents were also studied and modeled, as shown in Figure 5.3. We posit that technological culturation will impact the acceptance and use of IT in the organization as a whole. The more frequently (and/or intensely) that employees are exposed to IT, by such activities as training where the technology developed in another culture has been the subject, the more they should be influenced positively to use that technology.

Research method

The technique chosen to empirically test the two research models was a field study, instrumented via a questionnaire [32]. The questionnaire was filled out by managers and knowledge workers attending an annual regional conference on the Internet, CAINET. An annual event since 1996, the Cairo Internet Conference and Exhibition is the main Internet event in the region. There can be little doubt that this sample is a relatively savvy set of Internet users. Year to year, the conference program reflects an increasingly varied set of subjects and case studies of successful use of Internet capabilities.

Participants were asked their personal views and their perceptions of their respective organization's attitudes toward the use of the Internet. The total sample size was 100, or roughly 10% of the conference's registered attendees. As English was the working language of the conference, the research instrument was in English. The instrument was made available to attendees at the registration table and responses were solicited on a strictly voluntary basis.

We pointedly chose to examine the impact of culture on this sample of more sophisticated users. In the first place, the responses of actual users were more insightful, we felt, than would be the hypothetical reactions of nonusers. If we detected salient cultural factors affecting Internet acceptance among this group, then there is a strong likelihood that they would be even more pronounced among a group of technology laggards. The respondent firms were also likely to be leaders in the use of the Internet and, therefore, offer insights into their employees' usage that would be practically important to Arab practitioners. We sought, therefore, to examine the acceptance of the Internet by this group of individual respondents as well as that of their organizations. There were 100 returned questionaires, of which, 92 were individuals with a strong identity with Arab countries. Of the total, 89% were born in an Arab country, and 95% claimed nationality in an Arab country, with Egypt being the most common nation, reported by 85% of the respondents. Consequently, the researchers felt confident that the respondents were able to respond to questions concerning prevailing SNs in the Arab world.

Respondents

To further ensure that we were gathering and analyzing data only on Arabs, we checked self-reported nationality and cross-checked the number of years a respondent had worked in the Arab world against their age. Non-Arabs were not consciously used in the analysis. The majority of respondents were Egyptians (85%), although there were also citizens of Kuwait, Lebanon, and Saudi Arabia in the sample pool (7%; see Table 5.6).

Based on a MANOVA analysis in Straub *et al.* [4], it is reasonable to assume that the slight variation in Arab countries represented in our sample will not affect results. Straub *et al.* [4] found no relationship between country and their independent variables (IVs) and dependent variables (DVs) and since the same variables were used in the current study, we anticipated no problem in this respect.

Measures and instrumentation

Although major portions of the questionaire instrument had already been pretested and validated, as reported in Hill *et al.* [7], Straub *et al.* [4] and

Table 5.1   *Measures for constructs in model 1*

Constructs	#	Items	Type of Construct [α]
Technological Culturation	I.10a	Travel for business to non-Arab advanced technology countries [Degree scale]	Formative
	I.10b	Travel for pleasure to non-Arab advanced technology countries [Degree scale]	
	I.14a	Learned a lot through expert training in advanced technology from other countries [Likert scale]	
	I.14c	Learned a lot through visiting businesses in non-Arab advanced technology countries [Likert scale]	
Social Norms	I.12a	Extent of time employees spend on average using Internet [Degree scale]	Formative
	I.13d	Computers are well accepted in Arab society [Likert scale]	
Systems Outcome Behaviors: Internet Usage	I.11	Hours/day individual spends using Internet [Ratio scale]	Reflective [.61]
	I.12b	Perception of time individual spent on Internet [Degree scale]	
	I.13c	Use Internet for business purchasing [Likert scale]	
	I.13f	Use Internet for business information gathering [Likert scale]	

Hofstede [33], we fully tested the instrumentation in the current study, as recommended by Straub [34]. Appendix A shows the complete instrument. Measures for the constructs, with their corresponding reliabilities for the DVs, are shown in Tables 5.1 and 5.2. When the scale formats varied, normalized, or adjusted, Cronbach's α's were used. These statistics are acceptable by Nunnally's standards for exploratory research [35].

SNs were formative rather than reflective, and, for this reason, Cronbach α's were not deemed to be the appropriate test [36]–[38]. Although both "form" the latent construct "Social Norms," the time an employee spends on the Internet is not necessarily related to the perception that Arabs accept computers in their society. While it is possible to conceive of a possible linkage, the more conservative interpretation is to assume that the linkage is loose, at best, and that the construct is formative. The same logic applies to the technological culturation construct in both models, which we also designate as formative.

Table 5.2 *Measures for constructs in model 2*

Constructs	#	Items	Type of Construct [α]
Technological Culturation	I.15	% of employees in organization who have been trained by experts who learned in technologically advanced countries [Ratio scale]	Formative
	I.14e	Employees learned through experts trained in advanced technology of other countries [Likert scale]	
Systems Outcome Behaviors: Internet Usage	I.12a	Extent of time employees spend on average using Internet [Degree scale]	Reflective [.81]
	I.16	% of employees with access to Internet [Ratio scale]	
	I.17	% of employees who regularly use the Internet [Ratio scale]	

Validity of the instrument

To validate the instrumentation, including the constructs, i.e., to test the convergent and discriminant validity of the measures, a variation of Campbell and Fiske's [39] multitrait-multimethod (MTMM) analysis was employed. When partial least squares (PLS) is utilized as the analytical tool, it is standard practice to conduct a discriminant validity analysis by creating average variance explained (AVE) statistics and to compare these with the cross correlations of other measures in the instrument [38]. If an AVE is larger than correlations in its row and column, then this is *prima facie* evidence for discriminant validity. AVE analysis, however, depends on reflective measures, and we have adopted a conservative stance that none of the IVs in the current study are reflective.

In their argumentation on how researchers may test formative constructs, Diamantopoulos and Winklhofer propose that researchers correlate formative items with a "global item that summarizes the essence of the construct" [40, p. 272]. Other than this article, there is little guidance in the methodological literature on proper validation of formative constructs [40]. Accordingly, this recommendation, as well as techniques developed in Ravichandran and Rai's empirical study [41], were consulted for reasonable guidance in validating our formative constructs.

Given the paucity of methodological advice on how to validate formative measures, we developed a logically and methodologically consistent approach to validation. Whereas we did not have multiple methods for measuring the constructs, we were able to compare the traits (scale items) and the constructs due to the properties of formative constructs and PLS statistics available to us. In PLS, loadings represent the influence of individual scale items on reflective constructs; PLS weights represent a comparable influence for formative constructs [42].

To test the measurement properties of the instrument, we first transformed all data to a five-point scale to correspond with the most common scale in the instrument.[2] With all data normalized, we multiplied values by their individual PLS weights and summed them up for each construct, a formulation suggested by Bagozzi and Fornell [43]. In effect, then, we created a weighted score for each measure (termed "indicator" in PLS) and a composite score for each formative construct. Thus, using these values, we were able to run inter-item (that is, inter-measure) correlations as well as item-to-construct correlations and create a matrix of these values, as shown in Table 5.3.

Campbell and Fiske [39] argue that in a matrix similar to this, measures thought to be part of the same construct should correlate at a significant level with each other. By creating a composite construct value, we can extend this logic by arguing that the individual measures should also correlate significantly with their construct value. As can be observed in the matrix in Table 5.3,[3] the weighted and transformed formative measures all qualify by this standard. The inter-item correlations and the item-to-construct correlations for TC1, TC2, and SN are all significant, all but one at least at the 0.05 level. This is persuasive evidence for convergent validity of the instrument.

We also compared measures and constructs in the two TC variables in the two models. These are indicated in TC1 and TC2 in the matrix. With the exception of correlations between variable 10a (business travel in foreign countries) and the composite technological score for TC2, all of these correlations are significant at the 0.10 level. Using entirely different measures, TC1 and TC2 correlate at 0.390 at the 0.05 level. This comparison likewise suggests that the instrument has acceptable convergent validity.

The logic for discriminant validity is that the inter-item and item-to-construct correlations should correlate more highly with each other than with the measures of other constructs, and, in our case, with the composite constructs themselves [39]. By comparing values in the TC1, TC2, and SN rectangles with values in their own rows and columns, we can see that there are only a few violations of this basic principle. Campbell and Fiske [39] point out that normal statistical distributions in a large matrix will result in exceptions

---

[2]The formula for this conversion is [6-ABS (value to be transformed or highest value)/ ((difference between the highest value and the lowest value)/4) + 1].

[3]TC1 represents the construct as formulated in the individual model; TC2 represents the construct as formulated in the organizational model.

Table 5.3 *Inter-item and item-to-construct correlation matrix*

	V10A	V10B	V14A	V14C	TC1	V12A	V13D	SN	V15	V14E	TC2	YEARS	AGE	EMAIL	F2F	TEL	FAX
V10A	–																
V10B	.394**	–															
V14A	.221**	.279**	–														
V14C	.181*	.231*	.486**	–													
TC1	.410**	.673**	.772**	.761**	–												
V12A	–.095	–.033	.281**	.257**	.200*	–											
V13D	–.337**	–.292**	.074	.097	–.082	.332**	–										
SN	–.275**	–.181*	.210*	.170	.059	.792**	.801**	–									
V15	.076	.190*	.415**	.235**	.357**	.328**	–.034	.166	–								
V14E	.115	.192*	.613**	.458**	.543**	.371**	.064	.243**	.574**	–							
TC2	.098	.263**	.420**	.235**	.390**	.328**	–.050	.158	.995**	.577**	–						
YEARS	.568**	.024	.013	.078	.102	–.049	–.083	–.056	–.103	–.064	–.103	–					
AGE	.432**	–.017	–.033	.041	.046	–.177	–.130	–.166	–.160	–.141	–.165	.880**	–				
EMAIL	–.077	–.053	–.010	.017	–.045	–.094	.105	.008	–.177	–.113	–.183	–.037	.050	–			
F2F	–.024	–.139	–.113	.120	–.084	.012	.428**	.281**	–.112	–.145	–.120	.106	.160	.238**	–		
TEL	–.049	–.128	–.047	.201*	–.030	.068	.055	.062	.052	–.003	.039	–.099	–.066	.165	.597**	–	
FAX	–.061	.020	.063	.117	.084	.165	.182	.164	–.019	.069	–.025	–.193*	–.248**	–.049	–.312**	–.186	–

TC2 and Model 2. SN is the composite

N.B. TC1 is the technological culturation composite value for Model 1. Similarly with TC2 and Model 2. SN is the composite value for SNs.

**Correlation is significant at the .05 level (2-tailed).

*Correlation is significant at the .10 level (2-tailed).

that are not necessarily meaningful. They suggest that one uses judgment in determining whether the number of violations is low enough to conclude that the instrument items discriminate well.

Besides the variables of interest in the study, we included a series of other variables for the sake of comparison and contrast. In the smaller *Years/Age* rectangle, work year (Years) and Age are classic demographics that, in most cases, should not correlate with technological culturation or SNs, and in most cases, they do not. Two violations of the test (the correlations of both Years and Age with variable 10a: business travel in foreign countries) are higher than the corresponding correlations in the same row (0.568 and 0.432). Why would this be? Those who travel for business the most are likely to be the most experienced business persons, which is reflected in the number of years they have been working and their age. So this particular technical violation is easily explained by the nature of the data and actually reinforces the integrity of the data gathering.

Among the other comparison variables were *Social Presence Variables* (for email, fact-to-face communications, telephone, and FAX; see larger rectangle in Table 5.3). These measure the extent to which respondents feel that these media reflect the social presence of a human being [44]. Although not used specifically in the current study, these are validated items that have appeared extensively in the IS literature [45]. Again, for purposes of evaluating discriminant validity, these measures indicate that the TC1, TC2, and SN constructs have acceptable measurement properties. There were no violations in the matrix with respect to these variables.

The only other technical violations in the matrix that are worth noting are those between variable 10a (TC1), again, and several of the SNs items. V10A with V13D (SN) is higher (0.337) than the inter-item correlations of the TC1 variables V10A with V14A (0.221) and V14C (0.181). This means that this measure is not discriminating as well as we would like. Overall, as indicated, the construct has acceptable measurement properties, but there is no question that there are a few violations at an expected and acceptable level. What we can say is that V10A is not as strong as the other measures of the TC construct, which is a weakness that also emerged in Straub *et al.*'s work [4].

To ensure that the DVs were acceptable from a measurement standpoint, a factor analysis of the Model 1 DV (Internet usage) and other variables (Table 5.4) showed that Internet usage converged cleanly and at high loadings on a single factor (factor 2 in this case). The instrument also discriminated well, as the other variables loaded on separate factors.

Model 2 Internet Usage was also distinct from other variables, as Table 5.5 reveals. The first factor was this construct, which loaded cleanly, at high levels, and on different variables than the experience construct and a miscellaneous construct.

Table 5.4 *Factor structure for model 1 DV construct*

Measures	Factor 1: Years/Age Experience	Factor 2: Internet Usage	Factor 3: Misc.
YEARS	.977		
AGE	.977		
V11		.785	
V12B		.775	
V13F		.604	
V13C		.543	
V13A			.787
V13B			.736

Extraction Method: Principal Component Analysis; Rotation Method: Varimax with Kaiser Normalization; Rotation converged in 4 iterations

Table 5.5 *Factor structure for model 2 DV construct*

Measures	Factor 1: Internet Usage	Factor 2: Years/Age Experience	Factor 3: Misc.
V12A	.822		
V16	.809		
V17	.733		
YEARS		.971	
AGE		.970	
V13B			.887
V13A			.493

Extraction Method: Principal Component Analysis; Rotation Method: Varimax with Kaiser Normalization; Rotation converged in 6 iterations

Data analysis

The sample was comprised of middle and senior managers and knowledge workers in companies and organizations from both the private and public sector in the Middle East; there were also respondents from outside the Arab world, and these data were not used in the subsequent analyses.

Respondents were seasoned professionals, with a mean age of 31 and work experience of eight years (with a standard deviation of 8.7 yr). The distribution of educational levels also suggests that the respondents were fairly well educated (see Table 5.6). They reported on average 3.8 h of Internet use per day.

Table 5.6   *Descriptive statistics*

	Category	%	N	Mean	SD
Age	25–30	5%	90	30.98	9.13
	30–40	50%			
	40–50	25%			
	50–60	15%			
	60+	5%			
Nationality	Arab (non-Egyptian)	7%	100		
	Egyptian	85%			
	European	5%			
	American	2%			
	Asian	1%			
Education	Private Sector (BA, BSc, MA, MBA, MSc)	50%			
	Public Sector (BA, BSc, MA, MBA, MSc)	15%			
	Academics (PhD)	25%			
	Individuals (BA, BSc, MA, MBA, MSc)	10%			
Work Experience			90	8.16	8.64
Individual Internet Usage (I.11, Hours/day)			90	3.75	2.41
Employees' Internet Usage (I.12a, Hours/day)			90	3.19	.83
Gender	Male	70%			
	Female	30%			

The distribution shows that 50% of the respondents used the Internet from 2 to 5 h per day. How they use the Internet is informative (see Table 5.7). Less than 30% used the Internet to order goods and services for business purposes, and less than 2% use it for gathering business information, yet over 70% use it for email.

While this group does report significant exposure to technologies, such as the Internet, a strong majority of respondents also indicate that its acceptance is not without significant reservations. Forty-six percent expressed concern that family and community life may be threatened by the Internet; 58% disagreed that computers are well-accepted in Arab society, a necessary component for the Internet; and 40% disagreed that the Internet would have a positive impact on Arab family and community ties (see Table 5.7).

As previously argued, this sample profile is particularly suitable for this study as it represents a robust test of technological culturation. The respondents

Table 5.7   *Respondent profile and Internet usage*

Individuals

Travel	• Travel in non-Arab Industrialized world for business purposes	46% a great deal 24% a fair amount
	• Travel in non-Arab industrialized world for pleasure	30% a great deal 26% a fair amount
Internet savviness	• Daily time on the Internet	3.75 hours
	• Use for email	70% agree +
	• Use to order for business purposes	30% agree + 53% disagree + 2% agree +
	• Use for business info gathering	91% disagree +

Perceptions of Internet use by their peers in their organizations

Access	• % employees with Internet access	73%
	• % employees who use Internet regularly	62%
Acceptance of Internet	• Most feel threatened about how Internet will affect family & community life	46% agree + 23% disagree +
	• Internet is attractive to employees/orgs because computers are well accepted in Arab society	14% agree + 58% disagree +
	• Internet will strengthen Arab family & community ties	24% agree + 40% disagree +

are generally high on the scale of TC and so homogeneous that relationships will not be statistically significant unless the effect is large. Hence, findings of statistical significance, supported by the qualitative data, can be interpreted as providing strong evidence in support of the model.

To test the research models, PLS analyses and a qualitative assessment of the free-format data were conducted. Initially, we examined the descriptive statistics of the sample group, which offered insight into the character of Internet-savvy individuals.

Thus, while the respondent profiles indicate that the respondents were necessarily older, well educated, and computer proficient, they are the segment of the population most likely to be using Internet personally and in the workplace. Indeed, the average computer usage by organizational employees is also high (3.19 h/day), indicating that the firms and organizations sampled are likely on the leading edge of Internet deployment.

Is this data source appropriate for answering our research questions? We felt that cultural effects discovered among this group on IT outcomes

Table 5.8   *PLS composite reliability for models 1 and 2*

Construct	Model 1	Model 2
Systems Usage	.738	.760

would be even more pronounced among the general population. With such a homogeneous sample of high-end users, it is very possible that there would be insufficient variability to find significant effects for TC (and SN) on usage, but if the statistics are still significant, then we can say that the models are robust. With a more diverse sampling, the differences among heavy and light usage should be statistically even more striking.

PLS analysis

Using the data from the 90 Arab respondents only, the two models were tested using PLS. Because of the particular statistical techniques PLS employs, it can be used with sample sizes as small as 20 [18], which is far less than our sample size. The first model examined the links between SN, TC, and Internet usage for each respondent. The second model investigated links between TC and Internet take-up for the respondent's organization. As shown previously, the instrument demonstrated good measurement properties and significant loadings and weightings. Loadings and weights of the reflective and formative measures, respectively, indicate that the constructs generally demonstrate convergent validity. All were significant at the 0.05 level except for V10A and V10B, which is consistent with Straub *et al.* [4]. Given the problems with these measures, researchers need to explore other ways of tapping into the TC construct. Fortunately, the other measures were sufficiently powerful to produce the effect we posited. Table 5.8 presents the results of PLS composite reliability for the models. It offers evidence that the constructs are indeed reliable. They are both within accepted limits [38].[4]

Figures 5.4 and 5.5 display path coefficients and explained variance for the two PLS models. Results support both models, explaining, respectively, 47% and 37% of the variance.

The individual acceptance model found strong relationships between SNs and technological culturation and usage, in spite of the fact that two of the loadings on indicators were not significant. There were no such drawbacks or anomalies in the simpler organizational model. Employees apparently

---

[4]Least square techniques are generally robust to the violation of the need for interval data for the DV [46],[47].

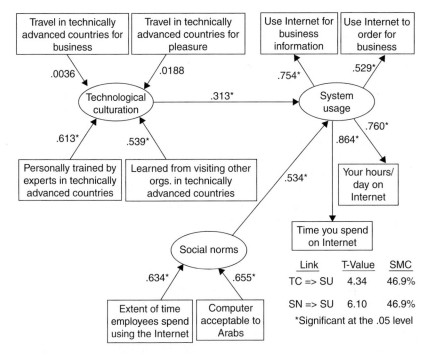

Figure 5.4 *Findings of PLS analysis for Model 1*

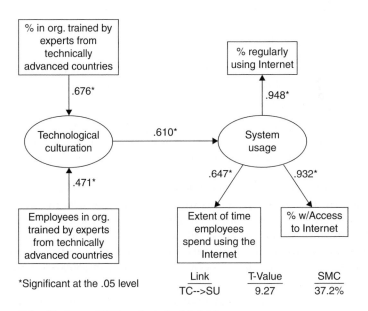

Figure 5.5 *Findings of PLS analysis for Model 2*

respond to the influence of experts from other cultures. The explained variance for Model 2 was lower, it is true, but still at a very acceptable level [48].

Qualitative analysis

Respondents were given an opportunity to address a free-format question, which asked what factors encouraged or discouraged the acceptance of the Internet in the Arab world. Over 38% of the respondents identified at least one factor that they felt either encouraged or discouraged the acceptance of the Internet. Tables 5.9 and 5.10 provide a summary list of discouraging and encouraging factors, respectively. Respondents were more inclined to list discouraging factors by 20%, perhaps indicative of the hurdles they believe they face.

Among the negative factors, socio-economic concerns were prominently mentioned, including the cost of computers, the lack of education in knowing how to use them, and the insouciance of "rural" people. There was a strong undertone in these free-format responses that a growing digital divide was continuing to separate the elite, well-to-do, and highly educated Arabs from the poor: the bulk of the population. Cultural barriers were also raised, especially language barriers. For many uneducated Arabs to use the Internet, there will have to be many more sites with Arabic content. Presently, there are a limited number of useful sites like this.

Other respondents were concerned about the differences in culture represented by the global connectedness of the Internet. General statements reflecting this concern included

"Some cultures [with presence on the Internet] affect our customs in a negative way ..."

Moral and religious cultural issues were also raised, one commentator finding there to be an "abrupt increase [in] unethical sites and locations." Another respondent expressed this as follows:

"[The Internet] can affect ... social life ... [and] face-to-face communication ... [It] can cause Internet addiction ... Non-ethical, non-religious sites ... can harm ... young children and youth ... and later [take] the place of sports and important activities and hobbies."

A few respondents focused on infrastructural issues in detailing discouraging factors. The lack of a pervasive, inexpensive and reliable telecommunications infrastructure in the Arab countries being reported was particularly stressed.

Encouraging factors included all of the key variables in our study. Numerous respondents mentioned the value of education and training in the hardware and software that originate in industrialized countries while still maintaining that more Arabic content was needed. Fear of other cultures needed to be overcome through awareness and government support for disseminating knowledge of the positive effects of the Internet.

Table 5.9   *Discouraging factors for the acceptance of Internet in the arab world*

Discouraging Factors	# Times Mentioned
Cost (high)	14
Lack of training and education (some misunderstanding)	13
Awareness	9
Culture conflict	9
Language	6
Inappropriate usage (waste of time)	5
Infrastructure	5
Technological barriers	5
Inappropriate contents	4
Security	2
Availability	2
A respondent may have had more than one response	93 total items listed

Table 5.10   *Encouraging factors for the acceptance of Internet in the Arab world*

Encouraging Factors	# Times Mentioned
Training and education	17
Organizational and managerial benefits	14
Awareness	13
Availability	12
Cost (decreasing cost of access)	11
Access more information	8
Easy to use	5
Technology innovation	5
Language	4
Infrastructure	3
Being an active participant	1
A respondent may have had more than one response	74 total items listed

Discussion

We asked questions to determine the extent to which referent groups, such as peers and society at large, might influence the attitudes and behaviors of the respondent toward the Internet. SNs (along with TC) explained 47% of the variance of the model. The responses to the free-format question "what factors encourage or discourage the use of the Internet in organizations," suggest the need to understand the peculiarities of the individual, as evidenced by microlevel cultural beliefs and behaviors of individuals in developing countries, and how they perceive their respective organization, as a key component in a successful transfer of information technology into an organizational and business environment. The respondents in our study were generally well-educated users, but there was enough variability in their background and attitudes to reveal that more education/training in these technologies by experts with experience in technologically advanced countries will result in greater acceptance of systems. Even with the numerous cultural barriers identified as problematic by the respondents, they can be mitigated, at least in part, through technological culturation.

Another contribution of the study was the qualitative findings. It is useful to know that lack of awareness of the Internet and its restrictiveness of language (that is, lack of Arab language sites) are barriers to adoption. These areas need further study to see how they can be mitigated, at the very least.

Limitations to the study

More data is always desirable. It would be useful to increase the sampling, both in terms of number but also with a more diverse sample profile. Based on our findings, one would expect to see greater explained variance with stronger cultural indicators. Technological culturation continues to be difficult to measure. One possibility is that the construct is recursive in nature. Most real-world processes are like this – exposure, response, further exposure, further response, and so on. Given the nature of our research questions, tools, and cross-sectional approach, we believe we are only able to capture the front-end of the process. In the case of this study, we believe the back-end is demonstrated through the evolution of SNs and the reported use of the Internet by the respondents. We suggest that a longitudinal study may allow a more complete examination of the recursive nature of this construct. Similarly, we wanted to measure the extent to which an individual's attitude is influenced by external referent groups. We attempted two measures of SNs which proved to be reasonable; however, there may be others that are preferred. We admit, however, to the exploratory nature of this effort. In addition, we did not include SNs as part of the organizational model because the theory of reasoned action, which provides the theory-base for this construct, does not posit how organizations react to their own SNs. Another possible limitation is nonresponse bias, which we did not have a means of testing in this study. Finally, this study examined one specific technology (the Internet) through the eyes of a primarily single-country population. Consideration of additional technologies and different and/or larger geographical representation would serve to build a more generalizable set of insights for international technology transference.

Implications for researchers

Specific contributions of this study provide scholars and managers with new insights. From the standpoint of theory, the data set suggests that technological culturation significantly affects Internet usage, which is another instantiation of the systems outcome/technology transfer construct in Straub *et al.* [4]. This relationship was held to be true in both the individual and organizational models.

SNs were also significant, indicating that some cultural factors beyond Straub *et al.*'s cultural influence modeling [4] may be having an impact. Together, these results support contemporary critical theory literature on Arab society and culture.

While the construct of TC was operationalized sufficiently in the current study, it is clearly not yet well enough defined for the research stream to adopt unreservedly. TC measures that were troublesome, but still significant, in Straub *et al.* [4] were insignificant in the current study (I.10a and I.10b) for the individual model and supplanted by alternate measures of the specific training and education received (I.14a) and visitations to sites where the technology was being used (I.14c). There is ample evidence that exposure to advanced technology from other cultures has a real effect. What seems appropriate at this point is for scholars to revisit the construct and redesign it with a refined theory base. The relationship of TC to theory-based familiarity constructs could be fruitful in this regard.

A methodological contribution in the study is the modified MTMM analysis, which can be used to explore measurement properties when the constructs are formative. To our knowledge, the modified MTMM approach is an innovation in the literature.

Finally, evidence was found in favor of Straub *et al.*'s cultural influence modeling [4], which attempts to represent the important cultural influences on the transfer of IT to developing countries. Two cultural variables were conceptualized in the present work, and relationships between two of these and IT systems outcomes (i.e., systems usage, in this case) were explored. Whereas the construct of national IT policies and infrastructure was not explored, future studies can and should study this key latent variable.

With regard to future research, we support Straub *et al.*'s position [31] that there are inherent dangers in assuming that cultural beliefs are universal and always must be measured in the aggregate, as in [33]. Measures in this study were styled to the cultural forces that expose people to technology in the Arab world. Many or most of these measures may be adaptable to other cultures, but they would need to be carefully applied. Future research should test how the TC construct can be operationalized in very different cultures. In this way, we can learn how generalizable the construct is.

Cultures have levels [49] – ethnic, organizational, and function (as in "IT culture") – and these should be studied for joint effects. Further work on SNs and cultural beliefs should also be pursued in this vein.

How different is Internet diffusion in developing countries from that in the developed world, and is it also different from other forms of technological innovation? These are interesting and useful questions to pursue.

Implications for practice

SNs were important in the individual model, and this is an attractive addition to the study findings of this research stream thus far. Individuals are apparently influenced by whether others are also using the Internet. This result suggests that leading edge firms will experience a strong take-up of information technologies, partly because of the highly social and family-oriented nature of Arab culture [50]. Arabs are high on Hofstede's collectivist dimension [33], and this is likely being reflected in the salience of SNs in impacting usage. Contrarily, if the top managers of an organization are Internet-averse and this is communicated to the middle managers, there will likely be an opposite reaction. The take-up will be stillborn and may never result in widespread usage in certain firms.

For managers, the study suggests that culture can be harnessed to encourage the adoption of IT. When possible, managers should creatively use prevailing SNs and related cultural attitudes for and against technological innovation. Merely legislating adoption will be even more of a failure than it is in the technically advanced cultures. Arab culture has a strong patriarchal, tribal, and collectivist strand [50], and, therefore, high-level supporters are even more critical [51] than they would be in Western, industrialized cultures, for example. In the technical world of engineering, and more specifically for managers of engineers, these findings may provide particular insights as the use of technology is so dominant. While the technology of focus in this study is the Internet, one might expect that SNs and related cultural attitudes will influence the acceptance of other technological innovations. As engineering managers become aware of these factors, they can take measures to mitigate the resistance and encourage adoption of the respective technology.

Indeed, managers need to be cognizant of cultural differences and adapt to cultural contexts, wherever possible. The significance of the TC variables indicates that training and education in the hardware and software from advanced technology sources can bolster the transfer process. Technological culturation comes from an individual's experiences, and, unlike Straub *et al.* [4], our research on Internet diffusion reveals that formal culturation can be effective. Individuals that hold cultural beliefs that detract from acceptance of the technology can be swayed, it appears, by personal and informal exposure to the technology of the non-Arab industrialized world and prevailing SNs that are conducive to that end.

Conclusion

Cultural obstacles to the diffusion of information technologies in the Arab world are significant, as noted by the respondents. However, there are many factors that are encouraging, as well. Technological culturation is a process that seems to overcome certain cultural inhibitors. When individuals are exposed to the beneficial uses of the Internet in other cultures, they are more favorably inclined toward adoption. This effect seems to occur whether the trainers are Arabs educated in these technologies or foreigners from the technology-originating cultures. Mass forms of technological culturation, however, will be difficult. In many Arab countries today, few have been trained on the use of the Internet. Private universities are well equipped with computing and networking facilities and literate Internet instructors, but it is the large public institutions that touch the masses and yet lack facilities and faculty with state-of-the-art training. To date, only a handful of institutions and training organizations formally provide open courses on the Internet.

This situation is changing rapidly in some Arab countries such as Egypt, though, with the recently created Ministry of Communications and Information Technology (MCIT). More top-level support from the government and the involvement of the private sector could spread knowledge of and ability to use the Internet to hundreds of thousands of new users.

SNs that demonstrate favorable reactions to the technology are also helpful in creating an atmosphere where new IT can be transferred. Managers can advance these SNs by such proven actions as encouraging opinion leaders to adopt the technologies [52]. This has the effect of spreading the news that the innovation has benefits that may outweigh cultural negatives. Organizational employees as a whole appear to also respond to this form of cultural exposure. Even visitations to other environments where the technology is appreciated may have an influence on adoption.

Since its establishment in October 1999, the MCIT has taken a lead role in establishing policies and supporting partnerships between the public and private sectors. A government initiative to offer the Internet for free, toward the end of 2001, is illustrative of steps taken by the government to promote Internet diffusion and thus to reduce the digital divide within. *Global Schools Online* is another initiative that pairs government, business, and civic leaders in an effort to integrate Internet technologies within the educational systems to strengthen the existing information infrastructure and to provide the means for community building. Such efforts by influential opinion leaders bode well for the future of Egypt and the ways Egyptians leverage technology. These, in our views, are exemplary policies for diffusion of IT throughout the Arab world.

Culture can be a barrier to IT transference in Arab cultures. We believe that it can also be overcome through certain critical mechanisms. This study is part of a stream of research investigating this phenomenon.

Appendix A

X INSTITUTE   **Y UNIVERSITY**
Cairo, Egypt   **City, State USA**

Research Questionnaire on Use of the Internet by Organizations in the Arab World

This is a research questionnaire dealing with how people feel about the Internet. Even if you yourself do not use the Internet, we are interested in your responses!

We are studying the use of Internet in Arab businesses and organizations, please fill out the questionnaire! This is for non-commercial purposes only.

Thank you.

The Research Team

Dr. A	*Dr. B*
A Department	*B Role*
A University	*B Institute*
City, State USA	*Cairo, Egypt*
A@A.edu	B@b.com.eg
Dr. C	*Dr. D*
C Dept.	*D Dept.*
D University	*D University*
City, State USA	*City, State USA*
C@c.edu	D@d.edu

Section I.   Personal Information. *All responses strictly confidential.*

1. How many years of working experience do you have? ____ years

2. Which best describes your current position? (*Please check one*)

   ❷ Top Management   ❷ Administrative staff
   ❷ Middle Management   ❷ Professional staff
   ❷ Supervisory Management ❷ Other (please specify): _____

3. Your country of birth: _____   4.   Current nationality: _____

5. How many years have you lived in each of the following Arab countries?

No. of Yrs		**No. of Yrs**		**No. of Yrs**	
Algeria	_____	Lebanon	_____	Saudi Arabia	_____
Bahrain	_____	Libya	_____	Sudan	_____
Egypt	_____	Mauritania	_____	Syria	_____
Iraq	_____	Morocco	_____	Tunisia	_____
Jordan	_____	Oman	_____	U. A. Emirates	_____
Kuwait	_____	Qatar	_____	West Bank	_____
				Yemen	_____

6. How many years, in total, have you lived abroad in ***non-Arab industrialized countries***? _____ (years)

7. Age: _____   8. Sex: Male ⑧ or Female ⑧

9. Education: High School ⑧   University bachelor's degree ⑧
                  Masters ⑧   Doctorate ⑧

	A great deal of travel	**A fair amount of travel**	**A small amount of travel**	**Have not traveled at all**
10a. How much do you travel in the ***non-Arab industrialized world*** for business purposes?	⑧	⑧	⑧	⑧
10b. How much do you travel in the ***non-Arab industrialized world*** for pleasure?	⑧	⑧	⑧	⑧

11. How many hours in a work day do you spend on work related activities on the Internet? _____Hours _____Minutes

12. How much time do?	**A great deal of time**	**A fair amount of time**	**A small amount of time**	**No time at all**
12a. people in your organization spend working on the Internet?	⑧	⑧	⑧	⑧
12b. you spend on the Internet at work?	⑧	⑧	⑧	⑧

13. Please indicate your agreement or disagreement with the following statements about the Internet by checking off the appropriate response:

		Strongly Agree	Agree	Neutral or Not Sure	Disagree	Strongly Disagree
13a.	Most people in my organization feel threatened by the ways the Internet could affect our family and community life.	⑧	⑧	⑧	⑧	⑧
13b.	Most people in my organization believe the Internet relates to how much human interaction takes place.	⑧	⑧	⑧	⑧	⑧
13c.	I use the Internet to order goods and services for business purposes.	⑧	⑧	⑧	⑧	⑧
13d.	The Internet is attractive to most employees of organizations because computers are well accepted in Arab society.	⑧	⑧	⑧	⑧	⑧
13e.	Most people in my organization feel that the amount of face-to-face contact at work and the use of the Internet are related.	⑧	⑧	⑧	⑧	⑧
13f.	I use the Internet very frequently for business information gathering.	⑧	⑧	⑧	⑧	⑧

14. Please indicate your own experiences and viewpoints by checking the appropriate response

	Strongly Agree	**Agree**	**Neutral or Not Sure**	**Disagree**	**Strongly Disagree**
14a. I have learned a great deal about the Internet from experts (Arab or non-Arab) trained in technologically advanced countries	⑧	⑧	⑧	⑧	⑧
14b. Most people in my organization feel strongly that the Internet will strengthen Arab family and community ties.	⑧	⑧	⑧	⑧	⑧
14c. I have learned a great deal about the Internet by visiting other businesses in the non-Arab industrialized world.	⑧	⑧	⑧	⑧	⑧
14d. A company or organization's rules should not be broken – even when the employee thinks it is in the organization's best interests.	⑧	⑧	⑧	⑧	⑧
14e. The employees in my organization have learned a great deal about the Internet from experts (Arab or non-Arab) trained in technologically advanced countries.	⑧	⑧	⑧	⑧	⑧

14f.   I plan to continue working for my organization until I retire.   ⑧   ⑧   ⑧   ⑧   ⑧

14g.   Given how Arabs feel about computers, I think most workers in organizations are going to find it difficult to accept the Internet.   ⑧   ⑧   ⑧   ⑧   ⑧

14h.   I feel nervous and tense at work very often.   ⑧   ⑧   ⑧   ⑧   ⑧

15.   What percentage of employees in your organization have received training from experts (Arab or non-Arab) trained in technologically advanced countries? _____%

16.   What percentage of employees in your organization have access to the Internet? _____%

17.   What percentage of employees in your organization use the Internet regularly? _____%

Section II.   Feelings about Media

Please indicate your feelings towards the following communication media by marking the appropriate number in each box. *Example:*

Costly 1??2??3??4??5??6??7 Not costly

Email	Face-to-face	Telephone	WWW	FAX
6	2	4	1	3

Personal 1??2??3??4??5??6??7 Impersonal

Email	Face-to-face	Telephone	WWW	FAX

Unsociable 1??2??3??4??5??6??7 Sociable

Email	Face-to-face	Telephone	WWW	FAX

Cold 1??2??3??4??5??6??7 Warm

Email	Face-to-face	Telephone	WWW	FAX

Sensitive 1??2??3??4??5??6??7 Insensitive

Email	Face-to-face	Telephone	WWW	FAX

Section III.   Questions about Your Ideal Job

Please think of an ideal job – disregarding your present job. In choosing an ideal job, how important would it be to you to (please circle one answer number in each line across):

	Of Utmost Importance	Very Important	Of Moderate Importance	Of Little Importance	Of Very Little or No Importance
1. Have sufficient time left for your personal or family life?	⑧	⑧	⑧	⑧	⑧
2. Have challenging tasks to do, from which you can get a personal sense of accomplishment?	⑧	⑧	⑧	⑧	⑧
3. Have good physical working conditions (good ventilation and lighting, adequate workspace, etc.)?	⑧	⑧	⑧	⑧	⑧

4. Have considerable ⑧   ⑧   ⑧   ⑧   ⑧
   freedom to
   adopt your own
   approach to the
   job?

5. Have training ⑧   ⑧   ⑧   ⑧   ⑧
   opportunities (to
   improve your
   skills or to learn
   new skills)?

6. Fully use your ⑧   ⑧   ⑧   ⑧   ⑧
   skills and abilities
   on the job?

Section IV.   Free Format Question
On the back of the questionnaire, please answer the following question.
Please write as much as you wish.

*   In your opinion, what factors *encourage* or *discourage* the use of the Internet in organizations in the Arab world?

Thank you very much for your time and participation. Please return to the registration desk.

The Research Team

References

[1] (2001) ASP Strategies and IT Markets in the Arab Middle East. Pyramid Research, Economist Intelligent Unit. [Online]. Available: www.pyramidresearch.com

[2] R. M. Davison, D. R. Vogel, R. W. Harris, and N. Jones (2000), "Technology leapfrogging in developing countries: An inevitable luxury?," *Electron. J. Inform. Syst. Develop. Countries*, Vol. 1, pp. 1–10.

[3] S. Kamel and M. Hussein (2001), "The development of e-commerce: The emerging virtual context within Egypt," *J. Logist. Inform. Manage.*, pp. 119–127.

[4] D. W. Straub, K. Loch, and C. Hill (2001), "Transfer of Information Technology to the Arab world: A test of cultural influence modeling," *J. Global Inform. Manage.*, Vol. 9, pp. 6–28.

[5] C. Avgerou (2000), "Recognising alternative rationalities in the deployment of information systems," *Electron. J. Inform. Syst. Develop. Countries*, Vol. 3, pp. 1–15.

[6] C. E. Hill, D. W. Straub, K. D. Loch, W. Cotterman, and K. El-Sheshai (1994), "The impact of Arab culture on the diffusion of Information Technology: A culture-centered model," in *The Impact of Informatics on Society: Key Issues for Developing Countries*. IFIP, Havana, Cuba.

[7] C. Hill, K. Loch, D. W. Straub, and K. El-Sheshai (1998), "A qualitative assessment of Arab culture and Information Technology transfer," *J. Global Inform. Manage.*, Vol. 6, pp. 29–38.

[8] I. Ajzen and M. Fishbein (1980), *Understanding Attitudes and Predicting Social Behavior*. Prentice-Hall, Englewood Cliffs, NJ.

[9] D. S. Bertolotti (1984), *Culture and Technology*. Bowling Green State Univ. Popular Press, Bowling Green, OH.

[10] M. Kransberg and W. Davenport (1972), *Technology and Culture: An Anthology*. Schocken, New York.

[11] S. Corea (2000), "Cultivating technological innovation for development," *Electron. J. Inform. Syst. Develop. Countries*, Vol. 2, pp. 1–15.

[12] A. Escobar (1994), "Welcome to Cyberia: Notes on the anthropology of cyber-culture," *Current Anthropol*, Vol. 35, pp. 211–231.

[13] T. Donaldson and T. W. Dunfee (1994), "Toward a unified conception of business ethics: Integrative social contracts theory," *Acad. Manage. Rev.*, Vol. 19, pp. 252–284.

[14] D. Hakken (1991), "Culture-centered computing: Social policy and development of new information technology in England and in the United States," *Hum. Org.*, Vol. 50, pp. 406–423.

[15] T. Ingold (1996), "Technology and culture?," in E. Levinson and M. Ember, Eds. *Encyclopedia of Cultural Anthropology*. Holt, New York, pp. 1297–1301.

[16] B. Pfaffenberger (1992), "Social anthropology of technology," *Ann. Rev. Anthropol.*, Vol. 21, pp. 491–516.

[17] W. Schaniel (1988), "New technology and cultural change in traditional societies," *J. Econ. Issues*, Vol. 22, pp. 493–498.

[18] D. F. Eickelman (1981), *The Middle East: An Anthropological Approach*. Prentice-Hall, Englewood Cliffs, NJ.

[19] N. Luhmann (1988), "Familiarity, confidence, trust: Problems and alternatives," in D. G. Gambetta, Ed. *Trust*. Basil Blackwell, New York, pp. 94–107.

[20] M. Wedel, M. Vriens, T. Bijmolt, W. Krijnen, and P. Leefland (1998), "Assessing the effects of abstract attributes and brand familiarity in conjoint choice experiments," *Int. J. Res. Market*, Vol. 15, pp. 71–78.

[21] C. W. Park and P. V. Lessig (1981), "Familiarity and its impact on consumer decision biases and heuristics," *J. Consumer Res.*, Vol. 8, pp. 223–230.

[22] M. Laroche, C. Kim, and L. Zhou (1996), "Brand familiarity and confidence as determinants of purchase intention: An empirical test in a multiple brand context," *J. Bus. Res.*, Vol. 37, pp. 115–120.

[23] R. Gulati (1995), "Does familiarity breed trust? The implications of repeated ties for contractual choice in alliances," *Acad. Manage. J.*, Vol. 38, pp. 85–112.

[24] R. H. Mendoza and J. L. Martinez Jr. (1981), "The measurement of acculturation," in J. A. Baron, Ed. *Explorations in Chicano Psychology.* Praeger, New York, pp. 1–83.

[25] D. Hakken (1990), "Has there been a computer revolution? An anthropological view," *J. Comput. Soc.*, Vol. 1, pp. 11–28.

[26] —— (1993), "Computing and social change: New technology and workplace transformation, 1980–1990," *Ann. Rev. Anthropol.*, Vol. 22, pp. 107–132.

[27] —— (1993), *Computing Myths, Class Realities: An Ethnography of Technology and Working People in Sheffield.* Westview, Boulder, CO.

[28] G. Rose and D. Straub (1998), "Predicting general IT use: Applying TAM to the Arabic world," *J. Global Inform. Manage.*, Vol. 6, pp. 39–46.

[29] S. Zaheer and A. Zaheer (1997), "Country effects on information seeking in global electronic networks," *J. Int. Bus. Stud.*, Vol. 28, pp. 77–100.

[30] P. Ein-Dor, E. Segev, and M. Orgad (1993), "The effect of national culture on IS: Implications for international information systems," *J. Global Inform. Manage.*, Vol. 1, pp. 33–44.

[31] D. W. Straub, K. D. Loch, R. Evaristo, E. Karahanna, and M. Srite (2002), "Toward a theory-based measurement of culture," *J. Global Inform. Manage.*, Vol. 10, pp. 13–23.

[32] M. Boudreau, D. Gefen, and D. Straub (2001), "Validation in IS research: A state-of-the-art assessment," *MIS Quart.*, Vol. 25, pp. 1–24.

[33] G. Hofstede (1980), *Culture's Consequences: International Differences in Work-Related Values.* Sage, Newbury Park, CA.

[34] D. W. Straub (1989), "Validating instruments in MIS research," *MIS Quart.*, Vol. 13, pp. 147–169.

[35] J. C. Nunnally (1967), *Psychometric Theory.* McGraw-Hill, New York.

[36] W. W. Chin (1998a), "The partial least squares approach to structural equation modeling," in G. A. Marcoulides, Ed. *Modern Methods for Business Research*, London, U.K., pp. 295–336.

[37] —— (1998b), "Issues and opinion on structural equation modeling," *MIS Quart.*, Vol. 22, pp. VII–XVI.

[38] D. Gefen, D. Straub, and M. Boudreau (2000), "Structural equation modeling and regression: Guidelines for research practice," *Commun. AIS*, Vol. 7, pp. 1–78.

[39] D. T. Campbell and D. W. Fiske (1959), "Convergent and discriminant validation by the multitrait-multimethod matrix," *Psych. Bull.*, Vol. 56, pp. 81–105.

[40] A. Diamantopoulos and H. M. Winklhofer (2001), "Index construction with formative indicators: An alternative to scale development," *J. Market. Res.*, Vol. 38, pp. 269–277.

[41] T. Ravichandran and A. Rai (2000), "Quality management in systems development: An organizational system perspective," *MIS Quart.*, Vol. 24, pp. 381–415.

[42] K. Bollen and R. Lennox (1991), "Conventional wisdom on measurement: A structural equation perspective," *Psych. Bull.*, Vol. 110, pp. 305–314.

[43] R. P. Bagozzi and C. Fornell (1982), "Theoretical concepts, measurement, and meaning," in C. Fornell, Ed. *A Second Generation of Multivariate Analysis*, Vol. 2. Praeger, New York, pp. 5–23.

[44] J. Short, E. Williams, and B. Christie (1976), *The Social Psychology of Telecommunications*. Wiley, New York.

[45] D. Gefen and D. Straub (1997), "Gender difference in the perception and use of e-mail: An extension to the technology acceptance model," *MIS Quart.*, Vol. 21, pp. 389–400.

[46] W. J. Conover and R. L. Inman (1981), "Rank transformations as a bridge between parametric and nonparametric statistics," *Amer. Statist.*, Vol. 35, pp. 123–129.

[47] S. Labovitz (1970), "The assignment of numbers to rank order categories," *Amer. Sociol. Rev.*, Vol. 35, pp. 515–524.

[48] R. F. Falk and N. B. Miller (1992), *A Primer for Soft Modeling*. Univ. of Akron Press, Akron, OH.

[49] J. R. Lincoln, M. Hanada, and J. Olson (1981), "Cultural orientations and individual reactions to organizations," *Administ. Sci. Quart.*, Vol. 26, pp. 93–115.

[50] R. Patai (1973), *The Arab Mind*. Scribners, New York.

[51] U. Yavas, M. Luqmani, and Z. A. Quraeshi (1992), "Facilitating the adoption of information technology in a developing country," *Inform. Manage.*, Vol. 23, pp. 75–82.

[52] E. M. Rogers (1983), *Diffusion of Innovations*, 3rd ed. Free Press, New York.

Reproduced from *IEEE Transactions on Engineering Management*, Vol. 50, No. 1, Feburary 2003, pp. 45–63. Reprinted with permission from IEEE.

About the authors

Karen D. Loch received the Ph.D. degree in management information systems from the University of Nebraska, Lincoln.

She is currently the Director of the Institute of International Business and an Associate Professor at Georgia State University, Atlanta. As Director, she provides guidance for program development at undergraduate and graduate levels, partner institutions, and professional and executive development offerings. Her current research interests include streams in international IT transfer and social and ethical concerns of information systems. She has published in leading journals including, the *European Journal of Information Systems, DATA BASE for Advances in Information Systems*, the *Journal of Global Information Management, Communications of the ACM, MIS Quarterly*, the *Journal of Business Ethics, Academy of Management Executive, Communications of the AIS*, and others. She is an Associate Editor for the *Journal of Global Information Management* and serves on the editorial board for *Information Resources Management Journal*. She was the first Vice President of International Relations for the Information Resources Management Association (IRMA). In this capacity, she established a network of IRMA world-wide representatives of research colleagues in over 25 countries. She has owned her own firm, providing IT consulting services to companies.

Dr. Loch is a member of ACM, AIS, INFORMS, the Society of Business Ethics, and the Academy of Management.

Detmar W. Straub received the Ph.D. degree in English from The Pennsylvania State University, University Park, and the D.B.A. degree in management information systems from Indiana University, Bloomington, IN.

He is currently the J. Mack Robinson Distinguished Professor of information systems at Georgia State University, Atlanta. He has conducted research in Net-enhanced organizations, computer security, technological innovation, and international information technology with over 100 publications in journals including *Management Science, Information Systems Research, MIS Quarterly, Organization Science*, the *Journal of MIS*, the *Journal of AIS*, the *Journal of Global Information Management, Communications of the ACM, Information & Management, Communications of the AIS, Academy of Management Executive*, and *Sloan Management Review*. He is currently an Associate Editor for *Management Science and Information Systems Research*. He was formerly an Editor-in-Chief of *DATA BASE for Advances in Information Systems*, a Senior Editor for *Information Systems Research* (Special Issue on e-Commerce Metrics), and an Associate Editor for *MIS Quarterly*.

Sherif Kamel received degrees from the London School of Economics and Political Science, London, U.K. and The American University, Cairo, Egypt.

He is currently an Assistant Professor of management information systems and an Associate Director of the Management Center at the School of Business, Economics, and Communication, The American University. From 1987 to 1991, he was the Training Manager of the Cabinet of Egypt Information and Decision Support Center, and from 1992 to 2001, he was the Director of the Regional information technology (IT) Institute. In 1996, he was one of the Cofounding members of the Internet Society of Egypt.

He has many publications in IT transfer to developing countries, electronic commerce, human resources development, decision support applications, and knowledge management. He serves on the editorial and review boards of a number of information systems and management journals and is the Associate Editor of the *Annals of Cases on Information Technology Applications and Management in Organizations.*

Dr. Kamel is currently the VP of Communications for the Information Resources Management Association.

Questions for discussion

1 What forms of technological culturation would you adopt if you are the CIO of a company in the Arab world to speed up the utilization of the Internet?

2 If you were the executive of a new Internet company in the Arab world, what social norms would you pay attention to in your infrastructure and marketing to effectively sell to the Arab cultural world? How would you emphasize the positives of the Internet while addressing the negative aspects with your mitigations?

3 How can you leverage technological culturation to take advantage of social norms of the Arab culture? What is the interaction between technological culturation and social norms? How do these interplays affect Internet adoption?

4 Imagine you are a government leading official in the Arab world. What policies would you suggest to promote the adoption of the Internet in your country? Who would you have to cooperate with in this effort in your country?

6 The Key Role of Organizational Culture in a Multi-system View of Technology-driven Change

Ángel Cabrera, Elizabeth F. Cabrera and Sebastián Barajas

Abstract: Organizations undergoing technology-driven change must understand that technology is only one of several inter-related components which drive organizational performance. A multi-system perspective of organizations highlights the interdependencies between an organization's technology, structure and culture and how these affect organizational processes and behaviors. Successful technological innovations require that either the technology be designed to fit the organization's current structure and culture or that the organizational structure and culture be reshaped to fit the demands of the new technology. Thus, the desired effects of new technology are most often realized in organizations able to implement the additional changes that are required to maintain overall fit. To illustrate these issues, this paper presents a case study based on a technology-driven change in a Turkish financial organization. Special attention is given to the role of organizational culture, which is often cited as the most critical factor in successful technology assimilation.

Introduction

Anyone who has lived through the implementation of a large-scale technological innovation in an organization has run at some point or another into the crude reality of major organizational and human, rather than purely technological problems. Those who have not had the experience firsthand can rely on a 1996 report by the OASIG group that summarizes the experiences of 45 UK leading information technology (IT) researchers and consultants.[1]

[1]OASIG is a Special Interest Group funded by the British Department of Trade and Industry which deals with Organizational Aspects of Information Technology. The referenced 1996 report, entitled "The Performance of Information Technology and the Role of Human and Organizational Factors", can be found at http://www.shef.ac.uk/~ iwp/publications/reports/itperf.html.

According to this report, about 80–90% of IT projects fail to meet their performance goals, and this is in part due to the fact that organizations give inadequate attention to the non-technical, i.e. human and organizational, factors which are critical determinants of the effectiveness of the new systems. IT projects are usually technology-led and address too narrow an agenda, often connected with cost savings. Generally speaking, managers fail to understand the links between technical and organizational issues and between the new technology and the strategic business goals and needs of their organizations.

The same report points out that successful IT implementation requires organizations to adopt an integrated approach to organizational change in which people and technical factors are viewed as inextricably linked and interdependent. In this sense, senior managers must take full responsibility in developing a long-term strategic view of change, and project managers must be given responsibility for managing change, for paying full attention to human and organizational issues, and, more concretely, for actively considering how the new technology may affect the way in which work is organized and jobs are designed.

The purpose of this paper is to present an integrative model to help both administrators and technology designers understand and manage the interconnections between technology and other human and organizational aspects of a business. The ultimate goal is to be able to efficiently manage the changes imposed upon the organization by the introduction of a new technology in such a way as to minimize the human costs of the transition while maximizing the benefits obtained from the technology.

Within this model we will pay special attention to the factors that determine the behavior of the group of people that form a particular organization. By understanding how human behavior is influenced by the particulars of an organization we might be able to clarify the potential impact of introducing a new technology. A useful way of understanding collective determinants of behavior is to appeal to the notion of *culture*. The first part of the paper is devoted to clarifying this concept, its operationalization, and its relationship with organizational change.

Technology and people, however, are only two of the several subsystems which are at work within the organization and which together define its performance. In order to understand the interconnections between technology and people we need a bigger picture which lays out the relationships between these two and other important subsystems such as organizational structure, business and management processes, and strategy. The second part of this paper presents a general multi-system framework that illustrates the most important dependencies among the major subsystems of the organization.

Finally, for this framework to be of any use, it should be able to help us deal with change. To illustrate how the framework can be used to effectively plan and manage technology-driven change, the last section of the paper describes an experience in which these concepts were applied in the context of a large-scale IT project in a financial institution.

Culture as a determinant of behavior

Culture can be broadly understood as "a set of basic tacit assumptions about how the world is and ought to be that a group of people share and that determines their perceptions, thoughts, feelings, and, to some degree, their overt behavior" (Schein, 1996). According to Hofstede (1991) there are three main factors that, at least to some degree, determine the behavior of a person in the workplace: national culture, occupational culture, and organizational culture.

National culture is based primarily on differences in values which are learned in early childhood from the family. These values are strong enduring beliefs which are unlikely to change throughout the person's life. *Occupational culture*, which is acquired through schooling and professional training between childhood and adulthood, is comprised of both values and shared practices. Shared practices are learned perceptions as to how things should be done in the context of some occupation and are, as such, more malleable than values. Finally, *organizational culture* is based on differences in norms and shared practices which are learned in the workplace and are considered as valid within the boundaries of a particular organization.

The relative influence that occupational and organizational cultures exert on people's behavior appear to vary significantly across occupations (Mintzberg, 1978; Schein, 1996; Trice & Beyer, 1993). Some professional groups (such as physicians) have acquired exclusive rights to perform certain kinds of work, to control the training requirements for performing that work, and to regulate how the work is performed and evaluated. Because the work of these professionals is so severely constrained by these rights, the occupational cultures associated with them are quite immune to administrative practice. The behavior of these professionals is more strongly determined by their occupational culture than by the culture of the organizations in which they practice. On the contrary, the behavior of other less regulated professionals (e.g. the administrative staff of a hospital) will be more prone to influences from the culture of the organization.

From the point of view of technology design and implementation, national culture can be an important issue in transferring technology across nations, designing systems with culturally diverse teams or deploying systems for users from different cultural environments. In terms of occupational culture, some researchers have found that dysfunctional interactions among the different professional groups involved in IT projects are often the cause of deficient implementation. Schein, for example, has observed some strong differences in basic assumptions held by engineers, operators and top executives.

Whereas engineers saw networking technology as an opportunity to eliminate cumbersome hierarchy, executives saw hierarchy as a necessary mechanism for control and coordination. Whereas engineers saw expert systems and MIS (management information systems) as excellent tools to improve management decision making, executives felt unnecessarily constrained by them. Being aware of existing occupational differences can help us manage implementation more effectively. As Schein has argued, "organizations will not learn effectively until they recognize and confront the implications of [their different] occupational cultures" (Schein, 1996).

Organizational culture

Organizational culture, which will be the focus of this paper, can be thought of as a pattern of basic assumptions and beliefs, developed by a given social group throughout its history of internal integration and external adaptation, that has worked reasonably well in the past to be considered by the group as valid and important enough to be passed on to new members as the "correct" way of interpreting the organization's reality (Schein, 1990).

Organizational culture comprises a set of social norms that implicitly define what are appropriate or inappropriate behaviors within the boundaries of the organization. Organizational culture is not necessarily homogeneous across all areas of the organization. While some of the norms will permeate the entire organization, different groups within the organization might develop their own sub-cultures.

Assessing an organization's culture is not an easy enterprise, due in part to the fact that the actual underlying values and norms do not necessarily correspond with the officially espoused ones, not even those espoused by the top executives (Argyris & Schön, 1978). Several methods have been devised to conceptualize and assess organizational culture. Here we will concentrate on the framework proposed by Hofstede. We justify this choice because (a) this framework is relatively easy to map onto organizational issues and is therefore useful for effectively managing change, and (b) because there are commercially available tools that allow practicing managers to apply this framework at a relatively low cost in real settings.

In one of their studies, Hofstede, Neuijen, Ohayv, and Sanders (1990) assessed the values and perceptions of daily practices of employees from 10 different organizations, five in Denmark and five in the Netherlands. A major finding of this research showed that, independently of observed national culture differences (which corroborated the results of an earlier study by Hofstede (1980)), organizations varied in the way their practices were perceived by their respective members. In-depth statistical analyses revealed six main dimensions of cross-organizational variability: (1) process vs. results orientation, (2) employee vs. job orientation, (3) parochial vs. professional identity, (4) open vs. closed communication system, (5) loose vs. tight control, and (6) normative vs. pragmatic mentality.

Process vs. results orientation refers to whether an organization is more concerned with the means and procedures that must be followed to carry out the work or with the goals that are pursued with that work. Process orientation is typical of mechanistic or bureaucratic organizations rich in rules and procedures, whereas results orientation is typical of organic, risk-taking organizations, in which mistakes are well tolerated and innovation is valued.

The *employee vs. job orientation* reflects whether the organization is more concerned with the well-being of the person or with getting the job done. Groups or committees often make the important decisions in employee-oriented cultures, and an effort is made to help new members adjust. On the contrary, job-oriented cultures tend to rely on individual, top-down decision making.

The *parochial vs. professional* dimension reflects the weight that is given to the occupational cultures of the members of the organization. In parochial organizations, employees identify strongly with their organization, whereas in professional cultures employees identify more with their profession. In hiring new employees, parochial organizations rely on social and family background information, whereas professional cultures hire on the basis of job competence alone.

An *open* or *closed* system refers to the communication climate within the organization. In an open system culture information flows easily through the organization, whereas closed cultures are more secretive. Interestingly, Hofstede et al. (1991) found that organizations with more women at the top management were more likely to have an open culture.

Organizations also vary in the amount of control they exert over individuals. *Tightly controlled* cultures, for example, may observe strict meeting times and show a strong cost-saving consciousness. *Loose control* organizations are more permissive about individual's preferences (e.g. public jokes about the company are accepted).

Finally, organizations vary in their degree of conformity to institutional pressures. *Pragmatic* cultures are more market driven and are open to ad hoc solutions, while *normative* cultures are more concerned with following institutional rules. Meeting customer needs is a major objective in pragmatic cultures while normative cultures are more interested in adhering to the "correct" procedures as a way of obtaining legitimacy (Hofstede, 1980).

The culture of an organization is initially connected to the values of its founders, as well as the socioeconomic, regulatory and institutional environment of the organization. Culture is maintained and transmitted through stories, rituals, symbols and practices. One of the key determinants of organizational culture is the way in which the organization manages its employees, or, in other words, the organization's human resource (HR) management practices (Cabrera & Bonache, 1998). The HR policies (staffing, training, compensation, performance appraisals, career management, recruiting, etc.) send messages to the employees as to what behaviors are considered desirable and, hence, they determine the shared practices which define, according to Hofstede, the organization's culture.

Unlike national and occupational cultures, organizational culture can be, at least to some extent, modified. By the time a person enters the organization, their national and professional cultures are already in place. Being aware of them can be helpful to better manage technological innovations, but there is nothing that we can do to change them. On the contrary, there are several levers that, given the need, the time and the resources, management can attempt to move in order to influence and shape the organization's culture (Miles & Snow, 1978). This potential manageability of organizational culture makes it particularly interesting from the point of view of implementing technology-driven change.

A multilevel view of organizational performance and change

Why is organizational culture so important from the point of view of implementing technological innovations? As we will see, a new technology can impact the very nature of the work being carried out to the point of imposing new requirements in the behaviors that are expected from users. Whether or not a technological innovation ends up yielding the intended results will in part depend on whether the behavioral requirements it imposes are compatible with the current culture or whether the current culture can be altered so as to become compatible with those requirements.

Aligning technology and culture is not an easy task, among other reasons because they both interact with other key organizational subsystems: the organization's formal structure and procedures, its processes and its strategic intent (i.e. the objectives it ultimately attempts to accomplish). The model in Figure 6.1 will help us to clarify these complex interconnections (Ruddle & Feeny, 1997). This model is a manifestation of the so-called *sociotechnical systems perspective* (Pasmore, 1988), an approach to organizational design according to which every organization consists of two complex and inter-coupled systems: the technical and the social system. Organizational effectiveness is considered to be a function of how well the social and technical systems are designed with respect to one another and with respect to the demands of the outside market. Our model, however, expands on this distinction by establishing three different levels of analysis of organizational performance: the strategic level, the capability level and the infrastructure (or architecture) level.

The bottom level, which we will refer to as the *infrastructure or architecture level* contains the long lasting pieces of the organization: the organization's

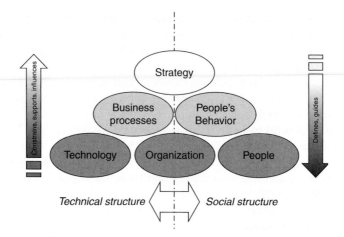

Figure 6.1   *A multi-system framework of organizational performance*

technology, its structure and its people (including the set of managerial practices that regulate the relationship between the organization and its members). This infrastructure supports the system of complex activities carried out by the organization and which include *business processes* and *behaviors.* The organization's processes and behaviors form the *capabilities* of the organization.

Finally, if we step back and take a more holistic view of the activity of the organization, we find the organization's strategy. Strategy refers to the way in which the organization sees itself in relation to its stakeholders (customers, providers, shareholders, employees, government) and to the ways in which the organization chooses to employ its resources in order to satisfy the needs of its stakeholders. The strategic level of analysis deals with questions such as what types of clients the organization tries to serve, what objectives of quality and/or cost the organization seeks to accomplish, what kind of value the owners of the organization expect to obtain, and what kind of work environment the organization is trying to provide for its employees (Porter, 1996).

In a sense, we can think of the organization as a real life theater play. The architecture level includes all the necessary components without which the play could not take place: the stage, the costumes, the script, the actors, the technicians and the director. When the curtain is raised and the actors and technicians engage in action, operating the different devices and prompts and interacting with one another as prescribed by the script, a flow of dramatic action emerges. These are the "processes and behaviors" of the play. Finally, one can step back and reflect on what the play is actually about. We can ask, for example, about the expected emotional response in the audience, about the level of technical and artistic mastery achieved by actors and technicians, and about ticket box outcomes. This level of discourse would correspond to what we have called the strategic level of analysis of organizational performance.

Whether or not the organization is able to achieve its strategic objectives will depend on whether it can deploy the right kinds of processes and behaviors, which are in turn determined by the organization's architecture. So, lower levels determine what can and cannot happen at upper levels. For example, a hospital group lacking digital communications *infrastructure* will hardly be able to develop the *capability* to carry out certain distance diagnoses. This limitation will in turn restrict the kinds of services that this group can offer patients attending its satellite units (*strategy*). If for some reason we introduce a change in one of the infrastructure subsystems (a change in technology, in organizational structure or in how the human resources are managed), we will impact the capabilities of the organization and, hence, the chances of the organization achieving its objectives. For this reason, *changes at lower levels should always be informed and guided by an analysis of implications at upper levels and should be ultimately linked to the organization's strategy.*

This does not imply that change initiatives must necessarily come from the organization's top management. New technological developments known to the technical staff can open up strategic opportunities that may have never been considered by the management alone (Kirn, 1997). What the model implies is that, even when the changes are initiated by a technological innovation, their successful implementation requires an analysis of the effects the changes may have on the capabilities and strategic intent of the organization.

In summary, the model underlines the importance of aligning the different subsystems of the organization along two complementary dimensions. On the one hand, there needs to be a coherent connection among strategy, capabilities and infrastructure. This is what we will call *vertical fit*. But at the same time, following the indications of the sociotechnical systems perspective (Pasmore, 1988), the model emphasizes the importance of aligning the social and technical components of the organization. This is what we call *horizontal fit*. At the capability level, horizontal fit implies integration between business processes and people's individual and social behavior. At the infrastructure level, horizontal integration implies integration among technology, organizational structure and people. For example, a new information system that automates administrative procedures and integrates client information could eliminate the need for back office administrative work while increasing the functions of current customer service jobs. In order to adapt to the new situation, current back office personnel could be transferred to customer service departments (an organizational re-arrangement). This, however, might create a conflict between the sub-culture of the former administrative people (not used to dealing with the end customer) and the service orientation that is required by the new jobs. In order to deal with this misalignment we might need to create specific training programs or redefine performance appraisal procedures (HR interventions).

The framework in action: managing change

Before engaging in any major change process, it is important to have a clear and integrated picture of (a) where the organization stands now, and (b) where we want the organization to be (Figure 6.2). We will call the current state of affairs the "as-is" organization, and the desired state of affairs the "to-be" organization. The definition of the "to-be" is fundamental in order to establish a clear direction for all changes. The analysis of the "as-is" is necessary for understanding the feasibility of the proposed changes and the most likely barriers. The comparison between the "to-be" and the "as-is" will help us identify and prioritize the interventions that will be necessary to make the transition: they will help us *navigate* through the transition. To illustrate how this framework can help manage change we will describe our experiences in a large-scale technology-led change at a financial institution in Turkey.

The context of the change

The organization that we will be referring to is one of Turkey's top five commercial banks in terms of number of branches, number of employees and net profit. As of 1995 this bank employed over 7000 persons divided between its head office departments (around 2000 employees) and a network of about 400 offices distributed throughout the entire country. In the 1970s and 1980s the banking sector in Turkey had been highly profitable due in part to protectionist regulations that limited competition. These regulations started being eased in the early 1980s under the influence of renovated European standards. This deregulation helped foreign banks to enter the market, which contributed to the creation of a more competitive environment and thus jeopardized historic profit margins. As a consequence of these changes, most Turkish banks were convinced of the need to streamline their processes so as to become more cost efficient and to reorganize in such a way as to improve their capacity to continuously adapt to future market evolutions.

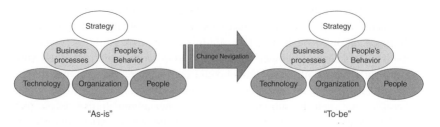

Figure 6.2   *Change management diagram*

Within this context, our Bank decided to put together a large, international team with the objective of designing and implementing whatever organizational and technological changes were necessary for the Bank to maintain and even improve its competitive position in the Turkish market. There was a shared understanding that these changes would most likely include a heavy IT component. In fact, the largest portion of the project budget was dedicated to upgrading the bank's information systems infrastructure from its current old-fashioned main-frame based systems to a state-of-the-art integrated client–server architecture.

However, given the magnitude of the changes that were expected, significant resources (about 20% of the total budget) were dedicated to anticipating and managing organizational and human issues. The fact that an expert in change management was appointed as leader of the entire project is a good indicator of the importance that was attributed to human issues. This leader emphasized that, independent of the magnitude of the resources dedicated to developing the IT, the project was about changing the organization to be more successful, and not about upgrading the technology for its own sake.

The project team was made up of an average of 120 people, including analysts from the Bank and outside consultants. The team was structured around three main groups: a group dedicated to redesigning the IT platform (the Technology group), a group dedicated to the reengineering of business processes and the functional design of the information systems (the Process group) and a group dedicated to organizational and human issues (the Change Management group). Whenever necessary, multidisciplinary teams were set up – including also line employees – to carry out specific tasks.

Strategy: setting up the master plan

Starting from the top of the model, we need to understand the main variables governing the strategic positioning of the organization in its market (Porter, 1980). Here are some questions that we might find useful to ask in order to reach a sufficient understanding of these issues.

*   *Positioning.*   What distinctive value is the organization trying to offer to its customers and how is it going to manage to survive to do so? Does the organization primarily focus on maintaining low costs, on providing a differentiated service, or on excelling in a particular niche? Knowing the general positioning of the organization can inform us about the organization's priorities, about what it expects from investments in technology and, hence, about how success will be measured.
*   *Perspective on innovation.*   Organizations vary in the way they face innovation (Miles & Snow, 1978). *Defenders* are organizations that focus primarily on improving the efficiency of their operations without actively

searching for new market opportunities. They compete by maintaining lower costs than their competitors. On the contrary, *prospectors* are organizations which are constantly innovating, experimenting, and trying out new products and services that give them a "first-to-market" advantage – privileges associated with offering unique products and services. Finally, *analyzers* are organizations that maintain a stable position in their core business while keeping an eye on competitors and trying to rapidly adopt those innovations that appear to have the greatest potential. Knowing where the organization stands with respect to innovation can also reveal important information about what the organization may expect from its investments in technology.

- *Current corporate plans.*   Are there any ongoing or upcoming corporate plans to expand or reduce services or client base? Corporate plans which may appear to be unrelated to our projects might actually have a great impact on our chances of success. An upcoming merger with another organization might cause prior systems integration efforts to become useless or even counterproductive. Geographic expansions may have implications for networking and communication requirements. Outsourcing plans might limit the interest in investing in certain types of systems. Because an organization's capacity to assimilate change is not unlimited, we need to make sure that the changes imposed by our new technology are not too overwhelming.

Unfortunately, finding satisfactory answers to these questions is not straightforward. Strategy is often only tacitly embedded in the actions of the organization and official documents and plans rarely capture the reality of what the organization is actually trying to accomplish (Mintzberg, 1978). So, in order to get a more realistic picture of the organization's strategic intent one has to dig a little deeper. From a methodological point of view, a possible action plan would include a few early strategy clarification sessions with top-managers and decision makers from each of the affected areas of the organization. Several group techniques have proved useful in guiding such sessions (see Higgins, 1996 for a review).

In the case of our Bank, several *strategy clarification* meetings were set up in which top executives discussed, with the assistance of an external facilitator, what they perceived to be the main threats and opportunities faced by the bank in the current market and in the immediate future. These discussions were guided by quantitative and qualitative data showing the Bank's performance in different areas as compared to that of key competitors. Members of each of the project's three groups also attended these meetings. These meetings helped clarify the bank's objectives. For instance, it seemed that the Bank was particularly interested in specific market segments and wanted to tailor their products and services to the needs of those segments. Also, they saw themselves as a quick and efficient bank (in terms of internal costs and customer convenience) and wanted to emphasize those strengths. Finally, they wanted to reinforce the consistency of their bank-wide services.

In addition to clarifying these goals, the meetings served to:

- Send a message to all project managers about the business objectives of the Bank for which the technical and organizational efforts would be instrumental.
- Reach a consensus among the Bank's management as to the Bank's priorities and expectations from the project.
- Document the Bank's vision for the immediate future in a way that could serve as a reference point for all the persons involved in the project (during the meetings the term "McBank" was coined to reflect the desired bank-wide service consistency and this term transmitted a very clear message to all team members about this particular expectation of the Bank's top management).
- Increase the level of commitment of the Bank's top management to the objectives of the project. This commitment was later key in obtaining their involvement and sponsorship for the implementation of the different interventions in their respective business areas.

Capabilities: laying out the play

Processes

The strategic expectations of the organization need to be translated into business process and behavior specifications. Bringing strategic intent down to processes specifications can be done according to widespread business process reengineering (BPR) techniques (Hammer, 1996; Hammer & Champy, 1993). Based on a specific strategic intent and knowledge of the opportunities offered by the new technology, BPR yields (a) a redefinition of key processes, (b) a set of functional requirements for the design or adaptation of the new technology, (c) a set of task descriptions that serve as input for the redesign of the organization's structure, (d) a set of measures of performance for evaluating the new processes, and (e) specific recommendations as to the kinds of behavioral patterns and attitudes required to carry out the new processes.

Knowing the strategic perspective of the organization with respect to innovation can be useful to determine which processes should receive more attention. "Defender" organizations will most likely be concerned with gradually decreasing costs and increasing efficiency of current processes, often through mechanization of practices (Miles & Snow, 1978). "Prospector" organizations, on the contrary, will be more interested in processes needed for the creation of new products and services and will probably be willing to trade process efficiency and routinization for flexibility. Finally, "analyzers" will be more concerned with processes underlying the efficient adoption, implementation and marketing of innovations that have proven valuable elsewhere.

In the case of our Bank, we were dealing with an analyzer profile. Market studies showed that clients saw the Bank as modern and innovative, but the top management thought of the bank more as a well oiled machine. The Bank was good at adopting new products and services, but it was best at efficient distribution. Given the strategic emphasis on efficiency, the process reengineering tasks focused on improving major commercial processes connected with customer service (automating administrative tasks, integrating operations and centralizing data), but some effort was also spent on improving product development processes.

Behavior

When we try to define optimal behavioral patterns based on strategic considerations the notion of organizational culture becomes most relevant. Initial accounts of organizational culture in the 1980s (Ouchi, 1981; Peters & Waterman, 1982) considered that there were particular cultural configurations which led to organizational success. For instance, it was believed that culture "strength" – the degree of consensus and identification of organizational members with the dominant norms – could lead to organizational success. These prescriptive views of culture have lost momentum over time, in part due to difficulties in explaining some renowned organizational failures. For example, IBM, a role model to early authors in terms of cultural strength and organizational "excellence", ended up experiencing great difficulties adapting to the dramatic changes in the computer industry in the late 1980s in part due, ironically, to the strength of its culture.

More recently, researchers have moved towards a contingent approach according to which a culture (weak or strong) will be an asset for achieving organizational success so long as it encourages the kinds of behaviors that are critical for the organization to successfully compete in its environment (Miller, 1993, 1994). So, whereas a process-oriented culture might be prescriptive for an organization following a defender strategic profile, that same orientation could be fatal for a prospector organization. The key is to find a cultural configuration that guarantees both *horizontal* and *vertical* fit.

Although there is still not a "behavior reengineering" methodology as well structured and tested as BPR, there are several things that we can do to try to identify the cultural profile that could meet the requirements of the "to-be" organization.[2] In our case, we expanded our strategy clarification meetings with

---

[2]The term "human reengineering" has appeared in the management literature (Cooper & Markus, 1995), however not with the meaning that is implied here, but rather as a reference to methods to overcome employee's resistance to change.

a series of sessions in which (a) we explored the concepts of culture and organizational culture, (b) we analyzed the connection between strategy and culture, (c) several sub-groups were identified within the organization as potentially requiring distinctive profiles, and (c) a consensus was reached as to what general cultural and sub-cultural profiles were most adequate in order to achieve the strategic objectives previously identified, given the user requirements that would presumably be imposed by the upcoming technology.

In particular, a distinction was made between central service departments in the head quarters and the activity of the branches. For example, head quarter departments were thought to require process orientation as a means to guarantee process efficiency and reliability, whereas the branches were seen as ideally risk-taking and commercially proactive, thus more in line with a results-orientation.

What is important at this point is not just to draw a picture of the ideal cultural profile of the organization but to draw this picture in reference to the current situation. In our case, we did this by applying Hofstede's model of organizational culture. The Bank was divided into 10 target groups that were considered a priori to be likely to show differences. The divisions were both hierarchical and functional. A random sample from each target group was tested with Hofstede's tools, yielding measures along each dimension. In addition to the current culture, respondents were also asked to assess their "desired" culture, i.e. what the culture of their *ideal* workplace would be.

This assessment of organizational culture was important for several reasons. First, it allowed us to detect possible misalignments between the current culture and the requirements of the to-be organization. For instance, the assessment revealed that administrative employees who had held back office jobs in the past had developed a strong means-oriented sub-culture. If these people were to be assigned to commercial positions requiring a results (rather than a means) orientation, some actions would have to be carried out to facilitate the transition.

Second, the culture assessment can help detect organizational strengths on which to rely during the change process. In our case, one such strength was detected along Hofstede's *parochial* vs. *professional* dimension. Following a tradition of strong investments in training and development, the Bank had achieved an overall positive attitude towards learning. In fact, working for the Bank was perceived among business school undergraduates as an excellent career opportunity. A positive attitude towards learning is usually associated with a professional (rather than parochial) culture, and our assessment confirmed this prediction. This information led us to believe that certain change management interventions would be more successful if framed in terms of professional development.

Finally, a culture assessment can help detect (and therefore prepare for) potential resistance to change. Alignment between the culture employees wished they had (the "desired" culture) and the culture the top management wished they had (the "optimal" culture) could reflect a predisposition by the people to change in the prescriptive direction. In other words, this situation would signal that employees agree with management about the changes that are to be undertaken and will therefore be open to any initiative that would make the change possible. On the contrary, if the "desired" and "optimal" cultures differ with one another, resistance can be expected.

Infrastructure: setting up the play

Technology: designing the stage

If one follows the steps that we have described, by the time one reaches this point, there are clear references as to what role the technology is expected to be playing in the to-be organization. Furthermore, one hopefully has a clear idea that technology alone may not suffice to enable the expected changes.

In terms of technology design, we must have collected several pieces of information that can be of great relevance. First, the new definitions of the work processes yield clear requirements for the design, in terms of the functionality that needs to be satisfied and in terms of how that functionality must be coordinated with existing processes and technologies. Second, our ideas about the strategic characteristics of the organization can give us clues as to what sorts of technologies might be better received. For instance, organizations with a defender profile – those seeking to provide services more efficiently – will tend to favor the development of a single, integrated core technology (Miles & Snow, 1978). Prospectors, on the other hand, will tend to avoid long-term commitments to a single technology because doing so could hinder their capacity to innovate. Prospectors will feel comfortable investing in prototypes of new technologies and maintaining a high mix of different technologies. Finally, analyzers will maintain a dual scenario with a core, integrated technology that guarantees process efficiency and a moderate amount of other, innovative technologies that can become integrated in the long run.

In the case of our Bank, the departing point was a high mix of technologies, which had resulted not from aggressive innovation, but from unfavorable historical evolution of computer technology. The proposed technological change included the integration of systems and data into a unified and efficient core information system built over a client–server architecture that would facilitate the adoption of future developments.

Organization: writing the script

The process modifications introduced by the new technology can have significant consequences for the nature of the tasks that need to be carried out and the distribution of responsibilities and definitions of jobs. So, we need to ask: Which old tasks have been automatized and are therefore no longer necessary? Which new tasks appear with the new processes? Which tasks will be qualitatively or quantitatively modified?

Tasks are the building blocks of job definitions. Any change in the nature of tasks requires a reevaluation of current job definitions. Organizational design requires the clustering of new tasks into jobs and the redefinition of report lines, especially if the new processes impact the distribution of decision making responsibilities. More often than not, organizational design results in a number of old jobs becoming obsolete, some new jobs being created and some others being significantly redefined. If these changes are significant, a transition plan should be devised. Based on the competence and cultural profiles of the old and the new jobs, the transition plan specifies what persons will be assigned to what jobs and what training actions must be carried out to facilitate the change.

In our case, the most important change in the structure of the organization was the fact that most administrative positions in the bank's branches were no longer necessary. In the "to-be" organization, the branches were considered as distribution channels with purely commercial responsibilities. So, consequently, most administrative tasks were either automated by the new systems or centralized at the headquarters. While the headquarters would be able to absorb some of the administrative personnel no longer needed in the offices, most of them had to be recycled to meet the needs of commercial positions.

A transition plan was elaborated in which the persons best prepared to change jobs were identified and the necessary training programs were developed. In addition, the definition of the new jobs and the demographics of the persons who were going to be holding those jobs suggested some additional design specifications for the information systems under way, especially in the areas of user interface design and on-line support. Notice that it is not until we have a clear idea of the nature of the new jobs and future job holders that we can actually complete the design of the user-oriented parts of the information systems. This further emphasizes the importance of the notion of *horizontal fit* discussed earlier.

People: casting the actors and rehearsing the play

Finally, we arrive at the most delicate and complex of the subsystems: the human resource architecture that sustains the people needed by the organization. Organizations try to deliberately influence their people in order to generate needed patterns of behavior. They do so by deciding how to recruit and select their employees, how to train and develop them, how to evaluate their performance, how to compensate them for their work, how to communicate with them, and how to manage them during their work hours.

For instance, a company that wants to emphasize efficiency and cost savings will tend to organize its staffing through internal recruitment, will help its employees gradually build their skills through extensive training programs and will base performance evaluations on efficiency measures (Miles & Snow, 1978). On the contrary, a company that lives off innovation will tend to use external recruitment of specialists, will spend time and resources identifying and recruiting people with the needed skills and will tend to rely on results-based evaluations of performance.

From the point of view of managing change, it is important to determine (a) which people in the organization will be most impacted by the upcoming changes, (b) how these people are currently being managed, and (c) which discrepancies might exist between the current state of affairs and the behaviors required by the to-be organization.

In our case, the evaluation of the people affected by the changes and the way they were currently being managed included, in addition to the aforementioned culture assessment:

- A demographic study by target group (back-office personnel, tellers, client-service representatives and marketing people) which included, among other data, age, sex, education level, time in the organization and in-company training. The importance of gathering this kind of information cannot be overemphasized. Without knowing what the target population is like it is impossible to know what we can reasonably expect from them. In our case, this study helped us elaborate an organizational transition plan that took into consideration the peculiarities of each target group.
- A study of the Bank's current communication architecture which assessed how much and how well information flowed through the different areas and levels of the organization. The assessment focused on employee satisfaction with the amount of information received, the perceived trustworthiness of information sources and the effectiveness of available channels (including anything from periodic meetings to e-mail). The survey prompted respondents to consider situations of prior technical or organizational change. Managing change is to a great extent about sending the right message to the right people at the right time. With an assessment like this we were able to identify not only what the most efficient communication channels were, but also who was the most trustworthy spokesperson for each group. This information helped us elaborate a detailed communication plan aimed at paving the way for the upcoming changes.
- An assessment of dominant leadership styles. Studies of organizational change reveal that some leadership characteristics, such as degree of involvement of subordinates in decision making, have a positive effect on the acceptance of change. Failure to solicit subordinates input in the planning of the changes and not informing them appropriately are common sources of

resistance toward change (Reichers, Wanous, & Austin, 1997). In our case, a survey was administered to test how employees in different units and at different levels perceived the effectiveness of the leadership style of their direct supervisors. Contrary to what the top management had anticipated, lower level employees saw their leaders as mostly autocratic and not very inclined to soliciting (not to mention accepting) subordinate input in major decisions.

• An assessment of current human resource practices. In order to figure out how to induce the necessary changes in behaviors, it is important to analyze what current practices might be influencing the behaviors and attitudes that need to be changed. If we want to increase the use of a certain technology, we need to determine which HR practices might be contributing to the currently low levels of utilization. Perhaps the technology is aimed at increasing customer service quality while current HR practices are rewarding workers for quantity and speed of services. Perhaps the HR practices are such that employees have nothing to win or loose by using the technology. It is very important to understand the main HR practices in place and how they relate to the behaviors we are trying to change. Finally, we need to have an idea of how easy or difficult it might be to alter these practices: very often we will find strong institutional pressures which will constrain our possible interventions (pressures from labor unions, general work regulations, government by-laws, etc.).

Changing the collective behavior of large groups is not an easy task. Few HR interventions take effect immediately. Behavioral changes rely on individual learning processes that take time. The bigger the change, the longer it takes. On occasion, the change would require so much time and effort that it might be easier to adapt other aspects of the organization to the current culture than the other way around.

If we decide that the current culture might be hindering the future of the organization and we are convinced of the need to adapt it, then it is important that we carefully plan a sequence of intermediate objectives and actions, as well as methods to evaluate our progress. That is, in addition to determining what river the organization needs to cross, we need to identify what stepping stones can help the organization cross it. Information gathered about the organization's current strengths and weaknesses can help us to identify how large a step the organization can take at one time, and this can help us to set up a realistic agenda of objectives and timing.

Conclusions

Organizational culture is a key construct in understanding and managing the behavior of people within the boundaries of an organization and in implementing organizational change. But organizations are complex systems that include several other interlocked subsystems. At first glance we can distinguish between a technical and a social subsystem. Then, at varying levels of abstraction we can look at the organization's infrastructure, its capabilities and its strategy. This paper has tried to provide a general view of the main interconnections between these subsystems and has tried to illustrate how this view can help an organization to more effectively manage change. Given the complexity of each of the subsystems, not to mention the complexity of the interactions, it seems unlikely that any single person can comprehend the whole set of implications that a given change project might precipitate. However, it is not only feasible, but actually highly recommendable, that all of the persons involved in any major change project (managers, physicians, engineers) have at least a broad systemic understanding of how their decisions might affect other subsystems of the organization.

The current work leads us to make the following recommendations regarding technology-led change:

1. Changes in technology have effects that go beyond the technology arena. A new technology can unbalance other key organizational subsystems. Successfully assimilating a new technology requires that these other organizational subsystems absorb these disruptions and adapt to a new equilibrium. Failing to achieve a new equilibrium will most likely result in a frustrating waste of time and resources. This equilibrium must be viewed along both *vertical* and *horizontal* dimensions.
2. Vertical fit refers to the alignment between the new technology, the capabilities of the organization and its strategy. There are no universally good technologies. A technological innovation will add value to the organization if and only if it can contribute to generating the capabilities that are necessary for the organization to achieve its objectives.
3. Horizontal fit refers to the integration between the social and technical subsystems of the organization. For an organization to be able to successfully *adopt* a new technology, it will have to *adapt* its structure and its human resource architecture in a way that allows the new technology to be used by the right people in the right way and at the right times.
4. As far as organizational structure, changes in the organization's core technology will often challenge existing procedures and decision making policies, and will force the modification of existing jobs and job assignments.
5. In relation to the people subsystem, we have argued that the concept of culture, understood as the norms, values and basic assumptions shared by the people in the organization, can provide a valuable medium to assess and manage change. There are three main sources of culture at work: national culture, occupational culture and organizational culture.

References

Argyris, C. and D. A. Schön (1978), *Organizational learning: A theory of action perspective.* Addison-Wesley, Reading, MA.

Cabrera, E. F. and J. Bonache (1998), "An expert HR system for aligning organizational culture and strategy," *Human Resource Planning*, Vol. 22, No. 1, pp. 51–60.

Cooper, R. and M. L. Markus (1995), "Human reengineering," *Sloan Management Review*, Vol. 36, No. 4, pp. 39–50.

Hammer, M. (1996), *Beyond reengineering*. HarperCollins, New York.

Hammer, M. and J. Champy (1993), *Reengineering the corporation.* HarperCollins, New York.

Higgins, J. M. (1996), "Innovate or evaporate: Creative techniques for strategists," *Long Range Planning*, Vol. 29, No. 3, pp. 370–380.

Hofstede, G. (1980), *Culture's consequences.* Sage, Beverly Hills, CA.

Hofstede, G. (1991), *Cultures and organizations: Software of the mind.* Sage, Beverly Hills, CA.

Hofstede, G., B. Neuijen, D. D. Ohayv, and G. Sanders (1990), "Measuring organizational cultures: A qualitative and quantitative study across twenty cases," *Administrative Science Quarterly*, Vol. 35, pp. 286–316.

Kirn, S. (1997), "Cooperative knowledge processing," in S. Kirn and G. O'Hare, Eds. *Cooperative Knowledge Processing.* Springer, Berlin.

Miles, R. E. and C. C. Snow (1978), *Organizational strategy, structure and process.* McGraw-Hill, New York.

Miller, D. (1993), "The architecture of simplicity," *Academy of Management Review*, Vol. 18, pp. 116–138.

Miller, D. (1994), "What happens after success: The perils of excellence," *Journal of Management Studies*, Vol. 31, No. 3, pp. 325–358.

Mintzberg, H. (1978), "Patterns in strategy formulation," *Management Science*, Vol. 24, No. 9, pp. 934–948.

Ouchi, W. G. (1981), *Theory Z.* Addison-Wesley, Reading, MA.

Pasmore, W. A. (1988), *Designing effective organizations: The sociotechnical systems perspective.* Wiley, New York.

Peters, T. J. and R. H. Waterman (1982), *In search of excellence: Lessons from America's best-run companies.* Harper & Row, New York.

Porter, M. E. (1980), *Competitive strategy: Techniques for analyzing industries and competitors.* Free Press, New York.

Porter, M. E. (1996), "What is strategy?," *Harvard Business Review*, Vol. 74, No. 6, pp. 61–78.

Reichers, A. E., J. P. Wanous, and J. T. Austin (1997), "Understanding and managing cynism about organizational change," *Academy of Management Executive*, Vol. 11, No. 1, pp. 48–59.

Ruddle, K. and D. Feeny (1997), *Transforming the organisation: New approaches to management, measurement and leadership.* Oxford Executive Research Briefing, Templeton College, Oxford University.

Schein, E. H. (1990), "Organizational culture," *American Psychologist*, Vol. 45, pp. 109–119.

Schein, E. H. (1996), "Three cultures of management: The key to organizational learning," *Sloan Management Review*, Vol. 38, No. 1, pp. 9–20.

Trice, H. M. and J. M. Beyer (1993), *The cultures of work organizations.* Prentice Hall, Englewood Cliffs, NJ.

Reproduced from *International Journal of Information Management*, Vol. 21, No. 3, June 2001, pp. 245–261. Reprinted with permission from Elsevier Ltd.

About the Authors

Ángel Cabrera is Professor of Organizational Behavior and Human Resource Management and Dean at Instituto de Empresa graduate business school in Madrid, Spain. He holds an engineering degree in Telecommunications Engineering from Universidad Politécnica de Madrid, and an M.S. and Ph.D. in Psychology from the Georgia Institute of Technology, which he attended as a Fulbright Scholar. Before joining Instituto de Empresa he worked as a consultant and manager at Andersen Consulting (now Accenture). His current research focuses on change and knowledge management.

Elizabeth F. Cabrera is Assistant Professor of Human Resource Management and Organizational Behavior at the Universidad Carlos III in Madrid, Spain. She received an undergraduate degree in Business Administration from Rhodes College and M.S. and Ph.D. degrees in Industrial and Organizational Psychology from the Georgia Institute of Technology. Her research interests include HR architectures, organizational culture, and the evaluation of HR systems and interventions. Her research is partially funded by the Spanish Ministry of Science and Technology research grant SEC2000-0395 and the Comunidad de Madrid research grant 06/0065/2000.

Sebastián Barajas is a Director at Deloitte Consulting. He received his undergraduate business degree from the University of Barcelona and his MBA from ESADE business school, also in Barcelona. He was a founding partner of the consulting firm CMC and later an Associate Partner with Andersen Consulting (now Accenture). His current interests focus on people centered business transformation.

Questions for discussion

1   There is a choice in` making culture and the macro environment fit the technology or in making the technology fit the culture and macro environment. Under what circumstances would you choose one over the other and why?

2   Imagine you are the CIO of a bank wanting to implement an IT project in accordance with your future strategic vision. What steps do you need to go through to implement this project according to the study to ensure success?

3   According to the study, what is the usefulness of an organizational culture assessment prior to IT project implementation?

4   Think of a company you have worked for. Of the three types of company mentioned in the study which type does it belong to? How does this classification influence the company's strategic vision, culture, and its IT project upgrade implementation?

5   How would you implement the organizational cultural change that is necessary to complement the new IT technology? What steps do you go through? Using the study's metaphor, how would you 'rehearse the actors for the play'?

6   As the CIO of the company, how would you think about the horizontal and vertical fit of organizational culture with technology?

7   Given that the effects of organizational culture and IT technology are organic, revolving, iterative, and ever changing according the changes in the business environment, how would you manage this ongoing process of change?

7 Dangerous Liaisons?
Component-Based Development and Organizational Subcultures

Jimmy C. Huang, Sue Newell,
Robert D. Galliers and
Shan-Ling Pan

Abstract: This paper presents an exploratory case study of the investment banking arm of a multinational banking corporation (Invebank) and its attempt to introduce component-based development (CBD). Based on a logic of opposition and utilizing literature on organizational culture and metaphors as an analytical device, issues confronting Invebank in CBD adoption are identified. In particular, problems in CBD implementation were encountered because, while CBD requires extensive knowledge sharing and collaboration, subcultural differences in Invebank meant that this proved difficult to enact. Thus, the paper considers the complexities of subcultural differences in firms and provides a salutary reminder that the implementation of corporate-wide integrative "solutions" such as CBD, may be problematic. Further, there is more to the issue of organizational subcultural differences than the oft-cited business-information technology (IT) divide. Nevertheless, the case demonstrates that subcultural differences should not simply be viewed as a threat. Rather, the recognition and discussion of these differences can provide a stimulus for identifying limitations of the policies surrounding technology implementation and use that if changed could help to maximize the benefits of the technology. Simplistic entreaties to knowledge sharing and the nurture of collaboration and consensus are, thus, brought into question. Implications for further research into the implementation of integrative software solutions like CBD in multifunctional and multifarious organizations are also considered.

I. Introduction

Attempting to achieve organizational renewal through information technology (IT) innovation is increasingly popular. Many organizations, for example, have undertaken business process reengineering (BPR) [13], [23] and, more recently, many have adopted corporate-wide integrative solutions, such as enterprise resource planning (ERP) systems [8] and component-based development

(CBD) [22]. Such initiatives are implemented on the premise that they will drive strategically important organizational change. However, as Robey and Boudreau [44] argue, the idea that IT "drives" or "forces" change is relatively simplistic and is unsupported by empirical evidence. Even the view that IT is an "enabler" of change is problematic since there is typically a complex relationship of reciprocal causality between IT and organization, with the outcomes emergent and difficult to predict in advance (e.g., [54] and [37]).

Noting this more complex relationship, Robey and Boudreau [44] argue that a useful way to consider the organizational consequences of IT is through oppositional logic (rather than the more typical deterministic logic). This approach focuses on opposing forces that promote and oppose social change simultaneously. They argue that this perspective is better able to account for contradictory outcomes of IT implementations. This perspective held promise for analyzing the case to be reported in this paper, where the expected consequences of a particular IT implementation did not occur.

The particular technology considered in this paper is CBD, as adopted in Invebank – the investment arm of a multinational banking corporation. CBD has been presented as a revolutionary approach capable of speeding up the technology development process, particularly in software engineering. Instead of developing new technology following the conventional end-to-end path, CBD reuses and assembles existing components to create a new system within an "evolvable environment," where new solutions can be effectively added on [22]. In addition to the resultant dramatic improvements in development efficiency, Due [18] argues that low development and maintenance costs have led to its increasing popularity. Comprehensive reviews about the benefits and challenges of CBD can be found in [8] and [39].

Conversely, it is also documented that CBD is no panacea. Bosch [5] reports that reusable components often require substantial modification to meet changing requirements. Vitharana and Jain [52] make the point that adequate testing is often ignored and underestimated. More importantly, from the perspective of this paper, Kunda and Brooks [27] argue that the human and social issues related to the introduction of CBD are typically overlooked as a result of an overemphasis on technological benefits. They suggest that the introduction of CBD is a sociotechnical challenge where group and organizational dynamics and technological advancement continuously and mutually shape and reshape each other. Despite Kunda and Brooks' study, a more detailed consideration of the impact of cultural factors on information system (IS)/IT implementation in general, and on CBD in particular, remains underdeveloped [2].

This paper focuses on research where the impact of cultural factors on the implementation of CBD has been specifically examined. The research is based on a single case study. Given the previous lack of empirical evidence covering the impact of cultural factors on CBD implementation, this is very much an exploratory case and, in the final section, we stress the importance of further research on this topic. This paper is structured as follows. We first turn to the organizational and suborganizational culture literature as a foundation for our case analysis and then deal with epistemological issues, including the research context and the data collection methods and analysis strategy employed. Next, we highlight the major research findings before drawing conclusions in light of extant theory.

II.   Organizational culture and subcultures

Robey and Boudreau [44] suggest four different theoretical approaches suitable for research employing a logic of opposition:

1) organizational politics;
2) organizational culture;
3) institutional theory;
4) organizational learning.

They stress that this list of approaches is not exhaustive. Nor are these different theoretical approaches, we would contend, mutually exclusive. In other words, employing a logic of opposition, it is possible to look at the same case from potentially each of these theoretical lenses and probably more beside. This is because there are overlaps between these different approaches. As Van Maanen and Barley [51, p. 48] indicate: "… the study of cultural organization is … closely bound to the study of organizational conflict." Here, we found it useful to employ a cultural theory lens to consider the implementation of CBD in a case organization.

Organizational culture has been shown to influence the process of how technology is adopted, embedded, and institutionalized within organizations. Davenport [14] and Powell and Dent-Micallef [41] both depict the need for an information culture that is open, flexible, and expansive in order to ease the implementation of technology. Similarly, Ruppel and Harrington [45] and El Sawy *et al.* [20] propose developing a culture that encourages trust and knowledge sharing. Sloan and Green [49] stress the importance of a culture favorably disposed to new IT, while Astebro's [1] empirical account explores the influence of culture from the perspective of managerial influence and resource availability.

All of these examples of IS research adopt what Martin [29], [31] describes as an integration perspective. They depict the organization as having a single culture that is unified and consistent; or failing that, one where the aim is to achieve this consistency. This perspective is only one of three perspectives identified by Martin [29], the other two being differentiation and fragmentation. Importantly, Martin argues that no single perspective should be seen as more appropriate than another, since in each case the perspective is "an interpretive framework that is subjectively imposed on the process of collecting and analyzing cultural data" [29, p. 12]. Empirical data can be interrogated from each or all of these perspectives and, if only one perspective is selected, this is done in order to help provide a "concise and coherent" account of a particular issue. In this paper, we adopt the differentiation perspective to bring into focus those aspects of culture that can help us in understanding the problems that Invebank was facing in introducing CBD.

The differentiation perspective focuses on differences within organizations and so describes organizational culture as a collection of subcultures. This perspective recognizes that there will always be conflicts of interests within organizations and recognizes the inevitable influence of power [40]. Those adopting the differentiation perspective do not usually deny that there may be some unity and consensus across an organization (the focus of the integration perspective) but argue that it is useful to explore ways in which different groups see things differently. Culture can be as much a fragmenting force as a unifying one [51]. Culture, from this perspective, is defined as that which is shared, recognizing that what is shared will differ in different organizational groups [28].

From the cultural differentiation perspective, Martin [29] emphasizes three key issues: inconsistency, subcultural consensus, and ambiguity. Inconsistency is a kind of oppositional thinking, where different groups have different interpretations of a particular phenomenon. These inconsistencies exist because of differences between tasks, expertise, and activities [14], [46] and because of differing demographic characteristics [29]. Such differences create paradigmatic diversity [15], which divides organizations into various informal groups with invisible boundaries [48] that inhibit cross-functional collaboration. While these inconsistencies may be apparent across group boundaries, within groups there is consensus – a coherent meaning system, which provides clear solutions to the problems shared by the group [51]. This means that the differentiation perspective excludes an analysis of ambiguity. Ambiguity is not part of culture, but is rather the "chaos underlying culture" [29, p. 93].

DiBella [17] discusses a failed planned organizational change program from a differentiation perspective and concludes that: "Problems in implementing change programs cannot simply be attributed to poor managerial communication or a generic failure to follow OD principles. Problems derive from the innate fragmentation of meaning that comes from cultural differences" [17, p. 369]. DiBella developed two theoretical propositions from his study: 1) the more cultural boundaries that span a change program, the more the change outcome will deviate from change plans or expectations and 2) the more cultural boundaries that span a change process, the greater the diversity of cultural dimensions that affect the change process [17]. Given that in this paper we explore a single case, we cannot specifically test these propositions. However, the intention is to see whether these propositions appear as relevant for IS/IT implementations as for other kinds of organizational change.

In research on IS/IT implementation, there have been a few studies that suggest the importance of subcultural factors. For example, Robey and Azevedo [43] conclude that, given that the same technology can acquire different meanings among different groups, contradictory consequences from that technology's adoption and use should be expected, rather than be seen as an aberration. Similarly, Cooper [9] discusses the inertial impact of culture on IT implementation. There have been few studies, however, that explicitly explore the degree to which subcultural organizational boundaries influence the adoption of a particular IS/IT.

In summary then, the literature not only highlights the distinctive characteristics and significance of subculture, but also suggests the need to take into account subcultural differences when exploring the process of IS/IT adoption within an organization [38]. Yet, our understanding of how organizational subcultures interplay with the process of technology development remains limited, with few studies specifically addressing this issue [25]. Thus, this paper addresses the extent to which subcultural inconsistencies and a lack of organization-wide consensus in a particular case organization limited the realization of benefits from a CBD implementation.

III.   Research considerations

Guided by the research focus of examining the impact of subcultural inconsistencies on the adoption of CBD, methodological concerns related to research design, data collection, and analysis are now outlined. An interpretative case study methodology [54], [26] characterizes the underlying research design. A case study approach is considered appropriate since it allows us to address "why" and "how" research question(s). Such questions are difficult to address by testing the relationship between dependent and independent variables [55]. According to Bryman and Burgess [6], a case study takes into account the context where social phenomena are constructed and embedded. Such an understanding helps researchers make sense of data without the risk of oversimplifying the social phenomena under investigation. Thus, an interpretative case study methodology allowed us to conceptualize subcultural differences within Invebank and their impact on the introduction of CBD.

Research context

Restructured in 1997, Invebank provides a range of financial products, including foreign exchange, currency options, and interest rate derivatives.

Operating in major financial centers including London, New York, Tokyo, and Hong Kong, a total of 1500 employees generated more than $2 billion gross profits in 2000, an increase of 6% compared to 1999. Invebank has several divisions, the largest being the Technology and Business Divisions, together accounting for more than 65% of the total workforce. The remainder is organized in various supporting divisions (e.g., Administration, Accounting and Legal). The Business Division is divided into small teams based on specific products (e.g., money markets, interest rate derivatives, currency options). The Technology Division is organized into ten subdivisions, two of which are further divided into eight different product-specific groups. The rest cover other aspects, such as IT security, Internet, credit risk, architecture, and infrastructure.

Data collection

Data were collected during April 1999–March 2001 from four sources: on-site observation, interviews, informal dialogue (conversations with employees via email, telephone, or conversation without any prior arrangement), and documentation. This provided a richness of findings and enabled triangulation [16], [55]. The research started with two months of on-site observation fulfilling two purposes: 1) the fostering of better understanding of the case company's structure, culture and subcultures, technology, business processes, and social setting and 2) the facilitation of interview question design [55]. Following this initial phase, 39 interviews were conducted with 32 members of staff in three different phases. Table 7.1 provides summary details. The rationale for having three rounds of interviews was threefold. First, conducting interviews at different times during CBD implementation facilitated an understanding of the process. Such process research [44] requires a longitudinal study [36]. Second, it facilitated the use of the "snowballing technique" [53] to identify potential interviewees for the second and third rounds. Third, it enabled those who joined Invebank during this period to be included in later interviews.

Interview questions were derived from the kind of oppositional logic discussed earlier [44, p. 179] with a view to identifying opposing forces that represented "the old and new guard or the privileged and the unprivileged." Questions were centered on each interviewee's involvement in, understanding of, and experience with CBD. Questions also focused on how interviewees perceived Invebank's organizational culture and their own group cultures, as well as their experience of other groups within the bank. Questions to top managers concentrated on Invebank's overall strategic direction and business and technology developments. Each interview lasted 90 min on average. All interviews and informal telephone conversations were tape recorded, with the interviewees' permission, and transcribed. Each transcript was approved by

Table 7.1   *Interviews and interviewees*

	07/1999–12/1999	02/2000–08/2000	09/2000–03/2001
Top management	1	1	1(1)
Group directors/sub-group managers (Business)	2	1	2(1)
Group directors/sub-group managers (Technology)	4	2	1(1)
Specialists (Business)	2	3	2(1)
Specialists (Technology)	5	3	6(3)
Other	2	1	0
Total	16	11	12

(*) refers to the number of follow-up interviews within each interviewee category

the interviewee concerned and used as a reference point for additional telephone and email discussion. Data were also collected from company documentation, including letters, written reports, administrative documents, newspapers, company archives, and its Intranet site.

Data analysis

Prior to data analysis, preparatory research activities included transcribing interview tapes, typing and filing research notes, summarizing documents, and clustering them into four groups – interview transcripts, research notes, photocopied documents, and information downloaded from the case company's Intranet and databases. The idea of "concept cards" [42] was used to outline the content of each file and identity potential linkages with other files. According to Yin [55], an analytic strategy is vital, not only to choose suitable analytic technique(s), but also to provide rigor to analytical outcomes. Two main techniques employed were "open coding" [50] and a "conceptually clustered matrix" [32]. Though this research was not designed for theory generation, the open coding approach associated with forms of Grounded Theory [50], was useful to synthesize the large volume of data collected. Data were sorted into various categories, such as the perceived potential of CBD and characteristics of subcultures. Use was also made of the kind of metaphorical analysis demonstrated by Morgan [33]. As a result, conceptually clustered matrices were developed displaying key themes representing the opposing forces of different groups [44] and to cross-examine categorizations generated from open coding. An innovation implementation process model [10] was incorporated into the conceptually clustered matrices to add further structure. The implementation process model consists of six stages:

1) initiation;
2) adoption;
3) adaptation;
4) acceptance;
5) routinization;
6) infusion.

Based on this framework, we were able to present subcultural differences as opposing forces, demonstrating how they influence the process and product at each stage of CBD implementation. Since the CBD project was not completely appropriated, we do not, in this paper, consider the infusion stage. More detailed analysis is presented in Section IV, which deals with case findings.

IV. Case findings

Organizational culture and subcultures

As indicated, instead of identifying the unifying characteristics of organizational culture, our analysis emphasizes fragmentation and differentiation as a means to explain how subcultural differences influenced each stage of CBD implementation. We are not arguing that there were no unifying elements to the culture of Invebank, only that focusing on the fragmented and differentiated elements helps in exploring the problems that were experienced during CBD implementation.

An initial problem was to find a means of identifying and describing different subcultures. Previous research provides little advice in this regard. Serendipitously, one of the interviewees described the fragmentation within Invebank in terms of "The Crusades." We found this metaphor helpful in thinking about the different subcultures within Invebank and, recognizing that metaphors are an established tool for describing different forms of organizing [33], we borrowed it for our analysis. According to the interviewee (the Technology Director), Invebank had several specialist groups with distinctive interests. Top managers represented *warlords* who had control over resources and formulated overall tactics. Ten out of 12 top managers had experience of the trading battlefield. Business users symbolized *the force,* which was responsible for victory or defeat, as they accounted primarily for Invebank's revenue. Front office traders (*frontline soldiers*) claimed more credit than the *rear echelons* because they were directly engaged in the fight. Technologists were characterized as *armorers* who designed and crafted weapons employed by the frontline soldiers. While all armorers appeared similar, in practice, those who produced weapons for the frontline, like front office technologists, had more glamor than those who produced logistical tools. These back office technologists might be described as *gloomy smiths*. The rest of Invebank staff were considered *serfs,* whose significance could easily be forgotten. Apart from the warlords, the above can be further divided into *loyal servants* (as the permanent staff positioned themselves) or *mercenaries* (the very word frequently used by permanents to describe contractors).

There have been several previous studies that have reported the impact of differences between user and technology communities on technology implementation (e.g., [47] and [3]). We argue, however, that to perceive each group as having a unified identity has oversimplified the differences within each, thereby underestimating the complexity of subcultural differences as they influence implementation. To overcome this simplification, we used differentiation within technologist and user groups, thereby exploring fragmentation further. Moreover, in addition to illustrating how individuals in Invebank saw their own subcultures, we also outline how they perceived others. Building on the crusade metaphor, we outline subcultural groups in Table 7.2. We acknowledge that this is not an exhaustive list. Nevertheless, the subcultural differences described in the following are appropriate and useful to depict each group's direct or indirect influence on CBD implementation.

1) *Frontline Soldiers*: Front officer traders are in charge of buying and selling, thereby determining Invebank's profit or loss. Traders work long hours to cope with the high volume of trading and the need to accommodate the time difference between London and New York. Taking risks is permitted, because time required to assess the risks is traded against greater trading

Table 7.2 *Intra-divisional subcultures*

Division	Intra-divisional subcultures
Business	Front office traders (**frontline soldiers**)
	Back office managers and administrators (**rear echelons**)
Technology	Front office technologists (**glamorous armorers**)
	Permanent staff (**loyal servants**)
	Contractors (**mercenaries**)
	Back office technologists (**gloomy smiths**)
Others	Central and regional supporting managers and administrators (**serfs**)

volume. Traders are perceived as being privileged, well paid, and having significant influence in Invebank. Their luxurious lifestyle is often the focus of informal conversation, a trait viewed by others as extremely annoying. Their influence lay in having the majority of seats on the board (12 out of 13) that controls all vital resources and decisions, including investing in CBD. Others see them as "racing horses," "fast moving," "dominating," and "arrogant snobs," and see themselves as "subordinates," "servants," or "less fortunate" in contrast.

2) *Rear Echelons*: Back office managers and administrators are responsible for settling the trades conducted by the front office. Despite the fact that financial products vary in nature, settling procedures remain largely the same. Trading settlement requires a high degree of accuracy: one minor error could substantially jeopardize Invebank's profit. In addition, procedural accuracy is vital due to monetary trading regulations. In contrast to the main headquarter (HQ)'s imposing modern City building, all back office functions, including Business and Technology, are located in a run down area in central London. They are perceived by others, in particular by front office traders, as being "nitty-gritty," "old fashioned," or "bureaucratic," because of their focus on detail and paperwork. They see themselves as being "reliable," "isolated," or "closer to the Group than Invebank."

3) *Glamorous Armorers*: Front office technologists design, develop, and maintain systems used by the traders. Located next to the traders, the job requires close collaboration with them and involves the same long working hours. Timeliness and innovation are vital. New products cannot be launched unless supporting systems are developed and tested. Front office technology has the highest concentration of contractors – almost 70% of total contractors – and accounts for a third of the Technology Division's head count. Contractors generally receive higher pay than permanent staff, but have fewer company benefits. Contractors are labeled by some of the permanents as "seasonal laborers" or "mercenaries" and see themselves as "flexible" but "unfairly treated" and "insecure." Contractors are viewed in the following terms: "they take the money, they take the chance," "I treat the permanents and contractors equally ... I encourage my people to take any available training ... except the contractors." Permanents are perceived by contractors as "unapproachable," "unfriendly," or "egocentric." They position themselves as "traders' dependable partners."

4) *Gloomy Smiths*: Back office technologists design, develop, and maintain systems to assist business users in the domain of settlement support and administration. Back office systems are expected to be reliable and accurate. Like their front office colleagues, the back office technologists work in close collaboration with users. The difference lies in focusing on system robustness, instead of continuous innovation. This is because the

basic process and functionality of back office systems is relatively stable. Back office technologists are regarded by their users as "extremely helpful" or "supportive" and perceive themselves as "perfectionists" or "the gatekeeper of the Group's tradition." Front office technologists consider them as "dinosaurs," "so 70s," and "Invebank's past."

5) *Serfs*: The rest, ranging from directors [e.g., of Legal, Estates, and Human Resources (HR)] to cleaners, represent the supporting functions at Invebank. Not having sufficient knowledge of either business or technology, it is unsurprising that these divisions are not included in major decision making. Dispersed across three floors on top of the trading floor, front office personnel, including traders and technologists, suggest Invebank should "outsource them;" some wonder "why they take up so much office space without producing anything." Such perceptions echo how *serfs* see themselves as "not in the mainstream" or "invisible."

Subcultural differences and their impact on CBD implementation

Based on the model proposed by Cooper and Zmud [10], the impact of subcultural differences at each stage of CBD implementation is discussed.

1) *Initiation*: There is a growing trend in developing and trading new financial products that cut across different product categories, such as interest rate derivatives and emerging markets. In Invebank, they were able to develop new products quickly, but the time required to develop supporting systems meant that it was often another 18 mos before the product was ready for trading. For front office traders, this time difference meant the loss of potential profit and the opportunity to be the first in the market. They were, therefore, keen to speed up system development. The General Manager's solution was to recruit technologists from competitors with leading edge skills. Many of these technologists had previous experience of CBD. More generally, these new technologists recognized the need to revamp outdated systems and architectures and revolutionize the way systems were developed. One of these new people was appointed in early 1997 as Global Head of Technology. He had 12 years experience in multinational investment banks, including J P Morgan and Kleinwort Benson. He recalled the time when he joined Invebank:

> When I first came in, Technology (Division) had an appalling reputation in the Business (Division), very poor. It (technology) was seen as a differentiator amongst our competitors, but it was also recognized we were pretty crap at it.

2) *Adoption*: Three months after he was appointed, the Global Head of Technology presented a proposal to implement CBD to the board. The board's initial decision was to reject the proposal, on a vote of nine to four. According to the General Manager, this was because the required

initial investment was too high while the expected return was uncertain. The Director of Front Office Business saw CBD as a "black hole." Not knowing when Invebank might make a return on the investment, he considered that it was sensible to invest in something else. As the Head of Technology recalled:

> People in the business environment tend to think that technology is toys for boys ... It's hard for us technologists to educate them and communicate with them, so that they can understand the value of CBD and understand what we've done well and that we need more money to do even better.

A series of meetings within the Technology Division was organized to inform specialists about CBD and its importance and to generate refinements to the proposal. Moreover, the Technology Division promoted CBD to business users, in particular those on the trading floor, who could then influence the board. A decision to implement CBD was made in September 1997.

Following this decision, there were clear differences between groups in terms of how they perceived CBD. Most front office technologists considered that its implementation was necessary, because a fundamental change in systems development was required to leverage support for new products. As the Head of Interest Rate Derivatives Technology noted:

> Because the industry is moving so fast you need to be light on your feet and ready to implement new parts quickly ... you need to put a technical infrastructure in place such that you can implement new things correctly.

Conversely, back office technologists, who faced few demands for continuous change, did not see its value. They wanted to concentrate on centralizing all regional trading settlements to ensure better control. Back office managers and administrators shared this view. In contrast, most front office traders welcomed CBD, as was evident by the fact that they had actively tried to persuade their representatives to reverse the board's initial decision.

3) *Adaptation*: Phase One of the adaptation stage, initiated in late 1997, focused mainly on laying the foundation for CBD by defining and delivering changes to core finance systems and processes. In particular, a component-based application architecture was installed. According to the Global Head of Technology:

> We had a significant number of disparate systems and we had five different FX systems, three Money Market systems. It was ridiculous ... so we had an extremely aggressive plan to hire the right people, which I did and then built and installed global solutions as quickly as we possibly could. That was all about implementing building blocks around the high-level application architecture.

Phase Two started in late 1998, focusing on implementing solutions based on the component-based application architecture for different business areas. For example, a financial architecture program was initiated to put various components in place for financial exchange related business, such as a repository of trades data and accounting events, a financial data warehouse and a reporting environment.

Headcount in the Technology Division grew significantly at this stage to accommodate CBD implementation. Many contractors with experience in financial systems were recruited. The rationale behind employing more contractors was twofold. First, it helped to bring in the required expertise without having to train staff. Second, it provided the flexibility. As the Global Head of Technical Architecture noted:

> When your project changes its shape, size and scale, you can bring in new contractors to meet the new shape, size and scale.

An impact of having larger numbers of contractors was that some permanent staff did not consider contractors as part of Invebank, arguing that they should not receive the usual benefits. It was Invebank's policy not to provide any training to contractors, simply because it was their responsibility to ensure their own market value. This antipathy was, partly at least, because the permanents' own career prospects were limited by employing contractors. Since contractors with required expertise could be relatively easily recruited, it was not economically sensible for managers to rotate permanent staff to enhance their skills. As the General Manager noted:

> This business is so complex it takes a very long time for people to truly become exceptional ... And how does he get that understanding when he works with that business for a year or eighteen months? Well, then how do you compensate that guy to stay on? Because he probably wants to diversify his product skill base or his technical skill base. So that's a real problem. In some ways it's more of a problem with permanent staff, because contractors are solely driven by money. So that's OK, pay more money and you retain the value. On the permanent side, it's more difficult because there are some guys who if they moved areas, we'd probably pay them a lot less because they move from a situation where they have all the valuable skill and knowledge to an area where they're learning from scratch. It's very, very difficult to keep the balance.

Technology contractors based in the front office indicated that they saw a different set of problems. First, they felt that the tension with permanents hampered their performance. Without their support, they could not obtain enough background information to understand systems that were unique to Invebank. Second, they recognized that it often took longer to develop a reusable component than to develop a system for a one-off purpose. Hence, on some occasions, they decided to ignore the reuse policy and develop components for one-off use.

In-house training programs, including basic finance and technology, were organized in an attempt to educate technologists with business knowledge and business users with technological knowledge. During the first half of 1998, 20 finance seminars were fully attended by staff from the Technology, HR, Legal, and Administration Divisions. In contrast, after only three sessions, the technology seminars were cancelled because of low attendance (in total, only 11 people attended). Even though the seminars were organized for business users, only one back office administrator attended the first seminar. While some front office users indicated that they had not attended because of time constraints, others considered attendance unnecessary. In particular, three traders argued that understanding technology was not part of the CBD rationale, which had been proposed by the technologists in the first place.

4) *Acceptance*: Differences in accepting CBD were observed between front and back offices. Reactions in the front office were comparatively positive. For example, front office traders reported that the impact of CBD was significant. As one trader noted in 1999:

> We used to spend a lot of time working on manually intensive and low-value adding stuff, like production of reports and reconciliation, because the core finance systems were not providing the required functionality … We can now focus our resources on higher value activities of analysis and business support.

In addition, front office technologists were delighted with improvements enabled by CBD, in particular the ability to provide better support to business users. One technologist from the Currency and Exotic Options group explained:

> It gives you the binding of the users since they're actually involved in the development of the program. It's a bit like prototyping. You can ask users how they like it and you can quickly move components around from there to there, or change screen colors and so on. It gives them the binding from the beginning, so they can't say "hey! we don't like the screen", because they were actually in on the design before it came into use.

In contrast to this, back office personnel – both technologists and users – did not want involvement in CBD. The consensus here was that CBD was not needed. Back office technologists, business managers, and administrators were involved in the centralization project during the second half of 1998 and no major change occurred around CBD. This led to conflict between front and back office personnel. Front office technology directors perceived back office technology directors as the major barrier to implementing CBD throughout Invebank. Back office directors argued that, given available resources and priorities, CBD was not top of their agenda.

There were also different interpretations of CBD policy between permanent and contractual front office technologists. Some contractors, in particular those with substantial experience in CBD, argued that the likelihood of reuse of some components was low. Also, tight deadlines became infeasible if all components had to be reusable. In contrast, the permanents with limited experience in CBD, were keener to follow the reuse policy. Consequences stemming from such a divergence were evident in the growing tension between permanents and contractors, with contractors often being blamed for failure by directors. The Director of Interest Rate Derivatives noted:

> We have a large number of contractors who do not want to share information and do not want to build systems in a way that is component-based, because they believe that their value is so rich ... they see things that run across products as a threat to their position and their stance.

5) *Routinization*: The two phases of CBD implementation illustrated in the adaptation stage were largely completed during the second quarter of 2000. The main goal, according to the Global Head of Technology, was to maximize the inventory of reusable components and reinforce the component reuse policy. By this time, for some front office technologists, CBD was seen as commonplace. For others, CBD was an ongoing nightmare. Various directors of the Technology Division complained about the difficulty of persuading technologists, in particular contractors, to follow policy. Some technologists argued that their directors did not trust their judgement about which components would not have much reusable value and, thus, should not be designed on CBD principles.

Pressure from the board to reduce IT expenditure was observed. When the CBD project was proposed, one of the key selling points was to have heavy investment in the first two years, then to reduce expenditure, particularly in terms of overall headcount. This had not happened. For instance, a 1999 internal report stated that capital investment required for CBD had exceeded 1998's annual IT budget by 240%. A 2000 report showed that IT expenditure remained 1.8 times higher than in 1998. The Global Head of Technology argued that a large portion of this expenditure had occurred because of Y2K compliance. However, he indicated that to reduce headcount even after this was infeasible. Rather, there was a need for another technology team to be responsible for managing the reusable components that had been developed. His view was that Invebank had not been able to significantly benefit from the CBD investment, because they did not have a collaborative culture:

> At the moment, we are trying to address this precise issue, because it's like having a Concorde running on one engine. The reason to develop a collaborative culture isn't just

about people who'll enjoy coming to work, but also to educate our people about the value of sharing knowledge with others. If you share information, the culture will move twice the pace it's moving today. If you break down those barriers where everybody thinks they're right, you'll move three times as fast.

Other front office technology personnel shared similar viewpoints. The Manager of Foreign Exchange Technology argued that sharing information across different teams was a problem:

> ... interaction between developments is minimal. It's on a need to know basis, so if there are requirements from other systems on our systems then we get involved. Why? Because I guess we're such a small team we just don't have the time ... to sit and converse ideas with other teams. We don't have that luxury ... I wouldn't say they try to keep (information). I don't think the interaction is there for them to divulge it. And because it's on a requirement basis, you'll only give it when they require it. And they would do the same. If they require it then that's not a problem, we provide it. That's how we see it ... From the people outside my control I have to demand (information), or make some kind of agreement whereby they provide services. In the past we've tried to do that and it hasn't worked.

Even though the impact of cultural fragmentation on CBD was recognized, a collaborative change project proposed by the Global Head of HR in early 2000 never reached the board. Criticisms raised by some business and technology directors were centered on the issue that he did not have sufficient knowledge of business or technology. Thus, he had no creditability in proposing anything that would impact other divisions. As he himself acknowledged: "Once a serf, always a serf".

Discussions and conclusion

In the discussion which follows, we present the lessons that have been learned from this exploratory case study and the managerial implications arising from these. These are summarized in Table 7.3.

As Martinsons and Chong [30] note, many IT systems fall short of performance expectations, despite rapid advances in these technologies. They argue that this is more often due to human social factors rather than technical ones. Our analysis reinforces the point by focusing on how cultural factors influence IS/IT implementation. Specifically, we explored different ways in which subcultural groups in Invebank viewed CBD and why and how this influenced the CBD process. Each subculture has its own values, norms, and practices. These differences exist because different groups have different tasks to fulfill and different relationships with the organization as a whole. These different tasks and relationships place different demands on the individuals involved and often require different orientations, approaches and outlooks [4].[1]

---

[1]It should be noted at this point that we are not claiming that ours is an exhaustive nor definitive set of subcultural groups as they existed in Invebank, only that our categorization helped in exploring different views about CBD that influenced the implementation process.

Table 7.3 *Summary of the lessons learned and managerial implications*

Lessons learned	Managerial implications
Demonstration of the usefulness of employing a logic of opposition to illustrate both the threat and value of subcultural differences during IT/IS implementation	Managers need to recognize the opportunities and potential provided by subcultural differences during an IT/IS implementation (as well as the threats)
The value of metaphor to conceptualize subcultural differences	Managers can use tools, such as metaphor analysis, as a vehicle for both understanding and communicating the subcultural differences which exist in a particular context
The multi-faceted nature of subcultural differences, which requires us to go beyond differences between technologists and business users	Managers need to identify the various stakeholder groups and understand the factions within as well as across these stakeholder groups
The importance of creating knowledge redundancies between different subcultural groups during an IT/IS implementation	Managers need to consider creating knowledge redundancy, through utilizing the expertise of the HR function, as a critical step in reducing conflict resulting from misunderstandings between and within stakeholder groups
The importance of improvisation within the context of CBD implementation and use, which implies the need to take into account the concerns of different stakeholder groups	Managers need to continuously evaluate their policies for developing and using the reusable components to reflect the concerns of different stakeholders and the general trend of technology development

We used a "crusade" metaphor to portray the various subcultures within Invebank and their different values and orientations. The idea of using metaphor in this study was actually suggested by comments from one interviewee and we found this to be very useful. Indeed, given the stimulation to organization theory that was prompted by Morgan [33], one conclusion from this paper is that metaphor may be a helpful tool for capturing and exploring subcultural fragmentation. Future research could usefully explore the potential of using metaphor to understand subcultural fragmentation in different IT/IS implementation contexts. Moreover, it would be useful if research focused on exploring the extent to which metaphors can provide managers with a practically useful tool to understand and manage the impact of subcultural differences.

The analysis has further demonstrated how subcultural differences impeded information sharing and collaboration, not only between technologists and business users but also between technologists themselves (contractors and permanents; front and back office technologists) and between business users (front and back office staff). Indeed, a key conclusion from our analysis has been that previous accounts of the influence of subcultural differences on IS/IT implementation that have focused on the different mindsets and orientations (i.e., different subcultures) of those working in IT and those in business functions (e.g., [11] and [21]) oversimplify the issue. In Invebank, differences between front and back office personnel meant that, while traders saw benefit in CBD implementation in providing them with faster IT innovation, administrators saw little, if any, value from this new approach, feeling that it was a distraction from their more pressing concern to improve control. Similarly, differences between permanent and contractor technologists were evident, with contractors at times ignoring CBD policy on reuse in order to ensure that they met development deadlines. This was more important for them since they were more eager to satisfy their client in order to ensure contract renewal. The permanents did not have this pressure. Instead, they viewed the contractors as a threat to their own promotion opportunities and so often withheld vital information that would help the contractors in their work. Moreover, given that the contractors were more experienced in CBD projects, being hired precisely because of this expertise, they were more aware of its limitations and so were more ready to accept that not all components needed to be developed as reusable. Permanents, with less experience, were less ready to accept this. Thus, there were significant differences within, as well as between, the technologists and business users. Indeed, in some cases, there was greater convergence of views and values between technologists and users than within each group. For example, back office technologists and administrators both felt that CBD was not a priority, while front office technologists and traders thought that it was. These results suggest future research might usefully explore how the benefits of CBD can be maximized once the technological infrastructure is in place. In particular, through evaluating the situations in which a component is best developed as reusable or for one-off purposes.

The outcome of these subcultural differences and lack of collaboration was that Invebank's CBD implementation had not achieved all its expected benefits, at least not to date. IT spending had increased, rather than decreased and few reusable components had been developed that could be used in both front and back offices. Management was aware of some problems, especially in relation to a lack of collaborative culture, but had so far been unable to overcome them. The literature on integrating technologies such as CBD (but also including ERP and BPR) would support the view that a key problem at Invebank was their lack of a collaborative or open culture [14] – one that encouraged trust and knowledge sharing [20], [45]. We might, therefore, argue that Invebank could usefully develop a unified collaborative culture to break down subcultural barriers. However, we believe that this is naïve, since it oversimplifies the cultural concept, adopting as it does an integrative perspective [29]. Moreover, it is based on the false assumption that culture is something that can be managed and changed to meet managerial needs [2]. As DiBella [17, p. 370] notes: "… the idea that cultural assumptions can be shared throughout an organization is a major (and false) assumption." By adopting the differentiation perspective, we have illustrated the existence, influence, and complexity of subcultural differences and thereby, the often utopian nature of the collaborative culture argument.

In adopting this differentiation perspective, we have also demonstrated the usefulness of employing a logic of opposition [44], which focuses on the opposing forces (here defined in terms of different subcultural groups) that promote or oppose change. Given a change initiative, like CBD, whose scope is wide involving diverse groups, it is perhaps inevitable that cultural differences will shape how change is implemented [17]. Indeed, prior to the CBD initiative, conflicts between these subcultural groups were minimized by structural separation. It is not, therefore, that the CBD project created conflicts, simply that these conflicts surfaced once intergroup collaboration was required. This is the case with any integrative technology like CBD. Humans appear to require boundaries in order to make sense of their role in organizations. Simply because integrative technologies *can* span boundaries does not mean that boundaryless organizations *will* arise as a result of such technologies [34]. It is only when basic assumptions are violated that culturally-based resistance becomes important and apparent [9]. In Invebank, these basic assumptions were violated with the onset of CBD and various dimensions of culture shaped the ensuing events, very much in line with DiBella's propositions [17].

In helping to understand the impact on the CBD initiative of the cultural diversity at Invebank, it is useful to consider the typology developed by Cooper [9]. He suggested that two primary conflicts are important for exploring the likely impact of cultural diversity – the relative emphasis on order *versus* flexibility and the relative emphasis on internal systems *versus* the external environment. Given back office concern for order and stability (internal environment) as against front office concern for flexibility and responsiveness (external environment), it is hardly surprising that these different subcultural groups viewed the CBD initiative differently. As Cooper [9] notes, different cultures require, process, and are satisfied with different kinds of information so that the validity of a specific IT system may differ for different cultures.

The literature on the need to develop an "open" and "collaborative" culture is not only based on a limited integrative perspective, it is also typically lacking in any concrete suggestions as to how such a culture should actually be developed. Where this issue is addressed, the key is usually seen to be to create some knowledge redundancy [35] so that those in different functions learn something about the work and activities of those elsewhere. This will allow them to appreciate the needs of others so that information sharing can occur. For example, in relation to the literature on technology adoption, Earl and Skyrme [19] argue that the solution to the problem of subcultural differences between technologists and business people is to create "hybrids" – technologists with business knowledge and business people with technology knowledge. While this "solution" clearly has some merit, the degree and complexity of subcultural differences in organizations like Invebank suggests that this solution would be rather expensive and not easily achievable, certainly not in the short-term. In fact, Invebank did attempt this through facilitating training programs, but these were not well received, especially by business personnel who saw no need to understand technology. Indeed, the very feasibility of the "hybrid" solution has been called into question in view of such problems (cf., [12]).

Perhaps a better approach, in the short-term at least, is to identify cultural differences and try to determine and constantly monitor how these differences may affect IS/IT implementation. This accords with Cooper's [9] view that, at least in the short term, culture should be viewed as a stable structure that constrains change rather than as something that can be readily changed. More fundamentally, as DiBella [17] argues, these differences should be accepted and understood from the perspective of each particular group so that adaptations to the system can be seen as acceptable and constructive, rather than as obstructive defiance and intransigence from particular groups. Such improvisation [36], tinkering, or bricolage [7] is, after all, a common occurrence in IT/IS implementations and is not inevitably counterproductive. Thus, in Invebank, it was perhaps unnecessary to enforce CBD on back office personnel who had a clear set of priorities and objectives that were not best met through the CBD initiative. Nor was it necessarily right to develop all systems according to the principles of component reusability. In this respect, listening to contractors' concerns might have helped Invebank decision-makers. Emphasis would, thus, be placed on ensuring that diversity is managed and celebrated rather than denounced. Notwithstanding, the purpose of this paper has not been to present generalizable solutions to this issue of contrasting subcultures, but to awaken interest in the complexities of the development and implementation of so-called corporate-wide integrative technologies such as CBD. To be forewarned is to be forearmed.

References

[1] T. Astebro (1995), "The effect of management and social interaction on the intra-firm diffusion of electronic mail systems," *IEEE Trans. Eng. Manage*, Vol. 42, pp. 319–331.

[2] D. Avison and M. Myers (1995), "Information systems and anthropology: An anthropological perspective on IT and organizational culture," *Inform. Technol. People*, Vol. 8, pp. 43–56.

[3] G. Baster, P. Konana, and J. Scott (2001), "Business components: A case study of Bankers Trust Australia Ltd," *Commun. ACM*, Vol. 44, pp. 92–98.

[4] F. Bladder (1995), "Knowledge, knowledge work, and organizations: An overview and interpretation," *Org. Studies*, Vol. 16, pp. 1021–1046.

[5] J. Bosch (1999), "Superimposition: A component adaptation technique," *Inform. Software Technol*, Vol. 41, pp. 257–273.

[6] A. Bryman and R. Burgess (1999), "Introduction: Qualitative research methodology—A review," in A. Bryman and R. Burgess, Eds. *Qualitative Research*. Sage, Newbury Park, CA.

[7] C. U. Ciborra (1994), "From thinking to tinkering: The grassroots of IT and strategy," in C. U. Ciborra and T. Jelassi, Eds. *Strategic Information Systems: A European Perspective*. Wiley, New York.

[8] "Special Issue on Component-Based Enterprise Frameworks," *Commun. ACM,* vol. 43, 2000.

[9] R. Cooper (1994), "The inertial impact of culture on IT implementation," *Inform. Manage*, Vol. 27, pp. 17–31.

[10] R. Cooper and R. Zmud (1990), "Information technology implementation research: A technological diffusion approach," *Manage. Sci*, Vol. 36, pp. 123–139.

[11] D. Couger (1996), "The changing environment for IS professionals: Human resource implications," in M. J. Earl, Ed. *Information Management: The Organizational Dimension*. Oxford Univ. Press, Oxford, U.K.

[12] W. Currie and I. Glover (1999), "Hybrid managers: An example of tunnel vision and regression in management research," in W. Currie and R. D. Galliers, Eds. *Rethinking Management Information Systems*. Oxford Univ. Press, Oxford, U.K.

[13] T. Davenport (1993), *Process Innovation: Reengineering Through Information Technology*. Harvard Bus. School Press, Boston, MA.

[14] ——— (1994), "Saving IT's soul: Human-centered information management," *Harv. Bus. Rev,* vol. 72, pp. 119–131.

[15] D. De Long and L. Fahey (2000), "Diagnosing cultural barriers to knowledge management," *Acad. Manage. Exec*, Vol. 14, pp. 113–127.

[16] N. Denzin (1988), *The Research Act*. New York, McGraw-Hill.

[17] A. DiBella (1996), "Culture and planned change in an international organization: A multi-level predicament," *Int. J. Org. Anal*, Vol. 4, pp. 352–372.

[18] R. Due (2000), "The economics of component-based development," *Inform. Syst. Manage*, Vol. 17, pp. 92–95.

[19] M. J. Earl and D. Skyrme (1992), "Hybrid managers: What do we know about them?," *J. Inform. Syst*, Vol. 2, pp. 169–187.

[20] O. El Sawy, I. Eriksson, A. Raven, and S. Carlsson (2001), "Understanding shared knowledge creation spaces around business processes: Precursors to process innovation implementation," *Int. J. Technol. Manage*, Vol. 22, pp. 149–173.

[21] D. Feeny and L. Willcocks (1999), "Rethinking capabilities and skills in the information systems function," in W. Currie and R. D. Galliers, Eds. *Rethinking Management Information Systems*. Oxford Univ. Press, Oxford, U.K.

[22] J. Grundy, W. Mugridge, and J. Hosking (2000), "Constructing component-based software engineering environments: Issues and experiences," *Inform. Software Technol*, Vol. 42, pp. 103–114.

[23] M. Hammer and J. Champy (1993), *Reengineering the Corporation: A Manifesto for Business Revolution*. Harper Business, New York.

[24] S. Harrington and C. Ruppel (1999), "Telecommuting: A test of trust, competing values and relative advantage," *IEEE Trans. Prof. Commun*, Vol. 42, pp. 223–239.

[25] M. Hauser (1998), "Organizational culture and innovativeness of firms – An integrative view," *Int. J. Technol. Develop*, Vol. 16, pp. 239–255.

[26] H. Klein and M. Myers (1999), "A set of principles for conducting and evaluating interpretive field studies in information systems," *MIS Quart*, Vol. 23, pp. 67–94.

[27] D. Kunda and L. Brooks (2000), "Assessing organizational obstacles to component-based development: A case study approach," *Inform. Software Technol*, Vol. 42, pp. 715–725.

[28] M. Louis (1985), "An investigator's guide to workplace culture," in P. Frost, L. Moore, M. Louis, C. Lundberg, and J. Martin, Eds. *Organizational Culture*. Sage, Newbury Park, CA.

[29] J. Martin (1992), *Cultures in Organizations*. Oxford Univ. Press, Oxford, U.K.

[30] M. Martinsons and P. Chong (1999), "The influence of human factors and specialist involvement on information systems success," *Hum. Relat*, Vol. 52, No. 1, pp. 123–152.

[31] D. Meyerson and J. Martin (1987), "Cultural change: An integration of three different views," *J. Manage. Stud*, Vol. 24, pp. 623–647.

[32] M. Miles and A. M. Huberman (1994), *Qualitative Data Analysis: An Expanded Sourcebook*. Sage, Newbury Park, CA.

[33] G. Morgan (1997), *Images of Organization*. Sage, Newbury Park, CA.

[34] S. Newell, S. Pan, R. Galliers, and J. Huang (2001), "The myth of the boundaryless organization: Limitations of collaborative technologies in global firms," *Commun. ACM*, Vol. 44, pp. 74–76.

[35] I. Nonaka (1994), "A dynamic theory of organizational knowledge creation," *Org. Sci*, Vol. 5, pp. 14–37.

[36] W. Orlikowski (1996), "Improvising organizational transformation over time: A situated change perspective," *Account. Manage. Inform. Techno*, Vol. 5, pp. 1–21.

[37] —— (2000), "Using technology and constituting structures: A practice lens for studying technology in organizations," *Org. Sci,* Vol. 11, pp. 404–428.

[38] W. Orlikowski and D. Gash (1994), "Technological frames: Making sense of information technology in organizations," *ACM Trans. Inform. Syst*, Vol. 12, pp. 174–207.

[39] C. Pancake (1995), "The promise and the cost of object technology: A five-year forecast," *Commun. ACM*, Vol. 38, pp. 32–49.

[40] J. Pfeffer (1981), *Power in Organizations*. Pitman, New York.

[41] T. Powell and A. Dent-Micallef (1997), "Information technology as competitive advantage: The role of human, business and technology resources," *Strat. Manage. J*, Vol. 18, pp. 104–375.

[42] P. Prasad (1993), "Symbolic processes in the implementation of technological change: A symbolic interactionist study of work computerization," *Acad. Manage. J*, Vol. 36, pp. 1400–1429.

[43] D. Robey and A. Azevedo (1994), "Cultural analysis of the organizational consequences of information technology," *Account. Manage. Inform. Technol*, Vol. 4, pp. 23–37.

[44] D. Robey and M. Boudreau (1999), "Accounting for the contradictory organizational consequences of information technology: Theoretical directions and methodological implication," *Inform. Syst. Res*, Vol. 10, pp. 167–185.

[45] C. Ruppel and S. Harrington (2001), "Sharing knowledge through intranets: A study of organizational culture and intranet implementation," *IEEE Trans. Prof. Commun*, Vol. 44, pp. 37–52.

[46] S. Sackmann (1992), "Culture and subcultures: An analysis of organizational knowledge," *Administr. Sci. Quart*, Vol. 37, pp. 140–161.

[47] G. Sanders and J. Courtney (1985), "A field study of organizational factors influencing DSS success," *MIS Quart*, Vol. 9, pp. 77–93.

[48] E. Schein (1996), "Culture: The missing concept in organization studies," *Ad-minist. Sci. Quart*, Vol. 41, pp. 229–240.

[49] R. Sloan and H. Green (1995), "Manufacturing decision support architecture," *Inform. Syst. Manage*, Vol. 12, pp. 7–16.

[50] A. Strauss and J. Corbin (1990), *Basics of Qualitative Research: Grounded Theory Procedures and Techniques.* Sage, Newbury Park, CA.

[51] J. Van Maanen and S. Barley (1985), "Cultural organization: Fragments of a theory," in P. Frost, L. Moore, M. Louis, C. Lundberg, and J. Martin, Eds. *Organizational Culture.* Sage, Newbury Park, CA.

[52] P. Vitharana and H. Jain (2000), "Research issues in testing business components," *Inform. Manage,* Vol. 37, pp. 297–309.

[53] A. von Meier (1999), "Occupational cultures as a challenge to technological innovation," *IEEE Trans. Eng. Manage,* Vol. 46, pp. 101–114.

[54] G. Walsham (1993), *Interpreting Information Systems in Organizations.* Wiley, New York.

[55] R. Yin (1994), *Case Study Research: Design and Methods.* Sage, Newbury Park, CA.

Reproduced from *IEEE Transactions on Engineering Management*, Vol. 50, No. 1, Feburary 2003, pp. 89–99. Reprinted with permission from IEEE.

About the authors

Jimmy C Huang received the Ph.D. degree in industrial and business studies from the University of Warwick, Coventry, U.K.

He is currently a Lecturer of IT and strategy at Nottingham University Business School, Nottingham, U.K. He had previously taught at the University of Aberdeen, Aberdeen, U.K. His research interests include the knowledge integration processes underlying the implementation of corporate wide technological initiatives, such as enterprise resource planning systems and component-based software development.

Sue Newell received the degree in psychology and the Ph.D. degree from Cardiff University, South Glamorgan, U.K.

She is currently a visiting Trustee Professor in the Department of Management, Bentley College, Waltham, MA. She is also a Professor of Management at Royal Holloway, University of London, London, U.K. She has published widely in a range of areas, with her main research focusing on innovation – exploring this in terms of the networking and knowledge sharing that can support (or impede) innovation processes.

Dr. Newell is one of the founding members of the ikon (innovation, knowledge, and organizational networking) research unit at Warwick University, Coventry, U.K.

Robert D. Galliers is currently Provost of Bentley College, Waltham, MA, while on leave of absence from the London School of Economics, London, U.K., where he directed the research program in the Department of Information Systems. Formerly Dean of Warwick Business School, U.K., and Head of the

School of Information Systems, Curtin University, Australia, he has published widely on a range of subjects concerned with the strategic and organizational change issues associated with the adoption and use of modern IT.

Dr. Galliers was a Co-Chair of the International Conference on Information Systems, Barcelona, Spain, 2002, a former President of the Association for Information Systems, and joint Editor-in-Chief of the *Journal of Strategic Information Systems.*

Shan-Ling Pan is currently an Assistant Professor with the Department of Information Systems, School of Computing, National University of Singapore, Singapore. His research interests include the recursive interaction of organizations and information technology (enterprise systems), with particular emphasis on issues related to work practices, cultures, and structures from a knowledge perspective. Some of his previous research has been published in *Communications of ACM, Journal of Strategic Information Systems, Journal of Organizational Computing and Electronic Commerce, European Journal of Information Systems,* and *Decision Support Systems.*

Questions for discussion

1   Imagine you are the CEO of Invebank. What would you do to achieve your CBD project's objectives knowing what you know about subcultures and the roles they play in the CBD adoption process?
2   How do you build consensus across different subcultures within an organization? Are consensus and unity necessary for a successful implementation of CBD?
3   Would you apply the "opposing forces" paradigm to a successful organizational launch of CBD? In that case, how would the "opposing forces" paradigm help you in the examination of subcultures and conflicts? How would this help in the examination of a successful adoption of CBD?
4   Could IT play a role in gradually changing the corporate culture?
5   What roles does communication with each subculture group play in the success of the CBD adoption process? Of what use is communication in a corporate culture trying to change in its adoption of CBD?
6   How can you sell CBD to each subculture and bring each on board in the case of Invebank?

8 Assimilating New Technologies

The Role of Organizational Culture

Norton Hoffman and Robert Klepper

Abstract: A technology may have met all the necessary user requirements, had buy-in from senior management, and yet be a resounding failure because the crucial role of organizational culture was overlooked. Like most social issues, organizational culture is amorphous, difficult to measure and quantify. This article helps IS managers analyze their own organization's culture to discover the role it will play in adopting a new technology.

With each new information technology that enters the marketplace, the trade press features exemplary IT departments that assimilate the new technology successfully. Much less attention is given to companies that struggle with new technology adoption, but many do. Why are some companies successful, and why do other companies have problems?

One answer undoubtedly lies in the specific steps taken by successful companies to implement new technology. Does this mean that every IT department that follows the script of a successful adopter of new technology will also succeed? Putting the question this way should immediately raise doubts in a savvy manager's mind. What if my application of the new technology is not similar to it's application in the exemplar company? What if my resources do not match those of the successful IT department? What if my company and the way it makes decisions affecting adoption of new technology are not parallel to those of the successful company? Behind every success story probably lies a multitude of factors and circumstances that are taken for granted by the managers in the successful company and escape exploration by the journalists.

Academics also have potential blind spots. Journal reviewers demand theoretically based analyses. Theories attempt to get at what are, hopefully, core issues in the explanation of a phenomenon. The explanatory variables suggested by a theory may prove to be statistically significant but leave a large "error" term that hides other factors of possibly equal or greater importance. Or the explanatory variables may be correlated with other factors that more accurately and fundamentally explain the phenomenon at issue.

What academics identify as success factors in new technology assimilation often boil down to good project management practices: sound planning, realistic risk assessment, adequate resources, good monitoring and control, and the like. But is good project management the only explanation as to why one company succeeds and another fails? Project management books and articles abound, and good project management skills are widely known. Why then are some companies able to apply good project management skills in new technology adoptions while others are not?

> Corporate culture is messy, imprecise, and not easily measured or changed, so it seems to have no practical value to an IS manager looking for quick answers.

Organizational culture and new technology assimilation

The authors contend that the culture of an organization is an often overlooked or underemphasized influence on the initial success or initial failure in new technology assimilation. Rarely does the trade press delve into issues of corporate culture. It is messy; because it is imprecise; it cannot be easily measured or changed, it seems to be of no practical value to a manager looking for quick answers. Academics are more likely to include organizational culture as an explanatory variable, but often in a way that gives organizational culture short shrift, either by taking a very narrow or an overly simplistic approach to culture.

At least two problems are involved in trying to use organizational culture to understand success and failure in new technology assimilation. First, organizational culture is a vast issue; the literature, both popular and academic, is huge. Where should one start? And second, the many extant conceptualizations of organizational culture lead to many possible explanatory variables that might be used to characterize an organization's culture. What in an organization's culture is important for technology assimilation?

This article draws on an organizational culture conceptualization and framework by Goffee and Jones (1996) that is recent, accessible, and relatively easy to apply. It is true that other organizational culture factors not captured by this framework could be important, but the case study evidence used here suggests that the framework is useful for understanding and managing some aspects of new technology assimilation.

Case studies of successful and unsuccessful adopters of client/server technology are used to illustrate the role of organizational culture in new technology assimilation. The success stories come from an article by Subramanian and Lacity (1997). The failure comes from a company in which one of the authors worked at the time client/server was being introduced. The remainder of the article presents an organizational culture framework, then a discussion of the initial difficulties with client/server technology, then the case studies. The article ends with warnings for managers of technology assimilation.

The Goffee and Jones organizational culture framework

In the Goffee and Jones framework, culture is community or the way in which people relate to each other. In their model they focus on two types of human relations and their consequences for organizations: sociability and solidarity.

Sociability can be defined as friendliness in relationships between people in an organization, it is valued for its own sake, independent of its impact on the performance of the organization. Through friendships, ideas, attitudes, interests, and values are shared. Reciprocity is a hallmark of friendship so that actions are taken that favor others with no expectation of immediate payback. Sociability has favorable consequences in the form of morale, creativity, teamwork, acceptance of new ideas, information sharing, and motivation to go beyond the stated requirements of a job. Sociability also has an unfavorable side in the sense of tolerance of poor performance on the part of friends, an "exaggerated concern for consensus" when friends are reluctant to disagree with or challenge or criticize one another, along with insufficient focus on mission, strategy, and goals. Organizations with high sociability tend to have cliques and informal networks that can subvert or replace decision-making through formal organizational processes.

Solidarity is the ability of people to pursue shared goals efficiently and effectively for the larger good of the organization without much regard for the impact on individuals and the relationships between them. Solidarity is favorable in the sense that it generates single-minded dedication to the organization's mission and goals, quick response to changes in the environment, and an unwillingness to accept poor performance. Work roles are defined and understood. With everyone working for the overall good and everyone held to the same high standards, people in high-solidarity organizations often trust their employers to treat them fairly, based on merit, with resulting commitment and loyalty to the firm. The downside of solidarity is the possibility of a single-minded focus on the wrong strategy, lack of commitment if individuals cannot see personal advantage in what the organization is doing, and disputes over responsibilities and roles as people and departments try to protect their turf from the aggressive efforts of others to achieve the organization's goals.

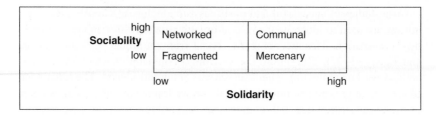

Exhibit 8.1   *Organizational culture framework*

When the two dimensions of sociability and solidarity are placed on the axes of a diagram like that in Exhibit 8.1, four cultures are defined by the quadrants of the diagram.

Communal/culture

The communal organization with high sociability and high solidarity is typical of new, small, fast-growing companies. People are driven by common goals, and at the same time are united by strong social bonds. Goffee and Jones find this organizational culture most often in political, civic, and religious organizations. It is a culture that is hard to maintain in medium- and large-scale profit-making firms. A single-minded drive for organizational goals often conflicts with the forgiving attitude that is part of sociability. Organizations that begin as communal usually migrate to another form as they mature.

Fragmented culture

Fragmented organizations would appear to be completely dysfunctional. The low sociability and low solidarity of this organizational culture seems to leave it rudderless and ungovernable. However, Goffee and Jones point out that organizations that house collections of professionals (e.g., doctors, lawyers, and academics) can be quite successful with fragmented cultures. Similarly, virtual organizations that outsource many functions can also succeed with fragmented cultures.

Networked culture

The networked organization has a culture of low solidarity and high sociability. High sociability is evident in the frequent water-cooler conversations and the many colleagues who go to lunch together and spend time in activities and social gatherings outside the workplace. Many decisions are made outside official hierarchical channels. Low solidarity manifests itself in poor definition of and focus on objectives, difficulty in agreeing on and sticking to priorities, and the highly political nature of decision-making. A networked organization can be successful, particularly when the nature of its work demands creativity. If strategies must play out over long periods of time, sociability maintains commitment, and it maintains overall commitment if overall success is a collection of divided and local successes. To be successful, however, an organization must find ways to cope with the informal decision processes and the low productivity that would otherwise result.

Mercenary/culture

Mercenary organizations with low sociability and high solidarity are focused on strategy and winning in the marketplace. They have clear priorities and act quickly in response to outside events. Persons who do not perform are let go if they are incapable of improvement. The downside is the lack of cooperation between organizational units in mercenary organizations, a defect that is a considerable liability when the market demands creativity and close cooperation between organizational units.

The communal and fragmented organizational cultures are not the norm in modern economies. Most profits making businesses have cultures that can be characterized as networked or mercenary or that lie on an axis between these two cultural types; the subsequent analysis concentrates on these.

Client/server as a new technology

Client/server (CS) is no longer a new technology, but at the time of the case studies – the early and mid-1990s – it was. In one of the many publications on client/server, Gagliardi (1994) stated why assimilation of client/server was such a formidable task.

1. The new technology required a new set of principles and different problem solving skills.
2. The new technology was neither mature, "self-managing," nor complete.
3. Barriers to new technology often existed in the form of incompatibilities with other technologies, legacy systems that did not work or did not work well with the new technology, and people who resisted it. Therefore, the adoption of CS was risky.

To this list can be added the authors' own observations on the sources of risk in CS technology when it was new.

1. CS was not one technology but several, which presented interface and compatibility issues and problems.
2. CS changed rapidly; evaluation of the technology was difficult; and evaluation of vendor products and how they relate to each other was also difficult.

3. CS was idiomatic and largely unpatterned; there was little standardization; the rules were few and the vocabulary was not yet standardized.
4. CS was focused on building systems, not on operations or producing
business value; no common methodology or approach for building CS
systems existed. Each new system demanded an endeavor in conceptualization, implementation and operation *at the level of technology* as well as
the *business level* and the *business technology interface.*

> There were numerous indicators of the high sociability; senior man-
> agers all were promoted from within, based on their political skills,
> past service, and intense loyalty.

Cases of client/server failure and success

As with all new technologies, some IT departments had successes in client/
server assimilation and others experienced failures. The case of failure is presented first, followed by the cases of success.

A client/server failure

Service, Inc. is a large U.S. services company with several interrelated service businesses. Information systems are critical to a number of the study company's services and can be considered strategic to the company. Service, Inc.
was a low-solidarity, high-sociability company at the time of the case study
in the mid-1990s. As such, it fit into the networked quadrant of the Goffee
and Jones organizational culture framework.

Sociability

There were numerous indicators of high sociability in Service, Inc. Senior
managers all were promoted from within, based on their political skills, past
service, and intense loyalty to the organization. Meetings were often attended
by 20 or more people, even for consideration of minor issues; exclusion from
a meeting caused great dismay. Agendas were rarely prepared; minutes were
often ignored; communication was largely oral. Meetings were considered
successful when everyone felt good about the outcome, causing older executives to call Service, Inc. a "feel-good" organization. It was difficult to raise
issues or handle conflict. To reverse an executive decision required the building of a broad base of consensus.

Important memos required multiple signatures. More than one author as
a signatory was a sure indicator that management felt the pronouncement
critical. The purpose of the multiple authorship and signing was to stress the

unanimity of management regarding the content of the memo. The effect was to quash discussion and dissent. The memos also relieved any one person of responsibility. The technique was that of a committee raised to a higher power.

Group decision-making was the norm; individual decision-making and risk taking were discouraged. Persons who took individual initiative, even when successful, were often ostracized and dropped from the social loop of lunches, meetings, and memo production.

Solidarity

Service, Inc. was a low-solidarity organization. This was not always the case, however. As one of the first firms in its industry, Service, Inc. had clear direction at the outset. It expanded from its original core business by developing and acquiring other related businesses in an expanding vision of its corporate direction and purpose. Employees were unified in this vision.

Now Service, Inc. faces strong competition in its original core business and in each of its related business segments. Profit margins have shrunk. Some business segments suffer losses. At the time of the case study, confusion reigned over what to do and how to proceed. Unity of purpose was gone; Service, Inc. was an organization with a decided lack of solidarity.

Client/server in service, Inc.

The case study concerns a client/server system designed to support customer service in one of Service, Inc.'s divisions. The system initially failed. Queries to support service representatives in phone conversations with customers took as long as 30 minutes to complete. Information systems personnel tried to fix the system and succeeded in making some improvements, but response-time problems persisted for almost a year.

Divisional managers were extremely upset, and in some cases their careers suffered. Manual workarounds were quickly devised, but the quality of customer service suffered and expenses soared. Business managers were immensely frustrated, and in some instances their careers suffered. On the other hand, managers in the information systems department responsible for the system endured some criticism from senior managers, but the high sociability in Service, Inc. blunted much of this criticism. None lost their jobs, and none were replaced as a result of the system debacle.

The high sociability and low solidarity of Service, Inc. directly contributed to problems with the client/server system in the following ways.

The Client/server solution choice

To choose a new-to-the-organization client/server technology for a mission-critical project presents high risk. A more traditional technological approach familiar to the information systems department was probably a better choice for such an important system at the time the choice was made. But the choice of a client/server solution to the customer service need was not seriously challenged. Client/server was chosen, in part, because it was the latest technology with great promise, but also because an executive in another division of the company with much influence in the information systems group of the division in question strongly advocated a client/server approach.

Low solidarity in Service, Inc. also contributed. Confusion and lack of focus on business objectives allowed a manager only distantly connected to the division in which the CS solution was implemented to have undue influence.

Poor staffing and training

Information systems management decided to staff the project with internal people supplemented by experienced external consultants. The project leader had no previous client/server experience, and a person new to database administration was made database administrator. The client/server application development tool and database were new to the project development team; no one on the project had experience with these. In response to time pressures to complete the project, information systems management gave project staff only one week of training in the new tools. The poorly trained and inexperienced internal staff never jelled as a team with the outside consultants, leading to communication problems and conflicts.

Corporate sociability norms played a role in these inappropriate staff appointments and also acted to quell concerns. A network of executives both inside and outside the division's information systems group were behind the selection of the inexperienced project leader and database administrator. Information systems managers led others to believe that the staff and training were adequate to do the project, and these assurances were accepted by other managers in line with corporate sociability norms.

Lack of corporate standards

Service, Inc. had no official technology or project development standards, not even standards for the use of such methods as entity-relationship diagrams in system design. Lack of corporate information systems standards played a role in the client/server problem, and lack of standards had a basis in the culture of the organization. A client/server application development tool and a database product were chosen as the client/server platform for the project at the suggestion of the influential executive in another division. The platform chosen was different from most of the new mid- and lower-tier systems being built in the organization at the time, which were implemented with another leading development tool and database. Service, Inc. did not capitalize on its limited knowledge and experience base. More fundamentally, Service, Inc. had no standards for new technology, nor did the organization move toward standards. Even when the project in question and other projects ran into trouble, the lack of standards was a precipitating factor in problems and the resolution of problems, was not addressed.

Committees were formed to study information systems standards issues, but no real progress was made. The information systems department did not feel at liberty to set standards, even in their own area of expertise, without input from other noninformation technology managers. Noninformation technology managers were incapable of giving good counsel in these situations, and decision-making ground to a halt. Decisions required consensus, and on technical matters that involved nontechnical outsiders, no consensus was possible.

Service, Inc.'s lack of solidarity also played a role. It was more difficult to appreciate the importance of corporate standards in an organization that lacked clear direction and purpose.

Inadequate testing

The system was "completed" with only a slight delay from the scheduled delivery date, but as soon as the system went into production, severe response time problems occurred. Testing under production conditions had not been properly and thoroughly done – a result of time pressures to complete the project, inexperience of the project team, and the absence of a thorough system development methodology. The role of corporate sociability in selection of the project team, training, and lack of a methodology have been addressed previously.

> Close vendor ties did not permit an honest appraisal of the lack of vendor success.

Inappropriate vendors

The development team made little progress in improving response time. Information systems executives then hired two consulting firms – the vendor that had sold Service, Inc. the hardware for the client/server system and the database vendor – to help solve the responses time problem. Both vendors made marginal contributions to improving performance, but neither had solutions that reduced response time to acceptable levels. Service, Inc. had brought in the wrong parties. Neither of the vendors supplying hardware nor the software vendors were in a position to be sufficiently critical of the technology they supported to address crucial underlying problems.

Again, sociability contributed to hiring the vendors as consultants to fix the system problem. The vendors were originally chosen because they had good relationships with persons in Service, Inc., both inside and outside of the information systems department. When the vendors failed to solve the performance problem, Service, Inc.'s management continued to retain them and pay them. Close vendor ties did not permit an honest appraisal of the lack of vendor success.

Deflection of feedback and criticism

Organizational sociability protected information systems managers from major criticism and the consequences of their performance for a long period. The database administrator for the project insisted on third normal form for database tables. When evidence accumulated that relaxation of the normalization rules could produce significant gains in system response time, the DBA refused to yield and insisted on retaining normalized tables in opposition to the project team. His allies among executives inside and outside the information systems department supported him in this controversy, and no change was made until much later.

Sociability insulated the project from users and the effect that users might have had on the correction of problems. Despite the fact that user managers were extremely dissatisfied with system performance and complained to their managers, information systems management and the project development team acted quite independently of users and customers. They enjoyed the support of the network of executives who put them in charge of the project and were immune from the wrath of users.

Had Service, Inc. been a high-solidarity organization, there would have been clear expectations of performance with little toleration for failure. Service, Inc.'s low solidarity resulted in a lack of standards for performance and contributed to toleration of poor performance.

The client/server system in Service, Inc. was eventually successful. At the initiative of managers from the user community, an experienced information systems manager was finally hired from outside and given a mandate to fix the system. He hired competent outside consultants. He forged the outsiders and the insiders into a cohesive team. He initiated a redesign of the user interface that reduced the number of windows and the demand on system resources for navigation. He established an ombudsman function so that users could effectively communicate with the system developers. The outside consultants identified other system problems – problems with clustered indexes, which when clustered differently – and normalized tables, which when denormalized appropriately – produced good response time. Finally, the new manager developed trainers on the new system from the ranks of the user department, which worked to move users rapidly up the system learning curve and helped establish user confidence in the repaired system.

Shortly after making the changes that solved the system response-time problems, the new manager was fired. His style and personality clashed with the sociability norms of Service, Inc.

> Concerns for the role of organizational culture do not enter the Subramanian and Lacity analysis, but their case study firms indicate a level of solidarity.

Client/server successes

Subramanian and Lacity (1997) present case studies of client/server success in three companies: a manufacturer of silicon wafers, a baking company, and an insurance company. Projects with new-to-the-organization client/server technology went smoothly in each company.

Subramanian and Lacity identified six critical success factors in the client/server projects they studied:

1. Secure the support of top management.
2. Redesign business processes before technology selection.
3. Provide adequate training, support, and maintenance.
4. Insource development but outsource to facilitate organizational learning or acquire vendor expertise.
5. Implement incrementally.
6. Include users on the development team.

Most of these factors were recognized as critical to success at the outset of the projects and were incorporated in the way the client/server projects were performed in all three companies. The authors of this study note that the factors they discovered are not new but are part of the standard repertoire of best practices in information technology project work.

Concerns for the role of organizational culture do not enter the Subramanian and Lacity analysis, but their case study firms are probably much higher in solidarity than our study company. (No evidence is presented as to the sociability in the organizational cultures of these companies.) All three firms were selling a fairly standardized product in competitive markets. To be successful in these business environments, the firms likely had corporate cultures with a relatively high degree of solidarity. Of the six Subramanian and Lacity critical success factors for client/server success, four suggest a singleness of purpose that is characteristic of organizations with high solidarity. The four are strong support of top management; redesigning business processes before technology selection; providing adequate training, support, and maintenance; and including users on the development team.

High solidarity unites the organization behind common goals; thus, new technology will be carefully scrutinized and evaluated for its ability to further those goals. Appropriate technology standards and development methods are more likely to be in place in high-solidarity organizations because managers are focused on success and appreciate their contribution to success. Similarly, appropriate resources, including staff resources and outside consultants, will be assembled to help assure success in the use of the new technology.

Conclusion

The role of organizational culture in new technology assimilation is an important but often neglected issue. One source of this neglect may be the difficulty in conceptualizing and applying constructs of organizational culture important for success and failure in new technology assimilation. The Goffee and Jones corporate culture framework can be used for this purpose. It is relatively easy to understand, and managers can fairly easily and accurately judge whether their corporate culture is high or low on the "sociability" and "solidarity" dimensions. Once managers understand their corporate culture in terms of sociability and solidarity, they can be on guard for potential problems in new-technology assimilation.

Managers of technology assimilation in mercenary organizations typically enjoy high solidarity with a clear vision of the future and a better chance of widespread agreement on the aims and objectives of new technology and the resources and governance necessary to reap the potential benefits. Persons in high-solidarity organizations are generally receptive to mastering new roles demanded by a new technology that supports corporate strategy. The low sociability of mercenary organizations also favors successful assimilation by blunting the influence of those whose opinions are tangential to the concerns of the new technology project.

On the other hand, networked organizations are particularly difficult settings for new-technology assimilation. Managers in networked organizations must be on guard and must anticipate the organization's reaction to impending change. Problems can arise from low solidarity in networked organizations. A lack of clear strategic direction often leads to conflicting agendas and difficulty in achieving unity of purpose on new initiatives. Chances of success with new technology may be undermined by disagreements and conflicts that result in poor requirements definition, inadequate allocation of resources, and failure to assign accountability and hold persons responsible. Furthermore, the high sociability of networked organizations may allow poorly informed and tangentially involved persons and factions to exercise a disruptive influence over good decision-making to the detriment of successful assimilation of new technology. High sociability may also act to bias reporting and obscure progress on new technology projects. Managers in low-solidarity or high-sociability organizations need to exercise strong leadership and obtain senior management support to overcome the degenerative effects that low solidarity and high sociability can have on decision-making when new technology is assimilated.

References

G. Gagliardi (1994), *Client/Server Computing, Killing the Mainframe Dinosaur and Slashing Runaway MIS Costs.* PTR Prentice Hall, Englewood Cliffs, NJ.

R. Goffee and G. Jones (1996), "What Holds the Modern Company Together?," *Harvard Business Review*, Vol. 74, p. 6.

A. Subramanian and M. Lacity (1997), "Managing Client/Server Implementations: Today's Technology, Yesterday's Lessons," *Journal of Information Technology*, Vol. 12.

Reproduced from *Information Systems Management*, Vol. 17, No. 3, Summer 2000, pp. 36–42. Reprinted with permission from Taylor & Francis.

Questions for discussion

1   It is people who implement the technology. Therefore, organizational culture matters in the success of IT's implementation. From the study, give examples of how these statements are true.
2   What are the Achilles heels in the combination of the challenges of implementing the server/client system and the corporate culture, which made the IT implementation fail at Service Inc.?
3   Imagine you were in charge of Service Inc. What mitigating things could you have done to counteract the corporate culture's effect on the IT project without changing the culture?
4   In the study the author has only used two elements to describe the corporate culture. Can you think of other elements of the corporate culture that would have an impact on the success of the IT implementation?
5   As the CEO of a company, how can you get to know your own company culture? Would a client/server project succeed or fail in the company you worked for previously?

9 A Qualitative Assessment of Arab Culture and Information Technology Transfer

*Carole E. Hill, Karen D. Loch,
Detmar W. Straub and
Kamal El-Sheshai*

Abstract: Information technology transfer is not an easy task, and seems to be particularly daunting for developing countries. As most technology is designed and produced in developed countries, it is culturally-biased in favor of those developed countries' social and cultural systems. This bias creates cultural and social obstacles for developing countries to transfer technology into practice. Based on focus groups, interviews of Arab–American business people, and a field study conducted in five Arab countries, this paper presents the findings of a qualitative progressive study to systematically examine the linkage between information technology transfer and sociocultural factors that support or impede a successful transfer.

In many countries, organizations experience difficulty and even failure in transferring information technology (IT) into practice. Despite receiving billions of dollars in products and information, this problem seems to be even more severe in developing countries (Atiyyah, 1989; Knight, 1993; Cuningham and Sarayrah, 1994). Why would this be the case? Much of the technology designed and produced in industrialized countries is culturally-biased in favor of their social and cultural systems; consequently, developing countries encounter cultural and social obstacles when transferring technology into practice. Cultural and social factors are a powerful explanation for why westerners, who attempt to implement technology transfer, are often challenged in terms of their own ideas, beliefs, and values about how technology "should" be utilized in developing countries, as the initiatives result in failure.[1] The intent of this paper is to report the progression of a study examining the role of culture in the transfer of information technology to Arab countries.

The study began with a series of focus groups of recently arrived Arab young adults living in a large metropolitan area in the U.S. Subsequently, structured interviews were conducted in the Arab–American business community using an instrument with closed- and open-ended questions based on the findings of the focus groups data set. The structured interviews, coupled with a critical literature review of key social-cultural components of Arab society, allowed us to delineate some salient features of Arab culture that supports or deters the transfer of technology. Finally, a larger sample of Arabs were interviewed in five countries using both qualitative and quantitative instruments. This paper will focus on the qualitative aspects of these research endeavors by reporting the respondents' ideas about the relationship between information technology transfer (ITT) and the sociocultural context of the Arab world.

Culture and information technology transfer

The body of literature which considers culture and technology transfer is disparate.[2] Much of the work has focused on economic factors that influence the transfer of technology (Contractor and Sagafi-nejad, 1981; Bond and Hofstede, 1989), or the organizational characteristics of the recipient organization rather than the characteristics of national cultural and their interplay with the transfer of technology (Cunningham and Sarayrah, 1994; Contractor and Sagafi-nejad, 1981). Kedia and Bhagat's study (1988) presented a conceptual model that advanced the field in that it (1) examined technology transfer across nations and (2) explicitly included societal culture as a key factor. However, the next logical step of delineating the sociocultural variables that foster and impede the adoption of new technology is not taken.

Ein-Dor et al. (1992) conducted a meta-analysis of the extant literature to create a list of national cultural variables affecting information systems and to propose a framework for future global information systems research and implementation. The fundamental questions of their work related to the "degree to which the specific characteristics of the adopting countries influence the desire to adopt and the success or failure of adoption, and to what extent do those differences render incorrect or irrelevant those models and prescriptions accepted in the technology-orienting countries" (1992: 34).

The concept of national culture is complex. They proposed a reasonable categorization of culture according to the degree of stability of the individual factors. Factors inherent to the culture over time, tending to dominate the culture and very resistant to change, are classified as constants'. Examples include geography, language, currency, social norms and traditions. Factors which are more readily changed include GNP, technology, employee morale, education level, and were termed changeables'. Ein-Dor et al. (1992) state that the constants are not within the control of IS designers. Accepting this as fact, the study of the sociocultural factors, termed cultural constants, and their role in ITT becomes even more vital as the trend in globalization marches forward.

Two more recent studies (Burn, 1995; Mahmood and Gemoets, 1995) both take steps in the right direction. Burn's work focuses on the transference of a specific technology, EDI, to a specific geographical region, Asia. While she discusses the interplay of cultural values with ITT, it is not the essence of the work nor is the phenomenon empirically examined. Mahmood and Gemoets (1995) posit that Mexico is a very attractive and likely receptive host for IT transfer. They argue that the economic, political, legal, and social environment of Mexico makes it ripe for such activity. They do not deal with the sociocultural elements, however, beyond the acknowledgment of their complicity in successful ITT.

It is true that the general issues and conflicts involved in information technology transfer to developing countries and regions, such as the Middle East, are being discussed in the literature more frequently. Two studies (Abdul Ghani and al-Sakram, 1988; Khan, 1991) examined the transfer of technology in Saudi Arabia and Bahrein respectively. While geographically of interest to us, these studies focused on organizational culture and structure issues rather than cultural values and beliefs. Atiyyah (1989) did find that ITT is often hampered by technical, organizational, and human problems in Saudi Arabia. Cultural conflicts between the organization and management style of western and Arab institutional leaders and workers have impacted the system development process and produced unsuccessful approaches to computer use and policy (Ali, 1990; Atiyyah, 1989; Goodman and Green, 1992). Furthermore, Al-Meer (1990) points out that differences in motivation of workers in the Arab world and the Western world is an important component for predicting organizational commitment to technological changes in Arab countries. All of these studies serve as examples of instantiations of sociocultural factors in Middle East countries impacting the diffusion of technology.

Our study is unique in that it (1) Focuses on the complex sociocultural construct, categorized as cultural constants by Ein-Dor et al. (1992), thereby extending previous research in this line of inquiry. (2) Is qualitative in nature, using focus groups, semi-structured interviews and field study methodology to gather data. Ein-Dor et al. (1992) found that almost all of the studies in their analysis were limited to survey methodology which limits the ability to probe the participant for underlying explanations and the like. (3) Affords an in-depth look at the cultural phenomenon in multiple Middle East countries, allowing comparison within the developing region as well as to developed regions, and (4) Is empirical, moving beyond frameworks and propositions to offer tangible insight into the dynamic relationship between culture values and beliefs and ITT.

Social and cultural characteristics of Arab society

In this section we attempt to provide the reader a thumb nail sketch of some of the key characteristics of culture and society in the Arab world. We acknowledge as well the theoretical and geographic pitfalls of generalizing about an area of 5.25 million square miles that encompasses 21 states inhabited by a mostly young population expected to number over 200 million before the end of this century.

Barakat (1993), in his recent book on the Arab world, delineates a number of features of their culture and society. An abbreviated list of his synthesis includes such social characteristics as: (1) social diversity; (2) hierarchical class structure; (3) patriarchal relations, particularly in the family; (4) primary group relations; (5) continuing dependency and underdevelopment.

Barakat (1993) furthermore, identifies a number of value orientations that, according to him, reveal conflicts among the various groups that makeup Arab society: fatalism vs. free will (Patai, 1973) conformity vs. creativity, past-oriented vs. future-oriented, culture of the mind vs. culture of the heart, collectivity vs. individuality, open vs. closed-mindedness, obedience vs. rebellion, charity vs. justice, and vertical vs. horizontal values.

These conflicting value orientations are a major indicator of the complexity and contradictory nature of Arab culture. Barakat (1993) argues that these conflicts are what makes Arab culture what it is today (181–205).

There are two other characteristics which receive a great deal of attention in the literature: gender relations and Islam. Two things to note regarding the literature on gender roles: (1) the focus seems to be on gender segregation in private lives and not professional; (2) there is little agreement regarding the effects of the segregation, i.e., domination or independence of action (Nelson, 1991; Abu-Ludhod, 1990).

Without a doubt, the literature portrays Islam as the dominant characteristic of Arab culture and society. While Islam is the dominant religion for all social groupings and is used to define the parameters for much of what constitutes the beliefs and actions in Arab society, its followers are counseled not to use it as the major organizing principle for Arab thought and action. Its influence is always changing as people "practice" their everyday life (Asad, 1986; Fisher, 1980; El-Guindi, 1981). While there is agreement that there is a God and that Muhammad is His Prophet, there is little agreement on the interpretation of other principles and ideas. Thus, Islam is not monolithic nor is it unchanging. Hence while a prevailing characteristic, we as researchers would be remiss to use Islam to singularly define the Arab group.

This brief description of the major characteristics of culture and society in the Arab world illuminates the complexity of the beliefs and actions that makes up Arab culture. Clearly it is not a monolithic structure or a mosaic of peoples, but a complex system that is always changing. Our approach, then, assumes that Arab culture and history, while selectively borrowing ideas and materials from the west, is an independent complex system filled with contradictions and opposing forces which, in effect, defines Arab culture and society (Abu-Lughod, 1990; Barakat, 1993).

We place ITT in the context of selective diffusion from the west. The transfer of technology does not transform Arabs into Westerners. On the contrary, ITT fits into their complex systems in a way that allows Arabs to remain independent. This study uses the critical approach as its conceptual framework in an attempt to factor out variables that will enhance or obstruct the transfer of technology in Arab countries. Clearly the Middle East region provides us with rich material to describe the influence of sociocultural factors on ITT.

Research methods and sampling

The research reported in this paper explores the development of a qualitative research strategy designed to determine the salient cultural and social variables for ITT among Arab-Americans business people and young Arab adults living in the U.S., and a sample of middle class Arabs living in five countries. The ultimate goal of the overall research project is to predict success and failure of information technology transfer to Arab countries using qualitative and quantitative research methods. The project uses several techniques to lay the foundation for a cultural influence model. We report here the findings of qualitative data collected in three distinct phases.

Cross-cultural research issues

Cross-cultural research presents special challenges which must be addressed in the design of the study. Much thought was given to this, especially in the areas of language and instrument administration. English was the language of choice for the pilot study. Since the respondents in this phase were all native Arabic speakers with a high level of competency in the English language, this seemed to be a reasonable choice. Language fluency questions verified our suppositions in this regard. Being sensitive to Arab cultural beliefs, we determined that mailed survey methodology would not be as desirable as administering the surveys in face-to-face meetings. This is consistent with our anticipation about how the survey would be administered in the target Arab countries, where we used two forms of the instrument, one in Arabic and one in English. The instruments were adjusted for the dialectical variations of the different countries. All instruments were back-translated for accuracy.

Focus groups

The first phase of the research program consisted of three focus groups of young Arab adults. Participation in the focus groups was voluntary; the research team members and the students did not know each other in advance. The students were contacted through the international students office. Due to the sensitive relations between some of the Arab countries, we placed the volunteers into separate groups by nationality: Palestinian, Lebanese, and Jordanian. The groups ranged from two to six participants.

We posed an evolving set of open-ended questions to each group. Our goal was to ascertain their beliefs, values, and attitudes about ITT and those of their families in their native countries. We chose this particular set of individuals because they had lived in the U.S. for less than three years, would reflect the perspectives of the younger generation of Arab adults, and made a reasonable surrogate for the type of individuals we expected to find in the field. An additional side benefit was that they represented different countries permitting the investigators to screen for intra-cultural variation.

The focus groups' participants were 90% male and 10% female, and ranged in age from 20 to 28 years. The average number of years they had lived in the U.S. was 2.6 years with frequent trips home. The participants responded to a series of questions regarding cultural and social factors surrounding the use of information technology and their respective native cultures. Hypothetical situations were presented to the participants with the intent of eliciting underlying cultural beliefs. Demographic information such as travel outside of the Arab world, family relations, and education was also collected. All sessions were tape-recorded and subsequently transcribed for analysis.

Pilot study

Transcripts of the focus groups were analyzed and used as the basis for the development of a semi-structured interview instrument consisting of a set of open-ended questions. We created four scenarios, each describing the development and implementation of different types of information systems and technologies in varying organizational settings. Participants were asked to read these scenarios and respond to a series of questions regarding their cultural beliefs and their assessment of the likely success or failure of the information system described in the scenario. The open-ended questions focused on reasons why IT would or would not be accepted in their native countries. The respondents were asked to list the most important cultural factors that they thought would support or impede the transfer of technology in organizations.

Twenty Arab–American business people comprised the pilot study sample. The voluntary sample was drawn from the membership list of a local Arab–American professional organization. While these respondents lived in the U.S., they maintained business and family associations in the Middle East. The study does not assume that fluency in English or a high level of education necessarily means Arabs are "westernized" in fundamental ways. They not only reflect the

Arab cultural perspective, they were able to reflect upon it having the status of both an insider and an outsider. Face-to-face interviews were conducted. Participants were asked to complete the structured instrument prior to the interview in order to ensure unbiased responses. The participants represented six nationalities in the Arab world. Fifteen percent of the participants were female. The average age was fifty and average educational background was 17.9 years. Participants had lived about half of their life in Arab countries and half in other countries.

Field study

This sample was drawn from knowledge workers in Jordan, Egypt, Saudi Arabia, Lebanon, and the Sudan. Within countries, samples were drawn from both private and public organizations. The total sample size of 270 was drawn from countries, and organizations across the spectrum of IT penetration. The average age of the respondents was 35 years (STD = 9.86). The educational level of the respondents varied from high school diploma to doctoral work (see Table 9.1). Twenty percent of the respondents have a master's degree or higher; of these, 93 percent earned their degree in a western-developed country. Conversely, 81 percent of the respondents earned their degree in an Arab country. They indicated their command level of English to be quite high, with ninety-three percent indicating that they can read it easily, seventy-four percent can speak it easily, and 88 percent can write it easily.

Research findings and discussion

Focus group analysis

The purpose of the focus groups was to ascertain participants' general ideas about information systems and to delineate cultural and social characteristics

Table 9.1 *Educational demographics field study participants*

	Education				
	Number of Degrees		*Location*	*Degree Conferred*	
High School Diploma	10.4%	(28)	Arab Countries	81.0%	(218)
Undergraduate	69.3%	(187)	Western Developed	19.6%	(51)
Masters	13.3%	(36)			
Doctorate	7.0%	(19)			

that support or impede the transfer of technology. Analysis of the transcripts of the focus groups revealed that most of the participants felt that there is a difference between Arab culture, in general, and the Western world. They believed that these differences certainly impact the transfer of technology to their native countries but that its importance varied according to social class. Overall, they felt that only upper level employees, who have been influenced by western technology, support ITT into the Arab world. Moreover, they reported that much of this support was stronger in principle than in action. Although organizations purchase information systems, many of the top managers do not personally use it. Nevertheless, the focus group members felt strongly that, given the hierarchal structure of Arab society, technological change must come from top management. In order for it to be successful, they felt that employees must perceive changes to be beneficial to them or to their families. The fear of unknown effects of technology on their personal and work lives make the labor force more resistant to technological change. Differences in world view and perception of technology between top managers and lower-level employees was a topic that was raised by multiple respondents.

Focus group members also noted that technological changes are most often brought into organizations by younger people who have studied in the Western world. They exhibit a different attitude towards technology, often perceiving technology as beneficial to the organization. In contrast, they felt that many employees consider themselves first over the company/organization and only think about how technological innovations will benefit themselves or their families. This discussion led us to hypothesize that primary and extended family obligations are often more important than organizational allegiance.

Indeed, all the participants in the focus groups agreed that the most outstanding cultural factor that distinguishes Arab society is the importance placed on the family. Extended kinship groups function as social, economic, and moral support for individuals. They stated that Arabs view the world in communal terms, rather than in individualistic ones. Their identity is more closely related to their feeling of unity in their kinship group. An individual does not make a decision by him/herself; rather they consult with members of their kinship group.

Group loyalty extends to their place of work. Even though larger organizations are considered a family unit, workers are more inclined to strengthen their standing in their immediate work group rather than labor toward the objectives of the organization. Work groups are often thought of as a kinship group with all the rights and obligations attached to specific types of social relationships. And, as with kinship groups, workers often do not like things to be highly structured. As one participant notes, they like "things just to happen rather than being pre-planned." The focus group members reasoned that a history of colonization in Arab countries made the workers passive and "laid back." Arabs generally do not like change, although they frequently talk about it. One participant remarked that: "Arabs often substitute words for action. That is, they talk about changes, but will not take actions required for change to take place." Consequently, they may say that they support techno-logical innovation while their actions may reject the use of it.

Participants also pointed out that Arabs share information with one another only if the individual thinks that by doing so, he/she will gain status or power or that their kinspeople or work group will gain by their actions. As a conse-quence, when workers make decisions about changing their behavior, the two most important reference groups that influence their decisions are their kin-ship groups and their specific work groups within the structure of the work-ers' organization. As a result, the goals and objectives of top managers are only peripherally considered in their daily lives. One participant said, "alle-giance to company growth is secondary to that of the family." All participants agreed, however, that social and cultural influences on decisions in the work-place depends upon the workers economic status. Social status notwithstand-ing, family and immediately peer influence is the strongest for most Arabs. In addition, they stress that workers' personal relationship with their superiors is deemed more important than the goals and objectives of the organization.

The participants in the focus groups indicated two additional cultural and social factors that influence organizational behavior particularly with refer-ence to ITT. They stated that religion plays a significant role in the lives of Arabs; it provides the basis for their values and moral restraints. It is inex-tricably related to the role family plays in their lives as well as more public behavior, such as dress. It is a fundamental organizing and motivating princi-ple for their lives and explains their loyalty to their family, their kin, and their work group, and less so, than their place of employment.

Education was delineated as another extremely important factor that moti-vates behavior in organizations, particularly the acceptance of changes in tech-nology. Focus group participants agreed that education is the most important avenue to improve social standing in Arab society. They especially mentioned the broadening of one's perspective due to studying abroad and learning for-eign languages. Ironically, they felt that once Arabs return to their respective country, the knowledge and skills they learned in other countries may not be accepted as viable alternative policies and procedures in businesses and organizations, including accepting new technologies. Indeed, the consensus of the focus groups was that some Arabs educated in the west, upon their return to their homeland, may find it difficult to use the knowledge they learned in foreign universities to create changes. Loyalty to religion, family and national traditions often outweigh accepting change from outside. Ambivalence toward the industrialized non-Arab world slows technological change. In addition, they felt that IT threatens jobs and, given a cultural aversion to physical labor, the diffusion of new technology is often seen as a threat to their entire way of life.

During the interviews, the participants in the focus groups repeatedly pointed out the variability of their statements according to social class. They felt that in most Arab countries the better educated people, not necessarily the leaders, would use computers and other IT. However, if the political leaders would set an example for the people by using IT, they would send a message to the workers in the countries to use IT also. One participant said that it is very prestigious to use computers in his country and that it is the young people from wealthy families who are constantly finding ways to use computers; they are the ones who know about the latest software. While the participants felt that generational differences are important for understanding variation in IT, they felt that class differences are even more important for predicting ITT.

Such consensual statements by the young Arabs who participated in our focus groups are consistent with the extensive literature on the key cultural and social features that influence changes in Arab countries. They also provided a basis for developing our structured interview instrument designed to test one component of our mode – the impact of cultural and social factors on ITT.

Analysis of Arab–American business people

A sample of Arab and Arab–American business people were interviewed using an interview instrument consisting of predominantly structured questions and scenarios designed to test for technological culturation and for the salient cultural and social factors for predicting ITT. In addition, the respondents were asked to discuss, in open-ended questions, the reasons why they would or would not use computers and other related technological equipment in their work or in their personal lives. Lastly, they were asked to discuss reasons why ITT may or may not be successful in Arab countries. Their responses mirrored those of the focus groups and the literature review.

Two-thirds of the respondents stated that computer use is important in their personal lives as well as in their work. Seventy percent did not discuss any reasons why they would not use them. Their reasons for using computers centered around the following functions: organizing capabilities, efficiencies, and importance for keeping their companies competitive. Thirty percent responded by discussing reasons they or people they knew would be reluctant to use computers.

These reasons centered around the following factors: financial costs, time costs in learning systems and programs, lack of knowledge about computer use, fear of computers, and problems attendant with comparable hardware and software packages. One respondent talked about the threat that computers may have on his family, meaning that computers may change his children's ideas about the importance of family (family-oriented as opposed to worldly-oriented). Another respondent stated "only if the work doesn't need a computer or computer skills which is rare in our times." Conversely, a respondent said that he could not afford a computer. Another stated that there are several reasons for not using computers in work or for personal use, including the huge time investment required to learn the hardware and software packages which are then rapidly replaced without backwards compatibility. In addition, the non-standard use of applications software packages and hardware among different levels in institutions and businesses often make data transfer unsuccessful. These comments reflect an extremely important social factor for ITT.

Several respondents commented on the importance of having computers at home for their children's education. They felt that "today computers are a necessity" for work and "for survival in the future workplace." The respondents discussed how using computers makes their work more efficient by being able to link to their workplace from home, by having access to public services and databases, and by aiding in the training and education of their children. All but two of the respondents said that if they did not already have a personal computer at home, they planned to purchase one. The two respondents who were not interested in purchasing a computer did not classify themselves as professionals. They worked in lower managerial jobs and, unlike the professional respondents, they did not think that knowledge of IT was critical for economic success. While the numbers are not sufficient to declare a pattern, we are hypothesizing that the higher the managerial rank of the respondents, the more they support the use of IT in both professional and private lives.

Several of the respondents discussed the importance of personal relationships in the workplace. They reported that most business in Arab society is carried out in face-to-face interactions. Communicating via computers, e-Mail, fax, etc. runs counter to the affective nature of communicating with a family member, peer, employer, or employee. They value face-to-face communication. Because of these cultural values, they encounter problems in motivating workers to accept new innovations – to learn new ways of working and communicating. One respondent stated that Arabs prefer direct human contact which "leads away from computer use."

In varying degrees, respondents discussed the differential use of IT according to the workers' position in the hierarchy of an organization or business. They said that top managers use computers or advocate using computers. If they do not use them, their action sends a strong negative signal concerning the use of technology.

Additional problems for ITT reported by the respondents were worker motivation, particularly in governmental and quasi-governmental organizations. Governmental and quasi-governmental agencies' propensity to purchase the most technologically sophisticated innovations which are then seriously underused is consistent with the literature.

Finally, several respondents discussed the wide variation of IT policy and IT diffusion in the Arab countries. One respondent divided the Arab world into "water people," referring to those countries along the Mediterranean coast that are more influenced by the west, and "landlocked" countries that are more conservative and traditional. Another respondent stated that gender would be a major obstacle for ITT in the traditional countries more so than in the more westernized ones. Several of the respondents statements bordered on "blaming the workers" in a particular social stratum, traditional cultural values, or lack of motivation for problems of ITT to Arab countries. Others attributed ITT problems to the lack of leadership of the professional and upper managerial levels or political leaders.

In general, participants felt that social factors such as class and education were key variables for explaining the success or failure of ITT. Several respondents discussed how the isolation of computing departments in organizations impede ITT. Computer departments are isolated from other departments, resulting in little or no communication between information systems personnel, managers, and workers. It is possible that such isolation may also be a function of the informal organizational culture and, indeed, reflects how organizations collectively think about IT.

The respondents were asked to evaluate the effect of particular cultural beliefs on IT outcomes in four different scenarios. Analysis of these scenarios indicates that two cultural beliefs tested for in the scenarios are considered important. They are the preference for face-to-face communication in personal interactions within an organizational setting and the primacy and importance of primary group relations in organizational decision making. These findings support the findings of the open-ended questions.

Analysis of field study

There are several salient themes in the responses to the open-ended questions asked on the qualitative section of the research instrument administered in the Arab countries. Perhaps the most evident is the overwhelming verbal acceptance of the use of computers in the workplace. Since the survey was given in workplace settings, the majority of our sample listed several benefits for using a computer in their daily work activities and for personally owning a computer (see Figure 9.1). Most of the responses to this question associated using a computer to help them in their work tasks, thinking that its use saves time in terms of data entry, storage and speed of access. They also mentioned benefits of decreasing the amount of time it takes to find and retrieve data in their work as well as the organizational benefits to using a computer. With better organization of data and people, most felt that planning is more efficient and simply better. All the information is available on which to make planning decisions. The ability to access information quickly was certainly an overriding theme in their responses. Being able to have large amounts of information in a short amount of time not only increases one's ability to plan more efficiently,

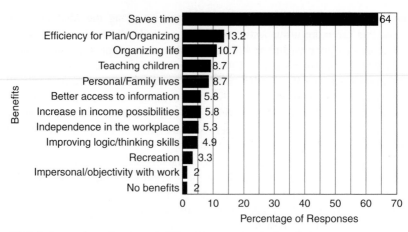

**Note that percentages do not sum to 100, as they are not mutually exclusive.

Figure 9.1   *Benefits to personally owning a computer (N = 140 responses)*

it also, according to some, increases one's thinking skills. Having to handle large amounts of data makes one think more logically and, as a consequence, improves business outcomes. It is significant that only 2% stated that the computer is not beneficial for work or for any other aspects of their lives.

Another theme involves the separation/integration of the computer in the workplace and at home. Much of the literature on Arab culture emphasizes the importance of home and the conservative nature of its influence on adopting new cultural forms including technology. Our findings indicate that, given our sample, Arabs, who have been exposed to technology and who work in organizations that use computers, are in the slow process of transforming these cultural forms not only in their workplace but also in their personal lives. A small percentage (8.7%) reported the benefits of using computers in their personal lives. Another 8.7% said that they are teaching their children about computers. What is clear is that a certain segment of the population appears to have transferred the benefits of using a computer from the workplace to their family.

Moreover, this finding suggests that family/household structure of the Arab is beginning to incorporate western-based ideas about the organization of information for their daily lives as well as for work. It appears that their thinking about work may be changing as well due to the adoption of ideas that include technology in their lives. Several respondents mentioned that the ability to use a computer increases and diversifies their chances for either supplementing their present employment or making their work more independent of a business organization. The changing work and personal lives of Arabs certainly reflect global trends in the use of information technology. A cautionary note must also be made. While we found evidence to support the belief

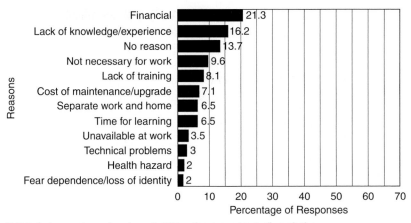

** Note that percentages do not sum to 100 as they are not mutually exclusive.

Figure 9.2   *Reasons for NOT using a Computer (N = 197 responses)*

that ITT is taking place in the Arab world, this is not to suggest that the manner of diffusion nor use of the technology mimics our western way. In fact, we would argue that in those organizations where ITT is most successful, it is because the transfer has taken place in sync with the cultural beliefs held by the respective organization. Moreover, even those that viewed computers in a positive light, expressed concern that, for example, computer use might take away from family time, a higher cultural value.

We then asked them to offer reasons for not using a computer. The comments reflect the answers of the first question. The most cited reason for not using a computer is financial (see Figure 9.2). If they could finance a computer either in their business or personal life, they would do so. It appears that, among our sample, the main reason for not using a computer is related to money and experience/training/access rather than culture. Only 6.5% felt that they should separate the use of computers in the workplace and in the home. This is a small percentage compared with other reasons which are more materialistic rather than idealistic. There is, however, some resistance to the use of computers. A few of our respondents' answers indicate a fear of losing independence or loss of identity at work. Informal interviews substantiated that there are workers who fear computers and sabotage them by entering false data into the computer. In other words, they fear that they will lose their power and/or autonomy at work by having less control over their job and their relations with their fellow workers and employees. Without specifically articulating it, they seem to recognize that information is power and that the computer makes information more readily available to a broader spectrum of people.

Other workers simply say that they do not want to put the time into learning the computer, indicating to us that they also are reluctant to use it. We suggest that these reasons for resisting using a computer and by extension, adopting information technology are driven by both social and cultural factors. They are not merely resisting technology but the idea of technology – what it represents to them and the meaning to them for adopting a new form of communication from a foreign source. The majority of our sample, however, appears to have made this transformation and readily accept new forms of technology. As we pursue this stream of work, we will press the respondents to go beyond their individual view of ITT to present an insider's assessment of ITT vis-à-vis the organization and society at large, and offer explanation for the state of ITT.

Conclusion

The successful transfer of IT into organizational/business workplaces in culturally and socially diverse countries requires an understanding of micro-level beliefs and behaviors within the framework of national and international macro-structures. Culture gives people the sense of order they have to their everyday social lives. The cultural beliefs and values of different occupational groups in the hierarchal social structure of Arab society differ markedly in terms of how they construct a meaning for technology in their everyday work and personal lives.

This paper has presented the findings of a qualitative progressive study to systematically discover the linkage between information technology transfer and the sociocultural factors that support or impede a successful transfer. These data indicate that most respondents in all three subsamples believe that specific components of Arab culture and society have an influence on how IT is viewed and the extent to which it is utilized (see Table 9.2). These variables certainly have an influence on the transfer of technology from non-Arab cultures to Arab ones. While there is some variation among the groups in regard to the specific components that will support or impede the transfer of technology to their native countries, they all agree that sociocultural factors are powerful for predicting the outcomes of technology transfer. In one sense, the most interesting group is the Arab–American business people. Many of them had lived in the United States or another "western" developed country for over 15 years, and were well-educated. They were primarily business owners who operate and compete in the Western world and clearly computers are an integral part of the model. Yet this group evidenced strong identification with their Arab culture. The fact that they articulated so clearly the Arab cultural perspective speaks to the depth at which people hold their cultural values and beliefs, and the risk we run should we consciously, or otherwise, choose to ignore their influence on ITT.

Table 9.2 Summary of respondents' views of cultural and social factors affecting ITT

	Focus groups	Arab–American business people	Field study
Social Influences	• Social class • Educational level • Organizational hierarchy • Personal relations in work group	• Status in organization • Leadership in organization • Personal relations between levels of organization • Personal relations in work group	• Social class • Personal relations in work group • Educational level
Cultural Influences	• Family and kinship obligations • Communal world view • Religion • Valuing the past	• Face-to-face interactions • Allegiance to family and kin group • Concept of time • Religion • Gender relations	• Face-to-face interactions • Allegiance to family and kin group • Concept of time • Religion
Impediments for ITT	• Loyalty to work group • Loyalty to national traditions • Attitudes toward outside influences • Fear of change • Lack of worker motivation • Words substitute for action • Generational & class differences	• Financial • Isolation of computing departments • Conflict with personal values (religious) • Incompatible hardware and software • Lack of worker motivation	• Financial • Conflict with personal values (religious) • Time constraints • Lack of education • Fear of loss of identity • Fear of being controlled
Impetus for ITT	• Educated in West • Power in younger generation • Action rather than rhetoric of top level managers • Political leaders set example for workers	• Keep business competitive • Imperative for younger generation • Top level managers as role models for workers • Link to world system	• Efficiency of organization • Teach children • Increase knowledge base • Improve business outcomes • Increase independence and opportunities • Link to world system

Social class and degree of non-Arab influence appear to be important factors for delineating the specific cultural beliefs that correlate with successful IT. The preferences in Arab culture for face-to-face dealings mitigate against technology interfaces as does the cultural tendency to build consensus and create family-like environments within organizations. The focus group sample and the Arab–American business people sample emphasized how traditional religious values and conservatism tend to reinforce resistance to IT among specific Arab subgroups, particularly those that associate IT with outside technological influences on Arab social structures that result in, in their opinion, less humane, more mechanistic milieus, and demand a change in workers' perception of time.

When individuals held cultural beliefs that were at variance with the dominant cultural beliefs and values, they were more often than not influenced by an external factor, such as a high level of education and/or long term exposure to the technology of the non-Arab industrialized world. This does not mean, however, that they have become western. Rather, all three subgroups demonstrated a very strong sense of identification with their Arab culture, evidence of their continuing to see ITT through an Arab culture-dominated lens. Simply put, the transfer of technology does not transform Arabs into Westerners.

Finally, while the subjects in our study understood that there were differences between themselves and other Arab groups, they appeared to be unaware of the complex interaction between ITT and culture. It is therefore our challenge, and this is the beginning of our efforts, to understand the manner in which ITT takes place within the Arab society, and the influence of sociocultural factors on ITT. Culturally appropriate IT design and implementation which considers the differential influence of culture on ITT may enhance its transfer. Instead of blaming the workers, or some cultural value, as singular explanations for ITT failure, we propose that a combinatory approach, perhaps incorporating the most salient factors of culture in designing transfer processes, might enhance ITT in organizations/businesses in Arab society.

Endnotes

[1] There are several studies conducted in Middle East countries that report anecdotes of attempts to transfer IT across cultural barriers and resulting in failure. See the following: Al-Hegelan, A. and M. Palmer (1985), "Bureaucracy and Development in Saudi Arabia," *Middle East Journal*, Vol. 39, pp. 48–68; Huxley, F. (1978), *Wasita in a Lebanese Context: Social Exchange Among Villagers and Outsiders*. Anthropological Papers #64, University of Michigan Museum of Anthropology, Ann Arbor; Zureik, E. (1978), "Values, Social Organization and Technological Change in the Arab World," in A. Zahlan, Ed. *Technology Transfer and Change in the Arab World*. Pergamon, London, pp. 185–199.

[2] See Segafi-nejad and Belfield (1980) for an extensive bibliography of works on international technology transfer during the 1960–70s. Much of Hofstede's work focuses on generalizable societal differences which allow comparison between cultures. Bond's work, in conjunction with Hofstede, adds to this stream of inquiry, cf: Hofstede, 1980, 1983, 1986; Hofstede and Bond, 1988. Nor is there clean delineation between the disciplines, mixing national cultural and organizational culture, and economic assessment, cf. Cunningham and Sarayrah (1994), Zaheer and Zaheer (1997), Hofstede, Bond, and Luk (1993), Bond and Hofstede (1989), Tung (1993).

[3] The dominance of primary group relations characterizes intimate, personal, informal, noncontractual, comprehensive and extensive relations. Once entering into a personal relationship, individuals engage in an unlimited commitment to one another. They are committed members of a group rather than independent individuals who constantly assert their apartness and privacy. Their affiliation to a group and group solidarity are thus primal.

[4] This latter feature of Arab society has a tendency to create "... a strong determination to adopt and imitate the most fashionable and technologically sophisticated innovations" although "the process of development continues to be hindered by prevailing socioeconomic and political structures and by a network of authoritarian relationships" (Barakat, 1993:26).

References

Abdul Ghani, J. and S. Al-Sakran (1988), "The Changing Data Processing Environment in Saudi Arabia," *Information & Management*, Vol. 14, No. 2, February, pp. 61–66.

Abu-Lughod, Lila (1990), "Anthropology's Orient: The Boundaries of Theory on the Arab World in Theory, Politics and the Arab World" *Critical Responses*. Sharabi. Hisham, Ed. Routledge, New York.

Ahmed, Akbar (1992), *Postmodernism and Islam*. Routledge, London and New York.

Al-Hegelan, A. and M. Palmer (1985), "Bureaucracy and Development in Saudi Arabia," *Middle East Journal*, Vol. 39, pp. 48–68.

Ali, Abbas J. (1990), "Management Theory in a Transitional Society: The Arab's Experience," *International Studies of Management and Organization*, Vol. 20, No. 3, pp. 7–35.

Al-Meer, A. A. (1990), "Organizational Commitment: A Comparison of Westerners, Asians and Saudis," *International Studies of Management and Organization*, Vol. 19, No. 2, pp. 74–84.

Asad, Talal (1986), *The Idea of an Anthropology of Islam*. Georgetown University Center for Contemporary Arab Studies, Washington, D.C.

Atiyyah, S. H. (1989), "Determinants of Computer System Effectiveness in Saudi Arabian Public Organizations," *International Studies of Management and Organization*, Vol. 19, No. 2, pp. 85–103.

Barakat, Halim (1993), *The Arab World*. University of CA Press, Berkeley.

Bond, M. H. and G. Hofstede (1989), "The Cash Value of Confucian Values," *Human Systems Management*, Vol. 8, pp. 195–200.

Bum, J. M. (1995), "The New Cultural Revolution: The Impact of EDI on Asia," *Journal of Global Information Management*, Vol. 3, No. 4, pp. 16–23.

Contractor, F. J. and T. Sagafi-nejad (1981), "International Technology Transfer: Major Issues and Policy Responses," *Journal of International Business Studies*, Fall, pp. 113–135.

Cuningham, R. B. and Y. K. Sarayrah (1994), "The Human Factor in Technology Transfer," *International Journal of Public Administration*, Vol. 17, No. 8, pp. 1419–1436.

El-Guindi, Gadwa (1981), "Veiling Infitah with Muslim Ethic: Egypt's Contemporary Islamic Movement," *Social Problems*, Vol. 28, pp. 465–483.

Ein-Dor, P., E. Segev, and M. Orgad (1992), "The Effect of National Culture on IS: Implications for International Information Systems," *Journal of Global Information Management*, Vol. 1, No. 1, pp. 33–44.

Fisher, M. J. (1980), *Competing Ideologies and Social Structures in the Persian Gulf in Wêe Persian Gulf States*, A. J. Cottrell, Ed. Johns Hopkins University Press, Baltimore, pp. 62–78.

Goodman, S. E. and J. D. Green (1992), "Computing in the Middle East," *Communications of the ACM*, Vol. 35, No. 8, pp. 21–25.

Hofstede, G. (1980), *Culture's Consequences: International Differences in Work-Related Values*. Sage, Beverly Hills, CA.

Hofstede, G. (1983), "Dimensions of national cultures in fifty countries and three regions," in J. B. Deregowski, S. Dziurawiec, and R. C. Annis, Eds. *Expiscations in Cross-cultural Psychology*. Swets and Zeitlinger, Lise Netherlands.

Hofstede, G. (1986), "Cultural differences in teaching and learning, International," *Journal of Intercultural Relations*, Vol. 10, No. 3, pp. 301–320.

Hofstede, G. (1991), *Cultures and Organizations: Software of the Mind*. McGraw-Hill Book Company, London.

Hofstede, G. and M. H. Bond (1988), "The Confucius connection: From Cultural Roots to Economic Growth," *Organizational Dynamics*, Vol. 16, No. 4, pp. 4–21.

Hofstede, G., M. H. Bond, and C. Luk (1993), "Individual Perceptions of Organizational Cultures: A Methodological Treatise on Levels of Analysis," *Organization Studies*, Vol. 14, No. 4, pp. 483–503.

Huxley, F. (1978), *Wasita in a Lebanese Context: Social Exchange Among Villagers and Outsiders*. Anthropological Papers #64, University of Michigan Museum of Anthropology, Ann Arbor.

Kedia, B. L. and R. S. Bhagat (1988), "Cultural Constraints on Transfer of Technology Across Nations: Implications for Research in International and

Comparative Management," *Academy of Management Review*, Vol. 13, No. 4, pp. 559–571.

Khan, E. H. (1991), "Organization and Management of Information Systems Functions: Comparative Study of Selected Organizations in Bahrein," *Information & Management*, Vol. 21, No. 2, pp. 73–87.

Knight, J. (1993), *Contumacious Computer in Informational Technology in Support of Economic Development*, W. W. Cotterman and M. B. Malik, Eds. Georgia State University Business Press, Atlanta.

Mahmood, M. A. and L. A. Gemoets (1995), "Information Technology Transfer and Diffusion to Mexico: A Preliminary Analysis," *Journal of Global Information Management*, Vol. 3, No. 4, pp. 5–15.

Patai, Raphael (1973), *The Arab Mind*. Scribners, New York.

Piscatori and James P. (1986), *Islam in a World of Nation-States*. Cambridge University Press, Cambridge.

Sagafi-nejad, T. and R. Belfield (1980), *Transnational Corporations, Technology Transfer and Development: A Bibliographic Sourcebook*. Book #3 in the Technology Transfer Trilogy. Pergamon, New York.

Tung, R. L. (1993), "Managing Cross-National and Intra-National Diversity," *Human Resource Management*, Vol. 32, No. 4, Winter, pp. 461–477.

Zaheer, S. and A. Zaheer (1997), "Country Effects on Information Seeking in Global Electronic Networks," *Journal of International Business Studies*, Vol. 28, No. 1, pp. 77–100.

Zureik, E. (1978), "Values, Social Organization and Technological Change in the Arab World," in A. Zahlan, Ed. *Technology Transfer and Change in the Arab World*. Pergamon, London, pp. 185–199.

Reproduced from *Journal of Global Information Management*, Vol. 6, No. 3, Summer 1998, pp. 29–38. Reprinted with permission from Information Resources Management Association.

About the authors

Karen D. Loch is an Associate Professor of Decision Sciences at Georgia State University. Her current research interests span international IT studies, security and ethical concerns, and knowledge management. Loch has published in journals such as *Communications of the ACM, MIS Quarterly, Information Systems Journal, Academy of Management Executive, Journal of Global Information Management*, and one book on International IT Education. She serves as AE for *The Journal of Global Information Technology Management*, and as review board member for *Information Resources Management Journal, The Journal of Global Information Management*.

Carole E. Hill is a Professor of Anthropology at Georgia State University. She has published research in the areas of health care policy, health behavior, and cultural knowledge in Costa Rica, the U.S. South, and the Middle East.

She has published 8 books and over 60 articles in journals such as *American Anthropologist, Social Science and Medicine, Human Organization,* and *Anthropological Quarterly.* She is an editor for the *Journal of Qualitative Research* and has served as President of the Society of Applied Anthropology.

Detmar W. Straub is a Professor of Computer Information Systems at Georgia State University. He has published research in the areas of technological innovation, computer security, and international IT studies. He has published over 60 papers in journals such as *Management Science, Organization Science, Information Systems Research, MIS Quarterly, Communications of the ACM, Journal of MIS, Computers & Security, Information & Management,* and *Sloan Management Review.* He currently serves as an Associate Editor for Information Systems Research and has held several editor and AE positions for other leading IS journals.

Kamal M. El-Sheshai is a Professor of Decisions Sciences and Interim Director for the Institute of International Business at Georgia State University. His principle research interests include international IT studies and forecasting. He has published in such journals as *Retail Management, Journal of Accounting Research,* and *Management Accounting.* He serves as reviewer for several journals, including *Decision Sciences, Accounting Review,* and the *International Journal of Forecasting.*

Questions for discussion

1   Imagine you are an Arab manager in charge of implementing an IT transfer for a multinational corporation. What salient cultural factors would you explain to your American superior to ensure a successful implementation of the IT transfer? How would you explain the IT transfer to your Arab co-workers?
2   How would you structure your IT transfer taking into account the importance of national culture?
3   How is the perception of technology influenced by the factors listed in Table 9.2? How does that perception affect a successful implementation of IT transfer?
4   Given the constants of national Arab culture, how would you shape the IT transfer to reflect the values, social and cultural norms of Arab culture in order for the IT transfer to be more successful?
5   Can you think of cultural differences between the American and Arab cultures that affect the IT transfer? For example, Americans value individualism, personal freedom and free access to information. How does that contrast with the Arab culture's emphasis on family, the kinship group, and Islam?

Part Three

The Role of Culture in IT Use and Outcomes

In this section, we include four readings that examine culture's influence on patterns of IT use and related outcomes among different cultural groups. 'IT use' relates to specific behaviors as it pertains to how certain groups and individuals interact with a given technology to achieve their desired goals. The first article examines culture's influence on IT use and outcomes from an organizational perspective while the other three do so taking a cross-cultural (national) focus. Of the national cultures, the following eight countries are studied: Egypt, Finland, Hong Kong, Korea, Mexico, Peru, Sweden, and the United States.

The reading selections by Calhoun et al. (2002), Leidner et al. (1999), and Rose et al. (2003) examine how national culture values shape individual attitudes and use patterns with respect to information technology. The fundamental question being addressed in such research is 'will the same patterns of use be evident across cultural groups or will use patterns vary based upon cultural differences?' The implication here is that designers of information technology must take into consideration the particular cultural context such technologies are embedded within. Cultural differences may influence how different groups actually use the technology – perhaps in ways totally unanticipated by its designers. Likewise, IT professionals and managers who are responsible for the deployment of information technologies must consider the cultural environment; particularly if such deployment takes place in a multi-national context. Under such situations, the implications for implementation strategy, change management, and training strategies may be far-reaching.

The article by Leidner et al. (1999) is a study of executive information systems (EIS) used among Mexican, Swedish, and US managers. Using Hofstede's dimensions of national culture, they studied national culture's moderating influence on the relationship between EIS use and senior management perceptions of EIS use outcomes. Specifically, they found that perceptions of certain EIS use outcomes (e.g. decision-making speed) were more favorably perceived in countries with lower power distance and uncertainty avoidance than in countries high in uncertainty avoidance and power distance.

The Calhoun et al. (2002) article examines the relationship between national culture and information overload from IT use. What is of particular interest with this study is their use of Hall's (1976) conceptualization of culture along the dimensions of being high versus low in context. A low context culture is one where individuals have a preference for quantifiable data and for information to be conveyed directly. In contrast, individuals from high context cultures prefer a communication style that is less direct where parties draw inferences from non explicit information. These researchers found that users from high context cultures (Korea) experienced higher levels of information overload from IT use than lower context cultures like the USA.

Thus, it appears that information systems users from high context cultures will be less likely to use a given IT, particularly if that system provides more information than individuals are able to cope with.

Rose et al. (2003) draw from Hall (1983) to examine how values relating to the use of time in performing tasks (polychronism vs. monochronism) were related to concern over website delays (an IT outcome). Cultures that favor polychronism will have a stronger preference for the performance of activities in parallel than will those in more monochronic (preference for performing single activities at a time) cultures. Using these dimensions of culture, they found that subjects from polychronic cultures (Egypt and Peru) tended to be less concerned with website delays as those from monochronic cultures (USA and Finland).

To summarize, three of the four readings (Calhoun et al., 2002; Leidner et al., 1999, and Rose et al., 2003) examine culture's influence on IT use and outcomes from a cross-cultural (e.g. national) perspective. This seems to be consistent with the historical trend of this vein of research. A subset of this research stream is one that uses national culture as a variable of interest in GSS research. Collectively, the GSS research (Chung and Adams, 1997; Mejias et al., 1996; Quaddus and Tung, 2002; Tan et al., 1998; Watson et al., 1994) provides strong evidence that the effect of computer-mediated communications tools on certain group processes and outcomes may be dependent to some extent on culture. In particular, Hofstede's values of individualism vs. collectivism and power distance figure prominently in these findings.

While there is a significant body of research examining culture's influence on IT use and outcomes from a cross-cultural perspective, research that examines similar questions from an organizational culture or sub-culture perspective seems to be less focused and a bit fragmented. There are, however, a number of excellent studies worth mentioning that investigate how values at the organizational or even sub-culture levels influence patterns of IT use and certain outcomes such as implementation success. For example, McDermott and Stock (1999) found group-oriented organizational cultures to be positively related to managerial satisfaction with advanced manufacturing technology (AMT) outcomes, while rational-oriented cultures were closely associated with competitive success in AMT implementation.

Another study by Harper and Utley (2001) showed that people-oriented organizational cultures tended to experience greater levels of implementation success than those with more production-oriented cultures, while Tolsby (1998) found that the cultural values of a military organization contributed to participants failing to take ownership of newly implemented information systems. Additionally, Kanungo (1998) found that computer network use was found to have a stronger impact on user satisfaction in more task-oriented as opposed to people-oriented organizational cultures.

Another theme of research at the organizational culture level is one that examines the relationship between organizational values and knowledge management (KM) use and outcomes. Several such studies were specifically interested in cultural values that are associated with knowledge management success. The common finding across these studies is that organizational values influence KM success (DeLong and Fahey, 2000), KM infrastructure capability (Gold et al., 2001), KM technology use (Alavi et al., 2005–2006; Leidner et al., 2006), and perception of individual ownership of information and knowledge (Jarvenpaa and Staples, 2001).

We've selected a study by Leidner et al. (2006) as a representative sample from this group of studies at the intersection of KM and organizational culture. In this study, the researchers use a case study approach to compare and contrast the cultures and knowledge management approaches of two global organizations. Whereas in one organization the KM effort became little more than an information repository, KM in the second organization evolved into a highly collaborative system fostering the formation of electronic communities. This article helps to illustrate how firms' attempts to launch corporate-wide KM initiatives may be strongly influenced by the organizational culture. Furthermore, it helps demonstrate how the use of KM technology and the outcomes of such use may evolve in unanticipated ways in response to the organization's cultural values.

References

Alavi, M., T. Kayworth, and D. Leidner (2005–2006), "An Empirical Examination of the Influence of Organizational Culture on Knowledge Management Initiatives," *Journal of MIS*, Vol. 22, No. 3, winter, pp. 160–191.

Calhoun, K. J., J. T. C. Teng, and M. J. Cheon (2002), "Impact of National Culture on Information Technology Usage Behavior: An Exploratory Study of Decision Making in Korea and the USA," *Behavior & Information Technology*, Vol. 21, No. 4, pp. 293–302.

Chau, P. Y. K., M. Cole, A. P. Massey, M. Montoya-Weiss, and R. M. O'Keefe (2002), "Cultural Differences in the Online Behavior of Consumers," *Communications of the ACM*, Vol. 45, No. 10, October, pp. 138–143.

Chung, I. K. and C. R. Adams (1997), "A Study on the Characteristics of Group Decision Making Behavior: Cultural Difference Perspective of Korean vs. U.S.," *Journal of Global Information Management*, Vol. 5, No. 3, summer, pp. 18–29.

DeLong, D. W. and L. Fahey (2000), "Diagnosing Cultural Barriers To Knowledge Management," *Academy of Management Executive*, Vol. 14, No. 4, November, pp. 113–127.

Gold, A. H., A. Malhotra, and A. H. Segars (2001), "Knowledge Management: An Organizational Capabilities Perspective," *Journal of Management Information Systems*, Vol. 18, No. 1, pp. 185–214.

Hall, E. T. (1976), *Beyond Culture*. Anchor, Garden City, CA.

Hall, E. T. (1983), *The Dance of Life: The Other Dimension of Time*. Anchor, New York, NY.

Harper, G. R. and D. R. Utley (2001), "Organizational Culture and Successful Information Technology Implementation," *Engineering Management Journal*, Vol. 13, No. 2, pp. 11–15.

Jarvenpaa, S. L. and S. D. Staples (2001), "Exploring Perceptions of Organizational Ownership of Information and Expertise," *Journal of Management Information Systems*, Vol. 18, No. 1, pp. 151–183.

Kangungo, S. (1988), "An Empirical Study of Organizational Culture and Network-Based Computer Use," *Computers in Human Behavior*, Vol. 14, No. 1, pp. 79–91.

Leidner, D. E., S. Carlsson, J. Elam, and M. Corrales (1999), "Mexican and Swedish Managers' Perceptions of the Impact of EIS on Organizational Intelligence," *Decision Sciences*, Vol. 30, No. 3, summer, pp. 633–661.

Leidner, D. L., M. Alavi, and T. R. Kayworth (2006), "The Role of Culture in Knowledge Management: A Case Study of Two Global Firms," *The International Journal of e-Collaboration*, Vol. 2, No. 1, pp. 17–40.

McDermott, C. M. and G. N. Stock (1999), "Organizational Culture and Advanced Manufacturing Technology Implementation," *Journal of Operations Management*, Vol. 17, pp. 521–533.

Mejias, R. J., M. M. Shepherd, and M. Morgan (1996), "Consensus and Perceived Satisfaction and Consensus Levels: A Cross Cultural Comparison of GSS and Non-GSS Outcomes Within and Between the US and Mexico," *Journal of Management Information Systems*, Vol. 13, No. 3, winter, pp. 137–161.

Quaddus, M. A. and L. L. Tung (2002), "Explaining Cultural Differences in Decision Conferencing," *Communications of the ACM*, Vol. 45, No. 8, August, pp. 93–98.

Rose, G. M., R. Evaristo, and D. Straub (2003), "Culture and Consumer Responses to Web Download Time: A Four-Continent Study of Mono and Polychronism," *IEEE Transaction on Engineering Management*, Vol. 50, No. 1, February, pp. 31–43.

Tan, B. C. Y., K. K. Wei, R. T. Watson, D. L. Clapper, and E. McLean (1998), "Computer-Mediated Communication and Majority Influence: Assessing the Impact in an Individualistic and a Collectivist Culture," *Management Science*, Vol. 44, No. 9, pp. 1263–1278.

Tolsby, J. (1998), "Effects of Organizational Culture on a Large Scale IT Introduction Effort: A Case Study of the Norwegian Army's EDBLF Project," *European Journal of Information Systems*, Vol. 7, No. 2, pp. 108–114.

Watson, R. T., T. H. Ho, and K. S. Raman (1994), "Culture: A Fourth Dimension of Group Support Systems," *Communications of the ACM*, Vol. 37, No. 10, pp. 45–55.

10 The Role of Culture in Knowledge Management: A Case Study of Two Global Firms

Dorothy Leidner, Maryam Alavi and Timothy Kayworth

Abstract: Knowledge management approaches have been broadly considered to entail either a focus on organizing communities or a focus on the process of knowledge creation, sharing, and distribution. While these two approaches are not mutually exclusive and organizations may adopt aspects of both, the two approaches entail different challenges. Some organizational cultures might be more receptive to the community approach whereas others are more receptive to the process approach. Although culture has been widely cited as a challenge in knowledge management initiatives and many studies have considered the implications of organizational culture on knowledge sharing, few empirical studies address the influence of culture on the approach taken to knowledge management. Using a case study approach to compare and contrast the cultures and knowledge management approaches of two organizations, the study suggests the ways in which organizational culture influences knowledge management initiatives as well as the evolution of knowledge management in organizations. Whereas in one organization, the KM effort became little more than an information repository, in the second organization, the KM effort evolved into a highly collaborative system fostering the formation of electronic communities.

Introduction

Knowledge management efforts are often seen to encounter difficulties from corporate culture and, as a result, have limited impact (DeLong and Fahey, 2000; O'Dell and Grayson, 1998). An Ernst and Young study identified culture as the biggest impediment to knowledge transfer citing the inability to change people's behaviors as the biggest hindrance to managing knowledge (Watson, 1998). In another study of 453 firms, over half indicated that organizational culture was a major barrier to success in their knowledge management initiatives (Ruggles, 1998). The importance of culture is also evident from consulting firms such as KPMG who report that a major aspect of knowledge management initiatives involves working to shape organizational cultures that hinders their knowledge management programs (KPMG, 1998). These findings and others (Hasan and Gould, 2001; Schultze and Boland, 2000) help demonstrate the profound impact that culture may have on knowledge management practice and of the crucial role of senior management in fostering cultures conducive to these practices (Brown and Duguid, 2000; Davenport et al, 1998; KPMG, 1998; Gupta and Govindarajan, 2000; Hargadon, 1998; von Krogh, 1998; DeLong and Fahey, 2000).

Studies on the role of culture in knowledge management have focused on such issues as the effect of organizational culture on knowledge sharing behaviors (DeLong and Fahey, 2000; Jarvenpaa and Staples, 2001) and the influence of culture on the capabilities provided by KM (Gold et al, 2001) as well as on the success of the KM initiative (Baltahazard and Cooke, 2003). More specifically, Baltahazard and Cooke (2003) ascertained that constructive cultures (emphasizing values related to encouragement, affiliation, achievement, and self-actualization) tended to achieve greater KM success. Similarly, Gold et al (2001) found that more supportive, encouraging organizational cultures positively influence KM infrastructure capability and resulting KM practice. Finally, Jarvenpaa & Staples (2001) determined that organizational cultures rating high in solidarity (tendency to pursue shared objectives) will result in a perception of knowledge as being owned by the organization, which in turn leads to greater levels of knowledge sharing.

While studies have shown that culture influences knowledge management and in particular, knowledge sharing, there is little research on the broader aspects of the nature and means through which organizational culture influences the overall approach taken to knowledge management in a firm. The purpose of this research is to examine how organizational culture influences knowledge management initiatives. We use a case study methodology to help ascertain the relationship of the organizational culture to the knowledge management approaches within two companies. The following section discusses knowledge management approaches and organizational culture. The third presents the methodology. The fourth section presents the two cases and the fifth discusses the case findings, the implications and the conclusions.

Knowledge management approaches and organizational culture

Knowledge management approaches

Knowledge can be defined as a form of high value information (either explicit or tacit) combined with experience, context, interpretation, and reflection that is ready to apply to decisions and actions (Davenport et al, 1998). While all firms may have a given "pool" of knowledge resources distributed throughout their respective organization, they may be unaware of the existence of these resources as well as how to effectively leverage them for competitive advantage. Therefore, firms must engage in activities that seek to build, sustain, and leverage these intellectual resources. These types of activities, generally characterized as knowledge management, can be defined as the conscious practice or process of systematically identifying, capturing, and leveraging knowledge resources to help firms compete more effectively (Hansen et al, 1999; O'Dell and Grayson, 1998).

There are two fundamental approaches to knowledge management: the process and the practice approaches. The process approach attempts to codify organizational knowledge through formalized controls, processes and technologies (Hansen et al, 1999). Organizations adopting the process approach may implement explicit policies governing how knowledge is to be collected, stored, and disseminated throughout the organization. The process approach frequently involves the use of information technologies, such as intranets, data warehousing, knowledge repositories, decision support tools, and groupware (Ruggles, 1998), to enhance the quality and speed of knowledge creation and distribution in the organizations. The main criticisms of this process approach are that it fails to capture much of the tacit knowledge embedded in firms and that it forces individuals into fixed patterns of thinking (DeLong and Fahey, 2000; Brown and Duguid, 2000; von Grogh, 2000; Hargadon, 1998).

In contrast, the practice approach to knowledge management assumes that a great deal of organizational knowledge is tacit in nature and that formal controls, processes, and technologies are not suitable for transmitting this type of understanding. Rather than building formal systems to manage knowledge, the focus of this approach is to build the social environments or communities of practice necessary to facilitate the sharing of tacit understanding (Brown and Duguid, 2000; DeLong and Fahey, 2000; Gupta and Govindarajan, 2000; Wenger and Snyder, 2000; Hansen et al, 1999). These communities are informal social groups that meet regularly to share ideas, insights, and best practices (see Table 10.1).

Drawing from this discussion, some key questions emerge. First, how does culture affect organizations' approaches (e.g. process or practice) to knowledge management and secondly; as organizations pursue these initiatives, how do cultural influences affect the KM activities of knowledge generation, codification, and transfer? To address these questions, it is necessary to explore the concept of organizational culture.

Organizational culture

Schein (1985) defines organizational culture as a set of implicit assumptions held by members of a group that determines how the group behaves and responds to its environment. At its deepest level, culture consists of core values and beliefs that are embedded tacit preferences about what the organization

Table 10.1 *The process vs. practice approaches to knowledge management*

	Process approach	Practice approach
Type of knowledge supported	Explicit knowledge – codified in rules, tools, and processes	Mostly tacit knowledge – unarticulated knowledge not easily captured or codified
Means of transmission	Formal controls, procedures, and standard operating procedures with heavy emphasis on information technologies to support knowledge creation, codification, and transfer of knowledge	Informal social groups that engage in story telling and improvisation
Benefits	Provides structure to harness generated ideas and knowledge Achieves scale in knowledge reuse	Provides an environment to generate and transfer high value tacit knowledge Provides spark for fresh ideas and responsiveness to changing environment
Disadvantages	Fails to tap into tacit knowledge. May limit innovation and forces participants into fixed patterns of thinking	Can result in inefficiency. Abundance of ideas with no structure to implement them
Role of information technology	Heavy investment in IT to connect people with reusable codified knowledge	Moderate investment in IT to facilitate conversations and transfer of tacit knowledge

should strive to attain and how it should do it (DeLong and Fahey, 2000). These tacit values and beliefs determine the more observable organizational norms and practices that consist of rules, expectations, rituals and routines, stories and myths, symbols, power structures, organizational structures, and control systems (Bloor and Dawson, 1994; Johnson, 1992). In turn, these norms and practices drive subsequent behaviors through providing the social context through which people communicate and act (DeLong and Fahey, 2000). Putting this into the context of knowledge management, organizational culture determines the social context (consisting of norms and practices) that determines "who is expected to control what knowledge, as well as who must share it, and who can hoard it (Delong and Fahey, 2000: 118)". Figure 10.1 illustrates this conceptual linkage between culture and knowledge management behavior.

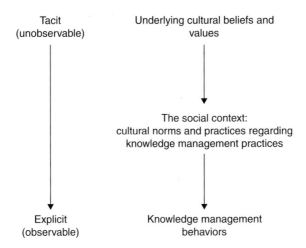

Figure 10.1   *The impact of organizational culture on knowledge management behaviors*

As Figure 10.1 depicts, the social context (consisting of norms and practices) is the "medium" for transmission of underlying values and beliefs into specific knowledge management behaviors. While Figure 10.1 is useful to explain the conceptual linkage between culture and knowledge management behavior, further explanation is needed to inform our understanding of the types of cultures that exist within organizations.

A number of theories have attempted to define culture at the organizational level. Wallach (1983) conceptualizes organizational culture as a composite of three distinctive cultural types: bureaucratic, innovative, and supportive. In bureaucratic cultures, there are clear lines of authority, and work is highly regulated and systematized. Innovative cultures are characterized as being creative, risk-taking environments where burnout, stress, and pressure are commonplace. In contrast, supportive cultures are those that provide a friendly, warm environment and where workers tend to be fair, open, and honest. From Wallach's standpoint, any given firm will have all three types of culture; each to varying levels of degree. Wallach's cultural dimensions were developed based upon a synthesis of other major organizational culture indices.

Wallach's cultural dimensions were applied by Kanungo et al (2001) to study the relationship between IT strategy and organizational culture. Part of the attractiveness of Wallach's dimensions, in comparison with other commonly used cultural indices such as the Organizational Culture Profile scale (O'Reilly and Caldwell, 1991), the Competing Values Framework (Quinn and Rohrbaugh, 1983), or the Organizational Value Congruence Scale (Enz, 1986) is that it is highly intuitive. Managers can readily identify with the descriptions of the three general culture types. Consistent with Kanungo et al

(2001), we will employ Wallach's approach to describe organizational cultures. Specifically, we are interested in the question: how does organizational culture influence knowledge management initiatives?

Methodology

A case study method, involving multiple (two) cases was used. The approach of the study is depicted in Figure 10.2. The figure, based on the work of Yin (1994), displays the replication approach to multiple-case studies. As illustrated in Figure 10.2, the initial step in the study involved the development of a theoretical framework on the relationship between organizational culture and organizational knowledge management (KM) strategies. This step was then followed by the selection of the two specific cases (the data collection sites) and the design of the data collection protocol. Following the case selection and data collection steps, the individual case reports were developed. A cross-case analysis of the findings was then undertaken. This analysis provided the basis for the theoretical and normative discussions and implications presented in the final section of the paper.

The two case studies involve two very large and global corporations: Company A and Company B. Company A is a global consumer goods company with 369 000 employees worldwide. The company is headquartered in the U.S. and operates in four other regions: Europe, Middle East and Africa, Central and South America, and Asia. The company revenues consistently exceed $20 billion. In Company A, large-scale knowledge management projects were initiated at the North American region in 1996. Company B is a high-tech global company with multiple product lines and services. Similar to Company A, Company B is headquartered in the U.S. and operates globally in other regions of the world. With approximately 316 000 employees, its revenues exceed $80 billion. Large-scale knowledge management projects were initiated in Company B in 1995.

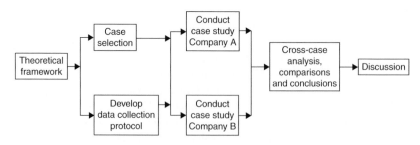

Figure 10.2   *Case study methodology adapted from Yin 1994*

These two particular companies were selected for the purpose of this study for the following reasons. First, significant opportunities and challenges are associated with knowledge management activities in large and geographically dispersed companies. Thus, identification of factors such as organizational culture that may influence KM outcomes in this type of organization can potentially lead to high payoffs. Second, considering the high levels of organizational resources required for implementation of large-scale knowledge management initiatives, these initiatives are most likely encountered in very large firms. Thus, the phenomenon of interest to these researchers could be best investigated in the context of very large firms with an established track-record in KM projects. Lastly, past contacts that one of the researchers had with these two firms facilitated their recruitment as case study sites.

Data collection

Data for this study were collected through semi-structured interviews with a small group of managers and professional employees at the two company locations in the U.S. Identical approaches to data collection were used at Company A and Company B[1]. Six individuals at each of the two companies were interviewed. In each of the two companies, three of the interviewees were the current or the potential users of the KM systems. The remaining three interviewees in each company were the KMS sponsors or supporters.

The interviews took between 45 and 85 minutes and were conducted between October 2001 and January 2002. All the interviews were tape recorded and then transcribed for data analysis. The interviews all followed the same protocol. The informants were first asked to characterize their organization's culture in their own words. The three cultures described by Wallach were then portrayed and the informants were requested to identify which one best described their organization. The interviewees were next asked to describe and characterize the KM practices in their company. A set of specific questions guided the discussions of these practices. For example, each informant was asked to describe the specific KM activities that he/she engaged in and to discuss the affects of these activities on the self and/or on the peers. Each informant was also asked to describe any resistance and impediments to KM that he/she might have noticed in the organization. The same interviewer, using identical data collection protocols, conducted all the interviews in Company A and Company B. The interviewer carefully read the transcripts to ensure accuracy.

---

[1]After this initial data collection, we returned to Company B a year later and conducted more widespread interviews across different business units. This data collection and analysis is discussed in Alavi et al (2005).

Data analysis

An author not involved in the interviews, and hence having no predisposed interpretation of the transcripts, conducted the data analysis. Based upon the transcribed interviews, twelve profiles were written, each one based upon the perspective of a single informant. These profiles described the informants' perspective of culture and their perspective of KM. The profiles of informants for Company A were compared and contrasted with each other, as were those of Company B. Cases for each company, reported in the next section, were then written based upon the within-case analysis. The cases for each company were then interpreted from the perspective of how the culture appeared to be influencing the organizational KM initiative. This is also reported in the next section. After the two cases and their within-case analysis were complete, a cross-case comparison and contrast was undertaken, leading to the formulation of the discussion section.

Case descriptions and analyses

Knowledge management at Company A (Alpha)

Knowledge management at Alpha began as a top-down idea, courted by senior management "as a way of helping the company become more leading edge" according to one informant. A small group of eight or nine individuals at the headquarters was charged with driving knowledge management and facilitating knowledge sharing. As a result of larger issues surfacing, most notably the economic downturn that rocked US-based businesses in early 2000, the top level initiative "fell into the background" and the small dedicated group was disbanded. Thus, at the organizational level KM was an idea that received neither funding nor action. However, at the business unit level, successful KM initiatives have been built around intranet or around Lotus Notes team rooms.

Intranet-based KM projects

One initiative in the marketing area of the corporate headquarters is called MIC – marketing information center. MIC serves the global marketing community of several thousand individuals around the world. It is an intranet-based library containing links to agencies, compensations, human resource information and contracts, among other things. MIC is opportunity-oriented rather than problem-oriented. The members did not use the community to post a problem inquiry and await responses, but rather to look for ideas performed in other parts of the company and think about adopting the ideas to their local group.

MIC is intended to be a catalyst for collaboration and to "propel a universal worldwide marketing community." Because the chief marketing officer no longer allowed the budgeting of glossy manuals or brochures, MIC was widely accepted as the primary means of obtaining such "static" information. In fact, as attempts were made to include best practices in MIC, the initiative encountered resistance. Explains one informant: "we could never nudge the culture enough to have people understand and be motivated to enter their information." Another informant felt that there were challenges in overcoming "people's fear of being judged for their ideas and their indifference to yet another information site."

CM connection (CMC) is another KM initiative within the North America marketing unit. This is a web-based marketing repository used to disseminate information such that wholesalers that are responsible for store level execution can have access to the most recent information on how to merchandise the latest promotions. As with MIC, the major impact of CMC has been the reduction of the number of printed catalogs, in this case by 80%. Among the challenges experienced with CM connection has been convincing content providers to own the information in the sense of both providing it and keeping it up-to-date. Another issue has been that CM connection is seen by some as distracting from their relationships with clients. Even while MCC may reduce the amount of time spent traveling, this is not necessarily welcome in "a sales and marketing-oriented relationship company because you are taking away relationship points."

The Human Resources unit, with the Corporate Functions unit, also has an intranet-based KM, referred to as My Career. My Career is designed for managers and employees to help provide information about what tools, classes, and coaching is available for development. One of the goals of My Career has been to merge all of the training information into one place.

Many such intranet-based KM projects have been developed throughout Alpha; so many that the "portal project" was initiated to alleviate the problem of "too much information in too many places, different IDs and passwords for each database, having to remember what is in the database to even go to get the information." However, despite some initial receptiveness to the idea from the head of the New Business Ventures unit, IT budgets were frozen and the project never got underway.

The common thread running through the intranet-based KM projects at Alpha is that they all are geared toward housing static information with the most major of impacts being the reduction in printed catalogs. Among the greatest resistances, according to informants, is that these KM projects appear to try to standardize work practices in a company comprised of "creative assertive people who want to do it their way and make their own individual mark."

Lotus-Notes-based KM

Lotus Notes forms the basis of other KM initiatives within Alpha. What distinguishes the Lotus-Notes-based KM projects from the intranet-based KM projects is the added focus on facilitating teamwork. The Lotus-Notes-based initiatives developed independently from the intranet-based initiatives. The North American marketing group developed a Lotus-Notes-based community of interest. The system contains examples of briefs, shared research, shared examples of different sites, and information on internal research. This micro KM has 50–60 regular users.

An important feature of the system is that whenever new information is added, community members receive an email. In this way, members visit the community when new information that is relevant to them has been posted. This KM project has served as a means of sharing best practices. For example, a marketing manager from the UK posted information concerning a successful auction initiative which was then emulated by five other countries. On an individual level, the KM has helped to increase the frequency of communication among members of the community. Similar, HR developed HR Source – a Lotus-Notes-based "general bulletin board" where meeting notes, follow-up action items, strategy documents, and work plans are placed. It is shared by the HR community on a global basis.

Lotus Notes is also the platform used to develop team rooms. The individual responsible for managing team rooms for North America has what he calls "the 6-month rule": if a team room is not getting regular utilization over 6 months, it is deleted so that they can save money on the server expense. He says that he deletes about 70–80% of team rooms. He thinks the lack of reward is the biggest barrier toward KM system usage:

> people who don't have technology in their title don't take it upon themselves and are not generally rewarded for exploiting technology.

Also, content management is a barrier: "this is the responsibility of the end user but it is perceived as the responsibility of the technology group." However, a marketing manager had another opinion, attributing lack of use of the team rooms to self-preservation:

> even if someone took the time to put something out there, even if I knew it was there, went and got it, had the time to review it, and understand it, I am going to create this other thing by myself. I might look at that as input, but then it is the new XYZ program and I created it.

Analysis of Alpha's knowledge management: the impact of culture on KM behaviors and outcomes

The perceptions of culture

While each individual interviewed gave their own perception of the culture at Alpha and the perceptions naturally contain some variance, there is a marked theme running through the individuals' views. Informants describe Alpha as "risk averse" and bureaucratic. They speak of an environment where people "don't want to be noticed," where direction is "unclear," and where "individual survival" trumps teamwork. Moreover, informants state that people "work in silos," "feel isolated," and "are afraid being criticized for their ideas." The "slow, bureaucratic, hierarchical" culture at Alpha has resulted in "silos of information." As a consequence, managers indicate that even though they have "great consumer and customer information," they "end up reinventing the wheel 1000 times." However, our informants also maintained that although they characterize the culture as bureaucratic, they also sense that Alpha is "striving" to become more innovative and supportive.

The possible impacts of culture on KM

The statements and observations of our informants point to two largely shared perspectives: (1) that the culture emphasizes the individual and (2) that the culture is in a state of transition. In understanding the impacts of KM, one can see the influence of the individuality within Alpha. Table 10.2 lists the characteristics of culture, characteristics of the KM initiatives, and characteristics of KM behaviors as expressed by the informants.

At work within Alpha seems to be a tension between a culture that demands individuality and the communal aspects of KM. The informants talk about a culture that is one of "individual survival" where individuals "fear being judged for their ideas" where there is individual "isolation" and where individuals try

Table 10.2 *Characteristics of culture, KM initiatives, and KM behaviors*

Culture characteristics	KM characteristics	KM behaviors
Dominant culture is Bureaucratic	Intranet-based "static" repositories of information	Individuals access information on "as-needed basis"
Emphasis on individual: • individuals are "risk averse" • individuals fear being criticized for ideas • individuals are uneasy and prefer to go unnoticed • individuals relationships externally, particularly within the marketing unit, are perceived as critical to their success	Failed top-down effort Bottom-up initiatives largely targeted creation of repositories Some use of Lotus Notes to create team rooms Team rooms have high failure rate	Individuals reluctant to contribute information Individuals reluctant to own and maintain content Individuals uncomfortable using ideas from the systems, since they do not own the idea Individuals use repository when rules prohibit printing brochures Individuals reluctant to use tools that would result in a loss of touch points with customers

to go unnoticed. The overall feeling is that of individuals trying to avoid being noticed. Such a culture does little to foster the sense of community that may be necessary to enable KM to move beyond static repositories of information into the kind of dynamic system envisioned by developers where ideas flow freely and where KM provides a catalyst for collaborative engagement. Not only are individuals reluctant to share their information for fear of "being criticized for their ideas," they are also reluctant to use information posted in a KM, for lack of credit for the idea. Such behaviors can spring from a culture that emphasizes individual ideas and contribution.

The individual aspects of the culture go well beyond individuals behaving a certain way because of a reward system, but reflects an underpinning notion that to succeed in a marketing-oriented organization, one must be creative and that creativity is perforce, of an individual nature so that to survive as an individual, one must capture ideas and only share them if they are going to be favorably judged. One must not look to others for learning or for problem solving, but might look to reuse creative ideas in some circumstances (like the auction site example from the UK) where one may tailor the idea to one's environment. It is telling that the informants speak of using outsiders (e.g. consultants) to assist with problem solving and learning, instead of attempting to use any of the existing KM to post queries, and this in spite of the fact that it is recognized that the company "reinvents the wheel 1000 times."

Another tension within Alpha seems to stem from the expectations of what "should" occur in a bureaucratic culture and what was occurring. The top-down approach to KM, an approach that would be consistent with a bureaucratic organization, had failed at Alpha. Yet despite the failure of the top-down approach to KM and the seeming success of several bottom-up approaches such as MIC and the marketing team room for the community of 50, one informant still proffered the need for top management leadership to be the key to success with KM. He considered the bottom-up approaches as "band-aid-approaches." In his opinion, power within Alpha comes "from knowledge hoarding not knowledge sharing." In order for KM to be assimilated in this environment, "behavior really has to come from the top. Leadership needs to walk the walk." In a bureaucratic culture, individuals become accustomed to clear guidance from senior management. The absence of clearly stated support from senior management may be sufficient to deter many from experimenting with the KM tools available to help them.

Summary

Alpha has many KM initiatives that have largely been developed as bottom-up initiatives. The KM tools seem well designed and housed with valuable information. The informants are able to use the tools to facilitate the retrieval of information they need in the performance of their jobs. However, the tools have not, as yet, progressed to the level of fostering collaboration. And while there are some successful communities from the standpoint of providing a place to share meeting notes and plans, the majority of team rooms remain unused and, if used, become as much a library of information as a communication tool. In some ways, the culture of Alpha appears to foster the types of KM behaviors observed, in that the individual is seen as the primary source of innovation and ideas, as opposed to the community being the ultimate source of success. Thus, individuals will use the systems as needed, but are mostly occupied with their individual roles and work and do not attribute value to the collaborative features of technology.

Knowledge management at Company B (Beta)

Beta is organized into seven major units. Our interviews were concentrated within the Innovations Services group of the consulting wing (referred to as Worldwide Services Group, or WSG) of Beta.

Knowledge management at Beta began in 1996 with the view that KM was about "codifying and sharing information," leading to the creation of "huge repositories of procedures and process approaches." It was assumed that people would go to a central site, called Intellectual Capital Management System (ICM), pull information down, and "would all be more knowledgeable." ICM is under the "protection" of the Company B Corporation. There is a process one must undertake to have information submitted and approved. The process is complicated by legalities and formalities. As a result, ICM is not used as widely as it could be. What was discovered from the initial foray into knowledge management was that the information was not being refreshed and that the approach was not complementing the way people really learned, which was through communities. Consequently, the KM initiative began to shift towards providing tools to communities that would help foster collaboration "both within teams and within locations and across the globe." Among the tools are team rooms and communities.

Team rooms

Lotus-Notes-based team rooms are widely used at Beta to coordinate virtual teams and to share important documents. Access to the databases of a team is limited to the members because of the confidential nature of a lot of the issues. The project manager, or someone delegated by the project manager, takes the responsibility of sanitizing the material and posting the most relevant parts to a community system such as OC-zone (to be discussed below) and or to the ICM, after the team's project has been completed.

The team rooms are valuable tools to help members keep track of occurrences as well as to help newly assigned members get quickly up to speed. Because of the itinerant nature of the Beta consultant's life, it is invaluable to have the documents they need stored in an easily accessible manner that does not require sending and receiving files over a network. Team room databases are also used for managing the consulting practices. It is important in helping new people with administrative tasks such as how to order a piece of computer equipment, how to order business cards, etc. The team rooms keep track of such metrics as utilization so that members of the team know "who's on the bench and who's not." One informant gave the example of a recent project she was put on at the last minute involving a selling project to a government department in another country. She was able to access all the documentation from the team room and was able to become a productive member of a new team very quickly:

> I can go in and start getting information about a particular topic and work with colleagues almost immediately. It allows me to work more easily with colleagues across disciplines.

Although the team rooms are invaluable in organizing and coordinating project teams, there are also some potential drawbacks. Some view the team rooms as engendering "a false sense of intimacy and connectedness." This sense of intimacy can be productive for the team as long as things are going well. However, "if things go south," says an informant, "you don't have the history or skill set to really deal with difficult situations." As a result, instead of "dealing with the conflict," the team is more likely to "just take someone off the team" and replace the person with another. In this sense, problems are not solved so much as they are avoided, and team members take on an expendable quality.

Communities

Communities serve members based not upon project or organizational position, but based upon interest. By 2000, a group referred to as "the organizational change (OC) group" had established a successful community of 1500 members cutting across all lines of business and was beginning to act as consultants to the other groups trying to set up communities. The OC community has gone so far as to quantify the business return of such a community, in terms of cycle time reductions and sophistication of responses to clients. The OC community is comprised of tools, events, and organization.

Tools: the technology tools at the disposal of the OC community are databases of information submitted by team rooms, including such things as white papers, projects and deliverables as well as client information. The databases also contain pictures of community members with personal information about the members.

Events: An important aspect of the OC community is the events that are organized for community members. These include monthly conference call meetings, which are generally attended by between 40 and 90 members, and the replay meetings, which draw another 40 to 70 members. In the past, the community has sponsored a face-to-face conference for members. Members often meet others for the first time, yet they already feel they know each other.

Organization: The organization of the community is managed by two community leaders. When someone requests information, or has a query to post to members, they send their message to one of the community leaders. The leader first tries to forward the message directly to a subject matter expert (SME). If the leader does not off-hand know of an appropriate SME, they will post the question to the entire group. In this event, the group members respond to the leader rather than to the community, in order to avoid inundation of messages. The leader normally receives responses within an hour and then forwards the responses to the individual with the query. The leader later sends an email to the person who made the inquiry, asking how the response was and how much time it saved. The leader says that they will receive as many as 28 responses to a particular inquiry. He or she has manually loaded a portion of what she's developed in the past seven months. There's 114 pieces of intellectual capital that they have loaded, and it is just a portion of what the leader has received.

The community has a structure that consists of a senior global board of 30 members representative of different parts of the business. There is a subject matter council that constantly scans the intellectual capital, as well as an expert council, and the health check team.

The health check team examines such things as how well members communicate with each other. They conducted an organizational network analysis to help better understand the communication networks. The team has a series of questions to help assess how they are doing in terms of high performance teaming. They use a survey that measures perceptions from the community members about what they see is happening and do a gap analysis on what is actually happening. Finally, the team does a self-assessment of where they are compared with the community maturity model developed by the OC community leaders. There is a community mission, vision and goals and they are working on capturing data to support the metrics to demonstrate value to the company and community members.

The goal is to attain level 5 maturity, considered "an adaptive organization." There are 13 areas of focus that the community leaders look at in building a sustained community. While communities are felt to be organic, there is also a community developers kit with an assessment tool to determine at what level of maturity a community is and what steps need to be taken to move the community forward. One community leader says that the purpose of the development kit "is not to confine, but to provide a road map in which to navigate and build." For this leader, the essence of "community" is "continuous learning". Of the initial KM efforts focused on information repositories, the leader says "I could see the technology coming that was going to enslave people, like an intellectual sweat shop." By contrast, the primary tools for a community are "passion and environment."

Impact of OC

One of the major impacts of the OC-zone is having a community that helps people "not feel isolated. People feel they are affiliated, that they are part of the company." Thirty percent of Beta employees do not have offices and work instead from home or from client sites. Such a work environment can easily be associated with isolation. However, the community is claimed by some to provide a clarity of purpose: "I see it as a conduit for both developing thought leadership and enabling thought leadership to get into the hearts and minds of the workers so that they all have a common vision, goals, and objectives."

Community members view the purpose of the community as a knowledge sharing forum and as a means of creating a sense of belonging. One member went so far as to suggest that she would "not be at Beta any longer if it wasn't for this community." The reason is that most of her connections at Beta have been made through the community. Also, being in the community helps her get assigned to projects. For example, the leader of a new project will call someone in the community and say that they are looking for a person with a certain profile. She finds that she gets asked to work on projects this way.

Other members refer to the community as "a supportive family" and state that within the community there will be someone who has already encountered any issue they will encounter on a project, and so the community keeps them from reinventing the wheel. The norms of operation exist to help OC-zone be as effective as possible. No one is under obligation to contribute, but individuals contribute in order to "help other people." One member credits the success of the community to the two leaders, whom she feels "in their hearts, care about the members of the community." She feels that the community is more than a community of people who like the topic of organizational change, but it is a community of people who support one another.

The primary resistance to the OC community has been the practice managers. Most of the community members report to practice managers. The practice managers are used to thinking in terms of billable hours. Indeed the performance evaluation system requires that an individual's goals support those of his or her boss. The community leaders hope that one day participating in a community will be included as a standard part of this evaluation system.

Analysis of Beta knowledge management: The impact of culture on KM behaviors and outcomes

The perceptions of culture

All of the respondents from Beta work within the same business unit. The respondents describe the culture of Beta as a blend of hierarchical and innovative. The hierarchical aspects are evident in that little innovation is undertaken until senior management has officially supported the innovation, but once senior management does give the green light to an idea "everybody jumps on it."

One aspect of culture that is highlighted by the informants is the importance of collaboration. Informants characterize the "street values" within Beta as "win, team, and execute." Beta informants recognize a duality of culture that on the one hand gives individuals control over their work and at the same time is highly supportive of the individual. The culture is autonomous in the sense of "not having someone looking over your shoulder and telling you what to do." And while there is certainly competition – everyone has objectives they are trying to meet – things "are always done in a collaborative helpful spirit."

The other dominant aspect of culture as related by the informants is that of hierarchy. The hierarchy is as much a hierarchy of experience as of structure. Community members, for example, proffered that becoming a subject matter expert is more about length of service to the company than to one's inherent knowledge. Another aspect of the bureaucratic culture is that "there is very much a correct way to do things."

Table 10.3 lists the characteristics of culture, characteristics of the KM initiatives, and characteristics of KM behaviors expressed by the Beta informants.

Beta's emphasis on collaboration seems to have enabled the progression of KM from a static information repository system into the development of active, vital communities of interest wherein individuals feel a sense of belonging to the extent that they identify themselves firstly with the community, and only secondly, if at all, with their actual formal business unit. One informant claimed to not identify herself at all with the Innovation Services unit. Of course, one could ponder whether such identity transfer from the business unit to the community serves the best interest of the unit.

At the same time, the bureaucratic and innovative aspects of the culture have also helped. Having senior management show interest in KM was a catalyst to individual groups undertaking KM initiatives with great enthusiasm. In addition, rather than ad-hoc communities that are entirely organic, the community model emerging at Beta is a relatively structured one.

While one can make the argument that Beta's culture influences KM development and use, one can also argue that KM at Beta is itself influencing Beta's culture. OC members claim that without a sense of "connection" provided by the OC community, Beta would be nothing but a "big and scary" company in which individuals "get lost." The community, though, allows and enables a culture of connection. In effect, one informant believes that the OC community attempts to shift a very technical, phone-oriented, work product-oriented way of communicating with each other into a more personal work-in-process movement towards what Beta refers to as "thought leadership."

Table 10.3   *Characteristics of Company B culture, KM initiatives, and KM behaviors*

Culture characteristics	KM characteristics	KM behaviors
Hierarchical, yet collaborative and innovative Individuals largely responsible for their own careers, yet competition is undertaken in a cooperative manner The team is the unit of success, more so than the individual Absence of extreme supervision of individuals' work – individuals have a sense of control	Company-wide information repository consisting of hundreds of information databases Team rooms used by project teams Communities of practice emerging. These communities include: tools, events, and structures The OC community is used as an example of a successful community and as a consultant to other emerging communities	Team members actively coordinate via the team rooms Community members obtain a sense of belonging to the community Community members post information from completed team projects to the community out of a sense of commitment, not coercion Community members are more loyal to the company (less likely to depart) because of their belonging to the community Assignments to projects made through community references

When asked why members take the time to participate in the community when there is no formal reward for so doing, one informant said simply, "it's just how we do business." Thus, the community has infused the culture of the members.

Yet this does not suggest that an organizational utopia has been, or will be, achieved. While the culture is becoming more connected, there is another angle. One informant believes that when you have widespread access to knowledge management you can also have a culture where people that know very little about something have access to enough information to be danger-ous. People get too comfortable with having access to knowledge and then they feel free to share it. This informant remained unconvinced that the knowledge one acquires through the network is as solid a foundation as the knowledge one has acquired through experience and traditional learning. Moreover, she feels that the notion of dialogue can get redefined in a way that you loose the quality of participation that one might be looking for.

Summary

Beta has many KM databases, collectively referred to as Intellectual Capital Management. While these databases serve an important role of housing and organizing information in a huge organization, they do not go so far as to foster collaboration. Instead, team rooms and communities of interest, largely left to the discretion of team members and community members, have proven to be vital tools to achieving collaboration, community, and belonging. And as the culture of Beta has been receptive to individual groups setting and pursuing their community agendas, the culture is also being subtly altered by the communities as members feel more of a sense of belonging to the community than to their business units.

Discussion of case study findings

The two cases offer insights into the role that organizational culture plays in the inception and maturation of knowledge management. This section summarizes the key findings that help us answer the question: how does organizational culture influence KM approaches? We suggest four responses to this question.

1. *Organizational culture influences knowledge management through its influence on the values organizational members attribute to individual versus cooperative behavior.* The two companies we examined share several similarities: both huge multi-national organizations are widely regarded by organizational members as being predominantly bureaucratic in culture, both organizations had initial KM approaches that were strongly supported by senior management, and both had initial KM approaches focused on the creation of a large centralized repository of organizational knowledge to be shared across the organization. These two large bureaucratic organizations began their KM quests with the process approach. The most striking difference between the organizational cultures of these two companies was the emphasis at Alpha on the individual, and the emphasis at Beta on the collectivity – the team or the community. This evinces itself even in the interpretation of innovation. While individuals at both companies spoke of the need for innovation in their organizations and of the striving of their organizations to develop an innovative culture, in the case of Alpha innovation was perceived as an individual attribute whereas at Beta innovation was perceived as a team-level attribute.

The individualistic view of innovation at Alpha seemed to militate against the requisite sharing and cooperation that makes the evolution of KM from process approach to a community of practice approach possible. In both companies, micro-level experimentation of the various possibilities of KM was undertaken within teams or business units. The value placed on individualism versus cooperativism seems to have played a significant role in the nature and form of the KM approach. The micro-level experimentations by teams or business units were carried out with their own assumptions about the usefulness of repositories of knowledge and the usefulness of communities or practice. We suggest that it is not organizational culture at the organizational level, or even the subunit level, that has the most significant influence on the KM approach, but organizational culture as embodied in the individualistic versus cooperative tendencies of organizational members. Thus, organizational culture influences KM approaches through its influence on individualism versus cooperativism. From a theoretical view, it seems that Wallach's (1983) cultural dimensions and those of Earley (1994) were both valuable at explaining organizational-level culture. However, Earley's cultural dimensions at the organizational level seem best able to explain why a KM approach tended to become more process or more practice based.

2. *Organizational culture influences the evolution of knowledge management initiatives.* Our findings suggest that firms do not decide in advance to adopt a process or practice approach to KM, but that this evolves. The most natural starting point is one of process, perhaps because the benefits seem more evident and because it can more closely align with the existing organizational structure. Moreover, the practice approach may not only fail to align with existing structure but it may engender a virtual structure and identity. It is interesting that at Beta, a culture dominantly viewed as bureaucratic, once the initial organizational change community was established, the evolution of the community then became a highly structured process of maturation.

The community leaders developed a tool kit to help other communities develop, which included a maturation model to help determine how mature a community was and to help develop a plan to move the community forward. What some might see as an organic process – that of establishing and developing a community or practice – became in a bureaucratic organization a structured process. Even if the idea for the community emerged from interested potential members, the evolution took on a structured form with tools, kits, assessments, and plans.

The cooperative aspect of culture at the individual level made the community possible; the bureaucratic elements of culture at the organizational level enabled the community to mature. Hence, the evolution of the community was highly dependent on the individual willingness of organizational members to sustain and nurture their community. This appeared tied to the importance they placed on cooperation with their community members, most of whom they had never met.

3. *Organizational culture influences the migration of knowledge.* In the case of Alpha, where as mentioned the informants seemed to identify the individual as the ultimate unit of responsibility in the organization, the individuals were also viewed as the owners of knowledge and had the responsibility to share their knowledge. This in fact created a major challenge since the individuals rejected this new responsibility.

At Beta, where the team seemed to be the focus of responsibility, knowledge migrated from the team to the community to the organizational level system and back down to the team. The leader of the team would take responsibility for cleaning the team's data and submitting it to the community and to the central information repository. Thus, knowledge migrated upward from the team to the central repository. Interestingly, the most useful knowledge was claimed to be that at the team and community level. Once the knowledge had completed its migration to the central repository, it was seen primarily as an item of insurance – for use in case of need. Knowledge sharing and transfer occurred primarily at the team and community level whereas knowledge storage was the function of the central repository.

The migration of knowledge is also influenced by the structural processes put in place to ensure that knowledge finds its way to the appropriate persons. Of key importance seems to be the way the queries are handled. The marketing group at Alpha adopted the approach of notifying individuals when new information had been added to the KMS. However, little interference was put in place to either guide people to the appropriate knowledge or encourage people to contribute knowledge. Contrarily, believing that the community should not become a bulletin board of problems and solutions, the leaders of the organizational change community at Beta worked arduously to learn who the subject matter experts were, so that queries would be submitted to the appropriate community leader who would serve as an intermediary between the individual with the query and the expert.

It has been widely reported that the use of knowledge directories is a primary application of KM in organizations. Our study suggests that the facilitated access to experts, rather than direct access via the location of an individual through a directory or via a problem posted to a forum, may lead to a more favorable community atmosphere.

4. *Knowledge management can become embedded in the organizational culture.* Over time, as KM evolves and begins to reflect the values of the organization, the KM itself can become a part of the organizational culture. At Beta, individuals spoke of their community involvement and their team rooms as simply the "way we work." In fact, the communities became so much part of the culture that even though they were not part of the organizational structure, they were part of individual's implicit structure. The "sense of belonging" that the individuals reported feeling towards their community suggests that the community had become an essential aspect of their value system, and hence had become part of organizational culture. The fact that the organizational change community members at Beta identified themselves first and foremost with their community, in spite of receiving neither reward nor recognition within their formal reporting unit for participating in the community, indicates the extent to which community participation had become a value and an aspect of the individual culture.

Implications and conclusion

The findings of our study suggest that a dominantly bureaucratic culture seems to tend toward an initial process-based KM approach. Furthermore, a bureaucratic culture seems to create the expectation among organizational members that senior management needs to provide a vision of purpose for KM, before the organizational members should embark on KM activities. In addition, the members view senior management support as validating any KM activities that they undertake. Innovative cultures, even if not the dominant culture at the organizational level, seem to enable subgroups to experiment with KM or create micro-KMs. In essence, in organizations having dominant bureaucratic cultures with traces of innovativeness, senior management support legitimizes KM but the innovativeness of the culture enables it to expand far beyond an organization-wide repository.

Specific KM behaviors such as ownership and maintenance of knowledge, knowledge sharing and knowledge reuse seem largely influenced by the individualistic or cooperative nature of the culture. Individualistic cultures inhibit sharing, ownership and reuse, while cooperative cultures enable the creation of virtual communities. Earley's (1994) work on organizational culture emphasized the individualistic and collectivistic aspects of culture. Organizations encouraging individuals to pursue and maximize their own goals and rewarding performance based on individual achievement would be considered as having an individualistic culture, whereas organizations placing priority on collective goals and joint contributions and rewards for organizational accomplishments would be considered collectivist (Earley, 1994; Chatman and Barsade, 1995). This dimension of organizational culture

Table 10.4   *Summary of organizational culture's influence on KM*

Cultural perspective	Influence of culture on knowledge management
Bureaucratic (Wallach, 1983)	Favors an initial process approach to KM Creates expectation among members that senior management vision is essential to effective KM
Innovative (Wallach, 1983)	Enables subgroups in organization to experiment with KM and develop KMs useful to their group
Individualistic (Earley, 1994)	Inhibits sharing, ownership, and reuse of knowledge
Cooperative (Earley, 1994)	Enables the evolution of process-oriented KM to practice-oriented KM Enables the creation of virtual communities

emerged as critical in our examination of the influence of culture on KM initiatives. These findings are summarized in Table 10.4.

This research set out to examine the influence of organizational culture on knowledge management approaches. Using a case study approach, we have gathered the perspectives of individuals in two firms that share some cultural similarities yet differ in other aspects. The findings suggest that organizational culture influences the KM approach initially chosen by an organization, the evolution of the KM approach, and the migration of knowledge. Moreover, the findings suggest that KM can eventually become an integral aspect of the organizational culture. Much remains to be discovered about how organizational cultures evolve and what role information technology takes in this evolution. This case study is an initial forray into a potentially vast array of research into the relationship between information technology and organizational culture.

References

Alavi, M., T. Kayworth, and D. Leidner (2005), Organizational and sub-unit values in the process of knowledge management. Working paper. Baylor University.

Baltahazard, P. A. and R. A. Cooke (2003), Organizational Culture and Knowledge Management Success: Assessing the Behavior-Performance Continuum Working Paper. Arizona State University West.

Bloor, G. and P. Dawson (1994), "Understanding Professional Culture in Organizational Context," *Organization Studies*, Vol. 15, No. 2, pp. 275–295.

Brown, S. J. and P. Duguid (2000), "Balancing Act: How To Capture Knowledge Without Killing It," *Harvard Business Review*, May, pp. 73–80.

Chatman, J. A. and S. G. Barsade (1995), "Personality, Organizational Culture, and Cooperation: Evidence from a Business Simulation," *Administrative Science Quarterly*, Vol. 40, No. 3, pp. 423–443.

Davenport, T. H., D. W. De Long, and M. C. Beers (1998), "Successful Knowledge Management," *Sloan Management Review*, Vol. 39, No. 2, pp. 43–57.

DeLong, D. W. and L. Fahey (2000), "Diagnosing Cultural Barriers To Knowledge Management," *Academy of Management Executive*, Vol. 14, No. 4, pp. 113–127.

Earley, P. C. (1994), "Self or Group? Cultural effects of training on self-efficacy and performance," *Administrative Science Quarterly*, Vol. 39, pp. 89–117.

Enz, C. (1986), *Power and Shared Values in the Corporate Culture*. The University of Michigan Press, Ann Arbor, MI.

Gold, A. H., A. Malhotra, and A. H. Segars (2001), "Knowledge Management: An Organizational Capabilities Perspective," *Journal of Management Information Systems*, Vol. 18, No. 1, pp. 185–214.

Gupta, A. K. and V. Govindarajan (2000), "Knowledge Management's Social Dimension: Lessons From Nucor Steel," *Sloan Management Review*, Vol. 42, No. 1, pp. 71–80.

Hansen, M. T., N. Nohria, and T. Tierney (1999), "What's Your Strategy For Managing Knowledge?," *Harvard Business Review*, March–April, pp. 106–115.

Hargadon, A. B. (1998), "Firms As Knowledge Brokers: Lessons In Pursuing Continuous Innovation," *California Management Review*, Vol. 40, No. 3, pp. 209–227.

Hasan, H. and E. Gould (2001), "Support for the Sense-Making Activity of Managers," *Decision Support Systems*, Vol. 31, No. 1, pp. 71–86.

Jarvenpaa, S. L. and S. D. Staples (2001), "Exploring Perceptions of Organizational Ownership of Information and Expertise," *Journal of Management Information Systems*, Vol. 18, No. 1, pp. 151–183.

Johnson, G. (1992), "Managing Strategic Change – Strategy, Culture and Action," *Long Range Planning*, Vol. 25, No. 1, pp. 28–36.

Kanungo, S., S. Sadavarti, and Y. Srinivas (2001), "Relating IT strategy and organizational culture: an empirical study of public sector units in India," *Journal of Strategic Information Systems*, Vol. 10, pp. 29–57.

KPMG Management Consulting (1998), *Knowledge Management: Research Report*.

O'Dell, C. and C. J. Grayson (1998), "If Only We Know What We Know: Identification And Transfer Of Best Practices," *California Management Review*, Vol. 40, No. 3, pp. 154–174.

O'Reilly, C. A., J. Chatman, and D. F. Caldwell (1996), "Culture as Social Control: Corporations, Cults, and Commitment," *Research in Organizational Behavior*, Vol. 4, No. 18, pp. 157–200.

Quinn, R. E. and I. Rohrbaugh (1983), "A Spatial Model of Effectiveness Criteria: Towards a Competing Values Approach to Organizational Analysis," *Management Science*, Vol. 5, No. 29, pp. 363–377.

Ruggles, R. (1998), "The State Of The Notion: Knowledge Management In Practice," *California Management Review*, Vol. 40, No. 3, pp. 80–89.

Schein, E. H. (1985), *Organizational Culture and Leadership*. Jossey-Bass, San Francisco, CA.

Schultze, U. and R. Boland (2000), "Knowledge Management Technology And The Reproduction Of Knowledge Work Practices," *Journal of Strategic Information Systems*, Vol. 9, No. 2–3, pp. 193–213.

von Krogh, G. (1998), "Care in Knowledge Creation," *California Management Review*, Vol. 40, No. 3, pp. 133–153.

Wallach, E. J. (1983), "Individuals and Organizations: The Cultural Match," *Training and Development Journal*, pp. 28–35.

Watson, S. (1998), "Getting To 'Aha!' Companies Use Intranets To Turn Information And Experience Into Knowledge – And Gain A Competitive Edge," *Computer World*, January 26, p. S7.

Wenger, E. C. and W. M. Snyder (2000), "Communities Of Practice: The Organizational Frontier," *Harvard Business Review*, January–February 63, pp. 139–145.

Reproduced from *The International Journal of Electronic Collaboration*, Vol. 2, No. 1, 2006, pp. 17–40. Reprinted with permission from Information Resources Management Association.

Questions for discussion

1 Describe the ways in which the organizational cultures of the two companies vary.
2 Which culture do you think provides a more attractive work environment and why?
3 What specific aspects of culture would you expect to influence the use of knowledge management systems?
4 How maleable do you feel the cultural characteristics are? Should the management of Company A decide to really push the idea of a KM system?
5 What are the pros/cons of a global KM versus a business-unit or team-unit KM initiative?

11 Impact of National Culture on Information Technology Usage Behaviour: An Exploratory Study of Decision Making in Korea and the USA

Kenneth J. Calhoun, James T. C. Teng and Myun Joong Cheon

Abstract: The globalization of world markets has led to the introduction of information technology, most often developed in western cultures, to other societies. Cultural values were embedded in the design and use of these technologies. Often, the receiving society did not embrace the technology because of culture. Examples of such behaviour include executive information systems and group decision support systems, which are cited later. This study examines the use of nonspecific applications of information technology for organizational decision making. A survey instrument was developed to measure decision makers' perceptions of the impact of information technology on the decision process. Decision makers in Korea and the USA indicated their perceptions of the extent information technology use impacted their decision making activities. The results indicated some behaviours appeared to change to take advantage of the technology, while others, particularly those associated with the cultural preference for communication, did not.

Introduction

The world is continuing to move toward global markets with the resultant interactions between members of different cultures. Many management and organization practices developed in western industrialized countries have failed when introduced to other cultures. Kim *et al.* (1990) showed that individual incentives used to motivate US workers were counter productive in collectivist cultures. With the widespread diffusion of information technology (IT) on a global scale, increasingly we are witnessing essentially the same technology being used in many different cultures. Hall (1976: 14) wrote 'there is not one aspect of human life that is not affected by culture'. While there are many examples of Anglo–American organization and management practices that clash with values of other cultures, it is widely believed that technology is universal. Trompenaars and Hampden-Turner (1998: 4) stated 'indeed, technologies do work by the same rules everywhere, even on the moon'. This is true of machines but not necessarily the human machine inter-action. While much technology is indeed culture free, it would seem that a technology, such as IT, that affects human behaviour may not be free of cul-tural influences.

Hofstede (1991: 5) defined culture as 'the collective programming of the mind that distinguishes the members of one category of people from those of another'. Much of the culture research in the literature is based upon the four factors defined by Hofstede. These factors are: power distance, uncer-tainty avoidance, masculinity and individualism. Power distance measures how a society accepts the unequal distribution of power. Uncertainty avoid-ance reflects the threatening feelings that members of a society experience when confronted by uncertain or ambiguous situations. Masculinity describes the extent that a culture values decisive, assertive behaviour vs. the feminine opposite where a society values modest behaviour. Individualism pertains to societies where loose relationships between individuals are the norm and the individual is expected to take care of himself/herself. Collectivism, the oppos-ite pole, reflects societies where social goals are paramount and in which from birth a person is integrated into a group. Hofstede and Bond (1988) described another factor, Confucian Dynamism, which determines the time orientation of a culture, either long term or short term. Hall (1976) described culture in terms of high and low communication context and monochronic or polychronic time orientation. High context communication reflects cul-tures where subtle clues and hidden meanings convey the bulk of the infor-mation whereas the explicit code of the message does not. Low context is the opposite, where the mass of information is in the explicit code. Monochronic time describes those societies that prefer to accomplish tasks sequentially and to adhere to schedules. Polychronic cultures are charac-terized by several activities occurring at the same time and little regard for schedules. More recently, Trompenaars and Hampden-Turner (1998) described seven cultural variables. Five of these are defined in terms of how people relate to each other. The other two are defined as how people manage time and how they relate to nature. All seven have counterparts in the vari-ables described above.

Theoretical foundations

In recent years, the application of IT in organizations has expanded further with the addition of communication functions such as e-mail, groupware, Internet, intranet and electronic meeting systems (Dennis *et al.* 1991). As

IT advances, the general notion of information technology has evolved to include telecommunication as a vital component in addition to computing. The growing dependence on both the computing and the communication dimensions of IT in the workplace has shaped a new environment. Prior to the emergence of this environment, the presence of IT in the organization typically took the form of specific computer application systems, such as accounts payable and financial reporting systems, which either automated specific operational procedures or supported certain managerial processes. In the new environment, however, access to computing and communication facilities is not only for predetermined management activities. Rather, such accesses are often attempted spontaneously to satisfy whatever decision and collaboration need exist at the moment. IT usage in such an environment is so embedded in work itself that the two become one. Applegate *et al.* (1991) have conceptualized this coalescence of computing and communication usage and organizational functioning as Organizational Computing (OC). Their notion of OC is described by organizations in which computing systems are explicitly recognized as integral elements of the organization process and not seen as exogenous artefacts.

The decision making process has been the subject of scholarly attention, which can be traced back to the dawn of the computer age (Leavitt and Whisler 1958). Dickson *et al.* (1977) conducted one of the first organized research programmes in IT, the Minnesota Experiments, aimed at the effect of computer-generated information on decision making and decision makers in the laboratory. A research tradition on IT and decision making has since developed within the IT field over the years resulting in a diverse array of literature that includes controlled laboratory studies (e.g. Davis and Kotterman 1994), field investigation (e.g. Sanders and Courtney 1985) and conceptual analysis (e.g. Huber 1990).

IT is an important component of the organizational decision process. Managers at all levels increasingly rely on IT to aid in making decisions. Research has demonstrated that there are national values that often inhibit the successful implementation of specific practices exported from one culture to another. Hofstede (1991) suggested that management by objectives (MBO) is more successful in countries with low power distance than in cultures where high power distance precludes the superior–subordinate negotiation necessary in the MBO process. Straub (1994) found that culture played a role in determining the kind of communication media selected. Technologies are developed with assumptions of what they are to accomplish but also how they are to be used. Kumar and Bjorn-Andersen (1990) found that system designer values vary across cultures. A great deal of the current knowledge concerning IT and the decision process is based on application specific systems. Ho *et al.* (1989) found the use of group decision support systems (GDSS) less successful in Singapore when compared to USA because there were different values concerning the expression of conflict. Leidner *et al.* (1999) describe different impacts on decision making between Swedish and Mexican managers in the use of executive information systems (EIS).

There is little doubt that many specific applications of IT, such as GDSS, EIS etc., are designed with embedded cultural values. Baligh (1994) suggested that trouble occurs when these embedded values conflict with the values of the adopting culture. The question we address is whether non-specific IT influences behaviour of decision makers in different cultures. Computers and communication devices are machines and, as such, would seem to be universal in nature. While it is true that these devices will operate in the same way, it is not clear that the data and information conveyed by them will be independent of national values.

National culture

Culture is a pattern of thinking, feeling and acting (behaviour) that is learned throughout a person's life, beginning in early childhood (Hofstede 1991, Trompenaars and Hampden-Turner 1998). The current study attempts to examine the evidence that IT use may indeed influence the behaviour of professionals and managers from two distinctly different cultures, Korea and the USA. Obviously, not all Koreans will have exactly the same values and beliefs, nor will the US respondents. Hofstede (1991) stated that his published research about cultural patterns only indicates what reactions and behaviours are likely and understandable, given one's past. There is likely to be variations in behaviour among the members of any culture.

Table 11.1 lists the rankings of Korea and the USA based upon Hofstede (1991), Hofstede and Bond (1998), Hall (1976), and Trompenaars and Hampden-Turner (1998). In the case of the culture factors of communications context and time orientation (Hall 1976), a ranking or score was not available, but the two subject cultures were classified as opposites.

The recent culture data from Trompenaars and Hampden-Turner (1998) identifies seven variables that distinguish one society from another. In four of these areas, Korea and the USA are directly compared. The first variable from Trompenaars and Hampden-Turner displayed in Table 11.1 is universalism–particularism. This variable, as are the other three, is measured by responses to several statements/scenarios. The agreement or disagreement to the statements or scenarios determines whether the respondents are universalists or particularists. The definition of this variable is whether relationships prevail over rules. A universalist would not break the rules for a friend while a particularist is more likely to do so. This variable is closely aligned to the individual–collective variable of Hofstede (1991). The rankings for the two countries were based upon two statements asking whether the respondent

Table 11.1   *Measures of culture (rank out of total countries surveyed)*

Culture variable	USA rank/N	Korea rank/N
Power distance	38/53	27.5/53*
Individualism	1/53	43/53
Masculinity	15/53	41/53
Uncertainty avoidance	43/53	16.5/53*
Long term–short term	17/23	5/23
Communications context	Low	High
Time orientation	Monochronic	Polychronic
Universalism–particularism*	27/31	3/31
Achievement–ascription*	43/46	14/46
Specific–diffuse*	37/45	10/45
Time present–past*	3/20	18/20

*In each variable, two statements/scenarios were employed. The data indicates an average ranking for the variable.

agreed or disagreed with stretching the truth for a friend. The USA is a universalist culture while Korea was particularist culture in the Trompenaars and Hampden-Turner research. Another variable, specificity-diffuseness, is also related to individualism–collectivism as well as power distance. The statements in this variable dealt with painting your superior's house and whether or not the company should provide housing. Specific cultures disagreed with both statements while more diffuse culture respondents agreed with the statements. A specific culture has little private space and a lot of public space. The USA is such a culture. The USA, which is a very individualistic culture, has a small private area consisting of one's self and one's family. The reverse is true for diffuse cultures where the large in-group and loyalty to the organization is private space. Korea is a strong collectivist culture. The third variable, time orientation, is related to the short–long term of Hofstede and Bond (1988). This variable was measured by having respondents answer questions about the importance of the past, present and future. The USA was more oriented to the present and less to the past and future than Korea. The final Trompenaars and Hampden-Turner variable is called ascription–achievement. This variable reflects the cultural value that status is awarded on achievement versus family background. This variable is related to power distance and individualism–collectivism. The USA was ranked among the achievement cultures while Korea was ranked as an ascription culture.

As is indicated in Table 11.1, the USA and Korea are quite divergent when assessed on a culture basis. Except for the power distance dimension, the country rankings of Korea and the USA are very widely dispersed. If one country is in the top one third of the countries measured, the other country is in the bottom one third. The substantial differences in culture between the USA and Korea make the two countries likely to expose behaviour changes due to IT. A similar study contrasting the UK and the USA would be unlikely to find differences as the two societies are very close in all the measures of culture.

Whether cultural variables will inhibit the use of non-specific applications of IT in decision making or enhance it, is not known. The culture variables defined by Hofstede, Hall and others describe likely behaviour in social contexts. They do not specifically refer to decision making and certainly not to the role of IT in the process. The effect of culture on behaviour is best understood by contrasting the likely behaviour between societies on opposite poles of the culture. For the most part, Korea and the USA represent very different cultures. A literature-based description of the culture variables identified earlier suggests the likely behaviours one could expect in the social context of life.

- Power distance reflects the degree to which a society accepts an unequal distribution of power. Strong power distance cultures tend to accept and follow orders from superiors without question. Superiors are expected to be autocratic, benevolent patriarchs. Superiors are expected to enjoy privileges and are accorded high status. This is what Trompenaars and Hampden-Turner describe as ascription. In low power distance cultures, subordinates are much more likely to question the reason behind the orders before accepting a task as legitimate. Superiors are not accorded special privileges, which is akin to the achievement pole of the ascription–achievement variable.
- Individualism. Collectivism reflects the basic beliefs of responsibility; individualism means the member of the society believes he or she is responsible for themselves and their immediate families. The rest of society is not given any special consideration. This is the universalism pole of the variable of Trompenaars and Hampden-Turner. In a collective society, the member is part of a large group of extended family, friends and firm all of which demand loyalty. The group welfare is paramount. This reflects the particularist pole.
- Uncertainty avoidance describes the society's tolerance for ambiguity. A society with strong uncertainty avoidance desires order. Rules and written procedures for dealing with situations are welcomed as a lack of such procedures induces stress. In weak uncertainty avoidance cultures, written rules and procedures are not sought or desired, as they imply unwanted control.
- Masculine. Feminine describes a view of social behaviour where being decisive and assertive is considered masculine and modest; demure behaviour is feminine. The masculine society hammers out problems in meetings, tends to be decisive and quick to judgment while the feminine

cultures are more likely to seek a harmonious solution than a fight and to be concerned with the impact of actions on others.

- Time dimensions include the Confucian Dynamism of Hofstede and Bond, the time dimension of Trompenaars and Hampden-Turner and the monochronic-polychronic variable of Hall. The short term and monochronic society, like the USA, is concerned with schedules, concentrates more on the immediate time frame and prefers to act on tasks sequentially using an analytic approach. The focus is on one task and there is emphasis on achieving resolution quickly. The long term and polychronic culture, like Korea, is less concerned with time constraints and acts upon several tasks at the same time employing an intuitive approach.
- Communication context describes the way cultures communicate. Low context cultures perceive the meaning of communication in the explicitly coded context of the message. The numbers, words and symbols encoded in the message convey the meaning. In a high context culture, the meaning is conveyed by subtle clues such as tone of voice, facial expression, body language, etc. The impersonal words and numbers of printed material do not convey much information in high context cultures.

There are no definitive answers to the question of which cultural trait will affect behaviour for non-specific applications of IT as there are for specific applications. The scholarly literature of culture suggests what type of behaviour one might expect from members of a culture. Korea is almost universally opposite to the USA in every measure depicted in Table 11.1. Even so, there may be a number of effects of IT use that would be simply machine processes and not subject to cultural influences. For example, Leidner *et al.* (1999) found a factor defined as data availability was perceived in the same way by Swedish and Mexican managers, who represent very different cultures. Our objective is to examine a number of non-specific applications of IT to see which, if any, suggest that behaviour has been influenced.

Research model

Teng and Calhoun (1996) measured two dimensions of IT and defined two types of decisions and demonstrated that IT influences decision making in a study of US managers and professionals. The respondents perceived that IT use impacted a number of factors associated with decision making and that the impact was often different for computing than communications and also different between the types of decisions. Operational decisions were defined as day-to-day decisions that are necessary for continued operation of the firm but are not the kind of decision that has significant use and commitment of resources. Examples would be handling a customer complaint, keeping a project on schedule, etc. Managerial decisions were defined as non-repetitive decisions

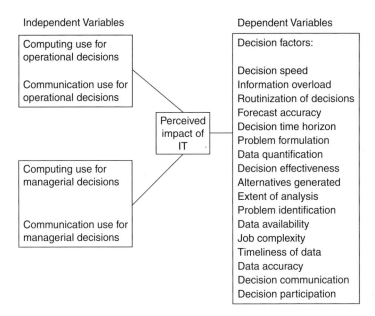

Figure 11.1   *Research model*

that have long run consequences. These decisions could involve the introduction of a new product, developing a new marketing programme, etc., where a large commitment of capital and personnel is required. In many respects, the definitions follow Simon's (1977) classification of programmed and non-programmed decisions. The research model is depicted in Figure 11.1.

Methodology and measurement of variables

The survey methodology was chosen to enhance the sample size of the research. It is difficult to physically observe a large number of decision makers in two countries to assess their behaviour. The research model is based upon established theories and/or empirical studies reported in the literature. The design of the survey instrument was based on the work of Teng and Calhoun (1996) with significant modifications. An extensive pre-test of the questionnaire was undertaken to enhance the validity of the instrument.

The survey questionnaire was distributed to a total of 142 employed decision makers in the USA and Korea, 77 in the USA and 65 in Korea. The USA sample came from a professional organization in a large mid-Atlantic city and part-time MBA classes in a major southern university. The Korean sample consisted of managers attending training seminars offered by a Korean university. Respondent profiles are displayed in Table 11.2. Although there are differences

Table 11.2 *Respondent profile*

Part a: industry profile

Industry	Number of respondents (%)	
	USA	Korea
Finance/insurance/banking	7 (9.1%)	5 (7.7%)
Manufacturing	24 (31.2%)	40 (61.5%)
Construction/engineering	5 (6.5%)	3 (4.6%)
Government/education	7 (9.1%)	6 (9.2%)
Energy/utilities	6 (7.8%)	2 (3.1%)
Professional services	4 (5.2%)	2 (3.1%)
Other*	24 (31.2%)	7 (10.8%)
Total	77 (100.0%)	65 (100.0%)

*'Other' includes retail, wholesale/distribution, transportation, etc.

Part b: management level

Management level	Number of respondents (%)	
	USA	Korea
Supervisory	9 (11.7%)	10 (15.6%)
Middle management	13 (16.9%)	2 (3.1%)
Top management	25 (32.5%)	37 (57.8%)
Professional (non-manager)	30 (39.0%)	15 (23.1%)
Total	77 (100.0%)	65 (100.0%)

Part c: functional area

Functional area	Number of respondents (%)	
	USA	Korea
Marketing/sales	7 (9.2%)	9 (13.8%)
Production/operations	11 (14.5%)	18 (27.7%)
Finance/accounting	6 (7.9%)	2 (3.1%)
Human resource mgt.	12 (15.8%)	2 (3.1%)
Mgt. information systems	6 (7.9%)	10 (15.4%)
General administration	6 (7.9%)	11 (16.9%)
Other*	28 (36.8%)	13 (20.0%)
Total	76 (100.0%)	65 (100.0%)

*'Other' includes R&D, purchasing, etc.

(Continued)

Table 11.2   *Continued*

Part d: respondent age

Age range	Number of respondents (%)	
	USA	*Korea*
Under 36	36 (46.8%)	23 (35.9%)
36–45	27 (35.1%)	35 (54.7%)
46 and above	14 (18.2%)	6 (9.4%)
Total	77 (100.0%)	64 (100.0%)

between the samples, they are not large and may be attributable to differences in the economies of the two countries. The Korean sample was more technically oriented due to a preponderance of manufacturing firms represented. The USA sample has more human resource specialists since the professional group sampled was a HRM organization.

Measurement of independent variables

The independent variable for this study is the intensity of IT use, both computing and communication, for operational and managerial decision making. The intensity of use is measured by the frequency of use and the level of sophistication of IT employed in decision making. These levels of sophistication were described as four modes of computing on the questionnaire as follows:

1. Use hard copy computer reports prepared by others and delivered to you;
2. Use software that offers a set of menu options for you to directly obtain information in predetermined formats;
3. Use software interactively through a series of menu-driven commands (e.g. Excel);
4. Apply software tools to solve business problems (e.g. using a spreadsheet macro).

As can be seen, the lowest level of computing use is restricted to getting computer-generated reports prepared by others. The other categories represent increasing sophistication in the use of IT. As a user progresses through the four modes, the extent of human–computer interaction increases. Frequency of computing usage is measured by frequency of use. For the four modes of usage, the respondent indicates how frequently that particular mode is utilized in operational as well as managerial decision making. For both, a five point frequency of use scale was used: infrequently (1), monthly (2), few times per week (3), few times daily (4), and many times daily (5). The intensity measure used in this study falls in the category of measures known as extent of system use, which has been used successfully in past studies in predicting system success (e.g. Thompson *et al.* 1991). A simple average of the four frequency scores was used as the measure for the intensity of computing usage in operational decision making. Likewise, a simple mean score was also taken to measure intensity of computing usage in managerial decision making.

We asked respondents to consider the use of computer-based communication to send and receive information in the coordination and decision making aspects of their job and presented the following four levels of communication applications on the questionnaire:

1. Local e-mail or voice-mail to communicate with members of your work group;
2. Organization-wide e-mail or voice-mail to communicate with total organization;
3. Accessing and updating a shared information repository (e.g. using Lotus Notes) with members of your work group or other members of the organization;
4. Telecommunication support for group decision making activities, such as electronic meeting rooms, teleconferencing and video conferencing.

For each of the four levels of communication applications, the frequency of usage measures were the same 5-point scale as those for the computing modes. Similarly, simple averages of the four scores were taken as the measures for level of communication usage in operational decision making and level of communication usage in managerial decisions.

Based upon a review of the literature, especially Teng and Calhoun (1996), we identified 17 decision attributes that were related to IT usage. These factors and the relevant literature citations are noted below:

- Decision speed (Huber 1984, Weizer 1992, Pelton 1993, Leidner and Elam 1995);
- Information overload (Huber 1990, Simon 1990);
- Routinization of decision making (Cheney and Dickson 1982, Huber 1984);
- Forecast accuracy (Kasper 1982, Yoo and Digman 1987);
- Decision time horizon (Rhyne 1985, Huber 1990);
- Problem formulation (Leidner and Elam 1995);
- Data quantification (Hohn 1986, Stevens 1990);
- Decision effectiveness (Sanders *et al.* 1984, Huber 1990, Belcher and Watson 1993);
- Alternatives generated (Alavi 1993, Gessner *et al.* 1994);
- Extent of analysis (Watson *et al.* 1991, Leidner *et al.* 1999);

- Problem identification (Leidner and Elam 1995);
- Data availability (Leidner *et al.* 1995);
- Job complexity (Hackman and Oldham 1980, Millman and Hartwick 1987);
- Timeliness of data (Rockart and Short 1989, Huber 1990);
- Data accuracy (Doll and Torkazahde 1988);
- Decision communication (Foster and Flynn 1984, Huber 1984, 1990);
- Decision participation (Huber 1984, Fried 1993, Gessner *et al.* 1994).

We incorporated these factors in the questionnaire. Respondents were asked to what extent does the use of information technology result in the following and indicated the extent of impact for both operational and managerial decisions according to the scale: 1 = none, 2 = little extent, 3 = some extent, 4 = large extent, 5 = great extent. Multiple items were used to measure each of the 17 factors. To test construct validity, principal components factor analysis was employed on each set of items and only one factor was determined. The items used for the constructs were taken from the literature and had been validated in prior research, lending some degree of content validity. Reliability was determined by Cronbach alphas for the seventeen decision factors. 'Churchill (1979: 70) stated that coefficient alpha is the basic statistic for determining the reliability of a measure based on internal consistency'. Nunnally (1967) suggested that alpha below 0.5 was insufficient for even exploratory research. The lowest alpha we found was 0.599 and most were in excess of 0.7 and almost half were above 0.8.

Correlation analysis was conducted to determine the relationships of IT and decision factors for both Korea and the USA. Since there are two dimensions of IT, two types of decisions and 17 decision factors, there are a total of 68 comparisons between Korea and the USA.

Results and conclusions

Table 11.3 contains the results of the correlation analysis for operational decisions. The correlations support the findings of Teng and Calhoun (1996) that decision makers perceive the impact of IT upon decision factors. For Korea, the correlation coefficients for computing are significantly different from zero at $p < 0.01$ or less for all 17 factors. For the USA, information overload, problem identification, decision communication and decision participation were not significantly different from zero. For the communications dimension of IT, Korea shows nine of the 17 coefficients as significantly different from zero, whereas the USA has only one, decision communications, as being significant. Given the high context nature of Korean culture, it is not surprising the respondents indicated much greater impact of the communications dimension of IT.

Table 11.3 *Correlation analysis: operational decisions*

(a) Computing dimension average n *for USA = 74, Korea = 63*

Decision factor	Correlation coefficient–difference		
	USA	Korea	Korea–USA
Decision speed	0.338*	0.352*	
Information overload	−0.013	0.469*	**
Routinization of decision making	0.297*	0.484*	
Forecast accuracy	0.258*	0.366*	
Decision time horizon	0.375*	0.519*	
Problem formulation	0.336*	0.567*	
Data quantification	0.427*	0.495*	
Decision effectiveness	0.225	0.357*	
Alternatives generated	0.335*	0.369*	
Extent of analysis	0.269*	0.509*	
Problem identification	0.161	0.328*	
Data availability	0.367*	0.525*	
Job complexity	0.330*	0.524*	
Timeliness of data	0.314*	0.466*	
Data accuracy	0.381*	0.416*	
Decision communications	0.216	0.553*	**
Decision participation	0.187	0.480*	

(b) Communications dimension average n *for USA = 63, Korea = 42*

Decision factor	Correlation coefficient–difference		
	USA	Korea	Korea–USA
Decision speed	0.205	0.272	
Information overload	−0.041	0.246	
Routinization of decision making	0.092	0.257	
Forecast accuracy	0.046	0.289	
Decision time horizon	0.137	0.354*	
Problem formulation	0.108	0.265	
Data quantification	0.190	0.289	
Decision effectiveness	0.135	0.417*	
Alternatives generated	0.118	0.368*	
Extent of analysis	0.079	0.121	
Problem identification	0.175	0.234	
Data availability	0.120	0.337*	
Job complexity	0.071	0.350*	
Timeliness of data	0.113	0.375*	
Data accuracy	0.038	0.436*	**
Decision communications	0.447*	0.494*	
Decision participation	0.218	0.377*	

*coefficient significantly different from zero at $p < 0.05$ or less;
**Korea–USA difference significant at $p < 0.05$ or less.

If we examine those correlation coefficients that were statistically differ-ent between the two countries, we can see that Korean managers found computing to cause much information overload for operational decisions. This is also consistent with a high context culture, more accustomed to inter-personal communication. The normal hard data output of computers does not match the communication form practiced in high context cultures. The US manager being used to and preferring hard data, reports no impact of com-puting on information overload for operational decisions. It is interesting to note that Korean managers do not see the communication dimension as caus-ing significant overload for operational decisions. While not as rich as face-to-face communication, voice-mail, teleconferencing and video conferencing all provide some subtle clues that convey the message to high context cul-tures that is not found in impersonal computer reports. Another significant difference is shown for data accuracy. Korean managers report a large impact of the communications dimension for operational decisions upon data accu-racy while US managers report virtually no impact, as they prefer the hard data form of the computing dimension of IT. Again, this is consistent with the high versus low context communication cultures. A more puzzling result is the significant difference about decision communication for the computing dimension. Korean respondents reported a strong impact on decision commu-nication from the managers while the US managers did not. Considering that Koreans also reported computing causing overload, it would seem the results are contradictory unless the overload effect of the computer output caused increased communications among colleagues in order to interpret the data.

The remaining correlation coefficients are generally of the same magni-tude. In itself, this is surprising since the culture values would suggest that there would be more differences. The similar perceptions concerning speed of decision making goes against the masculine-feminine positions of the countries as well as the time dimension of Korea and the USA. Even more surprising is the essentially equal perceptions concerning data quantification. As Hofstede (1991) stated, accounting (creator of hard data) is a ritual and the output of the accounting process is not used in decision making for long term, high context cultures which describes Korea. This result seems to indi-cate that non-specific IT can influence behaviour. Other results from Table 11.3 also indicate that IT changes behaviour. The extent of analysis factor shows that Korea reports a greater impact than the USA even though as a high-ranking country as measured by the Confucian Dimension, Korea would be expected to rely on intuition rather than analysis, which is the US approach to problem resolution.

Much the same results were reported for managerial decisions as operational decisions as depicted in Table 11.4. The computing dimension revealed that overload was significantly different between Korea and the USA as was deci-sion communication. The communications impact was not significantly dif-ferent for any of the factors although this may have been a result of smaller sample sizes. An example is the data accuracy factor. The US managers

Table 11.4 *Correlation analysis: managerial decisions*

(a) Computing dimension average n *for USA = 71, Korea = 53*

Decision factor	Correlation coefficient – difference		
	USA	Korea	Korea–USA
Decision speed	0.369*	0.392*	
Information overload	0.010	0.417*	**
Routinization of decision making	0.342*	0.539*	
Forecast accuracy	0.384*	0.344*	
Decision time horizon	0.324*	0.368*	
Problem formulation	0.325*	0.478*	
Data quantification	0.376*	0.343*	
Decision effectiveness	0.316*	0.420*	
Alternatives generated	0.360*	0.381*	
Extent of analysis	0.266*	0.444*	
Problem identification	0.274*	0.422*	
Data availability	0.349*	0.446*	
Job complexity	0.523*	0.470*	
Timeliness of data	0.352*	0.431*	
Data accuracy	0.360*	0.294*	
Decision communications	0.238*	0.627*	**
Decision participation	0.336*	0.581*	

(b) Communications dimension average n *for USA = 61, Korea = 36*

Decision factor	Correlation coefficient – difference		
	USA	Korea	Significanace
Decision speed	0.265*	0.178	
Information overload	0.026	0.277	
Routinization of decision making	0.080	0.347*	
Forecast accuracy	0.130	0.034	
Decision time horizon	0.177	0.393*	
Problem formulation	0.209	0.213	
Data quantification	0.235	0.259	
Decision effectiveness	0.182	0.345*	
Alternatives generated	0.202	0.304	
Extent of analysis	0.179	0.219	
Problem identification	0.266*	0.104	
Data availability	0.183	0.413*	
Job complexity	0.355*	0.300	
Timeliness of data	0.212	0.313	
Data accuracy	0.132	0.472*	
Decision communications	0.449*	0.558*	
Decision participation	0.398*	0.472*	

*coefficient significantly different from zero at $p < 0.05$ or less;
** Korea–USA difference significant at $p < 0.05$ or less.

reported a slightly larger impact of computing on data accuracy for the computing dimension than did Koreans but the reverse was true for communication where the Koreans reported a very strong influence on data accuracy. The same factors that were reported to have similar impacts for operational decisions were reported the same way for managerial decisions.

From the results contained in Tables 11.3 and 11.4, our research suggests that decision-making behaviour is changed by certain types of non-specific applications of IT, even those that incur human interaction that constitute a social situation. The cultural values that proscribe behaviour seem to be flexible when it comes to the use of IT in decision making. Our results indicate that the most resistant cultural value to the effect of IT is the communication context of the culture. The high context Korean managers consistently report more impact of communications on decision making than do the low context US managers. Several of the decision factors that deal with the effects of the communications dimension of IT show much more impact as reported by Korean managers, such as data availability, data accuracy, alternatives generated, and decision effectiveness, all of which contain an element of human interaction.

In summary, the non-specific use of IT seems to be more free of culture than the literature suggests is the case for specific applications, such as GDSS, EIS, etc. Adler (1983) suggested that the transfer of culture embodied technology depends upon the members of a culture having a capability to understand and use context free information. Low context communication is context free communication. Our results support Adler's contention that such transfer is very difficult to achieve when the recipient country is a high context communication culture.

Limitations and further research

Our objective was to explore the possibility that information technology in non-specific applications could alter the behaviour of decision makers. To achieve our objective, we surveyed managers from the USA and Korea to ascertain their perceptions about the impact of IT use for decision making. While our results suggested that such behaviour modification did occur, the sample sizes were too small for our results to be generalized. Our exploratory results certainly cannot be generalized to other cultures, as we only identified a few IT decision factors and a few combinations of cultural factors in the research. While the USA and Korea are quite different in culture, many cultures are individualist but are also feminine and many masculine cultures are collectivist.

Future research may replicate the study with other cultures and larger samples to see if the ability of IT to transcend national values as it appeared to do in Korea, also occurs in other Asian, Latin or European cultures. A significant improvement would be to include non-IT social items on the instrument in order to determine if the respondents were consistent with the general culture pattern of their society. If the social responses follow cultural expectations and the IT responses do not, it would be strong evidence that IT indeed affects the behaviour of decision makers.

References

Adler, N. (1983), "Cross-cultural management research: the ostrich and the trend," *Academy of Management Review*, Vol. 8, pp. 226–232.

Alavi, M. (1993), "An assessment of electronic meeting systems in a corporate setting," *Information and Management*, Vol. 25, pp. 175–182.

Applegate, L., C. Ellis, C. Holsapple, F. Radermacher, and A. Whinston (1991), "Organizational computing: definitions and issues," *Journal of Organizational Computing*, Vol. 1, pp. 1–10.

Baligh, H. (1994), "Components of cultures: nature, interconnections, and relevance to the decisions on organization structure," *Management Science*, Vol. 40, pp. 14–27.

Belcher, L. and H. Watson (1993), "Assessing the value of Conoco's EIS," *MIS Quarterly*, Vol. 17, pp. 239–254.

Cheney, P. and G. Dickson (1982), "Organizational characteristics and information systems: An exploratory investigation," *Academy of Management Review*, Vol. 25, pp. 170–184.

Churchill, G. (1979), "A paradigm for developing better measures of marketing constructs," *Journal of Marketing Research*, Vol. 16, pp. 64–73.

Davis, F. and J. Kotterman (1994), "User perceptions of decision support effectiveness: two production planning experiments," *Decision Sciences*, Vol. 25, pp. 57–79.

Dennis, A., J. Nunamaker Jr., and D. Vogel (1991), "A comparison of laboratory and field research in the study of electronic meeting systems," *Journal of Management Information Systems*, Vol. 7, pp. 107–135.

Dickson, G., J. Senn, and N. Chervany (1977), "Research in management information systems: the Minnesota experiments," *Management Science*, Vol. 23, pp. 913–923.

Foster, L. and D. Flynn (1984), "Management information technology: its effects on organizational form and function," *MIS Quarterly*, Vol. 8, pp. 229–236.

Fried, L. (1993), "Advanced information systems technology use," *Journal of Information Systems Management*, Vol. 10, pp. 7–14.

Gessner, S., M. McNeilly, and B. Leskee (1994), "Using electronic meeting systems for collaborative planning at IBM Rochester," *Planning Review*, Vol. 22, pp. 34–39.

Hackman, J. and G. Oldham (1980), *Work Redesign*. Addison Wesley Publishing Company, New York.

Hall, E. T. (1976), *Beyond Culture*. Anchor Press/ Doubleday, Garden City.

Ho, T., K. Raman, and R. Watson (1989), Group decision support systems: the cultural factor, *Proceedings of the Tenth Annual International Conference on Information Systems*, Boston, pp. 119–129.

Hofstede, G. (1991), *Cultures and Organizations: Software of the Mind*. McGraw-Hill Book Company, London.

Hofstede, G. and M. Bond (1988), "The confucious connection: from cultural roots to economic growth," *Organizational Dynamics*, Vol. 16, pp. 4–21.

Hohn, S. (1986), "How information technology is transforming corporate planning," *Long Range Planning*, Vol. 19, pp. 18–30.

Huber, G. (1990), "A theory of the effects of advanced information technologies on organizational design, intelligence and decision making," *Academy of Management Review*, Vol. 15, pp. 47–71.

Kasper, G. (1985), "The effect of user-developed DSS applications on forecasting decision-making performance in an experimental setting," *Journal of Management Information Systems*, Vol. 2, pp. 26–39.

Kim, K., H. Park, and N. Suzuki (1990), "Reward allocations in the United States, Japan and Korea: a comparison of individualistic and collectivistic cultures," *Academy of Management Journal*, pp. 188–198.

Kumar, K. and N. Bjorn-Andersen (1990), "A cross-cultural comparison of IS designer values," *Communications of the ACM*, Vol. 35, pp. 528–538.

Leavitt, H. and T. Whisler (1958), "Management in the 1980s," *Harvard Business Review*, Vol. 36, pp. 18–41.

Leidner, D. and J. Elam (1995), "The impact of executive information systems on organizational design, intelligence and decision making," *Organization Science*, Vol. 6, pp. 645–665.

Leidner, D., S. Carlsson, J. Elam, and M. Corrales (1999), "Mexican and Swedish managers' perceptions of the impact of EIS on organizational intelligence, decision making, and structure," *Decision Sciences*, Vol. 30, pp. 633–658.

Millman, Z. and J. Hartwick (1987), "The impact of automated office systems on middle managers and their work," *MIS Quarterly*, Vol. 11, pp. 107–124.

Nunnally, J. (1967), *Psychometric Theory*. McGraw-Hill, New York.

Pelton, J. (1993), "Toward a new national vision," *Telecommunications*, Vol. 27, pp. 7–42.

Rhyne, L. (1985), "The relationship of information usage characteristics to planning system sophistication: An empirical examination," *Strategic Management Journal*, Vol. 6, pp. 319–337.

Rockart, J. and J. Short (1989), "IT in the 1990's: Managing interdependence," *Sloan Management Review*, Vol. 10, pp. 7–17.

Sanders, G. and J. Courtney (1985), "A field study of organizational factors influencing DSS success," *MIS Quarterly*, Vol. 9, pp. 77–93.

Sanders, G., J. Courtney, and S. Loy (1984), "The impact of DSS on organizational communication," *Information and Management*, Vol. 7, pp. 141–148.

Simon, H. (1977), *The new science of management decision*, revised edn. Prentice-Hall, Englewood Cliffs, New Jersey.

Simon, H. (1990), "Information technologies and organizations by Ijiri and Sunders," *The Accounting Review*, Vol. 65, pp. 658–667.

Stevens, L. (1990), "Channeling the flood of data from outside online services," *Computerworld*, 25 June.

Struab, D. (1994), "The effect of culture on IT diffusion: e-mail and fax in Japan and the US," *Information Systems Research*, Vol. 5, pp. 23–47.

Teng, J. and K. Calhoun (1996), "Organizational computing as a facilitator of operational and managerial decision making: An exploratory study of managers' perceptions," *Decision Sciences*, Vol. 2, pp. 673–710.

Thompson, R., C. Higgins, and J. Howell (1991), "Personal computing: toward a conceptual model of utilization," *MIS Quarterly*, Vol. 15, pp. 125–143.

Trompenaars, F. and C. Hampden-Turner (1998), *Riding the Waves of Culture*, 2nd edn. McGraw-Hill, New York.

Watson, H., K. Rainer, and C. Koh (1991), "Executive information systems: a framework for development and a survey of current practice," *MIS Quarterly*, Vol. 15, pp. 13–30.

Weizer, N. (1992), "Videoconferencing comes of age," *Chief Information Officer*, Vol. 4, pp. 41–43.

Yoo, S. and L. Digman (1987), "Decision support system: a new tool for management," *Long Range Planning*, Vol. 20, pp. 114–124.

Reproduced from *Behavior and Information Technology*, Vol. 21, No. 4, July–August, 2002, pp. 293–302. Reprinted with permission from Taylor & Francis.

Questions for discussion

1   Discuss the difference between high and low context communication. Which characterizes your own type of communication?

2   Why would one expect communication style (high vs. low) to influence IT behaviour? And in what ways might the communication style exert an influence?

3   What types of IT would one expect the communication style to influence the most?

4   Do you think that the experiment was well conducted? How would you do it differently today?

12 Mexican and Swedish Managers' Perceptions of the Impact of EIS on Organizational Intelligence, Decision Making, and Structure

Dorothy E. Leidner, Sven Carlsson, Joyce Elam and Martha Corrales

Abstract: Although information technologies in business organizations around the world may be very similar, the meanings conveyed through the technologies may be dependent on managerial values and national culture. Cultural differences need to be understood before information technology developed for organizations in one country can be effectively implemented in organizations in another country. Drawing on survey responses from managers using Executive Information Systems (EIS) across many organizations in Mexico, Sweden, and the United States, the current study examined whether cultural differences influence perceptions of the relationship between Executive Information Systems' use and various outcomes related to decision-making behaviors and processes. The study found significant differences, predicted by cultural factors, in the impact of EIS use on senior management decision making. The findings confirm the notion that IT is used by executives to reinforce the decision-making behaviors valued in their culture.

Introduction

As the world increasingly moves toward more open, global markets, the need for timely, reliable, easily accessible information will be a key to effective decision making. Executive Information Systems (EIS) can be one means of providing this important information. Several benefits of EIS use have been suggested in the literature. Studies have suggested that EIS enable executives to focus more on analysis rather than the collection of data, to conduct more in-depth analysis, and to take action faster (Rockart & DeLong, 1988;

Watson, Rainer, & Koh, 1991), as well as to improve decision making and increase productivity (Belcher & Watson, 1993). Although originally seen in large U.S. organizations, the use of EIS as important management tools has also been reported in Australia (Pervan & Rhua, 1995; Pervan & McNeely, 1994; Hassan & Gould, 1994), Canada (Bergeron, Raymond, Rivard, & Gara, 1995), and the United Kingdom (McBride, 1995; Holtham & Murphy, 1994; Allison, 1996; Fitzgerald, 1992).

Yet, even as information technologies in business organizations around the world converge, the meanings conveyed through them as well as the outcomes of their use may remain culture specific (Limaye & Victor, 1991). For example, one study found that culture plays a role in the predisposition toward and selection of electronic communication media (Straub, 1994). This can be attributed to the fact that any information system is developed with a set of assumptions concerning how it should be used and what types of impacts should be anticipated; indeed, even designer values vary across cultures (Kumar & Bjorn-Andersen, 1990; Raman & Watson, 1994). For cases in which the use of the system requires adaptation of behavior to achieve benefits, adaptations that are consistent with core values in a culture will be more effective than adaptations incongruent with core cultural values (Baligh, 1993; Lachman, Nedd, & Hinings, 1994). Evidence of incongruence was revealed in a study that found that GDSS was not as well received in Singapore as in the United States, and even led to negative consequences because of different attitudes toward the appropriateness of the expression of conflict (Ho, Raman, & Watson, 1989).

EIS may be particularly culture specific in terms of the perceived outcomes of use in that these systems are: developed with individuals in mind, geared toward the provision of quantifiable information, and focused on providing daily or real-time information. These characteristics are highly valued in the culture of the United States but may not be as valued in other cultures. Such systems may meet with resistance when being implemented in cultures with different perspectives of time, individuality, and the importance and trustworthiness of quantifiable information. Even if successfully implemented, such systems may not yield the same benefits as they do in the culture from which the systems originally emerged. Much as universal statements about the effects of organizational structures on individuals cannot be made on account of national cultural differences (Lincoln, Hanada, & Olson, 1981), generalizations about the outcomes of using an information system on individuals cannot be made across cultures until research offers evidence of similar effects of IS use across cultures. The current study reports the findings of 184 EIS users from Mexico and Sweden and compares the current findings to the findings reported in Leidner and Elam (1995) of 91 EIS users from the United States in order to examine the following research question: Are there differences in the perceived outcomes of EIS use across cultures?

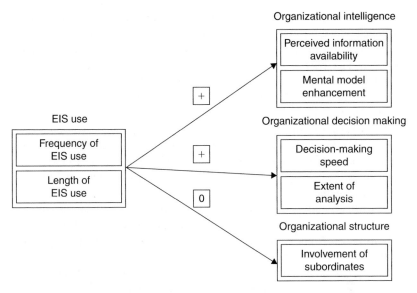

Figure 12.1 *Outcomes of EIS use for U.S. managers (Adapted from Leidner & Elam, 1995)*

The paper is organized as follows: The next section summarizes an existing theory of the impact of EIS on decision making based on a study of U.S. executives and presents the expected role of culture in explaining different outcomes of the theory in other cultures. The third section presents the methodology, and the fourth section presents the analysis and hypothesis testing. Finally, the fifth section presents the discussion of the findings, the limitations, and the conclusion.

Theoretical foundations and hypotheses

An EIS is a computer-based information system designed to provide senior, and in many cases middle and lower level, managers access to information relevant to their management activities. In a recent empirical analysis of 91 EIS users in the United States, Leidner and Elam (1995) examined the relationship between EIS use (measured as frequency of use as well as length of use) and outcomes related to organizational intelligence, decision making, and structure. Their findings, summarized in Figure 12.1, suggested that EIS use (frequency of EIS use, length of EIS use, or both) is positively related to increased information availability, enhanced mental models, greater analysis, and faster decision making. No relationship was found between EIS use and involvement of subordinates in decision making.

Because the Leidner and Elam (1995) research was based on a theory developed and tested on managers in the United States, it is neither possible to generalize to other cultures nor to ascertain the role that culture-based value systems play in influencing how EIS use will influence decision-making behaviors. Volonino, Watson, and Robinson (1995) suggested that EIS are used to the extent that they produce results valued by managers. We would suggest that anticipated and desired outcomes will vary across cultures because managerial values vary across cultures (Peterson, 1993; Boyacigiller & Adler, 1991). For instance, the fact that faster decision making is considered a desirable result may be culturally determined: The use of a system may not increase the speed of decision making in a culture that does not place an intrinsic value on fast decision making.

The current study extends research examining the outcomes of EIS to a multicultural context. Specifically, the research examines whether the same relationships between EIS use and five variables related to organizational intelligence, decision making, and structure identified in the aforementioned U.S. study will be found in cultures that are markedly different from the U.S., or whether these outcomes of EIS use are culturally independent. In the next section, we present the theoretical dimensions of culture. Based on this theory, we develop hypotheses of the outcomes of EIS use in Sweden and Mexico.

National culture

National culture has been defined as "the collective programming of the mind that distinguishes the members of one category of people from those of another" (Hofstede, 1991, p. 5). The most widely used constructs distinguishing national cultures in international business literature have been the constructs that emerged from Hofstede's study of 40 countries, from which he gathered over 100,000 responses to a questionnaire measuring values administered to employees of a single multinational organization. By holding the organization constant, Hofstede was able to isolate the differences attributable to national, rather than organizational culture. Exploratory factor analysis resulted in four dimensions with high reliability. These dimensions, defined briefly below, are: power distance, uncertainty avoidance, individualism, and masculinity (Hofstede, 1980, 1985). Hofstede and Bond (1988) later identified another cultural dimension, Confucian Dynamism, which was intended to uncover a cultural characteristic of the Eastern cultural clusters that did not emerge in Western cultural clusters – a society's search for virtue. The uncertainty avoidance scale, while appropriate in Western cultures, was less appropriate for Eastern cultures, as it presupposed a value attached to seeking and finding "truth." Eastern thought, however, does not emphasize truth as a goal but rather virtue. As the countries involved in our study are Western, we will not consider this dimension.

Power distance is the extent to which members of a society accept that power in institutions and organizations is unequally distributed (Hofstede, 1980). Power distance is related to the degree of centralization of decision making in organizations, with the higher power distance cultures accepting greater centralization than the lower power distance cultures (Hofstede, 1980).

Uncertainty avoidance is the degree to which members in society feel uncomfortable with uncertainty and ambiguity, which leads them to support beliefs promising certainty and to maintain institutions protecting conformity (Hofstede, 1980). Uncertainty avoidance is related to the degree of formalization in organizations and to the length of planning horizons, with higher uncertainty avoidance cultures having tighter controls and shorter planning horizons, over which there is presumably greater control than lower uncertainty avoidance cultures (Hofstede, 1980).

Individualism is the preference for a loosely knit social framework in society in which individuals are supposed to take care of themselves and their immediate family, as opposed to collectivism, in which there is a larger in-group to which is given unquestioning loyalty (Hofstede, 1980). Individualism is related to a low-context communication style wherein individuals prefer information to be stated directly and exhibit a preference for quantifiable detail, whereas collectivism is related to a high-context communication style in which individuals prefer to draw inferences from nonexplicit or implicit information (Hall, 1976; Gudykunst, 1997).

Masculinity is the extent to which society is achievement oriented, assertive, and competitive, as opposed to femininity, which is the extent to which a society values relationships, quality of life, and caring for others (Hofstede, 1980). Table 12.1 summarizes the differences in the cultural dimensions for the United States, Sweden, and Mexico using the scores and ranks as determined by Hofstede (1980).

Hypotheses

This section discusses how the above-described culture dimensions may affect the relationship of EIS use to perceived information availability, mental model enhancement, extent of analysis, decision-making speed, and involvement of subordinates.

Information availability

Information availability is the presence and accessibility of information relevant to managers. Prior research of U.S. executives has found positive and significant relationships between the frequency of EIS use and perceived information availability (Leidner & Elam, 1995). Since the purpose of EIS – to provide access to information – is not expected to vary systematically

Table 12.1   *Summary of theoretical cultural differences (from Hofstede, 1980)*

	United States	Sweden	Mexico	Mean score
Power Distance	Medium	Low	High	
Score*	40 (38)	31 (47)	81 (5)	57
Uncertainty Avoidance	Medium	Low	High	
Score*	46 (43)	29 (49)	82 (18)	65
Masculinity	High	Low	High	
Score*	62 (15)	5 (53)	69 (6)	49
Individuality	High	High	Low	
Score*	91 (1)	71 (10)	30 (32)	43
Communication Context	Low	Low	High	
Time Orientation	Monochronic	Monochronic	Polychronic	

*A score ranges from a low of 1 to a high of 100; values in parentheses represent rank out of 53 countries.

across cultures, EIS use is hypothesized to be perceived as making information available that was previously unavailable or difficult to obtain regardless of culture. Formally stated:

H1a: Swedish executives will perceive that EIS use leads to an increase in information availability.

H1b: Mexican executives will perceive that EIS use leads to an increase in information availability.

Mental model enhancement

Although there are not anticipated differences in the perceived information availability provided by the EIS, in some cultures the use of the information made available by the EIS may have different consequences than in others. For EIS to be useful in enhancing a manager's mental model, the type of information most readily available in EIS – daily financial performance figures – must be of particular value to the managers. We suggest that the degree to which EIS use is related to mental model enhancement may depend on whether the EIS user is from a collectivist, high-context culture or an individualist, low-context culture. Hall (1976) suggested that for top executives in a low-context office such as is typical in Sweden or the United States, most of the information that is relevant to the job originates from the few people the executive sees in a day. Because advisors and support personnel control the content and flow of organizational information, information is highly focused, compartmentalized, and controlled, and therefore not apt to flow freely. By contrast, executives in a collectivist, high-context culture such as Mexico have a preference for a multitude of informants at many levels. Hall (1976) suggested that in a high-context office, channels are seldom overloaded because people stay in constant contact. Thus, in a high-context culture such as Mexico, the additional information provided by an EIS is not likely to be as significant in enhancing one's mental model of the business as in the low-context cultures such as Sweden or the U.S., because executives in high-context cultures are accustomed to already receiving a wide variety of information from a multitude of sources. We therefore hypothesize:

H2a: Swedish executives will perceive that EIS use leads to an enhancement of their mental model.
H2b: Mexican executives will not perceive that EIS use leads to an enhancement of their mental model.

Extent of analysis

The extent of analysis in decision making is the "reflective thought and deliberation given to a problem and the array of proposed responses" (Miller & Friesen, 1980). Leidner and Elam (1995) found that for U.S. executives, the frequency and length of EIS use were positively related to the extent of analysis in decision making. The value placed on extensive analysis, and on the use of EIS to increase analysis, may be related to the uncertainty avoidance dimension of culture. Countries with very low uncertainty avoidance typically do not encounter anxiety related to an inability to accurately forecast all future factors that might be relevant to a decision. This helps explain why in low uncertainty avoidance cultures, longer term planning is undertaken as compared to high uncertainty avoidance cultures – the anxiety associated with an inability to predict important future factors inhibits the planning process in higher uncertainty avoidance cultures (Hofstede, 1985). Furthermore, data and information not coming from very trusted sources in a high uncertainty avoidance environment would be viewed with great skepticism. In practical terms, this suggests that high uncertainty avoidance cultures would not engage in as extensive an analysis of data before making decisions because the data may not be trusted or the data may not be viewed as predicting the future.

Moran and Abbott (1994) confirmed that in Mexico, a very high uncertainty avoidance culture, *proyectismo* – making decisions without critical analysis and assuming in time that all will be accomplished – is a common approach to decision making. Kras (1995) asserted that decision making and planning in Mexico has always been difficult because of the extreme fluctuations in the economic and political climate. Such fluctuations have led to a short-term focus and a lack of attention to detailed analysis. The short-term focus of Mexicans appears to be endemic to their political, economic, and cultural context (Ramos, 1962; Derossi, 1971). Derossi suggested that the historical instability in government and economics limits the range of forecasting and encourages private industry to behave negatively. A "predatory" attitude develops where immediate profit is sought because present favorable conditions are not expected to last. In addition to the political and economic situation which interacts with uncertainty avoidance to produce short-term planning, the educational system in Mexico encourages deductive reasoning and the pursuit of abstract concepts (Kras, 1995). Kras suggested that this results in managers with little inclination to carry out extensive analysis of detailed information. Condon (1985) echoed this view when he observed that Mexican managers prefer to entertain outlines of general principles supported by credible personal experience rather than getting mired in details.

Thus, analysis in support of decision making in Mexico and other high uncertainty avoidance cultures tends to involve an intellectual pursuit of abstract concepts as opposed to an analysis of detailed data (Kras, 1995), whereas in lower uncertainty avoidance cultures the decision-making and planning approach is largely empirical, making the analysis of operational and financial data valuable, such as that readily provided by an EIS. In the case of our study, the low uncertainty avoidant Swedish executives are expected to value extensive analysis prior to decision making whereas the Mexican executives are not expected to value in-depth analysis of data contained in an EIS, and are therefore not expected to experience an increase in the extent of analysis before decision making related to EIS use. Formally stated, we hypothesize that:

H3a: Swedish executives will perceive that EIS use leads to an increase in their extent of analysis in decision making.

H3b: Mexican executives will not perceive that EIS use leads to an increase in their extent of analysis in decision making.

Decision-making speed

The speed of decision making is defined as the lapse in time from when a decision maker recognizes the need to make some decision, to the point in time when he or she renders judgment (Stephensen, 1986). Leidner and Elam (1995) found support for the hypothesis that the frequency and length of EIS use would be related to the speed of decision making in their sample of U.S. executives. The degree of value attributed to fast decision making may be related to the dimensions of uncertainty avoidance and masculinity/femininity. Countries with high uncertainty avoidance may be expected to value fast decisions out of a concern that volatility in the environment might render decisions ineffective if they are not made immediately. Two decision-making patterns could result from high uncertainty avoidance – one, no decisions being made out of a concern that the decision would likely not fit the context once implemented; or two, continual rapid adjustments to the environment resulting in rapid successive decisions being made. We anticipate that in the business context facing Mexico in the 1990s, with the privatization of industries and the opening of the market, a pattern of making rapid decisions to ensure survival would be more likely than a pattern of continued waiting for more favorable circumstances.

The masculinity cultural dimension may also shed light on attitudes toward the importance of speed in decision making. Hofstede (1985) suggested that masculine cultures are more assertive, aggressive, and decisive than are feminine cultures. Assertiveness and decisiveness may reveal themselves in a tendency to make decisions quickly (although this says nothing about the time of implementing the decision). In summary, Sweden, ranking very low on masculinity and uncertainty avoidance, would not be predicted to value speed in decision making whereas Mexico, being very high on masculinity and uncertainty avoidance, would. Stated formally:

H4a: Swedish executives will not perceive that EIS use leads to an increase in their decision-making speed.
H4b: Mexican executives will perceive that EIS use leads to an increase in their decision-making speed.

Involvement of subordinates in decision making

Involvement of subordinates in decision making is the relying on subordinates both to bring to their superiors' attention potential problems requiring action and to analyze problems and alternatives. Leidner and Elam (1995) did not find a relationship between the frequency and/or length of EIS use with a change in the involvement of subordinates in decision making among U.S. executives. This may be because involving subordinates carries neither a consistent positive nor consistent negative connotation in the United States. Whether or not a positive or negative connotation is attached to involving subordinates in decision making may be related to the power distance dimension.

In high power distance cultures, centralized power and autocratic decision making is accepted whereas in low power distance cultures, power is decentralized and consensual decision making is preferred. The U.S., being in the middle of the power distance dimension, favors neither participatory nor autocratic decision making. Whereas a very low power distance culture such as Sweden would value consensual decision making, in high power distance cultures such as Mexico, the noninvolvement of subordinates in decision making is common and respected (Kras, 1995). Kras stated that in Mexico, there is no tradition of delegation of authority, and subordinates are expected

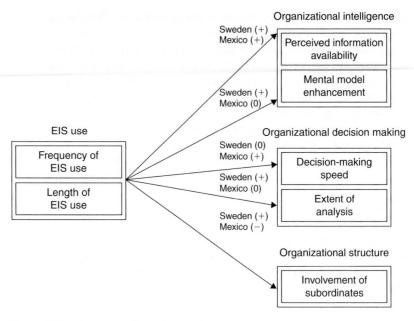

Figure 12.2   *Summary of hypotheses*

to accept unconditionally what their bosses say. Systems that enable delegation of responsibility may therefore be more readily embraced in cultures lower in power distance such as Sweden than in high power distance cultures such as Mexico. We thus hypothesize that:

H5a: Swedish executives will perceive that EIS use leads to an increase in their involvement of subordinates in decision making.

H5b: Mexican executives will perceive that EIS use leads to a decrease in their involvement of subordinates in decision making.

This section has presented hypotheses predicting that EIS users from Sweden and Mexico will respond in a systematically different way to the variables tested in the Leidner and Elam (1995) study of U.S. executives. Figure 12.2 summarizes the hypotheses.

Methodology

A survey instrument was used to gather data to test the relationships expressed in the hypotheses. The same survey used in Leidner and Elam (1995) was employed after having been translated into Spanish and Swedish. A native Swede translated the survey into Swedish and a native Mexican translated the survey into Spanish. Both translators had resided and worked in the United States. After the questionnaire had been translated, it was reviewed by individuals whose native tongue was Swedish for the Swedish version or Spanish for the Spanish version.

The items used to measure the five outcome variables are given in the Appendix. The variables measure the executives' perceptions of the outcome of EIS use. These were all measured on a 5-point scale, with 1 representing *to no extent* and 5 representing *to a great extent.* The operalization of the variables, having previously been described in Leidner and Elam (1995), will not be repeated here. EIS use was measured in terms of frequency (on a 5-point scale ranging from *monthly* to usage *several times per day*) and length (number of months) of use.

Data collection

Data collection in Sweden took place in 1992 and 1993. Through an extensive review of business, trade, and academic journals, and through contacting the major suppliers of EIS development shells and consultants for EIS development, the researchers identified companies in Sweden with EIS. Data collection in Mexico took place in 1994 and 1995. There were no references found in business, trade, or academic journals to Mexican organizations with EIS; nor were the authors able to glean information from U.S.-based suppliers or consultants. Instead, a database containing the names of the top managers and company addresses for all medium- and large-sized organizations in Mexico was obtained. The IS director in a random sample of the organizations was called and asked if the organization had an EIS.

A contact person was identified in each company and interviewed over the phone. The contact person was typically from the information systems department and had an important role in designing, developing, and/or maintaining the EIS. Interviewing the contact person was a means of ensuring that each of the companies participating in the study did in fact have an EIS as traditionally defined.

In addition, the authors visited several of the organizations in both countries and were given demonstrations of the EIS. Even though the authors did not personally use the EIS, the demonstrations they witnessed revealed no obvious differences in system features. The features of the EIS (drill-down analysis, status updates of information, graphical interface, access to an electronic news provider, etc.) appeared standard. In general, the systems from the Swedish sample were built in 1991–1992 and the systems from the Mexican sample in 1990–1991. By way of comparison, the systems from the Leidner and Elam (1995) U.S. study were built in 1989–1990. Considering that there is likely a lag in the time technology is developed in the U.S. to the time it emerges in foreign countries, the slight difference in time periods of EIS development was judged to be unimportant in influencing the equivalence of the samples.

The contact person was given a set of surveys to distribute to EIS users. If the number of users was less than 10, we requested that all EIS users be given a survey. If there were more than 10 EIS users, we requested that the contact person randomly distribute the surveys to EIS users. Because we were relying on a contact to encourage users to complete the survey and because the respondents would be high level, we considered it unrealistic to expect the contact to manage data collection of more than a small number (10) of users. In all cases except one, there were greater than 10 users. In the one company with less than 10 users, all completed the survey.

Care was taken in the handling of surveys to guarantee confidentiality for all respondents involved and thereby reduce the possible threat of respondents failing to respond at all or failing to respond honestly. Respondents were provided with private envelopes to seal and return to the researchers or to seal and return to the individual contact in the organization, who would then return the envelopes to the researchers. There was no code on the surveys to trace them to individuals. A cover letter to the participants explained the project, the voluntary nature of their participation, and the policies the researchers would employ to ensure their confidentiality.

Although senior executives were originally intended to be the users of EIS, these systems are now frequently used at lower management levels (Watson et al., 1991). Senior management can be considered as the president and one level below the president, whereas middle management is two levels below the president (Zaki & Hoffman, 1988). Using the Zaki and Hoffman classification, all of the Swedish respondents in the current study classify as senior managers, whereas half of the Mexican respondents were senior and half middle managers. We suggest that the samples are in fact comparable because Swedish organizations are much flatter than Mexican organizations. Hence, it is likely that many "senior" managers in Swedish organizations would be positioned at more than one level below the president (and hence defined as "middle" managers) were they in organizations as hierarchical as those in Mexico. Furthermore, Leidner and Elam (1995) found no difference in the outcome of EIS use for senior and middle managers, suggesting that the outcomes of EIS use are similar at both levels of management. In our study, all of the individuals were in middle- to high-level positions involving administrative responsibilities in their organizations, including supervising subordinates and planning, rather than in clerical, operational, or technical (such as engineering or computer science) positions. We therefore do not distinguish in this study between senior and middle managers, but refer to the EIS users as "managers."

Analysis and results

In total, 22 Swedish contacts and 24 Mexican contacts agreed during phone conversations to distribute surveys. Responses were returned from all 22

Swedish and 17 Mexican organizations. Among the original 24 organizations in Mexico that agreed to participate, it was determined during follow-up interviews that seven did not have working EIS but were in the stages of planning or developing an EIS. They were therefore disqualified from participating in the study. In total, 317 surveys were sent to the 39 organizations. Of these, 198 were returned for a response rate of 62% for total surveys sent. Of the 198 returned, 184 were usable: 95 from Sweden and 89 from Mexico. The industries represented by the Swedish organizations included construction, consumer products, transportation, manufacturing, petroleum, pharmaceutical, and telecommunications. The industries represented by the Mexican organizations included construction, consumer products, manufacturing, financial services, food products, and professional services.

Construct validity and reliability

Construct validity addresses the question of whether the constructs are real, as measured, or merely artifacts of the methodology. Eigenvalues greater than 1.0 and scree plots were used in determining the number of factors. For an item to be considered in the composition of a variable, it had to have a loading of at least .5 on the factor, with no loading exceeding .3 on another factor; had to conform to a priori assignments; and had to add to the variable's reliability. The mean of the items in each scale was used to combine the items into a variable score. Cronbach's alpha was used to assess the inter-item reliability of the final, multi-item scales. While a reliability score of .6 is usually considered acceptable (Nunnally, 1967), all of the variables' reliability scores exceed .8 except for one. The exception was the involvement of subordinates in decision making, with a reliability of .71. The factor loadings and the reliability scores for each variable are provided in Table 12.2. Table 12.3 presents the descriptive statistics for each variable by country.

Statistical analysis performed

MANOVA was run to test for an overall country effect on all the variables combined. The country effect is significant ($F = 4.56$, $df = 6$; $p = .000$). MANOVA was also run to test for an overall organizational effect. There was no significant organizational effect ($F = 1.47$, $df = 6$; $p = .159$); hence, the country differences overshadowed any organizational differences.

In order to test the hypotheses, the sample was divided by country. MANOVAs were run using frequency and length of EIS use as the independent variables; and information availability, mental model enhancement, extent of analysis, decision-making speed, and involvement of subordinates as the dependent variables. Because we are interested in the impact of EIS use on several outcome variables, conducting *t*-tests of differences in the outcome variables across the cultures would not provide insight into how

Table 12.2   *Results of the factor analysis and reliability tests*

Factor	Cronbach's Alpha	Factor loading
Perceived information availability	.86	
Availability of information that was previously unavailable except as a special request		.72
Information available in a more timely manner		.92
A single delivery source of important, frequently used information		.88
Mental Model Enhancement	.90	
Clearer sense of where things are going		.72
Sharper vision and increased comprehension of the business		.83
Better understanding of important trends		.84
Better insights into the problems and opportunities facing us		.85
Extent of Analysis in Decision Making	.90	
Spend significantly more time analyzing data before making a decision		.82
Examine more alternatives in decision making		.84
Use more sources of information in decision making		.82
Decision-making Speed	.88	
Make decisions quicker		.60
Shortened the time frame for making decisions		.67
Involvement of Subordinates in Decision Making	.71	
Many problems requiring organizational action are brought to my attention by subordinates		.52
I frequently involve subordinates in decision processes		.70

different levels of use in a country was related to various outcomes in that country. Therefore, we conduct our analysis by examining, within each culture, whether frequency or length of use have perceived impacts on the individual managers.

The results of the MANOVAs for each country are given in Tables 12.4 and 12.5. For Swedish managers, the MANOVA was significant ($F = 3.72$,

Table 12.3 *Descriptive statistics for Mexican and Swedish users of EIS by variable*

	Mean	SD	Min	Max	N
Descriptive statistics: Mexico					
Frequency of use	3.60	1.20	1	5	89
Length of use (Years)	3.37	1.38	1	5	82
Perceived information availability	4.22	0.81	1	5	87
Mental model enhancement	3.53	0.78	1	5	88
Extent of analysis	3.76	0.97	1	5	87
Decision-making speed	3.63	0.81	1	5	88
Involvement of subordinates	3.82	0.49	2.6	4.8	88
Descriptive statistics: Sweden					
Frequency of use	3.62	0.81	1	5	95
Length of use (Years)	2.59	0.96	1	5	95
Perceived information availability	3.81	0.61	1	5	95
Mental model enhancement	3.16	0.64	1	5	95
Extent of analysis	3.13	0.66	1	4.33	95
Decision-making speed	2.71	0.77	1	4.5	94
Involvement of subordinates	3.81	0.61	1	5	95

$p > 0$, $df = 10$). The frequency of EIS use was significantly and positively related to mental model enhancement and the extent of analysis in decision making; it was significantly and negatively related to the involvement of subordinates in decision making. For Swedish managers, the length of EIS use was significantly and positively related to perceived information availability, mental model enhancement, and decision-making speed. For Swedish managers, frequency of use was not significantly correlated with length of use ($r = .13$, $p < .09$). The Swedish managers tended to use the EIS at a fairly frequent level independent of the length of time they had had the EIS. For Mexican managers, the MANOVA was significant ($F = 1.835$, $p > .039$, $df = 10$). The frequency of EIS use was positively and significantly related to perceived information availability, the extent of analysis in decision making, and decision-making speed. The length of EIS use was not significantly related to any of the dependent variables. For Mexican managers, the frequency of use has a slight though weak positive correlation with length ($r = .19$, $p < .03$).

Table 12.4   *MANOVA for Swedish managers who use EIS*

	Regression coefficient	*T*	*P > T*
Information availability			
EIS use: Frequency	0.006	0.082	.935
EIS use: Length	0.129	2.279	.025
Mental model			
EIS use: Frequency	0.295	4.411	.000
EIS use: Length	0.175	3.204	.002
Extent of analysis			
EIS use: Frequency	1.680	1.958	.054
EIS use: Length	0.105	1.494	.139
Decision-making speed			
EIS use: Frequency	0.171	1.739	.086
EIS use: Length	0.216	2.686	.009
Involvement of subordinates			
EIS use: Frequency	−0.177	−2.700	.008
EIS use: Length	0.053	0.979	.330

Hypothesis testing

H1 predicted that Swedish and Mexican managers would perceive information availability with frequent and long-term use of EIS. This hypothesis is partially supported for both countries. The Swedish managers perceived increased information availability the longer they had used the EIS, whereas the Mexican managers perceived increased information availability the more frequently they had used the EIS. Swedish managers did not perceive increased information availability with frequent EIS use, and Mexican managers did not perceive increased information availability with length of time of EIS use.

H2 predicted that Swedish managers would experience an enhanced mental model from using EIS but that Mexican managers would not experience an enhanced mental model. This hypothesis was supported. Swedish managers who used EIS frequently or over time perceived an enhanced mental model. Mexican managers neither perceived an enhanced mental model with frequent EIS use nor with long-term EIS use.

Table 12.5 *MANOVA for Mexican managers who use EIS*

	Regression coefficient	T	P > T
Information availability			
EIS Use: Frequency	0.193	3.007	.004
EIS Use: Length	−0.096	−1.866	.066
Mental model			
EIS Use: Frequency	0.132	1.858	.067
EIS Use: Length	0.033	0.584	.561
Extent of analysis			
EIS Use: Frequency	0.215	2.273	.026
EIS Use: Length	−0.036	−0.480	.633
Decision-making speed			
EIS Use: Frequency	0.188	2.598	.011
EIS Use: Length	−0.036	−0.615	.540
Involvement of subordinates			
EIS Use: Frequency	0.072	1.243	.218
EIS Use: Length	0.022	0.468	.641

H3 predicted that Swedish managers would experience more extensive analysis resulting from EIS use but that Mexican managers would not experience an increase in their extent of analysis from EIS use. This was partially supported. The more frequent the use of EIS by Swedish managers, the greater the perceived extent of analysis in decision making; however, the relationship did not hold for the length of time of EIS use. A small but significant positive relationship was found between the frequency of EIS use and the perceived extent of analysis in decision making for the Mexican managers, but not with the length of time of EIS use.

H4 predicted that Swedish managers would not experience increased decision-making speed from EIS use but that Mexican managers would experience an increase in their decision-making speed related to EIS use. This hypothesis is also partially supported. Swedish managers did not perceive an increase in their decision-making speed associated with the frequent use of EIS; however, they did perceive an increase in decision-making speed associated with the length of time of EIS use. Mexican managers perceived an increase in decision-making speed associated with the frequent use of EIS but not with the length of time of EIS use.

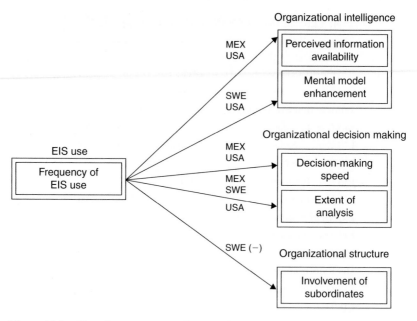

Figure 12.3   *Hypothesis testing results using frequency of EIS use*

H5 predicted that Swedish managers would associate an increase in their involvement of subordinates in decision making related to EIS use but that Mexican managers would associate a decrease in their reliance on subordinates in decision making related to EIS use. This hypothesis is not supported. In fact, Swedish managers had a significant negative relationship between the frequent use of EIS and the perceived involvement of subordinates in decision making. There was neither a positive nor a negative relationship between the frequency of EIS use or the length of EIS use with the perceived involvement of subordinates in decision making for the Mexican managers.

Figures 12.3 and 12.4 summarize the hypothesis testing results, including the U.S. results from Leidner and Elam (1995) for comparison. Table 12.6 presents the results as a comparison against the prior study of U.S. executives. Table 12.6 words the results in terms of the hypotheses used in Leidner and Elam (1995).

Discussion

This section discusses the major findings of the study and the implications of the findings for the theory of culture and for future research of EIS.

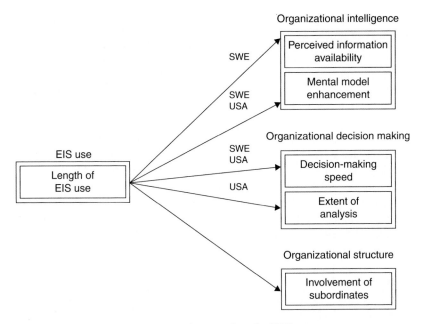

Figure 12.4   *Hypothesis testing results using length of EIS use*

Table 12.6   *Comparison of results against U.S. sample*

Hypotheses	USA	Sweden	Mexico
The more frequent the manager's use of EIS,			
the greater the perceived information availability	Yes	No	Yes
the greater the enhancement to his/her mental model	Yes	Yes	No
the greater the extent of analysis	**Yes**	**Yes**	**Yes**
the faster the decision-making speed	Yes	No	Yes
the less the involvement of subordinates in organizational intelligence and decision making	No	Yes	No
The longer the manager's use of EIS,			
the greater the perceived information availability	No	Yes	No
the greater the enhancement to his/her mental model	Yes	Yes	No
the greater the extent of analysis	Yes	No	No
the faster the decision-making speed	Yes	Yes	No
the less the involvement of subordinates in organizational intelligence and decision making	**No**	**No**	**No**

Note: Boldface indicates similarity across countries.

The major findings

Several points of interest were raised by the findings. Executives from both Sweden and Mexico, like the U.S. executives in Leidner and Elam (1995), perceived higher information availability when they used the EIS either frequently or over time. In other words, culture does not influence perceptions of information being made available by an EIS. Only in Sweden, however, was there a significant positive relationship between perceived information availability and length of EIS use. This may indicate that the Swedish organizations were continuously maintaining the information content of their EIS and adjusting the content over time to the needs of the executives. Future studies of EIS should examine such important design issues as how frequently to reassess information needs in order that the systems maintain value over time. While for Mexican executives there was not a significant positive relationship between length of EIS use and perceived information availability, neither was there a negative relationship. A negative relationship would indicate that, as with many technologies, there is a newness effect with the system in which users are initially pleased but the excitement wanes gradually over time. Most likely, the sample was selective in this sense – if the executives gradually perceived less information availability over time, they quit using the system and, hence, were not part of the sample.

In terms of achieving increased understanding of their organization from using EIS, Swedish managers, like the U.S. managers in Leidner and Elam (1995), reported enhanced mental models from frequent and long-term use of the EIS, whereas Mexican managers did not. This provides some evidence that certain types of information are more valuable in some cultures than others. Although the features and types of information in the EIS were very similar in each country, as revealed during interviews, the value of the information in the EIS toward helping managers understand their business was greater in Sweden and the U.S., based on the Leidner and Elam (1995) study, than in Mexico. This suggests that the Mexicans might have a greater unmet need for soft information in the EIS than the other two cultures. Adler (1983) suggested that the effective transfer of process and person embodied technology requires that members of a culture have the ability to absorb and utilize context-free information. This tendency is difficult to develop in cultures that function primarily by emphasizing context-dependent sources of information such as in Mexico.

Although the use of EIS was not perceived to enhance the executives' mental models in Mexico, the Mexican managers did perceive their decision-making speed to increase with the frequent use of EIS, similar to the U.S. managers in Leidner and Elam (1995). Contrary to the hypotheses, speed also seemed to be an important aspect of EIS in Sweden. Swedish managers, as did the U.S. managers in Leidner and Elam, associated decision-making speed with the length of use of the EIS. This might tentatively suggest that over time, the system influenced the Swedish managers to adopt a decision-making style – in this case fast decision making – that ran contrary to the dominant cultural pattern.

Managers from both Sweden and Mexico perceived more extensive analysis from using EIS frequently, but not from long-term use of the EIS. The Mexican managers were not expected to use EIS to increase their analysis. Indeed, it is interesting that while the Mexicans did not report an improved mental model, they did report more extensive analysis of data. This may tentatively suggest that the systems encouraged a decision-making behavior among Mexican executives – extensive analysis – that by itself did not alter the thinking of the managers.

Finally, contrary to the hypotheses, Swedish managers reported a decrease in their reliance on subordinates with frequent use of the EIS. One explanation might be that organizational power in Sweden is more equally distributed than in the U.S. or Mexico because of the lower power distance and, as a result, problems can be handled at a lower level in the organization; therefore, less interaction between upper level managers and subordinates is needed. Hence, the EIS could be used to distribute decision making downward rather than involving lower levels in upper level decision making. Also running contrary to the hypotheses was the finding that Mexicans did not report a decrease in their reliance on subordinates in decision making. Kras (1995) suggested that there is a new generation of managers in Mexico, which because of university training, strongly supports the delegation of responsibility together with the accompanying authority and accountability. Perhaps the results of this study suggest that they are in fact moving in this direction.

The cultural implications

Taken together, these major findings suggest that culture does play a role in the outcome of use of an information system. In 10 hypotheses comparing three cultures, agreement across all three cultures is found in only 2 of the 10 hypotheses (see Table 12.6). Moreover, there was no significant relationship between length of use of EIS in Mexico and any of the outcome variables. EIS, as are most common today, seem particularly well suited for cultures moderate or low in both uncertainty avoidance and power distance. In countries of extremely high uncertainty, the data in the EIS, though real-time, may still not be trusted, or may not be trusted to be indicative of future performance. Thus, while perhaps interesting, the information in the EIS may not be perceived as extremely valuable in decision making for the high uncertainty avoidance cultures. In high power distance countries, subordinates are wary of being checked upon. Kras (1995) suggested that subordinates in Mexico are inclined to feel that their superiors do not trust them if procedures are introduced that are designed to check on their performance. One might think that in high power distance cultures, subordinates would be accustomed to close scrutiny without complaint. However, it appears that subordinates in high power distance cultures accept mandates from superiors but then expect to be trusted to effectuate the work, whereas in low power distance cultures, subordinates are accustomed to more discretion in decision making but are not offended by superiors keeping posted of their performance. EIS also seem better suited to individualistic, low-context cultures in which hard, quantifiable information is valuable and trusted than to collectivist, high-context cultures, in which managers are accustomed to information flowing more freely, and being less locally owned, in the organization.

These generalizations are limited to the area of decision-making behaviors. It is very conceivable that other areas of EIS outcome not examined in this study are of particular value in a high-uncertainty, high-power distance, collectivist environments. The fact that the Mexican executives continued using the EIS over time despite not reporting significant relationships between the length of EIS use and any of the variables reported in this study suggests that they were perceiving benefits not addressed in this study, such as benefits in the area of communication or creating a shared vision of the organization. Such factors merit future research.

Lastly, it should be noted that several of the hypotheses were not supported and, in some cases, ran contrary to the predicted direction. The cultural dimensions proved insufficient in and of themselves to accurately predict all the outcomes of use. Other factors that were not considered in this study, such as the business, political, or economic environments of the countries, might interact with or supersede culture as a predictor of the outcome of EIS use. Another area for future research would therefore be to consider the relative importance of culture in interpreting systems' use and impacts.

Future research

EIS research does not yet have as longstanding a research tradition as do many systems, such as DSS, GSS, and electronic mail; yet the potential for organizational change when technology is used by senior managers is great and merits our attention. EIS research has evolved from case studies (Applegate & Osborn, 1988; Osborn & Applegate, 1989; Applegate, 1987; Rockart & DeLong, 1988) to descriptive studies of system features and success factors (Bergeron, Raymond, & Lagorge, 1991; Watson et al., 1991; Allison, 1996; Fitzgerald, 1992), to theoretical studies of the impacts of EIS on executives (Leidner & Elam, 1993–1994, 1995; Vandenbosch & Higgins, 1996). Although we know much about why and how EIS are used, we are only beginning to understand the long-term consequences of providing managers with ready access to detailed, daily information. Research is needed that examines the impact of EIS over time and, in particular, that examines the organizational consequences of EIS use. Furthermore, research is needed that examines the factors that contribute to the most effective uses of EIS. Carlsson, Leidner, and Elam (1996) proposed a framework for effective and ineffective EIS information design, but research is needed to consider the effective ways of using EIS and such issues as how widespread the EIS should be in the organization in order to achieve benefits. Although this study has attempted to expand our understanding of the impact of EIS on certain aspects of organizational decision making, structure, and intelligence, a plethora of issues merit attention, such as the implications of senior managers' use of IS on organizational communication, culture, and productivity. Future research can examine the effect of executives' monitoring organizational performance on subordinates' behaviors and the effect of such monitoring on perceived cultural changes. On a broader level, EIS represent less a class of separate systems than a philosophy toward information provision in organizations: the more timely, more readily accessible, more flexible, and more widespread the information, the greater the potential value of the system. This type of thinking is now seen with such systems as Intranets. Future research can examine various philosophies toward information provision and how these are manifested in system design and use.

Limitations and conclusions

Several limitations of the study need to be mentioned. One limitation is that the perceptions of managers from one culture reflecting upon their own behavior might be quite different than the perceptions of managers from a different culture reflecting on that culture. In other words, one must realize that just because one culture perceives their behavior to have been altered by a system, another culture observing the behavior might not notice the change. A second limitation is true of any multicultural research involving the replication of a study first carried out in one nation: The questions on the survey were originally intended for U.S. managers and were intended to reflect activities of importance to U.S. executives. It is possible that some questions may have been irrelevant to the Swedish and Mexican managers, but they answered them anyway. The corollary is also true: It is possible that some issues important to Swedish or Mexican managers may not have been included in the survey as they were not originally considered important to the U.S. managers. A third limitation concerns the sample: We neither controlled for geographical area within each country nor for system characteristics. Although the systems appeared to be quite similar across the countries, we cannot offer definitive proof of their similarity. A fourth limitation was our use of country as a surrogate of culture as is frequently done (Kim et al., 1990). Had we taken a direct measure of culture, this would have proven a stronger indication of cultural differences across the nations in our sample, but would have likely led to a lower response rate in that the survey would have been substantially longer. Lastly, perceptual measures were used for all variables except length of EIS use. The respondents were acting as informants of their own behavior. The use of perceptual measures need not be considered a weakness, but does suggest that the respondents' perceptions of the impacts of EIS use might not necessarily coincide exactly with reality. Le Blanc and Kozar (1990) found in one case that the perception of DSS success was low although objective measures indicated it was in reality high. Thus, the results must be interpreted within the context that perceptual measures were used. However, the perception of benefits through system usage may be sufficient justification in managers' minds for the system.

Despite the aforementioned limitations, this study makes a contribution to the growing knowledge of EIS as well as to the rudimentary field of cross-cultural IS studies. EIS are rapidly being adopted and used by organizations throughout the world. This study examined whether cultural differences influenced the relationship between EIS use and several aspects of decision-making behaviors and processes. In particular, we examined how executives in Sweden and Mexico perceived the outcomes of their EIS use and compared their perceptions with those of U.S. executives. We found that EIS have greater long-term relevance in low-context cultures such as Sweden and the United States. We also found that greater information availability does not necessarily improve general understanding of the business, as indicated by the Mexican sample of managers.

Kelley et al. (1987, p. 18) suggested that one perspective on culture and organizational adaptation is that "individuals irrespective of culture are forced to adopt industrial attitudes and behaviors such as rationalism, secularism, and mechanical time concerns in order to comply with the imperative of industrialization". This perspective ignores the longevity of basic cultural values and their influence on individual behavior. Although managers may be forced to adopt modern management technologies to survive in the global business environment, they are able to adapt the technology to their own cultural values rather than conforming their values to the assumptions of the technology. The adoption of management technologies designed to enhance individual performance, such as EIS, are context dependent, and culture is an important contextual factor to consider in anticipating potential benefits of information technology.

References

Adler, N. J. (1983), "Cross-cultural management research: The ostrich and the trend," *Academy of Management Review*, Vol. 8, No. 2, pp. 226–232.

Allison, L. K. (1996), "Executive information systems: An evaluation of current UK practice," *International Journal of Information Management*, Vol. 16, No. 1, pp. 27–38.

Applegate, L. M. (June 1987), *Lockheed-Georgia Company: Executive information systems. Harvard Case (9-187-135)*. Harvard Business School, Boston, MA.

Applegate, L. M. and C. S. Osborn (December 1988), *Phillips 66 Company: Executive information systems. Harvard Case (9-189-006)*. Harvard Business School, Boston, MA.

Baligh, H. H. (1994), "Components of cultures: Nature, interconnections, and relevance to the decisions on organization structure," *Management Science*, Vol. 40, No. 1, pp. 14–27.

Belcher, L. W. and H. J. Watson (1993), "Assessing the value of Conoco's EIS," *MIS Quarterly*, Vol. 17, No. 3, pp. 239–254.

Bergeron, F., L. Raymond, and M. Lagorge (1991), Top managers evaluate the attributes of EIS. *DSS-91 Transactions* (Ilze Zigurs, Ed.), 6–14.

Bergeron, E., L. Raymond, S. Rivard, and M. E. Gara (1995), "Determinants of EIS use: Testing a behavioral model," *Decision Support Systems*, Vol. 14, No. 2, pp. 131–146.

Boyacigiller, N. A. and N. J. Adler (1991), "The parochial dinosaur: Organizational science in a global context," *Academy of Management Review*, Vol. 16, No. 2, pp. 262–290.

Carlsson, S., D. E. Leidner, and J. J. Elam (1996), "Individual and organizational effectiveness: Perspectives on the impact of ESS in multinational organizations," in P. Humphreys, L. Bannon, A. McCosh, P. Migliarese, and J. C. Pomerol, Eds. *Implementing systems for supporting management decisions*. Chapman and Hall, London.

Condon, J. C. (1985), *Good neighbors: Communicating with the Mexicans*. Intercultural Press, Yarmouth.

DeRossi, F. (1971), *The Mexican entrepreneur*. Development Centre of the Organisation for Economic Co-Operation and Development, Paris.

Fitzgerald, G. (1992), "Executive information systems and their development in the U. K.," *International Information Systems*, April, pp. 1–35.

Gudykunst, W. B. (1997), "Cultural variability in communication," *Communication Research*, Vol. 24, No. 4, pp. 327–348.

Hall, E. T. (1976), *Beyond culture*. Anchor Books, New York.

Hasan, H. and E. Gould (1994), "EIS in the Australian public sector," *Journal of Decision Systems*, Vol. 3, No. 4, pp. 301–319.

Ho, T. H., K. S. Raman, and R. T. Watson (1989), Group decision support systems: The cultural factor. *Proceedings of the Tenth Annual International Conference on Information Systems*, Boston, MA, 119–129.

Hofstede, G. (1980), *Culture's consequences: International differences in work-related values*. Sage, Beverly Hills, CA.

Hofstede, G. (1985), "The interaction between national and organizational value systems," *Journal of Management Studies*, July, pp. 81–99.

Hofstede, G. (1991), *Cultures and organizations: Software of the mind.* McGraw-Hill, London.

Hofstede, G. and M. H. Bond (1988), "The Confucius connection: From cultural roots to economic growth," *Organizational Dynamics*, Vol. 16, No. 4, pp. 4–21.

Holtham, C. and C. Murphy (1994), "Executive information systems and senior management: Principles and practice," *Journal of Decision Systems*, Vol. 3, No. 4, pp. 259–276.

Jones, J. W. and R. J. McLeod Jr. (1986), "The structure of executive information systems: An exploratory analysis," *Decision Sciences*, Vol. 17, pp. 220–248.

Kelley, L., A. Whatley, and R. Worthley (1987), "Assessing the effects of culture on managerial attitudes: A three-culture test," *Journal of International Business Studies*, Vol. 18, No. 2, Summer, pp. 17–31.

Kim, K. I., H. Park, and N. Suzuki (1990), "Reward allocations in the United States, Japan, and Korea: A comparison of individualistic and collectivistic cultures," *Academy of Management Journal*, Vol. 33, No. 1, pp. 188–198.

Kras, E. S. (1991), *La administracion Mexicana en transición (Mexican management in transition)*. Grupo Editorial Iberoamérica, Mexico.

Kras, E. S. (1995), *Management in two cultures: Bridging the gap between U. S. and Mexican managers*. Intercultural Press, Yarmouth.

Kumar, K. and N. Bjorn-Andersen (1990), "A cross-cultural comparison of IS designer values," *Communications of the ACM*, Vol. 33, No. 5, pp. 528–538.

Lachman, R., A. Nedd, and B. Hinings (1994), "Analyzing cross-national management and organizations: A theoretical framework," *Management Science*, Vol. 40, No. 1, pp. 40–53.

Le Blanc, L. A. and K. A. Kozar (1990), "An empirical investigation of the relationship between DSS usage and system performance: A case study of a navigation support system," *MIS Quarterly*, Vol. 14, No. 3, pp. 263–278.

Leidner, D. E. and J. J. Elam (1993–1994), "Executive information systems: Their impact on executive decision making," *Journal of Management Information Systems*, Fall/Winter, pp. 139–156.

Leidner, D. E. and J. J. Elam (1995), "The impact of executive information systems on organizational design, intelligence, and decision making," *Organization Science*, Vol. 6, No. 6, pp. 645–665.

Limaye, M. R. and D. A. Victor (1991), "Cross-cultural business communication research: State of the art and hypotheses for the 1990s," *The Journal of Business Communication*, Vol. 28, No. 3, pp. 276–299.

Lincoln, J. R., M. Hanada, and J. Olson (1981), "Cultural orientations and individual reactions to organizations: A study of employees of Japanese-owned firms," *Administrative Science Quarterly*, Vol. 26, pp. 93–115.

McBride, N. (1995), "The role of executive information systems in organisations: An interpretive analysis," in J. F. Nunamaker, Jr. and R. H. Sprague, Jr., Eds. *Proceedings of the Twenty-Eighth Annual Hawaii International Conference on System Sciences*, Vol. III, 110–119.

Miller, D. and P. Friesen (1980), "Momentum and revolution in organizational adaptation," *Academy of Management Journal*, Vol. 23, No. 4, pp. 591–615.

Moran, R. T. and J. Abbott (1994), *NAFTA: Managing the cultural differences*. Gulf Publishing, Houston.

Nunnally, J. C. (1967), *Psychometric theory*. McGraw-Hill, New York.

Osborn, C. S. and L. M. Applegate (March 1989), *Xerox Corporation: Executive support systems. Harvard Case (N9-189-134)*. Harvard Business School, Boston, MA.

Pervan, G.P. and M. McNeely (1994), "Implementing and sustaining executive information systems: Influencing factors in mining industry context," in J. F. Nunamaker, Jr. and R. H. Sprague, Jr., Eds. *Proceedings of the Twenty-Eighth Annual Hawaii International Conference on System Sciences*. Vol. III, 101–119.

Pervan, G.P. and R. Rhua (1995), "Executive information systems in Australia: Current status and some historical comparisons," in J. F. Nunamaker, Jr. and R. H. Sprague, Jr., Eds. *Proceedings of the Twenty-Ninth Annual Hawaii International Conference on System Sciences*, Vol. II, 110–119.

Peterson, R. B. Ed. (1993), *Managers and national culture: A global perspective*. Quorom Books, Westport, CT.

Raman, K. S. and R. T. Watson (1994), "National culture, information systems, and organizational implications," in P. C. Deans and K. R. Kirwan, Eds. *Global information systems and technology*. Idea Group Publishing, Harrisburg, PA, pp. 493–513.

Ramos, S. (1962), *Profile of man and culture in Mexico*. University of Texas Press, Austin, TX. (translated by Peter G. Earle).

Rockart, J. and D. DeLong (1988), *Executive support systems: The emergence of top management computer use*. Dow-Jones-Irwin, Chicago, IL.

Straub, D. (1994), "The effect of culture on IT diffusion: E-Mail and fax in Japan and the U.S.," *Information Systems Research*, Vol. 5, No. 1, pp. 23–47.

Vandenbosch, B. and C. Higgins (1996), "Information acquisition and mental models: An investigation into the relationship between behaviour and learning," *Information Systems Research*, Vol. 7, No. 2, pp. 198–214.

Volonino, L., H. J. Watson, and S. Robinson (1995), "Using EIS to respond to dynamic business conditions," *Decision Support Systems*, Vol. 14, No. 2, pp. 105–116.

Watson, H. J., K. Rainer, and C. Koh (1991), "Executive information systems: A framework for development and a survey of current practices," *MIS Quarterly*, Vol. 15, No. 1, pp. 13–30.

Zaki, A. S. and R. C. Hoffman (1988), "Information type and its impact on information dissemination," *Journal of Information Systems Management*, Vol. 5, No. 2, pp. 71–82.

Reproduced from *Decision Sciences*, Vol. 30, No. 3, Summer 1999, pp. 633–661. Reprinted with permission from Blackwell Publishing.

Appendix: Items on questionnaire

Information Availability

Question: To what extent are the following benefits of your EIS use?
Availability of information that was previously unavailable except as a special request.
Information is available in a more timely manner.
A single delivery source of important, frequently used information.

Mental Model

Question: To what extent do you feel that the use of EIS has personally impacted you in the following ways?
I have a clearer sense of where things are going.
I feel I have a sharper vision and increased comprehension of the business.
I feel I have a better understanding of important trends.
I feel I have better insights into the problems and opportunities facing us.

Decision-making Speed

Question: To what extent has EIS helped you?
Make decision quicker.
Shorten the time frame for making decisions.
Spend less time in meetings.

The Extent of Analysis in Decision Making

Question: To what extent has EIS helped you?
Spend significantly more time analyzing data before making a decision.
Examine more alternatives in decision making.
Use more sources of information in decision making.
Engage in more in-depth analysis.

The Involvement of Subordinates

Question: To what extent do the following statements characterize your personal decision-making style?*
I personally identify most problems in my area of responsibility requiring organizational action.
Many problems requiring organizational action are brought to my attention by subordinates.

*Reverse Scored
*All responses were on a scale of 1 (*to no extent*) to 5 (*to a great extent*).

I rely on subordinates to keep me informed of daily problems.
I make many informal decisions that do not involve my subordinates.[*]
I frequently involve subordinates in decision processes.
I frequently involve subordinates in identifying and/or deciding upon courses of action.

About the authors

Dorothy E. Leidner is an associate professor of information systems at INSEAD in Fontainebleau, France. She received her PhD in information systems from the University of Texas at Austin, where she also obtained her MBA and BA. Dr. Leidner has published her research in many of the leading journals, including *MIS Quarterly, Information Systems Research, Organization Science, Decision Support Systems*, and *Journal of Management Information Systems*. Her research interests include executives' use of information systems, knowledge management systems, and electronic classrooms. Dr. Leidner has been a visiting professor at the Instituto Tecnologico y de Estudios Superiores de Monterrey (ITESM) in Monterrey, Mexico; the Institut d'Administration des Entreprises at the Université de Caen, France; and Warwick Business School, UK.

Sven A. Carlsson is an associate professor in the Department of Informatics at Lund University, Sweden. He has a PhD in informatics from the School of Economics and Management at Lund University. His research interests include the use of information technology to support both individual and group decision making, strategic information systems, and organizational transformation through information technology. He has been a visiting scholar at the University of Arizona, Tucson, and University of Southern California. His articles have appeared in *Journal of Management Information Systems, Information & Management, Journal of Decision Systems, Scandinavian Journal of Information Systems*, and international conference proceedings.

Joyce J. Elam is the James L. Knight Eminent Scholar in Management Information Systems in the Department of Decision Sciences and Information Systems, College of Business Administration, Florida International University, Miami, Florida. Before joining the faculty of Florida International University in 1990, she was an associate professor in the College of Business Administration at the University of Texas at Austin, and a Marvin Bower Fellow at the Harvard Business School. Dr. Elam earned her PhD in operations research from the University of Texas. She has served as associate editor for *MIS Quarterly* and is currently on the editorial board for *Information Systems Research*.

Martha Corrales is an assistant professor of information systems at the Instituto Tecnologico y de Estudios Superiores de Monterrey (ITESM), in Monterrey, Mexico. She received her PhD in information systems from

ITESM in 1997. Her dissertation research focused on Mexican managers' perceptions of the value of information technology.

Questions for discussion

1 Some would argue that cultures of business executives around the world are converging, as the technologies to support executive work become available everywhere. How does this article support, or contradict, this assertion?

2 Do the findings of this article suggest that if one attempts to implement the same system in business units in different countries, but in the same organization, that the business units in the different countries will use the system differently? Support your answer.

3 If you are managing a global rollout of a system for an organization, what steps could you take to try to ensure that the system would in fact be used in the same manner in the different locations?

4 Imagine that you have been asked to do a post-hoc justification of the value of the EIS for an organization in each of these three companies. In which country would the justification be easiest to make and why?

13 Culture and Consumer Responses to Web Download Time: A Four-Continent Study of Mono- and Polychronism

Gregory M. Rose, Roberto Evaristo and Detmar Straub

Abstract: Most e-commerce sites would like to include as much relevant and sales-inducing content on their pages as possible. Unfortunately, resulting download delays may lead to consumer frustration and a negative attitude toward the product or service displayed. But is frustration with download delay a universal problem or is it culture-specific? How should firms view this problem? These are the primary research questions investigated in the current study. An experiment conducted on four continents was selected as an appropriate research method to answer those questions. Country sites were selected for differing cultural senses of time and how this might affect individual responses to download delay. Our sample included the U.S. and Finnish cultures representing monochrome cultures and Egyptian and Peruvian cultures representing polychronic cultures. Consistent with the proposed hypotheses, subjects from polychronic cultures were significantly less concerned with download delays than subjects in monochrome cultures. Similarly, perceived wait times varied significantly between the mono- and polychronic groups. Practical insights derived from this study enable specific suggestions on customization of web page content richness as well as infrastructure requirements based on the cultural identity of the intended e-consumer. Moreover, results suggest theoretical implications for future research.

Introduction

The ability to effectively address the needs of customers through web technology has begun to differentiate service industries in the last decade [1]. Since many services have historically provided poor "service," the web offers one more way that forward-looking firms can expand their set of available channels and further outdistance competitors. Within a relatively short period of time, this electronic channel has changed from a novelty to a mainstream tactic for firms [2]. It seems inevitable that increasingly busy consumers pressured by time will opt for convenient technology-based solutions, and that such customer demand, therefore, will require even heavier firm investments in e-commerce (EC) technology [3]. Culture is undoubtedly a crucial issue in determining how firms will tailor their appeal to e-consumers, and it is a particularly important factor in situations where technological limitations are impeding the growth of the Web.

What are the key technological challenges that firms will have to address in order to fully exploit the inherent advantages of the Web channel, especially with respect to cultural issues? One of the most important is download delay [4], [5]. There are good reasons to believe that the wait time that customers face when requesting a web page from a server is one of the most serious impediments to rapid development of online business [4]. In fact, Khosrowpour and Herman's Delphi study identified download time as the single greatest problem for "the overall utilization and management of web-enabled technologies" [5, p. 1].

What are the crucial decision variables for managers? Which technological choices should be applied to result in faster downloads for their customers? How might both of these vary by culture?

First, firms have little to no control over the technology through which a consumer accesses the firm's websites. Narrow-band Internet connections on the consumer side mean that files sent by e-retailers cannot be downloaded quickly even if they arrive at the client end of the infrastructure in a timely fashion. This so-called client-side bottleneck cannot be eliminated by content providers and may only be resolved over time as broadband penetrates the world's markets [6], [7]. Other limitations include the geographical location of the server relative to the client, and even how aggressively content is cached on the consumer's machine or on an intervening proxy server.

Yet, managers currently do have some power to combat this impediment. Specifically, the firm's server-side technology and content is under their control. While sizable investments in industrial-strength servers, better compression algorithms, and server-side software can reduce the delay in sending content out to the consumer, server speed alone cannot eliminate delay. All other factors being the same, the more effective approach is reducing the amount of content on a web page. Lean content, including smaller (or nonexistent) multimedia and applet files, is the only way to reliably provide faster downloads through narrow-band, client-side connections. Reducing delay, however, has serious repercussions, as desired content is sacrificed.

Is the only solution for managers to limit client-side delay to "dummy-down" their web pages to the lowest common denominator of acceptable download delay? When is lean content a sensible strategy? Exactly how much of a capital investment needs to be made in rapid-response servers? Is millisecond response acceptable or does it have to be timed in nanoseconds?

One perspective on this question is to examine the current online infrastructure, especially on the client side. At the present time, even advanced technology countries like the U.S. and those in Northern Europe can be characterized as having a "slow" residential and small business infrastructure. Roughly 90%–95% of users in 2001 in these areas were connected to the Internet via narrow-band connections with throughput rates of 56 kb/s or less through dial-up modems [8], [9]. Further, slow connections are even more characteristic of emerging economies [8], [9].

Given that slow connections are now commonplace and likely to persist for some time to come, [6], [7], [10] are there any indications about how to select a reasonable level of investment based on client predilections? Anecdotes in the practitioner literature indicate that customers are frustrated when pages take a long time to download [11]. Empirical work has also uncovered a relationship between delays and negative reactions such as: increased intentions to abort EC web pages before they finish loading [12]; more negative user satisfaction, perceived ease of use, and intentions to use web applications [13]; and more negative attitudes toward brands included in a web page associated with the delays [14]. However, such studies have only begun to provide insight into exactly where the problems lie and with which customer base.

It is very likely, for instance, that certain groups of consumers will not react as adversely as others. From an international perspective, culture has been found to play a key role in determining what individuals perceive to be a "long" or a "short" time [15]. Are the download delays reported in the practitioner press of the U.S. and European countries an equally serious problem in countries where "time" is not so inextricably associated with money?

The research question explored in the current cross-cultural study is whether differing views of time have an impact on customer reactions to download delay. Our empirical approach involved gathering data from four countries located on four continents, each having a different cultural attitude toward time. We found strong support for culture as a significant factor in perceptions of download delay. Among the managerial implications of this finding is that culture-specific web pages can be designed to capitalize on the tolerance of certain cultures to longer downloads. This will enable managers to target their message to these groups through richer content. Likewise, results indicate that, depending on the targeted end user, firms can spend less on server technologies and still be viable e-service providers.

Literature review and hypotheses

One of the motivations behind the EC phenomenon is access to an even larger amount of information in a shorter time than is possible in a traditional bricks-and-mortar setting. The conundrum is that the very same promise that makes EC appealing, i.e., more in less time, can create severe negative perceptions of a product when the delivery of information is much slower than e-customers expect.

For an e-consumer, delays in downloading web pages may be due either to: 1) client processing limitations or 2) bandwidth limitations on the client-side; 3) intermediary infrastructure slow downs; and/or 4) server-side limitations. Although the firm can deal with server-side issues, the other three limitations are largely beyond its control. Particularly troublesome is the bandwidth used to connect to websites since most e-consumers are equipped with very slow connections.

Historically, increased response time has been perceived negatively in American studies of systems users [16], [17]. One can argue that the impact of the download time of web page content is analogous. Indeed, recent research has shown that in the U.S., download time has a negative impact on e-consumer web page and brand attitude formation, [14] can lead to aborted page loads, [12], and can reduce user satisfaction, perceived ease of use, and intentions to use web applications [13]. These findings likely offer some explanation for why more than 65% of e-shoppers abandon a sale before check out [18]. Moreover, other studies suggest that negative attitudes are subsequently transferred to objects associated with such delay leading to dissatisfaction with such objects as a software application [16] or a person's job [17]. To address such negative attitudes, many e-tailers have eliminated bandwidth-hungry content in order to reduce download times [19].

However, studies-to-date (reported previously) were conducted only in the U.S. Therefore, as a set, they raise the possibility that non-U.S. e-consumers may have different perceptions regarding download time. This is a nontrivial issue in that EC is increasingly becoming a global phenomenon, with Internet access being equally divided between English and non-English speakers [20]. Considering the relatively small penetration in countries like China and, therefore, the potential for explosive growth, this ratio is likely to be tipped even further toward non-English websites. In fact, Wood [21] suggests that Chinese will become the number one web language by 2007, a notion that was even featured recently in an Accenture (formerly Andersen Consulting) media advertisement in the U.S.

Hofstede [22] has suggested that management theories that apply to the U.S. may be ethnocentric and not apply well to other cultures. Indeed, although some models explaining computer behavior in U.S. or European countries do apply to general PC use in other cultures, [23] other research has been unable to so characterize such technology transfer between nations [24]. Similarly, there is support for the notion of culture-specific software. For example, software in China provides a culture-specific graphical user interface to Microsoft applications [2]. However, research has also found that some cultural differences lead to identical outcomes, albeit for different reasons. Specifically, differing motivations have been identified for the use of identical software applications across cultural groups [25]. Therefore, it seems reasonable to view contradictory findings to date as evidence that culture in-and-of-itself may not be the only, or even the decisive factor in explaining all systems outcomes. What this means is that, while culture may suppress or strengthen negative responses, it will not eliminate them.

While negative impacts of delay on attitudes toward delay are found outside of web-based services and systems [26]–[28], this relationship needs to be validated in EC environments. Likewise, the work to date has not validated this relationship within polychronic cultures. However, since studies investigating task delays have found attitude toward delay is consistently negative both in computer systems and services, [26]–[28] we posit that:

H_1: **Increases in download delay lead to a negative impact on attitudes toward delay, irrespective of culture.**

Cultural sense of time

One key cultural variable related to download delay is how people perceive time. According to Hall, [29] perceptions of time in different cultures are either monochrome or polychronic. Cultures that perceive events as unfolding in a linear fashion are said to be monochronic, a perspective common in most European/North American cultures. Monochronic cultures tend to be task oriented; they value promptness and typically do not change plans at the last minute [30]. Members of such cultures work on one issue at a time, and, therefore, delays in one task imply that others are, *per force*, delayed.

> "Monochronic people, like Scandinavians and North Americans, prefer to do one thing at a time. For instance, they do not book several meetings at the same time. Time is compartmentalized: there's time for everything and everything has its time [31, p. 89]."

Corroborating this, Hall [32, p. 6] suggests that "Americans think of time as a road [that] has segments or compartments that are to be kept discrete." Similarly, northern European Finland "is an extremely monochronic time-oriented culture" [33, p. 151].

On the other hand, events in polychronic cultures are not perceived as being tightly coupled to antecedents; they simply transpire. Examples of polychronic cultures include Latin American and Middle Eastern countries [15, p. 17] as well as Southern European cultures [15, p. 150]. Although events to polychronic unfold in complex ways, these events are seen as occurring mostly in parallel. Hall [34] suggests that polychronic groups tend to be involved in several tasks and processes concurrently, like jugglers. This may be due to the high extent of personal involvement within social groups. Tella [31] suggests that:

> "...polychronic people[s], represented by South Americans or Southern Europeans, tend to do several things at the same time or in parallel time segments. They do not think it odd to answer their phones while having a videoconference with foreign partners, or talk to a passing student by leaving the other videoconference partners to simply wait" [31, p. 89].

In fact, polychronic peoples are more likely to change plans and focus on relationships rather than tasks [30]. Some of the implications that may be gleaned, therefore, are that for polychronic peoples, this perception of non-linearity of time implies less urgency. This may be the case partly because one could turn his or her attention from a main task to another task being performed in a rough block of time (analogous to multitasking). Therefore, delays in a main task may be potentially played down.

In a manner similar to Hall, Nydell [35] observes these differences in chronism between polychronic Arabs and monochronic "Westerners"

> "...among Arabs, time is not as fixed and rigidly segmented as it tends to be among Westerners. It flows from past to present to future, and Arabs flow with it. Social occasions and even appointments need not have fixed beginning or endings. Arabs are thus much more relaxed about the timing of events than they are about other aspects of their lives [35, p. 27].

In sum, it appears that different regions of the world can be classified as being predominantly poly- or monochronic in culture. Further, these cultural differences correspond with a predictably more relaxed (polychronic) or less relaxed (monochronic) relationship with delays. Based on this line of reasoning, we posit that:

H_2: Effect of download delay on attitude toward download delay is less pronounced with polychronics than with monochronics.

Differences between mono- and polychronic cultures should not be limited to delay attitudes. Research shows that perceived wait time (PWT) is subjective and varies depending on circumstances, attitudes, and environment [26], [36], [37]. While no studies to date have measured differences in PWT between mono- and polychronic cultures, it seems likely that perceptions of passage of time would vary by culture. If cultural differences exist with regards to the perceived passage of time, evidence of cultural differences in attitude toward delay (as posited in H_2) would be further validated as well. Likewise, this finding would be very important to systems developers as many applications are designed expressly with reduction in PWT in mind [38]. Cultural differences in perceived delay would suggest new research into the predictors and outcome of PWT is needed for systems built for users of different cultural chronisms.

The ways individuals in cultural groups tackle tasks and tolerate task-induced delays suggest that they may perceive wait time duration differently. Similarly, relationships with time vary significantly based on cultural chronism. Our last hypothesis is a logical extension of these concepts:

H₃: Monochronics experience different levels of perceived delay time than polychronics.

No specific directional expectation was developed for this hypothesis on PWT. The aforementioned literature finds that actual delay has been shown to predict perceived delay, but not the predicted direction. Measured PWTs have been found to be greater than actual treatment times in some experimental groups and less than actual delay in others (see [26], [36], [39] for examples). Therefore, we limit our hypothesis to one of differences between cultures.

Methodology

Consistent with nearly all prior delay and computer response time studies, laboratory experiments were conducted to test the research hypotheses. Experiments have traditionally been used to test for impacts of delay in service settings, [26], [40] traditional computer systems; [17], [28] and web-based systems [12], [13], [41]. Experiments are also appropriate in download delay impact studies because the hypotheses imply a causal model [42].

For the experiment, validated artifacts, measures, and experimental procedures were faithfully adopted from Rose, *et al.* [12], Rose and Straub, [41], and Rose and Straub [43]. For detailed information on the validation process, please see these papers. In these studies, a mock web browser controlled the entire experience of the subject. The browser replicated the look and feel of Microsoft's Internet Explorer (as a screen shot of the artifact in Figure 13.1 shows). Although totally self-contained locally on an individual PC (i.e., not on the Internet or on a local area network), the mock browser appears to be retrieving and loading web pages from the Internet while, in fact, it is actually simulating and controlling the download times. Based on observations and pilot experiments, the artifact is built to simulate realistic variations of delay times and associated cues in the browser in order to increase the sense of realism. Exit interviews with over 100 test subjects in a variety of settings confirm that the mock browser and web pages appeared to be authentic to test subjects who believed they were examining actual web pages on the Internet.[1]

---

[1]To ensure that the interface as perceived across cultures was not a confound, we looked at typical catalog applications in many countries and discovered that the interface chosen is a format that existed in most countries. The design was simple and functional, and, therefore, avoided graphics preferences of one type or another. Moreover, the questions asked to test the hypotheses were not related to attitude toward the interface, but to functionality.

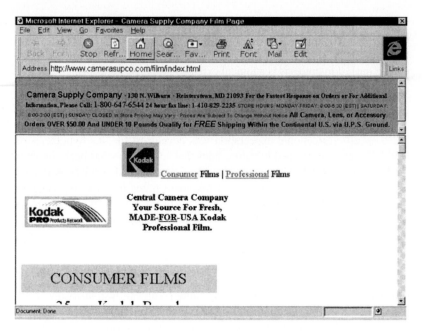

Figure 13.1   *Sample screen shot of the browser artifact*

Conducting the experiment required a lab of computers, with one PC for each subject. Although the hardware was different across the different sites, this created no noticeable differences in how the subjects viewed the software since, in pretests, the mock browser did not tax the performance of a basic test machine. In the prior studies, [12], [41], [43] browser artifacts were loaded onto university computer lab machines. As in Rose, *et al.* [12], Rose and Straub [41], and Rose and Straub [43], the current study was conducted with students enrolled in university information systems (IS) courses (third and fourth year undergraduates, and masters students, including M.B.A. students) in computer labs. These groups were appropriate because they were technically savvy and relatively young adults (average age of participants was 26 years). This profile is consistent with e-consumers as a whole [44]. Moreover, student subjects have been shown to predict results similar to "general" consumers [45] in situations like those being investigated here.

The repeated measures design in this study copes with the high cost in time and effort of setting up and conducting the experiment and the relative scarcity of appropriate subjects. In spite of the fact that these problems were exacerbated when the study was conducted in universities other than the U.S. institutions where the researchers teach, this repeated measures design allowed the capture of sufficient data for comparison across the four countries.

The browser artifact that allowed subjects to navigate through four different EC web pages presented multiple page views. The pages represented mock e-retailers selling a variety of camera films and VHS videotapes and supplies, with actual web pages and brand cue data adopted as templates for the experimental pages. Each page varied in trivial ways from other pages so as not to arouse suspicion [46]. Based on pilot studies documented in [47] it was determined that as many as five treatment pages could be observed (the first four pages shown were each unique and the fifth was a repeat) without making subjects wary about the reality of the experience. Likewise, with the instrument items being limited in number, the study could be conducted using five page views without excessive subject fatigue.

Four international locations were selected to run the experiments. The criteria for choice of location were twofold: First, we wanted to compare monochronic and polychronic cultures. Second, we wanted to ensure that the results were not otherwise culturally-idiosyncratic, and, thus, selected two countries for each of these views of time. In addition to the monochronic culture of the U.S., we conducted an experiment in Finland, which is also a monochronic country.[2] For polychronism, we selected Egypt and Peru. The classification of monochronic versus polychronic nations was based on Hall [15], [32]. Thus, we were able to compare results across four countries and four continents.

For these cultures, we did not expect other national differences like lack of economic development to affect results in that the subjects were drawn from a population base that was not affected in this experiment by that characteristic.[3] In other words, all subjects were similar with respect to economic and working status and access to computers. They differ, if the literature is correct, on chronism, which is why we manipulated download delay to test our predictions about their responses.

Identical experiments were conducted in each culture. All subjects were enrolled in an IS course. Personal computers at the universities all used an identical experimental artifact, and the experimental software randomly

---

[2] It is clear that countries do not always equate with "culture." Nevertheless, we used this as a rough approximation in lieu of more definitive work on how to specify an individual's "culture."

[3] Research colleagues in Finland, Peru, and Egypt helped us assess possible confounds such as number of disconnected internet calls, actual speed, etc. Internet access in Finland was similar to that of the U.S., if anything the Internet was more available to the subjects. In Peru, graduate students paid $20 000 (USD) annual fees to the Business School in a country where per capita income is around $2400 and, therefore, the subjects had internet access speeds and solutions not necessarily available to the rest of the population. This would make their situation more comparable to their counterpart shoppers in monochronic cultures, since actual access speed or other internet access characteristics appear not to be that different. In Egypt, subjects were working adults who had access to relatively high speed lines at work and in the university laboratories so the experience of the subjects was unlikely to be a factor in their responses.

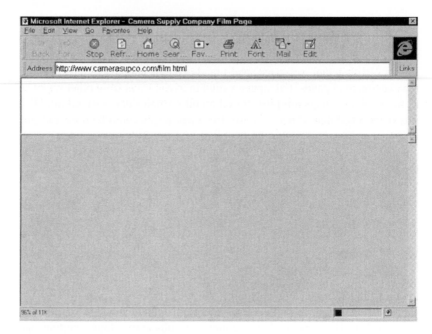

Figure 13.2   *Browser artifact showing status bar change*

assigned delay times and treatment pages. Treatment delays ranged from 15 to 90 s and were set at 15-s increments, for a total of six possible treatment levels. As noted, subjects were exposed to five page views and each of the five pages had a different delay treatment level. To increase the reality of the treatment, the status bar showed the loading time as well (as seen in Figure 13.2). In that treatment, delay levels were randomly assigned to subjects, the study demonstrates strong internal validity.

Subjects were given an instruction and questionnaire packet. The packet contained an overview of the study, an opt-out clause, and a login code for the browser (Appendix A includes excerpts from the packet). The login code determined the experimental treatment to which the subject was exposed. Instructions indicated how the users should navigate the web browser as well as how subjects should let each page load completely before answering post-test instrument items. After viewing an individual web page, subjects were instructed to answer questions related to that page.

All subjects were enrolled in courses conducted in English. Written materials were in English, and, without exception, comprehension of written English ranged from good to very good. For these reasons, the mock browser was not translated, but kept in English in all four countries. In fact, the browser included common and simple terms that subjects would come across frequently in their forays on the Web. The questionnaire was also kept in English for the Finnish and Egyptian samples because of their level of familiarity with sophisticated English texts.[4]

The first item was for attitude toward delay, adopted from prior download time studies [12], [41], [43]. This measure was a variation of the one adopted by Hui and Tse [48]. Attitude toward delay was ranked on a four-point scale: from "not significant delay," to "acceptable delay," to "excessive but still tolerable delay," to "intolerable delay." This measure of delay attitude has been shown to predict e-consumer intentions to abort EC web page loads, a very serious concern for e-retailers [12].

The second construct was PWT. Subjects were asked to indicate how long in seconds they perceived the download time delay to be for the page they viewed. An additional measure of attitude toward the web graphics was interleaved with attitude toward delay and PWT questions to counteract methods bias, and hopefully avoid fatigue and hypothesis-guessing [49].

Data analysis

Overview and demographic data

Results of the data analyses, detailed in the following, are summarized in Table 13.1.

Table 13.1 *Overview of findings*

Hypothesis	Short descriptor	Impact supported?
1	Actual delay affects system attitudes, irrespective of culture	Yes
2	Cultural chronism affects attitudes toward delay	Yes
3	Cultural chronism affects perceived delay	Yes

[4]It needs to be noted that in Peru, instruction was accompanied by simultaneous translation from English to Spanish, which was used by perhaps one third of the class. Similarly, some of the more complex teaching materials were translated to Spanish to ensure that even the small percentage of students who were not completely fluent in English would have no problems with comprehension. For this season, we decided to have the questionnaire translated to Spanish, something done in Peru by bilingual native speakers of Spanish. The Spanish version was then translated back into English by one of the authors, and final adjustments made.

Table 13.2 *Descriptive statistics*

	USA	EGYPT	FINLAND	PERU
N of trials (N = number of subjects * 5 trials/subject)	210	105	110	170
N of subjects	42	21	22	34
Home Internet connection	97%	86%	55%	74%
Broadband connection	2%	0%	33%	16%
56 k connection	58%	50%	50%	36%
33.6 k or less connection	40%	50%	17%	48%
Internet use per week (hrs.)	16	8	9	14
Average age (yrs.)	29	27	24	32
% who engage in e-commerce	80%	52%	91%	63%
Percent who use Internet	100%	100%	100%	100%

Sample sizes[5] and demographic information, including home Internet connection speeds, are shown in Table 13.2. As can be seen, subjects are fairly similar in age and all groups appear to be Web savvy. Demographic differences were not significant in the model tests detailed.[6]

[5]Sample sizes were appropriate for conducting multivariate regression analysis and ANOVA tests. For regression analysis, sample sizes should be 15–20 times the number of independent variables [50]. In this study, the sample size of 595 would allow for up to 40 independent variables to be included and still allow for generalizability. The tests conducted here had no more than 14 independent variables when all of the demographic questions were included. The primary tests included only two independent variables each and would have required a sample of only 30 for generalizability. Similarly, ANOVA tests should ideally be run with samples larger than 60 for tests of this type to have appropriate power levels [50]. The assumptions of the techniques employed were also met or can be ascertained to be high in statistical conclusion validity. Regarding multicollinearity, tests of the independent variables download delay and cultural chronism demonstrate the factors are not significantly correlated (VIF scores = 1.0, Pearson p-values = 0.824). These findings were expected because the delay treatment was randomly generated and assigned. Per assumptions of equal cell sizes and homogeneity of variances, multivariate analyses have been shown to be robust to violations of these assumptions [51].
[6]One difference between groups appears to be in home Internet connection speed. To see if this variable could be confounding results, it was included in a separate set of regression runs. In each case, home connection speed had no significant relationship with the outcome variable (p-values for connection speed were in excess of 0.27 in the tests). Likewise, demographic variables as control variables were examined in separate runs. While number of Internet hours was significant at the 0.05 level, it did not change the significance levels of the primary variables of interest. Further, the adjusted R^2 values for the models varied only by $+/-0.01$. Similar results were found for the attitude toward graphics measure. For reasons of parsimony and lack of theoretical grounding, these variables were omitted from the final reporting of results.

Hypothesis tests

The critical question in our study, of course, was whether there would be statistically significant variations in the attitude toward download delay across all cultures considered separately. To test this, chronism (dummy coded as 0,1) and actual download delay (see Table 13.3) were regressed on attitude toward download delay. As Table 13.2 shows, both variables were significant ($p = 0.000$). The negative value for the download delay suggests that the longer the download delay, the more negative the subjects' attitudes, holding chronism constant. This provides strong support for H_1.

The significance ($p = 0.000$) of cultural chronism implies that H_2 is also supported, and there are, indeed, cultural differences (as represented in this case by chronism) on attitude toward delay. Since cultural chronism was coded as a dummy variable ("1" for polychronism, "0" for monochronism), the positive regression beta indicates that polychronic subjects have a more positive attitude toward delay than monochronic subjects, as predicted by H_2.

Table 13.4 presents the ANOVA run used to test H_3. PWT was found to be significantly different between monochronic and polychronic cultures

Table 13.3   *Regression model summary: Test of impact of download delay and cultural chronism on delay attitude*

Predictor variables	β	T	p-value
(Constant)		44.868	.000
DOWNLOAD DELAY	−.643	−21.100	.000*
CULTURAL CHRONISM	.203	6.670	.000*

Table 13.4   *ANOVA model summary: Differences in perceived wait time between monochronic and polychronic cultures*

		Sum of squares	Df	Mean square	F	p-value
PERCEIVED WAIT TIME	Between Groups	12820.892	1	12820.892	11.237	.001*
	Within Groups	653738.59	573	1140.905		
	Total	666559.48	574			

Predictor: CULTURAL CHRONISM
Dependent Variable: PERCEIVED WAIT TIME
*Indicates Significance at the .05 Level

Table 13.5   *Descriptive statistics of average actual delay and perceived delay in all four cultures*

Culture	N	Average actual delay time	Average perceived wait time	Net difference (Actual delay – Perceived delay)
USA	210	51.93	37.88	14.05
Egypt	105	51.71	47.53	4.18
Finland	110	52.64	35.45	17.19
Peru	170	53.21	45.96	7.25
Total	595	52.39	41.32	11.07

($F = 11.237$, $p = 0.000$). This very interesting finding called for further analysis to see where the exact differences lie. Therefore, we examined actual delay and PWTs individually, for all four cultures (Table 13.5).

As can be seen in Table 13.5, PWTs did, indeed, vary among the cultural experimental groups. Likewise, these differences appear to vary greatly *between*, but very little *within* the cultural chronic groups. Monochronic cultures had average PWTs of 37.88 and 35.45 for the U.S. and Finland, respectively. In the polychronic groups, the times were 47.53 and 45.96 for Egypt and Peru.

The average *actual* delay treatment for all four sample groups was 52.39 s. These results indicate that all subject groups underestimated actual download delay, but monochronic culture groups underestimated by 14.05 s on average for the Americans and 17.19 s for the Finns. By contrast, Egyptians only underestimated the actual delay by 4.18 s and Peruvians by 7.25 s.

These facts suggested that *post hoc* analysis would be useful for further insights into the differences in PWT between monochronic and polychronic cultures. Table 13.6 presents the regression results. Again, both predictor variables were significant ($p = 0.000$). This significant finding for cultural chronism suggests that in polychronic cultures there is a perception of longer wait times than in monochronic cultures, in spite of experimentally identical actual delays.

What does this mean? Subjects from polychronic cultures believed that they waited longer than their monochronic counterparts did, even though both groups waited the same amount of time. Yet, considering the previous hypothesis tests, polychronic subjects also held a more positive attitude toward delay compared to members of the monochronic groups. In sum, it

Table 13.6 *Regression model summary for combined experiments: Differences in perceived wait time between monochronic and polychronic cultures*

Predictor variables	β	T	p-value
(Constant)		$-.706$	.481
DOWNLOAD DELAY	.559	16.360	.000*
CULTURAL CHRONISM	.123	3.586	.000*

Dependent Variable: PERCEIVED WAIT TIME
Overall F = 142.054 Adjusted R^2 = .330 Total df: 574
Overall Regression p-value = .000
*Indicates Significance at the .05 Level

appears that polychronics feel better about waiting and have more positive attitudes toward the delay even though they believe they have waited significantly longer than those in the monochronic group have.

Testing of potential confounds

To be assured that potential confounds such as user expectations are not affecting results, we examined these statistically. It was important to account for the possibility that instead of inherent cultural differences, monochronic users differ from polychronics with respect to acceptance of response times because they are accustomed to faster Internet connectivity speeds.

To test for the impacts of expectations of delay, analyses of differences in home Internet connection speeds were conducted. The logic behind these tests was that people accustomed to routinely waiting longer (i.e., if their home modem speeds are slower) might have better attitudes toward waiting than those who are accustomed to waiting less for page loads (i.e., those with faster home Internet connection speeds). Regression tests of reported modem speed home connection speeds on both dependent variables (PWT, $p = 0.675$; delay attitude, $p = 0.274$) found their influence to be insignificant, while the significance of download delay and cultural chronism were still significant ($p < 0.01$ for each). This result strengthens our argument that cultural differences, rather than other behavioral or experiential characteristics of a given group, affect their attitude or perception of delay in download times.

While there are differences between cultures, within-chronism groups' PWTs do not appear to vary significantly. An ANOVA test of differences between the U.S. and Finnish groups found no difference in PWT for the two chronic groups (*p*-value = 0.476) and an ANOVA between Egyptian and Peruvian subjects likewise found no significant differences (*p*-value = 0.756). It appears that within-chronism groups passage of time is viewed in a similar fashion. However, as noted earlier, there is a significant difference between attitudes toward delay for these monochronic and polychronic groups (see Table 13.3). In sum, these findings lend additional evidence to the theoretical proposition that cultural differences impact attitude toward download time but that these differences are minimal within cultures similar in chronism, even when members of these cultures are separated by thousands of miles.

Implications for practice, theory, and future research directions

Results of this research have several important implications, for both theory and practice. The four primary findings and associated suggestions are summarized in Table 13.7. Naturally, these possible interpretations are the result of a single study and as such will need to be supported with future work.

First, it is clear that our basic finding about cultural influence on IT/web usage agrees with the limited prior work in this area. Indeed, the current study suggests that there are good reasons to differentially customize content for cultures. Although there is a robust literature on how interface factors such as language, currency, colors, and other potential *faux pas* [52] need to be fitted to culture, we believe that the present study is able to take such recommendations one step further. In fact, because some more intuitively obvious customizations have already been implemented across the world (e.g., see Davis and Grimes [53]), our results may suggest critical yet-to-be-enacted changes in commercial web approaches as well as spark further research to refine the recommendations.

Armed with knowledge of this study, what should managers in charge of websites and web designers do with respect to cultural chronism and downloading? Specific implications for customization can be derived from how people perceive delays in download time as well as their attitude toward such delay. As predicted, we found that, irrespective of culture, all peoples would like to have download delays reduced. This finding is important because it validates this relationship within the world of web-based systems and extends prior monochronic findings to polychronic cultures. However, there are differences as to how much actual delay affects attitudes toward delay among different cultures, and we will draw implications from this finding, some of which are counterintuitive to some extent with respect to the extant literature.

Table 13.7 *Summary of primary findings and suggestions*

Finding	Details and suggestions
#1	The design of international websites needs to look beyond language, currency, and intuitive factors previously identified such as colors and pictures. Designers should not copy layouts and designs from other websites without careful deliberation.
#2	e-retailers need to manage download time for all e-consumers. This holds true for both monochronics and polychronics. All developers should be conscious of the file sizes web pages. Existing pages should be evaluated for size reduction.
#3	Customization of sites • There can be less concern with data reduction as a means of speeding page downloads for polychronics than there is for monochronics. The design decision may be to allow polychronic e-consumers to view more information-rich pages, which should improve site success. • There are lower barriers to entry when servicing polychronics due to more relaxed response time requirements. • There is no universal definition of what are appropriate server-side resources, because requirements vary based on culturally-suggested customizations. This is particularly important in the developing world. • Customization could include presenting different pages based on geographical location of top-level domain, language, and target markets.
#4	Perceived download time is not an appropriate surrogate for actual download time. The R^2 with both factors is only $= .330$. In addition, a significant cultural bias on perceptions of download time was found. Future work should utilize multiple measures of delay in addition to perceived wait time.

Polychronic cultures are typically more comfortable than monochronic cultures in performing more than one task or process in a given time block. We found, as expected, that this particular response of polychronics results in a lesser concern with longer download times than among the monochronic groups. What we did not predict was an interesting side finding. Polychronic people PWT to be considerably longer than the monochronic group.

This outcome is especially interesting because people in the experimental treatment were not as free as they would have been in their natural settings to be involved in other physical tasks during the same block of time. Yet, even when unable to freely multitask, polychronic subjects still reported significantly lower concern about longer downloads (with even longer PWTs) than monochronics. This finding may point to an even more basic structural issue. Relatively speaking, regardless of how many other tasks polychronics are involved in at a particular moment, it appears that they more willingly accept long downloads. In other words, they seem to have been "trained" by their culture to tolerate longer waits, so even in the absence of alternate ways to use their time, delays are less of a nuisance than they are for monochronic groups.

Future research may ascertain whether, in the presence of other tasks, polychronic peoples may be even less resistant to longer downloads and ascertain whether outcomes from delay are even less prominent when polychromes are free to multitask naturally. If polychronics viewing web pages outside of a laboratory setting are indeed less negatively impacted by delay, then even more desirable content can be included in pages for these groups than is currently indicated by the present analyses. Such analysis should include monochronics in their natural environment to allow them to multitask as well. Furthermore, it may be interesting to ask subjects their perceptions on waiting.

The ultimate design objective is to adjust extent of content to the needs and wants of specific cultures, even if that implies offering a much larger content set (pictures, video, sound, etc.) with their associated longer delays. People may still choose to use or not to use such content, but longer download times necessarily associated with richer content would be less likely to generate negative reactions from polychronic users. Future research must be conducted to understand how best to utilize the additional degrees of freedom developers have when creating systems for polychronic users. The data here offer no specific guidelines as to what delay-increasing characteristics should be added back to applications for a given polychronic audience. Our study does suggest that when building systems for polychronics, there are additional degrees of freedom available to increase wait times. Future research can identify what should be done with these extra degrees of freedom and in what ways developers should exchange greater delays for functionality when building systems for polychronics. At a theoretical level, this endeavor would enhance knowledge in contributing disciplines such as computer science and human computer interface studies.

In order to take full advantage of these findings, a multinational company must be able to identify the culture to which the customer belongs so that a given site offered may be appropriately customized. An initial approach is to associate web presentation language with cultural chronism. In this way, English content would assume monochronism, whereas romance languages could be geared to polychronic audience. Although crude, it may provide a higher level of fit than is current, and firms can go beyond this algorithm to offer an alternative to people who come to their site.

Currently, some firms like Amazon.com have completely separate websites for different countries, with language, prices and even functionality appropriately chosen. Similarly, others such as AOL.com offer different default languages and pricing based on originating internet provider (IP) address, but the defaults can be overridden. These are valid solutions. It may be that a combined approach would work best, addressing even the situation of an American expatriate living, say, in Lima, Peru. Since computer analysis of the IP address can identify the geographical area from which the request for a web page originates, the downloaded page can be offered in the major local tongue (such as Spanish, in this example) with an option to display in English. Since Spanish, a romance language, is associated with polychronic cultures, that set of pages could include richer content as deemed desirable by the content provider for that target group.

In contrast, if the customer requests content in English, which typifies many monochronic cultures, content could be reduced and a set of content-restricted pages with faster downloads could be served. This solution still does not cover polychronic but English-speaking cultures (e.g., black South Africans). So, it would need to be combined with top-level domains. Likewise, minority situations like native English-speaking polychronic Peruvians would not be covered. Future research could identify the relevancy and profitability of catering to overtly minority groups and would need to find whether language combined with national domain is indeed a stable culture identifier with respect to polychronism or monochronism.

A separate issue arises with localized EC sites. In principle, they would have the benefit of appropriate knowledge and would build a site culturally well suited to the needs of intended customers. Unfortunately, though, such sites are sometimes influenced by or modeled after English-language sites. As a result, even in polychronic cultures, such sites may have embedded monochronic principles. Therefore, even bringing the distinctions discovered in this paper to the attention of web designers could have considerable practical implications. Other studies could add to what we now tentatively believe about content-richness and download time. It would be interesting to investigate, for example, the proportion of locally built sites that "fit" their local culture, and whether that leads to higher site approval ratings and sales.

Another concept dealing with localization concerns the extent of appropriate investment of e-business resources. For polychronics, it appears that fewer resources need to be spent for fast servers on the server side, expensive broadband connections, and responsive applications. In brief, in order to have an acceptably responsive site, pages for polychronic cultures require smaller investments. The implication of this lower cost barrier is that limited-resources organizations selling in polychronic cultures may still be able to afford a viable web presence. This limitation on cost structures may be critical for organizations in developing countries where income levels are low and bandwidth and computer equipment costs are higher than in the developed world. Generally accepted e-business notions in the U.S. about needing the fastest servers connected to fat Internet pipes do not appear to apply equally to polychronic cultures.

While these findings indicate that polychronics are more tolerant of delay than monochronics, managers and software designers should be careful when interpreting these results. These findings do not imply that polychronics should be punished with unnecessary delay. Outcomes of this experiment allow us to better understand the relative cost of this impediment within each culture so that a culturally sensitive cost/benefit analysis can be conducted in the design or implementation of applications. These findings indicate that polychronics simply do not have the same level of dissatisfaction with increased delay when compared with monochronics. However, results clearly demonstrate that neither likes to wait.

In an ideal world, full functionality with near-zero delay would be optimal across both cultures. However, given that web applications routinely require tradeoffs between delay and other functionality, [19] and that applications are routinely built with less functionality than desired, [54] these findings indicate that polychronics would more willingly sacrifice speed for other functionality when compared with monochrome users. In contrast, it appears monochronics would see more value in eliminating delay at the expense of other desirable functionality when compared to their polychronic counterparts. In some instances in the developing world, where the cost of entry in providing web-based computing is so high, this inherent tolerance for waiting might make it possible to provide acceptable e-services where identical configurations would be unacceptable in the monochronic world. Therefore, these findings may open polychronic cultures to more services than would have been thought possible based on monochronic preferences.

The results of this study also have implications regarding the validity of the PWT construct for measure of web application success. Historically, PWT has been a measure of convenience for researchers and corporations trying to identify the impacts of delay in services and software. The appeal of this measure is that a consumer or client can be asked for their perception of delay (which is relatively simple to do). Managers or researchers do not need to physically capture the actual passage of time (which can be very difficult to do outside of a controlled laboratory setting).

While this measure has been deemed acceptable outside of web applications, it appears that PWT could be a fickle measure of delay for web services and may not be an appropriate surrogate. The significant but low explained variance between actual and perceived delay in this study ($R^2 = 0.330$) brings into question its usefulness as a surrogate. In addition, the significance ($p = 0.000$) of cultural chronism in Table 13.6 indicates that PWT is even less appropriate as a substitute for actual delay when one tries to generalize across cultures.

These findings support the recommendation in Rose and Straub [41] that, when testing for delay impacts, PWT should be used in combination with actual delay (as they seem to measure different aspects of waiting). Furthermore, additional delay constructs, such as attribution, [55] should be included. Each measure may lead to different outcomes and call for alternate preventive remedies.

While the experiment conducted here does provide a good deal of insight, it does have limitations that suggest future research. One of the potential limitations in this study relates to the choice of countries. Although our study compares two polychronic with two monochronic countries and the subjects within the four groups were very similar in real wealth and access to infrastructure, it also happened that the two polychronic nations were developing whereas the two monochronic countries were developed. This difference in national development creates an alternate explanation for the differences other than culture. The counter argument is twofold: 1) that some polychronic cultures are, in fact, in economically developed countries (for instance, France and Italy), and that 2) in the selected polychronic cultures, the researchers engaged subjects who were economically advantaged. The Peruvian sample was from an exclusive business school that has above-average income subjects and, therefore, subjects with better connectivity, almost like a highly developed neighborhood of Peru (something easily noticeable by high broadband penetration in the sample). In Egypt, the sample was working adults, the vast majority of whom had reasonable bandwidth connections to the Internet at work and who had a state-of-the-art computer lab at school. Therefore, in both cases the sample reflected a small stratum of the population, potentially nonrepresentative, something to be considered as well in a follow-up study. Ideally, a follow-up study should cross subjects from either a less developed monochronic culture, a well-developed polychronic culture or a combination of both, with particular care about the representativeness of the sample make-up with regard to the whole population.

In addition to extending this research into other nations and cultural groups, future research should investigate cultural differences for causes of PWT. These studies might lend insight into the ways polychronic and monochronic individuals respond to web-based delay and suggest possible design choices for website developers. Although the browser artifact did include a status bar as a potential PWT feedback mechanism, it is possible that future work will be needed to test the outcomes and antecedents for PWT under varied conditions. An additional possibility may be to manipulate displays of expected download time to identify variations in the PWT with all its implications.

Similarly, additional investigations are needed to understand the impacts of PWT when compared to actual delay impacts. Results from such studies would allow researchers and businesses to better understand which construct or constructs should be captured to measure and predict web application success. Moreover, these impacts and predictors need to differ by culture. In fact, future research should also investigate whether differences in chronism, delay attitude, and PWT translates into changes on success variables such as the actual buying decision.

Conclusion

This research sheds light on differences in delay attitudes and perceptions of web-based delay in monochronic and polychronic cultures. Results indicate that culture has a major impact on how e-consumers respond to websites. Managers who can tune their websites to general cultural dimensions, like sense of time, will have a freer rein to include rich content for polychronic cultures. On the other hand, monochronic cultures experience problems with long delays in general, and managers need to ensure that server-side delays are minimal and that web pages are lean for fast downloading.

In the previous section, we discussed several other important theoretical and practical implications of our work. In a nutshell, a major implication of our findings and the likely follow-up research suggests possible additions to the theoretical body of work on attitude toward delay, PWT and their respective impacts on e-retailing and web-based system success as moderated by culture. Furthermore, there are pragmatic implications, related not only to acceptable potential differences in EC infrastructure in monochronic versus polychronic cultures but also in the amount and type of content made available to users from various cultures.

Appendix A research instrument (English version)

Thank you for agreeing to participate

Part of this class session will be devoted to a research study. Results of this research will be used to understand attitudes toward delay and graphics in web pages. The activity conducted today will involve viewing a series of web pages and answering some related questions.

Final results from this research can be obtained by contacting [name withheld]. Please ask the research administrator for contact information if you are interested.

The total approximate time for participating in this research is 20 minutes.

Note: Please read the following statements and then sign on the line below if you wish to participate. If you have any questions, please ask the research administrator.

- I have freely volunteered to participate in this research.
- I have been informed in advance what my task(s) will be and what procedures will be followed.
- I have been given the opportunity to ask questions, and have had my questions answered to my satisfaction.
- I am aware that I have the right to withdraw consent and to discontinue participation at any time, without prejudice to my future treatment.
- My signature below may be taken as affirmation of all of the above statements; it was given prior to my participation in this research.
- I understand that all responses to this questionnaire are strictly confidential; only summary findings will be reported.

Signature: ———

(Next Step: Please enter in your login code (below) in the password box. This will start the special, customized web browser used for this research.

When done, please open this questionnaire to the next sheet and follow the directions...)

LOGIN CODE-[ ]

I. Web Page Evaluation

A. Web Page Section Instructions

The following section asks that you view a series of five web pages and answer some related questions.

The web pages contain content referring to brands of video cassettes and photographic film. Included among these are brands with which you are likely familiar: **Kodak** brand film and **JVC** brand video cassettes. Also included are two relatively new brands with which you are likely not familiar: **FilmTech** brand film and SCS brand video cassettes.

In the following section, *before answering any questions about a specific page*, please make sure the web page you are evaluating has completely downloaded. Once the web page has fully downloaded, please proceed as indicated.

(Next step: Please click on the yellow "Home" button in the browser. This will open the home page for this research which contains hyperlinks to the product pages you are to evaluate.

When that page has finished loading, please open this questionnaire to the next sheet to begin this study ...)

Note: this is only a subset of the research instrument: The actual instrument contained five iterations of the questions in Section I below.

(Next step: please go to the first web page available from the home page by clicking on the hyperlink for "Web Page #1".)

(let page download ...)

For Web Page #1

1. **Please indicate your attitude toward the download time delay for the page you just viewed** (choose one):
   [ ]   Intolerable delay
   [ ]   Excessive but still tolerable delay
   [ ]   Acceptable delay
   [ ]   Not significant delay
   (Next step: please open this questionnaire to the next sheet ...)
   For Web Page #2

2. **Please indicate how long you perceive the download time delay was for the page you just viewed:** _____seconds

   Instructions for question #3: Please review the graphics contained in this Web page. Indicate your attitude toward the graphics contained in the page you just viewed by checking one box of the scale below. The more strongly you identify with one anchor word on a scale, the more near that word you check a box on that line.

3. **Your attitude toward the graphics contained in the Web page you just viewed is:**
   Dislike very much -[]-[]-[]-[]-[]-[]-[]- Like very much *(Next step: Please click on the yellow "Home" button in the browser to return to the home page.*

   When that page has finished loading, open this questionnaire to the next sheet ...)

II. **Personal Information**

Please answer the following questions. Note that all responses to this questionnaire are strictly confidential; only summary findings will be reported.

16. **What is your sex?** Male [ ] or Female [ ]
17. **What is your marital status?** Married [ ] or Not Married [ ]
18. **What is your age?** _____ Years (optional)
19. **How many years of post-high school education do you have?** _____ Years
20. **Are you currently employed full-time?** Yes [ ] or No [ ]
21. **How many years of working experience do you have?** _____ Years

22. **Are you a [NATION NAME HERE] citizen:** Yes [ ] or No [ ]
23. **Do you generally view shopping as a source of pleasure (choose one)?** Yes [ ] Neutral [ ] No [ ]
24. **How many hours in a week do you spend on the Internet?** _____ Hours
25. **How often do you make purchases or gather information for shopping over the Internet?** _____ Per Month
26. **If you have Internet connection at home, please indicate your connection speed:** 33.6 k or slower [ ] 56 k [ ] High Speed (Cable Modem or DSL, etc.)[ ]

References

[1] A. Parasuraman (1996), "Understanding and leveraging the role of customer service in external, interactive and internal marketing," in *Proc. Frontiers in Services Conf.*, Nashville, TN.

[2] D. Amor (2000), *The E-Business (R)evolution*. Prentice Hall, Englewood Cliffs, NJ.

[3] M. L. Meuter, A. L. Ostrom, R. I. Roundtree, and M. J. Bitner (2000), "Self-service technologies: Understanding customer satisfaction with technology-based service encounters," *J. Market*, Vol. 64, pp. 50–64.

[4] G. Rose, H. Khoo, and D. Straub (1999), "Current technological impediments to business-to-Consumer electronic commerce," *Commun. AIS*, Vol. 1, pp. 1–74.

[5] M. Khosrowpour and N. Herman (2000), "Web-enabled technologies assessment and management: Critical issues, challenges and trends," in M. Khosrowpour, Ed. *Managing Web-Enabled Technologies in Organizations: A Global Perspective*. Idea Group, Hershey, PA, pp. 1–22.

[6] C. Platt (2001), "The future will be fast but not free," *Wired*, Vol. 9, p. 120.

[7] (2001) "Shakeout in fiber optics". *NY Times* [Online]http://www.nytimes.com/2001/07/29/opinion/29SUN2.html

[8] (2001) "U.K. behind broadband race". *BBC News*[Online]http://news.bbc.co.uk/hi/english/business/newsid_1258000/1258445.stm

[9] (2001) "Korea leads world in broadband usage". *NetValue Worldwide* [Online]http://www.netvalue.com/corp/presse/index_frame.htm?fichier = cp0028.htm

[10] L. Trager (2000), "Study: 56 K growing faster than broadband," in *Inter@ctive Week*.

[11] D. Lake (2001), "Quick and easy," *Ind. Stand.* [Online]http://www.the-standard.com/article/display/0,1151,22342,00.html

[12] G. Rose, J. Lees, and M. Meuter (2001), "A refined view of download time impacts on e-consumer attitudes and patronage intentions toward e-retailers," *Int. J. Media Manage.*, Vol. 3, pp. 105–111.

[13] J. Hoxmeier and C. DiCesare (2000), "System response time and user satisfaction: An experimental study of browser-based applications," in *Proc. 6th Americas Conf. Information Systems*, Long Beach, CA, pp. 140–145.

[14] G. Rose and D. Straub (1999), "The effect of download time on e-Commerce: The download time brand impact model," in *Proc. 9th Workshop on Information Technologies and Systems*, Charlotte, N.C.

[15] E. T. Hall (1989), *Beyond Culture*, 2nd ed. Anchor, New York.

[16] J. B. Wirtz and J. E. Bateson (1995), "An experimental investigation of Halo effects in satisfaction measures of service attributes," *Int. J. Serv. Ind. Manage.*, Vol. 6, No. 3, pp. 84–102.

[17] R. E. Barber and H. C. J. Lucas (1983), "System response time, operator productivity and job satisfaction," *Commun. ACM*, Vol. 26, pp. 972–986.

[18] J. Rewick (2000), "Clinching the holiday e-sale," *Wall Street J.*, Oct. 9.

[19] B. Tedeschi (1999), "Seeking ways to cut the web-page wait," *NY Times.* [Online]http://www.nytimes.com/library/tech/99/06/cyber/commerce/14commerce.html

[20] Anonymous. (1999) *Global Internet Statistics* [On-line]http://www.glreach.com/globstats/

[21] C. Wood (2000), "The future: Will it work? Amid smart robots and wireless wonders, some see a dark side," *Macleans.ca*, Aug. 21.

[22] G. Hofstede (1993), "Cultural constraints in management theories," *Acad. Manage. Exec.*, Vol. 7, pp. 81–94.

[23] G. Rose and D. Straub (1998), "Predicting general IT use: Applying TAM to the Arabic world," *J. Global Inform. Manage.*, Vol. 6, pp. 39–46.

[24] D. W. Straub, K. Loch, and C. Hill (2001), "Transfer of information technology to developing countries: A test of cultural influence modeling in the Arab world," *J. Global Inform. Manage.*, Vol. 9, pp. 6–28.

[25] R. O'Keefe, M. Cole, P. Chau, A. Massey, M. Montoya-Weiss, and M. Perry (2000), "From the user interface to the consumer interface: Results from a global experiment," *Int. J. Hum. Comput. Stud.*, Vol. 53, pp. 611–628.

[26] J. C. Chebat and P. Filiatrault (1993), "The impact of waiting in line on consumers," *Int. J. Bank Market*, Vol. 11, pp. 35–40.

[27] M. M. Davis and M. J. Maggard (1990), "An analysis of customer satisfaction with waiting times in a two-stage service process," *J. Oper. Manage.*, Vol. 9, pp. 324–334.

[28] J. L. Guynes (1988), "Impact of system response time on state anxiety," *Commun. ACM*, Vol. 31, pp. 342–347.

[29] E. T. Hall (1973), *The Silent Language*. Anchor, New York.

[30] A. Bluedorn, C. F. Kaufman, and P. M. Lane (1992), "How many things do you like to do at once? An introduction to monochrome and poly-chrome time," *Acad. Manage. Exec.*, Vol. 6, pp. 17–26.

[31] S. Tella (2000), "Achronos: Reflections on timeless time, media and communication," in S. Tella, Ed. *Media, Mediation, Time and Communication: Emphases in Network-Based Media Education*, Vol. 9. Media Education Center, Dept. Teacher Education, Univ. of Helsinki, Helsinki, Finland, pp. 83–100.

[32] E. T. Hall (1990), *The Silent Language*, 2nd ed. Anchor, New York.

[33] M. Karpinen-Shetta (1996), "Cultural analysis of working time in Japan and Finland," *Loisir & Société/Leisure and Society*, Vol. 19, pp. 151–167.

[34] E. T. Hall (1966), *The Hidden Dimension*. Doubleday, New York.

[35] M. K. Nydell (1987), *Understanding Arabs: A Guide for Westerners*. Intercultural, Yarmouth, ME.

[36] D. Leiser, D. Shinar, and J. Meyer (1995), "Time estimation of computer 'Wait' message displays computer systems: Interfacing with the user," in *Proc. Human Factors Perspectives on Human-Computer Interaction: Selections From the Human Factors and Ergonomics Society Annual Meetings 1983–1994*, G. Perlman, G. K. Green, and M. S. Wogalter, Eds., Santa Monica, CA, pp. 210–214.

[37] G. Tom, M. Burns, and Y. Zeng (1997), "Your life on hold: The effect of telephone waiting time on customer perception," *J. Direct Market*, Vol. 11, pp. 25–31.

[38] B. Shneiderman (1998), *Designing the User Interface: Strategies for Effective Human-Computer Interaction*, 3rd ed. Addison-Wesley, Reading, MA.

[39] (2001) *UIEtips E-mail Newsletter* [Online]. Available: http://world.std. com~uieweb/truth.htm

[40] J. C. Chebat, P. Filiatrault, C. Gelinas-Chebat, and A. Vaninsky (1995), "Impact of waiting attribution and consumer's mood on perceived qual-ity," *J. Bus. Res.*, Vol. 34, pp. 191–196.

[41] G. Rose and D. Straub (2001), "The effect of download time on consumer attitude toward the e-service retailer," *E-Service J.*, Vol. 1, pp. 55–76.

[42] E. F. Stone (1978), *Research Methods in Organizational Behavior*. Scott, Foresman, Glenview, IL.

[43] G. Rose and D. Straub (2001), *The Impact of Download Time on Brand Attitudes in B2C E-Commerce: The Download Time Brand Impact Model*. Georgia State Univ., Altanta, GA.

[44] Anonymous (1998), "GVU's 9th WWW user survey general demograph-ics summary," Georgia Tech. Res. Corporation, http://www.gvu.gatech. edu/user_surveys/survey-1998-04/re-ports/1998-04-General.html.

[45] S. Durvasula, S. C. Mehta, J. C. Andrews, and S. Lysonski (1997), "Advertising beliefs and attitudes: Are students and general consumers indeed different?," *J. Asian Bus.*, Vol. 13, pp. 71–84.

[46] M. T. Orne (1962), "On the social psychology of the psychological experiment: With particular reference to demand characteristics and their implications," *Amer. Psych.*, Vol. 17, pp. 776–783.

[47] D. Straub and G. Rose (2001), *Measuring inhibitors and responses to B2C e-commerce: An IS-marketing perspective.* Georgia State Univ., Atlanta, GA.

[48] M. K. Hui and D. K. Tse (1996), "What to tell consumers in waits of different lengths: An integrative model of service evaluation," *J. Market.*, Vol. 60, pp. 81–90.

[49] T. D. Cook and D. T. Campbell (1979), *Quasi Experimentation: Design and Analytical Issues for Field Settings.* Rand McNally, Shokie, IL.

[50] J. F. Hair Jr., R. E. Anderson, R. L. Tatham, and W. C. Black (1995), *Multivariate Data Analysis With Readings*, 4th ed. Prentice-Hall, Englewood Cliffs, NJ.

[51] H. R. Lindman (1974), *Anova in complex experimental designs.* W.H. Freeman, San Francisco, CA.

[52] A. Al-Arjani (1995), "Impact of cultural issues on the scheduling of housing maintenance in a saudi arabian urban project," *Int. J. Project Manage.*, Vol. 13, pp. 373–382.

[53] M. E. Davis and J. D. Grimes (1996), "Creating global software: Text handling and localization in taligent's commonpoint application system," *IBM Syst. J.*, Vol. 35, pp. 227–243.

[54] B. Tedeschi (2000), "E-Commerce report: Web sites redesign home pages". *NY Times* [Online]. Available: http://www.ny-times.com/2000/10/30/technology/30ECOMMERCE.html

[55] S. Taylor (1995), "The effects of filled waiting time and service provider control over the delay on evaluations of service," *J. Acad. Market. Sci.*, Vol. 23, pp. 38–48.

Reproduced from *IEEE Transactions on Engineering Management*, Vol. 50, No. 1, February 2003, pp. 31–43. Reprinted with permission from IEEE.

About the authors

Gregory M. Rose received the Ph.D. degree in computer information systems from Georgia State University, Atlanta.

After receiving Ph.D. degree, he was a Postdoctoral Fellow at the University of Jyvaskyla, Jyvaskyla, Finland. He is currently an Assistant Professor with the College of Business and Economics, Washington State

University, Vancouver. His research interests include the development, design, adoption, and use of web-based systems across various cultures in the Americas, Europe, and Africa. He has published in such journals as *Accounting, Management and Information Technologies, Information Systems Journal, Journal of Global Information Management, Electronic Markets,* and *Communications of the AIS*. He serves on the Editorial Review Board of the *Journal of Global Information Management*.

Roberto Evaristo received the Ph.D. degree in management information systems from the University of Minnesota, Minneapolis.

He is currently an Assistant Professor in the Information and Decision Sciences Department, University of Illinois, Chicago. He is involved in several projects related to the management of distributed projects in virtual organizations, with work done in Japan, the U.S., and Europe. He has published in journals including *Communications of the ACM, International Journal of Project Management, Database, Journal of Global Information Management, European Management Journal, Journal of Organizational Computing and Electronic Commerce*, and elsewhere, and serves on the Editorial Review Boards of the *Journal of Global Information Management* and the *Journal of Global Information Technology Management*.

Detmar Straub received the Ph.D. degree in english from The Pennsylvania State University, University Park, and the D.B.A. in management information systems from Indiana University, Bloomington.

He is currently the J. Mack Robinson Distinguished Professor of Information Systems at Georgia State University, Atlanta. He has conducted research in Net-enhanced organizations, computer security, technological innovation, and international information technology with over 100 publications in journals including *Management Science, Information Systems Research, MIS Quarterly, Organization Science, Journal of MIS, Journal of AIS, Journal of Global Information Management, Communications of the ACM, Information & Management, Communications of the AIS, Academy of Management Executive*, and *Sloan Management Review*. He is currently an Associate Editor for *Management Science and Information Systems Research*. He was formerly an Editor-in-Chief of *DATA BASE for Advances in Information Systems*, a Senior Editor for *Information Systems Research* (Special Issue on e-Commerce Metrics), and an Associate Editor for *MIS Quarterly*.

Questions for discussion

1　Do you consider yourself monochronic or polychronic? What is your attitude towards waiting? How long is too long for a download?

2   Are you willing to wait longer for different types of downloads (e.g., news story, a video, pictures from a friend, results from a search engine)? If so, what factors influence your willingness to wait?

3   What factors, aside from polychronism and monochronism, affect the willingness to wait? Do you consider the cultural factors more or less influential than the other factors you have identified?

4   Based upon the results of this study, what recommendations would you make to web designers?

5   What cultural differences besides polychronic/monochronic do you think should be taken into consideration in developing web content?

Part Four
The Role of Culture in IT Management

IT management involves the various aspects of management decision-making and strategy with respect to the effective management of firms' information resources. The subject of IT management is a broad topic that could include such topics as strategy, personnel, governance, and information ethics and privacy. The central question of this fourth part is 'how do variations in culture potentially influence how firms manage IT?' There have been a number of studies examining this issue from both the cross-cultural and organizational culture perspectives. The first two readings treat culture at the organizational level, whereas the third article by Slaughter and Ang (1995) examines the influence of culture on IT management from a cross-cultural (USA and Singapore) perspective. The fourth article takes a unique angle in trying to assess IT culture.

Those studies using the cross-cultural approach have been heavily biased towards the use of Hofstede's cultural value indices to examine how value orientations across countries can be used to explain differences in IT management practice across countries. A good example of this is Burn et al. (1993) who use Hofstede's dimensions of culture to explain differences in perceptions of critical IT issues by managers in the USA and Hong Kong. Likewise, Husted (2000) showed how levels of software piracy varied among individualistic vs. collectivist-oriented countries. Another study by Kettinger et al. (1995) demonstrates how differences in IT service quality (SERVQUAL) can be explained by differences in national culture.

Along this same theme, Milberg et al. (1995) examined how countries' approaches to regulating information privacy were influenced by power distance and individualism vs. collectivism value orientations. A later study by Shore et al. (2001) examines differences in student attitudes towards intellectual property rights across four countries using the power distance and masculinity vs. femininity dimensions of national culture.

The common theme among these articles is their comparison of a wide variety of IT management issues across two or more countries based upon one or more of Hofstede's dimensions of culture. As a representative sample, we have selected an article by Slaughter and Ang (1995) that follows this same theme. They conducted a longitudinal study to examine how differences in individualistic vs. collectivistic orientations between the USA and Singapore could be used to explain firms' information systems employment structures (e.g. choices to hire from within vs. externally). Not surprisingly, they found that more collectivist culture tended to use more internal employment structures (e.g. hiring from within) whereas more individualistic cultures placed less value on family orientation and loyalty, and hence used more external employment structures.

IS literature examining the influence of organizational culture on IT management practice is not as well organized around a consistent view of culture as it is for the cross-cultural studies discussed above, perhaps because the organizational culture literature itself is quite diverse, with little consensus on how best to define and measure organizational culture. Our first reading (Kanungo et al., 2001) draws from Wallach's (1983) taxonomy of organizational culture to explain how the type of IT strategy of given firms may vary based upon innovative, bureaucratic, or supportive value orientations. They conducted a nationwide survey of 72 public sector units in India and studied how particular organizational cultures of these firms related to their type of IT strategy.

Our second reading for this section is a study by Tomlin (1991) who surveyed 800 IT executives to better understand how their organizational culture related to their firm's competitive use of IT. Interestingly, the study showed that organizations using IT most successfully had developed strong internal information cultures that placed high value on the value of IT. The idea of firms having an information culture is an intriguing one that really focuses on how a firm's members value the technology artifact and the information it produces (Leidner and Kayworth, 2006). Future research could potentially seek to identify the various dimensions of information culture values and to examine how such values influence the adoption, use, and management of IT.

The final article in this part – that of Kaarst-Brown (2005) – focuses on the unique question of what makes an 'IT culture' and how does the role of the CIO vary in organizations with different IT cultures. Whereas the other articles in this book have looked at culture in terms of values, Kaarst-Brown digs deeply to focus on the assumptions about IT held by organizational members and uses these assumptions to decipher five distinct IT cultures. The article is delightfully insightful both for theory and practice, and is a marvelous way to conclude the book.

References

Burn, J. K., B. C. Saxena, L. Ma, and H. K. Cheung (1993), "Critical Issues in IS Management in Hong Kong: A Cultural Comparison," *Journal of Global Information Management*, Vol. 1, No. 4, pp. 28–37.

Grover, V., J. T. C. Teng, and K. D. Fiedler (1998), "IS Investment Priorities in Contemporary Organizations," *Communications of the ACM*, Vol. 41, No. 2, pp. 40–48.

Husted, B. W. (2000), "The Impact of National Culture on Software Piracy," *Journal of Business Ethics*, Vol. 26, No. 3, August, pp. 197–211.

Kaarst-Brown, M. L. (2005), "Understanding an Organization's View of the CIO: The Role of Assumptions About It," *MIS Quarterly Executive*, Vol. 4, No. 2, June, pp. 287–301.

Kanungo, S., S. Sadavarti, and S. Yadlapati (2001), "Relating IT Strategy and Organizational Culture: An Empirical Study of Public Sector Units in India," *Journal of Strategic Information Systems*, Vol. 10, pp. 29–57.

Kettinger, W. J., C. C. Lee, and S. Lee (1995), "Global Measures of Information Service Quality: A Cross-National Study," *Decision Sciences*, Vol. 26, No. 5, Sept/Oct, pp. 569–588.

Leidner, D. L. and T. R. Kayworth (2006), "A Review of Culture in Information Systems Research: Toward a Theory of Information Technology Culture Conflict," *MIS Quarterly*, Vol. 30, No. 2, June, pp. 357–399.

Milberg, S. J., S. J. Burke, J. H. Smith, and E. A. Kallman (1995), "Rethinking Copyright Issues and Ethics on the Net: Values, Personal Information Privacy, and Regulatory Approaches," *Communications of the ACM*, Vol. 38, No. 12, pp. 65–73.

Shore, B., A. R. Venkatachalam, E. Solorzano, J. M. Burn, S. Z. Hassan, and L. J. Janczewski (2001), "Softlifting and Piracy: Behavior Across Cultures," *Technology in Society*, Vol. 23, No. 4, pp. 563–581.

Slaughter, S. and S. Ang (1995), "Information Systems Employment Structures in the USA and Singapore: A Cross-Cultural Comparison," *Information, Technology, and People*, Vol. 8, No. 2, pp. 17–36.

Tomlin, R. (1991), "Developing a management climate culture in which information technology will flourish: how the UK can benefit," *Journal of Information Technology*, Vol. 6, pp. 45–55.

Wallach, E. J. (1983), "Individuals and Organizations: The Cultural Match," *Training and Development Journal*, February, pp. 29–36.

14 Relating IT Strategy and Organizational Culture: An Empirical Study of Public Sector Units in India

Shivraj Kanungo, Sanjeev Sadavarti and Yadlapati Srinivas

Abstract: This paper analyzes the relationships between selected aspects of organizational culture and IT-Strategy in public sector units (PSUs). Organization culture, which is treated as a shared set of norms and values, is analyzed with respect to IT-Strategies. Organizational culture is assessed in terms of innovative, supportive and bureaucratic cultures. IT strategy is viewed as comprising six generic strategies, namely, centrally planned, leading edge, scarce resource, necessary evil, monopoly and free market. The data on which conclusions were drawn arises from a nation-wide survey covering 72 public sector organizations in India. In addition to the survey research, we conducted an in-depth case study of State Bank of India. This yearlong study commenced in 1996. Statistically significant findings show that it is the innovative element of a PSUs organizational culture that is associated with a delineable IT strategy. Leading edge, free market, and monopoly IT-strategies are found to be related to innovative components of organizational culture. Monopoly and scarce resource strategies are associated with supportive and bureaucratic cultures, respectively. Our case study validates some of these findings in a large bank. Implications for practice as well as research are provided.

1. Introduction

Information, emerging within and outside the organization, takes its final form and is used according to the structural, socio-psychological and geographical setup of organizations. The socio-psychological setup, better known as 'organizational culture,' and its encounter with IT, results in unique uses, problems and intriguing issues. For linking IT use to organizational effectiveness the need arises for a well thought out and appropriate strategy. Until the early 1990s, public sector organizations or units (PSUs) in India dominated the Indian economy in almost all the core sectors. With the advent of economic liberalization, PSUs are facing stiff competition from the private sector that consists of both multinational as well as domestic organizations. In order to remain viable and competitive, PSUs have identified the role of IT (Kholi, 1994; Neogy, 1994; Kutty, 1994) as one of the key determinants of organizational renewal. While there is a comprehensive research base that documents the rationale for IT-enabled organizational effectiveness in the industrialized world, a more limited research base is available for the developing economies. Palvia et al., (1992) do provide a basis for this research and their research shows that strategic IT planning is considered among the least important elements of IS by managers in Indian PSUs. This research base suggests that, in most instances, investments in IT have not translated into organizational effectiveness and that there is plenty of scope for improvement. Studies from India (Gupta, 1996; Goyal, 1994; Rau and Rao, 1993) have also revealed that while some PSUs have used IT to drive productivity increases and derive organizational benefits, many are yet to use IT effectively.

While prior research shows us that the role and the nature of the association of IT with other organizational variables has not been studied in the PSUs of India (Bannet and Sicherl, 1992; Singla, 1992), organizational culture of public sector units (PSUs) in India has been used as an explanatory variable (Bhal, 1996; Sinha and Singh, 1993: Bhaduri, 1991) for organizational success or for less successful performance. Therefore, there is a felt need to develop a better understanding of the relationship between organizational culture and IT strategies.

Consequently, in this paper we have attempted to develop a better understanding of selected aspects of organizational culture and the strategies involved in the installation, implementation and use of computer systems. This is so because insights gained from IT experiences elsewhere (Heeks, 1995; Caudle et al., 1991; Mohan et al., 1990) cannot necessarily be translated directly into local Indian contexts. This is so because, while IT is argued to be culturally neutral, IT use is certainly not (Pacey, 1983). Pacey argues cogently to distinguish technology from technology-practice and relates culture, technology, and organizations to demonstrate the cultural influence on technology use.

This research is an attempt to map empirical relationships between organizational culture and IT strategy. Section 2 presents a review of the literature and the background for this study. In it we discuss the concept of IT strategy, organizational culture and the relationship between the two constructs. Section 3 is devoted to the research method adopted for this study and Section 4 contains the results of statistical analysis on the data collected. Section 5 provides a discussion of these results. Section 6 contains a case study that captures qualitative aspects of the relationship between IT strategy and organizational culture. Section 7 concludes the paper. In it we summarize the results and present the learning issues and implications for practitioners, and implications for theory.

2. Literature review

IT strategy

Researchers have shown considerable interest in various aspects of IT in organizations from formulation of IT strategies to planning approaches for IT to physical implementation of IT in organizations (Bakos and Treacy, 1986; Earl, 1993; Grover et al., 1993; King and Sethi, 1993; Markus and Keil, 1994; Venkatraman, 1994; Yetton et al., 1994). The focus of research on IT in organizations has shown considerable and significant change during the last decade. There has been a shift in focus from IT being conceived as a means of improving the efficiency of processes (Ein-Dor and Segev, 1978; Nolan, 1979; Rockart, 1979) to being used as a strategic tool in the hands of management and enabling re-engineering and transforming the ways organizations do business (Galliers, 1993; Venkatraman, 1994). Thus, over the last two decades, while IT has advanced so has the role that it is intended to carry out in organizations. IT is no longer considered as merely a supportive tool for existing organizational processes but is perceived as an integrating technology for initiating business changes and shaping structures in organizations to align them to business needs (Baets, 1992; Chan and Huff, 1993; Davenport, et al., 1989; Grover et al., 1993; Ward, 1987).

Besides the technological focus of IT practices in organizations, there are cultural and organizational factors that influence IT strategies and the way IT is planned. A study conducted by Premkumar and King (1991) provided empirical evidence linking organizational characteristics and IT performance in the organization. In this study a number of organizational variables, including culture and its role in IT planning were outlined.

Available literature on IT strategies in organizations seems to be influenced more by business strategies (Grover et al., 1993; Venkatraman, 1994) so much so that most of IT strategy categorizations tend to reflect a business orientation rather than having their own identity. Ward (1987) points out the fact that since the role of IT has been transformed considerably, traditional approaches to the management of IT are no longer appropriate for the determination of business strategies. He adds that generic business strategies related without analysis of ITs impact on the industry, competitive forces and the chosen business strategy will, by default, produce a non-specific IT strategy. He suggests that the stage of evolution in the business can be used to choose a specific IT strategy from available generic strategies. The dependence of an organization on existing applications also tends to force it toward a single generic approach (Ward and Griffiths, 1996).

For the survey part of this study we decided to adopt the classification of IT strategies provided by Parsons (1983). Generic strategies provide us with a basis for comparison across organizations based on broad criteria. Parsons describes five strategies in terms of general frameworks which guide the opportunities for IT which are identified, the IT resources which are developed, the rate at which new technologies are adopted, the level of impact of IT within the firm, etc. These generic strategies are explained further in Exhibit 14.1. While there have been other attempts at providing generic IT

Centrally planned: In a centrally planned IT strategy a firm attempts to integrate its corporate strategy and its information systems strategy. The firm will have focused on integrated systems so that maximum utilization is made of computer processing power. A centralized IT department will have used a top down planning approach.

Leading edge: This IT strategy implies that the firm continuously updates its hardware and software with the latest developments available in the market. In such a strategy, state-of-the-technology is continually acquired. Experimentation is encouraged in the hope that discoveries will lead to superior performance and the sustainable competitive advantage.

Free market: A free-market IT strategy assumes that the user is best qualified to determine his/her own needs. In such circumstances, the user is entitled to acquire hardware, software and services either from IT department or from any outside vendor. The only rule which is strictly applied is that the user obtain his IS services at a reasonable price.

Monopoly: Monopoly IT strategy rests on the premise that there should be one single source of computer services in the organization. The primary criterion for the success of monopoly strategy is the satisfaction of the user. In order to ensure this, there should be considerable excess capacity in the IT department to cope with the peaks in demand. One of the major difficulties facing the firm in implementing the strategy is the measurement of user satisfaction.

Scarce resource: Scarce resource IT strategy relies on the intensive control of money being spent on the IT department. Very strict budgets are set and the IT department is often simply not permitted under any circumstances to exceed the amounts laid down. A scarce resource strategy is based on the concept that administration is an unproductive cost and thus management must minimize all expenditure in this direction.

Necessary evil: Necessary evil IT strategy is based on the belief that the use of computers should be curtailed as much as possible. Only applications that cannot be performed without the use of a computer and which are very well cost justified are entertained. A minimum amount is spent on hardware, software and people. As a result firms pursuing this strategy often encounter a high turnover of their programmers, analysts and operators.

Exhibit 14.1　*Generic IT strategies*
(Source: Parsons 1983)

strategies (Das et al., 1991; Kim and Lee, 1991), Parsons' approach provides greater detail and coverage.

Organizational culture

Organizational culture can be defined as a set of norms, routines and myths specific to an organization. Deal (1982) considers culture to be a stable collection of values and symbols. Cooke and Lafferty (1983) consider organizational culture to be a reflection of shared values and beliefs that guide the thinking and behaviors of members. Additional definitions for organizational culture have been provided by Becker and Geer (1960); Louis (1983); Martin and Siehl (1983); Ouchi (1981); Uttal (1983); Van Maanen and Schein (1979). The multiplicity of the terms and concepts associated with organizational culture has contributed to conceptualizing the culture in different ways.

Consequently, the measurement or assessment of culture assumes significance. This is because culture can be conceptualized as having process dynamic properties as well as embedded or static characteristics. An analysis of the definitions and conceptualization of culture by different researchers reveals tremendous variety. For example, Schein (1985) emphasizes unconscious assumptions, Martin and Seihl (1983) emphasize stories and Smircich (1983) emphasizes meaning and context. While there is a broad agreement amongst culture researchers, they nonetheless emphasize different elements. Rousseau (1990) sums up this situation aptly by stating that it is not the definitions of culture that vary so widely across organizational researchers, but the type of data researchers collect (p. 156). Rousseau has provided a framework, shown in Figure 14.1, to choose data collection and analysis methods in this context.

An emphasis on the role of the unconscious, organizational uniqueness, epistemological bias toward social construction and subjectivism, and ethical concerns about data gathering (which purports to speak for respondents) tends to drive researchers toward the impressionistic and 'interpretive' boxes in Figure 14.1. When the focus shifts to the outer or manifest layers of culture, the epistemological issues (arising out of ontological differences) and

		Data	
		Data Collection	Data Analysis
Methods	Public	Standardized, Pre-specified	Standard, rules and heuristics
	Private	Impressionistic	Interpretive

Figure 14.1 *Public and private methods to study organizational culture (Delisi, 1990)*

ethical concerns become less compelling. In this situation a researcher can opt to operate from the 'standardized and pre-specified' and 'standard, rules and heuristics' boxes.

Since both approaches to the study of culture are appropriate, we chose to emphasize the 'public' notion of culture (see Figure 14.1) and to provide a balanced interpretation by incorporating a case study in our analysis.

Some of the culture assessment instruments that we reviewed include Norm Diagnostic Index (Allen and Dyer, 1980), Kilmann-Saxton Culture-Gap Survey (Kilmann et al., 1986), Corporate Culture Survey (Glaser et al., 1987), Organizational Beliefs Questionnaire (Sashkin and Fulmer, 1985), Organizational Value Congruence Scale (Enz, 1986), and Organizational Culture Profile (O'Reilly et al, 1991). Wallach (1983) identified and defined three separate organizational cultures covering almost all the parameters previous authors had identified. For this study we therefore used Wallach's approach to assess culture.

Linking organizational culture and IT strategy

There is abundant theoretical support for the culture-strategy nexus. Kitchell (1995) has been able to demonstrate empirically that corporate culture determines technology adoption strategies. Similarly, McRary (1995) has shown that corporate culture influences IT implementation strategies. Grover et al. (1998) show that a planning culture influences IT investment strategies. Additional support for linking corporate culture and IT investment strategies is provided by Hinton and Kaye (1996). Grote and Baitsch (1991) studied two groups within a communication network and found considerable cultural differences in network use for communication that could be attributed to cultural differences. Delisi (1990), as part of his strategic planning intervention at Digital, developed a list of critical issues or obstacles to the organization's achievement of strategic goals. He found that many of the critical issues concerning the organization came down to a choice between two different cultural approaches: entrepreneurial and professional.

While we acknowledge that the relationship between organizational culture and IT is reflexive in that IT can influence organizational culture as well as be affected by it (Grote and Baitsch, 1991; Robey and Azevedo, 1993), we have taken culture to be the antecedent (and more stable) variable. Since Robey and Azevedo (1993) emphasize the need to address aspects related to cultural persistence as well as change as a part of cultural analysis, we have chosen to concentrate on the persistence of culture. Given the nature of PSUs (particularly their large size and conservative work practices), organizational culture is more closely associated with depicting stable forces operating within an organization (Robey and Azevedo, 1993, p. 30). The lack of cultural dynamism in terms of cultural change is indeed a cause for concern for many policy makers. Whatever few cultural changes have been observed (Saxena, 1996) can be traced primarily to structural changes (e.g. reduced Government controls leading to greater autonomy) and can hardly be attributed to information technology (ibid). Additional support for cultural persistence comes from Bhal's 1997 study (Bhal, 1996) in which she observed that culture change in public sector organizations is extremely phlegmatic. Moreover Cooper (1994) provides additional support for assuming cultural antecedence in terms of IT implementation and how implementation strategies need to be formulated to report such linkages. Additional support for cultural antecedence in the culture-strategy relationship comes from Semler (1997), Tushman and O'Reilly (1996) and Vestal et al. (1997).

By far the most direct support for our study comes from Bates et al. (1995) who provided empirical support for a theoretical model that links manufacturing strategy to organizational culture. Related theoretical support, in the case of public sector organizations, is provided by Weber and Pliskin (1996) and by Kim et al. (1995) who show culture as a determinant of quality strategy in public sector organizations.

3.   Research methodology

Our unit of analysis was the organization since both organizational culture and organizational strategy have been conceptualized as organization level constructs. As both these constructs are complex phenomena, a research method based on a single data collection and analysis technique would have left out aspects of the research question. Therefore, multiple methods needed to be applied. In our research methodology, we adopted quantitative and qualitative methods we included testing research hypotheses using data collected through a questionnaire survey and have examined our findings in the context of an in-depth case study. The quantitative study enabled us to uncover and understand the broad nature of the relationship between organization culture and IT strategy. Taking off from where the survey research ended, the qualitative study not only validated some of these relationships but provided details of the relationships that were difficult to capture in the quantitative study or were not found as a part of the survey. The objective of using complementary data gathering and analysis methods was twofold. Firstly, this approach would allow us to collect broad-based as well as in-depth data. Secondly, the analysis of these data would provide generalizable as well as context-specific insights. Additionally, we could re-examine some of the context-specific data in the light of the survey results. The in-depth case study was conducted concurrently with the survey research. The latter part of the case was conducted with complete empirical results from the survey research. As a result, we were able to go back to organizations where we conducted the case studies and revisit some of the issues in the light of the survey findings.

Our research design is a response to what Robey and Azevedo (1993) call the paradox of cultural persistence and change. Both static analysis (using quantitative empirical data) and case analysis (incorporating organizational dynamics) are integrated to complement each other. A similar approach to research has been proposed by Gable (1994). In summary, we study culture in snapshot mode as well as a process. The next two sections describe how we operationalized the IT strategy and organizational culture construct.

Operationalizing the IT strategy construct

The set of planned organizational actions (i.e. strategy) is framed based on how people in the organization perceive a problem, find a solution to it and prepare themselves for future expected and unexpected problems. Perceptions may lead to top management taking the responsibility for IT in their own hands. Users may be allowed to do so on their own or to contribute to such efforts. Decisions are generally reached with the significant involvement of middle management. IT facilities can be developed by the organization itself, in consultation with external consultants, outsourced, or a combination of these options. Many such decisions are also determined by availability of resources, importance given to IT, nature of IT needs (perceived as well as real), and constitute the overall IT strategy of the organization. It has been argued that, for the most part, all key parameters are covered in six generic strategies, viz. centrally planned, leading edge, free market, monopoly, scarce resources and necessary evil IT strategies (Parsons, 1983).

Operationalizing the organizational culture construct

According to Wallach (1983) shared values, norms and beliefs of people in an organization can be mapped on to an innovative, supportive and bureaucratic culture. Wallach describes these as independent cultures. However, in order to describe an organizational culture completely, all three elements – present in varying proportions – are required. Culture is, therefore, measured in terms of parameters describing these three elements.

Covering almost all aspects of the organization culture, Wallach provides a validated instrument for empirically assessing three forms of organizational culture. The three forms are described in Exhibit 14.2. Survey items related to organizational culture and IT strategy are shown in Appendix A.

Research hypotheses relating organizational culture and IT strategy

The research hypotheses for this study are derived in this section. We have used the operationalizations in Exhibits 14.1 and 14.2 to deduce broad patterns

> **Bureaucratic cultures** have clear lines of responsibility and authority; work is highly organized, compartmentalized and systematic. The information and authority flow is hierarchical and based on control and power. Overall bureaucratic companies tend to mature, stable and relatively cautious. Adjectives used for describing this are culture-hierarchical, procedural, structured, ordered, regulated, established, solid, cautious and power-oriented.
>
> **Innovative cultures** are characterized by creative work environments. In such cultures challenge and risk taking are the norms. Stimulation is constant companion to workers, but innovative environment also take their toll on people who often are under great stress and burned out. Adjectives used for describing this culture are risk-taking, result-oriented, creative, pressurized, stimulating, challenging, enterprising and driving.
>
> **Supportive cultures** provide a friendly environment, and workers tend to be fair and helpful to each other and to the organization. An open, harmonious environment is encouraged and 'family' values are prompted. The adjectives used are supportive, trusting, equitable, safe, social, encouraging, relationships-oriented and collaborative.

Exhibit 14.2 *Organizational cultures*
(Source: Wallach 1983)

of relationships. For instance centrally planned IT strategy is characterized by the fact that it is integrated and interdependent with corporate strategy. Additionally it is characterized by large investments and centralized control over the IS function. However, to ensure initiatives from top management, IT requires a solid, established and cautious organizational setup. Therefore, we expect centralized planning to be associated with bureaucratic cultures.

People in an innovative culture tend to be self-generative and appear to thrive in a creative climate. A sociable atmosphere, personal freedom and high value for interpersonal relationships characterize a supportive culture. We would expect both these cultures to discourage centralized planning. People in an innovative culture are used to, and even thrive on, continuous challenges, a self-imposed pressure of a creative atmosphere, etc. and so discourage centralized planning. A supportive culture, which provides relation-orientation, personal freedom, sociable atmosphere, and the like, tends to be incompatible with centrally planned decisions being implemented successfully. So, both the innovative and supportive cultures discourage centralized planning.

We would expect innovative cultures to be most closely associated with leading edge strategies as they are equipped with the necessary creative and entrepreneurial outlook. Hierarchical and procedural work environments discourage people to think over and above what they are doing and the structural and solid nature of such environments may not facilitate the easy incorporation of new ideas. Hence, bureaucratic organizations are not likely to have leading edge IT strategies.

A free market IT strategy is determined primarily by the characteristics and culture of IT usage in the organization. People in the organization generally self impose some relationships and the duplication of technologies can be seen, due to lack of coordinated efforts. A supportive culture is also seen as discouraging this strategy. A bureaucratic culture does not allow the growth of this strategy through such inhibitors as hierarchy, rules and regulations, and power orientation. But the efforts through goal oriented, performance driven organizations stimulate this strategy in innovative environments.

Bureaucratic organizations would generally tend toward monopolistic IT strategies that develop a sole source utility service for IT owing to budgeting patterns and decisions. But effective use of IT in terms of cost reduction and increase in efficiency is seen when a concerted approach toward IT use is made, coupled with innovative and creative organizational changes. Typically, when IT investments are made by treating IT as a utility, innovative organizations can provide the framework to manage such investments and resultant risks creatively. A supportive culture would tend to dampen the effects of a monopolistic IT strategy by either avoiding significant organizational changes (reengineering or restructuring) or by going along with the IT department more in letter than in spirit to somehow preserve organizational harmony.

Finally, when an IT strategy is seen as a compulsion for organizational functioning then this may be seen as a necessary evil strategy. With ubiquitous IT use, few organizations consider IT to be an imposition. However, there could be instances, where large groups in an organization may posit a specific stance toward IT (e.g. clerks refusing to use PCs in a bank or insurance agents demanding special commissions when asked to use terminals to capture policy and policy-holder data). In such cases, acquiescence to management directives (by way of negotiated settlements), ostensively to ensure organizational performance and maintain harmony, may result in employees agreeing reluctantly to the implementation and use of such systems. Such scenarios are typical of supportive bureaucracies. Supportive cultures are expected to resist a top-down planning framework characterized by centrally planned IT strategies. On the other hand, they would encourage free market strategies.

Our expected findings are summarized in Table 14.1.

We expected to find that supportive aspects of organizational culture would demonstrate the highest levels of ambivalence with respect to IT strategy. We also expected to find that innovative and bureaucratic aspects of culture account for most of the IT strategies in organizations.

Sample size

For this particular study, the whole population of 210 PSUs in India was considered. The respondents from each organization included the CEOs

Table 14.1 *Hypothesized relations between organizational culture and IT strategies*
*(+ Supports − Discourages * Independent)*

	Innovative	Supportive	Bureaucratic
Centrally planned	−	−	+
Leading edge	+	*	−
Free market	+	−	−
Monopoly	+	*	+
Scarce resource	+	*	+
Necessary evil	*	+	*

(Managing Directors or Chairmen) and managers of different functional units at various levels including the IT manager. Only corporate offices were contacted and asked to complete the questionnaire. The average number of respondents per organization was five. Four organizations had three respondents while 16 organizations had more than seven respondents. The total useable sample size was 72. The response rate was therefore 32%. Responding organizations were distributed across size (turnover) and industry. All the responses came from the upper two revenue quartiles. Within these quartiles, the responses were evenly distributed between the first and the second quartile. The responses are biased toward larger organizations.

4.   Results

To analyze the relation between organizational culture and IT strategy, we first calculated correlation coefficients for each strategy and each cultural form. Following that, the relations found significant were analyzed further using their individual parameters. The second set of correlation values revealed additional insights into the relationship between organizational culture and IT strategy.

Table 14.2 shows the overall relationship between organizational culture and IT strategy. We see from Table 14.2 that the innovative dimension of organizational culture is significantly related to the leading edge, monopoly and free market strategies. The supportive dimension of organizational culture is related to the monopoly IT strategy and the bureaucratic dimension of culture is significantly related to the scarce resource strategy. The bureaucratic dimension exhibits the largest number of inhibitive influences also. We can see that the bureaucratic dimension is negatively correlated with leading

Table 14.2   *Correlation coefficients relating organizational culture and IT strategies*

	Centrally planned	Leading edge	Scarce resource	Necessary evil	Monopoly	Free market
Innovative	0.2805	0.3817*	0.0977	−0.0333	0.5606*	0.3447*
Supportive	0.2321	0.2468	0.2624	−0.0006	0.5623*	0.0606
Bureaucratic	0.0220	−0.2708	0.3601*	−0.0258	0.1005	−0.2423

*Significant to the level of 0.05.

edge and free market strategies. These relations, however, are not statistically significant. One way of using these results could be to treat organizational cultures as determinants of IT strategy. For instance, one could read from Table 14.2 that organizations that are innovative and supportive would tend to have a monopoly IT strategy. While we cannot make sweeping statements, our case study would help us to refine and elaborate on a specific organization. Our results are generally consistent with that which we had hypothesized (except for the supportive dimension of culture). Table 14.3 summarizes the survey results.

As expected, the results in the bureaucratic and innovative dimensions are consistent with our hypotheses. The significance of the results is higher in the innovative dimension (three out of the four results that agreed with the hypotheses are significant). In the bureaucratic dimension, only one of the five results that agreed with the hypotheses was significant. The absence of significance of central planning with the bureaucratic dimension was unexpected. As expected, however, the supportive dimension of culture remained ambiguous. For that reason, we took it up in the case study for further analysis.

Tables 14.4–8 show the relations between individual variables that made up the culture and strategy constructs. These results are discussed in Section 5.

5.   Discussion

As expected, organizations with an innovative culture showed significant positive relationships with leading edge, monopoly and free-market IT strategies. This indicates that such organizations with an innovative culture are most likely to develop an identifiable IT strategy. A better understanding of how specific factors are responsible for development of such strategies was developed using results in Tables 14.4–6.

Table 14.3 *Results compared to hypotheses (NA – We had not hypothesized any directional relationship. Hence significance is not applicable)*

	Innovative		Supportive		Bureaucratic	
	Directionality consistent with hypothesis?	*Significant?*	*Directionality consistent with hypothesis?*	*Significant?*	*Directionality consistent with hypothesis?*	*Significant?*
Centrally planned	No	No	No	No	Yes	No
Leading edge	Yes	Yes	Yes	NA	Yes	No
Free market	Yes	Yes	No	No	Yes	No
Monopoly	Yes	Yes	No	Yes	Yes	No
Scarce resource	Yes	No	Yes	NA	Yes	Yes
Necessary evil	Yes	NA	No	No	Yes	NA

Table 14.4   *Correlation coefficients relating innovative culture and leading edge IT strategy*

	Develop applications with no immediate use	State-of-art technology maintained
Risk taking	0.3598*	0.3296*
Results oriented	0.0786	0.2683
Creative	0.2314	0.4630*
Pressurized	0.3136*	0.0734
Stimulating	0.1073	0.5414*
Challenging	0.1246	0.2582
Enterprising	0.1592	0.2582
Driving	0.0173	0.0154

*Significance level of 0.05.

Table 14.5   *Correlation coefficients relating innovative culture and monopoly IT strategy*

	IT investments to improve internal efficiency of the organization	IT investment to differentiate product or service
Risk taking	0.4616*	0.3160*
Results oriented	0.4203*	0.2005
Creative	0.4072*	0.1582
Pressurized	0.0000	0.2980
Stimulating	0.6091*	0.2625
Challenging	0.4149*	0.1589
Enterprising	0.5645*	0.2495
Driving	0.3541*	0.2741

*Significance level of 0.05.

Table 14.4 indicates that maintaining state-of-the-art technology and development of IT without immediate applications involves an ability to take risks. Organizations that have the ability to absorb and utilize these technologies by fostering creativity tend to have leading edge IT strategies. High performing organizations where the work pressures are high, as well as those organizations which work in competitive environments, tend to develop IT applications that respond to future needs.

Table 14.6 *Correlation coefficients relating innovative culture and free-market IT strategy*

	Users determine need of IT	IS group/department within organization competes with outside vendors
Risk taking	0.0310	0.3007*
Results oriented	0.2194	0.0455
Creative	0.4267*	0.1837
Pressurized	0.3158*	0.1790
Stimulating	0.3395*	0.1102
Challenging	0.3354*	0.0652
Enterprising	0.3142*	0.0242
Driving	0.3880*	0.3519*

*Significance to the level of 0.05.

Table 14.7 *Correlation coefficients relating supportive culture and monopoly IT strategy*

	IT investments to improve internal efficiency of the organization	IT investment to differentiate product or service
Collaborative	0.3644*	0.3469*
Relationship-oriented	0.2857	0.2372
Encouraging	0.5157*	0.3105
Sociable	0.3191*	0.2929
Personal freedom	0.5322*	0.2177
Equitable	0.2843	0.0352
Safe	0.1666	0.1254
Trusting	0.3053	0.3909*

*Significance level of 0.05.

Table 14.5 supports the view that for IT to be used to improve efficiency of an organization a creative, stimulating, challenging, enterprising and driving culture is required. This implies that PSUs which display a monopoly IT strategy will have consolidated and channeled IT expertise, with centralized data allowing them to leverage investments in IT to make incremental

Table 14.8   *Correlation coefficients relating bureaucratic culture and scarce resource IT strategy*

	IT investment strictly on return-on-investment	IT budgets set before demand is placed
Hierarchical	0.3194*	0.2598
Procedural	0.1494	0.2981*
Structured	0.1333	0.2126
Ordered	0.0713	0.3788*
Regulated	0.0192	0.1193
Established, solid	0.1044	0.0349
Cautious	0.0745	0.3827*
Power oriented	0.1236	0.2340

*Significance level of 0.05.

improvements. While consolidation of expertise, hardware and other IT resources may be suitable, the results show that it is the task oriented dimensions of organizational culture that ensures IT resources for improvements in organizations. It is significant to note that except for risk-taking, no other cultural dimension is associated significantly with the need to differentiate a product using IT. This is a reflection of the monopolistic industry structure PSUs operate in as well as the lack of true autonomy that is required to make product/market related decisions.

From Table 14.6 we see that the free-market strategy, being essentially user driven, correlated more significantly with most of the aspects of innovative culture than any other factor. The results support the view that in an organization with a simulating, challenging, enterprising, driving, and creative culture the users tend to involve themselves in determining IT strategy. Due to the open-ended nature of this strategy, it is usually an interim strategy, wherein after consolidation and reorganization, organizations tend to migrate to either a monopoly or leading edge IT strategy. Importantly, it is only innovative culture that shows significant association with the above strategies. This leads us to conclude that leading edge, monopoly and free market IT strategies are all strongly associated with the innovative components of organization culture.

From Table 14.7 we see that organizations with a supportive culture show a significant correlation with monopoly IT strategy. It was hypothesized, however, that supportive culture is not associated with monopoly IT strategy. Analysis of Table 14.6 reveals possible reasons for supportive cultures to be associated with a monopoly IT strategy. Almost all the interpersonal factors described in the supportive culture show a strong association with decisions to develop monopoly strategy. Post survey interviews with IT managers revealed that supportive cultures tend to absorb group technologies like e-mail and groupware far more easily than other typical bureaucracies, especially in PSUs that have emerged recently in hi-tech areas like software development. Investments to improve internal efficiency of the organization require improvements in, and attention to, numerous human factors (such as nature of workplace interaction, hygiene factors, and degree of autonomy and empowerment), as can also be inferred from the results. Concurrent product differentiation through IT investments seems not to have much influence of this culture type. This finding also appears to be consistent with the fact that supportive cultures, which encourage consensual and pluralistic approaches, tend to engender IT strategies that do not 'rock the boat'. Such incremental improvements are not necessarily conducive to developing and implementing strategic information systems that have implications for an organization's competitive position. This is consistent with the nature of competitiveness in the PSUs of India that were (up until 1992) under no pressure to compete, and enjoying the financial support of the government.[1]

Results from Table 14.2 show that organizations with a bureaucratic culture show a significant correlation with scarce-resource IT strategy. When a scarce-resource strategy is opted for, it indicates either a paucity of resources for IT, which is perceived to be a cost center leading to fixed minimal IT budgets. A well-understood aspect of bureaucratic culture in India is to make safe decisions (Nigam et al., 1995; Lakshmipathy, 1985). In other words, while the reward structure is such that for excellent outcomes relating to IT decisions (or for that matter any decisions) the rewards are generally not forthcoming. Conversely, punitive measures for failures are more likely to be observed because establishing accountability, as a post facto exercise in decision-making, is endemic to any PSU in India. If we reflect on the results in Table 14.8, which shows the parameters of bureaucratic culture that correlate significantly with scarce resource strategy, it is seen that IT budgets show more correlation with the cautious, ordered and procedural nature of bureaucratic culture, thereby supporting our hypothesis.

In general there is no delineable process to chart an IT strategy as such in highly bureaucratic PSUs except for the budgeting process. It would be fair to say that IT budgets dictate the nature of investments. The over-cautious approach to IT-related decision-making is understandable since generalists are the decision-makers while IT specialists have to prove and ensure adequate returns on IT investments. By implication, the role of IT specialists is marginalized and hence, in some such organizations at least, the scarce-resource strategy changes into an unclear and ineffective strategy over time.

---

[1]The accumulated losses of PSUs, as of 1998 of 105 in number, is around Rs. 5000 crores. One crore = 10 million and 1 US Dollar ≈ 40 Rupees.

6.   Case study

In order to investigate some of the above results obtained from the survey research, we conducted a case study of the State Bank of India (SBI) over a period of three months in 1996–97 by interviewing senior managers and IT staff. SBI is a large bureaucracy and we were able to establish that the broad IT strategies SBI follows are consistent with that which our quantitative analysis had uncovered.

SBI is the largest commercial bank in India in terms of business, infrastructure and service. It has over 8800 branches spread all over the country. This bank has a history of over 200 years of operation. Increasing volumes of operations created a need in this bank to invest in IT in order to speed up its operations and thereby achieve higher efficiency in its operations. IT started proliferating in SBI as early as the 1970s. However, like in other public sector organizations, IT faced a lot of resistance from employee unions. The unions were opposed to computerization in SBI. This continued till as late as the mid-1980s when SBI reached some level of agreement with the unions. SBI since then has begun automating its operations, starting with back office computerization. The importance of IT is reflected in the fact that functional departments were created in the central office in the late 1980s with a top executive in charge of the Systems and Technology wing.

Starting with the introduction of data processing systems for administrative offices and transaction processing at some of the key branches at later stage, diffusion of technology in this bank has, however, remained a slow process. The main reasons for this were apparently political, attitudinal, cultural and environmental in nature.

While the impact of IT on organizational processes remained low, centralized planning for investing in IT continued. A cumulative expenditure of 129.60 crores in IT up to 1994 is an indication of this effort. However, this magnitude of IT investment had not, at the time of our study, been reflected in effective and efficient operations. Moreover, the strategic role of IT is not necessarily linked to the magnitude of investment made in IT. Since the number of branches of SBI is high, the allocation of budget in absolute terms for IT in SBI will have to be on the higher side. In order to make a visible impact on the operations of the bank, compared to other banks where the spread of the branches is less, the magnitude of IT investment will necessarily have to be greater.

SBI started investing in IT in the form of back office computerization of its operations in its branches with the objective of achieving a certain level of efficiency in its voluminous operations besides giving bankers in the branches a feel for the automated environment. The strategy adopted was to have back office IT systems in place first. Once these back office applications had stabilized and sufficient IT maturity levels attained, a switch over to online transaction processing systems would take place. A reflection on this strategy is the high number of back office automated branches and only around 27 branches with On-Line Transaction Processing Systems (OLTP). Branches are not as yet electronically linked to each other.

Thus the initial IS strategy of SBI can be identified as more operational and 'inside–out' in nature where focus was not as much on customer-oriented IT systems as much as on systems which could help the bank to handle higher volumes of business. Moreover, a more centralized approach to IT planning was adopted in order to provide standardized technological systems across all the branches. However, in its attempt to arrive at what they believed were the most appropriate IT systems, SBI went for different IT platforms and software platforms which were more proprietary in nature than open systems which led to systems operating in isolation rather than in an integrated manner.

Although SBI has, over time, attempted to develop a proactive approach to planning for IT, there is little evidence to support the notion that IT is playing a strategic role in the bank's operations or that the kind of applications which the bank is developing will have an impact on the strategic nature of IT systems. Moreover, the general trend is to follow in the steps of others. For instance, in its attempts to offer more customer-friendly systems (in order to respond to market trends in IT in the banking sector) SBI has also installed ATM systems in some of its branches without having efficient operational level information systems in place. This is expected to accelerate the integration of many bank systems since no organization can make its IT systems strategic in nature till effective operational systems are in place.

However, the lack of IT maturity in SBI coupled with its late emphasis on IT also cannot be overlooked. Consequently, the short lead times that are available to Indian organizations (SBI in particular, given the criticality of IT for its operations) would call for overlapping timelines for developing and implementing operational as well as strategic systems. Hence, a lopsided focus on any particular genre of information systems would not work for SBI. Thus what was required in SBI was to implement rapidly operational systems and strategic systems side-by-side. The approach adopted by SBI was more toward integration of systems rather than having isolated systems in the beginning, then replacing them with some other systems.

Budgetary resources for IT are not yet considered a constraint at SBI. Therefore, given the strategic importance of IT to India's largest bank, we found that it was a common perception within SBI that a dedicated planning group would be quite effective if a formal IT budget could be agreed to. In PSUs, like in other organizations, a budget formalizes what is generally considered implicit. In addition, since it was found that different regions in SBI showed differing abilities to utilize funds, it was still an open issue in terms of how much oversight or plan details are required for controlling and coordinating budgeted expenses. Significant organizational resources are expended on hardware procurement and infrastructure building. The scale of the organization, coupled with the lack of a coherent IS strategy (and a consequent lack of IS/IT plans), has led to a widespread belief that not all offices of SBI would ever get 'computerized', and that all of them need not be computerized. Given that individual's tasks in a bureaucracy are clearly delineated, technology deployment and implementation has required formal allocation of responsibilities in each office. In many instances, IT use takes place only after formal recognition of who the potential users would be and what, if any, additional responsibilities and remuneration they will be entitled to. Such work patterns and attitudes have delayed IT implementation and use significantly, in spite of management's espoused commitment to IT's role in SBI. However, even now, SBI scores low on the quality of facilitation mechanisms for IT. A facilitation mechanism is a driver or enabler. There is a recognition within SBI that if it can make up for this aspect by increasing interaction between its top management and IS planners, and by providing an increased role space for IS planners in strategic business planning, it will help to make IT systems in SBI more strategic in nature. In other words, these systems would be both operationally critical as well as a source of competitive advantage. It is not that SBI has not implemented systems comparable to those in other private sector banks or multinational banks, but the diffusion of such systems relative to SBI's scope and size is quite low. Sullivan (1985) uses the term 'diffusion' to denote the extent of IT deployment in businesses and the term 'infusion' to denote the impact of IT on businesses. In essence, while the strategic potential for IT use in SBI is high, the pressures to keep up with the present and increasing transaction load and match up to competitors' service levels have been the principal drivers of IT at SBI. We can thus classify SBI's IT strategy as necessary – which to many employees is 'evil' too.

Some other organizational attributes have also dampened the rate at which IT has diffused in the organization. They include the reward, promotion and the work culture. A majority of the promotions at SBI are made on the basis of tenure. The overall consequence of this framework is a loose result-orientation compared to other banks (typically private ones). Often delayed decisions and business outcomes are explained in terms of following 'due process' owing to the high procedure-orientation in SBI. In this context, the use of IT is widely believed to change the way things work in SBI. However, there is also a widespread belief that the way things work in SBI will not allow it to actualize the full potential of IT. In many ways, the use of IT is expected to usher in some, if not drastic, culture changes. This interplay between IT and culture and SBI can be described well by the 'dynamics between organizational culture and forces for cultural change to the interplay between the sand and the sea. Sometimes we notice the dominance of the tide as it affects the sand on the beach. Other times we notice the persistence of the beach in confining and defining the sea. Every management action is like a wave against the shore. Cultural transformation takes time and persistence. Erratic managerial intervention and periodic restructuring merely block the development and strengthening of culture (Howard, 1998, p.236)'. In SBI, cultural persistence is the more dominant phenomenon, with IT making limited inroads in specific situations (e.g. large bank branches in large metro areas). Past managerial initiatives regarding IT (many of which were disjointed) had reduced the efficacy of IT-enabled changes. However, there is an increasing pressure from the customers for SBI to use IT effectively. This is especially so since most other banks in the country have computerized their operations and have been able to demonstrate improved service capability.

A portfolio matrix of IT spending in the year 1992–93 (figures were made available by SBI Central Office, Bombay) is indicative of an attempt to keep up with increasing transaction load than to build information systems for competitive advantage in response to increasing competitive pressures.

- Mainframes have been installed at all the 13 Local Head Offices and 53 Zonal Offices for branch accounts reconciliation and performance monitoring.
- Back office systems for daily accounting jobs cover 300 branches.
- 800 branches are on OLTP.
- 28 service branches have been computerized thus computerizing the clearing operations of the branch.
- Basic infrastructure for communication is in place which includes Remote Area Business Messaging Network (RABMN) and membership of Society for Worldwide International Funds Transfer (SWIFT).

It can be seen from Table 14.9 that the bulk of the investment is on transaction processing and performance data processing, revealing the internal focus of SBI's management as contrasted with the external approach of more customer-oriented banks. Management policy seems to have been one of cost effective data capture and more expensive and technologically elaborate alternatives (like true OLTP on a centralized database using a robust private network) have not been tried out. This has made interfacing difficult for information consolidation at control points; with the result that optimization of information resource is not achieved. Considerable time is elapsed in compiling the overall picture of SBI's worldwide operations.

While there is agreement that the potential for using IS in SBI is tremendous, SBI's hierarchical and process-centric culture works against IT use. But for isolated efforts to create databases and customized packages, enterprise-wide information systems seem to be a remote possibility for SBI. Given the diversity of its activities, SBI's operations are not uniform across the enterprise. There are multiple multi-location organizations in SBI's umbrella. However, even stand-alone systems can make a real difference to the bank, as is evident from the instance quoted from Delhi Zonal Office of the Bank (Exhibit 14.3).

IT investments have not been pegged to ROI or related concepts (Willcocks and Lester, 1997) simply because the transaction load is increasing so fast that computerized information systems have become a necessity. In this instance, SBI behaves differently from what our quantitative data suggests – that is, there is a strong relationship between the depth of the organizational hierarchy and the need for ROI justification for information systems. There is support for the other finding that IT budgets are set up before demand is placed for systems. The centralized structure of the bureaucracy implies that budgets and targets are passed 'down' the organizational hierarchy. At this point in time, targets are technology focused. For example, a typical target reads: 'implement integrated back-office and front-office systems in 12 branches in this territory by year-end'. The internal budgeting process limits the evaluation of progress in IT development to monitoring system implementation progress and does not place importance on the impact of such systems on customer service.

While SBI has a predominantly bureaucratic culture, there are aspects that may superficially resemble a supportive culture. The resemblance to supportive aspects of culture stems from the fact that most employees of SBI (like any PSU) have a high need for security and are risk averse. In general, managers reported that personalized relationships were equally, if not more important than contractual or formal relationships and that work is performed as a part of a positive relationship. Loyalties to the unions are fierce and unions exist for operational, supervisory and some junior officer cadres.

Table 14.10 summarizes the comparative findings of the survey and the case study. We will now analyze these findings using the backdrop of a

Table 14.9   *Investment in IT for 1992–93 in SBI*

	Mainframe	Back office	OLTP	PCS	ATMS
Reconciliation	5.15%				
Performance data	22.13%				
House-keeping		15.21%			
Online transaction processing systems			42.43%		
Management information systems				11.89%	
Point of sale systems					3.17%

State Bank of India like all other nationalized banks stresses the concept of centralized profitability over that of profit generated by the branch unit. Though there has been in place the system of 'transfer pricing' to make each branch an independent profit generating unit, the need for each branch breaking even within a reasonable period was given a thrust only in the beginning of '90s. The Delhi module of the bank, which controlled over 200 branches had 22 loss making branches in 1991. Many were hard-core loss making branches. The first step in drawing out a strategy to turn around these branches, was to make a break-even model for the branch based on the business potential of the area where the branch was located. The controlling office used spread-sheet based sensitivity models to arrive at the break-even point of a loss making branch. The procedure followed was simple.

Step-1: The actual details of income and expenditure were entered into a spread sheet file and using the formulae for transfer-pricing the net-result of the branch was calculated.

These details were available from the monthly performance report sent by the branch each month.

Step-2: Monitoring this data at monthly intervals enabled the controllers to study the growth trends of the branch over a period of time.

Step-3: A meeting was arranged with the branch manager of the branch and the controller to facilitate the identification of potential areas of income and growth as well as predictable areas of expenditures.

Step-4: Sensitivity analysis was done for 12 items in the profit-loss statement to arrive at a number of ways to achieve break-even. The thrust areas for each branch were decided after a discussion with the branch manager and the number of variables in a branch were reduced to represent these thrust areas.

Step-5: A break-even model suitable for the branch was selected by the controller and a hard copy of this model was given to the branch.

Step-6: Over the next few months these branches were subjected to close scrutiny by the controller to see the progress of the plan of action arrived at to achieve the break-even figures for the variables. The freedom to change the model in case of rise/decline in a variable not anticipated earlier, was kept with the controller.

Results: Delhi module has four controllers. Only one controller, who had 12 of the 22 loss making branches in his region, took the follow-up action seriously and with conviction.

He managed converting 10 of his branches from loss making to profit making within a period of one year. These branches continue to make profits as initial slide backs were easily tided over by concentrating on the thrust areas.

The IS used in the case were sensitivity models developed on spreadsheets. But these were mere tools to support the controller and the manager. Making of a break-even model by itself did not result in any significant progress as was seen in the other three regions where there was no follow-up by the regional managers. There was no owner of the system apart from the "creator." The failure to institutionalize the system stemmed from a lack of processes to support end-user developed applications as also a lack of a shared understanding.

Exhibit 14.3 *Isolated use of spreadsheet application in the Delhi Zonal Office of SBI*

Table 14.10   *Comparison of major findings of survey and case study*

Attributes of interest	What the survey found	What we found in the case
Overall culture and strategy relationship	Significant relationship between bureaucratic culture and scarce resource strategy as well as supportive and monopoly IT strategy	SBI is a bureaucratic culture with a centrally planned and monopoly IT strategy. Aspects of supportive cultures are present.
Selected aspects of supportive culture	Collaborative, encouraging, sociable, personal freedom, and trusting components influence monopoly IT strategy	The lack of collaboration, encouragement, personal freedom and trust makes IT ineffective.
Selected aspects of bureaucratic culture	Hierarchical, procedural, ordered, and cautious aspects influence scarce resource IT strategy	Cautious and risk-averse approaches (in a very hierarchical and procedure-heavy environment) have limited the amount of investment that could have been made in IT

particular aspect of IT use in terms of credit management – since credit management is crucial to any bank.

With the majority of SBI branches handling large credits having computerized their transaction processing, information retrieval from branches has become expedient. Networking of branches is still to be done. Thus an on line credit processing system cannot be attempted at this stage. Conversely, the vast amount of historical data available at the local head offices (LHOs)[2] can be put to more productive use by creating a risk management system for the bank as a whole. The bank has already created special departments for recovery and rehabilitation of non-performing assets on their books. Alongside this effort, the bank needs to have a sophisticated risk management system at the corporate head office level as well as the LHOs, to estimate the default rate

---

[2]LHOs are typically located in state capitals. There are other regional head offices that also hold and generate vast amounts of historical data.

and potential default rate of current borrowers. This alone can help the bank in taking proactive steps to check the non-performing asset levels.

The absence of information systems in the credit management function can also be attributed to the bureaucratic setup that characterizes SBI. The functioning of the bank is extremely hierarchical and procedural. For example, when a request for a loan arrives, it may take several organizational levels (as many as six) and several weeks or months to process that loan. This is so because managers are risk-averse. Most managers accord higher priority to following due procedure than to expediting the process. This is mainly because positive results are not directly linked to reward structures. Secondly, the culture is highly power-oriented. There have been instances when a manager (with due authority) has taken the initiative and cleared a loan proposal. Subsequently, these individuals have been questioned by their supervisors regarding criticism. Hence, most managers tend to 'pass the paper up' the hierarchy to avoid such incidents. So, given the propensity of individuals to be less proactive compared to some of the other banks, the documentation that builds up with each case or transaction makes SBI data rich but information poor. In other words, processes in place lead to a significant amount of documentation and data collection – which, however, are not used for effective or timely managerial decision-making.

Given SBI's conservative character, a continuous debate regarding bankers and IT professionals has been taking place. The issue has to do with whether IT professionals need to be trained as bankers, thus resulting in a separate cadre, or to train bankers to manage IT. While many in SBI would like to believe that the debate has been resolved by way of training bankers to manage IT, environmental reasons coupled with internal compulsions have led to a consensus. Given the salary structure that SBI can extend to IT professionals, the likelihood of attracting high-quality IT professionals is low given the alternative available to IT professionals in terms of pay-scales and perks elsewhere. Secondly, SBI itself is considered over-staffed relative to the quantum of operations and personnel ratio in other banks. Further appointments lead not only to resentment (since this would imply IT professional making a horizontal entry) but would leave IT professionals with a techno-centric and limited role having a marginal role in banking per se.

Another determinant of SBI's culture is the belief system that is derived from SBI's historical role as a development bank too. SBI, for a long time, was assumed to have dual missions of corporate profitability and as an organization that would support social goals (in terms of alleviating poverty). This meant that dual sets of rules and procedures operated at SBI. For instance, soft loans were often extended to the poor (usually as a result of Governmental directives) while stringent analytical and data-based analyses were required to process other individual and corporate loans. This dichotomy has lingered on and has resulted in task and process fuzziness. High discretionary powers at higher levels and low levels of empowerment at the operational levels does not lend to meaningful computerization. There is an absence of process metrics and formal evaluation frameworks that can be used to track banking efficiency. One of the reasons cited for this specific issue is that for the price of banking services at SBI, such metrics may not add value. At specific branches, such metrics would be considered essential. However, because of the prevailing culture of uniformity and standardization, what is not applicable at one location is not applicable in another and vice versa.

7. Conclusion

As a result of this research, we have been able to demonstrate a relationship between innovative cultures and IT strategy. Innovative cultures tend to have well-defined strategies in place. Both innovative and supportive cultures are either positively correlated with IT strategies or show no relationship. On the other hand, the bureaucratic culture is associated with a scarce resource strategy. The bureaucratic culture should also be noted for showing negative (though not statistically significant) relationships with the leading edge and free-market strategies. This means that bureaucratic cultures have a tendency to discourage progressive IT strategies. The case study has aided in validating aspects of the quantitative findings.

Implications for research

By using both quantitative and qualitative research we were able to go beyond mere description and explore aspects of organizational dynamics and change. Quantitative assessment of culture accorded us the opportunity to explore and analyze the deduced relationship between organizational culture and IT strategy across different organizations. However, since a quantitative culture construct requires us to start with a set of constructs decided a priori, researchers will need to be aware of the inevitability of the exclusion of certain constructs of interest. This limitation of quantitative analysis – which is generally limited to answering the 'what' aspect of a phenomenon – can be compensated for by qualitative research that allows us to explore the meanings associated with significant relations from the more broadly-based quantitative studies. Qualitative research helps us answer the 'why' and 'how' (for a specific context) questions that underlie relations verified by broad-based studies. While results from quantitative studies can be generalized and replicated, it may not be desirable or possible to accomplish that using qualitative methods.

Our study has been able to demonstrate that culture is related to IT strategy. Past research has shown that formal strategic IT planning can be a crucial critical success factor for information systems within public agencies (Bajjaly, 1998). The eventual link between organizational culture and IS effectiveness is, therefore, open to further investigation. We believe that if researchers move away from focusing on specific culture themes and aspects of IS activities in organizations and attempt to cover a fuller range of cultural and IS constructs, the link between organizational culture and IT strategies and consequences of those strategies will be better understood. Our experience with using two research approaches was rewarding. While we were able to uncover both broad-based relations and SBI-specific insights, we believe that a significant amount of additional research is required to fully appreciate the relationship between culture and strategy and their interplay and the organizational consequences of that interplay. For instance, the bureaucratic and innovative dimensions of culture emerged as relatively clear correlates of selected IT strategies. However, we found that the supportive dimension of culture could emerge as an important co-determinant of IT strategy. In the case of SBI, selected aspects of the supportive dimension were evident. They included 'safe', (risk-averse in decision-making) 'equitable', (batches of employees, not individuals are promoted) and 'relationship-oriented' (strong unions at most levels). Additional research is required to investigate whether centralized planning at SBI was undermined by this particular strain of supportive culture.

Alternate culture constructs need to be used just as alternate conceptualizations of IT strategy need to be explored. Within the context of information systems, it needs to be recognized that culture includes cognitive, emotional and behavioral aspects. We believe, therefore, that other research approaches that incorporate these premises should be used. For instance, one approach could be treating culture as a metaphor for organizational life (Smircich, 1983) instead of treating culture as an intervening or causal variable. In using this approach, when looking at organizations as if they were cultures, symbols and meanings would be emphasized. Other approaches to find the hidden meanings, consequences, and motives behind acts, decisions and social behavior could include cultural anthropology, psychoanalysis, and hermeneutics.

Implications for practice

Most IT strategies in PSUs in India can be considered emergent. In other words, they have not been outcomes of proactive management concern that has led to formal deliberation and thought and resulted in a formal strategy document. On the other hand, the pressing need to computerize the organization (within the backdrop of governmental directives to improve productivity and organizational performance) has created pressures for most PSUs that typically result in the setting up of departments or responsibility centers for

IT at the corporate level. The major implication for PSUs is to formalize the presence of a coherent IT strategy.

Since the role of Indian PSUs is being radically redefined in the wake of economic liberalization (Singh, 1994) they are faced with the very real prospect of restructuring (Sushil et al., 1995). The Government of India has constituted a Disinvestment Commission with the primary aim of financial restructuring of PSUs through the sale of equity to both institutional investors (Krishna, 1996). Most opinion leaders and policy makers strongly recommend the need to break away from the system of bureaucracy (Singh, 1994) and suggest that PSUs should involve employees and the investors in the management of PSUs (Khatri and Macus, 1994; Biswas et al., 1994). The formulation of such implicit demands already started to result in a transformation of the organizational culture of PSUs. These directions of change appear to indicate an increase in the supportive and innovative components of organizational culture. One clear implication from this study is that Indian PSUs can no longer afford to neglect the cultural dimensions of their organization while formulating IT strategies. These strategies should be consistent with the culture of PSUs to successfully leverage IT resources for organizational effectiveness.

PSUs will have to develop clear-cut (formal and unambiguous) IT strategies as they are being forced to shed their bureaucratic style of functioning and

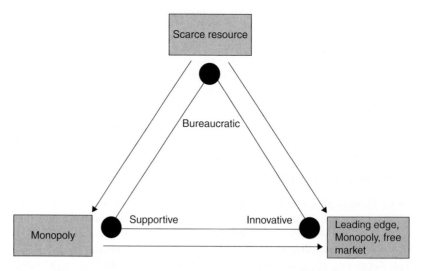

Figure 14.2   *Dimensions of cultures and suggested strategy directions*

change toward innovative and supportive cultures. A possible road map for IT strategies in these organizations would be to migrate from a scarce-resources strategy (associated with bureaucratic culture) to either a monopoly or a free-market IT strategy (associated with innovative and supportive cultures). PSUs that opt for free-market IT strategy are likely to migrate to a monopoly or leading edge IT strategy (associated with innovative and supportive cultures). This is shown in Figure 14.2.

The formalization of strategies is required to foster such cultural change, especially given the absence of security of tenure for individuals at the top levels in a PSU. This leads to short tenures for top management. Since PSUs are characterized by transferable jobs, a delineable and well laid out IT strategy will provide a sense a continuity and permanence for IT-related organizational processes and actions. The absence of an IT strategy encourages ad-hoc IT decisions and disoriented efforts. As Saxena (1996) reports, the transformation of PSUs requires a coordinated effort on the technological, structural, cultural and strategy fronts. Most PSUs are large multi-location organizations and the development of an integrated IT srategy will not only help provide a synergy for IT efforts but will also, in the longer run, enable cultural transformations in PSUs.

Given that IT is more 'interpretively flexible' (Robey and Azevedo, 1993) than some technologies, it may be reinterpreted and reinvented in its development and use. IT strategy formulation in an organization is a prime example of such technological interpretation. Hence organizational strategists should continuously look for meaningful linkages between aspects of culture that support IT use in addition to ensuring that IT is introduced and used such that unwanted aspects of cultural persistence are weakened. For example, it is clear that drastic IT-enabled reengineering approaches can come up against cultural blocks (Harrington et al., 1998). On the other hand, patient and longer-term approaches, which may appear to make incremental improvements, characterized by being non-threatening and meaningful to the eventual users may need to be given priority (Sauer Associates and Yetton et al., 1997). Therefore, those PSUs that can identify methods to nurture the innovative dimensions of their culture in a person-centered manner will be more likely to treat culture as a meaningful organizational process that fosters the concomitant growth of IT.

Acknowledgments

The authors thank the anonymous reviewers for their insightful comments and suggestions and also thank Professor Robert Galliers for his help and assistance in improving this manuscript substantially.

Appendix A.   Survey instrument

How does the following describe your organization	Does not describe my organization	Describes my organization a little	Describes my organization a fair amount	Describes my organization most of the time
(a) Risk taking	☐	☐	☐	☐
(b) Collaborative	☐	☐	☐	☐
(c) Hierarchical	☐	☐	☐	☐
(d) Procedural	☐	☐	☐	☐
(e) Relationship-oriented	☐	☐	☐	☐
(f) Results-oriented	☐	☐	☐	☐
(g) Creative	☐	☐	☐	☐
(h) Encouraging	☐	☐	☐	☐
(i) Sociable	☐	☐	☐	☐
(j) Structured	☐	☐	☐	☐
(k) Pressurized	☐	☐	☐	☐
(l) Ordered	☐	☐	☐	☐
(m) Stimulating	☐	☐	☐	☐
(n) Regulated	☐	☐	☐	☐
(o) Personal freedom	☐	☐	☐	☐
(p) Equitable	☐	☐	☐	☐
(q) Safe	☐	☐	☐	☐
(r) Challenging	☐	☐	☐	☐
(s) Enterprising	☐	☐	☐	☐
(t) Established, solid	☐	☐	☐	☐
(u) Cautious	☐	☐	☐	☐
(v) Trusting	☐	☐	☐	☐
(w) Driving	☐	☐	☐	☐
(x) Power-oriented	☐	☐	☐	☐

How IT issues are handled in your organization	To a very large extent	Most of the time	Around half the time	Not often	Rarely	Never	Can not tell for sure
(a) IS strategy integrated and interdependent with corporate strategy	☐	☐	☐	☐	☐	☐	☐
(b) Extremely large investments are made in IT	☐	☐	☐	☐	☐	☐	☐
(c) Developing applications that do not have immediate uses	☐	☐	☐	☐	☐	☐	☐
(d) State-of-art technology maintained	☐	☐	☐	☐	☐	☐	☐
(e) Needs of IT are determined by							
Top management	☐	☐	☐	☐	☐	☐	☐
Middle management	☐	☐	☐	☐	☐	☐	☐
Users	☐	☐	☐	☐	☐	☐	☐
Outside consultant	☐	☐	☐	☐	☐	☐	☐
(f) IS group/department within the organization competes with outside vendors	☐	☐	☐	☐	☐	☐	☐
(g) IS function and control centralized	☐	☐	☐	☐	☐	☐	☐
h) Investments in IT are based strictly on return on investment basis	☐	☐	☐	☐	☐	☐	☐
(i) IT budgets are generally set before demand for IT can be known	☐	☐	☐	☐	☐	☐	☐
(j) Investment in IT is made only when absolutely necessary	☐	☐	☐	☐	☐	☐	☐
(k) IT investments are made to improve internal efficiency of the organization	☐	☐	☐	☐	☐	☐	☐
(l) IT investments are made to differentiate product or service	☐	☐	☐	☐	☐	☐	☐

Application strategy	Not important	Slightly important	Important	Slightly important	Critically important	Can not tell for sure
Applications which are central to sustaining future business strategy						
Applications which may be important in achieving future success						
Applications on which the organization currently depends for success						
Applications which are valuable but are not critical to success						

References

Allen, R. F. and F. K. Dyer (1980), "A tool for tapping the organizational unconscious," *Personnel Journal*, pp. 192–199.

Baets, W. (1992), "Aligning information systems with business strategy," *Journal of Strategic Information Systems*, Vol. 1, No. 4, pp. 205–213.

Bajjaly, S. J. (1998), "Managing emerging information systems in the public sector," *Public Productivity and Management Review*, Vol. 23, No. 1, pp. 40–47.

Bakos, J. Y. and M. E. Treacy (1986), "Information technology and corporate strategy: a research perspective," *MIS Quarterly*, June.

Bannett, A. and A. Sicherl (Eds.), (1992), "Information systems of public enterprises in developing countries." *Public Enterprise* Vol. 12, No. 3, 4, pp. 173–380.

Bates, K. A., S. D. Amundson, R. G. Schroeder, and W. T. Morris (1995), "The crucial interelationship between manufacturing strategy and organizational culture," *Management Science*, Vol. 41, No. 10, pp. 1565–1580.

Becker, H. S. and B. Geer (1960), "Latent culture: a note on the theory of latent social roles," *Administrative Science Quarterly*, Vol. 5, No. 2, pp. 304–313.

Bhaduri, B. (1991), "Work culture: an exposition in the Indian context," *Vikalpa*, Vol. 16, No. 4, pp. 33–42.

Bhal, K. T. (1996), "Making sense of personal values and organizational cultue: towards indigenous management," *Report of The Dalmia Research Programme in Management in Asia*, IIT Delhi, New Delhi.

Biswas, D. K., P. K. Hota, and S. Khatri (1994), "Redefining the role of the public sector and strategic options for restructuring," *Public Enterprise*, Vol. 14, No. 1, 2, pp. 36–39.

Caudle, S. L., W. L. Gorr, and K. E. Newcomer (1991), "Key information management issues for the public sector," *MIS Quarterly*, June, pp. 170–188.

Chan, Y. E. and S. L. Huff (1993), "Strategic information systems alignment," *Business Quarterly*, Autumn.

Cook, R. A. and J. C. Lafferty (1989), *Organizational Culture Inventory: OCI*. Human Synergistics, Plymouth, MI.

Cooper, R. B. (1994), "The inertial impact of culture on IT implementation," *Information and Management*, Vol. 27, No. 1, pp. 17–31.

Das, S. R., S. A. Zahra, and M. E. Warkentin (1991), "Integrating the content and process of strategic MIS planning," *Decision Sciences*, Vol. 22, No. 5, pp. 953–982.

Davenport, T. H., M. Hammer, and T. J. Metisisto (1989), "How executives can shape their company's information systems," *Harvard Business Review*, March–April.

Deal, T. E. and A. A. Kennedy (1982), *Corporate Cultures: The Rites and Rituals of Corporate Life*. Addison-Wesley, Reading.

Delisi, P. S. (1990), "Lesson from the steel axe: culture technology and organisational change," *Sloan Management Review*, Fall, pp. 83–93.

Earl, M. J. (1993), "Experiences in strategic information systems planning," *MIS Quarterly*, Vol. 17, No. 1, pp. 1–24.

Ein-Dor, P. and E. Segev (1978), "Strategic planning for management information systems," *Management Science*, Vol. 24, No. 14, p. 1.

Enz, C. (1986), *Power and Shared Values in the Corporate Culture*. UMI, Ann Arbor, MI.

Gable, G. G. (1994), "Integrating case study and survey research methods: an example in information systems," *European Journal of Information Systems*, Vol. 3, No. 2, pp. 112–126.

Galliers, R. D. (1993), "IT strategies: beyond competitive advantage," *The Journal of Strategic Information Systems*, Vol. 2, No. 4, pp. 283–291.

Glaser, S. R., S. Zamanou, and K. Hacker (1987), "Measuring and interpreting organizational culture," *Management Communication Quarterly*, Vol. 1, pp. 173–198.

Goyal, D. P. (1994), *Management Information Systems: Concepts and Applications*. Deep and Depp Publications, New Delhi.

Grote, G. and R. Baitsch (1991), "Reciprocal effects between organisational culture and the implementation of an office communication system: a case study," *Behaviour of Information Technology*, Vol. 10, No. 3, pp. 207–218.

Grover, V., J. T. C. Teng, and K. D. Fiedler (1993), "Information technology enabled BPR: an integrated planning framework," *Omega International Journal of Management Science*, Vol. 24, No. 4, pp. 433–447.

Grover, V., J. T. C. Teng, and K. D. Fiedler (1998), "IS investment priorities in contemporary organizations," *Communications of the ACM*, Vol. 41, No. 2, pp. 40–48.

Gupta, M. P. (1996), "MIS at national level in India: analysis of problems and Issues," *Vikalpa*, Vol. 21, No. 3, pp. 3–15.

Harrington, B., K. McLoughlin, and D. Riddell (1998), "Business process re-engineering in the public sector: a case study of the contributions agency," *New Technology, Work, and Employment*, Vol. 13, No. 1, pp. 43–50.

Heeks, R. (1995), "Information systems strategy – a five-minute guide for public sector managers," *Information Technology for Development*, Vol. 6, pp. 139–143.

Hinton, C. M. and G. R. Kaye (1996), "The hidden investments in information technology: the role of organizational context and system dependency," *International Journal of Information Management*, Vol. 16, No. 6, pp. 413–427.

Howard, L. W. (1998), "Validating the competing values model as a representation of organizational cultures," *International Journal of Organizational Analysis*, Vol. 6, No. 3, pp. 231–250.

Khatri, S. and S. Macus (1994), "Strategic options for restructuring the public sector in India," *Public Enterprise*, Vol. 14, No. 1, 2, pp. 3–19.

Kholi, V. (1994), "Making the PSUs competitive – issues, problems and prospects," *Public Enterprise*, Vol. 14, No. 1, 2, pp. 278–286.

Kilman, R. H., M. J. Saxton, and R. Sepra (1986), "Issues in understanding and changing culture," *Calfornia Management Review*, Vol. 26, No. 2, pp. 87–94.

Kim, S. and J. Lee (1991), "A contingent analysis of the relationship between IS implementation strategies and IS success," *Information Processing and Management*, Vol. 27, No. 1, pp. 111–129.

Kim, P. S., W. Pindur, and K. Reynolds (1995), "Creating a new organizational culture: the key to total quality management in the public sector," *International Journal of Public Administration*, Vol. 18, No. 4, pp. 675–709.

King, W. R. and V. Sethi (1993), "Developing transnational information systems: a case study," *Omega*, Vol. 21, No. 1, pp. 53–59.

Kitchell, S. (1995), "Corporate culture, environmental adaptation, and innovation adoption: a qualitative/quantitive approach," *Journal of the Academy of Marketing Science*, Summer, Vol. 23, No. 3, pp. 195–205.

Krishna, Y. (1996), "Disinvestment the Indian way," *The Journal of Institute of Public Enterprise*, Vol. 19, No. 5, pp. 103–112.

Kutty, K. K. K. (1994), "Making the PSUs competitive – issues, concerns and prospects," *Public Enterprise*, Vol. 14, No. 1, 2, pp. 310–318.

Lakshmipathy, V. (1985), *Performance Appraisal in Public Enterprise – Patterns, Problems and Prospects*. Himalaya Publishing House, Delhi.

Louis, M.R. (1983), Culture: Yes, Organization: No. Paper presented at the Annual meeting of the Academy of Management, August, Dallas, Texas.

Markus, M. L. and M. Keil (1994), "If we build it, they will come: designing information systems that people want to use," *Sloan Management Review*, Vol. 35, No. 4, pp. 11–25.

Martin, J. and C. Siehl (1983), "Organizational Culture and counter culture: an uneasy symbiosis," *Organizational Dynamics*, Vol. 12, No. 2, pp. 52–64.

McRary, J. W. (1995), "Leveraging the power of information technology for sustained competitive success," *Engineering Management Journal*, Vol. 7, No. 1, pp. 3–4.

Mohan, L., W. K. Holstein, and R. B. Adams (1990), "EIS: IT can work in the public sector," *MIS Quarterly*, December, pp. 435–448.

Neogy, P. C. (1994), "Making the PSUs competitive – Issues, problems and prospects," *Public Enterprise*, Vol. 14, No. 1, 2, pp. 302–309.

Nigam, N. C., V. Gautam, and S. Kanungo (1995), "Report on the Role of Engineering Personnel in the Central Government, Research project sponsored by the Fifth Pay Commission," *Government of India*.

Nolan, R. L. (1979), "Managing the crises in data processing," *Harward Business Review*, Vol. 57, No. 2, pp. 8–27.

O'Reilly, C., J. Chatman, and D. F. Caldwell (1991), "People and organizational culture: a profile comparison approach to assessing person-organization fit," *Academy of Management Journal*, Vol. 34, No. 3, pp. 487–516.

Ouchi, W. (1981), *How American Business can meet the Japanese Challenge*. Addison-Wesley, Reading, MA.

Pacey, A. (1983), *The Culture of Technology*. The MIT Press, Cambridge.

Palvia, S., P. Palvia, and R. Zigli (1992), "Global information technology environment: key MIS issues in advanced and less-developed nations," in S. Palvia, P. Palvia, and R. Zigli, Eds. *The Global Issues of Information Technology Management*. Idea Group Publishing, Harrisburg, PA, pp. 2–35.

Parsons, G.L. (1983), Fitting information systems technology to the corporate needs: the linking strategy. Harvard Business School teaching notes June (9-183-176).

Premkumar, G. and W. R. King (1991), "Assessing strategic information systems planning," *Long Range Planning*, Vol. 24, No. 5, pp. 41–56.

Rau, P. R. and H. R. Rao (1993), "Management information technology: an Indian experience," *Journal of Information Science and Technology*, Vol. 2, No. 3, pp. 288–296.

Robey, D. and A. Azevedo (1994), "Cultural Analysis of the Organizational Consequences of Information Technology," *Accounting, Management and Information Technologies*, Vol. 4, No. 1, pp. 23–37.

Rockart, J. F. (1979), "Chief executives define their own data needs," *Harvard Business Review*, March–April.

Rousseau, D. M. (1990), "Assessing organizational culture: a case for multiple methods," in B. Schneider, Ed. *Organizational Climate and Culture*. Jossey-Bass, San Fransisco.

Sashkin, M. and R. Fulmer (1985), Measuring organizational excellence culture with a validated questionnaire. Paper presented at the August meeting of the Academy of Management, San Diego, CA.

Sauer, C., Yetton, P. W., and Associates (1997), *Steps to the Future: Fresh Thinking Based on the Management of IT-Based Organizational Transformation*. Jossey-Bass, San Francisco.

Saxena, K. B. C. (1996), "Re-engineering public administration in developing countries," *Long Range Planning*, Vol. 29, No. 5, pp. 703–711.

Schein, E. H. (1985), *Organizational Culture and Leadership*. Jossey-Bass, San Francisco.

Semler, S. W. (1997), "Systematic agreement: a theory of organizational alignment," *Human Resource Development Quarterly*, Vol. 8, No. 1, pp. 23–40.

Singh, R. (1994), "The role of public sector in the liberalized economy," *Public Enterprise*, Vol. 14, No. 1, 2, pp. 36–39.

Singla, M. L. (1992), *MIS in Public Sector*. Shipra Publications, Delhi.

Sinha, J. B. P. and S. Singh (1993), "Western organizations in Indian culture: principles for indigenous management," *Abhigyan*, pp. 15–22.

Smircich (1983), "Concepts of culture and organizational analysis," *Administrative Science Quarterly*, Vol. 28, pp. 339–358.

Sullivan, C. H. (1985), "Systems planning in the information age," *Sloan Management Review*, Vol. 26, No. 2, pp. 3–12.

Sushil, Bhal. K. T. and S. Kanungo (1995), "Report on Restructuring the Government Office," *Research project sponsored by the Fifth Pay Commission*, Government of India.

Tushman, M. L. and C. A. O Reilly III (1996), "Ambidextrous organizations: managing evolutionary and revolutionary change," *California Management Review*, Vol. 38, No. 4, pp. 8–30.

Uttal, B. (1983), "The corporate culture vultures," *Fortune*, Vol. 17, pp. 66–72.

VanMaanen, J. and E. H. Schein (1979), "Towards a theory of organizational socialization," *Research in Organizational Behaviour*, Vol. 1, pp. 209–259.

Venkataraman, N. (1994), "IT enabled business transformation: form automation to business scope redefinition," *Sloan Management Review*, Summer.

Vestal, K. W., R. D. Fralicx, and S. W. Spreier (1997), "Organizational culture: the critical link between strategy and results," *Hospital and Health Services Administration*, Vol. 42, No. 3, pp. 339–365.

Wallach, E. J. (1983), "Individuals and organizations: the cultural match," *Training and Development Journal*, February.

Ward, J. M. (1987), "Integrating Information Systems into Business Strategies," *Long Range Planning*, Vol. 20, No. 3, pp. 19–29.

Ward, J. and P. Griffits (1996), *Strategic Planning for Information Systems*. Wiley, New York.

Weber, Y. and N. Pliskin (1996), "The effects of information systems integration and organizational culture on a firm's effectiveness," *Information and Management*, Vol. 30, No. 2, pp. 81–90.

Willcocks, L. P. and S. Lester (1997), "In search of information technology productivity: assessment issues," *The Journal of Operational Research Society*, Vol. 48, No. 11, pp. 1082–1094.

Yetton, P. Y., K. D. Johnston, and J. F. Craig (1994), "Computer Aided Architects: A case study of IT and strategic change," *Sloan Management Review*, Summer.

Reproduced from *Journal of Strategic Information Systems*, Vol. 10, No. 1, March 2001, pp. 29–57. Reprinted with permission from Elsevier Ltd.

Questions for discussion

1   Using the organizational cultures discussed in the article, describe the culture of an organization in which you have worked. How easy, or difficult, is it to put the organization into one of the three cultural types?

2   How does the view of organizational culture in this article contrast with that of the Ngwenyama and Nielsen article (Article 4)?

3   Why have some PSUs used IT to drive productivity increases and derived organizational benefits while others couldn't achieve the same?

4   Is there an organizational culture type that you do not feel is effectively summarized by one of the three types discussed in this paper?

5   How can an IT strategy be planned to work in an organizational culture which is reluctant to a change?

6   Should any PSU pick up an IT strategy to the detriment of its cherished organizational culture? If yes, would it really work for them?

7   Describe what is meant by IT strategy. How might one expect IT strategy to be influenced by the three types of organizational culture?

8   The study looks at organizational culture. How might you expect the national culture of India to also have influenced the findings?

15 Developing a Management Culture in which Information Technology will Flourish: How the UK Can Benefit

Roger Tomlin

Abstract: This paper first reviews the potential strategic impact of information technology. Particularly important is the use of IT for competitive positions and the enabling role of an appropriate corporate culture for the delivery of effective IT. The need to move towards responsive holistic management approaches is discussed, together with the networked opportunities opened by IT. The paper highlights the strategic factors demanding positive attitudes to IT and shows how the UK is, so far, falling behind in the international IT competitive race. The paper concludes with an agenda for management action. Its arguments are based on the findings of several research surveys conducted by the author.

The strategic impact of information technology (IT)

IT moves to centre stage

Towards the end of the 1980s, the use of Information Technology (IT) in Europe reached a significant turning point. Corporate management began to view IT as primarily a strategic weapon 'critical to survival and success' rather than something 'necessary to run a business'. This clearly emerged from a three-year study completed by the author (Tomlin, 1990).[1] Responses

---

[1]This report draws on work by Roger Tomlin & Co for Amdahl Europe, including carrying out in-depth research about the management of IT in Europe and organizing three major international conferences. Full details are contained in the following books published by the Amdahl Executive Institute, Dogmersfield Park, Hartley Wintney, Hampshire RG27 8TE, UK – *Clues to Success: A Corporate Culture for Information Technology* (European Edition, 1990; Preliminary Edition, 1988), *Managing Change: Innovation through Information Technology* (1990), *Managing Information Technology in Europe: A British Perspective* (1989), *Business Success and Information Technology: Strategies for the 1990s* (1988), *Strategic Use of Information Technology* (1987).

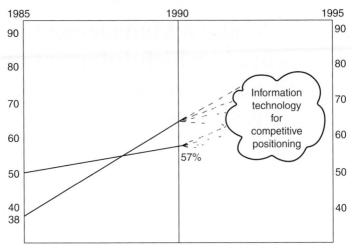

% Benefit from I.T. Investments

Figure 15.1   *From efficiency to competitive positioning*

from over 800 leading IT executives in Europe identified a distinct cross-over when the technology's main role became more focused on competitive advantage instead of inward oriented goals such as cost containment and administrative efficiency (see Figure 15.1).

IT is also becoming a key factor in the process of restructuring whole organizations and industries. Yet, over 70% of those interviewed felt they were not using IT sufficiently well to put them amongst the winners in the 1990s; British management emerged as being relatively poorly prepared to gain optimum business benefits from IT. No significant differences could be found between the levels of success with IT and the amount invested in the technology. In fact, top management in the organizations achieving least with IT felt the technology was just as important as those who were gaining the most.

Success is elusive, however, because management must deal with so many considerations in addition to implementing the technology effectively. This report analyses the nature of these complexities and describes how success can be brought within the grasp of any company. It argues that before considering how much more to spend on IT, every Board should ask: How can we not afford to spend the time and resources necessary to get our approach to IT, and the quality of our IT management, correct? In the words of a leading expert on competitive advantage, Michael Porter, 'The question is no longer whether IT will have a significant impact on a company's competitive position; it is how we take advantage of the opportunity' (Tomlin, 1988).

A corporate culture that breeds IT success

Our most recent study found that the most successful users of IT shared a distinct set of inter-related characteristics which define the corporate culture that produces the best results from IT:

(1) Co-ordinated leadership flowing from top executives, senior line managers and the experts in charge of IT resources, with each being allocated unambiguous roles in the management of IT initiatives and their associated implications;

(2) A common vision and shared values derived from an effective strategic planning process, and shaped by a proper appreciation of how best to serve the customer. This included a comprehensive business strategy for IT which lit the way ahead with beacon-like clarity, encompassing all aspects of the impact of IT: organizational change, new ways of running the business, integrated industry-wide networks, IT developments, personnel implications and so on;

(3) The right commitment and behaviour throughout the organization, based on respect for IT as one of the key aspects of the business and involving team work and partnerships across different groups. To achieve this, top management gave high priority to human and organizational issues and invested in excellent IT management. They also followed an open management style in which responsibility is delegated to levels where the work gets done.

(4) Good understanding and communication between general managers and IT specialists, resulting from co-ordinated and imaginative education, training and personnel practices. The potential and practical implications of IT were appreciated by everyone and people were given the skills to do the new jobs which arose.

(5) Confidence and trust cumulatively built from the progressively successful application of IT and mutual understanding, supported by continuous open publication of the results from organizational changes and IT investment.

The most important and urgent IT management issue, particularly in the UK, is to develop this cultural environment in which IT can flourish.

Creating the right cultural climate

There is nothing new in the notion that corporate culture has a great influence on how a business operates and the results it obtains. The problem is that many people regard culture as an intuitive factor in corporate life which is only about established ways of doing things. Nevertheless, many companies have found that a desired cultural climate can be created through policies involving systematic analysis, a clear understanding of what characteristics are needed and a well managed implementation.

The importance of corporate culture will grow in the 1990s. As Charles Hampden-Turner, (1990) a leading specialist on the subject, explains 'In the world of increasingly "flat" companies and sophisticated "knowledge-based" products, control and understanding of corporate culture are key responsibilities of leaders and a vital tool for management if it is to extract high performance and maximise share-holder return. A strong culture is necessary for both economic and psychological reasons in a looser style of organisation'. Many enlightened companies have implemented policies to revitalize their culture as the catalyst for making substantial progress. For example, between 1982 and 1988, British Airways went from being one of the least popular airlines, with year-end losses of £100 million to one of the busiest airlines with a profit of £320 million. This was due to a systematic programme of cultural change implemented under the direction of the Deputy Chairman and Chief Executive, Sir Colin Marshall. The goals instilled through the new culture were founded on a well-researched understanding of customer needs.

Within this culture, Sir Colin acknowledges that IT moved to centre stage because it empowered people lower down the organization to make decisions using accurate information. 'This leads to better service for our customers and a leaner organisation, which is a priority for any dynamic company in a competitive industry', he comments. He emphasizes that this success with IT did not come by accident. It was the product of a planned cultural framework which exhibits all the characteristics identified in our study.

Business innovation and IT

IT stirs the management melange

The prime rationale for IT was initially focused on internal efficiency, but during the 1980s it expanded into a complex fusion of four different dimensions (see Figure 15.2). As IT has evolved, differing emphases have increasingly been attributable to each dimension. The shift to a more competitive focus gathered momentum as technological, business, economic, social and political changes accelerated and converged. Such turbulence in the business environment is likely to intensify in the 1990s.

Amidst this volatility, a melange of management issues have become critical around the same time, such as:

(1) Controlling enterprises in a continuous state of flux;
(2) Ceaselessly improving productivity and quality;
(3) Keeping pace with market demands which create the need for shorter product life cycles and more customization;
(4) Co-ordinating integrated global operations;
(5) Introducing flatter, more responsive corporate structures;

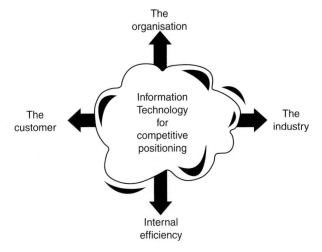

Figure 15.2   *The four dimensions of IT focus*

(6) Coping with demographic trends affecting workforce numbers and skills;
(7) Constantly seeking to reduce costs.

IT helps in each of these, providing scope for people to do entirely new jobs as well as improving performance in traditional ones.

Peters (1988) describes technology as '... a wild card affecting every aspect of doing business'. The leading industrialist Sir John Harvey-Jones has also pointed out that 'IT is undoubtedly the key technological enabler in terms of changing people and giving them the tools to allow the changes to take place'. At the same time as IT is becoming more central to business needs, the technology itself is posing more complex management challenges. When it had a more traditional cost-oriented focus, IT consisted of a number of discrete applications which were relatively easy to cost-justify and control (even though many mistakes were made). Now, information systems tend to form part of a seamless web of activities and interactions that are much more difficult to pin down accurately because they have broad-based strategic impacts on the whole spectrum of competitive positioning.

Cause or consequence of change?

IT has often been depicted as the sole engine for change. However, it is only one important ingredient in the modern management melange. IT is not a magic potion or panacea and unrealistic expectations, fuelled by IT hype, have often led to disillusionment among business executives.

IT can both stimulate and respond to rapid and far-reaching changes in the business environment. For instance, the trend towards flatter organizations has arisen from the need to cope with business turbulence by moving from rigid hierarchical organizational structures to more flexible approaches. IT can enable and stimulate this trend, but is not the reason why such a change should be made.

A vivid illustration of the interplay between business and IT innovation is that of a team at the Kodak photographic company who recently used a computer-aided design and manufacturing (CAD/CAM) network to develop a new product in response to a threat from a Japanese competitor. The results were very impressive. Development-to-shipping time was reduced to just 38 weeks, which is much less than previously achieved; overall costs were cut by 25% and product quality was greatly improved. Despite strong competitive pressures, the product gained an edge on rivals and became a profitable high-seller.

These achievements did not simply flow automatically from applying CAD/CAM. They depended crucially on innovations in how work was managed and organized. Decision-making was decentralized wherever possible, with team members having much autonomy within their spheres of expertise. Formal hierarchical lines of responsibility evaporated as part of this process. The team also agreed their own ways of rewarding people equitably for their joint efforts.

Instead of following traditional sequential development steps, all phases were worked on concurrently by people from many disciplines, including outside suppliers. Continuously open communications were maintained in order for everyone to have an opportunity to see what was currently happening on all parts of the design. The CAD/CAM network was essential in enabling the decentralization and openness to work effectively, unleashing a tremendous amount of creative energy. It provided the central information repository, rapid communications channels and management controls needed to ensure everyone worked to, and met, common targets. This enabled common planning formats to be used for strategic co-ordination without stifling local initiatives.

This kind of example highlights how IT makes it feasible, for the first time, to create more flexible networked organizations. In this context, 'networked' is defined as organizational behaviour based on a great deal of lateral communication and responsibility sharing, rather than the supporting IT networks (Scott Morton, 1990).

Adapting for success in the information age

All change for the future

As the focus of IT developments become more strategic, their reverberations throughout the organization increase. The more ambitious the system, and the higher the potential payoff, the more likely is it that IT innovation will have to be accompanied by fundamental alterations to established routines for running companies and doing business. The first wave of computerization was targeted at efficiency benefits which affected mainly clerical and factory-floor staff. In the future, the impacts will be universal.

The Management in the 1990s research project, directed by Scott Morton, concluded that the main barrier to gaining sustainable advantage from IT is getting individuals, and the overall human resource system, to respond at the required pace (Scott Morton, 1990). Management, at all levels, will have to make major adjustments in adapting to essential new organizational structures and working methods. The increased use of executive support systems and information networks offer organizations fresh options for their command and control procedures. Top management must decide how to re-orientate management approaches so as to take account of these opportunities, including their own decision-making and communications processes. Middle managers could be faced with particularly traumatic changes, including the slimming of the 'middle management bulge' which has been predicted for some time (*Business Week,* 1983). Many organizations arc now applying IT networks to cut management numbers as a way of improving business effectiveness.

Scott Morton (1990) believes a major constraint on progress in the future could come from middle management resistance. A key reason for this, he feels, is that many executives view the help of IT in restructuring organizations into smaller units as being primarily a diminution of their authority rather than a chance to build new business. 'Such middle managers are not foolish enough to give their chief executive an outright "No" when faced by change. But when someone comes to them with a new idea, a new system, or a new way of doing something, they are experts at prevarication'.

In order to benefit fully from IT, everyone in the organization must welcome and encourage innovation. The process of turning resistance into enthusiasm requires creative leadership coupled with a comprehensive education and training programme throughout the organization.

New ways of running a business

IT facilitates the restructuring of organizations to meet business goals. The Prudential insurance company, for example, has applied IT to decentralize its operations in order to enhance decision-making and administrative efficiency. 'Because of IT we have been able to break up our monolithic organisation. We have set up teams who can get closer to customers, keeping in touch with their changing needs. Each team has all the skills necessary to deal with a particular service or product.' Instead of having a few executives controlling the whole organization under the guidance of a Chief General Manager, the Prudential has established several Executive Directors in charge of their own business units.

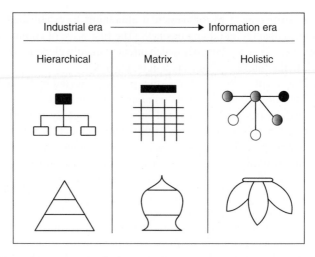

Figure 15.3   *Changes in management, organization and philosophy facilitated by IT*

Administration has also been decentralized using an information network to capture data at local offices rather than relying on a postage stamp and central mainframe.

IT networks, which cross organizational and national boundaries can stimulate new responses to the question – 'Should we make or buy in?' Sir John Harvey-Jones points out that when he became Chairman of ICI in 1982 the company was still tied to the traditional way of doing everything itself. 'Now, the trend is to dismantle this vertical structure and look for alliances which involve allowing partners right inside each other's organisations' he comments. Again, this is an IT-enabled advance, through techniques such as Just-In-Time (JIT) production and Electronic Data Interchange (EDI).

Networks also open up new choices about the places where work is carried out. Offices can be moved away from large urban conurbations such as London. People can work from home and keep in direct touch with colleagues and all necessary files and databases. Support can be brought closer to customers and distribution centres. Some support, e.g. for computer systems, can be carried out from a remote location anywhere in the world. There are many other examples of how IT networks have assisted enterprises to become more competitive. Thomson Holidays in the 1980s, for instance, exploited its leadership in online reservations to increase its market share by over 50%. It retained this lead for many years because rivals had great difficulty in matching the infrastructure of management attitudes, expertise and systems technology which it had nurtured for several years.

Moving towards holistic enterprises

From this management melange, IT is helping to lead business from an industrial age to an information era. The management structures and philosophies appropriate to the past are unlikely to be successful in the future. Therefore, successful enterprises are moving increasingly towards responsive holistic management approaches (as shown in Figure 15.3). The pyramid shape of hierarchical organizations has become ingrained in most corporate cultures. It offers easily understood lines of command from the top but is slow to respond to change – if it responds at all.

Many projects which cut across formal boundaries in pyramid structures have been controlled using matrix management methods involving people from many functions. The result has often been an uneasy blend between hierarchical and cross-functional structures. This makes people uncertain of their roles and responsibilities. Matrix techniques are likely to be a transitory phase. They provide an unclear organizational focus, undermining attempts to create a culture with which people can identify clearly.

A holistic management style is more suited to the information era. It looks at the way the total business operates as an integrated system, targeting corporate efforts towards discovering what customers really want and finding the best way of meeting their needs. Many autonomous, multi-disciplined teams can be built efficiently around a common cultural core in holistic enterprises thus encouraging greater flexibility and closer contact with customers. IT also allows such smaller business units to compete with larger monolithic organizations on cost and quality.

The networked opportunities opened by IT

Laying networked foundations

Technological price/performance improvements are continuing at about 25% per year in the totality of IT developments. This includes computers, workstations, local area networking, wide area telecommunications, information storage, robotics and 'smart' products. As a result, imaginative companies have been able to infiltrate IT into all areas of the workplace, within and between organizations. This is happening in all industry sectors, although there has been greater investment in areas where information is an intrinsic part of the end-product, i.e. financial services.

Most of the main strategic business benefits from IT come from services that combine computing and communications capabilities. For example, we found the highest application priorities in the 1990s were for networked services: executive decision support, office automation, EDI and international telecommunications in all sectors, and CAD/CAM, computer integrated manufacturing (CIM) and electronic point of sale (EPOS) for specific industries. These systems are building the infrastructure for the new kind of 'networked organization' identified by Scott Morton (1990). Soon more advanced technologies, including voice input, laser storage and parallel processors, will deliver products with impressive new business potential.

Enhancing information flows

At a corporate level, information networks give senior management the ability to have greater control over operations in real time. Alan Jacobs, Director of Information for the Sainsburys supermarket chain explains – 'We are operating our business in a totally different mode because managers can use our network to "plug into" individual stores to get up-to-date performance data. We are now able to spread our wings without worrying about the mechanics of information flows.'

Similarly, inter-organizational connections offer great potential for effective management co-ordination across an industry chain. In any consumer operation, for instance, suppliers, warehousing and distribution, retailers, financial services, databases and EPOS systems can be progressively linked via an integrated IT service (see Figure 15.4). Marks & Spencer has used EDI extensively – 'to keep the customer happy by putting the right merchandise on the right store shelf at the right time,' according to the company's IT Director Gareth Williams. This includes exchanging order and invoicing documents electronically with suppliers. An integrated network also links

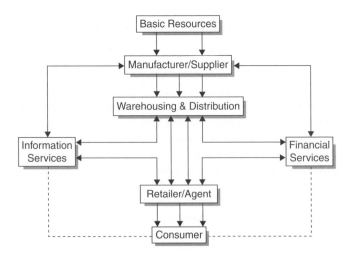

Figure 15.4   *Basic information flows between trading parties*

Marks & Spencer's EPOS terminals, in-store computers and corporate mainframes (Bradshaw, 1990).

The UK Government's Central Unit on Purchasing has estimated that the implementation of EDI could help save £500 million per year on non-defence purchases (EDI Analysis, 1990). A study of the logistics chain in the British National Health Service (NHS) show cost savings of £300 million per annum. It added that the number of suppliers to the NHS could be reduced from 500 to 50 by using EDI, which indicates how networked services can have major impacts throughout an industry.

In order to take advantage of these kinds of substantial benefits, many EDI networks are currently being used and developed in a variety of sectors, from air and shipping cargoes to insurance, vehicle manufacturers and book publishing. Although investments are necessary to establish such a service, paybacks can be substantial. For example, it was estimated that an EDI network for the British book publishing trade could be financed by the savings in postage stamps alone.

Real-time management across the globe

Networks shrink time and distance. This makes access to an effective integrated network essential for companies operating on a world-wide scale. 'Globalisation has made time a critical commodity' (Sir John Harvey-Jones). The Japanese, he says, were the first to realize this and have responded by deploying IT to introduce JIT techniques which have revolutionized attitudes to stock levels. When the Japanese began to challenge the Western motor industry, Ford had to radically rethink the way they made cars. It had to co-ordinate developments around the world, with much work being done concurrently. Using IT extensively to cut costs, improve quality and reduce the time taken from design to delivery, Ford took about a decade to catch up with the efficiency of equivalent Japanese operations. Ford of Europe now has a profit per worker twice that of its nearest European rival, Peugeot.

EDI is of major importance in global activities. For instance, networks covering clothing suppliers and stores allow data on customer purchases recorded on EPOS terminals in Europe to be fed directly to suppliers in the Far East, who can respond immediately to changing fashion and patterns of demand. OCL has become one of the largest container shipping companies in the world by exploiting its international network and IT knowhow. They enable customers to link directly with overseas suppliers for computer-to-computer order processing, and automatically arrange shipping and delivery as a 'transparant' service.

A computer link can also increase the negotiating power and reduce company costs of supporting a successful service because it can make others dependent on access to that service.

Strategic factors which demand positive attitudes to IT

The international competitive challenge

The evidence provided in this report demonstrates why positive corporate reorganizations are needed to make the best strategic use of key technical IT developments. This is essential if companies are to stay in business and improve competitive positioning. 'Critical technological transformations' and 'intense competition' were identified as the key characteristics of the 21st century business environment in a study by Korn/Ferry International (1990) and the Columbia University Graduate School of Business involving over 1500 chief executives in 20 countries.

Managers in all regions of the world regarded IT as the most important technology in its own right. IT is also a vital element in product and production technologies, which were the next two most significant areas of innovation they highlighted. Japanese executives were most aware of the likely intensity of international competition and, with a strategy based upon product enhancement through new technology, are getting ready for the roughest possible conditions. The single European market from 1992 is focusing West European eyes to the challenges of competing on a global scale.

The free movement of goods, services, capital and people within Europe after 1992 will have enormous impacts. Although this brings opportunities for some companies, the net result could be what Rajan (1990) calls a 'zero sum game'. He believes that the size of the economic cake will remain about the same but the new environment will accelerate the process of industrial restructuring through mergers, alliances, partnerships, joint ventures and much internal rationalization within organizations. In these conditions, only the fittest enterprises will survive. Rajan warns that only about a third of existing companies are likely to be among the winners. And Sir John Harvey-Jones has predicted that by the year 2000 half of Europe's factories will close and half its companies will either disappear or be taken over.

Demographic changes and the skills gap

While coping with stringent technological and competitive pressures, companies will have to deal with a demographic time-bomb that will explode in the (1990s). Since the middle of the 1960s, birth rates have slumped dramatically in the most developed countries, while more people are living longer.[2] The general ageing of the population in these countries will be accompanied by

[2]Statistical Office of the European Communities (Eurostat) (1989) *Europe in Figures: Deadline 1992*, HMSO and Macmillan Education.

a growing number of unemployed over-50s, many of whom have been made redundant by IT applications.

This is occurring during a period when IT is creating a demand for highly skilled professionals, especially 'knowledge workers', while cutting the requirement for less skilled work. The result is likely to be a growing army of relatively unskilled and untrained people, at the same time as there is an acute scarcity of the people actually wanted by companies. The workforce in the 1990s will have to be highly adaptable, often multi-skilled and with the knowhow to accelerate progress in a wide range of strategic activities. This will place a heavy responsibility on national education and training infrastructures.

These trends will cause a substantial increase in health and welfare costs for the elderly, but with fewer people available to generate the necessary wealth. There will, therefore, be extra pressure on companies to increase productivity, contain costs, enhance working flexibility and improve job satisfaction. The only way of doing this is to apply IT and other new technologies wisely.

How the UK compares

Falling behind in the competitive race

Britain entered the 1990s in a relatively weak position compared to its major international competitors. 1990 has seen a stream of gloomy economic news and the OECD predicts that by 1991 tie UK will have lower GNP growth, higher inflation and a larger balance of payments deficit than West Germany, France, Japan and the USA (The Economist, 1990). Such 'headline' figures are supported by evidence of deep-rooted reasons for this position. Douglas McWilliams says there is '… an inflationary psychology in pay bargaining …' which keeps wages, prices and unit labour costs on an upward spiral in the UK.[3]

Underlying failures in the education system and management attitudes to innovation are even more disturbing in view of the future challenges outlined above. 'The need to rebuild the British education system is urgent,' Porter (1990) commented after a detailed investigation into competitive advantage covering the USA, Japan, Singapore, Korea and a number of West European countries. 'It has badly lagged behind that of virtually all the nations we studied, Porter says that the education system both reflects and reinforces British tendencies towards non-competitiveness in personal terms. He points out that industry spending on training is less than 1% of revenues in the UK, compared to 2% in West Germany and 3% in Japan.

[3]CBI Economists See ERM Entry as Inflation Key, *The Times*, 5 September 1990, p.21.

German (Peters, 1990) and French (Rajan, 1990) education and training policies have strong cultural beliefs to support much larger and more structured investment programmes than in Britain. This helps to explain why only 38% of the UK workforce has had skilled vocational training compared to 67% in West Germany and 80% in France.[4]

Peters (1990) points out that having a highly skilled workforce has made an important contribution to the Germans becoming '. . . world leaders in applying high technology, including IT'. Technically skilled top managers, fewer middle management layers, and an orientation towards customization and harmonious labour relations are other reasons he gives for this success. On the other hand, Porter (1990) says that the underlying problems in the UK are exacerbated by what he describes as a British management culture which works against innovation and change because it is characterized by 'a penchant for tradition, a narrow definition of responsibility and a high level of concern for form and order'.

Other competitor nations also have their own special problems. For example, there are difficulties of reunification in Germany and more acute demographic and lifestyle pressures in Japan. Yet, these countries have better growth track records than Britain and sounder economic and educational infrastructures. Of course, there are many glittering examples of successful British companies that stand tall in the world arena. Porter's view, however, is buttressed by undeniable statistical evidence of faults in the national economic and human resource infrastructure, indicating that Britain is in a relatively unfavourable position to advance in the tough competitive environment of the 1990s.

Insufficient attention to the management of IT

Our study confirms that the general national problems are reflected in the way IT has been under-managed in the UK compared to its main European rivals, particularly West Germany.[5] Given the importance of IT to overall business success this lack of preparation could undermine British efforts to compete effectively in the single European market and the world at large.

UK companies performed particularly badly in many of the critical cultural areas including:

(1) Lack of top management understanding of how IT contributes to the business. Only 59% of executives in Britain felt top management understood

---

[4]see Rajan (1990), pp. 146–157 and 173–186 for a description of the French and British approaches. See also Agony of the Post-ERM depression, *The Sunday Times,* 9 September 1990.
[5]R. Tomlin & Co. (1989) *Managing Information Technology in Europe: A British Perspective,* Amdahl Executive Institute, Hampshire, UK.

how IT contributes to the business, compared to 83% in West Germany
and 72% in France;

(2) Inadequate appreciation by senior management of what is involved in
successfully deploying IT. Over 41% of respondents in the UK felt senior
management did not realize what was involved in successfully deploying
IT, against just 5% in Germany. The least successful users of IT in the
whole survey averaged 33% in this category, underlining Britain's apparently extremely weak position.

(3) Unwillingness of top management to devote sufficient time to make IT
projects a success. Top management devoted sufficient time to making IT
projects a success according to just 37% of replies in the UK, and 58% in
West Germany.

(4) Top management dissatisfaction with the present business contribution
from IT. Top management satisfaction with the IT contribution to business in the UK was just 27%, approximately half the levels found in West
Germany and France.

Not surprisingly, these attitudes have led to IT executives in Britain being
much less confident than their European counterparts that their companies
will gain as much benefits as they should from IT (see Figure 15.5). In the
UK, only 39% had any firm certainty that their organizations would get the
most from IT. In West Germany, the figure was an enormous 84% and in
France 56%.

Relationships between general management and IT specialists in the UK
are exacerbated by poor communications and insufficient opportunities for
IT staff to learn about the business. For example, 42% of British companies
said they were satisfied with communications between these groups compared
to over 60% in West Germany and France. All this contributes to the most
disturbing long-term conclusion about Britain's relatively weak IT management – many more British managers (31%) feel their companies will fail to
be leaders in IT innovation than their counterparts in West Germany (7%) and
France (16%). Education and training can improve the situation, but we found
that British management used fewer formal methods of training and education
than West Germany and France. This will be a major obstacle to catching up
with Britain's international rivals, given the strategic importance of IT to competitive positioning. Without the confidence and culture to apply IT effectively
to meet strategic goals, many British companies are likely to cut IT budgets
when the economic climate gets stormy rather than investing more in improving IT management (PA Consulting Group, 1990). Despite these background
difficulties, our study also produced a clear route out of this malaise. We
found many British companies who successfully used IT as a result of pursuing the correct management strategy. We also identified realistic practices
which can be adopted by any company wishing to achieve similar results.

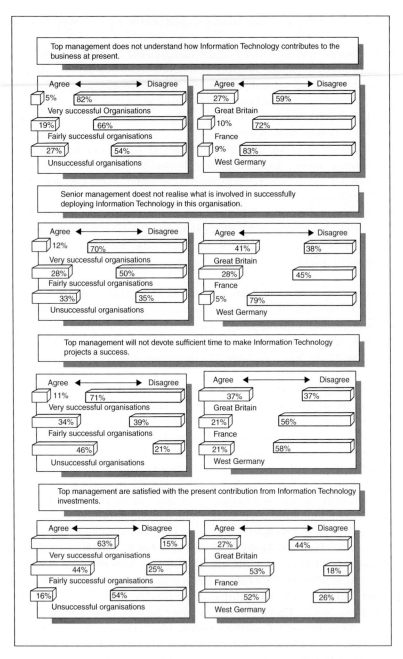

Figure 15.5   *Comparative views about IT in Britain, France and West Germany*

Creating a culture that breeds success with IT

Summary of objectives

Drawing on the practical experience of many executives responsible for major IT projects, this report explains why we have concluded that

(1) Excellent IT management is a competitive necessity;
(2) Without the right corporate culture, IT will never come close to achieving its full business potential;
(3) The organizations applying IT most successfully have distinctive cultural characteristics, as discussed earlier: leadership, a shared vision and values, commitment, understanding and confidence;
(4) To develop and sustain such a culture, top management must define a clear vision of their new 'organization of the 1990s' and the role of IT within it;
(5) IT should be integrated into the natural way the company competes and is managed.

The practical long-term vision should encourage everyone to understand and exploit the opportunities provided by IT, based on an appreciation that

(1) Business volatility and international competitiveness are likely to grow in the 1990s;
(2) IT can cause industry-wide changes in the relationships between suppliers, customers and service companies;
(3) There are likely to be substantial changes in how, where and by whom work is carried out;
(4) IT impacts can reverberate throughout the organization, requiring management to rethink traditional approaches to how they run their enterprises.

Using a corporate vision as a guiding light, detailed business-focused plans should be targeted along the four strategic IT dimensions identified in Figure 15.2. The plans should also facilitate the formation of necessary associated cultural changes, with top management providing the overall purpose and direction which helps everyone to work towards common goals.

IT projects, however, have often been hampered by a struggle for control. Our study shows that responsibilities for IT applications initiatives have been distributed among line managers, IT specialists, top executives and strategic planning functions (see Figure 15.6). Effective commitment to IT can be built only by forging constructive partnerships between these groups.

The partnership should be business-led, with strong IT involvement and cross-functional communication. This will avoid the danger of line managers, in charge of IT developments, making mistakes because of their technical inexperience. Top management can create the conditions for a co-operative team approach by insisting on education and training programmes

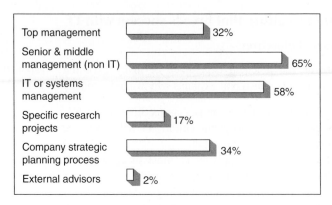

Figure 15.6   *Most frequent sources of IT initiatives in very successful organizations*

which ensure business executives appreciate the value and place of IT and IT experts understand the business in which they work.

Good project management of strategically significant IT applications, such as integrated networks, is crucial because they are usually complex to implement as well as being vital to business operations. Appropriate methods for controlling IT projects effectively should be established as a corporate priority in order to maintain the highest technical quality at all times.

An agenda for management action

Poor awareness of the importance of the prevailing culture is the most common management fault leading to IT delivering unsatisfactory results. To overcome this, top management must recognize that one of the most critical tasks for senior IT executives in the 1990s will be to take a leading part in creating suitable cultural climate.

We have found that a sound approach to developing the right IT policies is to undertake a systematic evaluation of existing attitudes and current practices. One of the first steps towards this should be an investigation to obtain a true picture of the company's aspirations for IT and the suitability of its existing culture to satisfy these ambitions. Our unique database of over 800 European companies is frequently used by managers as an objective yardstick for judging their company's readiness for IT success.

The assessment process would typically include:

(1) Establishing an agreed appraisal plan with top management, including the IT Director;
(2) Undertaking structured interviews with selected executives and staff;
(3) Completion of a questionnaire by participants in the survey;
(4) Analysis of survey results, e.g. comparing them to the most successful IT users, a complete industry sector, and particular countries (see Figure 15.7);

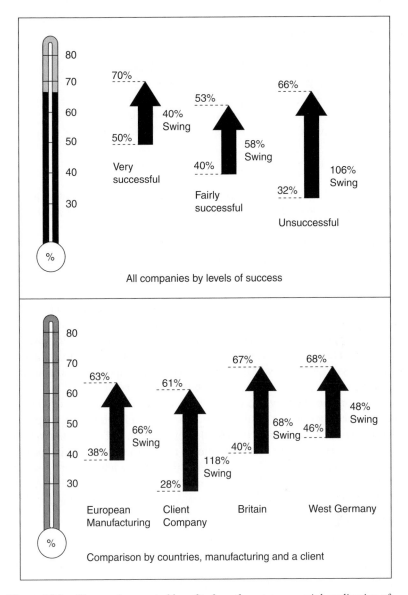

Figure 15.7 *Changes in expected benefits from the entrepreneurial application of IT, over the next three years*

Note: Figure. 15.7 illustrates the expected increase in business benefits from 'entrepreneurial' type applications of IT, under various categories. The lower percentage of each arrow represents the current degree of benefit being obtained; the arrow head is what is expected over the next three years. The illustration shows that 'very successful' past users of IT have less ambitious expectations than those who have not been as successful with IT. The full research study also clearly shows that those companies with greater expectations (i.e. degree of swing) do not usually have the right cultural characteristics to achieve their aspirations. These companies can take positive steps to develop the right managerial environment and consequently gain more and more benefits from future IT investments. Those who do not however, will fall further behind.

(5) Presentation of results in structured discussions designed to elicit feed-back and test reactions;
(6) Holding workshops with general and IT management to help build a widely-accepted vision and all-round commitment;
(7) Identification of the cultural characteristics required and how to achieve them;
(8) Presentation of results and plans to the Board for approval.

The outcome from an approach like this should be a plan representing a genuine consensus of views and experiences, indicative of the open and honest management style that should be sought.

Getting the culture right also optimizes returns on IT investments. Sir John Harvey-Jones has pointed out '… that hardly any companies are using more than about 50% of the available technology', which indicates there is much scope for making considerable IT improvements without spending a great deal on new technology. Time spent nurturing a culture for IT success will pay enormous dividends, but the process will not be easy or quick. As Sir John Harvey-Jones commented, 'Producing a corporate culture that encourages successful change can be a long haul of three to five years, or more. Nevertheless, companies will have every chance of getting ahead of competitors if they do this while staying in touch with advanced IT ideas.'

British organizations which heed this advice should be able to exploit the opportunities opened by a post-1992 'Europe without frontiers'. Being part of a strong Europe helps those who have the imagination and dedication to position themselves wisely to beat international rivals. The lengthy period needed to construct a culture that will respond effectively to the interwoven mosaic of issues outlined in this report means companies cannot afford to delay. Action should be taken now to secure business success with IT through this decade.

References

Bradshaw, D. (1990), "An outfit made of durable fibre," *Financial Times*, 6. 14th June.
Business Week (1983) A new era for management, 25th April, pp. 34–58.
EDI Analysis (1990) EDI could help save UK government £500 million a year, *EDI Analysis,* September p. 1.
The Economist (1990) Paris predicts, 30th June, p. 93. Korn/Ferry International (1989) Reinventing the CEO, 21st Century report, Korn/Ferry International, New York.
Hampden-Turner, C. (1990), *Corporate Culture for Competitive Edge,* The Economist Publications, London.
PA Consulting Group (1990) The impact of the current climate on IT – a survey report, PA Consulting, London.

Peters, T. (1988), *Thriving on Chaos*. Macmillan, London.
Peters, T. (1990), "The German economic miracle," in *Across the Board*. Conference Board inc, New York.
Porter, M. (1990), "Michael Porter's agenda for Britain," *The Director*, April, pp. 41–48.
Rajan, A. (1990), 1992: A Zero Sum Game. The Industrial Society, London.
Scott Morton, R. (1990), (ed). *Managing Change: Innovation through Information Technology*. Amdahl Executive Institute, Hampshire, UK.
Tomlin, R. (1988), *Business Success and Information Technology: Strategies for the 1990s*. Amdahl Executive Institute, Hampshire, UK.
Tomlin, R. (1990), *Clues to Success: A Corporate Culture for Information Technology*, European Edn. Amdahl Executive Institute, Hampshire, UK.

Reproduced from *Journal of Information Technology*, Vol. 6, 1991, pp. 45–55. Reprinted with permission from Palgrave.

Biographical notes

Roger Tomlin has spent over 30 years applying Information Technology in a variety of management positions. His early experience was gained with ICL, implementing automated information systems into companies such as Harrods, British Oxygen, Mathew Hall, Sun Life of Canada, British Broadcasting Corporation and others. In 1964 he undertook an applied research project to study management of the IT function. This resulted in the publication of five hand books, 'Techniques of Computer Management'. On leaving ICL to join John Hoskyns and Company in 1967, he was the youngest area manager in the company. He spent 3 years with Hoskyns initially responsible for a business providing turnkey computer systems for UK's manufacturing industries until it was taken over by GKN. He then became Managing Director of Computer Education in Schools. In 1970 he published 'Managing the introduction of Computer Systems' (McGrawHill: in French, German, Spanish and English). The book was given a merit award for original content.

He joined the Travel Division of International Thomson Organisation (ITO) to introduce systems into Thomson Holidays in 1970. As a group board Director he was responsible for the initiatives which resulted in Thomson Holidays becoming a world wide case study for the highly effective use of IT for competitive advantage. He was also responsible for extensive automation in the airline business, retailing, ITO corporate management systems and was the ITO adviser on IT in the USA and Europe. He introduced strategic planning into the travel division, integrating IT and strategic planning as a regular management activity. He was a non-executive Director of several companies.

In 1984 he started his own consulting business. This now specializes in the management of Information Technology. Clients include several multinationals.

Associate organizations have been established in West Germany, France, Italy and USA. Close ties have been created with several leading Business Schools and Universities in America and Europe. Mr Tomlin has spoken at management conferences around the world, and has sat on many conference panels with international business leaders. He is also an Honorary Visiting Senior Fellow at City University Business School, London.

Questions for discussion

1   Describe elements of a corporate culture in which IT can succeed. How does the lack of each of these elements impact IT success and how does it affect the business as a whole?

2   What is the relationship between corporate culture and IT implementation? How does one affect the other? How do both affect customer service?

3   What is IT's role in bringing a flatter company structure? What is IT's impact in Just In Time, Electronic Data Interchange, and internal communication on how people work?

4   How does communication and IT infrastructure affect the way we do business? What does 'networked' mean in this context?

5   Given the global competitive landscape for 'knowledge workers', how does the example of the UK inform you about the competitiveness of your country and the companies in your country in the future?

6   How do corporate and national culture affect IT success? What elements in the culture are necessary for a nurturing IT environment?

16 Information Systems Employment Structures in the USA and Singapore: A Cross-cultural Comparison[1]

Sandra Slaughter and Soon Ang

Introduction

According to the classic view of labour markets, workers move freely from job to job and firm to firm (Bakke, 1954). From the worker's perspective, this movement is governed by pressures to maximize the fit between worker skills and job requirements, with the objective of maximizing earnings. Historically, however, hierarchical (internal) control of labour supplanted the open labour market as a way of securing and controlling workers (Doeringer and Piore, 1971). More recently, there have been challenges to the historical perspective of internal labour markets as the primary structure of employment. Pfeffer and Baron (1988), for example, suggest that organizations increasingly are externalizing a buffer of workers against the core or permanent workforce. Externalization refers to the degree of attachment, or more appropriately, detachment of a worker to the organization. According to Pfeffer and Baron (1988) there are three dimensions of externalization:

(1) the physical proximity between the worker and organization;
(2) the extent of administrative control over the employee wielded by the organization; and
(3) the duration of employment.

Thus, externalization occurs where the worker is removed from the work-place for non job-related reasons, by diminishing the duration of employment

[1] The authors wish to express their appreciation to A. Teh, M.C. Ho, and F.B. Ahmad for their data collection effort in this research.

and by reducing administrative control over the employee (for example, where payment is done by another employer). Externalization is viewed by some as a necessary economic response to an environment which is becoming increasingly dynamic, competitive and uncertain (Handy, 1989; Scott-Morton, 1991).

Although organizations may be adopting forms of structuring their workforce which move away from the traditional internal structure (for example, by outsourcing activities), the assumption that work is subject largely to hierarchical/bureaucratic control appears to underlie much of the research concerning personnel, including information systems (IS) personnel. Many studies of IS personnel (e.g. Bartol, 1983; Ferratt and Short, 1986; Igbaria *et al.*, 1991) focus on examining issues relevant to the organization's permanent internal IS workforce (such as turnover and career pathing), and studies of temporary or contract IS workers are rare. However, in practice, since the late 1980s, many internal IS organizations have been undergoing continual "downsizing" of the traditional permanent workforce and experimentation with alternative forms of work structure (Ang, 1991; *Computerworld*, 1989; Korzeniowski, 1990). Thus, in light of more recent trends in the actual organization of IS work, it is important to gain an understanding of the evolution away from traditional work structures and to reassess and re-evaluate the implications of this phenomenon for managing IS personnel. Furthermore, it is instructive to examine whether trends towards more externalized employment structures are restricted to the USA or occur in other countries. Such an examination provides deeper insight into the antecedents of IS employment structures.

This study focuses on gaining an improved understanding of the externalization phenomenon in relation to the IS workforce in the USA and Singapore. These countries have been selected for analysis since they have very different forms of industrial economies (*Economist*, 1993) and cultures (Bunke, 1990), and should therefore provide unique insights into the externalization phenomenon. We propose two perspectives to explain preferences for externalization in these countries:

(1) a market perspective emphasizing economic factors; and
(2) a cultural perspective emphasizing values.

Our study investigates the extent of externalizing IS workers in both countries. The methodology employed in the study consists of content coding and analysis of advertisements for job positions in these countries over a three-year timeframe (from July 1990 to April 1993). Results indicate that, overall, the USA adopts more externalized IS employment structures than Singapore. Moreover, a trend towards increased externalization is more discernible in the USA only in the past year.

Results from this study provide preliminary evidence of the existence of external forms of employment structures in the USA, while suggesting that the traditional, hierarchic employment relationship is prevalent in Singapore. We suggest that these results can be interpreted from both market and cultural perspectives. Furthermore, our results have two implications for future studies of IS personnel:

(1) The results imply that future investigations should examine IS personnel and human resource strategies for managing external, as well as internal workers.
(2) Our results suggest the importance of sensitivity to the influence of cultural factors in explaining national preferences for IS personnel arrangements.

In the following sections of the article, we discuss the importance of employment structures for the IS workforce, outline employment relationship preferences from both a market and a cultural perspective, describe the methodology employed by this study, present detailed results and conclude with a discussion of results and suggestions for further research.

Employment structures and the information systems workforce

In a study of IS management issues for the 1990s (Niederman *et al.*, 1991), one of the top issues to emerge (ranked No. 4) is the management of IS human resources, in terms of specifying, recruiting and developing personnel. IS executives report that although the size of their department is being continually reduced, they are faced with an increasing number of projects which require greater and more specialized technological skills (Niederman *et al.*, 1991). At the same time, demographic trends are forecasted to result in acute shortages of skilled IS personnel by the year 2000 (US Department of Labor, 1989). In addition, technologies such as CASE (computer-aided software engineering) threaten to make the skills of many traditional analysts and COBOL programmers holding current IS positions obsolete (Rouzer, 1992). Thus, IS managers are faced with resolving difficult issues such as whether to retrain or replace their current permanent IS workforce, how to attract workers with skills in newer technologies, and whether to retain these workers as part of their permanent workforce. Compared with other occupations, managing the IS workforce is becoming particularly challenging because the underlying information technologies are changing rapidly and making the skills of the IS worker obsolete, and because economic conditions continually pressure for increased productivity in information systems work (Yourdon, 1992).

This requires the IS manager to weigh constantly the costs and benefits of motivating and attracting skilled IS workers and retraining or replacing them when their skills become obsolete.

Although prior research into IS personnel has provided valuable insights, it has focused, for the most part, on issues relevant to managing a permanent internal workforce. For example, past studies have examined topics such as job satisfaction of IS programmers and analysts (Goldstein and Rockart, 1989), differing levels of turnover among IS personnel (Baroudi, 1985; Bartol, 1983; Guimaraes and Igbaria, 1992), and career path planning, decisions and outcomes (Igbaria and Siegel, 1993; Igbaria and Wormley, 1992; Igbaria *et al.*, 1991). Another body of literature has examined potential differences between IS and non-IS workers in terms of how IS workers should be managed (Ferratt and Short, 1988), how to motivate IS workers (Couger and Zawaki, 1980; Ferratt and Short, 1986), and differing levels of social and achievement needs of IS versus non-IS workers (Bartol and Martin, 1982). Underlying these studies is the implicit assumption that IS workers are part of the internal permanent workforce of the IS organization. In general, issues such as how to motivate temporary IS workers, how to manage a contracted workforce, and how to allocate optimally tasks between temporary and permanent workers have not been addressed. However, press suggested that alternative organizational arrangements for IS work (such as outsourcing) have become increasingly popular in practice, and that IS executives need to understand how to manage and monitor these types of arrangements (Leinfuss, 1991). Thus, it is important to assess the extent to which externalized employment structures have been adopted in the IS workforce.

Furthermore, it is important to examine IS work arrangements in various cultures. Cross-cultural comparisons enable insights into the generalizability of the externalization phenomenon. In addition, examining different cultures provides insights into the relative importance of cultural as well as economic factors in motivating national preferences for employment structures.

As a precursor for further investigation into these issues, we begin by assessing the forms and extent of the externalization phenomenon in the IS function in multiple cultures. Thus, our study addresses the following general research questions:

- *R1*: what are the different forms of externalizing IS human resources?
- *R2*: what is the extent of externalizing IS human resources?
- *R3*: how does the extent of externalizing IS human resources differ across cultures?

It is important to examine these questions because how work is structured has implications for the conditions under which individuals work as well as for the skills, practices and structure required by organizations. To provide insights into these questions, we review existing literature on the evolution of internal and external labour markets, interpreting it from both a market and a cultural perspective. We then apply these insights to the IS employment situation.

A market perspective of work arrangements

In the labour market literature, there are various perspectives regarding the evolution of internal and external labour markets (Scott, 1992). One of the earlier challenges to the classic view of the open labour market was raised by Doeringer and Piore (1971) who observed that information, opportunities, mobility and rewards can be differentially structured and shaped by varying occupational, industry, and organizational arrangements. Thus, they argue that internalization via administrative governance structures emerged as a means of controlling or influencing the open labour market. The market-oriented view of organizational structure can be most closely associated with Williamson (1975; 1981; 1983; 1985). Building on the work of earlier economists (Coase, 1937; Commons, 1934), Williamson argues that the basic unit of economic analysis is the economic transaction – the exchange of goods or services across technological boundaries. Technological boundaries refer to technologically separable interfaces, i.e. points where one stage of activity terminates and another begins (Williamson, 1981). Every transaction contains costs associated with ensuring that each party to a transaction lives up to the terms of the agreement. Williamson argues that the more the uncertainty within the marketplace, the greater the likelihood that some parties will cheat, rendering the marketplace less reliable, less efficient and less profitable. Thus, businesses create governance structures to internalize transactions, reducing transaction costs and increasing efficiency.

In terms of the employer–employee relationship, transaction costs can explain the movement towards internal forms of governance. Internal forms of control lower transaction costs by reducing informational requirements and the need for recurrent contracting (Williamson, 1980). Under this view, where there is a monopoly situation of workers with firm-specific skills, the result is higher transaction costs because firm-specific skills and knowledge create small numbers of bargaining situations between employer and employee, favouring opportunistic behaviour on both sides. Thus, it is more advantageous for the organization to bring the worker under internal management, because the costs of contracting are high. Williamson further argues that the most important influence on the movement towards internal labour markets is the specificity of assets embodied in the worker. Human asset specificity is increased as the skills and knowledge of the worker become more specialized and less transferable to other employers. Thus, internal organization of labour benefits both worker and employer where assets are specific because it provides the employee with prospects of upward mobility through regularized career advancements and enables the employer to recoup investments in training the worker.

A related market explanation of the evolution towards internal forms of control is the size argument (Edwards, 1979). Where there are large, powerful firms which are in a monopoly situation, and as these firms grow in size and complexity, it is more cost-effective to shift towards bureaucratic control of employees. Thus, bureaucratic control becomes embedded in the social and organizational structure of the firm and establishes the impersonal force of company rules or policy as the basis for control. A common thread linking these arguments for internal labour market arrangements is the reduction of costs related to contracting and controlling workers.

Market arguments can also be made for the more recent shift towards external labour markets. Similar to internal markets, external markets can provide cost advantages in certain situations. In general, costs of permanent workers can exceed those for temporary workers because of the additional expenses for benefits, training and recruiting. For example, a recent bulletin on employee benefits published by the United States Chamber of Commerce indicates that while organizations reported paying health, retirement and vacation benefits to 100 per cent of full-time employees, only 17 per cent of part-time or temporary workers received paid benefits from these firms (Chamber of Commerce of the United States, 1991). In addition, the cost of these benefits for long-term workers, in particular, has been rising dramatically in recent years. The United States Chamber of Commerce also reports that employee benefits increased from 17.0 per cent to 37.9 per cent of total payroll costs from 1955 to 1990. This provides significant cost incentives for organizations to reduce the number of permanent employees by externalizing workers.

Thus, the market perspective suggests that costs of contracting and administering workers motivate the choice of appropriate employment structure. Because there are cost trade-offs involved with internal and external workers, an optimal employment structure strategy may be a "dual" form where organizations retain an internal "core" of permanent workers and a buffer of external workers to absorb environmental fluctuations (Mangum *et al.*, 1985). Such an arrangement allows organizations to adjust more easily the size of their workforce, enabling more flexible response to economy, industry and product demand variations. Cost arguments assert that the internal core of workers would most likely consist of those with firm-specific skills, involved in core or critical activities to the firm's survival, and in whom the firm has invested a significant amount of training. Externalized workers would tend to be those involved in less central activities, and would possess skills that are less firm-specific and more rapidly obsoleted.

A cultural perspective of work arrangements

A different perspective on the choice of work arrangements is the cultural explanation. According to Smircich (1983), culture may be viewed as a socially learned way of life of a people and the means by which orderliness and patterned relations are maintained in a society. While the market perspective views organizations as striving towards maximum efficiency, cultural theorists examine the non-rational, subjective aspects of organizational life. From the cultural perspective, organizations are expressions of the larger culture of the society (Gamst and Norbeck, 1976). Thus, organizational work arrangements reflect the cultural norms, ideals and values of the society in which the organization is embedded.

Under the cultural view, internal forms of work arrangements would likely be preferred in organizations where societal values favour such structures. For example, cultures in which the individual is subordinated to the group may prefer lifetime employment systems and seniority systems to maintain the integrity of the group. Internal employment structures would also be consistent with cultures that stress the importance of the family and obedience to authority. In contrast, external forms of work arrangements may be favoured by cultures which value individualism and free enterprise and fear the power of large, bureaucratic, governmental organizations. Thus, the cultural perspective suggests that societal values motivate the choice of employment structures, i.e. that employment structures result from cultural predispositions.

Of course, it is likely that neither economic nor cultural factors *alone* may suffice to explain national preferences for employment structures. A country's economy and culture may be closely intertwined. The economic structure may reflect the country's culture, and that culture may be generated in part by economic constraints. As Hamilton and Biggart (1988) argue, cultural values may influence the predisposition of nations to favour certain forms of organizational structure. However, value patterns provide only a general sense of why nations may favour certain employment structures. On the other hand, economic factors may be too specific and too narrow to account for organizational forms. Rather, Hamilton and Biggart suggest an integrated cultural and market view in which the patterns of authority relations in the society provide a more complete explanation concerning national preferences for employment structures as organizations adapt to changing economic conditions.

Application to the IS situation

Preferences for employment relationships in the general labour market have implications for the choice of management structure of IS work. In the IS arena, externalization of IS work can arise due to market considerations. As the costs of supporting permanent IS workers increases, organizations would favour externalization schemes to reduce the size of the internal IS work-force. This externalization of IS workers can be characterized by a diminished temporal duration of the relationship between the principal (the firm requiring IS services) and the agent (the worker providing the IS services) which would likely occur in the form of use of contract workers or consulting firms (Niederman and Trower, 1993). In addition, there would also be reduced administrative involvement of the principal in traditional duties of IS personnel management such as selection, recruitment, employee benefits, and compensation schemes by the use of employment agencies.

Similarly, we contend that cultural forces may play an important role in influencing the extent to which externalized IS employment structures are adopted. While cross-cultural research has been conducted on the differential use of advanced information technologies (Straub, 1994), cross-national dimensions of information management (Burn *et al.*, 1993) and the management of IS personnel (Tan and Igbaria, 1994), few studies have examined the impact of cultural factors on the externalization of IS workers.

In this study, we examine the externalization of IS work over three years and in two different countries – the USA and Singapore. The longitudinal design enables assessment of the tendency towards externalization of IS workers over a period of time, while the comparative design enables assessment of the generalizability of the externalization phenomenon. A comparative study of the USA and Singapore was chosen because, while both countries rely heavily on information technology, the industrial economies and cultures of these countries are very different and should therefore provide unique insights into the externalization issue. Singapore represents one of the countries with newly industrializing economies (NIEs) that rely heavily on information technology skills. Singapore experiences average annual growth rates in gross domestic product (GDP) per head of about 6–7 per cent (*Economist*, 1993). On the other hand, the USA is archetypal of mature industrial economies with similar heavy rehance on information technology, but with a more modest annual growth rate in the range of 2–3 per cent (*Economist*, 1993).

The labour market for IS workers is also very different in these countries in terms of demographics and supply and demand conditions. For example, a survey of Singaporean analysts and programmers (Couger, 1986) reveals demographic differences between IS professionals. In general, Singaporean IS workers are younger (70 per cent are under 31 years of age versus 36 per cent in the USA), less experienced (72 per cent have four years or less experience versus 55 per cent in the USA), and better educated (71 per cent have obtained a BS degree or higher versus 57 per cent in the USA) (Couger, 1986). In addition, the Singaporean government has the goal of becoming a software leader and has implemented considerable economic incentives to attract major software companies to the country. This has the effect of increasing demand for IS labour such that there are shortages of qualified IS workers (Neo, 1993).

Finally, there are interesting cultural differences between these countries which have implications for the IS workforce. Relative to the USA, Singapore stresses collectivism, belongingness, loyalty as reflected by the strong Confucian ethic (Bunke, 1990), and high power distances (Bond and Hofstede, 1989; Hofstede, 1991). Workers with these values may prefer to commit themselves to full-time employer–employee relationships rather than externalized forms of employment. The attractiveness of long-term employer–employee relationships is also enhanced by the use of seniority wage systems, especially in the public sector which forms the primary employer of IS workers in Singapore. In firms where seniority wage systems are used, wages are pegged at length of service, rather than any direct link to performance and productivity.

In contrast, the USA promotes societal values of individualism and free enterprise which are thought to lead to segmentalist organizations, and emphasize productivity and financial performance (Kanter, 1983). These values foster creation by market forces of independent economic "firms" which may be as small as an individual. Such a climate may be favourable to externalizing IS workers from large bureaucracies, since these workers can act profitably as individual economic agents in the marketplace.

Thus, given the differences in the nature of the industrial economies and the cultures of the USA and Singapore, this study will explore the generalizability of the externalization of IS work between the two countries. By assessing the extent of externalization in two different countries, we can determine whether the trend towards externalization is a phenomenon idiosyncratic to the USA or a phenomenon which may be generalizable to other nations.

In the following sections, we describe the methodology employed to study these issues and the results obtained.

Methodology

Method

A content analytic approach was adopted to analyse the employment structures found in the USA and Singapore. This method has the advantage of being unobtrusive, and enables making replicable and valid inferences from data in their context (Krippendorff, 1980).

Sample

Advertisements for IS jobs were gathered from two different sources: *Computerworld* from the USA, and *Straits Times* from Singapore;

Computerworld was selected as it is the premier national trade journal in IS where IS job opportunities are widely advertised [1]. *Straits Times* is the major English newpaper in Singapore and is the country's largest national source of advertisements for IS jobs.

To gather a sample of recent IS job advertisements, a stratified sampling strategy was adopted. Advertisements were sampled in each quarter beginning July 1990 and ending June 1993. For *Computerworld*, all advertisements appearing in the first week of each quarter were sampled. For *Straits Times*, all IS-related advertisements appearing in the first Saturday of each quarter were sampled [2]. In total, 12 issues of *Computerworld* and *Straits Times* were sampled. Table 16.1 provides the total number of advertisements found in the 12 issues of *Computerworld* and *Straits Times*, respectively.

Coding scheme

IS job advertisements were coded for their respective employment structures. The coding scheme is based, in general, on the types of administrative externalization in employment structures discussed by Pfeffer and Baron (1988), and on the types of IS work outlined by Niederman and Trower (1993). From these perspectives, we distinguish between internal and external IS work, and sub-classify external IS work into three different categories (contract work, quasi-contract work, and consulting/employment agency) (Ang and Slaughter, 1995). The coding scheme, therefore, describes four IS employment structures:

Table 16.1   *Total number of IS job advertisements found in 12 issues of* Computerworld *and* Straits Times

Journal/quarter and year	Computerworld *(USA)*	Straits Times *(Singapore)*
Q3 (July) 1990	35	34
Q4 (October) 1990	25	33
Q1 (January) 1991	41	27
Q2 (April) 1991	56	11
Q3 (July) 1991	31	34
Q4 (October) 1991	28	19
Q1 (January) 1992	58	27
Q2 (April) 1992	38	28
Q3 (July) 1992	29	14
Q4 (October) 1992	34	17
Q1 (January) 1993	52	36
Q2 (April) 1993	51	26
Total	478	306

(1) Full employment (Employ) where the potential job applicant enters into an employment relationship with a company whose main business is other than in IS consulting (Figure 16.1). An archetypal job is one where the IS worker is employed to work in the internal information systems department of a manufacturing or service firm.

(2) Quasi-contract (Quasi) where the potential job applicant enters into an employment relationship with a company whose main business is in IS consulting (Figure 16.2). A prototypical job is one where the applicant is employed by the consulting firm (e.g. Arthur Anderson), but his or her skills are employed by clients of the consulting firm.

(3) Employment agency (Agency) where the potential job applicant is hired by employment agency which either contracts the applicant out to client firms on a permanent basis; or contracts the applicant out to client firms

Source: Ang and Slaughter (1995)

Figure 16.1 *Traditional IS employment relationship (Employ)*

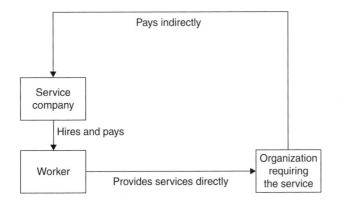

Source: Ang and Slaughter (1995)

Figure 16.2 *IS employee leasing work relationship (Quasi)*

on a temporary basis (Figure 16.3). In the case of contracting the applicant out to client firms on a permanent basis, the employment agency
acts on behalf of its client in the selection and screening process. In the
case of contracting the applicant out to client firms on a temporary basis,
the employment agency enters into a contractual relationship with each
potential applicant who, in turn, works for the client of the employment
agency. Thus, the job applicant is typically self-employed, using the
agency as a source of contract work.

(4) Contract work (Contract) where the potential job applicant is contracted
directly by a firm requiring his or her IS services (Figure 16.4).

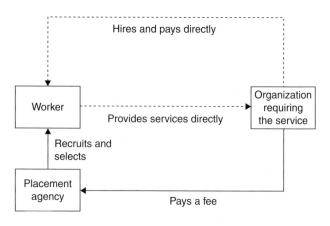

Source: Ang and Slaughter (1995)

Figure 16.3   *IS placement agency relationship (Agency)*

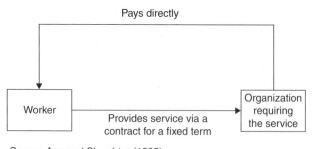

Source: Ang and Slaughter (1995)

Figure 16.4   *IS contract work relationship (Contract)*

Coding reliability

Two coders were given the above employment structure scheme and its description. Before the coders coded the stratified samples of advertisements from *Computerworld* and *Straits Times*, random samples of job advertisements from issues of *Computerworld* and *Straits Times* outside the July 1990–April 1993 period were used by the coders to achieve sufficient inter-coder reliability regarding the categories of employment structure. Initially the coders independently coded a random sample of ten advertisements each from *Computerworld* and *Straits Times*. After the independent coding, the Cohen coefficient of agreement for nominal scales was computed (Cohen, 1960) to assess the relative agreement between the coders. Differences in coding the employment advertisements were resolved, and the coders independently coded another round of ten advertisements each from *Computerworld* and *Straits Times*. After the second round of independent coding, agreement between the coders was 100 per cent with regards to employment structures. Subsequently, advertisements from *Computerworld* and *Straits Times* from the July 1990–April 1993 quarters were divided between the coders and the advertisements coded independently. Examples of coded advertisements are shown in Figure 16.5.

Results

Table 16.2 shows the number of advertisements in the different categories of employment structures across *Computerworld* and *Straits Times*. A chi-square analysis was conducted on the data in Table 16.2 to analyse if the proportion of employment structures found in *Computerworld* differed significantly from those in *Straits Times*. The chi-square of 84.7 (df = 1) was significant at $p < 0.0000$. Overall, *Computerworld* reflected a significantly greater proportion of non-Employ employment structures than *Straits Times*.

To assess if proportions within each individual employment structure differed across the two sources of advertisements, chi-square analyses were performed on each of the four employment structures independently. Tables 16.3–6 reflect the proportion of each employment structure in both *Computerworld* and *Straits Times*. The resultant chi-square analyses showed that, independently, the proportion of each employment structure in *Computerworld* and *Straits Times* differed significantly.

We then traced the pattern of each employment structure over the 12 quarters. From Tables 16.7 and 16.8 (illustrated graphically in Figures 16.6 and 16.7, respectively), the proportion of employ to other employment structures declined dramatically in the last three quarters in *Computerworld* (from an average of about 65 per cent from late 1991 to the middle of 1992, to about 48 per cent from late 1992 to the middle of 1993). In *Straits Times*, the

Employer

Senior
Programmer Analyst

Systems development and support, as well as operational responsibilities. Job requires extensive knowledge of PowerHouse, VAX VMS, DECnet and PATHWORKS in a financial applications environment. Operations and system management experience desirable. Minimum 7–10 years programming and analysis experience required. Call or write for application.

Pennichuck Water Works
DP Job Search, 4 Water St, PO Box 448
Nashua, NH 03061-0448
603-882-5191
Fax: 603-882-4125

Agency

No Downtime
One résumé – 100's of
Assignment Possibilities

Keep working by simply forwarding a résumé to our National Recruiting Center and The Experts will electronically distribute it to their national branches, network affiliates and franchise locations. Get a world of attention with just one contact.

Our programmers and software engineering employees enjoy weekly pay, a wide variety of projects, résumé and interview guidance, a star treatment. Many positions are salaried with benefits.

Here are a few of this week's requirements:

- HP 3000 Cognos
- AS 400 RPG III
- IBM IDMS/ADSO
- Power Builder
- SAS
- OS/2C
- CICS DB2
- IMS DB/DC
- INIX C & C++
- SOL Server
- VTAM, Netview
- APS
- VAX/VMS
- TOTAL/SUPRA
- SYBASE
- RS 6000/AIX/C

At the Experts – time is money!! Don't waste either – fax or mail résumé immediately to The Experts National Recruiting Center, 200 Reservoir St, Needham, MA 02194, (617) 444 716.

The Experts
... "It Takes One to Know One"

Quasi

PUT 20 YEARS
OF EXPERIENCE
TO WORK FOR YOU!

DataMasters, a dynamic employment consulting firm, has current contract requirements in the Southeast. Excellent oportunities exist within the following state-of-the-art environments:

VAX: ORACLE/UNIX/ C /SOL • FORMS • INGRES/UNIX/ C
BASIS PLUS

IBM: D82/ADABAS/NATURAL/TESSERACT
IMS D8/DC & DB2 • DB2/CSP • AS/400/RPG3
MS-WINDOWS • HOGAN or AFS

Other: POWERBUILDER • TERADATA • OBJECT VISION

DataMasters offers competitive rates and excellent benefits. Please call or send résumé to:

DM DataMasters®
P.O. Box 14548, Dept. CW6
Greensboro, NC 27415-4548
1-800-DataMasters
FAX 1-919-373-1501
Since 1971 Internationally Affiliated EOE

Contract

Software Consultant: Design, develop, test and implement financial and banking applications using Paradox 3.5 & 4.0. QuattroPro, Lotus Notes, Autotester, C++, PAL and Pascal on Intel 386/486 machines in MS-Windows environment. Consult with end users, perform systems analysis and prepare development specifications. Manage projects and direct applications training and maintenance (troubleshooting, modifications and documentation). Some projects performed at client site in various geographic locations. 40 hrs/week, 8.15 a.m. to 5.00 p.m. $42,000 per year. Minimum requirements: Masters in Business Administration in Computer Science, MIS or Finance. Must have at least 2 years' experience in a job offered or 2 years' experience as a Systems Engineer and/or Systems Analyst. Experience must include development, implementation and testing of financial applications (at least 1 year of which must be in banking applications) and project management. Must have completed project work in each of the following areas: 1) Cost-benefit analysis of MIS needs and development and presentation of recommendations for action; 2) Computer security in Networks; 3) Use of PAL, Autotester and Lotus Notes in Windows environment. Project work may be completed as a sole performer or as a team member. Must of completed one course in each of the following: 1) Distributed Processing and Telecommunications Systems 2) Computers Methods in Management 3) Computers and Microprocessors 4) Corporate finance. Must be willing to travel to client site for extended periods. Résumé required. Must have proof of legal authority to work permanently in the US. SEND 2 COPIES OF RÉSUMÉ TO THE ILLINOIS DEPARTMENT OF EMPLOYMENT SECURITY, 401 South State Street – 3 South Chicago, Illinois 60605. Attention: Len Boksa. Reference #V-IL 10335-B. NO CALLS. AN EMPLOYER PAID AD.

Source: Computerworld (1995b)

Figure 16.5 *Examples of advertisements coded for employment structure*

Table 16.2   *Overall counts and proportions of employment structures in the USA* (Computerworld) *and Singapore* (Straits Times)

Employment structure	Computerworld number	Computerworld (%)	Straits Times number	Straits Times (%)	Total number	Total (%)
Employ	291	0.609	278	0.909	569	0.726
Quasi	42	0.088	4	0.013	46	0.059
Agency	96	0.200	16	0.052	112	0.143
Contract	49	0.103	8	0.026	57	0.072
Total	478	1.000	306	1.000	784	1.000

Table 16.3   *Proportion of "Employ" structure across the USA* (Computerworld) *and Singapore* (Straits Times)

Employment structure	Computerworld number	Computerworld (%)	Straits Times number	Straits Times (%)	Total number	Total (%)
Employ	291	0.609	278	0.908	569	0.726
Not-employ	187	0.391	28	0.092	215	0.274
Total	478	1.000	306	1.000	784	1.000

Note: Chi-square = 84.2 (df = 1), $p < 0.00001$

Table 16.4   *Proportion of "Quasi" structure across the USA* (Computerworld) *and Singapore* (Straits Times)

Employment structure	Computerworld number	Computerworld (%)	Straits Times number	Straits Times (%)	Total number	Total (%)
Quasi	42	0.088	4	0.013	46	0.059
Not-quasi	436	0.912	302	0.987	738	0.941
Total	478	1.000	306	1.000	784	1.000

Note: Chi-square = 18.89 (df = 1), $p < 0.0009$

Table 16.5   *Proportion of "Agency" structure across the USA* (Computerworld) *and Singapore* (Straits Times)

Employment structure	Computerworld number	Computerworld (%)	Straits Times number	Straits Times (%)	Total number	Total (%)
Agency	96	0.201	16	0.052	112	0.143
Not-agency	382	0.799	290	0.948	672	0.857
Total	478	1.000	306	1.000	784	1.000

Note: Chi-square = 33.6 (df = 1), $p < 0.00000$

Table 16.6   *Proportion of "Contract" structure across the USA* (Computerworld) *and Singapore* (Straits Times)

Employment structure	Computerworld number	Computerworld (%)	Straits Times number	Straits Times (%)	Total number	Total (%)
Contract	49	0.103	8	0.026	57	0.073
Not-contract	429	0.897	298	0.974	727	0.927
Total	478	1.000	306	1.000	784	1.000

Note: Chi-square = 16.14 (df = 1), $p < 0.00006$

proportion of employ to other employment structures remained-stable at over 90 per cent across many quarters, dipping to about 80 per cent only in the last quarter – April 1993.

In absolute numbers, quasi, agency, and contract incidents remain relatively sparse in *Straits Times,* totalling only 28 out a total 306 employment structures. In contrast, the number of quasi and contract employment structures rose dramatically in *Computerworld*, especially in the last three quarters. The average percentage of quasi to total employment structures was about 18.6 per cent in the last three quarters compared with an average of less than 10 per cent in other quarters. The average percentage of contract to total employment structures was about 16.5 per cent in the last two quarters compared with an average of less than 10 per cent in other quarters. For the agency employment structures, the trend is less discernible, with peaks at quarters 3 (1/91), 5 (7/91), 6 (10/91), 9 (7/92), and 11 (1/93).

Table 16.7 *Pattern of employment structures across time in the USA (Computerworld)*

Quarter	1	2	3	4	5	6	7	8	9	10	11	12
E#	24	15	20	45	17	17	40	25	21	16	25	26
%	0.686	0.600	0.488	0.804	0.548	0.607	0.690	0.658	0.724	0.471	0.481	0.51
Q#	1	1	1	4	3	0	4	4	0	10	7	7
%	0.029	0.040	0.024	0.071	0.097	0.000	0.069	0.105	0.000	0.294	0.135	0.14
A#	7	4	13	5	9	8	11	6	7	5	12	9
%	0.200	0.160	0.317	0.089	0.290	0.286	0.190	0.158	0.241	0.147	0.231	0.18
C#	3	5	7	2	2	3	3	3	1	3	8	9
%	0.086	0.200	0.171	0.036	0.065	0.107	0.052	0.079	0.034	0.088	0.154	0.18
T#	35	25	41	56	31	28	58	38	29	34	52	51
%	1.00	1.00	1.00	1.00	1.00	1.00	1.00	1.00	1.00	1.00	1.00	1.00

Note: E = employ, Q = quasi, A = agency, C = contract, T = total; # = number of advertisements; % = proportion of total advertisements

Table 16.8 *Pattern of employment structures across time in Singapore* (Straits Times)

Quarter	1	2	3	4	5	6	7	8	9	10	11	12
E#	31	28	26	8	33	16	26	26	13	16	34	21
%	0.912	0.848	0.963	0.727	0.971	0.842	0.963	0.929	0.929	0.941	0.944	0.81
Q#	0	0	0	0	0	0	1	1	0	0	0	2
%	0.000	0.000	0.000	0.000	0.000	0.000	0.037	0.036	0.000	0.000	0.000	0.08
A#	1	4	1	3	1	3	0	1	1	0	0	1
%	0.029	0.121	0.037	0.273	0.029	0.158	0.000	0.036	0.071	0.000	0.000	0.04
C#	2	1	0	0	0	0	0	0	0	1	2	2
%	0.059	0.030	0.000	0.000	0.000	0.000	0.000	0.000	0.000	0.059	0.056	0.08
T#	34	33	27	11	34	19	27	28	14	17	36	26
%	1.00	1.00	1.00	1.00	1.00	1.00	1.00	1.00	1.00	1.00	1.00	1.0

Note: E = employ, Q = quasi, A = agency, C = contract, T = total; # = number of advertisements; % = proportion of total advertisements

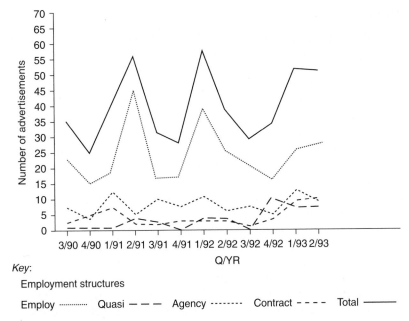

Figure 16.6 *Employment structures across time for the USA* (Computerworld)

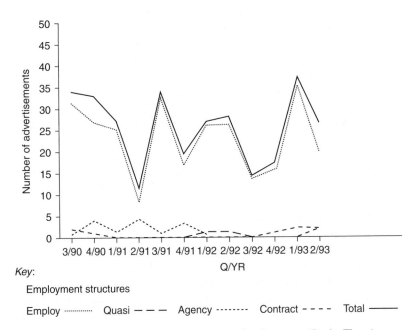

Figure 16.7 *Employment structures across time for Singapore* (Straits Times)

Discussion

Overall, we find that the proportion of types of employment structures differs between the USA and Singapore, as reflected by the job advertisements found in *Computerworld* and *Straits Times*, respectively, from July 1990, through April 1993.

IS jobs in the USA appear to be more varied in their employment structures than in Singapore. Specifically, the increasing use of more externalized forms of employment structures in the USA seems to confirm a general trend towards greater reliance on contracting for immediate IS skills requirements (such as using IS consultants from consulting firms, or direct independent contract workers) rather than retaining IS skills in the form of a more permanent employment relationship. This trend may be in response to an increasingly volatile environment where there is an economic imperative to acquire quickly the necessary skills at the lowest cost (Fierman, 1994; Tilly, 1991). In fact, externalized employment structures provide a more rapid and economic means of skill repositioning in light of short-lived technologies than internal efforts to curb skills erosion of incumbents (Powell, 1990). In addition, societal values of individualism and free enterprise in the USA favour externalized IS employment, because independent IS workers can function profitably as economic units. It may also be that a higher level of skills in entrepreneurship is prevalent among workers in the USA, enabling more independent contracting, or that the social network creates more opportunities for private consulting.

In Singapore, the traditional employment relationship for acquiring IS skills persists. One potential explanation is the force of cultural values of belongingness and loyalty which favour working as a group (as opposed to individually) as well as long-term employment relationships within a firm. Another possible explanation may be the general shortage of IS workers in Singapore (Neo, 1993) which causes firms to offer attractive compensation packages to induce IS workers to remain in full-time employment with the firm, rather than to be self-employed as contract workers or being employed via an employment agency. In addition to attractive compensation packages offered by independent firms, Singapore has a national savings scheme, the Central Provident Fund (CPF), for all employees. Employees can draw on the Fund on retirement or for a number of other long-term investments[3]. From the worker's point of view, the benefit fund may provide an incentive to prefer traditional permanent employment to independent work because of the increase in salary from the employer's contribution to the fund. Moreover, as uncertainty avoiders, workers in Singapore may be attracted to greater security of a long-term employment relationship with a firm rather than a series of short-term contractual relations with many firms (Chew and Chew, 1992).

These findings have implications for future directions in IS personnel research. Evidence of increased externalization in the USA suggests that issues such as how to manage and motivate external IS workers and how to allocate resources and tasks effectively between temporary and permanent IS workers may become significant and fruitful areas for further study. Additional study of the antecedents of the IS externalization phenomenon, including the impact of cultural factors, would also be instructive. For example, future studies could examine the critical dimensions of the cultural and economic environment and attempt to link them to evolving IS employment structures in different nations. These kinds of investigations could provide a better understanding of how and why differing employment structures emerge in the IS workplace and how they can be effectively managed.

Notes

1. *Computerworld* claims to reach more computer professionals each week than any other journal of its kind (*Computerworld*, 1992a). Job advertisements in *Computerworld* differ by region. For this sample, we used the Computerworld which reflected job advertisements in the Eastern portion of the USA. The Eastern region represents the largest number of *Computerworld* subscriptions for the USA (40 per cent of the total number of subscriptions). Thus, the sample is restricted only to advertisements pertaining to the Eastern region of the USA and may not necessarily reflect IS job advertisements in the Mid-western and Western parts of the USA.
2. *Straits Times* is a daily newspaper. More job advertisements appear on Saturday than on any other day of the week. Accordingly, Saturday was chosen as the day to sample IS job advertisements.
3. The CPF scheme is compulsory. The employer has to contribute an additional 20–25 per cent of the employee's salary to the fund each month. As the CPF contribution by the employer adds 20–25 per cent to the base salary received by an employee, it may therefore be more attractive for workers in Singapore to work as employees rather than as independent workers.

References and further reading

Ang, S. (1991), "The etiology of information systems outsourcing", paper presented at Information and Decision Sciences Workshop, University of Minnesota, 8 March.

Ang, S. and S. Slaughter (1995), "Alternative emloyment structures in information systems: a conceptual analysis", *ACM/SIGCPR Conference Proceedings,* April.

Bakke, E. W. (1954), *Labor Mobility and Economic Opportunity*. MIT Press, Cambridge, MA.

Baroudi, J. J. (1985), "The impact of role variables on IS personnel work attitudes and intentions," *MIS Quarterly*, Vol. 9, No. 4, December, pp. 341–356.

Bartol, K. M. (1983), "Turnover among DP personnel: a causal analysis," *Communications of the ACM*, Vol. 26, No. 10, pp. 807–811.

Bartol, K. M. and D. C. Martin (1982), "Managing information systems personnel: a review of the literature and managerial implications," *MIS Quarterly*, Vol. 7, No. 2, special issue, pp. 49–70.

Bond, M. H. and G. Hofstede (1989), "The cash value of Confucian values," *Human Systems Management*, Vol. 8, No. 3, pp. 195–199.

Bunke, H. C. (1990), "More about the United States and some about Singapore," *Business Horizons*, March/April, pp. 6–9.

Burn, J., K. B. C. Saxena, L. Ma, and H. K. Cheung (1993), "Critical issues of IS Management in Hong Kong: a cultural comparison," *Journal of Global Information Management*, Vol. 1, No. 4, Autumn, pp. 28–37.

Chamber of Commerce of the United States (1991), *Employee Benefits: 1991 Edition*, Report No. A3840-1, Publication No. 0289.

Chew, S. B. and R. Chew (1992), *The Singapore Worker: a Profile*. Oxford University Press, Singapore.

Coase, R. H. (1937), "The nature of the firm," *Economica*, Vol. 4, November, pp. 386–405.

Cohen, J. (1960), "A coefficient of agreement for nominal scales," *Educational and Psychological Measurement*, Vol. 20, No. 1, pp. 37–46.

Commons, J. R. (1934), *Institutional Economics*. University of Wisconsin Press, Madison, WI.

Computerworld (1989), "Outsourcing: the great debate," *Computerworld*, Vol. 23, No. 49, December 11, pp. 69, 72, 74.

Computerworld (1992a), "Computer careers section," *Computerworld*, Vol. 26, No. 40, October, pp. 99–100.

Computerworld (1992b), "Computer careers section," *Computerworld*, 28, December, pp. 120–131.

Couger, J. D. (1986), "Effect of cultural differences on motivation of analysts and programmers: Singapore versus the United States," *MIS Quarterly*, Vol. 10, No. 2, June, pp. 188–196.

Couger, J. D. and R. A. Zawacki (1980), *Motivating and Managing Computer Personnel*. Wiley, New York, NY.

Doeringer, P. B. and M. J. Piore (1971), *Internal Labor Markets and Manpower Analysis*. Heath, Lexington, MA.

Economist (1993), Special report, Vol. 329, No. 7833, 16 October, p. 80.

Edwards, R. (1979), *Contested Terrain: the Transformation of the Workplace in the Twentieth Century*. Basic Books, New York, NY.

Ferratt, T. W. and L. E. Short (1986), "Are information systems people different: an investigation of motivational differences," *MIS Quarterly*, Vol. 10, No. 4, December, pp. 377–387.

Ferratt, T. W. and L. E. Short (1988), "Are information systems people different? An investigation of how they are and should be managed," *MIS Quarterly*, Vol. 12, No. 3, September, pp. 427–443.

Fierman, J. (1994), "The contingency workforce," *Fortune*, Vol. 129, No. 2, January 24, pp. 24–29.

Gamst, F. C. and E. Norbeck (1976), *Ideas of Culture*. Holt, Rinehart and Winston, New York, NY.

Goldstein, D. K. and J. F. Rockart (1989), "An examination of work-related correlates of job satisfaction in programmer/analysts," *MIS Quarterly*, Vol. 8, No. 2, June, pp. 103–115.

Guimaraes, T. and M. Igbaria (1992), "Determinants of turnover intentions: comparing IC and IS personnel," *Information Systems Research*, Vol. 3, No. 3, pp. 273–303.

Hamilton, G. G. and N. W. Biggart (1988), "Market, culture and authority: a comparative analysis of management and organization in the Far East," *American Journal of Sociology*, Vol. 94, pp. S52–S94.

Handy, C. (1989), *The Age of Unreason*. Harvard Business Press, Cambridge, MA.

Hofstede, G. (1991), *Cultures and Organizations: Software of the Mind*. McGraw-Hill, New York, NY.

Igbaria, M. and S. R. Siegel (1993), "The career decision of information systems people," *Information and Management*, Vol. 24, No. 1, pp. 23–32.

Igbaria, M. and W. M. Wormley (1992), "Organizational experiences and career success of MIS professionals and managers: an examination of race differences," *MIS Quarterly*, Vol. 16, No. 4, pp. 507–529.

Igbaria, M., J. H. Greenhaus, and S. Parasuraman (1991), "Career orientations of MIS employees: an empirical analysis," *MIS Quarterly*, Vol. 15, No. 2, pp. 150–169.

Kanter, R. M. (1983), *The Change Masters: Innovation and Productivity in the American Corporation*. Simon and Schuster, New York, NY.

Korzeniowski, P. (1990), "MIS belt being pulled tighter," *Software Magazine*, August, pp. 45–50.

Krippendorff, K. (1980), *Content Analysis: An Introduction to Its Methodology*, Sage Commtext Series, Sage Publications, Newbury Park, CA.

Leinfuss, E. (1991), "How outsourcing impacts IS managers (Part I)," *Computerworld*, Vol. 25, No. 37, September, p. 113.

Mangum, G., D. Mayall, and K. Nelson (1985), "The temporary help industry: a response to the dual internal labor market," *Industrial and Labour Relations Review*, Vol. 38, No. 4, July, pp. 599–611.

Neo, B. S. (1993), "Development of IT human resources: trends and practices in Singapore," *1993 Pan Pacific Conference on Information Systems,* Kaoshiung, Taiwan, Republic of China, 30 May–1 June, pp. 107–112.

Niederman, F. and J. Trower (1993), "Influence of organization type on IS personnel roles and performance," *Proceedings of the 1993 ACM SIGCPR Conference,* March.

Niederman, F., J. C. Brancheau, and J. C. Wetherbe (1991), "Information systems management issues in the 1990s," *MIS Quarterly,* Vol. 15, No. 4, pp. 475–495.

Pfeffer, J. and J. Baron (1988), "Taking the workers back out: recent trends in the structuring of employment," *Research in Organizational Behaviour,* Vol. 10, pp. 257–303.

Powell, W. W. (1990), "Neither market nor hierarchy: network forms of organizing," *Research in Organizational Behaviour,* Vol. 12, pp. 295–336.

Rouzer, W. R. (1992), "Mainframe programmers look to avoid fate of the dinosaur," *Computerworld,* Vol. 26, No. 3, 26 October, p. 138.

Scott, W. R. (1992), *Organizations: Rational, Natural and Open Systems,* 3rd ed. Prentice-Hall, Englewood Cliffs, NJ.

Scott-Morton, M. (1991), *The Corporation of the 1990s: Information Technology and Organizational Transformation.* Oxford University Press, New York, NY.

Smircich, L. (1983), "Concepts of culture and organizational analysis," *Administrative Science Quarterly,* Vol. 28, No. 3, pp. 339–358.

Straub, D. (1994), "The effect of culture on IT diffusion: EMail and Fax in Japan and the US," *Information Systems Research,* Vol. 5, No. 1, March, pp. 23–47.

Tan, M. and M. Igbaria (1994), "Turnover and remuneration of information technology professionals in Singapore," *Information and Management,* Vol. 26, No. 4, pp. 219–229.

Tilly, C. (1991), "Reasons for the continuing growth of part-time employment," *Monthly Labour Review,* March, pp. 10–18.

US Department of Labor (1989), *Occupational Outlook Handbook.* Bureau of Labour Statistics, Government Printing Office, Washington, DC.

Williamson, O. (1975), *Markets and Hierarchies.* Free Press, New York, NY.

Williamson, O. (1980), "The organization of work: a comparative institutional assessment," *Journal of Economic Behaviour and Organization,* Vol. 1, No. 1, pp. 5–38.

Williamson, O. (1981), "The economics of organization: the transaction cost approach," *American Journal of Sociology,* Vol. 87, No. 3, pp. 548–577.

Williamson, O. (1983), "Organization form, residual claimants and corporate control," *Journal of Law and Economics,* Vol. 36, No. 1, pp. 351–366.

Williamson, O. (1985), *The Economic Institution of Capitalism.* Free Press, New York, NY.

Yourdon, E. (1992), *Decline and Fall of the American Programmer*. Yourdon
Press, Englewood Cliffs, NJ.

Reproduced from *Information Technology and People*, Vol. 8, No. 2, 1995,
pp. 17–36. Reprinted with permission from Emerald.

Questions for discussion

1   How do the cultural and economic influences theorized by the author in
the USA and Singapore comment on meritocracy, i.e. the best worker
should be paid the most money?
2   What other factors can you think of that might have contributed to the
difference found in the study result?
3   Consider the relative pay levels of the contract worker vs. the full-time
worker in each country. Would that have an effect on the study result?
Why or why not?
4   Consider the reputation of contract work vs. full-time work in each country. What is the social stigma attached to each type of work? Would that
affect the study result?
5   Which type of worker do you want to be? How does that reflect your values and how much you expect to be paid for each type of work?

17 Understanding an Organization's View of the CIO: The Role of Assumptions About IT

Michelle L. Kaarst-Brown

Executive Summary

At the 2003 Society for Information Management's (SIM) annual meeting in New York City, many of the sessions focused on what CIOs could do once they got a seat with their business peers at the executive meeting table. Heightened concerns about information security and legislative compliance have increased interest in the answer.

Despite the importance of IT to modern organizations, many IT executives are still not at that table because they are not viewed as equal to their business peers. Even elevating IT executives to C-level management and giving them the title of Chief Information Officer (CIO) do not guarantee that they are accepted and invited to high-level business meetings.

This article provides one perspective on why some organizations are more open than others to affording their CIO an effective, influential, senior executive role. Our conclusion: Dominant assumptions about IT in different areas of an enterprise can explain differences in CIO status. Five assumptions that matter are:

1. Who should control IT direction
2. How central IT is seen to business strategy
3. The value placed on IT knowledge
4. Justifications for investing in IT
5. Who are deemed winners and losers when a new IT system is installed.

This article explores these assumptions, and the IT clusters they form, to help CIOs and other senior IT executive better address the different "assumption environments" they face.

Why status matters

In 1985, Benjamin et al. wrote about the changing role of the Chief Information Officer (CIO).[1] They argued that the creation of the CIO position demonstrated that the status of IT executives was being elevated and integrated into top management. Paradoxically, twenty years later, one of the major problems many CIOs face is a lower perception of their IT function's status than other business units.[2]

Although there is little argument that IT has become integral to the strategic operation of most organizations, this in itself seems to have little to do with the status of the CIO (and the other senior IT executives) or the business' perceptions of the IT function overall. Status is more than a large office or special parking privileges. It is recognition from the organization, or at least key parts of it, of the IT function's capabilities and value.

A presentation at a recent conference was particularly telling. The CIO recounted the multi-million-dollar cost savings a new systems portfolio management program brought the company. But then he admitted that he was still working to get the top business people on his side. When asked "Why?" he replied, "IT is still not viewed as an equal at our firm, and we have to keep proving ourselves."[3] At another meeting, consultants, IT executives, and IT academics debated quite heatedly over whether the IT function was a second-class citizen and poor cousin to the business units. Sadly, the overwhelming consensus was that IT was all too frequently excluded or unwelcome in key decisions, such as setting organizational strategy.

The importance of status and credibility of CIOs and their IT organization go beyond job satisfaction. Status and credibility affect an organization's ability to extract value from its IT investments. Armstrong and Sambamurthy[4] found that a CIO's membership on the top management team and frequent informal interactions with business executives were almost as important to a firm's successful assimilation of IT as the other executives' level of IT knowledge. Business executives with greater IT knowledge can better assess a CIO's credibility and better leverage IT. Yet, having the CIO at the table was almost equally valuable.

Other researchers note similar findings. One is that CIOs who influence their executive peers using rational persuasion and personal appeal generated

[1]Benjamin, R.I., C. Dickinson, Jr., and J.F. Rockart, "Changing Role of the Corporate Information Systems Officer," *MIS Quarterly*, 1985, 9(3), p 177.
[2]Levinson, M., "CIO and CEO: How To Work With Your Boss," *CIO Magazine*, 2004, 18(1), p 1.
[3]2003, identity concealed.
[4]Armstrong, C.P. and V. Sambamurthy, "Information Technology Assimilation in Firms: The Influence of Senior Leadership and IT Infrastructures," *Information Systems Research*, 1999, 10(4), pp 304–327.

peer commitment, whereas those who used negotiated exchange or pressure encountered peer resistance.[5,6]

Business executives who view their IT peers as having lower status invite negative outcomes for their enterprise: IT executives may not be involved in IT-related planning, which can lead to important oversights. IT may not be able to align with business objectives because IT management is not privy to them. IT may not receive the critical resources it needs because top management does not fully understand IT's role. And, top executives may continue to question whether or not IT delivers business value because they do not realize that value creation requires their involvement as well.[7,8]

Achieving high status and a seat at the top management table does not solve a CIO's problems, however. In fact, it presents a different set of challenges that need to be managed. Nevertheless, the bottom line is that IT executives' status matters.

A cultural explanation of CIO status

There are many common explanations for the low status of particular IT executives. To name only a few, they include: personality conflicts, a lack of corporate technology vision, poorly aligned IT goals, lack of business knowledge, lack of IT awareness among the business executives, incorrect formal structure and reporting relationships, even the location of the CIO's office. Communication ability and relationship with the CEO can influence perceptions of the CIO and the IT function as a whole.[9,10] Organizational history with IT successes and failures, shared plans, and social factors can also affect relationships between CIOs and business executives.[11]

However, something deeper is going on here. CIOs' status may be low even when they are co-located with business peers, have an MBA degree, are

[5]Enns, H.G., S.L. Huff, and C.A. Higgins, "CIO Lateral Influence Behaviors: Gaining Peers' Commitment to Strategic Information Systems", *MIS Quarterly,* 2003, 27(1), pp 155–174.

[6]Chan, Y., "Why Haven't We Mastered Alignment? The Importance of the Informal Organizational Structure," *MISQ Executive,* 2002, 1(2), pp 97–112.

[7]Ibid.

[8]Wheeler, B.C., G.M. Marakus, and P. Brinkley, "From Back Room to Boardroom: Repositioning Global IT By Educating the Line to Lead at British American Tobacco," *MISQ Executive,* 2002, 1(1), pp 47–62.

[9]Stephens, C.S., "Five CIOs at Work: Folklore and Facts Revisited," *Journal of Systems Management,* 1993, 44(3), p 34.

[10]Op. cit. Enns, et al, 2003.

[11]Reich, B.H. and I. Benbasat, "Measuring the linkage between business and information technology objectives." *MIS Quarterly,* 1996, 20(1), pp. 55–81. Also see: Armstrong and Sambamurthy, 1999, and Enns, et al, 2003.

surrounded by tech-savvy business executives, and have great personal charisma.[12] What, therefore, is the underlying cause?

One explanation is that an enterprise's history with IT becomes embedded in its culture. Organizational culture can influence all aspects of IT development, implementation, and managements.[13,14,15,16,17] But culture is very difficult to define and assess. By focusing on the underlying assumptions that shape culture – specifically the assumptions related to IT – we can narrow our attention to a few key assumptions that provide insights into CIO status and the relationship of the IT function with the rest of the enterprise.

Assumptions about IT

Our research uncovered five categories of "underlying assumptions"[18] about IT that affect the status of IT executives and their IT function, and therefore affect the resulting strategic management of IT. Just as organizational culture can account for differential treatment of women in management,[19] so too can assumptions about IT account for differences in treatment of the IT function and its leaders.[20,21]

---

[12]A new CIO at a research site moved his office up to the executive floor to be co-located with his business peers and increase his informal interaction with them. His personal efforts went a long way to improve already good relationships, but his assumptions about the role of IT and the IT function conflicted with those held by those other executives and departments heads.

[13]Gordon, G.G., "Industry Determinants of Organizational Culture," *Academy of Management Review,* 1991, 16(2), pp 396–415.

[14]Gordon, G.G., "The Relationship of Corporate Culture to Industry Sector and Corporate Performance," in *Gaining Control of the Corporate Future,* R.H. Kilmann, et al. (Editors), 1985, Jossey-Bass.

[15]Kaarst-Brown, M., "A Theory of Information Technology Cultures: Magic Dragons, Wizards, and Archetypal Patterns," 1995, York University.

[16]Kaarst-Brown, M.L. and D. Robey, "More on Myth, Magic and Metaphor: Cultural Insights into the Management of Information Technology in Organizations," *Information Technology & People,* 1999, 12(2), pp 192–217.

[17]Kaarst-Brown, M.L. and J.R.E. Evaristo, "International Cultures and Insights Into Global Electronic Commerce," in *Global Information Technology and Electronic Commerce,* P. Palvia, S. Palvia, and E. Roche (Editors), 2002, Ivey Publishing.

[18]Underlying assumptions are what Edgar H. Schein, a well-known culture researcher, would refer to as the deep structure of culture. See also Schein, E.H., *Organizational Culture and Leadership: A Dynamic View,* 1985, San Francisco, CA: Jossey Bass, and Schein, E.H., *Organizational Culture and Leadership,* Second edition, Management Series, 1992, San Francisco: Jossey-Bass Inc.

[19]Hood, J.N. and C.S. Koberg, "Patterns of Differential Assimilation and Acculturation for Women in Business Organizations", *Human Relations,* 1994, 47(2), pp 159–181.

[20]Op. cit. Kaarst-Brown, 1995.

[21]Op. cit. Kaarst-Brown and Robey, 1999.

We uncovered these assumptions, and the clusters they form, mainly by studying IT-related assumptions in 31 departments or operating units of two large insurance companies. We recorded their history and experiences with IT from their first system through their recent exploration of Web-based applications.[22]

The two firms studied

The two firms – called "Alpha Corp." and "Gamma Corp." (pseudonyms) – had their first experiences with IT about the same time: the mid-1960s and early 1970s. However, they had very different experiences, as did their various IT leaders, due to the different dominant assumptions about IT that developed in them.

Alpha Corp. was established over one hundred years ago. Its earliest experience with IT came in the late 1960s when it acquired a smaller, but innovative, firm. Alpha moved deeply into IT in the early 1970s when it automated many of its policy issuing and administration processes.

Gamma Corp., on the other hand, was established in the early 1970s by government mandate. It relied on IT from the beginning.

From 1989–1992, Alpha had approximately one-third the revenue of Gamma. Alpha's IT department of 55 was about one-sixth the size of Gamma's at that time, even though it had about half the employees and a similar number of branch offices. Alpha's revenues were about $300 million versus $1.2 billion for Gamma in 1992. Since that time, Alpha has been involved in a steady series of mergers and acquisitions, with final revenues of both firms reaching $2.9 billion in 2003.

While the management environments differed for the IT leaders, both companies exhibited the same five clusters of assumptions about IT. Both had similar functional divisions. Yet, the relationships and status assessments of the IT function and the senior IT executives varied depending on the assumptions of the business units and the groups within the IT organization. An interesting point is that even though the personalities of the senior IT executives differed significantly throughout the years of our study, these differences did not change the consistency of the assumptions about IT nor the perceived stature of the senior IT executives. Also, the assumptions did not coalesce over time into a single dominant cluster at either firm; rather, all five clusters continued at both firms.

The five categories of assumptions about IT

The five assumption categories important to CIO status and IT management are:

1) Control assumptions – Who should control IT direction?
2) Centrality assumptions – How central is IT to business strategy?

---

[22]A description of the research is found in the Appendix.

Assumption category	Description
CONTROL Assumptions – Who controls IT direction?	Assumptions about organizational level or functional group that should control decisions about IT direction. These assumptions do not refer to a single individual, but rather to a position or group.
CENTRALITY Assumptions – How central is IT to business strategy?	Assumptions about the significance of IT to business strategy. These assumptions focus on past and future success or survival of either an entire organization or particular organizational units.
IT SKILLS VALUE Assumptions – What is the value of IT skills and knowledge?	Assumptions about the value or lack of value placed on IT skills and knowledge among different groups or levels.
JUSTIFICATION Assumptions – What justifies further IT investment?	Assumptions about the purposes for which IT should be used that justify further IT investment.
BENEFICIARIES of IT Assumptions – Who benefits or loses when IT is used?	Assumptions about who wins or loses as a result of IT development or adoption. Winners and losers are defined broadly, but cover the full range of stakeholder groups from employees to customers.

Figure 17.1   *Assumptions that influence CIO and IT status*

3) IT Skill Value assumptions – What is the value of IT skills and knowledge at different organizational levels?
4) Justification assumptions – What justifies further IT investment?
5) Beneficiaries assumptions – Who benefits and who loses when IT is used?

Figure 17.1 provides descriptions of each category.

Throughout our research, we heard a variety of assumptions that varied in wording and emphasis. We synthesized this into a spectrum of five dominant assumptions for each category.

Control assumptions. Given the volume of literature that links power with change or power with IT, it was not surprising that assumptions about control over IT direction emerged quite strongly at both companies.

The spectrum of five assumptions in this category were that IT direction should be controlled by the IT function, corporate executives, business units, IT and user groups together, or no one at all (because IT was already out of control); see Figure 17.2. This assumption category provides an initial clue about the status of the IT function and its leader.

Centrality assumptions. Control of IT direction was one issue. Importance of control was another. IT might or might not be viewed as strategic to the organization – that is, as being central and critical to achieving the organization's goals and business strategies. Despite being information intensive insurance companies, assumptions about the strategic significance of IT varied considerably across (and sometimes within) different divisions at Alpha and Gamma.

Assumption category	Spectrum of assumptions
Who should control IT direction?	<ul><li>*IT professionals* (IT) should control IT direction.</li><li>*Corporate business executives* should control IT direction.</li><li>*Business units* should each control their own IT direction.</li><li>Control should be *shared* between IT and users groups.</li><li>Let's *not control it*, let's avoid it because IT is out of control.</li></ul>

Figure 17.2   *Control assumptions*

Assumption category	Spectrum of assumptions
How central is IT to business strategy?	<ul><li>Embraced as *imperative* to corporate success</li><li>Significance *depends on whether a business leader is* sponsoring the IT project</li><li>*High level* of centrality to *operational and tactical goals* at the business unit level</li><li>*Selective centrality*, depending on nature of strategic business problems</li><li>*Not significant* at all unless required by external forces (industry standard; survival issue)</li></ul>

Figure 17.3   *Centrality assumptions*

The spectrum of assumptions about IT's centrality were that IT was imperative to success, depended on whether or not IT work was sponsored, was only central to operational and tactical goals, depended on the strategic problem being addressed, or was not significant at all, unless required by external forces; see Figure 17.3. The centrality assumption of a business group provided insights into the status of IT and the senior IT executives, and the relationship quality between IT and the business group. As one would expect, where IT was viewed as significant, the IT leader was also viewed as more important.

IT skills value assumptions. The companies demonstrated different levels of appreciation for IT skills and IT knowledge in general – that is, in business staff and in IT staff alike. The spectrum of assumptions were that IT skills and knowledge were highly valued and rewarded, not valued as highly as business skills, necessary for some people, neutral on their own but valuable when partnered with business skills, or not valuable at all and maybe even threatening; see Figure 17.4.

As expected, when a department placed a low value on IT skills, its managers assumed they didn't need these skills to be successful. A CIO working with these departments, whose business peers viewed him or her as too technical, would be at a perceptual disadvantage. A recent study found that technical ability did not *necessarily* undermine a CIO's ability to influence

Descriptive assumption	Spectrum of assumptions
What is the value of IT skills and knowledge?	• IT skills are *highly valued and rewarded*; may give one status regardless of position or gender. • IT skills are *not as important* as insurance skills, *but* people with IT skills can *be useful if directed* by business leaders. • IT skills and knowledge are *necessary* for certain business unit managers and staff. • IT professionals or skill holders are valuable when *partnered* with holders of business skills but neutral on their own. • IT skills are not valued and may be *threatening*.

Figure 17.4   *Value of IT skills and knowledge assumptions*

business peers.[23] However, if technical skills were viewed as *inferior* to core business skills, then the CIO could still face this disadvantage.

As an example, a new senior vice president of administration at Alpha, to whom the vice president of information systems reported, admitted that he downplayed his level of IT expertise out of concern that he would be branded as a "techie" and lose his business credibility. He felt he was especially vulnerable because he was new to the insurance industry. He lacked credibility by not having proven insurance skills. After joining the firm, he quickly became aware of the underlying assumption that business skills in general and insurance skills in particular were superior to technology skills. His interpretation was supported by several IT staff at Alpha who felt that their opinions were less valued because they were seen as not being part of the core business and not sufficiently knowledgeable about insurance.

Justification assumptions. Justification assumptions answer the question, "What opportunities justify the costs and risks of investing further in IT? Some assumptions lead to proactive investments; others lead to reactive investments. In the 31 business units in the two insurance firms, IT investments were justified based on a spectrum of assumed reasons: when they could lead to innovation, reduce staff or costs, increase unit level productivity, assist a strategy (such as increase quality), or only when there was no other choice to survive or stay competitive; see Figure 17.5.

These variations could be loosely linked to corporate strategy, such as low cost, product differentiation (focused), or innovation.[24] More specifically, however, the differences reflected distinct justifications for investment that provided important signposts for the CIO and his or her team.

Beneficiaries of IT assumptions. Adoption of a new technology leads to expected and unexpected consequences, both positive and negative. The

[23]Enns, H.G., S.L. Huff, and B.R. Golden, "CIO Influence Behaviors: The Impact of Technical Background," *Information & Management,* 2003, 40(5), pp 467–476.
[24]Porter, M.E., *Competitive Advantage: Creating and Sustaining Superior Performance,* 1985, New York: The Free Press, p 557.

Descriptive assumption	Spectrum of assumptions
What justifies further IT investment?	• Experimentation and research and development in IT provide opportunities for finding new or improved services (innovation) • Justified when IT will help reduce staff or operating costs (same output with less staff) • Justified when IT can support unit-level strategy or improve personal and unit productivity (i.e., more output of better quality with same people) • Justification varies depending on business problem or strategy and IT opportunity (cost, quantity, quality, variety, or innovation). • Investment in new IT is justified when there are competitive or survival pressures – that is, when there is no choice but to invest in IT to survive or stay current with industry standards.

Figure 17.5   *Justification assumptions*

"beneficiaries of IT" assumptions reflect expected outcomes, that is, which people are believed to win or lose from the new use of an information technology. These assumptions may be about individuals, the IT function, shareholders, customers, or even the organization as a whole.

This spectrum of assumptions reflects more than the expected business value of IT. It reminds us that technological change can produce fears about being on the losing side of change. Business groups that fear the effect of a potential IT investment on themselves are likely to view the CIO and the IT team negatively. On the other hand, technological changes pushed by some departments can take a heavy toll on the IT function itself, making IT staff feel like losers as they attempt to meet unreasonable expectations.

The two firms demonstrated a spectrum of five assumptions about beneficiaries: everyone wins, the organization and shareholders win but IT may lose, only certain business units win and IT may win or lose, selective loses are inevitable, or no one wins; see Figure 17.6.

Clustering the assumptions

Rather than assess each assumption individually, CIOs can gain greater insights by looking for dominant patterns, that is, clusters of assumptions. At the two insurance companies, we pattern-matched main assumptions of departments and groups. We found that the dominant assumption for each category clustered into discernable patterns of behavior toward information technology, the senior IT executive, and the IT function as a whole. We refer to these as clusters.

Here is an example of one cluster, which we call "IT Is Support, Not a Partner."

• *Control assumption:* IT should be controlled by the senior business executives.

Descriptive assumption	Spectrum of assumptions
Who wins and who loses with IT adoption?	• Everyone wins – IT, the IT professionals, the organization, shareholders, and customers. • The organization and shareholders win; IT and other staff may lose. • Specific business units may win; no one loses (except maybe IT). • The organization, shareholders, and customers win, but selective losses may be unavoidable. • No one wins; or non-technology staff lose.

Figure 17.6 *Beneficiaries assumptions*

- *Centrality assumption:* The significance of IT depended on whether or not a business manager championed the IT project.
- *Value assumption:* IT skills were not valued as highly as core business skills.
- *Justification assumption:* IT investments were justified only when they reduced either costs or staff.
- *Beneficiaries assumption:* The organization as a whole would benefit from IT, but some losses would be unavoidable. Generally, IT staff would lose because their job was to serve the business.

In this assumption cluster, the CIO and other senior IT executives have little status, and the IT function is treated as a second-class corporate citizen.

We found five such clusters of assumptions and gave each a name that reflects IT's implicit status in the eyes of the business group.[25] Figure 17.7 shows the five clusters.

Following are examples of each cluster of assumptions about IT, and the impact of the assumption cluster on CIO status. CIOs will likely recognize their enterprise or certain departments in these examples.

"IT is a necessary evil"

The human resources division of Gamma Corp. contained many different departments that provided a variety of corporate and employee services. One group was the benefits department. Although the CIO had an excellent relationship with the vice president of HR, his status, and the status of his team, was significantly less with the benefits department.

---

[25]These status patterns are based on the archetypal cultural patterns published by Kaarst-Brown, 1995, and Kaarst-Brown and Robey, 1999. In these papers, the cultural archetypes are called: the Fearful IT Culture, the Controlled IT Culture, the Revered IT Culture, the Demystified IT Culture, and the Integrated IT Culture.

Assumption clusters / Assumption categories	"A necessary evil"	"It is support, not a partner"	"IT Rules!"	"Business can do it better"	"Equal partners"
WHO SHOULD CONTROL IT DIRECTION	Let's not control it, let's avoid it because IT is out of control	Corporate business executives should control IT direction	IT professionals should control IT direction	Each business unit should control its own IT direction	Control should be shared by IT professionals and business units
CENTRALITY of IT to BUSINESS STRATEGY	Not assumed to be central to business strategy	Must have senior business champion or sponsor	Crucial at corporate (strategic) level	Important at operational or tactical levels	Balanced importance depending on issues
VALUE of IT SKILLS and KNOWLEDGE	Not valued; potentially a threat	Business knowledge superior; IT second class but used when needed	IT skills highly valued and rewarded	IT knowledge and/or skills REQUIRED at mid-managerial and staff business levels	IT skills valued as partnered with business skills
JUSTIFICATION for IT INVESTMENT	No choice but to adopt IT solution as a survival measure	To reduce costs and/or staff (or at executive decree of benefits)	R&D; innovation; to improve or create new services	Improved services; personal productivity and unit level services	Customer oriented; problem-specific
BENEFICIARIES of IT (Winners or Losers)	Non-IT staff will lose; no one wins	Staff may lose; organization wins; IT staff may suffer demands	IT staff win; organization and clients win	Business units win so organization wins; IT may lose if shut out of projects	Selective losses; organization and customers win

Figure 17.7   *Clusters of assumptions about IT*

The benefits employees did not question the CIO's competency or personality, but they did question everything else about IT. They saw IT as a necessary evil, so they were not welcoming to IT staff. They avoided IT at worst, and only "tolerated" IT staff at best. Employees in other departments fully recognized the benefits department's low view of IT. One employee in the department called his department "very cautious." An employee in another department called them "resistant."

Employees in benefits expressed strong concern that people would suffer once a new pension system was implemented. Rather than state their concerns directly, though, these concerns surfaced as complaints and challenges during implementation. These employees did not get involved during development. In fact, they opposed having to include their processes in the new corporate HR system. They lost that battle, so they dragged their feet throughout development.

This group also placed high value on their specialized skills, experience, and knowledge about benefits. They viewed IT staff as arrogant for not understanding the importance of these skills. In fact, the group unanimously assumed that if technology spread to all their tasks, their efficiency, effectiveness, and control over their work would suffer. They would also be subjected to increased monitoring. They might be let go. The director of another group that shared this set of assumptions, and also viewed the CIO and IT function as a necessary evil, explained:

> "Some people are scared to death. They say 'I love the feeling that you can give me all this information, but now you can measure me, too.'"

A potentially positive aspect of this group's concerns surfaced as zealous testing of the new pension module that automated a formerly manual process. Unfortunately, when the group found errors in the pension calculations, they viewed these errors as yet more proof that computers could not be trusted, and neither could the people who developed and managed them. The CIO's credibility suffered, even though the calculation errors were generally measured in cents.

This cluster of assumptions about IT is more common than expected and is perpetuated in many organizations by systems failures, media hype on security problems, and corporate downsizing after automation. The CIO should not expect a seat at the executive table when this cluster is dominant among senior management.

"IT is support, not a partner"

Alpha Corp.'s senior management viewed IT as support, not a partner, setting the tone for much of the company's view of IT. Because of this view, the CIO and his IT management team faced challenges on budgets, priorities, and resources every day. Senior management believed that IT needed to be almost totally directed by the business executives – *excluding* the vice president of IT – because they knew their business best. It did not matter that their knowledge or use of IT was limited.

Management also viewed IT folks as "different," which translated into "lower power status." IT even struggled to get resources for basic maintenance and upgrades. Technical problems were viewed as signs of IT's inferior abilities. None of the vice presidents of IT during the course of this study had high status with the executive group, even though one had been with the company for twenty years and was viewed as a highly competent executive by external peers.

The vice president of IT was not part of the strategic planning process and was often excluded from providing official input until the majority of project decisions had been made. In fact, when a special committee was formed to discuss the future of Alpha's most important information system, the new senior vice president of administration (to which IT reported) had to use considerable political maneuvering to get the vice president of IT on the committee. It was then stressed that the IT vice president's role was only to "clarify technical issues rather than serve as an equal member." The rationale for his secondary role was as follows:

"The vice president of IT might be biased about technology options, whereas the branch and head office end user members were not biased."

Another line executive reiterated this view, explaining that

"[The VP of IT] was on the committee as a technical expert, but he didn't try to guide their decisions. It was their business committee."

This cluster of assumptions was shared and reinforced by several other groups at Alpha Corp. Being the dominant cluster among the executives, it had a strong organizational impact at Alpha Corp. The CIO rarely reported to a senior executive with extensive computer knowledge. One senior vice president explained the history:

"Every senior [business] vice president has had IT at one time or another. There has been no continuity, no first-hand knowledge [with IT]. At senior levels there has been no representative who has been familiar with IT."

One vice president of IT noted his frustration:

"Our previous senior vice president was anti-computers, and we reported to him. No one understood us and so no one supported us. We (IT) were viewed as a cost, not an investment."

Many of the long-tenured IT staff were also frustrated that IT was viewed as not understanding the business problems or business strategy. Most had been with the company between ten and twenty years and did, indeed, understand company and industry issues. In fact, they were frequently highly respected outside their company, despite limited business credibility inside.

In line with these views, IT skills did not elevate a business unit employee's status. Employees could only expect to receive rewards if their IT knowledge led to significant benefits in the long term.

Alpha's IT group was expected to continually reduce and offset costs by saving money in the rest of the business through its services. Even the president focused on reducing IT expenses. The irony is that IT costs included all computer equipment costs and related office overhead and supplies – whether or not IT had any control over these expenditures.

Rather than focus on innovation or competitive new services, every IT project had to be cost-justified on reducing expenses. The senior vice president of insurance operations noted that he had been particularly vitriolic about the IT division a few years earlier due to their perceived lack of responsiveness to the business units. But he had since mellowed. His earlier frustrations were rather ironic, considering the line executives controlled how IT was used:

"The computer technology tail doesn't wag the company dog here!"

The result for the CIO and his team, however, was frustration.

"We work on something and it comes to a dead halt. … We don't know why. …"

"IT rules!"

One IT manager at Gamma stated:

"It is not part of our culture to criticize the technology."

While this acceptance of IT might seem to be every CIO's dream, "beware the company with a sacred cow at its helm. Sacred cows rarely make things happen. They want things to work the way they have always worked, and thus can be blindsided in a crisis.[26] We found pros and cons for CIOs who worked with departments that held the "IT Rules!" assumptions.

---

[26]Deal, T.E. and A.A. Kennedy, *Corporate Cultures: The Rites and Rituals of Corporate Life,* 1982: Addison-Wesley, p 55. This book was recently released in a second edition. It provides an interesting historical account of several high tech firms.

As noted earlier, Gamma was created during the early 1970s, when IT was beginning to move out of the back room and into the front line. PCs emerged a decade later and IT-based innovation has been a roller coaster ride ever since. Many Gamma employees saw IT as critical to company success, based mainly on the company's rocky start-up that had required the IT function to quickly develop many basic systems. IT staff appreciated others' recognition that the company's formation depended on IT:

> "We couldn't have been born without the technology. We saved the baby company."

The IT "old heroes" became part of the company's myths and, for many years, their dominance went unchallenged. Underwriting support services was one of the departments that held this view. It relied heavily on systems developed in the chaotic early years. The CIO and the IT function had high status with this department and with the large number of other departments at Gamma that also held the "IT Rules!" mindset.

Three "pros" we found with this viewpoint were as follows:

1) Business executives viewed IT as having strategic importance.
2) The organization placed a high value on IT skills and knowledge.
3) In some cases, business-unit champions had to have an IT sponsor for their projects to ensure that their IT development was consistent with the enterprise's overall technology strategy.

All three pros made the CIO's job much easier. In fact, in the cases where IT skills were seen as valuable, business employees aspiring to management had to spend some time in the IT department or be involved in a major IT project to advance in their career. One junior business employee commented that in her department,

> "People who can't or won't learn the technology and update their skills will find they don't have a job."

In addition, investment in IT research and development was an easy sell for IT, with support for exploration of emerging technologies. The senior IT executives and the CIO received considerable support for pilot project test sites not only in the underwriting support department but also in the other departments where managers believed that IT was the way to go and the IT function would lead the way. These groups' management believed it was IT's job to continually talk with vendors, evaluate the potential of new technologies, and determine their suitability and timeliness to Gamma.

During Gamma's first decade, the underwriting support group was highly tolerant of system errors and failures because they assumed the IT staff was doing its best under the challenging circumstances. Despite constant changes to fix premature systems, this group did not waver in its assumption that everyone ultimately wins through effective use of IT.

However, we also found three "cons" for IT functions dealing with departments with the "IT Rules!" assumption:

1) Departments sometimes did not question who should direct the future of IT. They defaulted to the CIO and the technical experts, sometimes missing the business strategy view – which was a significant oversight.
2) Some IT development units developed such a high sense of ownership of specific systems that they occasionally did not re-evaluate processes and systems that had outlived their usefulness. Those who believed that IT ruled did not question this judgment.
3) Management was complacent about the company's technological superiority. As one Gamma CIO noted, *"They have begun to believe their own press releases, which are not always true."*

Interviews in 2003 with a later CIO found that this perspective did, indeed, lead to system risks and significant financial losses prior to his arrival. He stated,

> "I had to clean house and rebuild a lot of bridges that had been burnt because prior IT managers had stopped listening to the users."

CIOs that can leverage the pros of the "IT Rules!" mindset, and avoid the cons, can use their trusted relationships with these groups to demonstrate the value of IT's potential to the other, less supportive, business groups.

"Business can do IT better"

Decentralization of control over IT has presented both opportunities and challenges for senior IT management. Decentralization to business units and smaller departments created tension between IT professionals and business managers, as well as between business managers who had different visions and resource requirements.

CIOs at Gamma and Alpha experienced such conflicts, not only because some departments fit in this cluster but because other departments fit in the other clusters. The result was various degrees of dispute over IT control. The view that business should control grew more common as a former IT manager (now working in HR at Gamma) noted,

> "It's not us (IT) and them. There isn't the awe anymore … The wall is definitely being broken down. IT is not an elitist thing anymore."

The actuarial/operations research department at Alpha exemplified the assumption that business units could – and should – support their own IT needs better. The department's vice president had been with Alpha for over eleven years, so he saw many of the largest system changes and upgrades. He noted,

> "Our work unit has to be very conversant with IT, but again, it's not a savior or a bane.... We just view it as a tool ... . If IT is viewed as a bane, it is when we can't make the changes ourselves. Within our department, we do have control ... . We do programming right to the level of JCL and rely on high level languages."

IT skills were assumed to be a requirement in groups that thought they could do IT better:

> "If we don't know how to run a computer, we don't have a job."

Some end users were even reported to be "at a technical level on par with the IT department." In fact, the demystification of computer technology appeared to demystify IT skills as well:

> "We are all computer people now, just like we are all telephone people now. ..."

By demystifying technology, they saw themselves gaining power over their own processes:

> "...When using a can opener, you don't think you are involved with mechanical engineering ... . To use a telephone, you don't think you are using information technology. ... I still think of IT in terms of interaction – the 'information' is more important than the 'technology' part of the term."

The "We can do IT better" cluster was among the more politicized because it was held by departments within larger divisions. They all seemed highly conscious of the power dynamics that revolved around who should control IT direction. They believed that IT was just a tool for business units to wield. Frequently, the end users in these departments were more frustrated with their own department executives than with the CIO, because the CIO often supported offloading work to them, if they were skilled. However, in dealing with these departments, the CIOs did face resource and standards challenges.

"Partners all the way"

People who viewed IT and the CIO as valued partners did so because they saw IT as an important asset to the organization. But they also realized that meeting expectations required collaboration, equal contributions of IT and business skills, and an understanding that IT might not always be the best solution.

Despite strong and dominant representation of the other four clusters, both Alpha and Gamma had several significant groups committed to building relationships between IT and the line. The information centers at both firms and the finance and planning division at Gamma[27] were in this partnering cluster.

The vice president of finance and strategic planning at Gamma, for example, firmly believed the business units and IT division had to work together to maximize the benefits of IT. He readily gave examples where working together had led to success in a finance and planning software project, in evaluating a new technology (imaging), and in pilot testing that technology in his department.

His department gained a reputation for cooperatively working with different IT functions, without being unduly influenced by them. He and his staff valued IT professionals' perspectives on business problems, but they made it clear to IT staff not to push technology on them:

"It was, in fact, a move from a world of technological dependence – which is seen as not being appropriate – to a view that technology was simply a tool for everyone to use…"

This vice president also saw value in the information technology steering committee (ITSC). It was a means to grow support for the collaborative view that the CIO wanted. Interestingly, the finance vice president, rather than the CIO, acted as the mediator on this committee to engender a balanced business-IT view of investments. As one member noted:

"Each area has a rotating member of the ITSC… I'm one… There is a buying into projects. If there is not a total buy-in, it is because there are some things we must do – such as a recent legislative change."

Some projects benefited from the integrated IT-business view; others did not. Committee members with IT knowledge were valued because they took a balanced view of the different roles IT could play in the business. Some departments wanted independence from IT. Others accepted the partnership view. As one executive explained,

"Self-sufficiency also means that I know when to ask IT. We both need to have skills."

Recommendations for CIOS

In this research, we found no ideal world for CIOs. For every example provided above, several more exist that illustrate both pros and cons for CIOs

---

[27]The CIO supported these assumptions and staffed the information centers with supporters. While one would expect such user support groups to be staffed with folks who believe in a partnership between IT and users, we also found this assumption cluster in other operational groups at both firms.

and their IT function. The five categories of assumptions cluster into distinct patterns that influence the status of the CIO and the IT function. Figure 17.8 summarizes the functional and dysfunctional impacts of each cluster.

What are the benefits of diagnosing the assumptions of your CEO, your executive peers, your own departments, and various business groups? One is for new CIOs. If they can quickly identify the dominant assumptions of important groups, they can predict potential relationship issues and act to address them. A second benefit is for all CIOs. They can use this perspective to identify potentially conflicting assumptions among multiple groups to head off these conflicts, and even stay out of the middle of them.

Cluster	Functional impact	Dysfunctional impact	Recommendations for CIO
"IT is a necessary evil"	CIOs can count on support for risk analysis. These individuals and groups are generally resistant to new IT and have low expectations of practical benefits from new technologies. These individuals or groups are risk-adverse and will be very cautious about new projects, expecting the CIO and his/her team to provide solid (and often additional) justification.	While personally well-liked, the CIO may not be accepted as a part of business. Negative attitudes towards CIO and IT function include tight budget constraints. CIO may Avoid planning meetings and/or fail to accept proposed IT solutions. Inconsistent diffusion of IT can result in mixed project results and therefore exacerbate low status of CIO and IT.	CIO may have to budget scarce resources (time and money) for education and training of key business management or users before moving forward on plans. CIO will need to provide lots of reassurance, including business plans that include risk assessments and contingency plans. CIO should encourage participation throughout various stages of R&D, pilot tests, systems development, and testing of products before deployment. Third-party endorsements from respected business leaders may be helpful. Internal success stories are also helpful, but not from those branded as "techies."
"IT is support, not a partner"	Business executives want to be highly involved in all IT decisions. Projects can move more quickly when working with a business sponsor, especially an executive-level sponsor or champion.	CIO is frequently viewed as a servant to the line rather than a peer. Despite low status with business executives, the CIO is called upon to deliver. The level of business executives' IT knowledge may constrain effective alignment and integration of IT. Regardless of skill or knowledge level, business executives may push "pet" projects that do not fit infrastructure plans, IT strategy, IT budget, or available IT manpower. Paradoxically, this mismatch can lead to even more executive business unit control over IT.	Make sure the CIO office is on the same floor as the other business executives. Be where you can participate in discussions. Recruit business-savvy IT staff or educate IT staff on business issues. Get them out in the business interacting with business staff. Educate the executive group on existing and emerging technologies, but be realistic about criteria for fit, risks and rewards. Market internally by promoting project successes and IT's contributions to the business. Cultivate a senior business-unit mentor who can speak for IT when the CIO is not invited. Require business plan justification that links IT and business, with a clear focus on how IT supports business goals.

Figure 17.8   *Functional and dysfunctional impact of clusters on CIO status*

Cluster	Functional impact	Dysfunctional impact	Recommendations for CIO
"IT Rules!"	CIO and IT have very high status and credibility in general, with CIO sharing an equal or elevated executive status. CIO has possible preferential status with CEO. CIO has high tolerance for IT risk and innovation, and anticipates positive outcomes from new IT and communication technologies. CIO can count on support for R&D investment, early adoption, and technical innovation. CIO supports IT championship behavior.	CIO and organization can become complacent and sit on their laurels during periods of rapid technology change. Other executives resent CIO's power and status with CEO. Conflicts occur over scarce resources Blind acceptance of IT value may lead to biased evaluation of ROI and other benefits of innovation that can come back to haunt CIO and successors. High (and unreasonable) expectations exist that CIO and IT function will have a technology solution for every business problem. Problems may be sought to take advantage of emerging IT solutions, putting pressure on CIO and IT to ride "bleeding edge" or lose image as technology leaders.	CIO must keep the focus on cost/benefit and IT business value. With power and status comes responsibility, creating a high pressure position. Management of expectations is critical. Communicate, communicate, communicate. Keep the IT function's focus on business processes and adding business value, not just on the joys of the technology. Since the buck stops in IT, the CIO needs to gain educated business supporters and business sponsorship for projects so that the business executives and other management are equally committed and accountable.
"Business can do IT better"	CIO will find a high level of IT knowledge among business colleagues. CIO will find support for IT innovation throughout the firm and IT champions at every level of the business. Assessment of IT projects will be seen on business unit level.	CIO status will vary depending on current level of conflict with various business units over business unit versus corporate IT plans and budgets. CIO and IT function may encounter resistance to standards and strategic IT planning. CIO may experience suboptimization of resources as business units seek to control their own IT spending and department level benefits.	CIO must work with various business units to educate and negotiate support for standards and internal controls. CIO should support training of business personnel on IT and IT development methodologies. Communicate and internally promote joint successes of IT projects. CIO and IT function should negotiate to play support roles in business-driven projects. Manage data as an organizational, not just a departmental, resource.
"Partners all the way"	The CIO has equal status and is involved as a partner and contributor to business strategy and goals. CIO will find balanced and realistic expectations of IT's role. CIO will find acceptance for IT solutions coming from either the business or IT function, and projects will be debated on their merit rather than politics or technocentricity. CIO will find collaborative and firm-wide benefits sought for new information and communication technologies.	CIO may find that rituals of collaboration may obscure problems with prioritization or assessment procedures. Individual power and prestige in groups, along with the usual turf battles, may supersede team processes and put the CIO in a position of choosing sides.	While seeming the ideal, having an equal role at the table puts the CIO on the same level as other executives, so good relations continue to be important. The CIO will want to allocate resources to keep the business folks up-to-date on IT and also to make sure IT staff are current on key business issues. There may be opportunities for IT staff to move laterally into the business and create cross-functional teams.

Figure 17.8   *(continued)*

"A necessary evil" recommendations. To make IT's working life bearable, let alone achieve strategic alignment, CIOs and IT functions viewed as "A necessary evil" need to expend large amounts of time and resources reassuring, educating, and meeting with the business units that take this view. It has been proven that assumptions can be changed when knowledge and skills are changed.[28] Such change can take time, but it is in the CIO's and the enterprise's long-term interest to move these recalcitrant units toward a more positive view of IT.

In some cases, IT projects may need to be "railroaded" through, especially when competitive advantage or organizational survival is at stake. However, it's better to encourage involvement and trust these business folks to see the weaknesses and risks in plans. They might even become strong supporters.[29]

"IT is support, not a partner" recommendations. CIOs who face assumptions that IT is only support, not a partner, need to cultivate business sponsors and senior line supporters who will either speak on IT's behalf or invite the CIO to meetings. Rather than resent IT's low status, these CIOs need to continually reinforce to key business supporters how IT supports business strategy.

Where formal structure fails – such as when the CIO is not part of the top executive team – CIOs need to leverage their personal savvy and informal networking. Informal relationships are necessary anyway to align IT with business goals.[30]

"IT rules!" recommendations. In the enviable situation where "IT Rules!," the CIO's seat at the executive table is fairly guaranteed. But our research and others' research show that these CIOs need to "manage expectations" and "communicate, communicate, communicate" what IT is doing and why,[31] because high expectations can quickly become seeds of dissatisfaction and criticism. Likewise, praise and support can lead to IT complacency and lack of responsiveness.

It is unwise to take one's technological superiority for granted, as various CIOs at Gamma learned. They enjoyed their place at the strategy table, but faced disaster when they could not manage the increasingly complex IT environment and live up to diverse expectations. As assumptions among business groups changed, some IT staff could not change their view to see IT as a tool of the business units. And several of the IT executives made enemies of business managers who felt that control over IT budgets and direction should be shared or in the hands of the business units.

---

[28]Sackmann, S., *Cultural Knowledge in Organizations: Exploring the Collective Mind*, 1991, London: Sage.
[29]Op. cit. Wheeler, Marakus, Brinkley, 2002.
[30]Op. cit. Chan, 2002.
[31]Op. cit. Sambamurthy and Zmud, 1999; Enns et al, 2003.

"Business can do IT better" recommendations. To harness the technological enthusiasm and independence of those who believe the business units can manage IT better, CIOs need to build their relationships with these units to negotiate a common infrastructure and technology standards. CIOs can also instill standards by supporting training in proven IT development methodologies and project management techniques. Sharing IT knowledge, building coordinating liaison mechanisms, and providing support to the business units will go a long way to keep the various units aligned.

"Partners all the way" recommendations. In situations where people congratulate themselves on how well IT and the business work as equal partners, CIOs need to beware of falling prey to blended roles and ritualistic interactions. These can mask poor communications, limited knowledge sharing, and failure to assess the true value of IT proposals.[32] As an example, one manager explained that after a successful joint development project, the system itself floundered. The reason:

> "ISD developed a wonderful piece of technology … . HR did not do as good a job implementing it."

This result is a reminder that partnering requires cross-functional teams with an eye to maximizing knowledge sharing, creative conflict, resource allocations, and cost/benefit analyses at all stages of projects.

Managing multiple assumption clusters

One of the biggest and most obvious challenges facing CIOs is managing multiple assumption clusters – such as where one group welcomes the CIO as a partner while another wants nothing to do with IT. Knowing what to expect from each group can go a long way to managing the diversity of assumptions that most CIOs face. We found all five clusters of assumptions in both companies, in this study and in dozens of other companies as well. Identifying the assumptions held by different groups can help mitigate potential conflict between groups with different views who are involved in the same corporate projects.

Different groups in the IT function may also hold different assumptions. At Gamma, for instance, the help desk and the security group held partnership assumptions. But one of the application development groups strongly held the "IT Rules!" assumptions. As noted earlier, this stance led to problems for various CIOs at the company.

Not all assumptions line up neatly into the five clusters described. Our research suggests that these clusters are actually "archetypal" patterns that

---

[32]Robey, D. and L.M. Markus, "Rituals in Information Systems Design," *MIS Quarterly,* 1984, 8(1), pp 5–15.

are fairly stable across a surprisingly large range of IT issues. But perhaps some groups may be fragmented, due to different, strongly held views of individuals. In these cases, it is best to try to find the dominant assumptions of the key decision makers and monitor those assumptions regularly.

Conclusion

Can assumptions about IT change? Do they change? We found the answer to be "Yes." People come and go, IT knowledge evolves, and project successes and failures become embedded in company history. All these influences on organizational culture and on assumptions about IT can change. That is why the best advice is to keep relationships strong, understand people's current assumptions (because they may have changed), and realize that beyond the boardroom table is the dining table. Make the time to socialize and uncover assumptions about IT. Listen to what is said and implied about the IT function and its leaders. Talk to the CEO, even when your assumptions about the role of IT differ.

Whether you are waiting for a seat at the strategy table, or have been there for years, using the five assumption categories and the clusters of assumptions to decipher the implicit status of IT may save you frustration and provide a strategy for managing critical relationships with business colleagues.

Appendix

This paper is based on an extensive study of assumptions about IT in 31 operating groups or smaller departments of two large insurance organizations. These departments include marketing, claims, human resources, finance, strategic planning, actuarial, underwriting, as well as various departments with IT and public affairs, to name only a few. The original study included 87 intensive interviews (1½ to 2 hours each) with members at all levels of the two firms, analysis of corporate and public documents, participant and direct observation, and dozens of follow-up interviews.

The time period of the study included significant on-site presence from 1989–1992 and ongoing follow-up from 1993–2003. It extended through the collective experiences of six CIOs and 11 other senior IT executives at these firms, as well as dozens of major systems development projects.

Results of this study have been presented in 25 academic settings with portions of the study published in *Information Technology and People* by Kaarst-Brown and Robey.[33] A full report on the early study is available in *A*

---

[33]Op. cit. Kaarst-Brown and Robey, 1999.

Theory of Information Technology Cultures: Magic Dragons, Wizards, and Archetypal Patterns.[34]

Additional experiences were informally collected from CIOs and IT executives in a variety of other organizations from 1993 to 2005, or as part of other research studies. Some of the other firm examples are included as anecdotal support, including IT executives' experiences gathered in a study published in *MIS Quarterly* by Reich and Kaarst-Brown.[35]

Reproduced from *MIS Quarterly Executive*, Vol. 4, No. 2, June 2005, pp. 287–301. Reprinted with permission from the University of Minnesota.

About the author

Michelle Kaarst-Brown

Michelle Kaarst-Brown (mlbrow03@syr.edu) is assistant professor at the School of Information Studies, Syracuse University. She received her MBA and Ph.D. from the Schulich School of Business, York University. Prior to joining academia, she worked in IT management, management development and strategic planning and as an executive consultant to the financial services industry. She has lived and worked in Canada, the U.S., and the Caribbean. She now specializes in how social, cultural and knowledge factors impact IT strategy, IT governance, and enterprise-wide risk management.

She completed one of the first organizational-level studies seeking to identify specific assumptions about IT, the influencers of these assumptions, how these assumptions shape organizational IT cultural patterns, and how they subsequently impact IT management at the organizational level.

She has published in a number of top academic and business journals including *MIS Quarterly, Information Technology and People,* the *Journal of Strategic Information Systems,* the *Journal of Organizational Change Management,* the *Journal of Global Information Management,* the *Journal of the American Society for Information Science and Technology* (JASIST), and *CIO Canada.* She serves as associate editor for *MIS Quarterly* and is on the editorial boards of *MISQ Executive* and the *Journal for Enterprise Architecture.*

Questions for discussion

1   Think of a firm you have worked for. Describe the firm's IT culture using the terminology of Kaarst-Brown's paper.

[34]Op. cit. Kaarst-Brown, 1995.
[35]Op. cit. Reich and Kaarst-Brown, 1999 and 2003.

2 Is it possible for a single organization to have multiple IT cultures (e.g., assumptions about IT)? Explain.

3 What factors, such as the economy or industry environment, might explain which of the IT clusters is seen in a particular organization? Is a certain cluster better in a certain situation?

4 Why would any CIO want to stay in an organization characterized by "a necessary evil" mentality or by an "IT is support, not a partner" mentality? Is one cluster by nature "better" than another?

Index